The Beauties of

Ebenezer Erskine

Selected by Samuel McMillan,
with an introduction by Joel R. Beeke

Reformation Heritage Books
Grand Rapids, Michigan 49525

Christian Focus Publications

© Reformation Heritage Books

ISBN # 1-892777-20-7

This edition published in 2001 by
Reformation Heritage Books, 2919 Leonard St., NE
Grand Rapids, MI 49525 phone 616-977-0599/
Fax 616-977-0889/e-mail: RHbookstore@aol.com
www.heritagebooks.org
and
Christian Focus Publications, Geanies House,
Fearn, Ross-shire, IV20 1TW, Scotland.
www.christianfocus.com

Cover design by Alister MacInnes

Printed and bound in Finland

First published in 1850 as
The Beauties of the Rev Ebenezer Erskine, being a
selection of the most striking illustrations of
gospel doctrine contained in his whole works with
copious notes from other eminent authors.

For additional volumes of Reformed persuasion,
both new and used, request a free book list from
Reformation Heritage Books at the above address

Foreword

The Beauties of Ebenezer Erskine offers the best portions of his sermons. Samuel M'Millan, who ministered at Aberdeen, selected these portions of Erskine's sermons in 1830. The present reprint is from an 1850 edition published in Glasgow by Blackie & Son. Subsequently, this volume went out of print. It has now become difficult to find, even on the used book market.

A lengthy introduction on the lives and preaching of Ebenezer and Ralph Erskine precedes the selected portions because these men deserve to be much better known than they are and because they have many lessons to teach us. The introduction is an expanded version of two addresses given at the 1999 Banner of Truth Conference in Pennsylvania and subsequently to the General Synod of the Associate Reformed Presbyterian Church, whose roots are in the Scottish Secession of 1733. I wish to thank my ministerial brethren at both gatherings for helpful suggestions. A special thanks to Phyllis Ten Elshof, Iain Murray, and Ray Lanning for their thorough proofing and valuable input.

A bibliography of additional sources on the Erskine brothers follows the sermons. If you know of additional sources, please send them to me at 2917 Leonard NE, Grand Rapids, Michigan 49525.

I am grateful for a resurgence of interest in the Erskine brothers. Free Presbyterian Publications is presently reprinting Ebenezer Erskine's three volumes of works. The publisher has done six of Ralph Erskine's seven volumes as well. Both sets are available in North America at a discount from Reformation Heritage Books. We hope that Samuel M'Millan's two-volume *Beauties of Ralph Erskine* will be reprinted in the near future.

Read this book as an act of worship. Read it with the goal of being elevated into the great truths of God. Some books may be tasted, while others should be chewed on before being digested. This volume belongs to the latter. I would suggest that you use it as a daily devotional. Read slowly, meditating, applying, and practicing its truths. May God's divine approbation rest richly upon this savory volume.

—JRB

EBENEZER AND RALPH ERSKINE:
Their Lives and Their Preaching

"Sir, you have never heard the gospel in its majesty," said Adam Gib to a young minister who had never heard Ebenezer Erskine preach. Ebenezer Erskine and his younger brother, Ralph, were great eighteenth-century Scots preachers. God used them to bring hundreds of people to conversion and thousands more to spiritual maturity through their lives, ministries, preaching, and writings.

The Erskines have many lessons to teach the contemporary church. The first part of this article is biographical and historical, showing that the Erskines were dissenters with a cause. The second part is homiletical and theological, showing that the Erskines were preachers who focused on the promises of God.

Dissenters with a Cause

Early Life and Ministry

Ebenezer Erskine was born in Dryburgh, Scotland, in 1680. Five years later, his brother Ralph was born in Monilaws, near Cornhill, Northumberland, the northernmost county of England. Their father, Henry, was a Puritan minister who had been ejected from his home and pastorate in Cornhill in 1662 by the Act of Uniformity. Their mother was Margaret Halcro, Henry Erskine's second wife. Both parents were of prestigious background and closely related to Scottish nobility.

The lives of the young boys were disrupted when their father refused to renounce the Solemn League and Covenant. The national government despised the preacher's Puritan principles. When Ebenezer was two years old, his father was arrested and sentenced to imprisonment on the Bass Rock for exercising his ministerial office illegally by "withdrawing from ordinances, keeping conventicles, and being guilty of disorderly baptisms." The Committee of Privy Council questioned Henry Erskine for hours, then finally asked if he would promise not to preach at any more conventicles. Erskine replied, "My lord, I have my commission from Christ, and, though I were within an hour of my death, I durst not lay it down at the feet of any mortal man."

Upon his request, Erskine's sentence to Bass Rock was commuted to exile, due to poor health. He and his family moved to England, and settled in Parkridge, near Carlisle. From there they went to Monilaws, where Erskine was arrested again and imprisoned for several months for preaching at conventicles. Erskine then preached in the border parish of Whitsome, where he helped lead Thomas Boston to Christ at age eleven. The king's indulgence of 1687 enabled him to continue his ministry without fear of arrest. In 1690, when Ebenezer was age ten and Ralph, five, their father was admitted to the parish of Chirnside, near Berwick, in southeastern Scotland, where he ministered until his death in 1696 at the age of seventy-two.

Ebenezer Erskine went to the University of Edinburgh, where he earned a master of arts degree in philosophy in 1697. He served as tutor and chaplain to the God-fearing family of the Earl of Rothes until he was licensed in 1703 by the Presbytery of Kirkcaldy and ordained to Portmoak, near Kinross, where he would minister for the next twenty-eight years. The year he was ordained he married Alison Turpie, a God-fearing woman who had a profound spiritual influence on him.

Erskine's first years at Portmoak were difficult, mostly due to a spiritual battle that he had with himself after overhearing a conversation on the "deep things of God" between Ralph and his wife. The discussion convinced Ebenezer that he was not yet converted. After a year of spiritual struggle, he finally began to experience what he called "the true grace of God." In the summer of 1708, Erskine wrote in his voluminous diary that he finally "got his head out of Time into Eternity." On August 26 he said that God had "brought my heart to give a consent to Him" and that he was now sure that God could never "deny His own covenant" with him. In turn, Erskine made a covenant with God. He wrote:

> Lord, if I have done iniquity, I am resolved through thy grace to do so no more. I flee for shelter to the blood of Jesus and his everlasting righteousness; for this is pleasing unto thee. I offer myself up, soul and body, unto God the Father, Son, and Holy Ghost. I offer myself unto Christ the Lord, as an object proper for all his offices to be exercised upon. I choose him as my prophet for in-

struction, illumination, and direction. I embrace him as my great priest, to be washed and justified by his blood and righteousness. I embrace him as my king to reign and rule within me. I take a whole Christ with all his laws, and all his crosses and afflictions. I will live to him; I will die to him; I will quit with all I have in the world for his cause and truth.

Life Transformed

Erskine's encounter with God transformed his life and ministry. After that summer of 1708, Erskine's diary entries reveal a man who walked with God, was fully satisfied with Christ, and was deeply humbled by his sinfulness. They show us a man who knew the sanctifying power of Christ's death and who was constantly amazed at the generosity of God's sovereign grace. They show a man steeped in Scripture, immersed in fervent prayer, and inspired by lofty and biblical views of God.

From the time of his conversion Erskine became more diligent than ever in preparing sermons. His delivery also improved; instead of fixing his attention on a stone in the rear wall of the church, he now looked straight into the eyes of his hearers. "The great desire and ambition of my soul, and that which I desire to aim and level at in all my ministerial work, is to commend Jesus Christ to immortal souls," he wrote.

The results were dramatic. Thousands of people flocked to hear him, coming from as far as sixty miles, particularly during Communion seasons. Hundreds of people were converted to Christ. Many members of his congregation began to take notes of his sermons. Erskine sometimes addressed the note-takers publicly as his "scribes."

Early Commitment

Ebenezer's younger brother, Ralph, showed evidence of piety at a very early age. According to the notebooks he kept, Ralph believed the Lord began His saving work within him when he was age eleven and his father died. "Lord, put thy fear in my heart," the young boy wrote. "Let my thoughts be holy, and let me do for thy glory, all that I do. Bless me in my lawful work. Give a good judgment and memory — a belief in Jesus Christ, and an assured token of Thy love."

Ralph experienced a profound sense of sin and of deliverance in Christ as well as remarkable answers to prayer. With this conviction he made excellent progress at school. He entered the University of Edinburgh at the age of fifteen to study theology. During his holidays Ralph stayed with his brother Ebenezer at Portmoak. After earning a master's degree in theology in 1704, Ralph worked for five years as a private chaplain for his relative, Colonel John Erskine. The Colonel had written to Ralph, saying, "I beg earnestly, that the Lord may bless your good designs to my children; and am fully persuaded, that the right impressions that children get of God and the ways of God, when they are young, is a great help to them in life." The Colonel's son, John, would later become a professor of Scottish law.

By 1709, Ralph was old enough to be licensed as a preacher, but he felt unworthy of the task. The Colonel did all in his power to persuade him to seek licensure. So did his brother, Ebenezer, who had secretly heard Ralph practice preaching. The Dunfermline Presbytery agreed to try Ralph Erskine out, and after a short time its members became convinced that this young man was sent by God to preach the gospel. Erskine was ordained to the second charge in Dunfermline in 1711 and promoted to the first charge in 1716.

After Erskine was settled in Dunfermline, he was overcome by doubts about his Christian witness and calling. He began scouring the works of godly men to find comfort. Thomas Boston's work on the covenant of grace finally brought him relief. After reading Boston, Erskine was able to plead the promises of God and regain peace of heart.

The assurance gleaned from that experience energized his ministry. So intent was Erskine on studying the Word, praying, and preaching, that he ignored sleep and worked long into the night. His motto became, "In the Lord have I righteousness and strength." A typical entry in his diary during this time reads like this:

> This morning, after reading, I went to prayer, under a sense of my nothingness and naughtiness, vileness and corruption, and acknowledged myself "a beast before God." Yet looking to God as an infinite, eternal and unchangeable Spirit, who from everlasting to everlasting is God, and always the same, and who manifests himself in Christ . . . he allowed me some communion with him in a way of believing, and I was made to cry with tears, "Lord, I believe, help thou mine unbelief." I was led, in some suitable manner, under a view of my nothingness,

and of God's all-sufficiency, to renounce all confidence in
the flesh, and to betake myself solely to the name of the
Lord, and there to rest and repose myself.

Fruitful Ministries

Ralph Erskine served the Dunfermline congregation for more
than forty years until his death in 1752. God mightily blessed
that work. Within two years of his ordination, the Spirit was
working so powerfully through his preaching that worshipers
filled the church and church yard. A previously dead church
came alive. After the evening service, prayer and thanksgiving
went on in small groups, sometimes until after midnight. One
seeker rose at 2:00 a.m. to pray in secret and found so many people in town on their knees that the countryside hummed like a
gigantic hive of bees. Hundreds of penitent sinners were pouring
out their hearts to God. The revival proved to be genuine and
abiding, though it remained largely confined to Dunfermline.

Ralph Erskine married Margaret Dewar, a gentleman's
daughter, in 1714. Margaret was noted for her kindness. She
served at Ralph's side for sixteen years, bearing him ten children, five of whom died in infancy. Erskine was shattered by her
death at the age of thirty-two. He wrote to a friend:

> Her last words expressed the deepest humiliation, and
> greatest submission to the sovereign will of God, that
> words could manifest, and thereafter, she concluded all
> with — "O death, where is thy sting? O grave, where is
> thy victory? Thanks be to God who giveth us the victory
> through Jesus Christ our Lord!" — which she repeated
> two or three times over. And yet, even at this time, I knew
> not that they were her dying words, till instantly I per-
> ceived the evident symptoms of death; in view whereof I
> was plunged, as it were, into a sea of confusion, when
> she, less than an hour after, in a most soft and easy man-
> ner, departed this life.

He did not remain alone for long, however. Two years later,
he married Margaret Simson of Edinburgh. In June 1732 Erskine
wrote, "I was made to bless the Lord for His goodness in providing me a wife whose character was so pleasant and peaceable."
He and his wife were greatly blessed as they taught their children
of the mercies of God in Christ, but they also experienced sorrow.
Three of four sons born to them died in childhood.

While Ralph's ministry was thriving, his brother Ebenezer

was called to a new charge in Stirling (1731), where he would serve for twenty-two years. Andrew Muirhead, who wrote a master's thesis on social and ecclesiastical life in the town of Stirling, concluded that Erskine's "religious impact was great,…and permeated every facet of life in Stirling." Hundreds of people from neighboring parishes joined Erskine's congregation. Professions of faith became so numerous and the Lord's Table so crowded in the churches of both Erskines that the brothers began to admonish the people in order to remove the chaff from the wheat. Very little chaff existed, however; most of the converts proved to be genuine, as evidenced by the fruits that their lives brought forth.

The Erskines sometimes served more than thirty tables at Communion. Ralph wrote on July 18, 1734, "There being such a multitude of people, and thirty-three tables, the service was not over at twelve o'clock [midnight,] and I began to preach betwixt twelve and one on that text, 'Behold, thy time was the time of love,' and the congregation was dismissed betwixt one and two in the morning." A year later he administered the Lord's Supper to thirty-eight tables of communicants.

The Erskines longed for more fruit upon their preaching, however. They grieved over how many of their parishioners remained unconverted, even apathetic. After thirty years of preaching in Dunfermline, Ralph Erskine wrote to his flock: "Where is the fruit that might be expected to follow thirty years of labor? Who has believed our preaching? How few among you were drawn to Christ!" When preaching about the "tabernacle of David that is fallen" (Amos 9:11), Ebenezer Erskine complained, "Oh, what barrenness and unfruitfulness is found under the preaching of the gospel!"

Those whom God greatly blesses He also tries, to keep them humble, or, as Elihu put it, to "hide pride from man" (Job 33:17). The troubles for the Erskines would come in four major waves, beginning in the early 1720s and continuing for more than two decades.

The Marrow Controversy
The first major trial, which became known as the Marrow Controversy, stirred the Scottish Church from 1717 to 1723. The controversy centered on the Auchterarder creed. In 1717, William Craig, a divinity student, complained to the General

Assembly about one of the propositions that the Presbytery of Auchterarder required all candidates for ordination to sign. The proposition, intended as a guard against preparationism, read: "I believe that it is not sound and orthodox to teach that we must forsake sin in order to our coming to Christ, and instating us in covenant with God." The Assembly sided with Craig, declaring the proposition to be "unsound and most detestable." It also said the statement tended to "encourage sloth in Christians and slacken people's obligation to gospel holiness."

The Assembly's commission somewhat softened the harshness of the General Assembly's pronouncement by stating in its report to the 1718 Assembly that the Presbytery was sound and orthodox in its intent, though the word choice was "unwarrantable" and should not to be used again. In the context of that debate, Thomas Boston told John Drummond of Crieff that he had received aid years ago on the disputed issue from a relatively unknown book titled *The Marrow of Modern Divinity*, written in 1645 by a certain Edward Fisher, who was probably a Presbyterian from London. Drummond mentioned the book to James Webster of Edinburgh, who told James Hog of Carnock about it. Hog wrote a preface for a reprinting of the book in 1718.

Fisher's book largely reflected the orthodox Reformed thought of its time, despite some Amyraldian overtones. It emphasized an offer of immediate salvation to sinners who looked to Christ in faith. This view was avidly supported by Boston and the Erskines, leaders among the Church's evangelical minority. Fisher's emphasis, however, raised the opposition of the controlling party of the Church, which contained many "neonomians" who held that the gospel is a "new law" *(neonomos)*, replacing the Old Testament law with the legal conditions of faith and repentance that must be met before salvation can be offered. These neonomians, who became known as the Moderates, maintained the necessity of forsaking sin before Christ could be received, whereas the Erskines and their evangelical friends said that only union with Christ could empower a sinner to truly forsake sin from the heart.

The Moderates considered a call to immediate trust in Christ and to assurance of faith to be dangerously antinomian *(anti*=against; *nomus*=law). An antinomian believes that the law of God is no longer the believer's rule of life. James Hadow of St.

Mary's College in St. Andrews identified a number of sup-
posedly antinomian statements in Fisher's book, including one
that he thought stated that the believer is not subject to the divine
law as a rule of life and another that seemed to suggest that holy
living was not essential to salvation. Hadow also said that the
book taught that assurance is of the essence of faith, and that the
fear of punishment and the hope of reward are not proper motives of a believer's obedience. Finally, Hadow claimed that
Fisher's book taught universal atonement because it asserted that
Christ's death was "the deed of gift and grant to mankind lost."

Led by Hadow, the General Assembly of the Church of Scotland condemned *The Marrow of Modern Divinity* in 1720 and
required all ministers of the church to warn their people against
reading it. The Erskines, Boston, and nine of their colleagues who
became known as the Marrowmen or Marrow Brethren for their
defense of Fisher's book, protested this action but without avail.
They were formally rebuked by the General Assembly in 1722.

The Marrow Controversy quieted down by 1723, but its effects lingered. The Marrow Brethren suffered continuing
rejection in the Church of Scotland. They lost many friends and
opportunities to move to more important parishes. In 1724, Ebenezer Erskine was a candidate for a call to the first charge in
Kirkcaldy but, when people opposed his candidacy because of
his participation in the Marrow controversy, the Assembly's
commission of 1725 refused to let his name stand. In some presbyteries approval of Assembly acts against Fisher's book was
even made a qualification for ordination.

The Erskines and the other Marrow Brethren, however, continued to teach and write on the doctrines the Assembly had
condemned. Thomas Boston published his copious notes on *The
Marrow of Modern Divinity* in the 1726 edition, and Ralph Erskine
wrote several tracts defending Marrow theology. The Marrow
Brethren also presented additional formal protests in a vain
effort to the Assembly to reverse its judgment on Fisher's book.

The Marrowmen were convinced that the Assembly, in condemning Fisher's book, condemned gospel truth. Doctrinally,
the controversy centered around various aspects of the relationship between God's sovereignty and human responsibility in the
work of salvation and on justification by faith alone. The Marrow Brethren emphasized God's grace, and the Assembly

insisted on what must be done to prepare oneself for grace. The Marrow Brethren described the covenant of grace as a testament containing God's promises of grace in Christ, which is freely offered to all. Assurance is found primarily in Christ and His work. A believer's response to this is love and gratitude, they said. Their opponents viewed the covenant as a contract with mutual obligations. The gospel is offered only to the prepared or "sensible" sinner and assurance focuses on the good works of the believer. Obedience is a response to threats of God's wrath as much as it is to His love.

Theological divisions in the Marrow controversy reflected similar divisions in Reformed thought. The Marrow Brethren were more in harmony with the Reformed orthodoxy of the sixteenth and early seventeenth centuries, codified in the Westminster Confession of Faith and catechisms. Marrow opponents, though representative of the majority of ministers in the early eighteenth-century Church of Scotland, reflected the legalistic tendencies of a part of Reformed theology that developed in the late seventeenth century.

Patronage and Secession
The second major trial that affected the Erskines centered around the issue of patronage. The 1731 Assembly, in dealing with an overture "concerning the Method of Planting Vacant Churches," legalized the appointment of ministers by patrons (wealthy landowners) rather than by the vote of church members. The church members called this "settlement by intrusion," for the unwelcome minister "settled" in the congregation as an "intruded" pastor. Both of the Erskines spoke out against the proposal, arguing strenuously for the right of the people to choose their ministers. Ralph Erskine refused to acquiesce in the settlement of a minister at Kinross against the will of the people, and took an active part in defending the Presbytery before the Commission for having refused to ordain the minister.

The 1732 Assembly reaffirmed support of patronage, even though the majority of presbyteries that responded had problems with it or were firmly opposed to it. In this, the Assembly violated the so-called Barrier Act of the 1697 Assembly, which protected inferior church courts from the imposition of superior church courts by stating that "before any General Assembly shall pass any Acts which are to be binding [they were] to be remitted to the consideration of the several Presbyteries [and] their opinion and consent reported to the next General Assembly." Furthermore, the 1732 Assembly refused to receive one petition signed by 2,000 people and another signed by forty-two ministers, including the Erskines, against the evils of patronage.

Ebenezer Erskine preached against the 1732 Act when he returned to his own congregation in Stirling. He also preached a strong sermon titled, "The Stone Rejected by the Builders, Exalted as the Head-Stone of the Corner," before the Synod of Perth and Stirling, which denounced the evil of patronage and the growing defections in the church in matters of doctrine and government. Erskine drew a parallel between the wicked conduct of the priests and rulers during Christ's earthly ministry and the recent transactions of the General Assembly. Though carefully worded, the sermon roused so much discussion that the Synod voted to rebuke Erskine. Synod took issue with Erskine's statement that "God's promise of guidance is given not to heritors or patrons, but to the Church as the body of Christ."

"As it is a natural privilege of every house or society of men to make the choice of its own servants or officers," Erskine said, "so it is the privilege of the house of God in a particular manner." When the 1733 Assembly supported the rebuke of the Synod, Erskine and three of his colleagues lodged a protest. The Assembly responded by insisting that the four repent of the protest. If they refused to do so, a higher censure would be passed against them.

The Assembly later that year carried out that threat by a majority of one. It suspended Erskine and three other ministers from their parishes, declared their churches vacant, and prohibited them from being employed by any Church of Scotland ministers.

The four ministers (Ebenezer Erskine, James Fisher, Alexander Moncrieff, and William Wilson) met at Gairney Bridge, near Kinross, in December 1733, where they renounced the jurisdiction of the General Assembly as it then existed, and founded the Associate Presbytery, giving birth to the Secession Church. They then drafted "A Testimony to the doctrine, worship, government, and discipline of the Church of Scotland," which set forth five reasons for the Secession:

- The prevailing party in the Church was pursuing

measures that undermined the presbyterian constitution of the Church.

- The measures adopted by the majority "do actually corrupt, or have the most direct tendency to corrupt, the doctrine contained in our excellent Confession of Faith."
- "Sinful and unwarrantable terms of ministerial communion are imposed, by restraining ministerial freedom and faithfulness in testifying against the present course of defection and backsliding."
- "These corrupt courses are carried on with a high hand, notwithstanding that the ordinary means have been used to reclaim them, and to stop the current of the present defection."
- The seceding ministers were "excluded from keeping up a proper testimony against the defections and backslidings of the prevailing party, by being denied ministerial communion with them."

Ralph Erskine, who was at the Gairney Bridge meeting, continued to fellowship and correspond with the other ministers, though he did not join the Associate Presbytery at that time. Meantime, his brother, Ebenezer, carried on his ministerial duties as if no sentence had been passed. Most people in the Presbytery of Stirling responded sympathetically to Ebenezer Erskine and felt alienated from the higher Church courts. Many ministers, including Ralph Erskine, allowed Ebenezer to preach from their pulpits.

In 1734 the General Assembly softened its stand against the suspended ministers. In 1735 it invited Ebenezer Erskine to serve again as moderator of the Presbytery of Stirling. That was "too little, too late," according to Ebenezer Erskine. After lengthy deliberations, Erskine and his three friends declined to return, stating that none of their grievances had been addressed. Moreover, several more parishes had been filled by heritors and patrons against the wishes of the people. The main issue for Erskine was honoring Christ's sole headship of the church and the sanctity of the relation between pastor and people. Erskine felt that sanctity could only be realized by Christ Himself. He differentiated between the established Church of Scotland and the Church *of Christ* in Scotland, stating that "the last is in a great measure driven into the wilderness by the first." When his colleagues pleaded with him to return to the Church of Scotland, he said they would better preserve the Lord's work and testimony if they would leave the Church as well.

After much inner conflict Ralph Erskine formally joined his brother in the Secession. He wrote in his diary on February 16, 1737, "I gave in an adherence to the Secession, explaining what I meant by it. May the Lord pity and lead."

On May 12, 1740, both of the Erskines and their colleagues were deposed by the General Assembly. The Seceders protested that they had not broken from the Church of Scotland, but only from the current prevailing party in the established Church.

Most of Ralph Erskine's congregation left the established Church with him. "I know not of seven or eight persons, among all the 8,000 examinable people of this parish, but seem to be still satisfied to subject themselves to my ministry in peace," he wrote. For nearly two years he preached one sermon each Sabbath under a tent and one sermon unmolested by civic authorities in the parish church. A new building seating 2,000 was completed in 1741. In 1742, a new minister was ordained in the parish church, all ties were broken, and several hundred people drifted back to the parish church.

In the end, fourteen of Erskine's twenty-six elders and deacons joined the Secession, five continued in the established Church, and seven stayed neutral. Ralph Erskine's church grew quickly, however. He continued to be the leading minister in the community.

Unlike Ralph, Ebenezer Erskine was immediately shut out of his church after he was deposed. Instead of letting his congregation break down the doors, Erskine began preaching outdoors. His congregation grew rapidly in the ensuing months. The Erskines became busier and busier. As they ministered to their own large churches and a variety of other parishes throughout Scotland, the Secession cause, which promoted Marrow theology, grew dramatically.

The Assembly continued to criticize the Erskines and the Seceders for making justification the goal of faith rather than Christ, and for showing disrespect to its authority. The Erskines, in turn, believed that the Assembly mistook anti-Baxterianism and anti-neonomianism for antinomianism and showed undue respect for "persons of quality" by endorsing patronage. For the Erskines, both the heart of the gospel and the biblical faithfulness of church government were at stake. Marrow theology became the hallmark of the Secession churches, which continued to grow and exert their influence in Scotland and elsewhere.

Whitefield and the Erskines

The next trial for the Erskines was their quarrel with George Whitefield. In 1739 Ralph Erskine and Whitefield began corresponding after Whitefield spoke of Erskine as "a field preacher of the Scots Church, a noble soldier of Jesus Christ, a burning and shining light who had appeared in the midnight of the Church." The two men highly respected, encouraged, and prayed for each other.

Ralph Erskine proposed that Whitefield visit Scotland and advised him how to proceed with that ministry. He said it would be best to join with the Associate Presbytery; to do otherwise would unduly comfort the Seceders' opponents. Whitefield replied that he could not do that, for he was coming as a visiting preacher to any who would hear him regardless of denominational affiliation.

On July 30, 1741, Whitefield arrived in Dunfermline, and the next day he preached for Ralph Erskine. Then the two men went into Edinburgh, where Whitefield preached at Orphan-house Park and Canongate Church. The following week Whitefield met with the Associate Presbytery at Dunfermline.

According to Whitefield's account, he and the Presbytery discussed church government and the covenant. Whitefield said that he was not interested in those subjects but only in preaching. Ralph Erskine said Whitefield should be given time to become better acquainted with those subjects since he had been reared in England and was not familiar with them. But others, who were not so charitable, argued that Whitefield should hold correct views on church government since "every pin in the tabernacle" was important. Whitefield became frustrated with the prolonged discussion on church government. He laid his hand on his heart and said, "I do not find it here." Alexander Moncrieff responded, rapping on an open Bible, "But I find it here."

Whitefield asked what the Presbytery wanted him to do. He was told that he didn't have to subscribe to the covenant immediately but to preach only for them until he had further light.

"Why preach only for you?" Whitefield asked. Ralph Erskine's answer, according to Whitefield, was "We are the Lord's people." Whitefield then said that if others were the devil's people, he had more need to go to them. The meeting was adjourned.

Whitefield's account was based on misunderstanding. Whitefield apparently attributed to Erskine what was said by someone else. Erskine sought to right the injustice the next Sunday by condemning an opinion he had heard that "none have Christ's image who have not just our image." Moreover, in a letter to Whitefield that Erskine wrote ten days later, he said: "Your refusing a close communing on this head [of church government and covenant] seemed to me so far unlike the disposition which our former correspondence made me think you were of, that I was willing to ascribe it rather to the hurry of temptation for the time, amidst the ringing of bells for sermon, and some rash words uttered in your hearing, than to any contrary bias that now you have got." Erskine went on to express anxiety that Whitefield might gain such a wrong impression of the Secession so as to be lost to them. He also congratulated Whitefield on the welcome he was receiving and on the liberality shown towards his burden for orphanages.

Whitefield continued to associate with the ministers of the established Church, however, so the break with the Associate Presbytery was inevitable. Both condemned each other. Ralph Erskine even went public with his stinging criticism. In *Faith No Fancy* and *Fraud and Falsehood Discovered*, Erskine denounced the Cambuslang Revival, calling its emotionalism the devil's work and Whitefield the devil's agent. Whitefield, in response, accused the Erskines of "building a Babel." He wrote to Gilbert Tennent, "The associate brethren are much to be blamed; I never met with such narrow spirits."

Though tension was high for a time, the Erskines and Whitefield later reached a peaceable accord of sorts. Whitefield later wrote in his *Journal*, "I have met and shaken hands with Mr. Ralph Erskine. Oh when will God's people learn war no more!" The following year, when Ralph Erskine died, Whitefield cited him in a sermon as one of "God's triumphant saints."

The Burgher Conflict
The last major trial for the Erskines involved the so-called Burgher conflict. This proved to be more heart-breaking and bit-

ter than any previous dispute. The Burgess Oath of 1744 was required of all citizens of Edinburgh, Glasgow, and Perth. The oath stated, "Here I protest before God, and your lordships, that I profess, and allow with my heart, the true religion presently professed within this realm, and authorized by the laws thereof: I shall abide thereat, and defend the same to my life's end; renouncing the Roman religion called papistry."

The oath was important because only burgesses (duly acknowledged citizens of these cities or boroughs) were permitted to vote, engage in commerce, or belong to a trade guild. Some members of the Associate Synod (the Seceders) objected to the oath, saying it endorsed the established Church. Others, including the Erskine brothers, regarded the oath as an approbation of the Reformed faith, intended only to exclude Roman Catholics from becoming burgesses. The Erskines affirmed the right to take the burgess oath, believing that an antiburgher position would lead to the abandonment of civic and political duty. Ralph Erskine wrote a greater number of pamphlets than any other member of the Burgher Synod in defense of this position.

After three years of synodical meetings, the issue split the young denomination. Twenty-three church leaders of the Antiburgher party, under the leadership of Adam Gib and Alexander Moncrieff, constituted themselves as the Antiburgher Synod, avowing that they were the rightful continuation of the Secession. Gib and Moncrieff were godly and conscientious men, but at times overly zealous in their conservatism. As one of Moncrieff's children put it, "Father hates everything new except the New Testament."

What made the split particularly heart-breaking for Ralph Erskine was that his son John sided with the Antiburghers and even participated in their Synod's decision to excommunicate the Erskines along with other members of the Burgher Synod. The Antiburgher Synod declared that the Erskines should be "holden by the faithful as heathen men and publicans."

Excommunication prompted Ralph Erskine to do some serious soul-searching, particularly on how the Seceders had behaved toward those left behind in the Church of Scotland. In examining how God must be regarding this new denominational split, Erskine admitted "untenderness towards those we left in the judicatories, when we made secession from them, without dealing more kindly with them, praying more for them, and bearing more with them, especially such as were friends to the same Reformation cause, though not enlightened in the same manner of witnessing for it."

That kind of soul-searching bore fruit. In the years following the controversy, the Burgher Synod redefined its position in a revised Testimony, gradually dropped the practice of covenanting, and resumed friendly relations with evangelical ministers in the established Church. When John Willison of Dundee (1680-1750), an influential Church of Scotland minister and author, was dying, Ralph Erskine was with him. A woman tried to revive the old quarrel by saying there would be no Secession in heaven, but Erskine would have no part of it. "Madam, in heaven there will be a complete Secession — from sin and sorrow," he said. Willison nodded assent.

The Work Goes On
Though the Erskines were deeply affected by controversy, that was not a priority for them. Their work centered on establishing congregations, winning souls, and training young ministers. When Alexander Moncrieff joined the Antiburgher Synod, Ebenezer Erskine was asked to teach divinity for the Burgher Synod, but served in that capacity only until 1749 when he resigned for health reasons. Ralph Erskine spent more time training men for the ministry. His vision of the ministry is compelling. Typical of his views are the comments he made on Luke 14:23 relative to the evangelistic work of ministers:

> Their work is not only driving work, while they preach the law as the schoolmaster to lead to Christ; but it is also drawing work, while they preach the Gospel of Christ, who was lifted up to draw men to Him by His love and grace. Their work is winning work, seeking to win souls to Christ, compelling them to come in; and their work is filling work, that their Master's house may be filled; and that every corner, every seat, every chamber, every story of His house may be filled. As long as the gospel is preached, His house is filling; and as long as there is room in His house, there is work for the minister; his work is never over, so long as His Master's house is empty; compel them to come in, that my house may be filled.

In the autumn of 1752 Ralph Erskine's wife begged him to slow down and spend more time with the family, for he was now sixty-seven years old. He promised to do so, but in October he became convinced that his work was nearing an end and that he should prepare to depart in peace. The following month he became very ill. His last sermon was on the text, "All her paths are peace." He was so weak that most of his death-bed words were difficult to understand, but people near him heard him say: "I will be forever a debtor to free grace." His final words were unmistakably clear. He shouted for all to hear, "Victory, victory, victory!"

When Ebenezer Erskine heard of his brother's death, he said quietly, "He has twice got the start of me; he was first in Christ, and now he is first in glory."

Ebenezer Erskine would soon follow. Because of his frail health Erskine had already ordained his nephew James Fisher as his sucessor in January 1752. The Sabbath after his brother's departure, Erskine struggled out of bed to preach his last sermon. His text was, "I know that my Redeemer liveth" (Job 19:25).

Erskine lived eighteen months longer. As death became imminent, one of his elders asked him, "Sir, you have given us many good advices; may I ask what you are now doing with your own soul?" Erskine replied, "I am just doing with it what I did forty years ago; I am resting on that word, 'I am the Lord thy God.'"

When a friend asked him if he, like Samuel Rutherford, was now and then receiving a *blink* (a brief glance from Christ) to bear him up in pain, Erskine said, "I know more of words than blinks: 'Though He slay me, yet will I *trust* in Him.'" He went on to say, "The covenant is my charter. If it had not been for the blessed Word, my hope and strength had perished from the Lord. I have known more of God since I came to this bed than through all my life."

Erskine's last words were to his daughter. When he asked what she was reading, she said, "Your sermon on 'I am the Lord thy God.'"

"Oh," he said, "that is the best sermon ever I preached." With that, he passed into the presence of the Lord his God. He died on June 1, 1754, at the age of seventy-three, after nearly fifty-one faithful years in the ministry and twenty years of guiding town affairs in Stirling.

Lessons for Today
The lives of the Erskines have many lessons for us:

1. The value of cultivating a growing relationship with God. In all the busyness of their ministries, the Erskines did not forget to seek nourishment for their own spiritual lives. They prayed morning, noon, and evening. Ralph Erskine made it his practice to read a portion of Scripture, often on his knees, before every private prayer. On occasion he would appoint a special day for prayer or humiliation in his family, keeping his children home from school on those days. The family would pray, talk, and walk together, and he would speak with them about the gospel and the ways of God with His people.

The Erskines radiated warm, experiential, Christ-centered Christianity. That was the heartbeat of their ministry. Their diaries show that there was no disparity between their personal relationship with God and the message they proclaimed. They lived in obedience to Paul's injunction to Timothy, "Take heed unto thyself and unto the doctrine; continue in them: for in doing this thou shalt both save thyself, and them that hear thee" (1 Tim. 4:16).

Will others also say of us that there is no disparity between our lips and our lives, between the doctrine we profess and the doctrine we act out in our daily lives? Scripture clearly assumes a cause-and-effect relationship between the character of a Christian's life and the fruitfulness of his life. That is particularly true for those of us who are ministers. We as ministers must seek grace to build the house of God with two hands — the hand of sound preaching and doctrine and the hand of a sanctified heart.

Ebenezer Erskine once said: "The ministers of the gospel, when dispensing the truths of God, must preach home to their own souls as well as to others; and truly it can never be expected that we should apply the truth with any warmth or liveliness to others unless we make a warm application thereof to our souls. And if we do not feed upon these doctrines, and practice the duties which we deliver to you, though we preach to others, we ourselves are but castaways."

Our sermons will not be dry or insipid if they are infused with the freshness of our own growing relationship with God. Let us never forget that we preach most when we live best. Our ministry is as our heart is. No minister rises much above the level of his own habitual godliness. John Owen put it negatively: "If a man teach uprightly and walk crookedly, more will fall down in the night of his life than he built in the day of his doctrine."

Perhaps Robert Murray M'Cheyne said it best, "A minister's life is the life of his ministry.... In great measure, according to the purity and perfections of the instrument will be the success. It is not great talents that God blesses so much as likeness to Jesus. A holy minister is an awful weapon in the hand of God."

2. *The way Christians should endure hardship.* The Erskines endured much tribulation before they entered into glory. In addition to the religious controversies that dampened their joy in ministry for twenty-five years, they endured much domestic grief. Ebenezer Erskine buried his first wife when she was thirty-nine; his second wife, three years before his own death. He also lost six of fifteen children. Ralph Erskine buried his first wife when she was thirty-two and nine of thirteen children. The three sons who reached maturity all entered the ministry, but one helped to depose his own father.

The Erskines well understood the adage that "God has only one Son without sin but none without affliction." Their diaries are filled with Christ-centered submission in the midst of affliction. Here is what Ebenezer Erskine wrote when his first wife was on her deathbed and he had just buried two children:

> I have had the rod of God laying upon my family by the great distress of a dear wife, on whom the Lord hath laid his hand, and on whom his hand doth still lie heavy. But O that I could proclaim the praises of his free grace, which has paid me a new and undeserved visit this day. He has been with me both in secret and public. I found the sweet smells of the Rose of Sharon, and my soul was refreshed with a new sight of him in the excellency of his person as Immanuel, and in the sufficiency of his everlasting righteousness. My sinking hopes are revived by the sight of him. My bonds are loosed, and my burdens of affliction made light, when he appears.... "Here am I, let him do to me as seemeth good unto him." If he call me to go down to the swellings of Jordan, why not, if it be his holy will? Only be with me, Lord, and let thy rod and staff comfort me, and then I shall not fear to go through the valley of trouble, yea, through the valley of the shadow of death.

We have much need to learn how to profit from affliction.

We need affliction to humble us (Deut. 8:2), to teach us what sin is (Zeph. 1:12), and to bring us to God (Hosea 5:15). "Affliction is the diamond dust that heaven polishes its jewels with," wrote Robert Leighton. Let us view God's rod of affliction as His means to write Christ's image more fully upon us so that we may be partakers of His righteousness and holiness (Heb. 12:10-11). Let our afflictions move us to walk by faith and to wean us from the world. As Thomas Watson wrote, "God would have the world hang as a loose tooth which, being twitched away, does not much trouble us." May we, like the Erskines, allow affliction to elevate our souls to heaven and pave our way to glory (2 Cor. 4:7).

3. *The importance of Christ's rule over His church.* Today, patronage no longer rules in most church circles. But do we really wish Christ to rule in the church? Do we wish for unanimity in our churches *in Christ,* or is Christ's rule impeded by church politics? Do some congregations exalt their ministers into a position that only Christ should occupy — and do not some ministers enjoy such treatment? Do some elders think they have been called to run the church as *they* think best without asking what Christ thinks best? And do many people in a congregation vote for office-bearers according to worldly standards rather than according to the criteria stated by Paul in 1 Timothy 3 and Titus 1?

What about the relationship between the minister and his congregation — is it not violated by search committees and congregations who seek to satisfy human expectations rather than God's? Are too many churches today disregarding the need for *God* to send a particular minister to their congregation? Have we lost sight of the supremacy of Christ in calling and sending His ambassadors to whomsoever *He* will?

4. *The value of conducting regular family visitation, catechetical training, and prayer meetings.* It was Ralph Erskine's custom, together with his colleague, to visit every home in his parish of 5,000 people once a year for spiritual examination and instruction. He also taught catechism to young children every week and wrote a catechism for their use. The catechism was direct and personal. It began with these questions: "Are you so young that you may not be sick and die? Are you so young that you may not go to hell?" He also encouraged fellowship meetings for prayer and fellowship.

Ebenezer Erskine had the same pastoral concerns. At Portmoak he met with the children of the parish each Sabbath to instruct them in the catechism as well as the day's sermons. He raised the standards of the parish school and started prayer meetings in various parts of the parish. In 1714 he wrote guidelines for praying societies that all members were expected to observe. During his many pastoral visitations, he began by saying, "Peace be to this house," then proceeded to question the adults about their spiritual condition. He also examined and encouraged the children. He closed with warm and affectionate prayer.

Do we who are ministers show such devotion to our flocks? Do we realize the value of habitual family visitation — often called "soul visitation" by our forefathers — to meet individually with members of our congregation? Richard Baxter came to the painful conclusion that "some ignorant persons, who have been so long unprofitable hearers, have got more knowledge and remorse of conscience in half an hour of close [private] disclosure, than they did from ten years of public preaching." Do we keep our hearts and homes open for people who may need opportunity for such disclosure?

Do we, like the Erskines, use the catechism to examine our parishioners' spiritual condition and to encourage them to flee to Christ? When we teach the young, do we, like the Erskines, explain the fundamental teachings of the Bible and urge young people to commit the Bible to memory? Do we make sermons and the sacraments more understandable to prepare covenant children for confession of faith and to teach them how to defend their faith against error?

Do we encourage our people to meet regularly for prayer? Do we lead them in those meetings, patiently guiding them to deeper levels of prayer and supplication?

Let us carry on our pastoral work patiently, not looking for quick and easy conversions with people. Rather, like the Erskines, we should be committed to build up believers so their hearts, minds, and souls are won to the service of Christ.

5. The importance of Christlike thinking in controversy. The Reformers often advised: "In essentials, unity; in non-essentials, liberty; and in all things, charity." During the Marrow and patronage controversies, the Erskines defended the gospel heroically, but at times an uncharitable, sectarian attitude crept into that defense.

Surely there was fault on both sides of the Whitefield-Erskine conflict. It was difficult for the Seceders, who had developed strong views of church government during their conflict with the General Assembly, to tolerate Whitefield's lack of concern for church government. Whitefield's biographer, Erasmus Middleton, even recognized that in Whitefield. He wrote, "Most certainly, he did not care for all the outward church government in the world, if men were not brought really to the knowledge of God and themselves. Prelacy and presbytery were indeed matters of indifference to a man, who wished 'the whole world to be his diocese' and that men of all denominations might be brought to a real acquaintance with Jesus Christ."

Sadly, in campaigning for their own right to dissent, the Erskines refused Episcopalian dissenters the same right. In denouncing the prevailing evils, the Seceders lost a measure of propriety. Their zeal at times ran ahead of their charity and their understanding. They certainly failed to distinguish essentials from non-essentials in the Associate Presbytery's official tract of 138 pages listing the Church of Scotland's sins in 1744. The tract included the statement: "The sins and provocations of this land are further increased by the kind reception that many, both ministers and people, have given Mr. George Whitefield, a professed member and priest of the superstitious Church of England; and by the great entertainment that has been given to latitudinarian tenets, as propagated by him and others; whereby any particular form of church government is denied to be of divine institution." In the heat of debate, these men forgot John Howe's warning that "the main inlet of all the distractions, confusions and divisions of the Christian world hath been by adding other conditions of Church communion than Christ hath done."

On the other hand, Whitefield showed little sensitivity for the difficulties that the Erskines were experiencing in the Church. By moving back and forth from Seceder to established Church, Whitefield added to the pain of pastors and congregations who had recently separated from each other, no matter how ill-advised the Seceders may have been to "unchurch" the Church of Scotland. The Seceders had been maligned and wounded in the house of friends. They experienced the profound cost of holding to their principles. They had stood against a disorderly church government that threatened the pure preach-

ing of the Word and they had lost much in the process.
Whitefield did not understand the ecclesiastical battles of the
Erskines against the growing evil of Moderatism that was casting spiritual death over the established Church. To his credit,
Whitefield acknowledged that the Erskines were more charitable
in their opposition to him than most of their colleagues. Whitefield wrote to one of Ebenezer Erskine's sons, "I wish all [the
ministers of the Associate Presbytery] were like-minded with
your honoured father and uncle; matters then would not be carried on with so high an hand."

Let us attempt to take the high road in church conflicts — the
road of principle that defends confessional fidelity and purity of
worship and polity *with Christlike charity*. It is not Christlike to see
only the worst faults of our opponents. True humility magnifies
our own flaws and diminishes the sins of others. Let us pray for
love that covers a multitude of sins as we stand for the essentials
of the faith.

We must avoid two extremes. The call to unity and charity in
Christ should help us avoid the kind of denominationalism pro-
duced by splits over non-essential doctrines and mere egotism.
Such splits violate the unity of the body of Christ. As Samuel
Rutherford warned, "It is a fearful sin to make a rent and a hole
in Christ's mystical body because there is a spot in it." Such dis-
unity offends the Father who longs to see His family living in
harmony; it offends the Son who died to break down walls of
hostility; and it offends the Spirit who dwells within believers to
help them live in unity.

On the other hand, the church should avoid any call to unity
that would tamper with her confessions of faith and disregard
purity of worship. Some divisions are essential to keep the true
church separate from the false. "Division is better than agreement
in evil," George Hutcheson once said. Those who support spuri-
ous unity by tolerating heresy forget that a split based on biblical
essentials helps to preserve the true unity of the body of Christ.

In the final analysis, the Erskines were dissenters with a
cause. They challenge us, for the most part, to better things.
They challenge us to consider Christ in all our afflictions. They
challenge us to crown the Redeemer as Head of the church and
to have a high view of the calling of the ministry. They challenge
us to pursue intimate acquaintance with God. We would do well

to make Ebenezer Erskine's personal covenant our own: "I will live to Christ; I will die to Him; I will quit with all I have in the world for His cause and truth." But perhaps most of all, they challenge us to proclaim and live a rich gospel message centered on the promises of God in Jesus Christ. The Erskines were pre-eminently preachers of the promises.

Preachers With a Message of Promise

When Samuel M'Millan published *The Beauties of Ralph Erskine* in 1812, followed by *The Beauties of Ebenezer Erskine* in 1830, he was not thinking of the faces of those great Scottish divines but of the spiritual gems in their Christ-centered sermons. The three volumes of Ebenezer Erskine's sermons and the six volumes of Ralph Erskine's sermons, together with Ralph's volume of *Gospel Sonnets,* profoundly influenced ministers and lay people of the Reformed faith in several countries. We are grateful for the reprinting of Ralph Erskine's sermons by Free Presbyterian Publications in 1991, and anticipate that Ebenezer Erskine's sermons will be reprinted as well. These sermons deserve a new hearing.

After showing how influential the preaching and writing of the Erskine brothers have been over the years, I will then offer highlights of their preaching derived from its major emphasis: God's promises in the gospel to sinners.

Influence in Scotland

The preaching and writings of the Erskines affected tens of thousands of people in Scotland for more than a century. Their preaching gave direction to the Secession movement. It assimilated and passed on the essence of Marrow theology to subsequent generations. Ebenezer Erskine's sermons, first printed as *Whole Works* in Edinburgh in 1761, were reprinted six more times in Scotland. Ralph Erskine's writings, first published in 1764, were reprinted four times in Scotland, and his *Gospel Sonnets* forty times in the eighteenth century. Scottish preacher William Taylor of New York, who lectured at Yale in 1886 on the history of Scottish preaching, recalled that the poems of Ralph Erskine were recited at communion celebrations when he was young. John Ker wrote in 1887 that the sermons of the Erskines were scattered throughout Scotland "in almost every farmhouse and cottage where there was an interest in religion."

The Free Church of Scotland was also influenced by the Erskines. George Smeaton, an eminent Free Church scholar, warmly introduced a reprinting of *The Beauties of Ralph Erskine*. Robert Candlish, a leading preacher in the Free Church, recommended reading the Erskines, as did the Free Church minister and theologian Hugh Martin, who wrote in 1875 that the Erskines were still loved by the Scottish people.

Influence in England, Wales, and Ireland
In England men of such stature as George Whitefield, Augustus Toplady, and James Hervey lauded the Erskines for preaching the gospel freely without sacrificing experimental depth. Hervey kept a copy of *Gospel Sonnets* on his desk for study until the end of his life. One of Hervey's last tasks was to dictate a preface to a new edition. In that preface he wrote that he had found in his lifetime no human works "more evangelical, more comfortable, or more useful" than those of Ralph Erskine. Dutch scholar P. H. van Harten, who wrote his doctoral dissertation on the preaching of Ebenezer and Ralph Erskine, said the writings of the Erskines helped strengthen Reformed thinking in and beyond the Church of England. Ralph Erskine's literary works were so treasured that as late as 1879 they were still selling well in London.

Many of the sermons of the Erskines as well as the *Gospel Sonnets* were translated into Welsh. Those writings helped shape the preaching of two eighteenth-century Welsh preachers, Howell Harris and Daniel Rowland, whose messages were instrumental in the conversion of thousands. The Calvinistic Methodists of Wales "read, borrowed, translated, used and commended the Erskine brothers," wrote Eifion Evans. The Erskines influenced people in Ireland as well, particularly through the ministries of John Erskine, Ralph Erskine's son, and James Fisher, Ebenezer Erskine's son-in-law, who labored there for some years.

Influence in The Netherlands and America
From 1740 on, the writings of the Erskines were translated into Dutch and received a ready welcome throughout the Netherlands. On a typical eighteenth-century market day in Rotterdam, farmers inquired at bookstalls for sermons of "Erskeyna," as they pronounced it. Alexander Comrie and Theodorus Van der Groe, two great leaders of the *Nadere Reformatie* (the Dutch variant of sev-

enteenth and eighteenth-century pietism, usually translated as Dutch Second Reformation), were greatly influenced by the Erskines. Comrie was catechized by both Erskines as a boy and later referred to Ralph Erskine as "my faithful old friend, whom God used as the guide of my youth." Van der Groe introduced several translated books of the Erskines, though he had a more restricted view of the promises of God than the Erskines. By the time of Van der Groe's death in 1784, the sermons of the Erskines were outselling those of any other Scottish or English divine in the Netherlands.

In the 1830s Hendrik Scholte, a well-known Dutch Secession leader who helped establish the Christian Reformed Church in America, published a number of Ralph Erskine's sermons. In the mid-nineteenth century volumes of the Erskines' sermons were published three times, finding a ready market among Dutch Reformed Church believers as well as among those who had seceded. Among the Seceders those who approved of the sermons of the Erskines defended an unconditional, free offer of grace; those who opposed the sermons judged them to be tainted by Arminianism. In 1904 Herman Bavinck, prominent Dutch theologian and professor at Kampen and the Free University of Amsterdam, wrote a largely commendatory foreword to a compilation of Ebenezer and Ralph Erskine's sermons. He wrote that their sermons contained a biblical, "spiritual psychology lacking in our day." He then added perhaps the harshest word he ever wrote: "It seems that we no longer know what sin and grace, guilt and forgiveness, regeneration and conversion are."

Throughout the twentieth century the writings of the Erskines have been reprinted frequently in the Netherlands. They continue to prompt discussion in Dutch Reformed circles, particularly in subjects such as how to preach grace to the unsaved and how to teach people about God's promises.

In America, the ministry of the Erskines bore considerable fruit. Converts of the Great Awakening became avid readers of the Erskines. Jonathan Edwards recommended the *Gospel Sonnets* in a letter to James Robe in Kilsyth. About 30,000 copies of the Erskine-Fisher *Catechism* for children were sold in America by the Presbyterian Board of Publications in Philadelphia. John Mason, Scottish preacher in New York and leader in the Associate Reformed Presbyterian Church, which he helped establish, was nourished by the Erskines.

Ecclesiastical Influence

The body founded by the Erskines and their colleagues quickly grew in size. What began as the Associate Presbytery soon became the Associate Synod. Congregations were established in many parts of Scotland and then in Northern Ireland. The Secession churches remained a factor in Scottish Church life until well into this century.

From these two homelands members of the Associate Church, sometimes called the Secession Church, and its people, the Seceders, migrated to the new world. Their influence was felt in many places. Some Associate Presbyterians held steadfastly to their own course, and as late as the 1960s there were some remaining Associate Presbyterian (AP) congregations which finally united with the Reformed Presbyterian Churches in North America (RPCNA) at the end of that decade.

Other Associate Presbyterians joined forces with Reformed Presbyterians at an early point to form the Associate Reformed Presbyterian Church (ARPC) in 1782. The Synod of the South separated from the main body in the 1820s, and continues as the present day ARP Church. The ARPs founded a college in 1837, and later a seminary (1857) in Due West, South Carolina, named in honor of the Erskine brothers.

In 1858, the ARPs in the North joined forces with the largest part of the remaining APs to form the United Presbyterian Church of North America (UPCNA). For one hundred years this small but vital denomination spread over the country, establishing churches, schools, colleges, seminaries and other institutions, as well as supporting a vigorous foreign missions program. The UPs were prominent in the cause of abolition before the Civil War, and in missions among the freedmen afterwards. For many years the UPs adhered to exclusive Psalmody, and took the lead in producing *The Psalter* of 1912, still used today in many Reformed churches.

The influence of the Associate Presbyterians was a potent factor in the history of Christianity in Canada as well. They were the first preachers on the field in many parts of Ontario and the Maritime Provinces. They were leaders in the union movement which gave birth to the Presbyterian Church in Canada in 1872.

The missionary work of the ARPs and UPs led to the planting of the ARP Church of Pakistan, the UP Church of Pakistan,

the United Evangelical Church of Egypt, and the ARP Church of
Mexico. Churches were also planted in Ethiopia and the Sudan.

Prominent AP, ARP, and UP scholars and writers include
such men as Jay Adams, John Anderson, Thomas Beveridge,
John Brown of Haddington, John Dick, John Eadie, James Fisher,
John Gerstner, James Harper, James Hog, James Kelso, John Ker,
Melvin Kyle, George Lawson, Addison Leitch, John Mitchell Ma-
son, John McNaugher, William Moorehead, James Orr, John T.
Pressly, and G.I. Williamson. Presbyterians such as Andrew
Blackwood, John Leith, Robert McQuilkin, James R. Miller, and
John Calvin Reid were UPs or ARPs by birth and upbringing.

Why have the Erskines been so influential? Why are they
still important for us to read today? Answers to these questions
should become clear as we examine the content of Ebenezer and
Ralph Erskine's sermons.

Two as One
In a sense the sermons of Ebenezer and Ralph Erskine could
have been written by the same hand. The brothers differed, of
course. Ebenezer's gifts were not as striking as Ralph's, but Ebenezer had a calm, sure strength that made him a better leader.
Ebenezer preached in a more stately style than his brother but
with less eloquence. Ralph was more self-effacing, more devout,
and more experimental than his brother, and looked more to the
Puritans for guidance. Nevertheless, the substance and spirit of
their sermons are so similar — and remained so throughout
their careers — that they may be examined together without
causing a disservice to either.

Exegesis and Homiletics
The Erskines leaned on the Reformers and Puritans for exegetical help. Luther and Calvin were their favorite commentators
among the Reformers, James Durham and Matthew Henry
among the Puritans. Some scholars have criticized the Erskines
for focusing more on the doctrines flowing out of a text than on
the exegesis of a text, wandering at times beyond the boundaries
of the text so that they lost its original intent. More commonly,
however, the Erskines showed considerable exegetical skill in
their sermons, particularly in expounding texts about salvation
in Jesus Christ.

Homiletically the Erskines followed the Puritan "plain" style
of preaching (cf. Westminster's *Directory for Public Worship* on "Of

the Preaching of the Word"). This style of preaching, according to William Perkins, did three things:

1. It gave the basic meaning of a text of Scripture within its context;

2. It explained points of doctrine gathered from the natural sense of the text;

3. It applied the doctrines "rightly collected to the life and manners of men."

The first part of an Erskine sermon was thus exegetical, usually providing a short analysis of the text; the second, doctrinal, stating and expounding some doctrine or "observation"; and the third, applicatory. The Erskines usually divided the third part, often referred to as the "uses" of doctrine derived from a text, into sections such as information, trial (self-examination), comfort, exhortation, and advice. For example, in a sermon titled "Present Duty Before Approaching Darkness," based on Jeremiah 13:16 ("Give glory to the Lord your God, before he cause darkness"), Ralph Erskine offered six points of information, two points of self-examination, five points of exhortation, and six points of advice. Because of the nature of the text, no section was offered for comfort.

This homiletical method often led to a lengthy series of sermons on one text. For example, Ralph Erskine delivered fourteen sermons on prayer based on Romans 12:12; thirteen sermons on Christian living based on Colossians 2:6; nine sermons on self-conceit based on Proverbs 30:12; and eight sermons on "The Happy Congregation" based on Genesis 49:10.

The Erskine sermons were a combination of doctrinal and experimental exposition. Doctrinally they focused on the great, central themes of Christianity: the person and work of Christ, sin and salvation, faith and hope, and God's grace. Experimentally they dealt with such matters as comfort, assurance, assistance in trials, and the privileges of being a Christian.

Centered on the Promises

The Erskines are best-known for sermons that focus on the promises of God. That was in keeping with Scottish tradition. For example, The Scots Confession of 1560 spoke of an "assured faith in the promises of God." Writings such as George Hutcheson's *Exposition of the XII Small Prophets*, Andrew Gray's *Great and Precious Promises*, and Thomas Halyburton's *Great Concern of Sal-*

vation made much of God's promises. "God binds Himself to us with His promises," Halyburton had written.

But the Erskines emphasized the promises even more than those writers. "What is the gospel but a word of promise?" Ebenezer Erskine asked (*The Whole Works of Ebenezer Erskine*, vol. 1, p. 262; hereafter 1:262). "Take away the promise out of the Bible," wrote Ralph Erskine, "and you take away the gospel" (*The Sermons and Other Practical Works of Ralph Erskine*, vol. 5, p. 118; hereafter 5:118), for "the gospel and the promise is one and the same thing" (5:235).

The Erskines never tired of preaching on the promises of Scripture. Ralph Erskine wrote, "I will look to the promise, and lay stress upon it, and upon a God that promises" (5:236). They found promises everywhere in the Bible, even in texts such as John 17:17, which says, "Sanctify them through thy truth; thy word is truth" (5:103). As Ebenezer Erskine wrote, "All the histories, prophecies and shadows, and types of the Word — what are they but an opening and an exposition of the promises?" (1:512).

Let us consider now how this centering on God's promises impacted the theology of the Erskines at a number of key doctrinal points.

1. Eternal Promises
The Erskines preached about promises spanning from eternity past to eternity future. Ebenezer Erskine defined God's promises as the "revelation of His counsel and purpose of grace before the world began" (1:431). Ralph Erskine personalized that, saying God's promises are a "revelation of His grace and good-will to sinners in Christ" (5:192).

All of God's promises proceed from an act of His sovereign will. "Hence, all the promises of the new covenant are so many *I wills*," said Ralph Erskine. "'I will be your God; I will take away the heart of stone; I will put my Spirit within you'" (5:375). From God's eternal perspective, those promises may only be claimed by the elect; but from man's perspective, they must be preached to all men, for whoever responds to the promises in faith will become recipients of them. The promises are *made* to the elect but are *endorsed* or *directed* to all "who hear the gospel, with their seed," the Erskines said. Every hearer has *the right of access* to the promises, therefore, but only the elect have *the right of possession*.

They alone will embrace the promises of God by faith (*Exposition of the Shorter Catechism,* Questions 81-84 on Question 20).

The God who makes promises from eternity also fulfills them in time. "God is not a speaker only, but a doer," wrote Ralph Erskine (2:308), "giving a being [or existence] to His promises" (5:382) in this life through His Word. The Erskines were fond of quoting Romans 10:6-8, stressing that sinners do not have to ascend into heaven to lay hold of the promises because the Word is near us, even in our mouth and heart (EE, 1:435-36; RE, 5:278). Ralph Erskine illustrated that by saying that as water flows from a distant source to a city by water mains and is brought so close to people's mouths that they can drink it from a faucet, so the water of life flows from the triune God as the fountainhead in heaven through the pipes of His promises in gospel preaching right to our mouths (5:278).

The nearness of God's promises eliminates any excuse for unbelief. In his sermon on John 3:18 ("Unbelief Arraigned and Condemned at the Bar of God"), Ebenezer Erskine said, "I am convinced that if sinners would know how closely Christ is brought to us by the gospel in the salvation He has wrought, there would not be so many unbelieving sinners among us" (1:358).

The promise endures into the future. The glorified Christ is God's eternal promise for now and the future, for He has ascended and will reign forever. Heaven is where God's promise will reach full perfection (RE, 2:519ff).

2. The Gospel as Promise

The promises of God are a means of salvation, the Erskines taught. Since the promise and the gospel coincide, the promise is as much a power of God unto salvation as is the gospel. Ralph Erskine explained this in his sermons on Galatians 4:28, titled "The Pregnant Promise." He said just as Isaac was born more of the power of promise than of nature, so believers are "children of promise" through God's eternal promise in Christ (5:96). God's "powerful and prolific promise" is thus the channel of saving power (5:108). In God's mind, spiritual conception took place in eternity, since the elect were Christ's seed promised to Him in the Counsel of Peace (Is. 53:10), but spiritual birth takes place in time. The pregnant womb of God's promise, which can never be aborted, is opened in the hour of regeneration by His own power. While God's pleasure is the ultimate, "moving cause" of that new birth, the promise of God is its means — the "instrumental cause."

3. Promises in Christ

The promises are inseparable from Jesus Christ, the Erskines taught. The promises were made to Christ in the Counsel of Peace, but He is also their content. Ralph Erskine illustrated the relation of Christ to the promises by saying the promise is like a cup, but Christ is the drink held by the cup. Faith doesn't just take hold of the cup of promise and look into it; it is satisfied only when it drinks Christ. Similarly, a nursing child is not satisfied with the breasts of a mother, only with the milk drawn from those breasts. So, too, a believer is not satisfied with the promises until he drinks freely of the milk of those promises, which is Jesus Christ and Him crucified (5:212).

Sipping the cup of Christ by Spirit-worked faith enlightens the mind and moves the will to seek more after Christ, Ralph Erskine said (1:126). The glory of Christ fills the soul as Christ appears in all His beauty as Savior and Lord. Natural enmity is broken; the will and affections are renewed, and the sinner cries out that Christ is altogether lovely, the chief among ten thousand.

The Erskines' preaching was thus, in keeping with pristine Reformation preaching, thoroughly Christ-centered. Preaching for them was "the chariot that carries Christ up and down the world," as Richard Sibbes wrote. "Christ is the Head, and centre of all gospel-truth, and we ought to hold by the Head; and so we shall hold by the truth," Ralph Erskine proclaimed (4:491). Elsewhere he said, "Whatever manifold articles of truth there be, yet truth itself is but one; and Christ the centre is but one" (4:246).

The Bible is a wellspring for preaching Christ, the Erskines believed. To be Word-centered and Christ-centered are synonymous since the Word proclaims Christ and Christ proclaims the Word. As Ebenezer Erskine said to his congregation: "All prophecies, promises, histories, and doctrines of the Word point us to Him, as the needle in the mariner's compass points to the pole-star.... Our preaching, and your hearing, is in vain, unless we bring you to the knowledge of Christ and an acquaintance with Him.... All the lines of religion meet in Him as their centre" (2:7-8).

The Erskines presented Christ in His ability and willingness to save, and preciousness as the Redeemer of lost sinners.

Preaching Christ with theological articulation, divine grandeur, and winsome passion was their greatest burden and most essential task. They chose texts to preach on from the Old and New Testament that centered on Christ and the gospel (RE, 5:88). They believed that every text led to Christ, either directly or indirectly, but it was the minister's responsibility to focus on texts most full of Christ, for "the more of Christ [there] be in any text, the more marrow and fatness, the more savour and sweetness, will be in [the sermon] to the soul that knows Him," Ebenezer Erskine wrote (2:8).

4. Promises of the Father and the Spirit

The promises are also inseparable from the Father and the Holy Spirit, the Erskines taught. For in Christ, God Himself comes to us as the Triune Redeemer, declaring "I am the LORD thy God." In such promises, the Father gives Himself with all of His divine attributes to save and help us. But so does the Spirit, for Christ promised to send the Spirit to believers to abide with them (John 16:7; RE, 5:101).

Notwithstanding their christocentricity, the Erskines were not christomonistic. They devoted considerable attention to the person and work of the Father, whose attributes are represented in Christ; and to the presence and work of the Holy Spirit, through whom Christ works out in sinners what He has merited for them. They extolled the Triune God and abased man the sinner. They did not worry about injuring the self-esteem of their listeners in the process, for they were far more concerned about esteeming the Triune God: the Father who created us in His image, the Son who restores that dignity to us through redemption and adoption, and the Holy Spirit who indwells us and makes us His temple. The Erskines would have viewed messages that build up self-esteem rather than center upon the Triune God as messages of self-deceit. We have nothing to esteem in ourselves apart from God and His grace, they would have said. Apart from His grace, we are fallen, wretched, unworthy, and hell-bound.

5. Promises of Every Kind

God comes to us in Christ, and Christ comes to us in a dazzling wealth of promises. Those promises meet any condition of any believer. In one sermon, Ralph Erskine listed fifty aspects of salvation contained in the promises and claimed that he could list a thousand more (5:259-60). "What can you desire that is not in the promise?" he asked. He then answered:

> The promise contains salvation from sin, from the guilt of sin, from the filth of sin, from the power of sin, from the sting of sin, from the stain of sin, from the fruit of sin, from the fountain of sin, and from the very being of sin at length. Here are promises of salvation from wrath, from the law, from justice, from death, from hell, from the world, and from the devil and unreasonable men. Salvation from troubles, and reproaches, and fears, and doubts, and faintings; salvation from desertion and despondency, from wants and weakness, from wrongs and injuries done to your names or otherwise; salvation from all woes and weariness; salvation from backsliding and apostasy; salvation from plagues and all imperfections; innumerable positive salvations and mercies; pardoning mercy, sin-subduing mercy, healing mercy, conquering mercy, comforting mercy, upholding mercy, grace increasing mercy, and perfecting mercy; sanctifying mercy, to sanctify all providences, all crosses, all relations; defending mercy, strengthening mercy, helping mercy, following mercy, enlightening, enlivening, enlarging mercy; mercy for supplying your wants, dispelling your fears, covering your infirmities, hearing your prayers, ordering all things for your good; and salvation to everlasting life, glory and immortality (5:259).

Ebenezer Erskine was also impressed by the variety of God's promises. In preaching on Revelation 22:2 ("the leaves of the tree were for the healing of the nations"), Erskine said that the promises, like leaves on a tree, are so diverse, that there is no ailment that they cannot heal. "What is your disease, O sinner? Whatever it may be, you will find a leaf on this tree that can heal you," he said (1:502). Ralph Erskine concurred: "Tell me one case that the promise does not reach," he asked (5:118).

People must be caught like fish by gospel promises. As Ralph Erskine said, the preacher, as a "fisher of men," must let down "a bundle of promises" as hooks on a line to catch people. The hooks are of various sizes to catch every kind of person. "Do you say, 'I am a poor insignificant worm?'" he asked. "Well, there is a hook for you. 'Fear not, worm Jacob, I will help thee.' Are you poor and needy? There is a hook for you: 'When the poor and needy seek water, ... I the Lord will hear them.' Are you a poor, blind creature, that knows not what way to go? There is a hook for you, 'I will bring the blind by a way they know not.'

"If one promise does not fit you, go to another," Erskine went on. "If one hook is too large for you, another will suit you better. O happy soul, if you be taken! For the hook will not hurt you, but only hale you to the same happy shore with all the children of promise" (5:128-30).

6. Unconditional Promises

To encourage sinners to grasp hold of the promises, the Erskines stressed the unconditional nature of those promises. In opposition to growing forms of legalism, neonomianism, and Arminianism, Ralph Erskine had complained already in 1720 that "the glorious gospel is much clouded at this day, with legal terms, conditions, and qualifications" for coming to Christ and embracing the promises (1:52). He recognized that hearts inclined toward legalism reach for the law or other conditions, including faith, repentance, mourning, and prayer, in hope of pleasing God and effecting peace with Him (1:168).

All conditions of the promises are already met by God, the Erskines argued. Either Christ meets those conditions for the sinner, or the condition of that promise is offered by God in some other promise. In every case, God meets the conditions for sinners who receive the promises by faith. Thus no sinner may reject any promise of God due to conditions he cannot meet. As Ralph Erskine wrote, "There is no conditional form put upon any promise in the Bible, to keep back a soul from applying and taking hold of the promise, but [rather] to draw it in to embrace the condition, either by taking Christ for the condition, or running to an absolute promise, where that condition is promised" (5:129).

To teach otherwise is to mingle the covenant of works with the covenant of grace, or to mix law and gospel, the Erskines said. The distinction between the law and the gospel must be guarded like a treasure. The law is a precept; the gospel is a promise (RE, 5:164-65). "How miserable are you that are gospel hearers, if you can never come to understand what is the gospel, and what is the law!" warned Ralph Erskine. "The law runs always in a mandatory strain; that is, in commands and threatenings: but the gospel runs in a promissory strain; the law begets fear and dread, and the gospel begets hope; and happy they, who, being terrified by the law, are made to flee away to the gospel...for there lies all your salvation" (5:193).

7. Faith: No Condition for the Promises

Even faith is not a condition for the gospel. The Erskines concurred with Robert Traill, who wrote: "Faith in Jesus Christ in justification is neither condition nor qualification, but in its very act a renouncing of all such pretences." Hence the Erskines wrote of "the grace of faith." Faith is one of the primary effects in the elect when they are effectually called (RE, 1:257).

Faith is "the way of the gospel," given by God, not a condition merited by man. The receiving hand of faith presupposes the giving hand of God (RE, 3:9; 5:16). Faith does nothing but receive Jesus as He is offered in the gospel, as the Shorter Catechism says. As Ralph Erskine wrote, faith is the "most uniting grace.... It makes us spiritually and mystically one with Christ" (3:475, 477). Because of faith's intimate union with Christ, the believer has a right to Christ and all His mediatorial work (RE, 2:172). Faith brings Christ and His salvation home to the soul; it is an excellent, a "leading and commanding grace," yet in its receiving character "it seems the poorest and weakest grace, the most beggarly of all the graces."

In describing the woman who anointed Jesus (Luke 7:36-50), Erskine wrote, "Love brings ointment to Christ's head, and repentance tears to wash his feet; but faith gives nothing, and brings nothing to Christ; yet it is designed to a higher office than any other grace: [for] it is the hand that receives Christ, and receives all from Him" (3:476).

Faith is not conditional to the gospel; rather, faith itself is promised in the promises of God, such as Psalm 110:3 ("Thy people shall be willing in the day of thy power"). Such texts, Erskine said, are "absolute," that is, they have no conditions attached to them (5:239). Were this not so, then no one would be able to believe. If faith was a condition, people could object against the gospel by saying, "But I cannot believe!" If faith was itself not unconditionally promised, the gospel would not be good news for sinners who mourn their lack of faith (5:107).

Erskine was aware that preachers such as Robert Rollock, Samuel Rutherford, and David Dickson spoke of faith as a condition. But he argued that when they did, they did not view faith as a condition in the proper sense of that word (5:107). Erskine would have approved of what Robert Shaw would later write: "Some worthy divines have called faith a condition, who were far from being of the opinion that it is a condition properly so called, on the performance of which men should, according to the gracious covenant of God, have a right to justification as their reward. They merely intended, that without faith we cannot be justified — that faith must precede justification in the order of nature. But as the term *condition* is very ambiguous, and calculated to mislead the ignorant, it should be avoided."

According to the Erskines, the act of faith by which we receive Christ is an act that utterly renounces all our works and righteousness as a condition of salvation. Faith is the cessation of all merit and utter abandonment to and acceptance of what Christ has done for us, completely and forever. It is venturing our soul, understanding, will, affections, and very life upon the blood of Christ alone (RE, 1:116, 301).

The Erskines used the word *condition* in a carefully defined context. Along with Andrew Gray, they taught that some promises had conditions or were conditional. Conditional promises, however, do not detract from the unconditional character of the gospel; rather, one covenant blessing is bound to another as links in a chain. There is an order in God's covenant blessings. Faith is given as a part of God's promise (RE, 4:128), then by faith other blessings are received through conditional promises. If conditional promises such as Malachi 4:2 ("But unto you that fear my name shall the Sun of righteousness arised with healing in his wings") frighten us, we should flee by faith to the absolute promises of God such as John 12:32 ("And I, if I be lifted up from the earth, will draw all men unto me") to obtain the condition of the conditional promise (5:106).

We must never confuse the right to believe and the power to believe, Ralph Erskine taught. The right to believe is based upon the offer of grace and the command of the gospel to believe. The power to believe is the gift of the Holy Spirit. Thus, whoever believes credits his faith to the internal work of the Spirit as a result of God's electing grace.

The believer must thus pray for the work of the Spirit. Nevertheless, as Erskine said, that does not mean that the sinner must feel the Spirit's power in order to believe. When the gospel call is pressed upon our heart, we may believe without feeling the Spirit's internal power. Such faith is not audacious, for how could obeying God's command ever be audacious? It is more audacious to say that a sinner cannot believe until he feels the power to believe. Such a response ends in unbelief or in pride. When it ends in unbelief, it leads to destruction. When it ends in pride, it brings its power to God as a reason to believe. True faith, by contrast, confesses, "I have no power; hence I flee from myself to Christ and the Word of promise to embrace His promised power" (2:307-322).

To the sinner who asked, "What if I am not elected?" Erskine responded: Don't meddle with that secret. If your heart goes out to the offer of grace, and you make Christ your choice by faith, then your election is sure. If you say, "All shall not be saved — and perhaps not I?," we answer, "Some shall be saved, and why not you?" (1:55, 157).

"Why is it that all who hear the gospel are not saved?" Erskine asked. "Is it not because they will not give employment to Christ to save them by faith? If you do not receive Christ, you will be damned for your neglect of Him — not because you were not elected (1:99; 2:408). We cannot say you are an elect man or woman, therefore believe. We have no such commission. God says by this gospel, 'Whosoever will, let him take,' and in taking he shall have proof of his being an elect vessel (2:182-83). But you say, 'If I am not elected, I will not get grace to come.' We answer that you could better begin on the other end: if you have no will to come, you have no grace to come. And if you have no will to come, who can you blame but yourself that you will not come? Will you complain that you have no grace to come and still reject the gospel of grace which alone can make you willing? If you end in hell one day, it will be because of your unbelieving rejection of the gospel. Non-election, therefore, can be no hindrance to you, for it is a secret with which you are not now to be concerned" (3:312-13; 5:224-25). The Erskines concurred with George Whitefield who advised, "Go to the grammar school of faith and repentance before you attend the university of election."

8. Repentance, Conviction, and the Promises
Repentance is not a condition of salvation, either, the Erskines said. Like Calvin, the Erskines taught that repentance is not a cause of grace nor a condition of grace but always a consequence of grace. Repentance derives from faith, not vice versa. If repen-

tance preceded faith, then sanctification, of which repentance is a part, would be indispensable for justification. That's what Roman Catholicism teaches. Repentance, rather, is a turning from sin to God through Christ by faith.

The goodness of God, perceived by faith, produces evangelical repentance. That, not legal repentance, is the kind of repentance we need. "Legal repentance," which tries to qualify the heart before God by remorse not rooted in the gospel and its promises, must be distinguished from "gospel repentance," which by faith views Christ as totally qualified for sinners and grieves that the heart has sinned against the gospel and its promises. Whatsoever is not faith is sin (1:433-34).

The convicting power of the law in the soul is anything but superfluous, however. The Erskines taught that God normally uses the law to convict a sinner prior to comforting him with the gospel. The Spirit of God uses the law in all of its righteousness to persuade the sinner of how deeply he has broken the law and how utterly unable he is to obey it (RE, 2:279-81; 3:10). The sinner loses all hope of being justified by the law or his own works (RE, 1:134) and confesses that God could rightly send him to hell (RE, 1:70).

Under the tutelage of the Spirit, conviction of sin by the law augments rather than detracts from free grace, the Erskines taught. Conviction is not a condition for the gospel, however, nor does it fit the sinner for the gospel. Here is why:

• Genuine humiliation under the law's curse and God's judgment makes us less fit in our own estimation for salvation. This is God's way of leading the sinner to a more profound need for Christ. Since the Spirit's purpose in bringing sinners to despair is to prompt them to flee to Christ, ministers must blow on two trumpets, Ralph Erskine said. The trumpet of the law must be blown so that the trumpet of the gospel may be heard (RE, 2:648-49). Preaching must convict the sinner of the wrath of God and the torments of hell that are due to him if he persists in unbelief and impenitence. Conviction under the law then leads the sinner to receive the gospel by sheer grace. As Erskine wrote, "The needle of the law is followed by the thread of the gospel" (2:41).

Conviction is not preparatory grace as much as it is humbling, stripping, killing grace. It puts to death self-righteousness and pronounces a curse upon the sinner (Gal. 3:10). The law is a hard, merciless taskmaster. It terrifies us and drives us to Christ Jesus, who is our only righteousness before God (Gal. 3:24). The law does not lead us to a saving knowledge of God in Christ; rather, the Spirit uses the law as a mirror to show us our guilt and utter hopelessless and to induce repentance, thereby creating and sustaining the sense of spiritual need that He uses to give birth to faith in Christ.

The Spirit thus uses the law to lead the sinner to renounce all assets and to flee to Christ, to turn all merits into demerits before the meriting Redeemer. The Spirit does not use the law to prompt a certain degree of conviction of sin, which is then used as an asset for pleading for grace. Every degree of conviction is adequate if the sinner flees to Christ, Ralph Erskine said. "The soul is sufficiently melted, when it runs into the mould. What is the gospel-mould? It is Christ; and when the melted soul runs into this mould, there does it get the right shape and form, and there only," he explained (4:526).

• Conviction of sin under the law is not a condition for salvation because it is not a human work. It is a divine work, sown in the heart by the Word and Spirit. The sinner's acceptance of the curse of the law is an act of Spirit-worked faith (RE, 2:197). Humiliation through the law usually precedes the sinner's knowledge of salvation through the gospel, but it does not precede the manifestation of Christ's grace. Christ, as the executor of the covenant of grace, convicts men of sin through the law, thereby paving the way for Himself (RE, 5:26).

Sinners, then, must flee to Christ with all their sin. They must be told that the gospel is free to sinners as sinners. The Erskines taught that the Lord wants us to relinquish all conditions for coming to Christ alone for full and free salvation. "He seeks that you come down from all terms, conditions, and personal qualifications; to a renunciation of your all, which is nothing, and to an embracing of Christ's all, which is 'all in all,'" Ralph Erskine wrote (6:470-71). He added that if you wait to enter into covenant with God "till you be in a better condition...you will wait to the day of judgment, and in the mean time inevitably perish at death; and all your terms, conditions, and good qualifications, will perish with you" (1:148).

9. The Free Offer and God's Promises
Like the Reformers, the Erskines advocated the free offer of the

gospel. The gospel was extended to everyone without conditions or reserve. Ebenezer Erskine wrote, "Oh, invite others to come to the Tree of Life and to see that His fruit is good, pleasant, profitable and plenteous. Tell the hungry what excellent fruit is here; tell the weary what glorious rest is here; tell the diseased souls what healing leaves are here. Let your resentment run against those who would hew down the Tree of Life." Ralph Erskine added, "There are many pipes full of water for refreshing, full of wine for cheering, full of milk for nourishing souls. And we are come to set the pipe to your mouth: 'Ho, everyone that thirsteth, come to the waters.' Here is a pipe for every mouth, by which you may draw Christ to your heart, though He be in heaven, and you on earth."

Biographer A.R. MacEwen wrote of Ebenezer Erskine's preaching: "Of all the sermons which have been preserved by his 'scribes,' as he affectionately styled the short-hand writers who clustered round his pulpit, not one fails to repeat the free offer of grace to all without distinction." The Erskines protested against the kind of extreme Calvinism that offered the gospel only to the elect. They believed that such a limited offer displaced the heart of the gospel message. As Ralph Erskine wrote to John Wesley: "The true spirit of God within a believer leads him to a dependence upon Christ *without* him, and not upon a Christ *within* him, not upon any created or communicated graces, gifts, experiences, tears, sorrows, joys, frowns, feelings, or whatever else."

The finished work of Christ is the heart of the gospel, the Erskines said. And that work must be freely and unconditionally offered to sinners. The Erskines offered the whole Christ, prophet, priest, and king, to all who would have Him. They did not separate Christ's benefits from His person or present Him as Savior from sin apart from His claims as Lord. They encouraged listeners to appropriate, or "close with," a freely offered Christ by faith, then to enter into "covenant with God" by drafting a document in which they promised to surrender their entire lives to Him. The Erskines would have been appalled at the evangelistic notion of rescuing sinners from hell without demanding their immediate submission to the sovereign lordship of Christ.

Predestination is no obstacle in proclaiming the gospel, the Erskines said. They opposed those Moderates who confessed a doctrine of unconditional election but preached a doctrine of conditional grace. The Erskines said such preaching contradicted the fullness and freeness of the gospel. Syllogistically, the major premise of such Moderates was that the grace of God in Christ saves the elect. Their minor premise was that the elect are known by their forsaking of sin. They therefore concluded that grace is given to those who forsake sin. Sinclair Ferguson says that such teaching includes four errors:

• Such preaching separates the benefits of the gospel from Christ, who is the gospel. These Moderates reasoned that since the benefits of Christ's works belong only to the elect and no one else appropriates the saving benefits of the cross, the benefits of the gospel must therefore be offered only to those to whom they belong, namely, the elect. The elect are thus known by signs that show they belong to the elect, such as their forsaking sin. How different such preaching is from that of the Erskines, John Calvin, and most of the Puritans who offer Christ with all His benefits to the greatest of sinners.

• Such preaching promotes a conditional offer of the gospel. If Christ's benefits are offered without Christ, those benefits must be offered on condition. For example, you may receive forgiveness *if* you have sufficiently forsaken sin. You may know grace *if* you have received a certain degree of conviction. Such conditions, of course, turn the gospel upon its head. The Erskines were adamant that only the grace of Jesus Christ enables a sinner to forsake sin.

• Such preaching distorts the character of God and the salvation that He offers. The Erskines taught that the free offer of salvation emphasizes the great work that God has done, out of which flows the great imperatives on how we are to respond. They said that to make the offer of grace dependent on anything, even upon graces received, distorts the true nature of grace. It distorts salvation because no man dead in trespasses and sins, as we all are by nature, can ever meet a single condition of God. And it distorts the character of God because our God deals with man on the basis of free, unmerited grace rather than presents conditions to lost sinners by which they may be saved.

• Finally, such preaching distorts the nature of pastoral ministry. One who has only a conditional gospel to offer knows only conditional grace. And one who knows only conditional grace knows only a conditional God. And one who knows only a conditional God will, in the final analysis, only be able to offer others a conditional ministry. He will give his heart, life, time, and devotion to people, but only on condition. He may master the mechanics of the great doctrines of grace, but until grace in God Himself masters him, that grace will not flow from him to his people. He will be a modern Jonah, sitting under his tree with a heart closed to sinners because he thinks of God in conditional terms.

What the Erskines taught is illustrated in the parable of the prodigal son, or as we might call it, the parable of the father of free grace. The homebound prodigal might have asked himself, "Have I felt sufficient sorrow for my sin and repented enough for my father to take me back?" Yet it was knowing the grace in the house and heart of his father that brought the young man to himself in the first place, then began to draw him home. Any thought of conditions that had to be met before qualifying for his father's love were silenced by his father's loving embrace.

Ministers must treat sinners like the father treated his wayward son. They must view people with eyes of mercy, approach them with feet of mercy, evangelize them with words of mercy, and love them with the Father's heart of mercy. Surely the beginning and end of the pastoral vocation is simply this: to know and love Christ, then to strive to be like Him by loving those whom He has entrusted to their care.

The father who loved the prodigal son was still concerned about his firstborn son, however. When the eldest son complained, "Didn't I meet all the conditions? Haven't I merited the ring, the robe, the fatted calf, and the feast?" the father responded as if to say, "It is all yours, unconditionally and freely, but your legalistic heart won't free you to enjoy my gifts. You will only accept grace on the condition that you merit it. On that condition, you can never have it."

May God prevent us from allowing the spirit of the Moderates, the neonomians, and the legalists to affect our preaching of God's free grace and the application of that grace to the flock of God. The offer must be presented to sinners without conditions. The Erskines agreed with Samuel Rutherford who stated, "The reprobate have the same warrant to believe in Christ as the elect."

God presents His gospel offer to sinners, even to Jerusalem sinners whose hands are filled with the blood of Jesus Christ.

Ebenezer Erskine wrote, "God speaks to every sinner as particularly as though he named him by his name and surname" (1:265). The gospel is God's letter of promise to every sinner. It says, "To you is this word of salvation come," and the word is Jesus Christ who has come to save sinners. God is not willing that any should perish, hence His gospel offer to all is sincere. "God is hearty and in good earnest when He offers us Christ and salvation in Him; it pains Him at His heart when sinners don't come to Him," Ebenezer Erskine said (2:497).

There is no excuse for rejecting such an invitation. Unbelief is always the culprit. As Ralph Erskine stated in a post-communion sermon: "Christ as the covenant is offered to you, man; to you, woman; to you that are before me, and behind me, and round about, in every corner of this place.... God's giving him in this gospel is your warrant for taking him: and if you will not hearken to this gospel offer of Christ for a covenant to you, I charge you, in God's name, and as you will answer at his tribunal, to declare before him and your own consciences, what ye have to say against him" (1:182).

The Erskines appealed to sinners, yes, even commanded them (1 John 3:23) to flee to Christ and His promises, knowing that the Holy Spirit blesses such preaching. "The promises are flying about your heads and ears," Ralph Erskine said to listeners. "Is there none of them flying into your hearts? Have you no use for any of these promises? If you be for the promise, then take it, and God's blessing with it, and Christ in the bosom of it; for the promise is the place where the Lord lies" (5:120).

When some parishioners pleaded their inability to embrace the promises, Erskine acknowledged that "faith is not a flower that grows in nature's garden" (4:321), but then advised them to attempt the impossible. Ebenezer Erskine used two illustrations to reinforce that advice. As Jesus told the lame man to stretch out his hand and the Lord gave him strength to do so, so sinners must attempt to believe in Jesus, trusting that God will give them the strength to do what is natively impossible for them to do. Likewise, as a child who is too young to read is sent to school with a primer he is asked to read and does so as he learns how to read, so God commands us to believe, then helps us to believe.

Sinners must seek God by waiting on Him. That means they must strive to remove every impediment to faith and to diligently use the means of grace, such as the preaching of the Word, learning the Scriptures, meditation, prayer, conversing with the godly, reading orthodox literature, and self-examination (RE, 3:195; 5:248). Those who neglect such means are so far out of God's way that they exclude themselves, Ralph Erskine said (3:467; 4:125). The poor beggar who stays at the wayside where the king passes is closer to God than the man who ascends a distant mountain where the king never passes (4:315).

Erskine advised sinners to neglect no duty or ordinance in which God may be found (6:426). "We never heard of any that got this disposition, but they found their waiting on the Lord was not in vain; the Lord pitied them, and gave them a heart to believe and receive Christ," he said (4:37).

10. Self-examination and the Promises
The Erskines were well aware that the promises of God can be abused. As Ralph Erskine said, "People may take and apply a promise amiss, and ruin themselves in their way of taking, when they take the promise to themselves, not of faith, [or] not out of God's hand, [or] not for the end and design for which it is given" (5:247).

How should the minister address this problem? Not by restricting the invitation of the gospel, the Erskines said, but by calling sinners to self-examination. Ralph Erskine explained that as a gardener waters both good plants and weeds, so a minister must water the garden of God's church that includes the good plants of the elect as well as the weeds of the reprobate. The offer of grace comes to both so that no one has any excuse for unbelief. Furthermore, the Holy Spirit will bless the offer of grace to deliver the elect from condemnation (5:109).

The faithful minister must offer grace to all his hearers, but he must also explain what a life of faith consists of, separating the precious from the vile. According to Ralph Erskine, he must ask questions, such as:

• What think ye of Christ? Has the Holy Spirit ever worked within you to extol Christ and to debase you at His feet?

• Have you experienced the promises of God?

• Have you partaken of Christ's humiliation, exaltation, righteousness, and strength? (5:193-235)

The faithful preacher must also present the clear marks of grace that meet the test of the Word of God. According to Ralph Erskine, you are a child of God, if:

- You strive to walk as Christ walked (1:134-36);
- Your heart is rent by and away from sin (1:104-105);
- You long for Christ's second coming (1:138);
- You diligently use the means of grace (1:357);
- You are making progress in the Christian life (1:356);
- You no longer enjoy the company of sinners (2:46);
- You seek to bring others to Christ (3:445);
- You regularly have God in your thoughts (9:94);
- You strive against temptation (5:219).

Such marks of grace are offered not to destroy but to strengthen the faith of the believer. Self-examination must be done by faith, depending on Scripture, Christ Jesus, and the Holy Spirit for enlightenment. If the believer can embrace by faith only a few evidences of salvation, he has good reason to be satisfied, Erskine said. By implication, the rest of the evidences will be there, for God does a full work in His people even when they can't see it. "If a child cannot go, yet if it can suck; if it cannot suck, yet if it can cry; if it cannot cry, yet if it can breathe, it is a mark of life: so, there may be breathings in the soul, that are evidences of life and faith, when other things are hid," Erskine explained (4:270).

Self-examination is crucial for the believer. As Ralph Erskine said, if all that you owned in the world was one precious stone, you would not regard its examination by a competent jeweler with indifference. Rather, you would wonder, "Can it withstand the blow of a hammer, or will it be smashed to powder?" Likewise, all that we have in this world and the next depends on whether or not we are saved in Christ. So we must examine ourselves to see whether our faith in Christ can endure the hammer blows of God's Word or if it will be smashed to pieces by those blows (4:522).

Proper self-examination is helpful for checking false assurance, which rests outside of Christ. It will also assure the true believer that his salvation is based on the right foundation, Jesus Christ. Self-examination should be a positive, growing experience. In seeing our faults, we will look more to Christ.

11. Assurance and the Promises

Proper self-examination helps the believer grow in assurance and sanctification. The Erskines differentiated between the assurance of faith that rests in the promises of God and the assurance of sense, or feeling, that rests in inward evidences of God's grace. The former works justification; the latter, consolation. By assurance of faith, we receive Christ as ours; by assurance of sense, we know Him to be ours. Assurance of faith says, "I am sure because God says it," while assurance of sense says, "I am sure because I feel it."

Ralph Erskine said that every believer must experience some assurance of faith but that not every believer has assurance of sense (3:28-29, 348; 4:184). In his famous sermon "The Assurance of Faith," Ebenezer Erskine said,

> There is a great difference betwixt the assurance of *faith*, and the assurance of *sense*, which follows upon faith. The assurance of faith is a *direct*, but the assurance of sense is a *reflex* act of the soul. The assurance of faith hath its object and foundation from *without*, but that of sense has them *within*. The object of the assurance of faith is *a Christ revealed, promised, and offered in the word*; the object of the assurance of sense is *a Christ formed within us by the Holy Spirit*. The assurance of faith is the *cause*, that of sense is the *effect*; the first is the *root*, and the other is the *fruit*. The assurance of faith eyes the promise in its *stability*, flowing from the *veracity* of the promiser; the assurance of sense, it eyes the promise in its *actual accomplishment*. By the assurance of faith, Abraham believed that he should have a son in his old age, because God who cannot lie had promised; but by the assurance of sense, he believed it when he got Isaac in his arms (1:254).

Assurance of sense, experiential piety, sanctification, and communion with God were highly treasured by the Erskines. Ralph Erskine spoke of "experimental sense and feeling" as a foretaste of heaven and an important means of glorifying God on earth. But he also warned against making the assurance of sense and experimental feelings the ground of faith, saying, "They are ebbing and flowing, up and down, it may be twenty times, in the space of one sermon; and your faith that is built thereupon, will be up and down therewith" (5:35). If we depend on our feelings rather than upon God's promises, the water in our cistern will soon be used up, Ebenezer Erskine said. We must go daily to the spring for fresh water. What we receive today cannot help us tomorrow (2:155). That means that if we wish to recover our certainty and comfort if it should be lost, we must go out of ourselves by a direct act of faith, taking "Christ a-new" (1:166).

The Erskines' stress was thus on a life of faith. The believer cannot live without some assurance of sense, they said, but he finds true stability through faith in Christ. The supreme act of faith is the appropriation of God's promises in Christ. That is the nature and marrow of faith (RE, 2:200ff). As Ralph Erskine said, "The sinner must be brought off from confidence in, or dependence upon frames, enlargements, influences and attainments, to a solid life of faith, upon the grounds that are unchangeable." Ebenezer Erskine offered nine points of comparison between a life of faith and a life of sense:

1. Sense regards only what a man presently enjoys, whereas faith regards what a man has in Christ and in a well-ordered covenant.

2. Sense tends to judge the love of God by circumstances or conditions, and whenever God seems to frown or hide, it cries out, "The Lord hath forgotten to be gracious." Faith sees the love of God in the face of Christ Jesus and in the declarations, offers, and promises of the Word. "In his word will I hope," faith says.

3. Sense and sight vary and fluctuate, but faith is steady and fixed, like Abraham, "who against hope believed in hope, and staggered not at the promise through unbelief."

4. Sense and sight focus on things that are present, whereas faith, like a prophet, looks at things to come.

5. Sense and sight are superficial and easily deceived with appearances, but faith is a meditative grace that goes deep into things.

6. Faith is the leader, while sense is a follower; faith is the duty, and sense the privilege connected with it.

7. Sense is hasty in judgment, whereas faith patiently waits to the end. Sense draws rash conclusions in the midst of difficulties, but faith waits until the cloud passes.

8. A life of sense is dangerous, but a life of faith is safe and sure.

9. The foundation of sense is within; it trades in the shallow waters of created grace, experimental attainments, marks of grace, and the like. The foundation of faith, by contrast, is in Christ, God's covenant, and the great and precious promises of God's Word. When the mariner keeps his ship in shallow waters,

he is in continual fear of rocks and sand-banks, but when he launches out into deep waters, he is safe. Likewise, faith trades in the deep waters of God's fulness in Christ, rising above doubts and fears of shipwreck (1:254ff.).

Where do we who are ministers lead people in our preaching? Do we keep them in shallow water by focusing on the assurance of sense, or do we lead them into deeper waters to challenge them to trust Christ and His promises? Spiritual experience is important, but experience is not the foundation of our salvation. Rather, faith in the promises of God in Christ should be the foundation of spiritual experiences. Like Richard Baxter, we should say, "For every look you take inside yourself, be sure that you take ten looks to Christ."

12. Sanctification and God's Promises

Faith alone justifies, but justifying faith is never alone. As surely as the rising sun brings forth light, faith in God's promises produces holiness, love, and obedience, Ralph Erskine said (2:36). Sanctification is the native, necessary, and inseparable fruit of justification; it is the justified man's way of living or walking to heaven (RE, 2:318, 3:240). To illustrate, Erskine said the believer is like a woman spinning at the wheel. One of her hands holds and the other works. One holds the thread and draws it down, and the other goes round and about the wheel. The holding hand is the hand of faith that clings to God's promises, and the working hand is the hand of obedience (3:425).

Christ in His obedience purchased the Holy Spirit to work both faith and sanctification in believers (1:150-51). The believer is like a ship, Erskine said. The sails of grace are not enough to move that ship; they must be filled with the winds of the Spirit in order to progress towards the heavenly port (3:109).

Sanctification receives Christ not only as Savior from hell but also as Lord of deliverance from sin. Sanctification carries faith beyond the cross to heaven, Erskine said (3:15; 1:96). No one can know Jesus as Savior who does not also receive Him as Lord of sanctification (3:38).

Sanctification transforms a believer's nature into the image of God through Jesus Christ by the power of the Holy Spirit (6:6; 1:312, 318). The believer is freed from the power and dominion of sin (2:269). A new heart produces a new walk (6:335). Sanctification bends the will, inclining it to obey God's will (1:361). The believer's goal is to be purged from sin, to kill sin, to be done with sin once and for all (1:68), and to serve God forever (2:306). He sees the law as a rule of life to obey out of love to God (2:269; 1:406) but realizes he will never fully obey that law in this life. Sin and corruption, darkness and ignorance, rebellion and unbelief will not be completely removed this side of the grave. We will still sin, but we will hate it more and more (1:102, 105).

The believer dies daily to sin and strives to live in grateful obedience to the promises of Christ. He cannot cease repenting until he has ceased sinning, and he cannot cease sinning until he has ceased living. Sanctification will become complete only when we die and enter into the presence of Christ (4:389; 1:326).

Concluding Lessons
The Erskines never lost confidence in the plain interpretation of Scripture. Neither should we. They believed in the perspicuity of Scripture, never forcing Christ out of a text where He is not. But they did go into each text with a kind of flashlight to look for Him and draw Him out. So should we. Let us preach Christ from the Old Testament as well as the New, from the law as well as the gospel, from warning texts as well as texts of encouragement, from the Psalms and history as well as prophecy and epistles. Let us preach Christ to sinners even if we cannot preach sinners to Christ.

The Erskines preached Scripture with an incredible array of illustrations. So should we. After all, Scripture is fascinating. It is attractive. It elevates, stimulates, challenges, and exhorts. Let its text ruminate in your mind and soul and live in your thinking, speaking, and acting.

The Erskines preached the big texts of Scripture with warmth and freshness. So should we. As Henry Venn wrote to his son, "I am persuaded we are very negligent in selecting our texts. Some of the most weighty and striking are never brought before the people, yet they are the texts that speak for themselves. You no sooner repeat them, then you appear in your high and holy character as a messenger of the Lord of hosts."

Like the Erskines, let us preach the whole counsel of God. Let us preach every doctrine to the full. Preach man's depravity and the spirituality of the law. Show people the fearful nature of their human predicament. Unveil their bad hearts and their bad records before God. Do not offer a quick fix — let the sinner know his plight, and offer him no escape from his dire need for Jesus Christ. Do not comfort him short of Christ.

Preach the love of God expressed through His promises. The love of God is the most powerful message that people can ever hear. Liberal preachers may steal fruit from our trees with that message, but do not neglect to preach it yourself. The heart of the gospel is God's immeasurable love. Show your people what God is like. Show them Jesus on His knees with a basin of water and a towel over his arm, washing the feet of men who are too proud to humble themselves. That is the heart of God. Tell your people that their Supreme Maker is so loving a God through Jesus Christ that He is willing to wash sinners from their filth and adopt them into His family as children of God. Teach them about the Triune heart of love.

Then, too, be sure to plead for the power of the Holy Spirit to speak about the things of God. We need the Spirit twice in every sermon — once in the study and once again on the pulpit. The Erskines worked hard and long on sermon preparation. With few exceptions, their sermons were fully written, wrestled out, and prayed over. They stayed close to their notes on the pulpit. Ralph Erskine is often portrayed with a sermon book in hand.

Later in life, the Erskines learned to speak more extemporaneously. At times, however, they struggled for a text. Ralph Erskine wrote in his diary one Sunday in 1731, "My eyes were towards the Lord for a word this day, having to preach, and not yet knowing what to think of for the subject." When they had little time to prepare, they leaned heavily on the Spirit. "Though I had studied little," Ralph Erskine wrote in 1739, "I preached on that word Zechariah. 8:19, 'Love the truth and peace.'"

We need to work hard at sermon preparation. We need to agonize for souls in our studies if our ministries are to be blessed from the pulpit. Of course there are times when God knows that we don't have adequate time for preparation, not because of slothfulness but because of a multitude of pastoral duties that press us throughout the week. During such times, we will experience, after heart-felt prayer, that the Lord will intervene for us, enabling us to preach with little preparation, sometimes better than we do with much preparation. But the Erskines would warn us not to make that the norm. There is little excuse for not preparing for the pulpit. Pulpit ministry is our primary task. Fail in that, and we fail in all. God will not keep assisting a lazy preacher.

Once on the pulpit, let us not overly rely on our notes. Regardless of how many notes you take to the pulpit, allow yourself freedom to deviate from them under the promptings of the Spirit of God, and pray for wisdom to know when to revert back to your notes. One of the greatest problems that many of us have in preaching is that when we move spontaneously from our notes, we fail to understand when to return. We are prone to begin extemporaneous speaking in the Spirit and to end in the flesh.

Finally, the Erskines challenge us to ask ourselves what is the heart of our evangelistic message. We are called to proclaim to all the inexhaustible riches of God's grace; to declare that in the cross and the resurrection of Christ, God has won the victory over everything that could keep sinners from Him. Sin and grace are vanquished only because of God's free grace, not because of our merit. Do we preach that? The Erskines proclaimed the gospel message indiscriminately to all. Do we? They preached the richness of Christ to bankrupt sinners. Do we?

The Erskines also spoke to the hearts of God's people. An aged saint said of Ebenezer Erskine's preaching: "Mr. Erskine had a peculiar talent of entering into the heart and conscience of sinners, and into all the hopes and fears, the joys and griefs, the very life and death of saints; I never heard one preach, who could so well as he, bring, as it were, the Savior and the sinner together."

The Erskines viewed the inner chamber and the pulpit as a wrestling arena. Everything they wrote or preached had a compelling, earnest, beseeching, inviting power. Listen to one of Ralph Erskine's closing appeals after preaching Christ to his flock:

> Woe will be to you, if you live and die without a due improvement of this glorious gospel, which is the doctrine of a God in Christ reconciling the world to himself. God worshipped out of Christ is an idol, and all hope of acceptance out of Christ is a dream. O then let Christ, above all things, have the preeminence among you. What doth God care for your coming to church, if you will not hearken to what he says, and come to his Son?... The Lord is my witness, that it is the desire of my soul that you may be convinced and converted, and brought to Christ.... Little matter what you think of me or my preaching. Let me decrease in your esteem as much as

you will, but let Christ increase among you, and then in the close of the day, I shall have you, and you will have advantage.... O go to God this night, and never give him rest, till you be brought, in some measure, to behold his glory in the face of Jesus, who is the "image of the invisible God."

The Erskines were no armchair petitioners, pulpiteers, or theologians. Do we likewise wrestle with God and men for the souls of men and women, boys and girls? Like the Erskines, let us take the kingdom of heaven by violence and the souls of men by divine allurement.

—Joel R. Beeke

2919 Leonard, NE
Grand Rapids, Michigan
January, 2001

CONTENTS.

MEMOIR

OF THE

REV. EBENEZER ERSKINE.

EBENEZER ERSKINE, the more striking passages of whose works it is the object of the following volume to display, was son to the Rev. Henry Erskine, by his second wife, Margaret Halcro, a native of Orkney, whose father was lineally descended from Halcro, Prince of Denmark, and whose great-grandmother was the Lady Barbara Stuart, youngest daughter to Robert, Earl of Orkney, son to James V. of Scotland. The place of his birth has not been certainly ascertained. One account states it to have been the Bass, where his father was at the time a prisoner for his attachment to presbyterial church government; another states it to have been the village of Dryburgh, where a house, said to have been the scene of his birth, is still pointed out, and has been carefully preserved. Wheresoever was the place, the day of his birth was the twenty-second of June, 1680, and the name Ebenezer [the stone of help] was given him by his pious parents, in testimony of their gratitude for that goodness and mercy, which, under their multiplied persecutions, had still attended them.

Of his early years nothing particular has been recorded. The elements of his education he received at Chirnside, Berwickshire, under the eye of his father, who was settled pastor of that parish, after the glorious Revolution, 1688. He afterwards prosecuted his studies at the University of Edinburgh, where he was regularly educated for the office of the holy ministry. During a portion of the time in which he was a student, he was employed as chaplain and tutor to the family of the Earl of Rothes, at Leslie House, which lying within the bounds of the presbytery of Kirkaldy, he was by that court taken upon trial, and licensed to preach the gospel in the year 1702. In the following year, having received an unanimous call from the people, he was in the month of September ordained pastor of the parish of Portmoak, Kinross-shire. It was in the retirement of this sequestered spot that Mr Erskine, by the assiduous discharge of the duties of his high calling, laid the foundation of his future eminence and usefulness in the church. Anxious to enlarge and to correct his views of divine truth, he spent a great proportion of his time in perusing the Scriptures, with some of the most approved expositors, as Turretine, Witsius, Owen, &c. He was also careful to improve by conversations on religious topics with persons of piety and intelligence, by which his views of the gospel, which at his first outset were considerably dark and confused, became accurate and luminous in no ordinary degree. Shortly after his settlement in the parish of Portmoak he was united in marriage with a young woman, Alison Turpie, of singular piety, and possessed of more than ordinary abilities. To this excellent woman, as an instrument under God, he was accustomed to confess that he was indebted in a particular manner for his first clear apprehension of the mystery of the gospel, her great proficiency in which he is said to have discovered by overhearing her in a con-

examinations, which he always followed up with suitable exhortations and prayer. Sometimes, instead of waiting at the school himself he sent for the scholars to wait upon him at the manse, which they were always forward to do, knowing that he never entered upon serious subjects with more endearing familiarity, or discussed them in a more animating manner than in his own house. In these benevolent intentions towards the rising generation, he took care to be happily seconded by teachers who were alike distinguished for piety and talents ; and to promote order and preserve good government in his parish, he had (a very general desideratum in our own days) a sufficient number of active and intelligent ruling elders in every quarter of it. Fellowship meetings for prayer and religious conference, was another mean which he employed for promoting the increase of knowledge and the growth of piety. For meetings of this sort he compiled a set of rules, in the year 1714, which every member of them was required to subscribe, and he was careful to direct them by his counsel, and to encourage them by his presence, once a month, as often as his other avocations would permit.

The consequences of so much diligence, as might reasonably have been expected, were an attention on the part of his parishioners of the most gratifying description, with the most indubitable proofs of many of them having received the truth in the love of it. Not only was his church crowded on the Sabbaths and at the weekly lecture on the Thursdays, but even his diets of examination drew together large audiences, his people being at once distinguished by a thirst for knowledge, by a spirit of devotion, and by the propriety of their general conduct. A gale of the Spirit seemed indeed to be upon all their assemblies ; and, especially in the exercises of praying and praising, the hearts of the worshippers appeared to be deeply affected. Speaking of the latter exercise, an old and pious member of his congregation was accustomed to exclaim, "Never again can I hear such delightful melody, till I get to heaven," and the remark has been frequently made, that under the pious labours of Mr Erskine, the parish of Portmoak became like a field which the Lord had blessed. It has even been affirmed, that to this day, the fruits of his labour are visible in the superior intelligence, and the marked veneration for godliness and honesty, by which the people of that parish continue to be characterised. Nor was the benefit of his labours confined to the people of his immediate charge. The celebrity of his character as a faithful preacher, attracted many serious Christians from other parishes, and on sacramental occasions he had numerous communicants from sixty and seventy miles distance. So great was the concourse of hearers on these occasions, that it was frequently necessary to have two separate assemblies for the preaching of the word, besides that in the church which was employed in the proper business of the day. His ordinary assistants on these occasions, were men for the most part highly esteemed in their day for soundness of principle and purity of practice : Messrs Wardrope of Ballingray, Gib of Cliesh, Macgill of Kinross, Bathgate of Orwell, Shaw of Leslie, Currie of Kinglassie, Gillespie of Strathmiglo, Hogg of Carnock, and his brother Ralph Erskine of Dunfermline. To these were added on more special occasions, Messrs Moncrief of Largo, Pitcairn of Dysart, Kidd of Queensferry, Webster of Edinburgh, and Williamson of Inveresk. The labours of all of these men were remarkably blessed, and perhaps in few places more than in Portmoak, which many savoury Christians on their death-beds spoke of with transport as a Bethel, where God had favoured them with renewed manifestations of his glory, and of the riches and the perpetuity of his love.

In consequence of his great and growing popularity, several attempts, as was to have been expected, were made to remove him to a wider sphere of action. After the death of Mr Macgill, he received in 1728, an unanimous and urgent call to Kinross, and shortly after, another equally so to the parish of Kirkaldy, both of which, from his great affection to the people of Portmoak, he refused; but it having been resolved to plant a third minister at Stirling, the Rev. Alexander Hamilton, with the whole population of that town and parish, gave him a pressing and unanimous call, which, after maturely weighing all the circumstances of the case, he judged it to be his duty to accept. He was accordingly translated to Stirling in the beginning of autumn, 1731, having lived on the best terms with the people of Portmoak for twenty-eight years. There was something ominous in the subject of his farewell sermon to his parishioners at Portmoak. The text was Acts xx. 22. "And now behold I go bound in the Spirit unto Jerusalem, not knowing the things that shall befall me there." The day has been recorded by one of his parishioners, as a sorrowful one, both to them and him. Of the parishioners he says, " the retrospect of twenty-eight years of great felicity which were for ever gone, and the uncertainty of what might follow, bathed their faces with tears, and awoke the voice of mourning and woe throughout the congregation, for the loss of a pastor, the constant object of whose ministry was to recommend to their souls the exalted Redeemer, in his person, offices, and grace ; who had laboured to rouse the inconsiderate to repentance and serious concern, and who had not failed, when religious impressions took place, to preserve and promote them with unwearied diligence. So much was the minister himself affected, that it was with difficulty he could proceed till he reached the end of the doctrinal part of his discourse, when he was obliged to pause, and, overcome with grief, concluded abruptly, " My friends, 1 find that neither you nor I can bear the application of this subject." Several individuals removed from Portmoak to Stirling, along with Mr Erskine, that they might still enjoy the benefit of his ministry; and the inhabitants of that parish continued to cherish the highest respect for his character, which he repaid by reciprocal esteem and by frequent visits, till circumstances unhappily shut the doors of every parish church in Scotland against him.

Though Mr Erskine had lived in the greatest harmony with his congregation, and was generally respected very highly as a man and a minister, he had not been without his trials, both of a public and of a private kind.   In the year 1713, he was deprived of three sons, Henry, Alexander, and Ralph, the first being in his eighth, the second in his fifth, and the third in his second year, and in the year 1720, they were followed by their excellent mother, Alison Turpie, whose death could not fail most sensibly to affect him.   About the same time he was brought to a considerable degree of trouble, for his attachment to the purity of gospel doctrine, which began to be violently impugned, not only by gross heretics, (such as Professor Simpson of Glasgow, who continued to trouble the church from the year 1714 to the year 1729, when the General Assembly of the Church of Scotland closed the process against him by a sentence of suspension) but by the General Assembly itself, which, in the year 1717, took the Neonomian errors of Baxter under its protection, by passing a vote of censure against the presbytery of Auchterarder, for a proposition which they had framed for checking the progress of that heresy, which was abounding both in the synods of Perth and Fife. Mr Erskine, who had escaped with difficulty from that plausible but dangerous and ensnaring system of doctrine, and who now on all occasions, with irresistible force of argument, held forth the pure gospel of the grace of God, in which Christ and all the blessings of the new covenant are freely and unconditionally exhibited for the sinner's acceptance, the everlasting righteousness of the Son of God being the alone ground of his justification, became particularly obnoxious to the more forward of the Baxterian brethren. In the memorable controversy respecting the well-known book, The Marrow of Modern Divinity, he had his full share, having put the finishing hand to the Representation and Petition, begun by Mr Thomas Boston, to the Assembly, 1721, respecting the act condemnatory of that book, which had been passed the previous year. He also prepared the first draught of the Answers to the Twelve Queries, which were afterwards completed by Mr Gabriel Wilson of Maxton ; and along with his eleven brethren, was solemnly rebuked and admonished for giving in their remonstrance, which was sound and seasonable, and still continues to reflect the highest honour upon their memories. All of these brethren were reviled in various publications of the day, as men of wild and

Antinomian principles, innovators in religion, who were attempting to overturn the Confession of Faith and Catechisms, enemies to Christian morality, with many other sage *et ceteras* of similar import. But perhaps not any one of them suffered more in his individual capacity than Mr Ebenezer Erskine. He was not only, along with so many of them as belonged to the synod of Fife, called on to subscribe anew the Confession of Faith, (not as it had been received by the church of Scotland, in the year 1647, but as explained by the obnoxious act condemnatory of the Marrow, in 1722, which they with one voice refused to do,) but his discourses were judicially complained of to the synod of Fife, in 1721 ; and in the month of May, 1725, he was arraigned before the commission of the General Assembly, by the Rev. Andrew Anderson of St Andrews, whom he had formerly numbered among his most particular friends. Mr Anderson's complaint was preferred in Mr Erskine's absence, and referred to no less than seven sermons, one of which had been preached ten years before, and, as the accuser alleged, was pointed against such as had taken the oath of abjuration.

Under all these irritating circumstances, Mr Erskine, while he displayed an unshaken attachment to the important truths for which he had been called in question, displayed also in no common degree that meekness and candour, which is in every case the result of these truths being truly received into the understanding, and being allowed to operate upon the heart. Of the Act of Assembly, 1720, he spoke always as (it really was so with numbers who supported it) an oversight, rather than any fixed purpose to establish a system of heterodoxy ; and of the disputed book, though he prized it highly and adhered to its doctrine to his dying day, he never hesitated to admit, that there were in it some expressions that were unguarded, and for which others might have been substituted with advantage. To those churchmen too from whom he had received the most injurious treatment, he manifested nothing but gentleness and forgiveness. These rude attacks upon his public discourses, were also over-ruled, by him who maketh the wrath of man to praise him, and restraineth the remainder thereof, for greatly advancing the interests of divine truth, and adding to the celebrity of the man from whose merit they were intended to detract. In a short notice to the first sermon which he published, he himself says, " It is very probable that this, and some other sermons now designed for the press, had slept in perpetual silence among my short-hand MS., if holy and wise Providence which overrules us in our designs and inclinations, had not in a manner forced me to yield to their publication for my own necessary defence, when the earnest entreaty of some dear to the Lord, could not prevail with me to fall in with any such proposal. The conduct of adorable Providence has brought me under such a conviction of culpable obstinacy in this matter, that I sincerely resolve, through grace, not to be so shy in time coming especially if I find these sermons, which are almost extorted from me, shall prove useful and edifying." Of his Rev. brother, Mr Anderson, whose uncharitable conduct had reduced him to the necessity of thus vindicating himself from the press, he is so far from speaking with any bitterness, that he says, " his name, if it were practicable, I have all the inclination in the world to conceal." He had indeed no real cause to

be offended, as whatever might be the motives of Mr
Anderson's conduct, the sermons were made, and still
continue to be extensively useful, and they added greatly
to the growing celebrity of the author.   But to return
to the narrative of Mr Erskine's life.—In the new and
important sphere of ministerial exertion which he now
occupied, he did not disappoint those high expectations that had been formed of him.   In discharging
the public and private duties of his office, he manifested the same unwearied assiduity he had exercised at
Portmoak, and his ministrations seemed to be still more
acceptable, and if possible still more successful.   He
had been only a short time settled in Stirling, however,
when matters came to a crisis in the national church, the
circumstances of which placed him in the forefront of the
battle, and he was subjected to years of contention,
which must have been painful to him, and which it is
painful to every lover of the prosperity of Zion, to con-
template.   Upon that important and often controverted
subject, however, the limits of this brief Memoir will
not allow us to enter.

   That his fair reputation as a Christian and a minister, was not in the least tarnished by these disputes
in the estimation of those who had the best opportunities of observing his conduct, is evident, from the
following testimonies from the presbytery, the kirk
session, and the town council of Stirling, given into
the commission of the General Assembly, which had
been appointed to proceed against him with the cen-
sures of the church in 1733.   "Mr Erskine's charac-'
ter," say the presbytery, "is so established among
the body of professors in this part of the church, that
we believe, even the authority of an Assembly condemning him, cannot lessen it."   " We beg leave to ob-

serve," say the kirk session, " that having had a trial of
Mr Erskine's ministerial gifts and labours these two
years bygone, we cannot but own, according to our dis-
cerning and experience, his Lord and Master hath endowed him with a very great gift of teaching and preaching the gospel, and many other good qualifications,
&c. &c., all attended with a very tender walk, wise and
prudent behaviour, which hath made him most acceptable to us, and persons of all distinctions in this place."
The town council, along with all that is above stated,
say, " that after two full years' acquaintance, we find
him to be a man of a peaceable disposition of mind,
and of a religious walk and conversation, and to be
every way fitted and qualified for discharging the offices
of the ministry among us."   To these very urgent re-
monstrances, the commission paid no attention, and
Mr Erskine, and his brethren in return, protested
against the sentence of suspension passed upon them,
the former continuing to officiate in the parish church
of Stirling to an undiminished audience, till the sentence of deposition was passed against him in the year
1740, after which he preached to his congregation in
the open air, till a meeting-house was built for him,
where he ministered as occasion offered to the inhabitants
of Stirling and many others from the adjoining country
until his death, which happened on the second day of
June, 1754, in the seventy-fourth year of his age.

His colleague, the Rev. and venerable Mr Alexander
Hamilton, though he did not join the Secession, never
ceased, during the short time he lived, to show both to
him and the associate presbytery the warmest regard,
and was accustomed to pray publicly for them.   In
preparing and passing the public papers emitted by the
Secession, Mr Ebenezer Erskine had a principal hand,

and particularly in that invaluable one, entitled, "Act Anent the Doctrine of Grace," which has been eminently and extensively useful. In constituting the associate presbytery at Gairney Bridge on the 25th of December, 1733, he was the mouth to his brethren, and in all the transactions of the Secession body was an influential member, till the day of his death. In the memorable breach which happened in that body, in the year 1747, he took the part of the Burghers, was appointed professor of theology to the body, and the Rev. John Brown, afterwards professor in the same chair, commenced his theological studies under him. Owing to increasing infirmity, however, Mr Ebenezer Erskine held the place only for one year. But of these important transactions, the history is too complex to be brought out in such a Memoir as the present.

We have already made mention of Mr Erskine's first wife, Alison Turpie. He was, three years after her death, married a second time to a daughter of the celebrated James Webster, one of the ministers of Edinburgh, who lived with him till the month of March, 1751, when he was again left a widower. He left behind him several children, one of whom, a daughter, died so late as the year 1814. Mr Erskine enjoyed excellent health till a few years before his death, when his bodily vigour began gradually to fail, and in 1752, Mr James Erskine, his nephew, was settled his assistant and successor. Though he was thus relieved in some degree from his pastoral cares, his infirmities continued rapidly to increase. It was his happiness, however, to experience the most tender sympathy from an extensive circle of relations and Christian friends, and, what was of far greater consequence, he enjoyed much of divine consolation, and

he was enabled to exemplify under acute pain and pro-
tracted debility, the power of that living faith he had so
often inculcated upon others. In compliance with the
wishes of his people, after he was almost completely
confined to bed, he was helped to the pulpit, where
he preached to them a short sermon from Job xix.
25, " I know that my Redeemer liveth," &c.—His
last sermon he preached from his bed in his own
room, on occasion of the baptism of a child, from
Psalm xlviii. 14, " This God is our God for ever
and ever, He will be our guide even unto death."
According to his own request, he was interred in the
middle of his meeting-house, where a large stone, on
which is inscribed in Latin, the time of his decease,
the duration of his ministry, his pastoral fidelity, and
his wish to be buried in the church, covers his grave.

After the rather minute account which we have
given of the life and the ministerial labours of this eminent servant of Jesus Christ, the reader, we should
think, will be able to appreciate his character without
any laboured summary. As a preacher he was certainly endowed with very superior talents. His sermons were rich with evangelical truth, which a dic-
tion, simple and nervous, enabled him to bring home
to the conscience and the heart. He had the advantages of a manly prepossessing countenance, an
easy elocution, and his whole demeanor in the pulpit was characterized by a singular dignity, which
made a strong impression on his hearers. The Rev.
Adam Gib himself, one of the first of preachers, was
accustomed to say, that he who had not heard Ebenezer Erskine, had never heard the gospel in its majesty. As an author, his sermons are the only productions
that can be called exclusively his own, and the nu-

merous impressions they have run through, may be taken as the surest test of their merits. Of these sermons the judicious Mr Thomas Bradbury has said, that " in them the reader will find a faithful adherence to the design of the gospel, a clear defence of those doctrines that are the pillar and ground of truth, a large compass of thought, and a happy flow of words both judicious and familiar." Mr James Hervey's encomium on these discourses is too well known to require repetition; and no less an authority than the Rev. Augustus Toplady says of them, " These sweet discourses were wonderfully blessed to my soul. The Lord was gracious to my soul this afternoon. The Spirit was my comforter, and Mr E. Erskine's two sermons on the rainbow of the covenant were the channel through which that comfort was conveyed." To multiply testimonies in favour of the sermons of Ebenezer Erskine, however, we reckon altogether superfluous. No pious man, we believe, ever read one page of them without feeling that they are the production of a mind richly embued with the love of God, and strong in the faith of Christ Jesus.

BEAUTIES

REV. EBENEZER ERSKINE.

Hebrews x. 19—22. *Explained.*

" HAVING therefore, brethren, boldness to enter into the holiest by the blood of Jesus, by a new and living way, which he hath consecrated for us, through the vail, that is to say, his flesh ; and having an high priest over the house of God : let us draw near with a true heart, IN FULL ASSURANCE OF FAITH," &c.

These verses contain the apostle's transition from the doctrinal to the practical part of the epistle. Having at great length discoursed upon the priestly office of Christ, in the foregoing part of the epistle, he sums up, in a few words, the scope and substance of all he had been saying, ver. 19—21., and then deduces a very natural inference from the whole, ver. 22., " Let us draw near with a true heart, in full assurance of faith." Like a wise builder, he first digs till he come to the foundation, and then calls himself and others to build upon it with confidence.

That we may have the more distinct view of the words, it is expedient that we observe in general, the apostle here very elegantly expresses New Testament privileges, in an Old Testament style and dialect. The highest privilege of fallen man, is to have access into the presence of God, his offended Lord and Sovereign : the only way of access is Christ, of whom the temple of Solomon was an illustrious type. And with allusion unto that typical temple Christ is presented to our faith under a threefold view, ver. 19—21.

1.

1. As a gate or door, by which we may enter into the holiest, and that with boldness, by virtue of his atoning blood, ver. 19. Under the Mosaic dispensation, Aaron alone, and not the Israelites, could enter into the holy of holies, and that but once a year, with the blood of beasts sacrificed for himself and them. But now, under the New Testament, through the death and satisfaction of the Son of God, the way of access to friendship and fellowship with a holy God, both here and hereafter, is made open and patent to every sinner, who by faith comes in under the covert of the blood of Jesus. No sooner had Adam sinned, but the door of access to the majesty of God was bolted against him, and all his posterity; the cherubim with the flaming sword stood in his way. But now the flaming sword of justice being quenched in the blood of the Surety, the door of access is again wide opened. I remember, the woman of Tekoah, 2 Sam. xiv. 14. in her parabolical address unto David, on Absalom's behalf, makes use of this argument with David, to persuade him to bring home his exile son, "God," says she, "doth devise means, that his banished be not expelled from him." This is remarkably true in the case in hand; God, in his infinite wisdom, has devised a way how his banished may be brought home again to his presence; and that is, through the blood and satisfaction of Christ, John x. 9. John xiv. 6.

2. To encourage us in our approaches to God through Christ, he is presented to us under the notion of "a new and living way, consecrated for us, through the vail, that is to say, his flesh," ver. 20. The inner vail, that separated between the holy place, and the holiest of all, in the temple of Jerusalem, was a type of that body of flesh assumed by the Son of God, whereby his Deity was vailed; and through the breaking or rending of this by his death on the cross, the way to God and glory becomes open and patent. And this is called a new way, either in opposition to Adam's way by a covenant of works, which is shut up ever

since the fall of man ; or because it never waxes old,
but is ever fresh, green, and fragrant, unto the believing soul. And it is called a living way, because,
though Christ was once dead, yet now he is alive, and
lives for evermore, to give life to every soul that comes
to God through him. And then, he is a way consecrated for us, he is dedicated for the use of sinners in
their dealings with God : " For their sakes," says he,
" do I sanctify myself." And O what can be more
encouraging to a lost sinner, to make use of Christ by
faith, than to know that he is just devoted for this
work of saving that which was lost !

3. Whereas the sinner might object, That though
the door be opened, and the new and living way consecrated ; yet he is either so ignorant, that he knows
not this way ; or so impotent, that he cannot walk in
it ; or so guilty, that he dares not venture to go into
the holiest : therefore, to obviate all these, Christ is
presented to us as " a great High Priest over the house
of God," ver. 21. O what noble encouragement is here
for believing ! Christ, as a High Priest, " is ordained
for men in things pertaining to God," Heb. v. 1.
And seeing he is ordained for men, may not men make
use of his mediation with confidence and boldness ?
Heb. iv. 14, 16. And then, by his office, he is obliged
to execute the duties of his office toward every soul
that employs him therein : he is obliged, as a High
Priest, to instruct the ignorant, to strengthen the weak,
to confirm the feeble, and " to make reconciliation for
the sins of the people." And therefore let us take
courage to employ and improve him, especially considering that he is both " a merciful and faithful High
Priest," Heb. ii. 17 ; and also " a High Priest who is
over the house of God ;" i. e. he has full power and
authority from his eternal Father, to negotiate our
affairs, and to render both our persons and performances acceptable unto him. In a word, the whole
management of the offspring and issue, and of all the
vessels of cups and flagons, is committed to him ; yea,

"all the glory of his Father's house hangs upon him, as upon a nail fastened in a sure place," Is. xxii. 24. And therefore, "seeing we have a High Priest (of such authority and interest), let us come boldly unto the throne of grace, that we may obtain mercy, and find grace to help in time of need," Heb. iv. 14—16. Whenever we have any business with God, whenever we would enter into the secret of his presence, or enjoy fellowship with him, let us go in at the back of our great High Priest, who has led the way before us, and is appearing in the presence of God for us.

Now, I say, the apostle having thus presented Christ under the most encouraging views, as the object of our faith, trust, and confidence in our dealings with the majesty of God, he proceeds to recommend and inculcate a correspondent duty in the words of my text, ver. 22. "Let us draw near with a true heart, IN FULL ASSURANCE OF FAITH, having our hearts sprinkled," &c.

Before we proceed to the more particular consideration of the words, it is very much worthy of our notice, to observe the apostle's order and method of doctrine, and how he knits the believer's privilege and duty together. He would have the privilege first believed, and then the duty performed : he would have us first believe, that "the door of the holiest is opened by the blood of Jesus," that there is "a new and living way consecrated for us," that "we have a High Priest ove. the house of God," ready to introduce us into his p·e-sence ; and, upon these grounds of faith, he presses and inculcates the duty, "Let us draw near," &c. It is pleasant hence to observe, how the method and order of the covenant of works is just inverted in the covenant of grace. In the covenant of works, duty was the foundation of our privilege ; man was first to perform duty, and upon his doing of that, might expect the privilege in a way of pactional debt. But now, I say, the very reverse of this is God's order and method in the covenant of grace ; for here we are first to believe the privilege, or to receive it as a grant of sove-

reign grace, and upon that ground we are to go on to
duty. This is a thing that needs to be adverted to
with the utmost attention, in regard the very bensil of
nature runs in the way of the covenant of works,
namely, to expect the privilege on the score of duty,
and to fancy that God is a debtor to us, when we have
done this and the other duty required in the law:
whereas the stream of nature runs quite cross to the
order and method laid in the covenant of grace, namely, first to receive the privilege in a way of grace, like
beggars receiving God's alms; and then to perform
duty, as a testimony of gratitude for the privilege received, without expecting any thing from the Lord
upon the account of duty done by us. This is what
proud nature spurns against with the uttermost reluc-
tancy. What? To take all freely, "without money
and without price," and to reckon ourselves unprofitable servants when we have done all, is what depraved
nature cannot yield to, till the heart be new-moulded
by sovereign and efficacicus grace. "Will the Lord
be pleased with thousands of rams, or with ten thousands
of rivers of oil?" &c. "Wherefore have we fasted,
and prayed, and thou takest no knowledge?" is expres-
sive of our natural way of thinking. But though this
way lie cross unto nature, yet this is the way in which
God will have sinners saved, or else they shall never
share of his salvation: he will have them to receive
eternal life begun here, and consummate hereafter, as
"the gift of God through Jesus Christ our Lord,"
without regard to any of our doings as a foundation of
our claim or title thereunto. Boasting must be for
ever excluded, that the glory of our salvation may redound allenarly unto grace, which "reigns through
imputed righteousness unto eternal life, by Jesus Christ
our Lord." And therefore, I say, study to rivet upon
your minds the order and method laid by God in the
covenant of grace, where privilege received by faith is
made the foundation of duty, and not duty the foundation of our claim to the privilege. This is the

scheme or order laid in our Lesser Catechism, by the Westminster Assembly; where, in answer to the 3d question, we are told, that " the scriptures principally teach," first, " what man is to believe concerning God, and then what duty God requires of man." And, according to this order, we have, first, the objects of faith, and privileges of believers explained; and then, the duties of the moral law inculcate upon that ground. And if this order of doctrine be inverted, we destroy the covenant of grace, and return to a covenant of works. So much for the connection.

I proceed to the words themselves. Where we may notice, 1. The grand duty the apostle urges upon the foregoing grounds, " Let us draw near." 2. He gives particular directions how we are to manage in our approaches unto God, through the new and living way, viz. " With a true heart, in full assurance of faith," &c.

As for the first, viz. the general duty that is pressed, " Let us draw near." The apostle does not tell us expressly, whither, or to whom, we are to draw near; but it is plain from the whole drift of the text and context, that he invites us to draw near to God: not to God absolutely considered, for thus he is inaccessible by guilty sinners; but to " God in Christ, reconciling the world unto himself." This is that throne of grace to which he had invited us to " come with boldness, that we may obtain mercy, and find grace to help in time of need," chap. iv. 16. The Greek word is the very same both there and here.

It is considerable, in the manner of the apostle's exhortation, that, when he is calling others to draw near he comprehends himself; it is not, " Do ye draw near," but, " Let us draw near." Ministers of the gospel, when dispensing the truths of God, must preach home to their own souls, as well as unto others. Sirs, we do not deliver truths or doctrines to you, wherein we ourselves have no manner of concern; no, our own souls are at the stake, and shall either perish or be saved eternally, as we receive or reject these precious truths which we deliver unto you. And truly, it can never be expected, that we will apply the truths of God with any warmth or liveliness unto others, unless we first make a warm application thereof to our own souls: and if we do not feed upon these doctrines, and practise these duties, which we deliver to and inculcate upon you, though we preach unto others, we ourselves are but cast-aways.

The exhortation, " Draw near," supposes our natural distance and estrangement from God : " All we like sheep have gone astray," says the prophet Isaiah, ch. liii. 6. When Christ would describe our apostate and lapsed state, he doth it under the notion of a " prodigal going into a far country," Luke xv. There are three things we all lost and forfeited in the first Adam, viz. the " image of God," the " favour of God," and " fellowship with God :" yea, so much have we lost them, that the apostle plainly tells us, that we are " alienated from the very life of God" in our natural state. This God intimated unto Adam immediately after the fall, in that question he propounded to him, when hiding himself from his presence among the thickets of Paradise, " Adam, where art thou?" Gen. iii. 9. *Non es ubi prius eras*, as Austin, one of the ancient fathers, glosseth it ; ' Thou art not where thou wast before.' What is become of the late friendship and fellowship that was betwixt me and thee ? Of a son of God, thou art become a child of the devil ; of an ally of Heaven, turned a confederate of hell. Thus the breach and rupture is wide like the sea. Can ever parties betwixt whom there is such a natural and moral distance be brought together again ? Yes ; the apostle's exhortation to draw near plainly bears, that the offended and affronted Majesty of heaven is accessible " by the blood of Jesus, by the new and living way." It was the great plot of Heaven from eternity, to bring fallen man back again into fellowship with his Maker. Infinite wisdom, animated by infinite bowels of mercy, has found the way, and the way is CHRIST, John xiv. 6

The main intent of his incarnation, and of the whole of his mediatory work, was to "bring us to God," 1 Pet. iii. 18. To bring strangers and enemies to amity and unity, is a great and mighty work; yet this work he accomplishes and brings about by the ransom he has paid for us, and by the operation of his Spirit in us.

This "drawing near to God," it does not consist in any approach unto the essence of God; for, essentially considered, "he is not far from every one of us: in him we live, and move, and have our being." Neither does it lie in an external or bodily attendance upon him in the duties of his worship, "Bodily exercise profiteth little:" many draw near to God with their mouths and lips, while their hearts are far removed from him. Neither does it consist in a moral seriousness; though, alas! it is much to bring some people even that length. People may be morally serious about eternal concerns, in a legal way, like the Pharisee, who came to Christ, saying, "Good Master, what shall I do to inherit eternal life?" Yea, Heathens, and Mahometans, and Jews, may be morally serious in their own way, but they cannot be said to draw nigh to God. What is it then, say you, to "draw near to God?" I answer, It is an act of the heart or mind, whereby the soul, under the influence of the Spirit, sweetly and irresistibly returns to a God in Christ as its only centre of rest. The poor soul having tried Adam's way of access, and finding that door bolted by the law, justice, and holiness of God, despairs of ever entering thereby. At length the man, when he has wearied himself in the greatness of his way, finding the door of the holiest opened by the blood of Jesus, the new and living way being discovered to him in the light of the word and Spirit, he cries out at the sight of it; O! "this is the gate of God," by this door will I enter into his presence; yea, "this is my rest, here will I dwell, for I desire and like it well." O what a sweet acquiescence of soul is there in God's device of salvation through

Christ! The man cannot but applaud and approve of it, as a device every way worthy of infinite wisdom, crying out with the apostle, O! "it is a faithful saying, and worthy of all acceptation, that Christ Jesus came into the world to save sinners." This ordinarily is the soul's exercise, both in its first and after approaches unto God, in any duty of worship. There is a constant improvement of the merit and mediation of Christ in every address the man makes to the Majesty of heaven; he, as it were, fixes himself in the clefts of the Rock of ages; he gets into the secret places of that blessed stair, by which we ascend unto heaven; and then he shows his countenance, and lifts up his voice, in drawing near to God, by the new and living way. We, as it were, take up the propitiation which God has set forth, in the hand of faith, hold it up to God, saying, "Behold the blood of the covenant: Behold, O God, our shield, and look upon the face of thine Anointed." We go quite out of ourselves, when we draw near to the holiest by the blood of Jesus; we overlook our own duties, graces, frames, attainments, grounding our hope of access and success only upon the merit ·and moyen of our great high priest, God having "made us accepted in the Beloved." And, in this view of things, the soul will readily express itself, as David did in the like case, saying, "I will go unto the altar of God, unto God my exceeding joy." And if God hide his face, the soul will wait, and bode good at his hand, saying, "Hope in God, for I shall yet praise him: he will command his loving kindness in the day-time, and in the night his song shall be with me." And if the Lord smile, and grant an answer of peace, he will not ascribe his success to his own faith, frame, fervency, but unto Christ alone, saying, "Not unto us, O Lord, not unto us, but unto thy name be the glory" Thus much for the main duty, of drawing near.

The apostle next proceeds to direct as to the manner of our approach. And,

First, He directs us to draw near "with a true heart." This is a word fitly spoken. If he had required us to draw near with a heart perfectly clean and pure, he might as well have bidden us fly without wings ; but he bids us draw near with a " true heart," *i. e.* with a heart truly concerned about acceptance with God, a heart truly approving of, and acquiescing in the new and living way. In short, a true heart here, is opposed to a double, doubting, distrusting, and hypocritical heart. All dissimulation is to be avoided in our dealings with him, who "trieth the hearts and reins, and whose eyes are as a flame of fire, searching Jerusalem as with candles." Psal. li. 6. " Behold, thou desirest truth in the inward parts." Whereas the hypocrite, who draws near with his mouth, and honours God with his lips, while his heart is far removed from him, shall not stand in his presence. Take care then that your hearts be honestly minded toward God when you draw nigh to him. But I pass this also, and go on to that which I have principally in view, *viz.*

The *second* direction or advice the apostle gives, in order to our successful approach unto God by the new and living way, and that is, to draw near " IN FULL ASSURANCE OF FAITH." The original word signifies to be fully persuaded, or assured of a thing ; and is opposed to wavering, doubting, and uncertainty. The apostle having laid a firm foundation of access in the preceding verses, he bids us trust to it, and rest upon it, with an unshaken confidence, and certain persuasion of success.

The Faith of God's Elect.

OUR inquiry at present is particularly anent " the faith of God's elect," which is well described in our Shorter Catechism, thus : ' Faith in Jesus Christ is a saving grace, whereby we receive and rest upon him alone, for salvation, as he is offered to us in the gospel.'

For clearing of which description, I offer the few following considerations.

1. That faith is a saving grace. And it is so designed, because it is "the free gift of God," Eph. ii. 8. It is not the product of free-will; such a flower never sprung out of the soil of depraved nature; no, it is one of the prime operations of the Spirit, in effectual calling, upon the souls of God's elect. It is not bestowed upon any upon the account of good dispositions or qualifications antecedent to itself; faith is the first grace, or the first act of spiritual life, and, as it were, the parent of the other graces, because it roots and graffs the soul in Christ, of whom alone our fruit is found. Before the implantation of faith, nothing but atheism, enmity, ignorance, and unbelief, overspreads the face of the soul, "being alienated from the very life of God, through the ignorance that is in us." And therefore, faith must needs be a grace, or free gift of God, bestowed without any antecedent merit, good disposition, or qualification in us. Faith is a saving grace; because, wherever true faith is, there salvation is already begun, and shall certainly be consummate in due time. There is an inseparable connection stated, by the ordination of Heaven, between faith and salvation : John iii. 16. "God so loved the world, that he gave his only begotten Son, that whosoever believeth in him, should not perish, but have everlasting life." Mark xvi. 16. " He that believeth, shall be saved." When we preach the everlasting gospel, making offer of Christ and his salvation unto every creature, we are at the same time to declare, that whosoever he be that gives faith's entertainment unto this gospel of the grace of God, shall be saved. So that this promise, establishing the connection between faith and salvation, is as extensive as the offer of the gospel, and is not made to believers exclusively of others. It is certainly true of every son of Adam, lying within the joyful sound of a Saviour, that if he believe, he shall be saved And this we are allowed to

declare in the name of God, as an encouragement to
every sinner to receive and entertain our message.

2. I remark from this description of faith, that it
hath Christ for its main and principal object; for it is
a faith in Jesus Christ. There is such a sibness betwixt Christ and faith, that they cannot be separate.
Take away Christ from faith, then faith is but a cypher,
and stands for nothing; nothing can fill the eye or
hand of faith, but Christ only. Christ is the bread of
life, faith is the mouth of the soul that eats and feeds
upon him : Christ is the mystical brazen serpent, faith
the eye of the soul that looks to him for healing :
Christ is the stronghold cast open to the prisoners of
hope, faith the foot of the soul that runs in to him for
shelter : Christ is our living altar, his satisfaction and
intercession like the two horns of the altar, and faith
flees in thither for safety from the law and justice of
God, which pursue the sinner for his life : Christ is the
bridegroom, and faith, like the bride, takes him by the
hand, saying, "Even so I take him." In a word,
faith slights and overlooks every thing else to be at
Christ, saying with David, Psal. lxxiii. 25. "Whom
have I in heaven but thee? and there is none upon
earth that I desire besides thee;" and with Paul, "I
desire to know nothing but Jesus Christ, and him crucified. Yea doubtless, I count all things but loss, for
the excellency of the knowledge of Christ Jesus my
Lord."

3. I remark, that faith is here described to be a receiving of Christ, according to what we have, John i.
12. "But as many as received him, to them gave he
power to become the sons of God," &c. For understanding this, you would know, that Christ, the ever-
blessed object of faith, is presented to us in the gospel under a great many different views and aspects,
in a correspondence unto which faith receives its denomination. For instance, Is Christ presented under
the notion of meat to the hungry soul? then faith is
expressed by eating. Is Christ held out under the

notion of living waters ? then faith is called a drinking.
Is he held out as a refuge ? then faith is called a fleeing to him, Heb. vi. 18.   Is he held out as a garment
to the naked ? then faith is a putting him on for clothing.   Thus, I say, according to the aspect in which
Christ is presented, faith receives its name ; as the
sea receives its names according to the different countries or shores it washes.   Just so here, when Christ
is presented under the notion of a gift, then faith is
called a receiving him ; for giving and receiving are
correlates, as you see, John iii. 27. " A man can receive (or as in the margin,' take unto himself') nothing, except it be given him from heaven."   Receiving, or taking of a thing, is but stealth or robbery,
where it is not warranted by an antecedent giving or
granting : so our receiving Christ would be but presumption, and a vicious intromission, if he were not
given of God to be received.   And this giving of
Christ in the revelation and offer of the gospel, is common to all, and warrants all to receive him.   John vi.
32. says Christ unto a promiscuous multitude, the far
greater part of whom were unbelievers, as is evident
from Christ's character of them, " My Father (says he)
giveth you the true bread from heaven," meaning himself.   We read, Psal. cxv. 16. that " God hath given
the earth to the sons of men," *i. e.* he made a grant of
it unto them, to be used and possessed by them ; and
by virtue of this deed of gift or grant, before the earth
came to be fully peopled, or stocked with inhabitants,
it was lawful for a man to take possession of it, and
use it as his own.   Just so here, " God hath so loved
the world of lost mankind, that he hath given his only
begotten Son, that whosoever of mankind lost believeth
in him, or receiveth him, should not perish, but have
everlasting life," John iii. 16.   This will not infer an
universal redemption : for I do not now speak of the
purchase or application of redemption, which, without
all doubt, is peculiar to the elect ; but of that giving
of Christ in the word, which warrants our receiving

of him. And this, past all peradventure, is common
to the whole visible church, yea, to all to whom the
revelation of Christ comes ; for if there were not such
a giving of Christ as warrants all to receive him, the
unbelieving world could not in justice be condemned
for rejecting him. O then " let mount Zion rejoice,
and let the daughters of Judah (I mean the visible
church) be glad," and receive it as " a faithful saying
and worthy of all acceptation," that " unto us a child
is born, unto us a son is given, whose name is called
Wonderful, Counsellor, The mighty God, The everlasting Father, the Prince of peace :" for these are
" good tidings of great joy to all people," Is. ix. 6.
Luke ii. 10. Receive this Saviour who is given to
you ; and receive him with gratitude and praise, warb-
ling out that doxology with heart and lip, " Thanks
be unto God for his unspeakable gift." And if you do
not, remember I tell you, you will follow after lying
vanities and slight your own mercy.

4. Upon this description of faith, I remark, that faith
is called not only a receiving, but a resting upon
Christ : Psal. xxxvii. 7. " Rest in the Lord, and wait
patiently for him." We are not, in my opinion, to think,
that receiving is one act of faith, and resting another
act of it ; they are only different expressions of the
same applicatory, justifying faith, or (as some will have
it) the rest of faith is a continuation of the reception.
There are a great many denominations of faith, of the
same divine authority with these two mentioned in
the answer of the Catechism, such as, eating, drinking, fleeing, entering, coming, trusting, &c. But these
are not different acts, but only different expressions of
the saving act of faith, making use of or applying
Christ in a suitableness unto the view wherein he is
presented in the word of God. Now, as to this expression of resting, it leads us to conceive of Christ as a
rock or a strong foundation, upon which we may,
and still ought to lay the weight of our everlasting concerns, with the greatest confidence. When we lay

our weight upon a rock, we are not afraid that the rock
sink or fail underneath us : so, in believing, the poor,
weary, burdened soul, finding itself unable to stand
upon its own legs, leans and rests upon this Rock of
ages, being confident that this Rock will not fail.
Or the expression of resting may allude unto a man's
resting upon a charter for an estate, a bond or bill for
a sum of money ; he rests upon it as good and sufficient
security : so the soul, in believing, rests upon the fidelity and veracity of a God in Christ, pawned in the
covenant of grace and promises thereof. He looks
upon the fulness of grace and truth, of merit and spirit
treasured up in Christ, as they are laid out in the word
of faith, saying, with David, " This is all my salvation,
and all my desire." On which account, faith, Heb. xi.
1. is called " the substance of things hoped for ;" because it rejoices in the promise, as though it had the
thing promised. This resting is equivalent unto trusting, as is evident from all these scriptures cited in the
Catechism upon this head. I shall notice further, before I
leave this point, that both these expressions of receiving
and resting, whereby faith is here described, do, in the
very nature of the thing intended, carry an application
and appropriation in them : for when I receive a gift,
I take it as my own property ; and when I rest upon a
charter or bond, I rest on it as my security : and if
this be not allowed, the relieving and supporting nature of faith is in a great measure lost ; without it we
could never be " filled with joy and peace in believing."
I shall only add, that both these expressions, pointing
out the nature of faith, do so describe it, as to put it
out of the rank or category of works ; for when a
poor man receives his alms, or when a weary man rests
him, he cannot in any propriety of speech be said to
work. God will have man saved, under the new
covenant, by such a mean and instrument, that so works
and boasting may be for ever excluded, and grace alone
for ever exalted.
    5. I remark, that faith receives Christ, and rests

upon him alone. The poor soul, before the saving
revelation of Christ, was grasping at empty shadows,
trusting in lying refuges ; and, like the men of the old
world, when the waters of the deluge were upon the
increase, was running to this and the other mountain,
where he might be safe from the swelling deluge of.
God's wrath ; but finding the waters to overflow his
hiding-places, he quits them, and flees to the Rock of
ages, saying, " In vain is salvation hoped for from the
hills, and from the multitude of mountains : in the
Lord only is the salvation of his people. There is
none other name under heaven given among men whereby to be saved, but the name of Jesus." Every man
by nature being married to the law in Adam, is attempting to climb up to heaven upon the broken ladder of
the covenant of works, and to pass the deluge of God's
wrath by the fallen bridge of the law. But as sure as
the Lord lives, your attempts this way will fail you ;
for " by the works of the law, no flesh living shall be
justified." God has established a bridge of communication between heaven and earth, by the obedience,
death, and intercession of his eternal Son ; and every
other passage to heaven but this, is stopped by the
justice and holiness of God. John xiv. 6. says Christ
there, " I am the way, and the truth, and the life ; no
man cometh unto the Father, but by me."

6. Faith receives Christ, and rests upon him alone
for salvation. This points at the end the sinner has
before him, in his first closing with Christ; he flees
unto him for salvation : Acts xv. 11. " We believe,
that, through the grace of the Lord Jesus Christ, we
shall be saved." By salvation here, we are not simply to understand an eternity of happiness in the enjoyment of God after time, but a salvation begun in
this present life ; salvation from the beginning of it in
regeneration, till it be consummate in glory. The soul
in believing, rests upon Christ for pardon, which is salvation from the guilt of sin, and condemnatory sentence
of the law : it rests on him for sanctification, which is

a salvation from the filth and power of sin ; for glorifi-
cation, which is a salvation from the very inbeing of
sin.   Alas ! the greatest part of the visible church have
no other notion of Christ, but only as a Saviour to keep
them out of hell, and to deliver them from vindictive
wrath.   It is true indeed, our Jesus saveth from the
wrath that is to come.   But how does he that ?
He does it by saving from sin in the first place : " His
name (saith the angel) shall be called Jesus ; for he
shall save his people from their sins."   His first and
great business was to " condemn sin, that arch-traitor,
and first-born of the devil, Rom. viii. 3. " to finish
transgression, and make an end of sin."   And therefore it is a salvation from sin, in the guilt, and filth,
and power of it, for which faith receives Christ, and
rests upon him.

7. I remark, that faith receives and rests upon Christ,
" as he is offered to us in the gospel."   This offer of
Christ, though it be last named in this description of faith,
yet it is the first thing, in the order of nature, that
faith believes : for unless one believe that Christ is
offered to him in particular as the gift of God, and as
a foundation of hope and help, he will never receive
him, or rest on him for salvation.   This is a believing
in order to believing ; a believing that Christ, and salvation in him, is really offered, in order to his being
accepted and received.   And therefore be verily persuaded, that Christ is yours in the offer, and " that
God hath given to you eternal life in his Son ; for this
is the record of God," 1 John v. 11.   And unless you
believe this, you " make God a liar, because you believe not the record that God hath given of his Son,"
ver. 10.   O Sirs, believe it that " unto you a child is
born, unto you a son is given, whose name is called
Wonderful," &c. ; and that God hath given him to a
lost world, in the gospel offer and revelation, that " whosoever believeth in him, should not perish, but have
everlasting life," John iii. 16.

Next, you may observe, that it is in the gospel that

this offer is made, and this gift of God is presented
unto you. What is the gospel, but a word of grace,
a word of promise, a word of faith, a word of life and
salvation ? and " to you is the word of this salvation
sent." And in this word, Christ and his everlasting
righteousness, and all sufficient fulness, is brought near
to you, in order to your receiving and applying him
to your own souls by faith. You need not climb up
to heaven, or dig into hell, in quest of a Saviour ; for
" the word is nigh thee (and Christ in the word), even
the word of faith which we preach," Rom. x. 6—9.
As a sum of money is brought nigh to a man in a
bond that is offered him, so is Christ brought nigh in
the word of promise unto us, Acts ii. 39. " The promise
is unto you," &c.   And without this word of grace and
promise, believing were a thing impossible, in regard
faith could never fasten on Christ, or on God in him,
without this word of faith.   If I should bid you believe
that such a man will give you a sum of money, you
would think me ridiculous, unless he had given his
word that he would do it ; your faith or trust could
not fasten upon him without his word or writ as the
immediate ground thereof : so here, our faith, trust,
or confidence, could never find a foundation without
God's word of grace and promise ; and in receiving
his word, you receive himself and all the treasures of
his grace laid up in Christ, and laid out to your hand
in the word.

    Next, it is considerable in this branch of the de-
scription that faith's reception and application of Christ
must be regulated by, and bear a proportion unto, the offer that is made of him in the gospel ; for here we are
told, that faith is a receiving and resting upon him *as*
he is offered, &c. This qualifies our reception of
Christ, and distinguishes the faith of true believers,
from that of hypocrites and formalists.   And therefore
notice this as a thing of the last moment and consequence, whether your faith comes up to the offer, and
corresponds thereunto.   I shall illustrate this in the
four following particulars.

1*st*, Christ is freely offered in the gospel : Is. lv. 1. " Ho, every one that thirsteth, come ye to the waters; and he that hath no money; come ye, buy, and eat. yea, come, buy wine and milk without money, and without price." Rev. xxii. 17.—" Whosoever will, let him take the water of life freely." So faith receives and embraces him as the free gift of God. Beware of thinking to buy the pearl with the money and price of your works, duties, and good qualifications; as if by these you were fitted for receiving Christ, or as if God made you the more welcome, on the account of these, to receive his unspeakable gift : no, no, remember that, in the matter of believing, you are to shake your hands from holding of such bribes; for the pearl of great price cannot be bought in such a way. It is true, believing is called a buying, Is. lv. 1. Rev. iii. 18. But then let it be remembered what sort of a buying it is; it is a buying without money, and without price. God's price in the market of the gospel is just nothing: and yet this is so great a matter with man, that the pride of his heart will not allow him to tell it down. We cannot think of coming up, I should rather say, cannot think of coming down to God's price ; I mean, of taking Christ and salvation in him and through him for nothing. Many say to God as Abram said to the king of Sodom, Gen. xiv. 23. " I will not take any thing that is thine, from a thread even to a shoe-latchet, lest thou shouldst say, I have made Abram rich." Just so does the proud self-righteous sinner upon the matter say unto God. God comes in a gospel-dispensation, saying, Come, sinners, I see you are " wretched, miserable, poor, blind, and naked :" you have nothing to give me as an equivalent for life, righteousness, and salvation ; and therefore I seek no money or price from you, but make a free gift of my Son, and his whole fulness, for nothing ; only take him as my free gift, and he and all that comes along with him is your own for ever. No, says the pride of the heart, " I am rich, and increased with goods, I stand in need of no-

thing" at God's hand : if God will give me life upon
the terms of the first covenant, as it was granted to
Adam ; or if (because I am already a sinner, and incapable of yielding a perfect and sinless obedience)
God will lower the terms of the covenant of works,
and grant me an interest in Christ and salvation for
my act of believing, or on the score of my honest aims
and good meanings, or sincere endeavours, I am well
content. But to take Christ and eternal life for nothing is what the proud legal heart cannot stoop to.
O what a cursed aversion is there in the heart of man
against his being a debtor unto grace, and grace only!
To buy without money, and without price, is a mystery which the selfish heart of man cannot comprehend.
But, Sirs, faith is a grace that comes to get, and not
to give : or if it give any thing, it is the ills of the soul;
but nothing of good does it pretend to give. The sinner, in believing, upon the matter says, Lord, I give
thee my folly, and take thee for my only wisdom ; I
give thee my guilt, that thou may be the Lord my righteousness ; I give thee my defilements, and take thee
for sanctification ; I give thee my chains and fetters,
that I may be indebted to thee for redemption and
liberty ; I give thee my poverty, and take thee for my
only riches ; I give thee my wicked, wandering, hard,
and deceitful heart, that thou mayst give me the new
heart and new spirit promised in thy covenant. Thus,
I say, Christ is freely offered, and must be freely received.

2dly, Christ is offered wholly, an undivided Christ
is offered, and thus also he must be received. There
are some who, in their professed and pretended way
of believing, do as it were halve and divide Christ.
Some do so far receive him as a prophet, that they
submit to the teaching of his word, and thereby come
to acquire a great deal of speculative knowledge in
the things of God ; but, being unacquainted with the
teaching of his Spirit, they never come to the knowledge of the truth as it is in Jesus. And hence it

comes that they never flee to him as a propitiation, or
submit unto his authority as a King and a Lawgiver:
for the execution of the prophetical office, paves the
way for his reception both as a Priest and King. Some
again professedly receive Christ as a Priest, to save
them from hell and the curse ; but, by continuing in
their ignorance under a gospel-revelation, and walking
according to the course of this world, and not according to the laws of Christ, they do evidently reject him,
both as a Prophet and King. Others again, and I
fear too many in our day, do professedly receive Christ
as a King and Lawgiver, to the prejudice of his priestly office, while they imagine, by their obedience to his
law, particularly the new gospel-law of faith and repentance (as some call it), to purchase a title to salvation ; by which means they either totally exclude the
righteousness of Christ, or mingle in their own acts of
faith and repentance with the righteousness of Christ,
in the affair of acceptance and justification before God:
in both which cases, " Christ can profit them nothing;
they are fallen from grace," as the apostle expressly de-
lares, Gal. v. 2, 4. Thus, I say, many pretended believers halve and divide the offices of Christ. But "is Christ
divided ?" No ; a whole, an entire and undivided
Christ must be received, or no Christ at all; there is nothing of Christ that a believing soul can want. It is true
indeed, the first flight of a poor awakened soul, fleeing
from the face of the law and justice of God, is to
Christ as a Priest ; because here, and here only, it finds
relief and shelter under the covert of everlasting righteousness. But at the same moment in which it receives
him as a Priest for justification, it submits unto his kingly authority, saying, as the men of Israel did unto
Gideon, " Rule thou over us :—for thou hast delivered us out of the hands of our enemies. O Lord our
God, other lords besides thee have had dominion over
us : but by thee only will we now make mention of
thy name."

   3dly, Christ is offered particularly unto every one

of the hearers of the gospel ; and accordingly faith receives him with particular application. The general
call and offer reaches every individual person ; and
God speaks to every sinner as particularly as though
he named him by his name and sirname : Remission
of sin is preached to you ; we beseech you to be reconciled ; the promise is unto you. And, for my part, I
do not know what sort of a gospel men make, who do
not admit this. Now, I say, faith, which is the echo
of the gospel offer and call, must needs receive an
offered Christ and salvation, with particular application
to the soul itself. For a person to rest in a general
persuasion that Christ is offered to the church, or offered to the elect, or a persuasion of God's ability and
readiness to save all that come to Christ, is still but a
general faith, and what devils, reprobates, and hypocrites may have. Man, woman, Christ stands at thy
door, thou in particular, even thou art called and commanded to believe in the name of the Son of God.
Here lies the great pinch and strait of believing ; the
convinced and awakened soul, through the policy of
Satan, and the workings of a deceitful heart, thrusts
away the word of grace and faith, as not pertaining unto it ; till God, by the power of his Spirit, irradiate
the word, and irradiate the mind of the sinner, letting
the man see that to him the word of this salvation is sent:
and then he believes with particular application, not
only good-will to man upon earth, but good-will to me;
Christ is offered to me, and therefore I take him for
my own Saviour ; the promise and covenant is directed
unto me, and therefore I embrace it as my security.
But, perhaps, more of this under the second general
head.

4*thly*, God is hearty, and in good earnest, in his
offers of Christ, and his salvation. O Sirs ! do not
think that a God of truth dissembles with you, when
he makes offer of his unspeakable gift, or that he offers
a thing to you which he has no mind to give. He
says, yea, he swears with the greatest solemnity, by

his very life, that he is in good earnest, and has no
pleasure in your death. And after this, to think that
he is not in earnest, what else is it, but to charge a
God of truth with lying and perjury? There cannot
be a greater affront offered to a man of common veracity. How criminal then must it be to impute such
a thing to him, for whom it is impossible to lie, and
who hates all fraud and dissimulation in others with a
perfect hatred? Thus, I say, God is in good earnest
in his offers of Christ; so faith is hearty, and in good
earnest in receiving and applying him: " with the heart
man believeth unto righteousness." God's whole
heart and his whole soul is in the offer and promise of
the gospel, Jer. xxxii. 41; and is it not reasonable that
we should give him a meeting, by believing with the
whole heart and soul? It is not one faculty, but all
the powers of the soul do jointly concur in this business of believing; though, indeed, to speak accurately,
with the learned and judicious Dr Owen, ' Faith is in
the understanding in respect of its being and subsistence, in the will and heart, in respect of its effectual
operation.*

* The term faith or belief, is not obscure in its meaning, but is in
common speech readily understood. In its largest sense it denotes
a persuasion of the mind as to the reality of objects existing, or of
the truth of propositions, of whatever kind these objects may be,
or by whatever means the knowledge of them may be imparted.—
But faith strictly taken, respects what is made known by testimony
alone.

Faith as saving is versant in a special manner about the character
and counsels of God as manifested in Christ, and the truths of revelation in their immediate connection with salvation. As a divine
grace, it is wholly the supernatural gift of God, and must proceed
from a divine cause and principle, and so must be of a higher nature
than any common act of the human mind arising in a natural course
of operation, or from the influence of any ordinary mean.

Saving faith has an immediate respect to the Lord Jesus Christ
as its special and personal object. All truths relating to salvation,
and consequently, the faith that views them, have an inseparable connection with him who is the Saviour.—Faith's chief and proper
business is to apprehend Christ, and to receive a full and free salvation through him.—A. Bruce.

The Assurance of Faith.

THERE is a twofold certainty or assurance, viz. of assent and application. The former necessarily supposes an assurance of understanding, or of knowledge, Col. ii. 2. The apostle there speaks of 'the full assurance of understanding,' which every Christian ought to breathe after, and which every believer hath in a greater or lesser measure ; for it is only "they that know his name that will put their trust in him," Psal. ix. 10. This assurance of understanding, as I take it, lies in an uptaking of the reality and excellency of things divine and supernatural : there is a beam of the glorious Sun of righteousness darted in upon the man's soul, who before was sitting in darkness, and in the regions of the shadow of death ; whereby he that was darkness in the abstract, becomes light in the Lord. He comes now to see things spiritual in another light than formerly ; he enters, as it were, into a new world of wonders, upon which account we are said to be "called out of darkness into God's marvellous light." Perhaps the man had before this, some dreaming, floating, superficial notions of these things ; he heard of them by the hearing of the ear : but now his eyes see them ; and he sees as great a reality in things invisible and eternal, as though he saw them with his bodily eyes.

Faith includes the knowledge of the mystery of God and of Christ in the light of grace, and the full assent of the mind to the truth of this mystery on account of the authority of God by whom it is attested. Nor is this all ; the believer also loves the truth, exults in it, and glorifies God ; he is ardently desirous of fellowship with the Saviour, that those doctrines which are true in Christ may be true to himself for his salvation ; consequently when Christ is offered to him by the word and Spirit, he receives him with the greatest alacrity of soul, rests and leans upon him, surrenders and yields up himself to him ; after which he now glories in him as his own, and delights in him exceedingly, reclining under the shadow of the tree of life, and satiating himself with its delicious fruits. This is the faith of God's elect, an invaluable gift, the bond of our union to Christ, the scale of Paradise, the key of the ark of the covenant by which its treasures are unlocked, the permanent spring of a holy, tranquil, and blessed life.—*Witsius.*

This is called by the apostle, Heb. xi. 1 " the evidence
of things not seen. There is such a certainty here, as
amounts to a demonstration ; so that you may as soon
persuade a man that it is midnight, when the mid-day
sun is shining upon him in full splendour, as persuade
a man in the lively exercise of faith, that there is not
a reality and excellency in things supernaturally revealed. This is so essential to faith, that very commonly under the Old Testament, and frequently also
under the New, faith receives its denomination therefrom, Is. liii. 11. Jer. xxxi. 34. John xvii. 3.

But, to come a little more close to the purpose in
hand, 1st, There is, I say, in faith an assurance of
assent, whereby the man assuredly believes whatever
God has said in his word to be true ; and that not
upon the testimony of men, of ministers, or angels,
but upon the testimony and authority of the God of
truth, for whom it is impossible to lie, speaking in
his own word, and saying, " Thus saith the Lord."
But in a particular manner the soul gives its assent
unto the truth of the gospel, and the revelation of the
word, concerning the person, natures, offices, undertakings, and performances of our Lord Jesus Christ,
as the Redeemer, Surety, and Saviour of lost sinners.
The man's understanding being enlightened with the
knowledge of Christ, and having got a view of him by
the Spirit of wisdom and revelation, he finds it to be
all true that God has said of Christ in the word ; so
that he cannot shun in this case to join issue with the
apostle, " This is indeed a faithful saying, that Christ
Jesus came into the world to save sinners," 1 Tim. i.
15. He sees the truth and veracity of God so much
engaged in the covenant and promises thereof,
that they are more firm than the everlasting mountains
and perpetual hills. Is. liv. 10.   Now, this certainty
of assent is, in scripture dialect, called a " believing the
report of the gospel," Is. liii. 1 ; a "receiving the record
of God," 1 John v. 10, 11 ; a " setting to the seal that
God is true," John iii. 33.

2dly, There is in faith an assurance of application,
or appropriation, expressed frequently in scripture by
a resting, a trusting or confiding in the Lord, and the
veracity of his word of grace and promise. By this
act of faith, the soul takes home the promise, and embraces it as good and sufficient security to itself. It
is said of the Old Testament worthies, Heb. xi. 13.
that they were "persuaded of the promises, and embraced them." Their faith in the promise was a persuasion, or assent with appropriation thereof to their
own souls, insomuch that they looked upon the promise
as their substance : and hence is that which we have
in the 1st verse of that chapter, " Faith is the substance
of things hoped for." This applicatory act of faith,
wherein the very life, soul, and sweetness of faith lies,
is pleasantly expressed and illustrated in David. God
had made a promise to him of the crown and kingdom
of Israel, which bore up his spirits, when, through the
rage and fury of Saul, he was hunted like a partridge
upon the mountains ; and viewing the promise, and
the fidelity of the promiser, he cries out, Psal. lx. 6.
" God hath spoken in his holiness, I will rejoice :" and
because I have the security of his promise, I dare say
it with confidence and assurance, " Gilead is mine,
and Manasseh is mine." In like manner, true faith, it
appropriates the mercy of God in Christ to the soul
itself in particular, upon the ground of the free and
faithful promise of God. I might here demonstrate,
that the stream of our best Protestant divines concur
in their sentiments as to this matter : I shall only at
present quote the definition of faith given by the great
and judicious Dr Owen, in his Catechism, or " Principles of the Doctrine of Christ;" where, having moved
the question, ' What is justifying faith?' His answer
is, ' A gracious resting on the free promises of God
in Christ Jesus for mercy, with a firm persuasion of heart
that God is a reconciled Father to us in the Son of
his love.' For proof of which he cites 1 Tim. i. 16.
John xiii. 15. John xix. 25. Rom. iv. 5. Heb. iv. 16.

Rom. viii. 38, 39. Gal. ii. 20. 2 Cor. v. 20, 21. And on the margin he has these words,——' Of this faith the Holy Spirit is the efficient cause, the word the instrumental, the law indirectly, by discovering our misery, the gospel immediately by holding forth a Saviour. Faith (adds he) is in the understanding in respect of its being and subsistence, in the will and heart in respect of its effectual working. According to this account of faith, this assurance I speak of, viz. a persuasion of the promise with appropriation (as the judicious Calvin speaks), can no more be separate from faith, than light can be separate from the sun. It takes home the grace and mercy of God to the soul in particular, which before lay in common in the offer of the gospel. And without this particular application, the offer and promise of the gospel can stand us in no stead; but is like a price put in the hand of a fool, who has no heart to it. Our meat set before us will never feed us, unless it be applied by eating it; so " except we eat the flesh, and drink the blood of the Son of man," by an applying faith, " we have no life in us." Whatever excellency there be in Gilead's balm, it will never recover the hurt of the daughter of Zion, unless it be used by faith. Faith answers and corresponds unto the word of faith, as the seal and the wax answer to one another, Zech. xiii. 9. " I will say, It is my people; and they shall say, The Lord is my God." Faith will not quit its MY's, though all the world should say against it. The marrow of the gospel (as Luther observes) is in these pronouns, MEUM, NOSTRUM, my and our. He bids us read these with great emphasis. Tolle meum, et tolle Deum, says another, " Take away property, and you take away God, take away Christ." It is the common dialect of faith in scripture, to vent itself in words of appropriation; it has a peculiar pleasure and satisfaction in these words, my and our, and rolls them in its mouth like a sweet morsel. See how sweetly David harps upon this string, Psal. xviii. 1, 2. no less than eight times in a breath does he repeat his appropriating my, " My strength, my rock, my fortress, my deliverer, my God, my strength, my buckler, the horn of my salvation, and my high tower." Yea, so tenacious is faith in this matter, that it will maintain its my's in the face of a hiding and frowning God : Psal. xxii. 1. " My God, my God, why hast thou forsaken me ?" My is a word of faith, says Flavel on the text. So Is. xlix. 14. " Zion said, the Lord hath forsaken me, and my Lord hath forgotten me." But I need not stand to offer more instances of this kind, seeing, as one observes, faith in scripture expresseth itself by these two words, my and our, no less than about three hundred times.

Thus you see what kind of assurance there is in faith, namely, an assurance or certainty of assent and application. The first may be found in a great measure, and in some sort, in devils and reprobates : the last is of a distinguishing nature, and peculiar only to the faith of God's elect, and of his operation ; though indeed some shadow of it also may be found in the presumptuous faith of hypocrites ; of which we may speak afterward. Knowledge and assent are preparatory toward that application, wherein the very soul of saving and justifying faith doth lie. And when we speak of them one after another, it is not as if they were really separate in the soul's exercise ; for I take them up as one complex undivided act of the soul. In the very first view and relation of Christ by the word and Spirit, the soul cannot shun to cry out with Thomas, " My Lord, and my God." I do not mean that the soul always, in the first moment of believing, runs that length, as to express itself so with the mouth ; but I mean, this is what faith would say, could it get up its head from under the load of unbelief and indwelling corruption, wherewith it is overpowered.*

* There is in justifying faith (required in the Scriptures, and wrought by the Spirit) an assurance of application, or appropriation by which act, the thing granted (Christ and his salvation) is received and taken into possession.
This is antecedent to all acts of reflection, that I am a believer

The Difference between the Assurance of Faith and the Assurance of Sense.

THERE is a great difference betwixt the assurance of faith, and the assurance of sense, which follows upon faith. The assurance of faith is a direct, but the assurance of sense is a reflex act of the soul. The assurance of faith hath its object and foundation from without, but that of sense has them within. The object of the assurance of faith is a Christ revealed, promised, and offered in the word; the object of the assurance of sense is a Christ formed within us by the Holy Spirit. The assurance of faith is the cause, that of sense is the effect; the first is the root, and the other is the fruit. The assurance of faith eyes the promise in its stability, flowing from the veracity of the promiser; the assurance of sense, it eyes the promise in its actual accomplishment. By the assurance of faith, Abraham believed that he should have a son in his old age, because God who cannot lie had promised, but by the assurance of sense, he believed it when he got Isaac in his arms. By the first, Noah was sure that he and his family should not perish in the waters of the deluge; but by the last, he was assured of it, when the ark rested upon the mountains of Ararat, and the waters were withdrawn again into their proper channels. By the former, the believing Israelites were assured, that Canaan should be their possession, because God had made a

and to all assurances thereon, and is therefore carefully to be distinguished from them. It is not the assurance that I have come up to certain terms required, or am endued with certain entitling qualifications, but an assurance of application of what is freely given.

This faith may be defined, a persuasion of the truth of the divine promises, and an appropriation of the divine blessings: or such a real persuasion of the fulness and freeness of salvation by Christ, or in other words, of the report of the Gospel, as effectually induces the soul to appropriate Christ, and all the salvation included in him; which appropriation is a farther real persuasion, grounded upon the grant that is in the word to sinners, that Christ is mine,—his death is mine, &c.—*Aphorisms Concerning the Assurance of Faith.*

grant and a deed of gift of it to them in his promise ;
by the latter they were assured of it, when they passed
Jordan, overthrew the old inhabitants, and divided the
good land by lot, as the inheritance of the tribes or
Israel. Time would fail me, to illustrate this matter
by instances that stand upon record in the sacred
oracles. Faith asserts its interest in a future good,
because promised ; sense asserts its interest in a present
good, because possessed. Faith says, " My God will
hear me ;" sense says, " My God hath heard me."
Faith says, " He will bring me forth to the light, and
I shall behold his righteousness ;" sense says, " He hath
brought me forth to the light, and I do behold his
righteousness." Again, faith is conversant about
things that are not seen, and hoped for ; sense is conversant about things seen, and actually enjoyed. Faith
says, " He is my God, because he has said in the covenant, I will be their God ;" sense again says, " He
is my God, because I know my soul has said unto the
Lord, He is my Lord." Faith assures the soul of
the remission of sins in the blood of the Lamb, because God has said, " I will be merciful to their unrighteousness, and their sins and their iniquities will I
remember no more ;" sense again assures the soul of
remission, because of the intimations of pardon in
some sensible smiles of the Lord's countenance, and
some saving operations of his grace. By faith I believe
my salvation, because it is purchased, promised, and
possessed by my glorious head Christ Jesus: but by sense
I believe my salvation, because I find this salvation
already begun in a work of regeneration, and advancing in a work of sanctification, " being confident of
this very thing, that he which hath begun the good
work, will perform it until the day of Jesus Christ."

The assurance of faith will stand its ground when
the assurance of sense is quite lost and gone. A clear
instance of this we have in Christ, when there was a
total eclipse of sensible manifestations, yea, nothing
but a lowering cloud of vindictive wrath surrounding

and breaking upon him as our Surety; yet, at that
same time, the assurance of faith maintains the claim,
and repeats it, saying, "My God, my God ;" upon the
ground not only of his eternal Sonship, but of the promise the Father had made to him, Psal. lxxxix. 26.
" He shall cry unto me, Thou art my Father, my God,
and the rock of my salvation." And lest you should
think this was a thing peculiar unto the Head, see an
instance of it also in the church, which is his body, Is.
xlix. 14. "Zion said, the Lord hath forsaken me, and
my Lord hath forgotten me." Upon which the holy
Rutherford sweetly glosses to this purpose : " He may
be a forgetting and withdrawing God to my feeling ;
and yet to my faith, MY GOD, and MY LORD : even as
the wife may believe the angry and forsaking husband
is still her husband." Heman, Psal. lxxxviii. is so far
deserted as to sensible presence, that he is, as to his own
feeling, "laid in the lowest pit, in darkness, in the
deeps," ver. 6. Yea, ver. 7. he adds, "Thy wrath lieth
hard upon me ; and thou hast afflicted me with all thy
waves." And, ver. 15, 16, 17. " While I suffer thy terrors, I am distracted. Thy fierce wrath goeth over me,
thy terrors have cut me off. They came round about me
daily like water, they compassed me about together."
What lower could a child of God be brought, on this side
of hell ? and yet faith, amidst all these clouds, steps in
with its appropriating my, ver. 1. "O Lord God of my salvation." And truly, if there were not some exhilarating
certainty in faith, acting upon the unalterable covenant,
in such cloudy and dismal dispensations, I know not
what could keep the believer from running into utter
despair. But the grace of faith will venture the soul's
safety upon the strong plank of the promise, even
when sensible consolations are quite dashed to pieces,
by the angry billows of outward and inward trouble,
like two seas, meeting upon the believer. David had
the experience of this, Psal. xxvii. 13. " I had fainted,
unless I had believed to see the goodness of the Lord
in the land of the living." Hence also it is, that the

Lord directs his people to the exercise of faith in such a case, Is. l. 10. " Who is among you that feareth the Lord, that obeyeth the voice of his servant, that walketh in darkness, and hath no light? let him trust in the name of the Lord, and stay upon his God."

Concerning the Doubting which often troubles Believers.

WHEN we speak of the assurance of faith, it is not to be so understood, as if every one that has faith were perfectly free of doubting. This, I apprehend, is what scares many at this doctrine of the assurance of faith. They think, that if there be an assurance in the essence of faith, then it would follow, that every true believer behoved always to have such assurance as to be free of doubting; which lies cross to the experience of the generation of the righteous. But this objection goes upon a palpable mistake, as if faith and a believer were one and the same thing. We do indeed assert, that there is no doubting in faith; for faith and doubting are commonly in scripture directly opposed one to another : but though there be no doubting in faith, yet there is much doubting in the believer, by reason of prevailing unbelief and indwelling sin. If it were true that assurance is not of the nature of faith, because the believer is not always assured ; by the same way of reasoning it would follow, that resting is not of the nature of faith, because the believer is not always actually staying and resting himself on the Lord ; or that trusting is not of the nature of faith, because the believer is not always trusting. It may be as well urged, that seeing is not of the nature of the eye, because sometimes the eye-lids are closed ; or that heat is not of the nature of fire, because its heat is not perceptible by reason of the ashes wherewith it is covered ; or that light is not of the nature of the sun, because sometimes it is eclipsed by the interposing moon. Remove the ashes, and the heat of the fire will apear ; remove interposing bodies, and the sun will have light ; open the eye-lids, and the eye will see : so do but remove ignorance, unbelief, and other incumbrances of corruption from faith, and see what the nature of it is then.   For it is of the nature of faith in the abstract, that the present question is, and not what lodges in the believer who hath faith.   In the believer there is "as it were the company of two armies," grace and corruption, love and enmity, repentance and impenitence, faith and unbelief; but these are not to be confounded together, because they are in the same subject.   We must not exclude complacency and delight in the Lord out of the nature of love, because, through remaining enmity and corruption, his love is so overpowered, that ne cannot perceive any such thing in him, but rather the reverse of love.   The same may be said of other graces.   So here we must not conclude, that there is nothing of this applicatory assurance in faith, because of prevailing unbelief, and doubts flowing therefrom.

The Difference between true Faith and mere Presumption.

As there is a great difference betwixt the my of faith, and the my of sense; so there is yet a far greater difference between the my of faith, (or of true sense flowing from it) and the my of presumption.   Presumptuous confidence has its my's, as well as faith and well-grounded experience; as we see plain in the case of Balaam, Num. xxii. 18.   "If Balak would give me his house full of silver and gold, I cannot go beyond the word of the Lord my God."   Now, say you, since a presumptuous confidence may speak in the dialect of true faith and experience, wherein lies the difference?   This is a very material and momentous question; and, with a dependence on the Father of lights, I shall attempt a resolution of it in the few following particulars.

1*st,* The assurance of faith receives and applies Christ to the soul in particular, as he lies in the revelation and grant that is made of him to sinners in the word, which is the immediate ground of faith; where-

as presumptuous confidence, though it claims an interest in him, yet does it not upon this bottom, or in
God's method and way of conveyance. The apostle
tells us, Rom. x. 8. that Christ, and his righteousness
and salvation, is brought nigh unto us " in the word of
faith." What is the design of a covenant of grace, and
of these declarations, offers, and promises of grace,
that are made to us in the glorious gospel, but just to
bring Christ so near to us, as we by believing may
come to apply him and his whole fulness to our own
souls ? John xx. 31. " These things are written, that
ye might believe that Jesus is the Christ the Son of
God, and that believing ye might have life through his
name." If we would find Christ, and eternal life in
him, we need not " ascend into heaven, or descend into
hell," in search for him, as the apostle speaks, Rom. x. 6,
7. But we are to search for him in the " scriptures,
for they are they which testify of him." Christ is
brought near to us in the testimony or record of God
in the word, where " he gives us eternal life, in his
Son Christ Jesus," 1 John v. 11. Now, faith, in its
direct act, I say, takes Christ, and claims him upon
this grant and gift that is made of him in the word of
grace ; and upon no other foundation will it adventure
to assert its interest in him. Like an honest man,
who will not intermeddle with goods, money, or the
estate of another, unless he have a charter, bond, testament, promise, or some such security, upon which
he may do it warrantably, without vicious intromission:
whereas the thief and robber puts to his hand, without
looking after any such warrant ; if he gets what he has
a mind for any how, he is easy. Here lies a fatal flaw
in the faith of many hearers of the gospel ; they grasp
at Christ and his salvation, but they overleap the gift
and grant of him in the word, as the immediate foundation of their faith. If we consult the experience of
the saints in scripture, we shall find their faith termi-
nating immediately upon the word : " In his word do
I hope," says David. " Remember the word upon

which thou hast caused me to hope. I rejoice at thy word, as one that findeth great spoil." Their faith did come by hearing or reading the word. This is the chariot in which the Lord rides, when he presents himself to us as the object of our faith and trust : and therefore that faith which overlooks the promise and offer of the gospel, is but a presumptuous faith. " Gilead is mine, and Manesseh is mine," says David, in that forecited lxth Psalm, because " God hath spoken in his holiness." So says an applying faith, pardon is mine, peace is mine, grace is mine, glory is mine in Christ, yea, God himself is my God ; because God hath made over himself, and all these things in Christ to me, in the covenant of promise, or testament of my elder Brother, sealed and confirmed by his blood. But, say you, may not a presumptuous hypocrite pretend to bottom his faith upon the promise, and claim an interest in him, even upon that ground ? An answer to this, leads me to a

2d Difference between the my of faith, and the my of presumptuous confidence, namely this, That though the presumptuous person may run away with the promise, yet he does not embrace the promise as it is in Jesus, or as Jesus is in it. This is a mystery which only can be explained to purpose by him who " openeth the book, and looses the seven seals thereof." The view I have of it, you may take up as follows. The covenant, and all the promises of it, are made to Christ as the first heir, both by birth and purchase : he is God's first-born, and therefore the heir of the inheritance of eternal life. But besides, as the second Adam, by his obedience and death, having fulfilled the law, and satisfied justice ; the promise of life, which was forfeited by the sin and disobedience of the first Adam, comes to be settled upon him, and his seed in him. Now, matters standing thus, the soul, in applying of the promise, takes its title thereto, not upon the ground of any thing in itself, but comes in only upon Christ's right and title ; his righteousness is the only

proper, entitling, meritorious condition of the covenant
and of all the promises thereof. Here lies the failure
in presumptuous confidence, that the man being never
cleanly beat off from Adam's covenant, he is always
seeking to found his title to the promise in himself,
some good condition or qualification wrought in him,
or done by him. Thus many attempt to enter themselves heirs to the promises, and to eternal life, but
shall never be able : Why? Because they do not by
faith enter themselves heirs in Christ, or upon his right
and title : and "another foundation can no man lay; for
the gift of God is eternal life, through Jesus Christ
our Lord." Thus, I say, presumptuous faith does
not embrace the promise " as it is in Christ, in whom
all the promises of God are yea, and in him amen."
And then, I say, he does not embrace the promise as
Jesus is in it; for as all the promises are in Christ, so
Christ is in all the promises. What is it that is be-
queathed in his testament, but himself and all his fulness ? He was the great mercy promised to the fathers.
When the covenant was promulgate unto Adam, and
afterwards unto Abraham, what else was it, but just a
promise of Christ? And when, in process of time,
the covenant of grace came to be further opened, in
a variety of promises, what were they all, but Christ,
and the grace that is in him, parcelled out to us, that
we by faith might apply him, with the grace that
is in him, according to our need? And hence it
is that the believer, in applying the promise, finding Christ in it, he eats it, and it is to him the
"joy and rejoicing of his heart;" he finds the Lord
in his own word of grace, and this makes it relieving and comforting to his soul ; he drinks in " the
sincere milk of the word," because therein he "tastes
that the Lord is gracious." But now presumptuous faith
is more taken up with the naked promises, than with
feeding the soul with Christ in and by the promise.
A man that is possessed of Christ by faith, he has not
Christ and his promise by him, as a man has money

lying by him in his coffer; he has not the covenant
and promises, as a man has his bonds and charters in
his cabinet, which perhaps he will not look to once in
a year: no, but he has Christ in the word of grace, as
a man has his bread by him, which he is daily feeding
and living upon: hence this applicatory faith is called
an "eating the flesh, and a drinking the blood of
Christ;" which expression implies such an application
of Christ to ourselves, as carries soul-nourishment
along with it. True faith roots the soul in Christ, just
as a tree is rooted in the ground; the prolific virtue of
the earth enters into the tree, and the tree at the same
time strikes and spreads its fibres into the earth, and
draws sap and moisture therefrom, sending a digested
nourishment through the whole, whereby it is made
to grow and bring forth fruit. So here, in believing,
the Spirit of life which is in Christ Jesus enters into
the soul; and at the same time, there is as it were a
sprig and fibre passing from every faculty of the soul,
striking into Christ, and drawing a digested sap from
him, whereby the soul is made to grow and flourish in
grace and holiness. Hence we are said to be "his
workmanship, created in Christ Jesus unto good works."
And, "Those that be planted in the house of the
Lord, do flourish in the courts of our God."

3dly, True faith receives and applies Christ according to the order that God has laid in his offices; but
presumptuous faith inverts that order. The order
that God has laid in the execution and application of
the offices of Christ, is this: Christ comes by his word
and Spirit, as a Prophet, enlightening the sinner's
mind with the knowledge of his lost estate by nature,
and the way of his recovery through his atoning blood
and satisfaction: upon which the soul, by faith turns
in to him as a Priest, taking sanctuary under the covert of his everlasting righteousness; and so submits
unto him as a King, receiving the law from his mouth,
and yielding itself unto his government, from a principle of gratitude to him who has bought it with a

price. But now, the presumptuous faith of the legalist inverts and disturbs this comely order laid by infinite wisdom among the offices of Christ : for in his
way of applying Christ, he begins with the kingly
office, pretending to obey him as a Lawgiver ; and,
upon this ground, expects that Christ will save him as
a Priest by his righteousness ; and thus makes his own
obedience the ground of the imputation of the righteousness of Christ. And what else is this, but to bring
money and price, contrary to the express command of
God, Is. lv. 1 ? Nothing can be of a more pernicious
tendency toward the overthrow of the freedom of
God's grace, in the great affair of justification and salvation. Hence it is the apostle so much inveighs
against this method of seeking justification, in the Galatians ; insomuch that he tells them expressly, that by
this way they made themselves " debtors to do the
whole law ; yea (says he), Christ is become of no effect
unto you, whosoever of you are justified by the law ;
ye are fallen from grace," Gal. v. 2—4. This method
of inverting the order of Christ's offices, and making
the first act of faith to terminate upon him as a King,
as it is a way of thinking most agreeable to nature,
which runs with a mighty bias towards Adam's covenant ; so, I judge, nature is much fortified in this way
of taking up the method of salvation by Christ, by the
strain of some men's doctrine in our day, who inculcate faith and repentance as new precepts given out
by Christ in the gospel, which were never required in
the moral law of the ten commandments. For if this
be so, then inevitably we must first obey Christ as a
King, by repenting and believing, in order to our being
justified by him as a Priest ; besides many other dangerous consequences which are unavoidable upon this
new law-scheme. All which are avoided, by teaching,
with the strain of orthodox divines, that there are no
precepts in the gospel strictly taken ; and that Christ
in the gospel giveth no new laws, but enforceth the
old law, viz. the moral, which being adopted into the

gospel-dispensation, obligeth us to believe in Christ upon his being revealed to us in the gospel, and consequently to repent also in an evangelical manner. For that these duties of faith and repentance, as to their essence, are required in the very first commandment of the moral law, is indisputably evident; and I do think it strange, to find it controverted by any who embrace and own the doctrine of the church of Scotland, particularly the Larger Catechism, where that point is plainly determined, in the explication of the foresaid first commandment. But it is not proper to insist on this controversy in a discourse of this nature; if need be, it may be discoursed apart.

4*thly*, Another difference betwixt the my of faith, and the my of presumption, is this, That the assurance of faith will maintain its claim, and humble confidence, even under sad challenges, and a deep and abasing sense of much prevailing iniquity; whereas presumptuous confidence succumbs and fails upon the prevalency of sin. The reason of this is, because the ground of presumptuous confidence is within the man; some good disposition and qualification which he finds within him, as he apprehends, which being dashed by the eruption of his reigning lusts, he has no more to look to, the foundation of his confidence is gone. But now, faith builds and bottoms its confidence, not within, but on something without, namely, the everlasting righteousness of the Lord Jesus, and the mercy of God running in this channel, exhibited in the word of grace. Here it is that faith sets down its foot, and upon this foundation it stands, against which the gates of hell cannot prevail. And thus, having the ground of its confidence from without, it is not shaken with every insurrection from within. An instance whereof we see in David, Psal. lxv. 3. The holy man, in the first part of the verse, cries out, under a sense of the strength, power, and guilt of sin, " Iniquities prevail against me." Well, but what says faith in such a case? " As for our transgressions, thou shalt purge them

away." Another instance of the like nature, we see
in the same holy man, Psal. cxxx. We find him, ver. 3.
under such a sense of sin and guilt, that, viewing himself as he stood in the eye of the law and justice, he
cannot shun to own, " If thou, Lord, shouldst mark
iniquities, O Lord, who shall stand?" Well, but
where does David's faith find a standing in such a
case? Only in the mercy and grace of a reconciled
God in Christ; and therefore he adds, ver. 4. " But
there is forgiveness with thee, that thou mayest be feared ; and plenteous redemption, that thou mayest be
sought unto." I do own, that a real believer may be
sadly shaken, as to the confidence of his interest in
Christ, under prevailing iniquity ; but this certainly is
his infirmity, and not his faith. Many real believers
live more by sense than by faith ; and hence it comes
that they are soon shaken, whenever sensible experience
is overclouded, under the sense of prevailing iniquity ;
though the pain of it is a just correction of their folly.
Whenever faith recovers from under the fit of unbelief,
and views what the soul is, and has, in Christ, and in
the covenant, it recovers its stability and confidence,
and withal, brings into the soul strength against corruption, so that it goes out against it like a giant re-
freshed with wine. But, say you, may not presumptuous faith recover its confidence also ? I answer, No
doubt it may : but then the difference lies here—True
faith goes to work in a quite different way, in order to
the soul's recovery, from that which the presumptuous
legalist takes. When the terrors of the law, or challenges of conscience, have at any time battered down
presumptuous confidence, the man goes to work, and
fills up the hole that the law has made in his soul,
with the new earth of his own obedience, reformation,
duties, and the like, and with this untempered mortar
he daubs and makes up the breach made in his conscience. But, on the other hand, though the believer
be as diligent in the way of duty as the other, yet nothing in heaven or earth can satisfy him under chal

lenges, or afford him ease or quiet, but Christ himself,
and his righteousness apprehended and applied by faith:
no balm but that of Gilead can cure his wound; he
fetches his healing only from under the wings of the
Sun of righteousness; all is but loss and dung in comparison of this, Phil. iii. 8, 9.

There are several other differences might be given
between the my of faith, and the my of presumption,
if I were not afraid of being tedious. Only, in short,
the more of the assurance of faith, or yet of well-
grounded experience, the more lowliness, humility,
and self-abasement. The higher that the soul is exalted
in and by Christ, the lower does it sink in its own
eyes, saying with David, when God promised to build
him a sure house, and that the Messiah should spring
of his loins, "Who am I, O Lord God? and what is
my house, that thou hast brought me hitherto?" The
poor believer, in this case, sees himself to be such a
miracle of rich and sovereign grace, that he is even
wrapped up in a silent wonder, and put to an everlasting stand, that he knows not what to say, "And is this
the manner of man, O Lord God?" And what can
David say more? But now, the more of a presumptuous confidence, the more pride and self-conceit, like
Laodicea, "I am rich, and increased with goods, and
have need of nothing;" accompanied with an under-
valuing of others in comparison of themselves, like the
proud Pharisee, "God, I thank thee, that I am not as
other men, or even as this publican."

Again, presumptuous assurance cherishes some secret
and beloved idol: the man spares some right-hand or
right-eye sin; and commonly his deceitful heart argues
for its being spared, because grace doth abound. But
now, true faith and experience purifies the heart, and
engages the man to an impartial and universal opposition to all sin, as dishonourable to God, and grieving
to his Spirit; and readily he bends his principal force
against these sins, which receive the greatest advantages against him, by interest, custom, constitution,

or education: and the consideration of abounding grace is so far from encouraging him in sin, that it teaches him to " deny all ungodliness and worldly lusts, and to live soberly, righteously, and godly in this present world."

Lastly, The my of faith, or solid experience, is always accompanied with much love to the person of Christ, and resignation of soul to him ; for " faith worketh by love." And therefore, at the same time, that the soul is enabled to say, " My beloved is mine," it cannot shun to add, " and I am his." " One shall say, I am the Lord's." The man presents himself " a living sacrifice, holy, acceptable unto God, which is his reasonable service." But now, as one well observes, presumption is lame of one hand : it has a hand to take pardon, to take heaven, and the benefits of Christ ; but as it has no true love to his person, so it has not a hand to give or resign the whole man to the Lord, to be for him, and not for another : and the plain reason of this is, that the power of natural enmity was never broken, and the man is married to the law, and to his lusts also.

Concerning a Weak and a Strong Faith.

OBSERVE 1. that the faith of every believer is not of the same size and strength. Some have a strong, and others have a weak faith : yea, the faith of the strongest believer, like the moon, has its waxings and wanings ; or, like the sea, its ebbings and flowings. Although every believer be in Christ, yet every believer has not the same measure of faith ; as every star is in the heavens, though every star be not of the same magnitude. The rounds of Jacob's ladder were not all at the top, though every round was a step towards heaven ; so, though every faith be not triumphing in a full assurance, yet every true faith is bending towards it. You may see one believer under a gale of the Spirit of faith, crying, with Job, chap. xix. 25. " I know that my Redeemer liveth :" while another labours under such discouragements, that, like the publican, he "stands afar off," with the tear in his eye, crying, "God be merciful to me a sinner." You may see one saying with Paul, " He loved me, and gave himself for me :" another, through the prevalence of unbelief, saying, Is his mercy clean gone for ever? Hath he forgotten to be gracious?" Perhaps you shall find one believer surmounting all fears, saying with the apostle, " Who shall separate me from the love of Christ ?" &c. while another is combating with many doubts, ready to raze foundations, saying, " I am cast out of thy sight ;" and all men are liars that will say otherwise, the prophets of God not excepted. It is with believers, as it is with children in a family ; one perhaps is lying in the cradle, another led by the mother or nurse, another can walk alone, a fourth comes to such full strength that he is able for work and business. Thus in the household of God there are babes, young men, and fathers. 2. That it is the duty of every believer, yea, of the weakest, to press after faith in the highest degree of it. Hence it is that Christ frequently checks his disciples for the weakness of their faith, " Why are ye fearful, O ye of little faith? O thou of little faith, wherefore didst thou doubt?" True faith is a pro- gressive thing, it goes on from one degree to another : hence is that expression of the apostle, Rom. i. 17. " The gospel is the power of God unto salvation ; for therein is the righteousness of God revealed from faith to faith." Faith in its first and weaker, and faith in its repeated and stronger actings, feeds and centres upon the righteousness of God's operation and imputation, for acceptance, pardon, and salvation. It is of the nature of all true grace, particularly of the grace of faith, to breathe after its own increase and perfection : hence is that prayer of the disciples, " Lord, increase our faith ;" and that of the poor man in the gospel, "Lord, I believe ; help thou mine unbelief." We must forget things that are behind, and reach forth unto things that are before : " The path of the just is as the shining light, that shineth ' more and more unto the perfect day." 3. That the certainty or assurance of application, as explained above, ebbs or flows according to the strength or weakness of the assent of faith. That there are degrees of assurance, will be controverted by none, who have any knowledge either of divinity or philosophy. The very words of the apostle in the text import, that we are not to rest in a lower, but ought to press after the highest degree of the assurance of faith : and the apostle accounts it a great blessing to the Thessalonians, that they had much assurance, 1 Thess. i. 5 ; plainly intimating, that some true assurance might be in a less degree. Now, I say, this assurance of application bears a proportion unto faith's assent, and waxes or wanes as it is strong or feeble ; so that a strong assent has a strong application, and a weak assent a weak application.*

In what the Full Assurance of Faith Consists.

In one word, I conceive it lies in such ' a firm and fixed persuasion, confidence, or trust in the faithfulness of a God in Christ, pledged in his covenant or promise, as overcomes and tramples upon all difficulties and improbabilities, all doubts and fears as to the actual

* The grace of God in the soul may be exceeding low, as to its life and exercise, yet the truth and reality of it, may be in the heart ; as there may be fire in the grate, when there is little appearance thereof, it being hid and covered with ashes. So the grace of God, the root of the matter, may be in the heart, when there is no appearance of it either to themselves or to others ; it is with them at times, as it is with the earth in the winter season, when at a remote distance from the sun ; the trees and vegetables wear the aspect ot death ; yet they have life in the root ; so it may be with the Christian, he may wear the aspect of death to himself and others, insomuch that he may write bitter things against himself, and ye have the life of grace in his soul ; the cause of the Christian's distress may be owing entirely to his looking for that joy and life in himself, that are only to be found in Christ who saith, Hos. 14. 8. " I am like a green fir tree ; from me is thy fruit found."—*Allen's Spiritual Mag.*

performance of what is promised in God's time and way; and all this with particular application to the soul itself." This description I would illustrate and explain in its several branches, were it not done upon the matter on the former two heads, this being nothing but a higher degree of the self-same faith formerly described. Such an act of faith we find put forth by Abraham, Rom. iv. 20, 21. where we are told that " he staggered not at the promise of God through unbelief; but was strong in faith, giving glory to God : being fully persuaded that what he had promised, he was able also to perform." This full assurance of faith, though mountains of impediments were in its way, yet it makes no more of them than if they were a plain; it overleaps and overlooks them all, fixing its eye only upon the power and faithfulness of the blessed Promiser; as we see clearly exemplified in the case of Abraham. His own body was dead, and incapable of procreation; Sarah's womb was barren, and incapable of conception: sense and reason in this case would have been ready to conclude, that it was impossible ever Abraham should have a son. But we are told, ver. 19. that he entirely abstracted from all considerations of that kind. " Being not weak in faith, he considered not his own body now dead, when he was about an hundred years old, neither yet the deadness of Sara's womb." He would not so much as listen unto the surmises of carnal reason; flesh and blood are put out of doors; and he rests with an assured confidence, without any doubting or hesitation, upon the fidelity of the Promiser, being certain that God would do to him in particular as he had said, when the time of the vision should come. In like manner we find, that after Abraham had gotten his beloved Isaac, the son of the promise, what a terrible shock, may one think, would it be to his faith in the promise, when God commanded him to take Isaac, of whom the promised seed (Christ) was to come, and offer him upon one of the mountains of Moriah! Gen. xxii. Reason here might be ready to object, and that not without great colour of religion, Can God, who has so severely forbidden murder, require me to imbrue my hands in the blood of my own son? Will not such a thing be an eternal reproach to Abraham and his religion? What will the Egyptians say, and the Canaanites, and the Perizzites, which dwell in the land? What will Sarah say, and how shall I ever look her in the face? But especially what shall become of the promise, and the veracity of him that made it, saying, " In Isaac shall thy seed be called?" Surely might unbelief and sense say, either this command is a delusion, or else the promise is a lie. But Abraham had a full assurance of faith as to the stability of the promise; and therefore he would upon all hazards obey the command of a promising God : he was fully persuaded, that though Isaac were sacrificed and burned into ashes, yet out of the very ashes of his sacrificed son, God could, and actually would raise up Isaac again, and so accomplish his own word of promise. Abraham, on the account of this his noble and gallant faith, is fitly called " the father of the faithful," his faith being proposed as a pattern to all others for their imitation ; and every true believer is on this score a child of Abraham. And let none imagine that they are not obliged to believe with such a faith as Abraham had ; for the apostle expressly tells us, that the history of his faith stands upon record in scripture, " not for his sake alone, but for us also," that we, after his example, may be encouraged to " believe on him that raised up Jesus our Lord from the dead," Rom. iv. 23, 24.

Object. O say you, if I had as good a ground for my faith as Abraham had; if I were as sure that the promise were to me, as Abraham was, I think I could believe with a full assurance of faith, as he did : but there lies the strait. I answer, You and I have as good a ground of faith as ever Abraham had. Abraham had a promising God in Christ to trust, and so have we : you have the same God, the same Christ, the same covenant, the same promise, as Abraham had. But, say you, God spake to Abraham, in particular, by name, when he gave him the promise, saying, " In thy seed shall all the nations of the earth be blessed." I answer, although you be not designed by name and surname, as Abraham was, yet a promising God in Christ addresses himself as particularly to you in the word of grace, and dispensation of the covenant and promise, as though he called to you out of heaven by name and surname, saying, " To you (i. e. to you sinners of Adam's race) is the word of this salvation sent. The promise is unto you that are afar off," &c. And not only is the promise presented, but an express command of believing superadded, requiring and binding every particular person, to take hold of it, and embrace it : so that, whatever shifts and evasions the unbelieving and deceitful heart may make, the promise of God comes as close and home to every individual hearer of the gospel, as that promise did to Abraham, when God bespoke him with an audible voice out of heaven ; yea, " we have a more sure word of prophecy, unto which we would do well to take heed, as unto a light that shineth in a dark place." Further, let it be considered that that promise was first presented unto Abraham as the object and foundation of his faith, before he could believe it ; and by believing it, became his in possession ; or in believing it, he was possessed of it as his own ; for, upon a supposition that he had not believed, he had never been possessed of the promised blessing. In like manner, the promise is presented to you as the immediate ground of believing ; and in believing, you come to be possessed of the great things contained in the promise ; but if you do not believe, you shall not see the salvation of God. Thus you see that you have the same ground of faith, and the same warrant for believing, that Abraham had : and there is nothing to keep you from a full assurance of faith, or a believing without staggering at the promise like Abraham, unless it be your own ignorance and unbelief.

I do own, as was hinted already, that every true believer does not come the length of Abraham, to believe without staggering ; but that is not the question. The present question is, If we have not now as good and firm a ground, and as good a right to believe the promise as Abraham had? If Christ, and his salvation and righteousness, be not brought as near to us in the word of faith, as it was unto him? This is what none, who understand the privilege of a New Testament dispensation, will adventure to deny ; yea, I will adventure to say, that the ground of faith, is laid before us under the New Testament, with a far greater advantage than ever Abraham had ; inasmuch as the gospel-revelation is much more clear, and brings Christ and his salvation much nearer to us, than ever he was under any period of the old Testament dispensation. " Abraham saw his day only afar off ;" whereas we live in that very day which he saw at such a prodigious distance : and therefore we have much more ground to believe without staggering than he had. And therefore, " seeing we have boldness to enter into the holiest by the blood of Jesus ; and seeing we have a new and living way consecrated for us, through the vail of his flesh ; and seeing we have an High Priest over the house of God : let us draw near with a true heart, in FULL ASSURANCE of faith," &c.

The sure and solid grounds of Faith's Assurance.

1. THE grace, mercy, and goodness of a promising God revealed and proclaimed in the word, is a noble ground for sinners, and yet more for saints, to trust him, and draw near to him through Christ, with a full assurance of faith : Psalm xxxvi. 7. " How excellent is thy loving kindness, O God ! therefore the children of men put their trust under the shadow of thy wings." It is cross to the very dictates of nature, for a man to trust one whom he apprehends to be an enemy ; yea, if we have but a jealousy that one bears us an ill-will

or designs our hurt, we will not trust or confide in him : but persuade a man once that such a one is his friend, that he hath an entire love and kindness for him, and wants only an opportunity to do him the greatest services he is capable ; in that case, he will trust him without hesitation. Just so is it in the case in hand : so long as we conceive God to be an implacable enemy, our prejudice and enmity against him will remain ; and while enmity against God stands in its full strength, it is absolutely impossible we can have any trust or confidence in him ; instead of drawing near to him with full assurance of faith, we flee from him like our first parents, under the awful apprehensions of his wrath and vengeance : but let us once be persuaded that he is a God of love, grace, pity, and good-will in Christ, then, and never till then, will we put our trust under the shadow of his wings. And therefore, to break the strength of our enmity and prejudice, and so to conciliate our trust in him, he is at the greatest pains imaginable to persuade us, that he bears a hearty liking and good-will toward us in Christ. And there are more especially these three ways God takes to convince us of his good-will toward men upon earth.

1*st*, By solemn proclamations and declarations of his mercy and grace : Exod. xxxiv. 6, 7. there the Lord passed by Moses, and proclaimed his name to him ; and what is it ? " The Lord, the Lord God, merciful and gracious, long-suffering, and abundant in goodness and truth, keeping mercy for thousands, forgiving iniquity and transgression, and sin, and that will by no means clear the guilty ;" or, as some read it, " in clearing he will clear," i. e. in clearing the sinner of guilt by pardoning grace, he will clear himself of injustice ; he will make it appear that he is just, when he is the justifier of him that believes in Jesus. Every where in scripture is the pardoning mercy of God proclaimed and presented as an encouragement to sinners to trust in him, Psal. cxxx. 7. " Let Israel hope in the

Lord : for with the Lord there is mercy, and with him is plenteous redemption."

2dly. By solemn oath. Lest we should disbelieve his word, he superadds his oath, to convince us that he has no ill will, but a hearty good-will toward our salvation and happiness, through the new and living way ; Ezek. xxxiii. 11. " As I live, saith the Lord God, I have no pleasure in the death of the wicked, but that the wicked turn from his way and live : turn ye, turn ye from your evil ways ; for why will ye die, O house of Israel ?"   " An oath among men is for confirmation of a controverted truth, and is to them an end of all strife," says the apostle, Heb. vi. 16.   Well, Sirs, shall the oath of a man be so much regarded, as to determine controversies among men ? How much more is the oath of the great God to be regarded, pawning his very life upon it, that he is not willing that any should perish, that he bears a hearty good-will toward our salvation through Christ ? Shall this be any more a controversy with us ?   To entertain a doubt or jealousy of what he says, is to make him a liar ; and to doubt and disbelieve what he swears, is to charge a God of truth with perjury.   And beware of looking upon it as a matter of indifferency, whether you believe this declared good-will, mercy, and grace of God, or not ; for it must needs be a matter of vast importance, wherein God interposes the solemnity of an oath ; and to think otherwise, is to charge the eternal God with a profanation of his own name, which he will not suffer in others without the highest resentment.

3dly, As if his word and his oath were not enough to convince us of his mercy, love, and good-will toward us, he hath given the most convincing and practical demonstration of it that was possible for God to give, and that is, by giving himself, in the person of his eternal Son, to be incarnate, or manifested in our nature ; yea, to be made like unto us in all things, sin only excepted.   O how great is this mystery of godliness, God manifested in the flesh !   Without contro-

versy, great and unsearchable is the mystery of love
and good-will that shines with a meridian lustre in an
incarnate Deity. If God had not loved us, and borne
such a hearty desire after our happiness and salvation,
would he even made such a near approach to us as to
dwell in our nature, when he passed by the nature of
angels? Yea, he was not content to become one with
us in nature, but he goes further, and becomes one in law
with us ; he puts his name into our debt-bond, and becomes "sin for us, that we might be made the righteousness of God in him ;" he becomes " a curse for us, that
we might inherit the blessing." It was a view of this design of love to man, shining in the incarnation of the
Son of God, which made the angels at his birth to
break forth with that celestial anthem, " Glory to God
in the highest, and on earth peace, good-will towards
men," Luke ii. 14. Now, this love, and good-will
of God toward man, in the incarnation of his eternal
Son, is proposed in the gospel revelation, as the greatest encouragement imaginable for guilty rebellious sinners to lay aside their enmity and prejudice against
God, and so to put their trust and confidence in him ;
as is plain, like a sunbeam, from that great text, John
iii. 16. " God so loved the world that he gave his only begotten Son :" Why, what was God's design in
all this good-will ? " That whosoever believeth in
him, should not perish, but have everlasting life." Because of the excellency of this love, the sons of men
do put their trust under the shadow of his wings. Now,
I say, faith, in drawing near to God, it takes a view
of this mercy and love of God in Christ, and upon
this ground raises itself up sometimes so high, as to
draw near in full assurance of acceptance : for still it
would be remembered, that faith, under the conduct
of the Spirit, takes up this revealed love and mercy of
God to sinners, with particular application there of to
the soul itself, as was before hinted. And what can
be more encouraging to a trust, without doubting of
acceptance ? O then, " let Israel hope in the Lord ;

for with the Lord there is mercy." O do not entertain jealousies of a God of love, as though he were displeased or dissatisfied with you for your trusting in his
mercy ; for " the Lord taketh pleasure in them that fear
him in those that hope in his mercy."

2. Faith grounds its assurance upon the infinite power of a promising God. Being once persuaded of his
love, mercy, and good-will in Christ, it proceeds to
fasten its foot upon everlasting strength, as fully able
to fulfil what he has promised, saying, I know that thou
can do every thing, and " there is nothing too hard for
thee. " Indeed, infinite power, armed with wrath and
fury, is the terror of a guilty sinner ; but infinite power, animated with infinite love, proclaiming, " Fury is
not in me," through the ransom that I have found, is
a noble ground of trust, and may embolden a guilty
sinner to " take hold of his strength, that he may make
peace with him." Hence it is, that the power of God
in Christ is frequently presented in scripture as a
ground of trust, Is. xxvi. 4. " Trust ye in the Lord
for ever : for in the Lord Jehovah is everlasting
strength." The faith of Abraham founded itself upon
this rock of the power of God, in that forecited instance, Rom. iv. when he believed without staggering
at the promise. Being first persuaded of God's good-
will toward him, in giving him a promise of the Messiah to spring of his loins, " in whom all the nations of
the earth should be blessed ;" he next fixes the eye of
his faith upon the power of this promising God, and
was " fully persuaded, that what he had promised, he
was able also to perform." So, Matth. ix. 27, we read
of two blind men following Christ, sending their cries
after him, " Thou son of David, have mercy on us."
They first believed that Christ was the promised Messiah, the son of David ; and in this they saw mercy and
good-will to man upon earth, he being the seed of
the woman, that should bruise the head of the serpent.
Well, Christ leads them on next to take a view of the
power of God in him, as a further ground of trust and

confidence, ver. 28. " Jesus saith unto them, Believe ye
that I am able to do this ?" They answer, "Yea, Lord :"
and thereupon Christ says unto them, ver. 29. " Accord
ing to your faith, be it unto you." Thus, I say, faith
grounds its trust, confidence, or assurance, in drawing
near to God through the new and living way, upon
the power of a promising God.

O, Sirs, there is no such distance betwixt God's saying and his doing, as there is among men ; for his saying is doing: Psal. xxxiii. 9. " He spake, and it was
done ; he commanded, and it stood fast." There is
an omnipotence or almightiness both in his word of
command, and in his word of promise ; therefore it is
called " the word of his power," Heb. 1. 3. And by
this powerful word, he upholds the great fabric of
heaven and earth, that they do not return unto their
original nothing : and may not our faith venture to
stand upon that bottom, on which heaven and earth
stands ? We are not afraid that this ponderous globe
of earth, which hangs in the liquid air, slide away from
under our feet with its own weight: Why ? Because
we believe that the word of God's power has fixed it
in its proper place, that it shall not be removed for ever.
Why should we not rest with as much assured confidence, as to everlasting concerns, upon God's covenant
and promise, seeing the same power of God is in the
word of promise, as in that word which upholds the
earth ? Yea, " the fashion of this world passeth away,
but the word of the Lord," his word of grace and promise, the foundation of faith and trust, " endureth for
ever." This is a consideration which at once removes
the principal discouragements that faith labours under.
What is it that weakens our faith, and keeps it from
arriving at a full assurance, as to the performance of
the promise, but one of these two? Either we look
upon the performance of the promise as difficult, or
uncertain. Now, faith eyeing the power of a promising, reconciled God in Christ, can easily surmount
both, and conclude, that the performance of the pro-

mise is both easy and certain. (1.) It is certain, for it depends upon the will of an unchangeable God, the promise being a declaration of God's purpose or will of grace; he was willing to promise, for he has actually done it, "the word is gone out of his mouth:" and he is willing to perform, for he is a God of truth, always yea, and amen. (2.) Faith viewing the power of God, sees the performance to be easy. What more easy than a word speaking? and yet one word from the mouth of God, can give being and accomplishment to all the promises, without any pain, cost, trouble, or hazard. The covenant of grace may be resembled unto a tree, the promises to the branches of the tree, loaden with all manner of precious fruit. Now, the least word, the least breath from the mouth of God, shakes the tree, and makes all the fruit of it to drop down, as it were, into the believer's bosom. And O, may the believer argue, will not he, who "so loved a lost world, as to give his only begotten Son, and who loved me, and gave himself for me," will not he ware a word, or the breath of his mouth, on me? Believe it, there is nothing but a word between you and all the sure mercies of David: yea, the word is already passed out of his mouth, I mean, the word of grace and promise; and there remains nothing but for you to believe, trust, and confide in it, and him that made it; and, in your so doing, all the sure mercies of the promise are your own in Christ. I suppose you do not doubt, but that God who cannot lie has promised. Now, there is as much reason to believe that he will perform, as to believe that he has passed his promise; for, as was hinted above, to promise and perform, to say and to do, are all one thing with him. Indeed when men promise, there is much ground to doubt the performance, because frequently things cast up afterward, which render it impracticable for them to do as they have said. But no such thing can happen unto him, who perfectly foresees all future events, and who commands things that are not, as if they were. Now, I say, faith sees

all this, and thereby raises itself up unto a full assurance, at least there is ground here for a full assurance
of faith, and no ground at all for doubting and wavering. And were not our faith pinioned with ignorance
and unbelief, it could not miss to believe without staggering upon this ground, as did the faith of Abraham.
3. The veracity and faithfulness of a God in Christ,
pawned in the promise, is another ground upon which
faith builds, when it draws near with a full assurance.
Faithfulness in God, and faith in man, are correlates;
and there is such a sibness and relation betwixt these
two, that our faith cannot subsist without faithfulness
in God. And, on the other hand, a revelation of God's
faithfulness would have been needless, if there were not
some to believe him. The light would be useless, if
there were not an eye to see it; and the eye would be
useless, if there were no light. To an unbelieving sinner, the revelation of the divine faithfulness is as unprofitable, as light is to a blind man; and our faith
would be like an eye without light, if there were not
faithfulness in God. Yea, faithfulness in God is the
very parent of faith in man. Faith is at first begot
and wrought in the soul by some discovery of the divine
faithfulness in the word of grace; and it is maintained
and increased in the same way and manner. Whence
is it that some do believe, and others not, who equally
enjoy the same revealed warrants and grounds of faith?
The matter is this, the faithfulness of God in the covenant and promise is revealed by the Spirit to the one,
and vailed and hid from the other, "the god of this
world blinding the minds of them which believe not."
And whence is it, that at one time a believer is "strong
in faith, giving glory to God;" and at another time,
"staggers through unbelief?" The reason is this, the
faithfulness of God at one time is so visible to him,
that he sees it to be like a mountain of brass under
him: at another time his light is so dark and dim, that
he imagines the promise, and the faithfulness of the
Promiser, to be but like a broken reed, not able to bear

his weight. But, O Sirs, what can be ground of assurance, yea of the highest and fullest assurance of
faith, if not the veracity of that God, who hath "righteousness for the girdle of his loins, and faithfulness for
the girdle of his reins?"

Let us but take a view of the high securities by which
the divine faithfulness is engaged, as to the outmaking
of his promise, and see if there be not ground for a
full assurance of faith. The most jealous and suspicious
heart in the world, could not desire greater security
from the most treacherous person on earth, than a God
of truth has granted unto us, for our encouragement
to believe.

1st, Then, Let it be considered, that the bare promise, though there were no more, is abundance of security, especially if we consider whose promise it is;
it is "God that cannot lie, who promises." A grace-
less Balaam gives him this testimony, "God is not a
man, that he should lie, neither the son of man, that
he should repent; hath he said, and shall he not do it?
or hath he spoken, and shall he not make it good?"
We will adventure to trust the word of a man like ourselves, especially if he be a man of integrity and
honesty, who, we think, will not falsify his word: and
shall we have trust and credit to give to a man that
may lie and repent, and yet no credit or trust to give
to him "for whom it is impossible to lie?" God has
so great a regard to his word of promise, that it is of
more worth in his reckoning than heaven and earth,
and all the visible creation; yea, "Heaven and earth
shall pass away, but one jot or one tittle of what he
hath spoken shall never fall to the ground." Yea, I
will adventure to say further, that the divine faithfulness is so much engaged in the promise, that his very
being is concerned therein. Man may break his word,
and continue to be man still; but God could not be
God, if he were not faithful and true, because faithfulness is essential to his very nature and being. Now,
is not that word a sufficient ground of faith, and of full

assurance, as to the performance of which the very be-ing of a God of truth is so much concerned? But this is not all; for,

2dly, Not only is the word of promise passed out of his lips, but it is entered and registrate in the volume of his book. You know, the bare word of an honest man is good, but his written and registrate word or promise is better. When we put a man's bond in the register of human courts, it is in order to our better security, and getting the more speedy diligence there-upon. Now, God has consented to the registration of his word of promise, yea, it is actually enrolled and registrate in the scriptures of truth ; and is not this a high engagement of the faithfulness of God? Perhaps you may think, if you had voices, visions, and revela-tions from heaven immediately, you could believe ; but I can assure you, in the name of God, that the Bible, the book of God, which you have among your hands, is a far better, a much more solid ground of faith and trust, than any thing of that kind. The apostle Peter tells us, 2 Pet. i. 17. that he was taken up into mount Tabor, at Christ's transfiguration, and there he heard a voice coming forth from the excellent glory, saying, " This is my beloved Son, in whom I am well pleased." This was a rare privilege, and a notable encouragement to believe : but yet, says he, ver. 19, " We have a more sure word of prophecy : whereunto ye do well that ye take heed," &c. O, Sirs, think on this, and prize and improve your Bibles.

3dly, The faithfulness of God is so much engaged in the promise, that it is a sealed deed. The great and infinite JEHOVAH, in the person of his eternal Son, has sealed the promise, yea sealed it with his blood. Dan. ix. 27. we are told concerning the Messiah, that he should " confirm the covenant with many." And how doth he confirm it, but by his death? Hence the blood of Christ is called " the blood of the covenant :" so Heb. ix. 16, 17. " Where a testament is, there must also of necessity be the death of the testator. For a testament is of force after men are dead : otherwise it is of no strength at all whilst the testator liveth." Thus, I say, the promise is sealed and confirmed by the blood of the Lamb, the most valuable seal that ever was appended to any deed in the world. And, in token and testimony of its being sealed by a Redeemer's blood, God has appended two other visible seals unto his covenant of promise, viz. baptism and the Lord's supper, which are " seals of the righteousness of faith ;" that is, as I take it, seals of that covenant where God promises peace and pardon, grace and glory, on the score of the imputed righteousness of Christ, apprehended by faith. And whenever these sacraments are dispensed to us, according to God's appointment, we have a sealed and confirmed promise and testament put into our hands, for our faith to feed and feast upon.

4*thly*, The faithfulness of God is so far engaged in the promise, that his oath is interposed : Heb. vi. 13. —18. there we read of " two immutable things, in which it is impossible for God to lie." His word is immutable, for it is always yea. But that we might have strong consolation, by having a strong ground of faith and confidence, he superadds his immutable oath : he not only speaks, but swears. Now, observe how the apostle speaks of the oath of God, ver. 13. " Because he could swear by no greater, he sware by himself;" q. d. If God could have gone higher in his oath, he would have done it. The form of God's oath is peculiar to himself, " As I live ;" he swears by his life, he swears by his holiness, he swears by his being and Godhead. As true as I am God, " I will bless thee," says the Lord to Abraham, ver. 14. But, may a poor soul say, what is that to me ? what interest or concern have I in God's oath to Abraham ? O yes, says the apostle, this concerns you and me, " who have fled for refuge to lay hold upon the hope set before us," ver. 18. Q. d. This concerns every poor soul, that has a mind for salvation in the " new and living way consecrated for us." He may say, and should say in himself, As sure as God said and sware to Abraham, so surely hath God said and sworn that I shall be saved, in fleeing for refuge to Christ, who is our hope. As if the Lord should say, O sinner, I set my own Son before thee in the gospel, as thy only refuge and sanctuary; I set him forth as a propitiation through faith in his blood; O flee, flee to him for thy life, " Turn ye to your strong hold, ye prisoners of hope;" for as sure as I am God, thou shalt be saved in him : " Israel shall be saved in the Lord with an everlasting salvation." O what a great matter is this, the oath of God! What will we ever believe, or whom will we believe, if we do not believe a God of truth swearing by his life? Do not say, you are not concerned with his oath; for as by believing you set to your seal, that he is true in what he says and swears; so by your unbelief you call him a liar, and, upon the matter, charge him with perjury, as was already hinted. And for you who have actually fled by faith unto his Son, you shall be as sure of God's blessing through eternity, as ever Abraham was, when he heard God swearing to him, " Surely, blessing I will bless thee, and multiplying, I will multiply thee."

5thly, The faithfulness of God is yet further engaged to believers in the promise, by giving a pledge or arls of the full performance : and the pledge he gives, is of more worth than heaven and earth. O, say you, what is that? I answer, It is the " Holy Spirit of promise, which is the earnest of the inheritance," Eph. i. 13, 14. If ever thou felt the Holy Spirit breathing on thee, by his saving influences and operations, thou hast the earnest of the inheritance, a pledge that all the promises shall be fully accomplished in God's time. You know, if a man give a pledge, it is a security for the full bargain; and if a man do not fulfil his bargain, he loses his pledge : so here, God will as soon forfeit his Spirit, as break his word. And is not this notable security to the believer ? Is not this a high engagement of the faithfulness of God ?

6thly, The faithfulness of God is yet further engaged in the promise, by the concurring declaration of the most famous witnesses that ever bore testimony in any cause, jointly attesting the truth of the promise, and veracity of the Promiser, 1 John v. 7. " There are three that bear record in heaven, the Father, the Word, and the Holy Ghost : and these three are one." The eternal Father attests the truth of the promise with a " Thus saith the Lord." The Son attests it, who is the essential and substantial Word ; for he is " the truth, the Amen, the faithful and true witness, who speaks in righteousness." The Holy Ghost attests it ; for he is " the Spirit of truth, leading into all truth ;" he is the holy Spirit of promise, not only because he himself is promised, but because he testifies of the truth of the promise, and faithfulness of the Promiser ; and, by his power and efficacy, seals and stamps these upon the soul, whereby he works faith or believing. Now, all these three witnesses are one ; not only one in essence, but one in their testimony. And what is the testimony and record of a Trinity ? It is this, ver. 11. " That God hath given (i. e. granted in his covenant of grace and promise) to us eternal life ; and this life is in his Son." And when this record or testimony of a Trinity is not believed, we make God a liar. From the whole, you see what high and deep engagements the divine faithfulness is come under for the outmaking and accomplishment of the promise. O, then, " Let us draw near with a true heart, in full assurance of faith ; for faithful is he that hath promised acceptance in the beloved."

But now, after all that has been said, some may be ready to object, It is true, the good-will, power, and veracity of the Promiser, are excellent encouragements to these who have a right to the promise to draw near to God in Christ with full assurance of faith : but that is my strait and difficulty, I doubt and fear, lest I have no claim or title to the promise of welcome into the holiest by the blood of Jesus, by that new and living way. An answer to this leads me to,

4. A fourth ground (taken in connection with the former) upon which faith may build its assurance, in drawing near to God by the new and living way, and that is, the indorsement or direction of the promise of welcome through Christ. To whom, say you, is the promise indorsed? I answer, It is directed to every man to whom the joyful sound of this everlasting gospel reacheth, John iii. 16. There you see that the promise of acceptance, and of eternal life through Christ, reaches forth its arms to a lost world; " Whosoever believeth in him, shall not perish, but have everlasting life." So here, Whosoever draweth near to the holiest by the blood of Jesus, by the new and living way, through the mediation of the great high priest, shall obtain grace and mercy to help them in time of need. The covenant of grace, and promises thereof, are so framed by Infinite Wisdom, in the external dispensation of the gospel, that they look to every man and woman, and, as it were, invite them to believe, and encourage them to enter into the holiest. He that sits on a throne of grace, calls every one within his hearing, to come for grace and mercy, assuring them, that come to him who will, " he will in no wise cast out." And we that are the heralds and ministers of the great King, whose name is " the Lord, merciful and gracious," have warrant and commission to proclaim, that to you, men, and the sons of man, is the word of this salvation sent : The promise is directed unto you, as a ground of faith, even " to you, and to your seed, and to all that are afar off, even as many as the Lord our God shall call." There is not the least peradventure, but the call or command of believing is to every one, otherwise unbelief could not be their sin. Now, the promise, in the indorsement and direction thereof, must be as extensive as the command : these two are inseparably linked together, both in the external dispensation, and in the inward application of the Spirit ; insomuch that whosoever is commanded to believe, has right to

the promise, as the immediate ground of his faith; and
whosoever actually believes, and builds upon this ground,
has the promise in his possession. Take away the promise from the command of believing, you separate
what God has joined together, and, in effect, command men to build without a foundation. It is true,
Christ is the object of faith ; but it is as true, that he
can only be the object of faith to us, as he is brought
near in the word of faith or promise, Rom. x. 8. And
therefore, seeing the promise is to you and me, and
every one who hears this gospel, I may warrantably
say with the apostle, Heb. iv. 1. " Let us fear, lest
a promise being left us of entering into his rest, any
of you should seem to come short of it." From
which text it is plain, that the promise of an everlasting
rest, in and through Christ, is left even to those who, like
the Israelites, may come short of it through unbelief.
And how is it left us, but to be applied by faith ?
Christ our elder brother has left his confirmed testament in our hands, to be improven and used in a
way of believing, in order to our being actually entitled to, and in due time, fully possessed of that rest,
which is the purchase of his death and blood. O,
then, let us fear, lest, when the promise is thus left us,
we should seem to come short of the possession ; for
the promise can never be ours in possession, though
left us, unless we believe ; as is plain from the words
immediately following, ver. 2. where it is added, concerning the unbelieving Jews, " The word preached
(viz. the promise of entering into his rest, as is plain
from the connection) did not profit them, not being
mixed with faith in them that heard it." A king's
proclamation, and promise of pardon to a company
of rebels, cannot profit any of them but such as accept of it. A legacy left by latter-will of a rich and
wealthy friend, to a certain family, without specifying
one individual person of the family, can only profit
that person, or these branches of the family who claim
right to the legacy, upon their friend's testament ; but

to the rest it is unprofitable, because, through pride or ignorance, or sloth, they forsake their own mercy. Or, suppose a letter should come indorsed to me, containing a bank-note of 50, 100, or 1000 pounds sterling, or more if you will ; the indorsement of the letter to me, gives me a right to carry the bill to the bank, and ask payment : but if, through pride and conceit that I am rich, and increased with goods, I will not receive the letter, nor ask payment of the sum, in that case I come short of my own privilege, and it becomes unprofitable to me. I own, that in every one of these similitudes, there is a dissimilitude ; the only use I make of them is, to show how near Christ and his salvation is brought unto us in the word of faith or promise, that thereby we may be encouraged to draw near by the blood of Jesus, with full assurance of faith, seeing he is faithful that hath promised acceptance in this new and living way. To all that is said, I shall only add,

5. Let it encourage us to draw near in full assurance of faith, that there is no lawful impediment to hinder our access and success, in entering with boldness into the holiest by the blood of Jesus. Every bar and hinderance that stood in our way is mercifully removed by our " great High Priest," who is " over the house of God." All the impediments that can be pleaded on God's part, are the law, justice, and holiness of God ; and all the impediment that can be pleaded on our part is sin. Now, none of these ought to hinder our drawing near in this new and living way, with full assurance of faith.

As for the law, that cannot be a just impediment to hinder our access ; for that moment the soul enters by Christ, as the way to the Father, the law gets its end, Christ being " the end of the law for righteousness to every one that believeth." Now, can the law be against its own end, or that which gives it its due ? All that the law demands is a perfect and sinless righteousness; give it that, and it has no more to seek. Now, this the law gets, that moment that a sinner believes, or draws near by the blood of Jesus. "What the law could not do, in that it was weak through the flesh, God sending his own Son, in the likeness of sinful flesh, and for sin condemned sin in the flesh : that the righteousness of the law might be fulfilled in us, who walk not after the flesh, but after the Spirit," Rom. viii. 3, 4. From whence it is plain, that every soul that believes in Christ, is that moment vested, by imputation, with the righteousness of the Son of God, whereby "the law is magnified, and made honourable." And therefore, in drawing near by the blood of Jesus, instead of having the law against us, we have the law for us, and on our side ; we have a perfect law-righteousness to plead upon.

Again, as for the justice of God, this is ready to scare us, who are guilty sinners, from so much as looking to-ward the holiest, or the place where God's honour dwells. But this can be no impediment either to our drawing near by the blood of Jesus, with full assurance of faith : Why ? That which justice demands, is a complete satisfaction for the injury done to the honour and authority of God, by the breach and violation of the holy and righteous law, which was a transcript of the purity and equity of his nature: now, when a sinner draws near, or enters into the holiest by the blood of Jesus, he gives justice that which it wants also, namely, a ransom of infinite value, even the ransom that God has found, the propitiation that God has set forth in the gospel, to be received by faith. The man, in be-lieving, he, as it were, presents this ransom unto justice for the sin of his soul : and whenever justice sees this ransom of the blood of Jesus in the hand of faith, it assoilzies and acquits the soul from all law-penalties, declaring that "now there is no condemnation to that man," Rom. viii. 1. Let none from henceforth "lay any thing to his charge : for it is God that justifieth; who then is he that shall condemn ? It is Christ that died, yea rather, that is risen again, who is even at the right hand of God, who also maketh intercession."

Thus justice, instead of barring our way to the holiest, becomes our friend, and casts open the door of access to us : for God is just, when he is "the justifier of them that believe in Jesus."

As for the holiness of God, that seems to stand as an insuperable bar in our way of entering into the holiest, by reason of the blot, defilement, and pollution of sin, which renders us utterly loathsome in the sight of the holy One of Israel. But, glory to God in the highest, this bar is also removed by the blood of Jesus ; for, that moment a sinner comes under the covert of this blood, and draws near to God under this covering, he hath his heart thereby " sprinkled from an evil conscience, and his body washed with pure water." That same moment that the righteousness of the second Adam is extended to us for justification, his Spirit enters into us for sanctification, renewing us in the whole man, after the image of God. And the blood of Jesus not only cancels the guilt of sin, which made us obnoxious to the law and justice of God ; but it hides and covers the filth of sin from the eyes of immaculate holiness. Yea, holiness is so much the sinner's friend, in drawing near through the blood of Jesus, that this attribute of the divine nature is pawned in the promise of acceptance made to Christ and his seed, Psalm lxxxix. 2, 35. On which account I may exhort all true believers, in the words of the psalmist, Psalm xxx. 4. " Sing unto the Lord, O ye saints of his, and give thanks at the remembrance of his holiness." Thus then, I say, all impediments and bars on God's part, that might hinder our access into the holiest, are removed by the blood of Jesus : and therefore, " let us draw near with a true heart, in full assurance of faith."

As for impediments on our part, they may be more particularly spoken to in the application. I shall only say at the time, that the sum-total of them all amounts to this, that we are sinners, and so wretched, miserable, poor, blind, and naked, that we cannot think that ever

God will receive or welcome us. But at once to roll away this impediment, let it be considered,. that this new and living way of access into the holiest, is only calculate for sinners : " Christ calls not the righteous (or innocent), out sinners," to enter by him, as the way to the Father. If you were not sinners, but righteous, as Adam was before the fall, you would not need to enter "by the blood of Jesus." But seeing the way and door to the holiest is just shaped and cal- culate for the sinner, let not the sinner scare to enter by it into the presence of God ; especially when he calls us, who are sinners, to " draw near with a true heart in full assurance of faith." Faithful is he that hath pro- mised acceptance in the beloved.

The Great Mystery in Believing.

THERE is a mystery in believing, which the world does not understand, yea, which none can know with- out " that Spirit which is of God whereby we know the things that are freely given to us of God." The apostle, 1 Tim. iii. 9. speaks of the mystery of faith. And indeed every thing about it is a mystery. The way of its production, or how it is wrought in the soul, by the power of the eternal Spirit, is a mystery : " Who can tell how the bones are formed in the womb of her that is with child?" far less are we capable to account for the way and manner of the Spirit's operation in forming and creating us in Christ Jesus by faith. Hence is that of Christ to Nicodemus, John iii. 8. " The wind bloweth where it listeth, and thou hearest the sound thereof, but canst not tell whence it cometh, and whither it goeth : so is every one that is born of the Spirit." How the Spirit of God drops into the heart the incorruptible seed of his own word, and impregnates it there, so as to turn it, though in itself but a dead letter, into a living principle, purifying the heart, de- basing self, and carrying the soul directly into Christ for all, is a mystery which we cannot comprehend or account for. And then the object of faith is a great mystery. God, the ultimate object of it, is an awful mystery : " Who can by searching find him out," either in his essence, operations, or manner of his existence, one in three, and three in one ? Christ, the more immediate object of faith, is a great mystery, an incarnate Deity : " Without controversy, great is the mystery of godliness : God was manifest in the flesh." The gospel-covenant, by which we believe in Christ, is a " mystery which hath been hid from ages, and from generations, but now is made manifest to the saints." And, lastly, the actings of faith upon its objects is a great mystery : how the poor believer on earth can receive Christ in heaven, at the right hand of God : how he applies him as his own Saviour, his own Prophet, Priest, and King, upon the indefinite grant that is made of him in the new covenant, where the man is neither designed by name or surname : how faith makes use of Christ and his fulness, with as great freedom as a man makes use of meat and drink that is set before him, on which account it is said to " eat the flesh and drink the blood of the Son of man :" how it puts on the righteousness of Christ, and glories in the obedience of another, as though the man had fulfilled the law in his own person : how it draws forth the fulness of the Godhead, dwelling bodily in Christ, and thus fills the soul with the " fulness of God :" how it will take a bare word, dropping from God's mouth, and rejoice in it as one that findeth great spoils : how it will take this word, and draw near to him in the new and living way, with full assurance of acceptance. These things are mysteries which flesh and blood cannot reveal : and yet to every true believer it is given, in less or more, to know these mysteries of the kingdom.

The Great Excellency of the Grace of Faith.

WHEN faith takes a view of the " blood of Jesus," of the "new and living way," and of the " High Priest over the house of God," it can "draw near to the holiest with

full assurance of welcome." And it is not without
warrant that faith promises itself welcome from the
Lord in its approaches to him through Christ : God
nas made the same, yea, much greater grant to the
grace of faith, as Ahasuerus made unto Esther, chap,
ix. 12. " What is thy petition ? and it shall be granted
thee : or what is thy request ? and it shall be done."
Compare this with John xiv. 13, 14. " Whatsoever
ye shall ask in my name, that will I do, that the Father may be glorified in the Son. If ye shall ask any
thing in my name, I will do it." So Mark xi. 24.
" What things soever ye desire when ye pray, believe
that ye receive them, and ye shall have them." As
Ahasuerus put a peculiar honour upon Esther, and
preferred her above all the maids in his kingdom ; so
God, the King of kings, stamps a peculiar honour and
excellency upon the grace of faith, preferring it above
all the other graces ; on which account it may say with
Mary, Luke i. 48. " He hath regarded the low estate
of his hand-maiden." Though God be high, yet hath
he a respect unto the lowly : though he be the high
and lofty One that inhabiteth eternity, yet he dwells
with the humble: he delights to choose, and put honour
upon the foolish, weak, base, and despised things of
this world ; yea, he chooses " things which are not, to
bring to nought things that are." Faith is the meanest
and lowest, the poorest and most beggarly of all the
other graces; for all the other graces they give something unto God, whereas faith, like a mere beggar,
comes not to give any thing, but to get and receive
all : and yet God takes this beggar, and sets it among
princes, to allude unto that expression, Psalm cxiii. 7,
8. Such honour and preferment does God put upon
this grace, that though he has said, " He will not give
his glory to another ;" yet so little jealousy has he of
the grace of faith, that he, as it were, sets it upon the
throne with himself, ascribing things to it, which are
proper and peculiar unto himself only : he sets the
jewels of his crown upon the head of faith. The sal-

vation of a lost sinner is God's prerogative ; he alone is
" the God of salvation, to whom belong 'the issues
from death ;" and yet we find this attributed unto the
grace of faith, " Thy faith hath saved thee, (says
Christ) ; go in peace." Justification is peculiar unto
God only, " It is God that justifieth," says the apostle ;
and yet the same apostle ascribes the justification of a
sinner unto faith. " A man is justified by faith without the deeds of the law." God alone is " the Lord
of life," who " kills, and makes alive ;" and yet life is
ascribed unto faith, " The just shall live by his faith."
Omnipotency is God's peculiar prerogative, he is the
Almighty ; and yet there is almightiness attribute unto
faith, " All things are possible to him that believeth."
" If we have faith as a grain of mustard-seed," we may
say unto this and the other mountain, Be thou removed,
and it shall be done. If we read the 11th chapter of
the Hebrews, we shall find things ascribed to faith,
which nothing but Omnipotency itself could effect,
such as the " stopping the mouths of lions, quenching
the violence of fire, raising the dead," and the like.
Now, would you know why God doth thus attribute
works and perfections to faith, which are proper to
himself alone ? The plain reason is, because faith is
such a low, mean, self-denied grace, that it is just the
genius and nature of it to exclude self, yea, to exclude
itself, to glory in the Lord alone, and to give him the
glory due unto his name, saying, " Not unto us, O
Lord, not unto us, but unto thy name be the glory."
Does faith save us ? Yes it does : but then it turns the
glory of salvation over upon the author thereof, saying,
" Our God is the God of salvation." Does the just man
live by faith ? Yes : but then faith steps in with " It is
not I :" Gal. ii. 20. " I live ; yet not I, but Christ liv
eth in me." Does faith justify ? Yea, it doth : but then
its language is, " Surely in the Lord have I righteousness, in him will I be justified, and in him alone will I
glory." Can faith do every thing ? Yea, but it is by
leaning on the arm of omnipotency. " I can do all

things through Christ which strengtheneth me." Thus, I say, faith arrogates and claims nothing to itself, but gives unto the Lord the glory due unto his name. And so zealous is faith to have God alone exalted, particularly the freedom of his grace in the justification and salvation of a sinner, that, though believing be the highest and greatest act of obedience that a person can yield unto the moral law, yet that boasting may be for ever excluded, it excludes and shuts out itself from the rank and category of works, or acts of obedience, Rom. iv. 5. "To him that worketh not, but believeth in him that justifieth the ungodly, his faith (objectively considered) is counted for righteousness." It is the peculiar excellency of faith, that it sinks its own act, that its blessed object, CHRIST, may be "all in all; it rejoices in Christ Jesus, and triumphs always in him." And though, as I was saying, it be the poorest, lowest, and most beggarly of all the other graces ; yet it is a grace that prides itself in the Lord Jesus, and by his blood enters with boldness into the holiest.

Reigning Unbelief a contradiction to the revealed will of God.

I say, reigning unbelief in the wicked is a flat contradiction to the will of God. The man under the power of unbelief, instead of drawing near with the assurance of faith, departs from him, through a distrust and jealousy of his grace, power, and veracity. Solomon tells us, Prov. vi. 34. "Jealousy is the rage of a man." If we shall entertain and express a jealousy or distrust of a man's veracity, it is enough to exasperate and enrage him against us : why? when we express a jealousy of him, we in effect call him a liar. And if man who is vanity, and the son of man who is a lie, reckon it such an indignity to have their veracity or kindness called in question ; how much more is it an indignity done to him, for whom it is impossible to lie? O Sirs! unbelief offers the most signal affront to a God of truth, that is possible for a creature to do.

God, as you were hearing, to encourage our faith and
confidence toward him, has given all the securities
which he could possibly grant ; yea, the most jealous
heart in the world could not ask better security from
the most treacherous person on earth, than God has
granted in his word : for though his bare word of promise be enough to command faith from all mankind,
yet, beside his word, he has given his writ ; beside his
writ, he has given his sacred oath ; beside his oath, he
has given a Surety ; beside a Surety, he has appended
solemn seals, and ratified all by the joint testimony of
the three that bear record in heaven, Father, Word,
and Spirit. Now, after all these securities, to entertain
a jealousy of him, as if he were not faithful to his promise of welcome and acceptance in the beloved, what
else is this but to make him a liar ? Faithfulness and
truth are "the girdle of his loins and reins ;" but unbelief does its utmost to strip him of his girdle, charg-
ing him with treachery and unfaithfulness. You would
reckon it an imputation of a very high and horrid nature, for any man to charge you with blasphemy against
God : and yet I will be bold to say, every unbeliever
is a blasphemer of God. Why, can there be greater
blasphemy under heaven, than to make God a liar ?
It is indeed most certain, that God will be found true,
and every man a liar : but yet the unbeliever does his
uttermost to make him a liar, by refusing credit to his
word. And, after all, is it any wonder though a holy
and jealous God be so enraged against the sin of unbelief, as to declare, that "he who believeth not, is
condemned already, and the wrath of God abideth on
him ?" Believe it, Sirs, if you continue to blaspheme
God by your unbelief here, you shall have time to
blaspheme him in hell with devils and damned spirits,
through the endless ages of eternity : John viii. 24.
"If ye believe not that I am he, ye shall die in your
sins." John xv. 22. "If I had not come, and spoken
unto them, they had not had sin : but now they have
no cloak for their sin."

In what the Unbelief of Sinners discovers itself.

1*st*, IT discovers itself in their frequent pleading the cause of unbelief, and that under the specious pretext of humility. O, will the man say, it would be too great a thing for the like of me to venture into the holiest; it would be presumption in me to draw near with full assurance of faith, asking peace and pardon, grace and glory; I dare not meddle with the gift of God, or take hold of his covenant; my fingers are too foul to touch such holy things. Here indeed is a fair mask and show of humility. But, Sirs, it is nothing else than the devil of unbelief wrapped up in Samuel's mantle; it is a pleading the cause of unbelief, and a refusing to obey the express command of God, under a pretence that you are not fit enough for believing, that you want this and that and the other qualification: and what is this but a tang of the old Adam, a tincture of the covenant of works? Whatever carnal reason may imagine, true faith, though it be the boldest, yet it is the most humble and self-emptying thing in the world; and the more of the boldness and assurance of faith, always the more humility. And the reason of this is plain, because faith in its dealings with God, despises so much as to cast an eye upon any grace or qualification in the soul itself, excepting it be its emptiness, misery, poverty, &c. and builds its whole confidence upon a ground without itself, namely, the noble qualification of the great High Priest over the house of God.

2*dly*, The unbelief of believers discovers itself in a faint, languid, and timorous way of believing, as if the ground they stand upon were not able to bear them. Much like a man walking upon weak ice, though he ventures his weight upon it, yet every moment he is afraid lest the ice break underneath him, and leave him in the deep. Just so is it with many believers, they venture upon Christ, upon his righteousness, and upon the faithfulness of God pawned in the promise, with a kind of erphing, as though they would fail underneath them, and leave them to perish for ever. And what else is this but unbelief, or a secret distrusting of the sufficiency of God's faithfulness, or of Christ's righteousness to bear up the soul in its eternal concerns?

3dly, The unbelief of believers appears in their being too much addicted to a way of living by sense. Sense, unless it have the stock in its own hand, it does not reckon the promise of God worth a farthing; but faith, it rejoices in the promise as its subsistence even when sense is out of doors. The believer who lives by sense, he will not believe the promise, or credit the veracity of the Promiser, unless he be hired and bribed with sensible consolations and manifestations; much like Thomas, John xx. 25. " Except I shall see in his hands the print of the nails, and put my finger into the print of the nails, and thrust my hand into his side, I will not believe." It is with many believers, as it is with some unskilful swimmers, they will venture into the deep waters if you will undertake to bear their heads above, but not otherwise; but this is not true swimming; true swimming is for a man to venture the weight of his body into the water, and by the strength of the water, and the waving of his hands and limbs, to bear himself up from sinking. So true believing is not for a man to trust God and his promise only when he is borne up with sensible consolations; but for a man to rest, stay, and bear up his soul upon the bare promise of God, even when these props are withdrawn; it is to " trust in the name of the Lord, and to stay ourselves upon him as our God, when we walk in darkness, and see no light."

Evidences of a Strong Faith.

1. THE more that the legality of the heart is overcome, the stronger is a man's faith. Every man is naturally married to the law as a covenant; and while there is any thing of nature in the believer, he will

find a strong bias in his heart, turning him into the
works of the law, as a ground of acceptance before
God. And O, how easily and insensibly do our spirits
glide into this old covenant-channel, imagining that
God accepts of us the better, on the score of our inherent holiness, or external acts of obedience! Now,
I say, the more that this bias of the heart is conquered, the stronger is our faith. A vigorous and lively
faith, it overlooks all graces, duties, attainments, and
experiences, as grounds of acceptance ; and founds its
confidence allenarly upon the blood of Jesus, the merit and mediation of the great high priest over the
house of God, by virtue of the covenant of grace, and
free promise of acceptance in him. The strong believer casts out the bond-woman, and her seed of legal
works and doings, owning himself only a son of the
free-woman, an heir of the promise of grace and glory,
through Christ and his imputed righteousness. Upon
this rock he drops his anchor, upon this foundation
he builds his hope, disclaiming his goodness as a thing
that extendeth not to the Lord, accounting his own
righteousness, whether legal or evangelical, before or
after conversion, as " loss and dung, that he may be
found in Christ, having the righteousness which is
through the faith of Christ." He will not take so
much as a stone or little pinning of the works of the
law, to help up the new fabric of grace ; no, it
shall be all grace from top to bottom, and through
every part of it, and grace reigning through imputed
righteousness alone : Eph. ii. 8, 9. " By grace are ye
saved, through faith ; and that not of yourselves : it
is the gift of God : not of works, lest any man should
boast."

2. Strong faith will build its confidence, as to great
matters, upon a naked word coming from the mouth
of Christ, even though sense and reason, yea, the ordinary course of providence, be against it. This we
see exemplified in the case of Abraham, formerly mentioned, Rom. iv. Though every thing seemed to

make against him, yet " He staggered not at the promise through unbelief, but was strong in faith, giving
glory to God." Yea, strong faith will catch at the
least hint of encouragement from the Lord, and build
its assurance thereupon, as to the desired event: Mat.
viii. 5—13, the centurion comes to Christ on behalf
of his servant, who was stricken with a palsy, and
grievously tormented. Christ answers, ver. 7. " I will
come and heal him." Well, the man's faith fixes upon
this simple word of promise, and is so much assured
of the good-will, power, and faithfulness of the Promiser, that he makes no more doubt of his servant's
recovery, than if it were already done, being persuaded, that diseases and distempers were as much at
Christ's beck, and much more, than his soldiers or
servants were at his; and that Christ's word of command could as effectually heal at a distance, as though
he were present : whereupon, ver. 10. we are told, that
Jesus marvelled, saying, " I have not found so great
faith, no not in Israel."

3. Strong faith is ordinarily attended with a firm
and fixed resolution to hang on the Lord, till it get
the errand it comes for : and no supposable discouragements shall make it quit its gripe. Jacob was a strong
believer, and, by the strength of his faith, " he had
power with God ; yea, he had power over the angel,
and prevailed." We read, Gen. xxxii. after a long
night's wrestling, the Lord says to him, " Let me go,
for the day breaketh :" Jacob answers, " I will not let
thee go, except thou bless me." This, one would
think, looked like rudeness and ill manners in Jacob,
to speak so to God : no, it was not rudeness, but only
the resolution of his faith. Lord, might Jacob say,
if thou ask my leave to go, I can by no means yield
to it ; let the day break and pass on, let night come,
and the next day break again, lame Jacob, and the
living God, shall never depart, till I get the blessing :
and his resolute faith like a prince prevailed. O let
all the true seed of Jacob follow his example, and they

shall be fed with the heritage of Jacob their father. The like instance we see in the Syrophenician woman, Mat. xv. 22—28. Her faith breaks through all dis-couragements, yea, improves seeming discouragements as arguments to fortify her suit ; whereupon Christ at length answers, " O woman, great is thy faith." Strong faith will rather die upon the spot, than quit its gripe : " Though he slay me (says Job), yet will I trust in him."

4. Strong faith, though it may be troubled at the hiding of the Lord's countenance, yet it will not be cast down at every cloud, as though the Lord had for-gotten to be gracious : no, it presently casts its eyes on the covenant, and reads love in God's words, when it cannot see them in his looks ; saying with the church, in Mic. vii. 8, 9. " Though I sit in darkness, the Lord will be a light unto me :—he will bring me forth to the light, and I shall behold his righteousness." Why ? He has said, and his word is sure, that " his goings forth are prepared," or secured, as the outgoings of the morning-light, Hos. vi. 3 ; and therefore I no more doubt of the Lord's return, than I doubt of the re-turn of the sun in the morning, when he sets out of sight in the evening. However dark the night may be, yet the day will break, and the shadows will fly away : " Weep-ing may endure for a night, but joy cometh in the morning." And, as strong faith keeps up the heart from sinking under the clouds of desertion, temptation, and inward trouble ; so it keeps the spirit of a man in an equal poise, under all the vicissitudes of time, so that " he shall not be afraid of evil tidings, his heart being fixed, trusting in the Lord. Although the fig-tree should not blossom, &c. yet will he rejoice in the Lord, and be glad in the God of his salvation," Hab. iii. 17, 18. Heroic faith hath the moon of this world under its feet ; it tramples upon all the changes of time, say-ing with the apostle, " I have learned in whatsoever state I am, therewith to be content," &c. However matters may be situate in the conduct of providence,

yet, a lively faith can see that there are no changes in God's covenant, no change of his love or purpose of grace.

5. The more fruitful a person is in the exercise of other graces, the stronger is his faith. You know the plenty and bigness of the fruit of a tree, flows from the abundance of sap and strength in the root : so here, faith is the radical grace, the root upon which the other graces grow ; and therefore, the more that a person abounds in love, hope, repentance, meekness, humility, and other graces, the more vigorous is his faith: for as the tree strikes its roots into the ground, and from thence draws and sends a digested nourishment through the several branches, whereby they are made to blossom and bring forth ; so faith unites the soul to Christ, through the word of grace, and fetches out sap and strength from that true olive, whereby the soul is made to "revive as the corn, to grow as the vine, and the scent and savour thereof to be as the wine of Lebanon."

Usual Attendants of a Weak Faith.

1. FREQUENT doubting, staggering, and wavering of the heart, is a concomitant of weak faith. You know, there is a great deal of smoke goes up from the fire, while it is weak, not thoroughly broken up ; so the more of the smoke of unbelieving doubts, fears, and jealousies, there is the less faith. Hence doubting and believing are opposed, " Wherefore didst thou doubt, O thou of little faith ?" A staggering at the promise through unbelief is opposed to the strength of faith, Rom. iv. 20. The word is borrowed from a man walking, whose feet through weakness hit one another, which makes him alter his pace, one step is quick, and another slow : so here, the way of weak faith is not equal. Perhaps, under a sensible enjoyment, he is this hour triumphing in his high places ; but anon the enjoyment is withdrawn, and he alters his pace, and

staggers through unbelief, saying, " His promise fails
for evermore ; he hath forgotten to be gracious."

2. The more hasty and impatient the soul is under
delays, the weaker is its faith. This I gather from Is.
xxviii. 16. " He that believeth shall not make haste."
Weak faith is so hasty, that it will allow of no time to
intervene betwixt the petition and its answer, betwixt
the promise and the accomplishment : If the answer
do not come presently, the man is ready to conclude,
" The Lord doth not hear, neither doth the God of
Jacob regard." But now, strong faith makes the soul
to wait God's time and leisure, saying, " I will direct my
prayer unto thee, and will look up. I will look unto
the Lord : I will wait for the God of my salvation :
my God will hear me."

How true Faith may be known, though very weak.

1. TRUE faith, even in the weakest measure, will
look on sin as an enemy, though it perhaps dare not
lay claim to Christ as a friend. True faith is said to
"purify the heart;" Acts xv. 9. It is a living principle in the soul, which is always opposing the motions
of indwelling corruption. Although indeed, sometimes,
through the prevalency of sin, it cannot be discerned,
more than the living spring at the bottom of the well,
when the waters are muddied ; yet like the living
spring, it is always working out the mud and filth, till
the waters be perfectly clear. Perhaps the soul is so
far from perceiving any real grace, any actual interest
in Christ, that it can see nothing but atheism, enmity,
unbelief, ignorance, pride, and such vermin of hell,
crawling in every corner ; and yet at the same time
the living principle of faith at the bottom of the heart
will be working and wrestling against these, sometimes
by groans, " Wretched man that I am, who shall deliver me ?" sometimes by complaint, " Iniquities prevail
against me :" sometimes by looks to heaven for relief,
" I know not what to do, but mine eyes are upon thee :"
sometimes by cries to heaven, " I am oppressed, under-

take for me:" sometimes by breathing desires after
more holiness, "Create in me a clean heart; Let my
heart be found in thy statutes; O that my ways were
directed to keep thy statutes!" By such things as
these, the truth and reality of faith may be discovered,
even in its weakest measure and degree.

2. True faith, though never so weak, will have a high
estimate and valuation of Christ, and the habitual bent
and bias of the soul will be toward him, 1 Pet. ii. 7.
"Unto you which believe, he is precious." Is. xxvi. 8.
"The desire of our soul is to thy name, and to the remembrance of thee." Weak faith perhaps dare not go
the length of saying with the spouse, "My beloved is
mine, and I am his:" yet it will be often saying, O
that he were mine! "O that thou wert as my brother that sucked the breasts of my mother!" And
if it could get out its breath, it would even cry, "Abba,
Father; My Lord, and my God:" but it is, as it were,
suppressed and smothered, when it would say so, with
prevailing unbelief. Where true faith is, there is a
void, emptiness, and restlessness of the soul, like the
fish out of its element, or a bone out of joint, till some
view of Christ come, and then indeed it returns unto
its rest. I remember, after the creation of Adam,
God caused all the creatures to pass before him : but
among them all there was not found an help meet for
him : there was something disagreeable and unsatisfy-
ing in all the inferior creatures ; so that though he had
them all at his command, yet still man was in a solitary
condition, Gen. ii. 20. But so soon as ever the woman
was present to him, he says, ver. 23. "This is now
bone of my bone, and flesh of my flesh ;" this indeed
is a help meet for me. Just so is it with the soul in
whom there is a principle of true faith : present riches,
profits, pleasures, and all worldly contentments to him,
he still finds something unsuitable and unsavoury in
them all ; but let Christ be revealed to him, immediately he cries out, O this is a help meet for me indeed!
Is. xi. 10. "To him shall the Gentiles seek, for his

rest is glorious." Psalm lxxiii. 25. " Whom have I in heaven but thee ? and there is none upon earth that I desire besides thee."

3. True faith, though in the lowest degree, will not rest there, but breathes after higher degrees of faith. Set the highest degree of faith before a weak believer, tell him of the faith of Abraham, how he believed without staggering; the man will indeed be humbled under a sense of his shortcomings, and lament his own unbelief; yet, at the same time, he will find a breathing, and eager desire in his soul to win such a length of believing. Thus, like Paul, he " forgets those things which are behind, and reacheth forth unto those things which are before," &c. When the weak believer hears of the full assurance of faith, his language is, " Lord, help my unbelief; Lord, increase my faith." I might tell you of many other evidences of faith in its truth and reality, though weak, as, that it works by love ; it empties the soul, and humbles it ; though the man cannot see himself great in God's eyes, yet he sees himself nothing in his own eyes ; as he values Christ highly, so he values himself less than the least of all God's mercies.*

Comfort to the weak in faith.

1. Know, for thy comfort, that the weakest believer is as nearly related to God as a Father, as the strongest believer is. The weakest and youngest babe in a family is as sib to the father as the first-born, or the son who is come to his full strength and stature. Every branch of a tree is not alike strong or big; and yet the tenderest twig is as really united to the root, and as really partakes of the sap of the root, as the strongest and most principal branch. So here,

* Now faith is hereby discerned when the heart of the believer contents itself only with Christ, the matter of salvation ; and doth believe not only that there is a remission of sins in general, but that his sins are forgiven to him in particular.—*Perkins.*

the weakest believer is in Christ, and partakes of his Spirit, as well as the strongest.

2. The weak believer is clothed with the white raiment of Christ's righteousness, and is as much justified thereby, as the strongest. Our great High Priest is clothed with a garment down to his feet, whereby every member of his body mystical is equally covered. It is equally true of every believer, that "there is no condemnation to them which are in Christ," Rom. viii. 1.

3. The least and weakest degree of faith shall hold out to the end. They are all "kept by the power of God, through faith unto salvation." He will not break the bruised reed, nor quench the smoking flax ; where the good work is begun, his faithfulness is engaged to carry it on to the day of Christ. The weakest degree of faith has glory and salvation knit to it by God's promise, as well as the strongest : It is not, He that believes strongly shall be saved ; but, He that believes indefinitely, whether his faith be weak or strong.

4. Our blessed Redeemer for ordinary vents his affection in a more tender and sensible manner toward weak believers, than toward the strong. The good Shepherd of Israel, he "carries the lambs in his bosom, and gently leads them that are with young." Hence it comes, that weak believers have commonly more sensible ravishing joys and consolations than strong believers. Much like a wise and affectionate parent, who will take his young infant on his knee, dandle it, and hug it in his bosom, while he will not allow his affections to run out after such a manner toward his son of age and stature, for that were to make a fool of him.

May the poor weak believer say, These are strong consolations indeed, if I might lay claim unto them : but that is what I still fear, that I have no faith at all, no, not like a grain of mustard seed. Beside what was said to this in the former part of the discourse, I shall only ask these two questions : 1*st*, Does not thy heart throb and faint within thee, when thou thinkest of a parting with the Lord Jesus ? If so, this says, that his love is shed abroad in thy heart by the Holy Ghost, and consequently a root and principle of faith, from whence it flows, cleaving to the Lord like the iron touched with the loadstone. And I tell thee good news, that as thou hatest to be put away from him, so " he hates putting away ;" and therefore there never shall be a separation. 2*dly*, Dost thou not find a restlessness in thy spirit, an uneasiness in thy bosom, when the Lord withdraws, like a bone out of joint, or a fish out of its element ? If so, the root of faith is within ; Christ has been with thee in a way of grace and love, otherwise thou couldst not distinguish between absence and presence. And if ever Christ made thee a visit, his first visit shall not be his last ; for " his goings forth are prepared (or secured) like the morning."

Advices to weak Believers.

1. BE humbled under a sense of remaining unbelief, and the weakness of your faith ; for "the Lord giveth grace (and more grace) to the humble." The more that self is pulled down, the higher is Christ exalted in a way of believing.

2. Be greedy of more faith. Covetousness in other things of this world is idolatry : but this is among the best things which you are allowed earnestly to covet ; and the more you covet and desire of the Spirit of faith, the more you shall get ; for " he satisfieth the longing soul, and filleth the hungry soul with goodness. Open thy mouth wide, and I will fill it."

3. Be well acquainted with the grounds of faith, as they are laid in the gospel-revelation, some of which I have pointed at in the preceding discourse. I am persuaded, that one great reason why so many do not believe at all, and why the faith of many real believers remains so weak, is their unacquaintedness with the

strong and sure grounds that their faith has to build upon. Weak timorous believers, fixed upon the foundation God hath laid in Zion, are just like a man standing on a firm immoveable rock, his head turns giddy, and he imagines that the rock is turning upside down with him, while the failure is not in the rock, but in his own head. Our faith fails us, through our unacquaintedness with the stability of God's covenant and promise. And therefore, I say, study to be better acquainted with the promise and faithfulness, power and love, of the Promiser.

4. If you would have weak faith increased and strengthened, then be frequently exercising any weak faith you have ; for gracious as well as natural habits are increased and improven by repeated acts : " To him that hath," and improveth well what he hath, " shall be given." This is the way to have your mite turned into a talent ; and your talent of faith, by frequent exercise, shall in due time become as ten talents.

5. When you get any sensible experiences of the Lord's love, improve them, not as the grounds of your faith, but as encouragements to go on in trusting and believing, upon the grounds of faith laid before you in the word. These sensible tastes of the Lord's loving-kindness are given you, not that you should doat upon the sweetness of them, but to encourage and further you in trusting and believing : Psalm xxxvi. 7. " How excellent is thy loving-kindness, O God! therefore the children of men put their trust under the shadow of thy wings." It is a common fault among many believers in our day, when they find any thing of sensible presence, then indeed they rejoice, and they have good reason so to do ; but no sooner doth a cloud come, but their faith, as well as their joy, evanishes, and they have as little trust to put in the word and promise of the God of their life, when his back is turned, or he out of their sight, as though they never had received a kindness at his hand. And this

is a reason, I am convinced, why it fares so ill with
many of us at this day ; and therefore let us amend it.
And what comfort and joy we find in his presence,
let it encourage and engage us to trust, and hope,
and wait, and believe in him, when absent to our sense.
And if we thus improve the marks of grace and consolations of his Spirit, the joy of the Lord shall be our
strength ; and our path shall be indeed " as the path
of the just, and as the shining light, which shineth
more and more unto the perfect day."

On the Lamp which God hath ordained, mentioned Ps. 132. 17.

By the *lamp* then I understand the word of God,
and particularly the word of the truth of the gospel.
You know the use of a lamp is to give light to men in the
dark, and to let them see their way.   All mankind,
ever since the fall, are in darkness, yea darkness itself.
They have lost their way, and are walking upon the
ridge of hell and utter destruction.   Now, the gospel,
or word of faith which we preach, is a light or a lamp
as it were, which God hath set up to discover to the
children of men how they have lost their way, and let
them see that new and living way of his own devising,
by which they may come back again to God and glory.
" We have a more sure word of prophecy : unto which
we do well that we take heed, as unto a light that shineth in a dark place, until the day dawn, and the day-
star arise in our hearts," 2 Pet. i. 19.   The dark place
that the apostle is speaking of, is this dark world, and
the heart of man is the darkest place in the world.
God who is the Father of lights, he has given his word,
the scriptures of truth, as a lantern or lamp, to direct
us how we are to glorify God, and to enjoy him for
ever.   To this light, or lamp, we do well to take heed,
as David did, the man according to God's own heart :
" Thy word (says he) is a light to my feet, and a lamp
unto my paths."   Now, the lamp of the word of God
casts a twofold light among the children of men, name-

ly, a law light and a gospel light. A law light, to discover sin and misery ; for by the law is the knowledge of sin : " The law was added because of transgression. I had not known sin (says Paul), except the law had said, Thou shalt not covet. And when the law of commandment came (says he), sin revived and I died." But then there is a gospel light, which serves to discover the remedy. And this I take to be principally understood in the text : " I have ordained a lamp for mine Anointed." I the eternal JEHOVAH have appointed the preaching and publication of the gospel as the great mean for bringing lost mankind unto the knowledge of that mighty One on whom I have laid their help. " It hath pleased God by the foolishness of preaching to save them that believe. Go ye into all the world, and preach the gospel to every creature," Mark xvi. 15.

Now, concerning this lamp of gospel light, which God has ordained, for the glory of his anointed, if time allowed, I might, 1. Premise a few things about it. 2. Tell you of some great and glorious discoveries that are made by it. 3. Give a few of its properties.

First, I would offer you two or three propositions about it.

1. This lamp was first set up in the purpose of God from eternity, or in the council of peace, when the whole plan of salvation through Christ was laid. " I was set up from everlasting, from the beginning, or ever the earth was : before the mountains were settled : while as yet he had not made the earth, nor the highest part of the world. When he prepared the heavens, I was there : when he set a compass upon the face of the depth : when he appointed the foundations of the earth (says Christ), I was by him,—rejoicing in the habitable part of his earth, and my delights were with the sons of men," Prov. viii. 23—31.

2. This lamp was first lighted in this lower world, immediately after the fall in paradise ; when a dark and dismal night of woe and misery was spreading itself

over our first parents, then a gleam of light began to break out in the first promise, Gen. iii. 15. : and afterwards unto Abraham ; " In thy seed shall all the nations of the earth be blessed."

3. The lamp of the gospel shone, typically and prophetically, during all the Old Testament period, before the coming of Christ in the flesh. It shone, as it were, under a vail, and only among the Jews. As for the Gentiles, except a few proselytes, they were aliens and strangers to the covenant of promise; they sat in darkness, and in the regions of the shadow of death.

4. After the coming of Christ in the flesh, and his resurrection and ascension into heaven, the lamp of gospel light was brightened, and the light of it was made more general and extensive. The vail of types, ceremonies, and prophecies, was rent, and by the commandment of the everlasting God, carried unto all nations for the obedience of faith, Christ being given of God for " a light to enlighten the Gentiles, and for salvation to all the ends of the earth."

5. Ministers of the gospel are, as it were, the lamp bearers. They are commissioned by Christ to preach the gospel, to teach all nations. To them the word of reconciliation is committed ; and as the heralds of the great King, they are to lift up their voice like a trumpet, and proclaim the salvation of God to the ends of the earth.

Glorious discoveries made by the Gospel Lamp.

I SHALL tell you of some discoveries that are made by the light of the gospel-lamp. Only in general remember that all the discoveries it makes are wholly supernatural ; the world by all its wisdom could never have found them out. Here vain man would be wise, yet he is born as void of gospel wisdom, as the wild ass's colt. Proud men may, and no doubt will, boast of their natural or acquired wisdom and penetration, as though, by the means of these, they could ransack and unfold the secrets of heaven ; and yet even when they are revealed, they cannot know, cannot receive them ; the things of the Spirit of God are foolishness to them ; hence is that of Christ, " I thank thee, O Father, Lord of heaven and earth, because thou hast hid these things from the wise and prudent, and hast revealed them unto babes. Even so, Father, for so it seemed good in thy sight, " Matth. xi. 25, 26.

I shall only mention a few things among many, that the gospel discovers, which nature's light could never have discovered, and which proud nature cannot receive when revealed.

By the gospel-lamp then, 1. We have discovered a Trinity of persons in one God, Father, Son, and Holy Ghost, three distinct persons, and yet but one God : "There are three that bear record in heaven, the Father, the Word, and the Holy Ghost : and these three are one," 1 John v. 7. This is such a hard doctrine to human reason, that Arians, Socinians, and Deists, they will reject the whole scriptures of truth before they entertain it ; or if they acknowledge the scriptures, they fall awork to prevent scripture-light, in order to bring Christ down from his supreme Deity in among the rank of created beings ; for between the Creator and a creature there is no middle being : and if Christ be a creature, I would ask what way any creature can make itself, seeing " without him was not any thing made that was made ?" John i. 3. So then, I say, the gospel-lamp discovers the mystery of the Trinity ; and how each person acts his part in the glorious work of our redemption.

2. By the light of this lamp we can look back to eternity past, and see what God was a-doing before the foundations of the world were laid ; how a council of peace was held with reference to the recovery and salvation of fallen men ; how an overture being made, that the Son of God should undertake the work of our redemption, that the different claims of mercy and justice might be fully satisfied in the salvation of fallen man ; and how the Son of God heartily agreed,

saying, " Lo, I come : I delight to do thy will, O my
God. He rejoiced in the habitable parts of the earth,
and his delights were with the sons of men." Without
the gospel men could never have known this ; but the
Lion of the tribe of Judah, he opened the book, and
disclosed the grand secret, and orders it to be published unto the ends of the earth.

3. The gospel-lamp discovers the glorious mystery
of the incarnation of the Son of God in the fulness of
time. In consequence of this glorious transaction, angels
they admire and adore a God in our nature. " When
he bringeth in the first-begotten into the world, he saith,
And let all the angels of God worship him," Heb i. 6.

4. By the gospel-lamp we have another mystery
opened, even the substitution of the Son of God in the
room of the guilty sinner, by which means our iniquities
come to be laid upon him. " The just suffered for the
unjust." He is the ram caught in the thickets, and
sacrificed in the room of the sinner. The sword of justice
awakes against the man that is God's fellow, who thinks
it no robbery to be equal with God. "He was wounded
for our transgressions, bruised for our iniquities, the
chastisement of our peace was upon him, and by his
stripes we are healed."

5. By the gospel-lamp only we know of a law-fulfilling
righteousness brought into this world, where " there is
none righteous, no not one. Seventy weeks are determined—to finish the transgression and to make an
end of sins,—and to bring in everlasting righteousness,"
Dan. ix. 24. " What the law could not do, in that it
was weak through the flesh, God sending his own Son,
in the likeness of sinful flesh, and for sin condemned
sin in the flesh ; that the righteousness of the law might
be fulfilled in us," Rom. viii. 3, 4. " Christ is the end
of the law for righteousness to every one that believeth,"
Rom. x. 4. " For he hath made him to be sin for us,
who knew no sin ; that we might be made the righteousness of God in him," 2 Cor. v. 21. O what a high
discovery is this for us, especially considering, that this

righteousness of the surety Christ is brought near to every one in the everlasting gospel, that they may put it on, and improve it for their justification before God! "Hearken unto me, ye stout hearted, that are far from righteousness. I bring near my righteousness : it shall not be far off, and my salvation shall not tarry," Is. xlvi. 12, 13.

6. By the gospel-lamp, we shall see great and glorious mysteries in the death and blood of Christ. As Samson found a honey-comb in the lion that he had slain, so may we find the great and soul nourishing mysteries of the grace, love, mercy, and wisdom of God in the death and blood of the Lamb of God. Here we may see the justice of God satisfied for the sin of man, by a sacrifice of infinite value, the anger of God turned away, and God declaring himself to be a God of peace through the blood of his eternal Son. Here we see the head of the old serpent bruised, that leviathan slain, and given to be meat to those who inhabit the wilderness of this world. Oh! meat indeed, and drink indeed. Here we may see a new and living way opened and consecrated, that we may enter into the holiest with full assurance of acceptance, &c.

7. The gospel-lamp discovers a mystery in the resurrection of Christ from the dead. There is more of God, and of his infinite power and wisdom, in the resurrection of Christ, than if all Adam's posterity were raised out of their graves in the twinkling of an eye. Christ is said, by his resurrection, to be " declared to be the Son of God with power," Rom. i. 4. And that power of the Father, whereby he was raised, had an "exceeding greatness" in it, and was a "mighty power," Eph. i. 19. The load of sin and wrath that lay upon the grave of our Surety, would have sunk all the angels in heaven, and men upon earth, to the lowest hell ; yet Christ, by his divine power, rises from under this load, and so bears away our iniquities, and leaves them buried in his grave behind him, and death itself swallowed up in victory, &c.

8. The gospel-lamp lets us see a mystery in his ascension into heaven, the most glorious solemnity that
ever the inhabitants of the spiritual world saw, which
made them all cry out, and shout, " God is gone up
with a shout, the Lord with the sound of a trumpet,"
&c. This world saw little solemnity in Christ's returning to heaven after he had finished the great work
of man's redemption. But, Oh! angels and glorified
saints, who were then arrived at heaven, they saw his
chariots of state attending him. " The chariots of God
are twenty thousand, even thousands of angels : the
Lord is among them as in Sinai, in the holy place.
Thou hast ascended on high, thou hast led captivity
captive : thou hast received gifts for men," Psal. lxviii.
17, 18.

9. The gospel-lamp lets us see a mystery in his appearance for us in heaven ; how he appears there as our
Representative and High Priest within the vail, with
much incense offering up the prayers of all saints, &c. ;
how he states himself as our Advocate with the Father,
to plead our cause, and to agent our business for us,
and to repel all complaints given in against us by the
accuser of the brethren. " He is able to save to the
uttermost, seeing he ever liveth to make intercession
for us, " Heb. vii. 25. " And if any man sin, we have
an Advocate with the Father, Jesus Christ the righteous." He appears for us before the bar, not as a sup-
pliant, but as one having authority : " Father (says the
Advocate), I will that they also whom thou hast given
me, be with me where I am ; that they may behold
my glory which thou hast given me, " John xvii. 24.

10. By the gospel-lamp there is a discovery made of
a new and better covenant established in Christ as a
second Adam, than that which was made with the first
Adam, even a covenant of grace and promise ; which
being confirmed by the death of Christ, is now set
out in its last and best edition, viz. as a testamentary
deed. Every thing in and about this covenant is wonderful and mysterious. The Trinity transacted in it

with Christ as a second Adam from eternity : "I have made a covenant with my chosen ; I have sworn unto David my servant," Psal. lxxxix. 3. The gradual manifestation of this covenant unto us, and the variety of dispensations that it has undergone under the Old and New Testament, and yet still the same covenant. The absolute freedom of this covenant unto us, no conditions or qualifications required on our part to interest us in it, the proper condition of it being already fulfilled in the obedience and death of Christ, it comes out to us absolutely free, "I will be their God. I will sprinkle them with clean water, and they shall be clean. I will take away the heart of stone," &c. The way how a sinner is brought within the bonds of this covenant is only owing to the gospel-lamp or light, namely, by faith, not of the operation of man, but of the operation of God in a day of power. He just makes the sinner willing to be saved without money and without price, upon the footing of free grace reigning and through an imputed righteousness, &c.

11. By the gospel-lamp we come to know the mystery of regeneration, or the new birth ; which so started and confounded Nicodemus, a teacher in Israel, that he babbles and speaks stark nonsense, when Christ proposes it to him. "Can a man (says he) be born when he is old ? can he enter the second time into his mother's womb, and be born ?" John iii. 4. The case is just the same with a great deal of men in our day, who set up for wits. They are ready to brand the doctrine of conversion and regeneration with the character of enthusiasm : but let such remember, that the God of truth has said it, with a verily, verily, except they know and feel it on their own souls, they "cannot enter into the kingdom of heaven."

12. The gospel-lamp discovers the way of justification for an ungodly sinner, by an imputed righteousness. This discovery is wholly supernatural, which the apostle Paul valued so highly, and gloried so much in, that when compared with the knowledge

hereof, he reckoned every thing else as so much dross and dung, &c.

13. The mystery of sanctification is discovered by the gospel-lamp; how Christ is made of God unto us sanctification; and how, by the great and precious promises, we are made partakers of the divine nature; and by beholding the glory of the Lord in the glass of the gospel, we are changed into the same image: how the heart is purified by faith in Christ, our old man crucified in him, and the body of sin destroyed, &c.

In a word, to shut up this head, by the light of the gospel-lamp, we may see in through the vail of death and mortality, and behold life and immortality brought to light: "For (says the apostle), we look not at the things which are seen, but at the things which are not seen: for the things which are seen are temporal; but the things which are not seen, are eternal." By the gospel-lamp, and the eye of an enlightened understanding, we may see the Jordan of death divided, and a passage opened for the Israel of God into the promised land of glory, where we shall be for ever with the Lord. By this lamp we may look to the end of time, and see Christ coming to judge the world. He will "descend from heaven with a shout, with the voice of the archangel, and with the trump of God. Behold he cometh with clouds; and every eye shall see him, and they also which pierced him; and all kindreds of the earth shall wail because of him. Verily, verily, I say unto you, the hour is coming, in the which all that are in their graves shall hear the voice of the Son of man, and shall come forth," &c. By this gospel-lamp we may see all that sleep in their graves raised up again, some to the resurrection of eternal life, and others to the resurrection of everlasting damnation; some are seen like condemned prisoners, brought out of gaol unto the place of execution, and whenever they see the judge upon his white throne, crying to the rocks and mountains to fall on them, to hide them from his angry face; whilst others are be-

held lifting up their head, because the day of their redemption is come, and crying to one another, " Let
us be glad and rejoice ; for the marriage of the Lamb
is come," Rev. xix. 7. By this lamp we may see the
righteous like so many suns shining in the kingdom of
their father, with robes made white in the blood of the
Lamb, crying, " Salvation to our God that sits upon the
throne, and to the Lamb for ever and ever."

Rev. vii. 1—3, explained.

It is agreed amongst the generality of interpreters
whom I have consulted, that in those three verses I
have now read there is a prediction of some awful
spiritual judgments to fall upon the visible church, together with the care that the Lord takes of his own
faithful remnant, by separating them from others, that
they might not be hurt thereby.

These spiritual plagues are expressed under the notion of four winds, ver. 1, which drive away unstable
professors ; who are not rooted by faith in Christ, just
as the wind drives loose and light things before it.
Those winds are said to be four, with allusion to the
four quarters of heaven, east, west, north, and south ;
implying, that the devil sets upon the church of Christ
from all airths at once, so that she is like a city besieg-
ed by enemies from all quarters. The instruments in
the hand of God, for plaguing the visible church with
those spiritual judgments, are four. Some say they
were four evil angels, like those that were sent to be
a lying spirit in the mouth of Ahab's prophets, to persuade him to go up to Ramoth-Gilead, to his destruction. Others think that they were good angels, because they restrained the winds until the saints were
sealed. But we need not insist to determine this difference, seeing we find God, the great Lord and Sovereign, sometimes making use of good, and sometimes
of bad angels, as the executioners of his wrath.

But now in the 2d and 3d verses follows the consolation of the saints of God, his little remnant, who are keeping their garments clean, and keeping the word of his patience. The eyes of the Lord are running to and fro through the whole earth to show himself strong in their behalf, and his care about them is thus expressed. "And I saw another angel ascending from the east, having the seal of the living God : and he cried with a loud voice to the four angels to whom it was given to hurt the earth and the sea, saying, Hurt not the earth, neither the sea, nor the trees, till we have sealed the servants of our God in their foreheads." Where, for explication, we may notice these following particulars.

1. The great agent that interposes for the safety of the saints, when the four noxious winds are blowing away the generality of professors ; and that is " another Angel :" not any created angel, like the four mentioned in the 1st verse, but the glorious Angel of the covenant, Jesus Christ, who was sent before Israel to open the way into the land of Canaan, concerning whom God says to Israel, Exod. xxiii. 21. " Beware of him, and obey his voice : for my name is in him." This I say is the Angel here spoken of, for he is the head that looks to the welfare of his members, " And he is given to be the head over all things unto the church, which is his body ;" and all the saints are in his hand, and none "shall pluck them out of his or his Father's hand."

2. We may notice from what airth this Angel doth arise and appear ; he ascends from the east, with allusion to the natural sun in the firmament, who arises from that airth, and spreads his light and influences toward the west. The coming of Christ is compared to lightning coming from the east. He is " the light of the world, the true light, which lighteth every man that cometh into the world." Some observe that the entry of the temple, by which the prince was to ascend, was upon the east ; and so it may signify, that when Christ comes, for the help and relief of his church, he appears in a princely character and sovereign way ;

and when he doth so he acts like himself, " the Prince of the kings of the earth."

3. This Angel is the lord-keeper of the privy seal of heaven, for "he had the seal of the living God." This shows that he is his Father's great trustee, who has all power in heaven and in earth committed unto him. On the same account the keys of the house of David, or the government, is laid upon his shoulders : Is. xxii. 24. " He shall hang upon him all the glory of his Father's house, the offspring and the issue, all vessels of small quantity : from the vessels of cups even to all the vessels of flagons." The care of God's particular kingdom, of his chosen generation, royal priesthood, peculiar people, and holy nation, is committed to him.

4. We may observe how Christ executes his authoritative trust; he cries with a loud voice to the four angels, to whom it was given to hurt the earth and the sea. His crying may signify Christ's authority, the imminency of the danger, and his care to have the hurtful winds restrained for a season. Those to whom he directs his cry, are " the four angels, to whom it was given to hurt the earth and the sea ;" whereby we are made to understand, that all the angels, both good and bad, are subject to the authority and command of him, who is " the head of all principalities, and power, and might, and dominion," &c. None of them all can act but by orders from him. Christ in heaven is looking to the welfare of his church and people upon earth in time of danger, when they themselves have no thought about their own hazard.

5. We have the particular charge given to the angels by Christ, which I have mainly in view, ver. 3. he said to them, " Hurt not the earth, neither the sea, nor the trees, till we have sealed the servants of our God in their foreheads."

Where we have, 1*st*, A prohibition. 2*dly*, The party immediately concerned in the prohibition. And, 3*dly*, The reason thereof.

1*st*, The prohibition : " Hurt not the earth, neither

the sea, nor the trees, for a time. Where you see the
judgment is not absolutely averted nor discharged,
but only suspended, until provision be made for the
safety of God's peculiar people. Observe, that any
favour showed unto the wicked, or any suspension of
divine vengeance with respect unto them, is owing unto
the truly godly that live among them ; if it were not
for the elect's sake, God would make short work with the
rest of mankind : " Except the Lord of hosts had left
unto us a very small remnant, we should have been as
Sodom, and we should have been like unto Gomorrah."

2dly, We have the party immediately concerned in
the prohibition ; "the earth, the sea, and the trees."
By whom in general we are to understand professors of
different kinds, against whom the bensil of those hurtful winds was levelled, and who were to sustain great
hurt and injury thereby to their souls, when God's time
of loosing them should come.   What sort of professors
of religion are particularly pointed at by "the earth, the
sea, and trees," shall be declared afterwards.

3dly, We have the reason of the restraint that is
laid upon the hurtful winds, that they are not suffered
to blow for a while, viz. "Until we have sealed the
servants of our God in their foreheads."   Where we
have,

(1.) The objects of the divine care, " the servants of
our God."   It is Christ that is speaking, and he speaks
in the capacity of a public head, in his own name, and
in the name of all his faithful friends and followers,
saying, Our God, because he is the head of the whole
mystical body, and stands in a joint relation to God with
his members and people, according to John xx. 17.
" I ascend unto my Father and your Father, and to
my God and your God."   The character that he gives
them is, that they are the servants of God ; and the
reason of this designation is, because they were such as
feared his name, Neh. i. 11. and because they " kept
the commandments of God, and the testimony of Jesus,"

whenthe flood cast out of the mouth of the old serpent was sweeping away the bulk of visible professors unto a course of apostasy.

(2.) We may notice what was to be done to or for the servants of God ; why, they are to be sealed, i. e. they are to be separate or distinguished from others that were to be doomed to destruction ; much like that, Ezek. ix. 4, 6. Says the Lord to the man who had the writer's inkhorn by his side, " Go through the midst of the city, through the midst of Jerusalem, and set a mark upon the foreheads of the men that sigh, and that cry for all abominations that be done in the midst thereof ;" and then, it is added, " Come not near any man upon whom is the mark." In short, this discovers the particular care that God has of his own remnant, and the special providence that God exercises about them, when his judgments are in the earth.

(3.) Notice the visibility of this seal ; they are sealed on their foreheads. Thus, Rev. xiv. 1. the hundred forty and four thousand who stand with the Lamb on mount Sion, they are said to " have his Father's name written in their foreheads ;" i. e. they had a visible profession of the name of God in the world, and were not ashamed to confess him before men. So here this seal is set on the foreheads of the servants of God ; i. e. as they had been faithful to his cause and interest, when others had deserted him and his truth ; so he would visibly own them as his before the world, and would not be ashamed of them, and would make his regard for them evident to all men, by the singular care he took of them, when his destroying judgments were in the earth.

(4.) The reason of their being thus sealed is here implied, viz. that they might not be hurt, i. e. that they might be preserved from the danger and hazard of these pestilential winds that were to blow in a little upon the visible church.

How to know whether we be among the sealed servants of God.

1. ALL God's faithful servants they have had their bands loosed : Psal. cxvi. 16. "Oh Lord, truly I am thy servant, I am thy servant, and the son of thy hand-maid : thou hast loosed my bonds." All are by nature held fast in the gall of bitterness, and bonds of iniquity : they are lawful captives. Now, has the Lord in a day of power loosed your bands, and proclaimed liberty to you, and made you free indeed ?

2. All God's servants have seen their Master's glory, beauty, and excellency ; 2 Cor. iv. 6. "God, who com-manded the light to shine out of darkness, hath shined into your hearts," &c. Have you seen the Father in the Son ? and has the sight transformed you into his image ?

3. The first-born of the family will be very dear unto you, " more glorious than all the mountains of prey," and that will be the language of your heart, " My be-loved is white and ruddy, the chiefest among ten thou-sand."

4. They are all very sensible of their inability to serve him as they ought ; yea, they are ready to ac-knowledge, that without him they can do nothing ; they will not brag of their services, as the proud Pharisee, " God, I thank thee that I am not as other men," &c.

5. They have all a great regard for his authority, and will obey God rather than man, as the apostles of Christ, Daniel, and the three children, &c. Every one of them is ready to say, " Lord, what wilt thou have me to do ?" Give strength to obey, and command what thou wilt.

6. They are all for the standing of their Master's house, and stand up for their Master's honour. It goes nearer the hearts of his faithful servants to see him in-jured, or his crown profaned, than any private interest of their own ; it grieves them to see their Master's house invaded by thieves and robbers ; and they will not take

them by the hand, but bear faithful testimony against them. They cannot part with the least hoof that pertains to their great Master.

7. All God's faithful servants have his seal set upon them, as you see in the text, " Hurt not the earth, neither the sea, nor the trees, till we have sealed the servants of our God in their foreheads." O, say you, how shall I know if I be among the sealed ? Answ. You may know it by the print of the seal. You know the print of the seal upon the wax, is an exact transcript of the graving that is on the seal. Just so is it here, when Christ seals, or sets his mark upon the soul, he just by the power of his Spirit puts the print of his own grace upon it, John i. 16. " Of his own fulness have all we received, and grace for grace ;" i. e. the grace that is in the believer, just corresponds unto the grace that is in Christ. As in nature, so it is in grace; the child receives from the parent by natural generation, member for member, eye, for eye, hand, legs, limbs, just like its parent that begat it ; so it is in supernatural things, or in regeneration, we receive from him, who of his own will begat us by the word of truth, grace for grace. The Spirit shows the things of Christ unto us, and we, by beholding thereof, are " changed into the same image from glory to glory, as by the Spirit of the Lord."

So then, see whether you have the following prints of Christ's seal upon you.

1st, The print of his life : " Because I live, ye shall live also." It is the life of Christ that is in the soul of the believer : " I live ; yet not I, but Christ liveth in me; and the life which I now live in the flesh, is by faith in the Son of God." Where notice, the believer does not live upon his own feelings, or grace in him, but on Christ the fountain of life.

2dly, The print of his light; " for he enlighteneth every man that cometh into the world." So then, have you in his light seen light? If so, then you will know the difference between light and darkness, day and night; and when it is night, you will long to see the sun again, and go mourning without the sun, &c.

3dly, A print of his love; for " God is love," and he " draws with the cords of love ;" he kindles a fire of love in the heart, the sparks of which are always flying upwards toward heaven.

4thly, A print of his holiness ; " Be ye holy, as I am holy." And this is it that makes the soul to groan under a body of sin and death, to war against it, and to long to be fully like him in holiness.

5thly, A print of his faithfulness in the word of truth : " Of his own will begat he us by the word of truth." What is faith, but just the impression of God's faithfulness made on the soul by the word of truth ; insomuch that, whenever the soul hears the record of God concerning Christ, it cries, O " this is a faithful saying, and worthy of all acceptation ? "

6thly, The soul gets a print of his seal for the honour and glory of God, so that the man cannot but stand up for the house of God, and the concerns of his glory. "The zeal of thine house hath eaten me up," says Christ ; and therefore, like him, the man that is sealed, he cannot endure to see the house of God turned into a den of thieves, robbers, and hirelings, buyers and sellers, and he is far from joining hand with them.

Isa. xxii. 24. *explained.*

In this chapter, from ver. 20. we have an illustrious prophecy of the kingdom and government of the glorious Messiah, under the type of Eliakim's preferment and promotion in the kingdom and government of Judah, as appears by comparing ver. 22 with Rev. iii. 7, where Christ applies this passage to himself. More particularly we have,

1. Eliakim's call unto his honourable employment, whereby is represented Christ's call unto his mediatory work and office : ver. 20. " And it shall come to pass in that day, that I will call my servant Eliakim the son of Hilkiah." Christ did not run unsent, like many in our

day, who intrude themselves into the office of the ministry, Is. xlii. 6, Heb. v. 4, 5, he did not take the honour unto himself, but was called of God, as was Aaron.

2. We have the badges of honour bestowed upon him in consequence of his call ; ver. 21, 22. " And I will clothe him with thy robe, and strengthen him with thy girdle, and I will commit thy government into his hand, and he shall be a father to the inhabitants of Jerusalem, and to the house of Judah. And the key of the house of David will I lay upon his shoulder: so he shall open, and none shall shut, and he shall shut, and none shall open." (1.) He is clothed with a royal robe. So Christ is clothed, Rev. i. with a garment down to the foot, that serves to cover and adorn himself and all his members ; and his robe is so odoriferous, with the holy anointing oil of the Holy Ghost, that they perfume the ivory palaces, Psalm xlv. 8.

(2.) He is strengthened with a girdle, a girdle of truth and faithfulness ; he is always ready girded for the execution of his work. (3.) He hath the keys of the house committed to him, and the sole government; he opens, and none shuts, &c. the keys of the heart, and the keys of hell and death are in his hand.

3. We have his confirmation in his honourable office and station ; he is " fastened as a nail in a sure place ;" ver. 23. "And I will fasten him as a nail in a sure place," &c. Christ is nailed in his mediatory work and office by an eternal decree, Psal. ii. 6. and by the oath of God, Psal. cx. 4 ; and all the powers of hell and earth shall never loose this nail. Many attempts have the powers of hell and earth made to loose this nail, but the gates of hell could never, and never shall accomplish their design.

4. We are here told to what advantage he should discharge his trust : " He shall be for a glorious throne to his Father's house." God mamifested in the flesh, or God reconciling the world to himself in Christ, is the throne of grace to which we are called

to come with boldness, that we may obtain mercy, and find grace to help in time of need : and this may well be called " a glorious throne," because there is, in this dispensation of grace, the brightest display of the glory of God ; the views of which made the angels, Is. vi. to cover their faces with their wings, and, Luke ii. to tune their harps at his incarnation and birth, crying, "Glory to God in the highest." Christ is the ornament of his Father's house, the brightness of his glory, and the brightest crown that ever adorned the human nature. Heaven and earth has credit by him. Solomon tells us, Prov. xxvi. 6, that " he who sends a message by the hand of a fool, cutteth off the feet, and drinketh damage ;" i. e. he sullies his own character, ruins his business, and is a reproach to him that sent him. But Christ, the Sent of God, the great Apostle and High Priest of our profession, he managed the affair of redemption, in which he was employed, to such advantage, that all parties concerned in his embassy to this lower world, reap advantage and honour by him ; he restores what he took not away, even glory to God, and salvation and happiness to lost mankind.

5. We have Christ's pre-eminence in God's family, and the dependence of all the domestics upon him : ver. 24, " And they shall hang upon him all the glory of his Father's house," &c.

Where we have, 1st, The designation given unto the church of God ; it is called, " The house of God and Father of Christ." God has a higher and a lower house. His higher house is heaven, where is the residence of the church triumphant, Is. xiv. 2. His lower house is the church militant : 1 Tim. iii. 15, we read " of the house of God, which is the church of the living God." See Heb. iii. Christ was sent and received gifts for men, that the Lord God might have a house wherein he might dwell with men, Psalm lxviii. 18.

2dly, We have the nature and quality of the house;

it is glorious, there is glory in it : Is. iv. 5, where the prophet, speaking of the church of Christ under the New Testament, says, " The Lord will create upon every dwelling-place of Mount Zion, and upon her assemblies, a cloud and smoke by day, and the shining of a flaming fire by night : for upon all the glory shall be a defence." And Psal. lxxxvii. 3. " Glorious things are spoken of thee, O city of God." There is a visible glory in the church visible, of which we read, Rom. ix. 4. " To them belonged the adoption, and the glory." Some view of this glory and majesty made Balaam, when he saw the comely order of the tents of Israel, and God's tent, or tabernacle, in the midst of them, to cry out, " How goodly are thy tents, O Jacob, and thy tabernacles, O Israel ! The Lord his God is with him." There is such a divine majesty in the church of Christ, when her doctrine, discipline, worship, and government, is ordered according to the pattern showed in the mount, and so much of a divine lustre, as strikes beholders both with terror and admiration ; for then it is that " she looks forth as the morning, fair as the moon, clear as the sun, and terrible as an army with banners," unto all the enemies of Christ ; so was it in our own land, in our reforming period. And as there is a visible glory in the church visible, so there is an invisible glory in the church invisible. God communicates something of the divine glory and image unto every one of his children : " The King's daughter is all glorious within." Through justifying and sanctifying grace, they who had " lain among the pots," become like " the wings of a dove covered with silver, and her feathers with yellow gold."

3dly, We have the high and honourable station that Christ hath in his Father's house ; he is the great Master-household, and the holy family is committed to him, and is said to " hang upon him as a nail fastened in a sure place." Of which more afterward.

4thly. We have the common consent of the whole family unto his management : " They shall hang upon him all the glory," &c ; *i. e.* the Father of the family and the whole offspring of the house, concur amicably that he should have the sole management. God the Father cries, " He is mine elect in whom my soul delighteth; and I have laid help upon one that is mighty ;" and all the family in a day of conversion, having the light of the knowledge of the glory of God in the face of Christ darted into their hearts, unanimously cry, every one, Approve, approve, approve!

5thly, We have some account of the furniture of the house, committed to the management of the great New Testament Eliakim. (1.) The glory. (2.) The offspring and issue. (3.) " The vessels of small quantity, from vessels of cups, even to all the vessels or flagons." By which, we are to understand believers, for they are the children of God, and the seed of Christ by regeneration ; and likewise called vessels, because they are the recipient subjects of divine grace, which is the wine, milk, and honey of the house.

Marks of our belonging to God's house or family.

1. ALL the offspring and issue of God's family, they have passed through the strait gate of regeneration, or the new birth ; for says Christ, "Except a man be born again, he cannot enter into the kingdom of God." But, say you, how may I know if I be a partaker of the new birth ? I answer, The new birth brings a new state or standing with it. You have quit your standing upon the law bottom of works, and all foundations of sand, and taken up your only stand upon the foundation laid in Zion, which is Christ Jesus. The new birth brings a new heart along with it : Ezek. xxxvi. 26. " A new heart will I give them," &c. The new birth brings with it new principles of action, a principle of life, of faith and love ; new motives and ends ; self-love constrains the sinner, but the love of Christ, and the glory of God, constrains the true convert to duty. The new birth makes a man to affect the new covenant, even a covenant of rich grace and promise,

" saying, this is all my salvation." The new birth makes a man to affect new laws. He was formerly under the law of sin and death ; but now he delights in the law of the Lord, and approves of it, as holy, just, and good ; he delights in the law of the Lord, after the inner man. The new birth brings a new language along with it ; the man gets a new tongue ; formerly he spoke the language of Ashdod, but now the language of Canaan. The new birth produceth new views, both of things temporal and eternal. So then, try yourselves by these whether you be among the true off-spring and issue of the house of God : for " he is not a Jew, who is one outwardly ; neither is that circumcision, which is outward in the flesh : but he is a Jew, who is one inwardly ; and circumcision is that of the heart, in the Spirit, and not in the letter, whose praise is not of men, but of God."

2. All the offspring and issue of the house have seen their Father's countenance ; and they are always glad at the sight of it, like David, " Thou hast put more gladness in my heart by thy countenance, than they when their corn, wine, and oil did abound."

3. All the offspring of God's family, each one of them resembles the children of a king, because they bear a likeness unto their Father and his first-born Son : " By beholding his glory, we are changed into the same image." And they hate themselves, because of their dissimilitude through remaining sin and indwelling corruption ; saying, with Paul, Rom. vii. 24. " Wretched man that I am, who will deliver me from this body of sin and death !'

4. All the offspring of God's family, they have great trust and faith to put in Christ the great Manager of the family : hence called believers, because they believe in, and believe on his name : John i.12. " But as many as received him, to them gave he power to become the sons of God, even to them that believe on his name." The very name of Christ is so sweet to them, that it is like ointment poured forth ; and if they had all the

souls that ever sprang of Adam dwelling in their bodies,
they could commit the keeping of them all to him.

5. All the offspring of the house are acquainted with the
Manager's voice, the voice of his word, and the voice
of his rod, " My sheep know my voice." When they
hear his promising voice, they are filled with joy and
peace in believing it. When they hear his commanding voice, they are ready to say, I will run the ways of
thy commandments : only give grace to obey, and command what thou wilt. When they hear his threatening
voice, they tremble at his word. When they hear his
correcting voice, in worldly trials and crosses, they
are ready to say with David, " I was dumb with silence, I opened not my mouth, because thou didst it."

6. All the offspring and issue of the family, they love
to lisp out their Father's name, crying, Abba, Father,
Rom. viii. It is true, through the prevalency of unbelief, and a sense of guilt and filth, they blush when they
speak to him as a Father ; but yet, now and then, as
faith gets up its head, they will be ready to cry, as the
church, Is. lxiii. 16. " Doubtless thou art our Father,
though Abraham be ignorant of us, and Israel acknowledge us not : thou, O Lord, art our Father, our
Redeemer, thy name is from everlasting."

7. If you be the true offspring of this family, your
Father's presence will be your delight, and his absence
hiding, and frowns will be an intolerable affliction. Christ,
the first-born of the family, he never complained so
much of all his other troubles, as when his Father
looked down upon him, Psal. xxii. 1. " My God, my
God, why hast thou forsaken me ?" Just so is it with
all the genuine offspring, as you see in David, Asaph,
Heman, and others.

8. You will dearly love all that bear their Father's
image, and the image of him who is the express image
of the Father; and the more resemblance they have unto
him, you will love them the better ; 1 John iii. 14.
" By this we know that we have passed from death
unto life, because we love the brethren." You will

esteem them, as David, the excellent ones of the earth; with them will be all your delight.

Lastly, All the offspring and issue of God's house, they have a zeal for the standing of their Father's house ; they " love the habitation of his house, and the place where his honour dwells ;" and therefore will have something of the Spirit of the first-born, of whom it is said, " The zeal of thine house hath eaten me up." Is it possible that a true child of a family can be unconcerned, when he sees robberies committed on his house, or the house of his father turned into a den of thieves ? Or will a true born child herden and associate himself with such, without opposing them, and witnessing against them ? A true child of the family will be ready to say of such, as Jacob said of Simeon and Levi, " They are brethren in iniquity : O my soul, come not thou into their secret," &c. Thus I have given you some marks which have a relation to the first character given to believers in the text.

I come next to pursue a trial, with an eye toward the second character or designation of vessels of different sizes, vessels of cups, and vessels of flagons, all hanging upon the nail fastened in a sure place. In the church, which is the house of the living God, there are vessels of mercy and vessels of wrath, vessels of honour fitted for the Master's use, and vessels of wrath fitted for destruction.

Now, here some may readily put the question, How may I know if I be a vessel of mercy and honour ? For clearing the way to the answering of this question, you will consider, that all the children of men sprung of Adam by natural generation, the elect of God as well as others, are, in the eye of the law, vessels of wrath fitted for destruction, through the pollution and guilt of original or actual sin. And until God come in a day of power, and dig the vessel of mercy from under the filth and rubbish of the fall of Adam, no man can make a difference betwixt the vessels of mercy, and of wrath,

because this is among secret things that belong to the
Lord.

But if the question be, How may a person know if
he be yet a vessel of mercy fitted by regenerating and
sanctifying grace for the Master's use? Hath God
yet formed me for himself? Hath he taken me out of
nature's quarry, out of the miry clay, and washed, and
justified, and sanctified me in the name of the Lord
Jesus, and by the Spirit of our God? Now, I say, if
this be the question, I will give you a few marks of the
vessels of mercy and honour.

1. Every vessel of mercy in the house of our God
(whether they be vessels of cups, or vessels of flagons),
has seen himself to be a vessel of wrath by nature,
condemned already, full of the vermin of sin and corruption, treasuring up to himself wrath against the day
of wrath. Hence all God's Israel are ready to take
up that melancholy song, "A Syrian ready to perish
was I: At that time I was afar off, an alien to the
commonwealth of Israel, a stranger to the covenant of
promise, without God, without Christ, and without
hope in the world." Hence,

2. All the vessels of mercy are taken up in admiring
the rich and free mercy of God, in taking up the like
of them from among the pots. "Not by the works
of righteousness, but according to his mercy he saved
us, by the washing of regeneration," &c. Oh, says
Paul, "I was a blasphemer, a persecutor, an injurious
person, but I obtained mercy. He took me (says David) out of the horrible pit, and miry clay, and set my
feet upon a rock, and put a new song in my mouth,
even praises unto our God."

3. All God's vessels of mercy have undergone the
hammer of the law in a greater or lesser measure: "Is
not my word as a hammer, saith the Lord, that breaketh the rock in pieces?" The law is a school-master,
to lead us unto Christ. So much hammering by the
law is necessary, and no more as serves to beat the heart
and hands of a sinner off from the broken nail of the

law, in point of righteousness. " I through the law (says Paul), am dead to the law." So much of this hammer is needful, as to beat down the vain and towering imaginations of our own goodness, holiness, wisdom, and righteousness ; the Dagon of self, in all the shapes and forms of it, must be broken down for ever. The vessel of mercy shall never more say with the proud Pharisee, " God, I thank thee, that I am not as other men ;" or, with Laodicea, " I am rich, and increased with goods, and stand in need of nothing."

4. All the vessels of mercy are made heartily content to change their holding. All mankind have their holding either on the first or second Adam ; they are either hanging by the broken nail of the covenant of works, or by the gospel-nail of the covenant of grace ; they are either seeking life and righteousness by the works of the law, or by the grace of the gospel. Now, in a day of conversion, the sinner having his hands knocked off from his first holding, he, by the hand of faith, which is God's gift, receives Christ, and takes hold of that covenant whereof he is head, saying, " In him will I be justified, and in him will I glory ; for in him have I righteousness and strength ; he is to me the end of the law for righteousness ; for he was made sin for us, though he knew no sin, that we might be made the righteousness of God in him ;" so Paul, Phil. iii. 8, 9.

5. All the vessels of mercy are melted in the fire of gospel grace and love, and made pliable to the will of God. The heart of stone is melted into a heart of flesh, Ezek. xxxvi. 26. The iron sinew of the obstinate will, through the heat of divine love, is made to give way, and yield unto the divine will, Psalm cx. 3; the language of every vessel of mercy, is, " Lord, what wilt thou have me to do ?" The adamantine heart is dissolved into evangelical repentance, so that the man now looks on him whom he had pierced, and mourns," Zech. xii. 10.

6. All the vessels of the house are washed, and will

be frequently washing themselves, in the fountain of a Redeemer's blood, from sin and from uncleanness, Zech. xiii. 1. The vessels of the house, through remaining corruption, temptation, and frequent falls into the puddle of actual sin, gather dust, and become dim and unfit for the use and service of the great Father and Manager of the house ; and therefore he will have them sprinkled with clean water ; he will have their hearts sprinkled· from an evil conscience, and their bodies washed with pure water ; " Except I wash thee (says Christ to Peter), thou hast no part in me." And this washing is what they themselves cry for, especially when defiled with any fall : hence they cry, with David, Psalm li. 2. " Wash me throughly from mine iniquity, and cleanse me from my sin. And, ver. 7. Purge me with hyssop, and I shall be clean : wash me, and I shall be whiter than snow."

7. All the vessels of the house, from the least to the greatest, have the name of the Father of the house, and of the Manager of the house, and of the house or city they pertain to, engraven upon them. It has been, and still is, the custom of great men, to have their names and arms graven on their gold and silver vessels ; so is it in the house of our God. All the vessels of mercy have his name and motto engraven upon them : Rev. xiv. 1. " Lo, a Lamb stood on the Mount Sion, and with him an hundred forty and four thousand, having their Father's name written in their foreheads." They have the name of Christ, the great Manager of the house, written on them, particularly that name, Jer. xxiii. 6. " The Lord our righteousness ;" and in this name of his do they rejoice all the day long, for in his righteousness are they exalted. And then, as we are told, Rev. iii. 12. the name of the new Jerusalem, which cometh down from God out of heaven, is engraven on them ; for they prefer Jerusalem unto their chiefest joy. In a word, God's name, his glory, honour, and authority, his truth, his worship, his cause, and interest,·the word of God, the testimony of Jesus,

the prerogatives of his crown and kingdom, every true believer hath these, as it were, engraven on his heart, and will study to profess and maintain them before the world.

8. If you be the vessels of mercy and honour, the Master of the house will now and then be making use of you, by pouring the wine, the oil, the water, or milk of his grace and Spirit into you : "For out of his ful ness do we all receive, and grace for grace." Every vessel of the house is anointed with the fresh oil of the Holy Ghost : "We have an unction from the holy One." And they that want this anointing of the Spirit, in one degree or another, the Manager of the house will not own them as his : "If any man have not the Spirit of Christ, he is none of his." They will be found among the foolish virgins, whose vessels had no oil, when the mid-night cry was heard, "Behold, the bridegroom cometh, go ye out to meet him." But, I say, all the vessels of mercy have a greater or smaller measure of the anointing of the Spirit ; and every anointing of the Spirit, enlargeth the vessel to hold more, insomuch, that through the frequent communications of the Spirit, a cup vessel at first becomes a large vessel, or a vessel of flagon, until it be ready to be transported from the lower to the upper storey of the house, where every vessel shall be filled brimful of God.

Quest. Some exercised soul may be ready to say, O how happy would I be, if I knew that I were but the least vessel in the house of God, hanging on the nail fastened in a sure place ! but, alas ! I am such a poor, worthless, useless creature, that I am afraid I am none of them.

Answ. It is the nature of all the vessels of mercy in the house of God, yea, of the great flagons, to esteem themselves worthless, and among the least, yea, less than the least of all the vessels of the house. Eph. iii. 8. says the great apostle Paul, "I am less than the least of all saints." And the lower that they sink in their own eyes, the higher do they rise in the esteem of the great Lord of the house, Is. lvii. 15. and the more of his grace and favour do they receive, for " he giveth grace unto the humble."

Object. 2. May another say, I am so broken and tossed with worldly trials, that I am ready to think I am none of the offspring or vessels of his house. *Answ.* " Many are the afflictions of the righteous, and through many tribulations we must enter into the kingdom." Christ himself suffered before he entered into his glory, and so have all the cloud of witnesses, Heb. xi. And therefore it is a false conclusion to think you do not belong to the Lord, because of multiplied roots of affliction ; for " if we be without chastisement, whereof all are partakers, then are we bastards and not sons. Whom the Lord loveth, he chasteneth." God's gold and silver vessels go frequently into the furnace, and there is a need-be for it, to purge away their dross ; and therefore learn to say with Job, " When thou hast tried me, thou shalt bring me forth as gold."

Object. 3. I am such a vile polluted creature, that I cannot think I am one of his offspring by regeneration, none of the vessels of honour, but rather a vessel of wrath, fitted for destruction. *Answ.* God will not cast away his gold and silver vessels, because of the dross and alloy of sin and corruption that is about them. A man will take up a vessel of his house, though it be lying in a dunghill. So here ; David, Solomon, Peter, and many others of the saints, fell into the mire of sin, and yet the Lord took them from the dunghill, and made them like the wings of a dove. And therefore, seeing God will not cast off for ever, do not you cast off yourself.

Object. 4. I am so harassed with Satan and his fiery darts, that I am afraid I am none of God's children, none of his vessels ; I am tempted to evils and abominations that I am afraid to name to any in the world. *Answ.* Christ himself was tempted in all things as we are, that he might be a merciful high priest, to simpathize with them that are tempted. Again, consider, for thy encouragement, that usually the devil gives the sorest pulls and pushes at the offspring of God's house, at the gold and silver vessels of his family : and if you did not belong to God, Satan would not pursue you so much. When Israel came out of Egypt, then Pharaoh and his host pursued most vigorously. Again, "The God of peace shall bruise Satan under your feet shortly."

Object. 5. I am none of the offspring or vessels : for God is hiding, and carrying to me as an enemy, insomuch that the very remembrance of him is a terror to me. *Answ.* This is no unprecedented case among God's children. David, when he "remembered God, he was troubled ;" Asaph cries, "Is his mercy clean gone ?" Heman, Psalm lxxxviii., "While I suffer thy terrors; I am distracted." Yea, Christ, the first-born and beloved Son, is under such agony of soul, that he cries out, "I am exceeding sorrowful, even unto death." It is hard to tell how far fatherly displeasure and chastisement may be carried ; but this is an uncontroverted truth, that the foundation of God standeth sure, and God will never disinherit any of the offspring and issue, or cast away any of the vessels that hang, by a faith of his operation, upon the nail fastened in a sure place.

Exhortation to men in general to rest all upon Christ.

THEN let every man and woman, that has a soul to be saved, come to him in a way of believing, and lay the stress of their eternal salvation upon the great manager of the house. This is a business of everlasting concern, and therefore allow me to enforce the exhortation a little.

There is no help for you in heaven or in earth ; all other nails are weak, broken, or crooked, but this of God's fastening ; and therefore to the bottom of eternal woe and misery you must go, unless you hang your salvation upon it. No name given under heaven whereby to be saved, but by the name of Jesus ;

neither is there salvation in any other : all refuge fails, and proves only a refuge of lies : " In vain is salvation expected from the hills, or multitude of mountains :" and therefore I may put that question to you in this case, " Whither will you flee for help ? or where will you leave your glory," if you do not " commit the keeping of your souls unto him as unto a faithful Creator."

This Manager is a person of great skill and experience in the business of saving souls that are lost by the fall of Adam ; it is his trade and business upon which he came into the world ; no case is desperate to him, for he is able to save to the uttermost, and he has been occupied in the work of saving the lost, ever since sin entered into the world. Many, many have gone through his hands, and he has made a good account of every one of them ; the innumerable company that are about the throne, singing the song of Moses and the Lamb, are all standing monuments of his skill and experience : every one of them cries, " Worthy is the Lamb that was slain : for thou hast redeemed us, and thou hast washed and saved us by thy blood."

The great Manager has not only skill, ability, and experience, but he is most willing to be employed. " To you, O men, doth he call, and his voice is to the sons of men. Come to me who will, I will in no wise cast out. Come, and let us reason together, saith the Lord : though your sins be as scarlet and crimson, I will make them white as snow and as wool." And to put the matter out of doubt, and beyond all controversy, he assures you of his willingness with the solemnity of an oath, Ezek. xxxiii. 11. " As I live, saith the Lord, I have no pleasure in the death of the wicked, but rather that they turn unto me, and live," &c. He is so willing and desirous of having the management of thy salvation committed to him, that it is the joy of his heart when a lost sinner comes to him for this end, as see cleared in the three parables, Luke. xv.

You are well warranted to hang your all upon this nail, for it was fixed in a sure place. For this very end he was set up from everlasting, from the beginning, to be the Saviour of lost sinners ; he is ordained for men in things pertaining to God : and it is the command of God, that you believe in him to the saving of your souls, that you receive and rest upon him, 1 John iii. 23. And therefore you must either trust this great Manager with your salvation, otherwise you counteract the authority of heaven in the greatest command that ever was issued out from the excellent glory.

Let nothing then scare you from coming to the great Manager by faith, or from hanging your justification, sanctification, and salvation, upon this nail fastened in a sure place. " Take heed, brethren, lest there be in any of you an evil heart of unbelief, in turning you away from the living God ; and let us fear lest a promise of salvation being left us, any of us should seem to come short of it ;" the consequence thereof will be fatal through all eternity.

Do not say, I am not prepared for coming to him ; for I know of no preparation a sinner can make for Christ, but that of his seeing himself lost and undone without him. What preparation had the man-slayer, besides danger from the avenger of blood, when he fled to the city of refuge ? What preparation has a drowning man to make for taking hold of a strong rope cast in to draw him ashore ? Is not the sick man prepared for the physician ? the man starving through want prepared for meat ?

Do not say, that the fiery law, and its curse, stands in your way ; for the law condemns you because you do not improve the remedy presented to you in the gospel. The thunders of the law are hushed into a pleasent calm, whenever the sinner comes unto mount Zion, and to Jesus the Mediator of the new covenant. Christ is " the end of the law for righteousness to every one that believeth ; and therefore no condemnation to them that are in him."

Do not say, that the decree of God is any obstacle in your way of coming unto Christ, and hanging your eternal salvation upon him ; for as the decree of God is secret, and does not belong to us, so, in the decrees of Heaven, the end and the mean are connected together, and the one made subservient unto the other. Does any man concern himself with God's decrees in the ordinary affairs of life ? Does the merchant argue, If God has decreed that I shall be rich, it shall come to pass, though I never go to the market and buy and sell ? Or doth the husbandman argue, I shall have a plenitful crop, if God has ordained it, although I neither plant nor sow ? Men will not venture their worldly affairs upon such a foolish way of arguing ; why then should any argue at that rate in matters wherein their precious souls are concerned, and lie at stake ?

May some poor soul say, O, gladly would I come to the great Manager Christ, and hang my soul's eternal salvation upon him, as on a nail fastened in a sure place ; but, alas ! I find such an utter impotence and inability to believe in him, that all exhortations are in vain, until the power of God be put forth to enable me ; " No man can come to Christ, unless the Father which sent him, draw him." *Answ.* (1.) The soul that is truly sensible of its own inability to believe, or do any thing for itself, is in the fairest way of believing ; for faith springs out of a thorough conviction of its own impotence and inability, either to will or to do. And therefore, (2.) From a sense of your own impotence, look up to him that giveth power to the faint, and increaseth strength to them that have no might; for he who commands you to believe, is the Author and Finisher of faith, ready to fulfil in you all the good pleasure of his goodness, and the work of faith with power. (3.) I would say to you that are in good earnest in making this objection, and complaining of inability to believe, that the power of God is exerted in a very silent and imperceptible way in bringing the sinner to believe in

Christ, therefore likened unto the falling of the dew, the growth of the corn, or a grain of mustard seed, or the gradual working of leaven in a measure of meal, which are best known by the effects ; and therefore observe and see if you can perceive any of the effects of the Spirit of faith in or about you, such as, a prizing of the word and ordinances, a drinking the sincere milk of it, a valuing of Christ, a renouncing of our own, and a leaning only to a Surety's righteousness, heart-love to all that bear the image of God ; these, or the like fruits of faith, may be sometimes found in the soul that is complaining of its own inability to believe ; and if so, it is a hopeful evidence that the good work is begun, and so you may be " confident of this very thing, that he who hath begun the good work, will perform it against the day of Jesus Christ."

I shut up this exhortation with two or three advices, in order to your committing your all into the hand of the great Manager of the house of God.

1. Study to be in good earnest in the matter of believing ; for it is with the heart that man believes unto righteousness. Faith is not a dreaming, sleeping work, as you see in the case of Peter's hearers, Acts ii. the jailor, Acts xvi.

2. Consider well the worth of the soul, and what danger it is into of being lost for ever. " What is a man profited, if he gain the whole world, and lose his soul ?"

3. Be frequently viewing the majesty of that infinite God, with whom you must have to do for ever and ever, and what a fearful thing it is to fall into the hands of an implacable and eternal enemy. " Who knows the power of his wrath ? Who can dwell with devouring fire ?" &c.

4. Be convinced, that, by the breach of the holy law in Adam, your federal head, and also in your own persons, you are liable to the wrath and displeasure of God, yea, *condemned already.*

5. Be convinced of the utter insufficiency of all those nails that you have been formerly trusting to. Perhaps you have been trusting to the nail of a general mercy in God. But this will not hold ; for God himself has declared, that he who " made sinners, will have no mercy on them ; that he will by no means clear the guilty," without a satisfaction to his justice, and faith's improvement of that satisfaction set forth in the gospel-revelation. Perhaps you are leaning to the nail of gospel-church-privileges, or receiving the seal of the covenant in baptism, or the Lord's supper. But this nail will give way : " Unless you be baptized with the Holy Ghost, and eat the flesh, and drink the blood of the Son of man, you have no life in you." Perhaps you are leaning to the nail of a blazing profession. But, alas ! this will fail you, as you see in the case of the foolish virgins, and those Matth. vii. 22, to whom Christ says, " Depart from me, I never knew you." Perhaps you are leaning your weight upon the nail of some common attainments under the drop of the gospel, such as, a common knowledge, a common faith, a common reformation, a common zeal for the public cause of Christ, without an actual taking hold of God's covenant of grace and promise. All these will give way. That knowledge that does not humble and sanctify, that faith that is not accompanied with a humble sense of unbelief, that reformation of life that does not begin at the heart, that zeal that is not founded on knowledge, will never abide the trial. Perhaps you are laying your weight upon the law or the works of it, either in part or in whole ; your morality, civility, delight in duties, or your own good meanings and endeavours. But, alas! this nail will break also : for the law is weak through the flesh, and there is no law given, since the fall of Adam, that can give life, otherwise righteousness would come by the law. The Jews leaned to this nail, and went about to establish their own righteousness, as it were by the works of the law. But what came of it ? The nail broke, and fell under

the condemnatory sentence of that law to which they leaned ; and there they lie, and will lie till their eyes be opened. Now, I say, study and be fully persuaded of the utter insufficiency of all these, or other nails you are venturing your salvation upon. The hail shall sweep away all these refuges of lies.

6. Turn away your eyes from all these, and take a view of the strength, sufficiency, and excellency of the nail that God has fastened in a sure place. Study the excellency of Christ in his person as Immanuel, God man ; the validity of his commission as the sent of God; the sufficiency of that righteousness he has brought in for justifying of the ungodly by his obedience unto the death ; the stability and freedom of the covenant whereof he is Head, Surety, and Mediator; the prevalency of his intercession, by virtue of which he is able to save to the uttermost all that come to God by him : I say, be much in viewing and meditating upon these things.

7. With these join earnest and importunate prayers in the name of Christ, that he, who is Father of light, Author of every good and perfect gift, may send forth his light and truth, that in his light you may see light; that it may be given you, by his word and Spirit, to know the mysteries of the kingdom of heaven, particularly that leading mystery of a God in our nature, "God manifested in the flesh, justified in the Spirit," &c. And while you are praying for these things, study to believe, and be confident toward him, that he will hear you, and that he doth hear you, because these things are agreeable to his will, Mark xi. 24. 1 John v. 14.

A word of advice to several sorts of believers as described in Isai. 22. 24

1. A word to weak believers, who are designed vessels of cups. I only suggest these two or three things unto you. (1.) It is a high privilege to occupy the least room in the house of our God. The prodigal son, when he came to himself, only begged of his father that he might have the place of a hired servant ; he

was glad to be under his father's roof, and to eat in his
father's house, at any rate.   (2.) God has service for
the least vessel of his house, as well as for the largest.
God never made a useless creature, and he does not
form any useless vessels ; no, every vessel is formed of
himself, to show forth his praise.   (3.) The least vessel
is God's property, and he will not disown, but maintain
his property, and own it before men and angels, saying,
" They are mine," in the day when he makes up his
jewels.   (4.) The bands, by which you hang upon the
nail fastened in a sure place, are as strong as those by
which the vessels of flagons are secured ; for he has
said as to both, " They shall never perish, neither shall
any pluck them out of my hand."   (5.) The weakest
measure of grace is a pledge of more ; for " to him that
hath shall be given."   What grace you have got is the
arles-penny of more a-coming, for " his goings forth
are prepared as the morning," as the break of day is
a pledge of more light to follow : " The path of the
just is as the shining light, that shineth more and more
unto the perfect day."   The least measure of grace
has glory connected with it, according to the order of
the covenant, Psalm lxxxiv. 11. " The Lord God is a
sun and shield, he will give grace and glory ;" first
grace, and then glory.

I next offer a word of advice unto the vessels of cups,
I mean weak believers.   Although you are not to envy
or grudge at God's bounty or liberality to others, in
making them vessels of flagons, yet you may and ought
earnestly to covet more grace than you have yet received ; and therefore we are commanded to " grow
in grace, and in the knowledge of our Lord and Saviour Jesus Christ."   In order to which, be humble under a sense of your own weakness and emptiness ; for
" he giveth grace to the humble."   Be diligent in the
improvement of what grace you have received ; for
" the hand of the diligent maketh rich."   Be frequently coming to the Manager of the house for more grace :
" To whom coming, as unto a living stone,—ye also,

as living stones, are built up," &c. Improve all the means of God's appointment for your edification, such as, the word, sacraments, prayer, Christian conference, that you may " add to your faith, virtue; to virtue, knowledge; to knowledge, temperance; to temperance, patience; to patience, godliness ; to godliness, brother-ly kindness ; and to brotherly kindness, charity ; for if these things be in you, and abound, they make you that ye shall neither be barren, nor unfruitful in the knowledge of our Lord Jesus Christ," 2 Pet. i. 5—8.

2. A word to the vessels of flagons, believers of a higher stature. To you I would say,

1*st*, Be not proud of grace received, but walk hum-bly with your God. " Who made thee to differ ? and what hast thou that thou hast not received ? His soul that is lifted up is not upright in him." True grace, where it is genuine, the more a man receives of it, he is always the more humble and empty, as you see in Paul, Eph. iii. 8. " Less than the least of all saints." To keep your sails low, consider that the most eminent saints have discovered the greatest weakness, even in the graces wherein they most excelled ; as we see in the case of Abraham, Moses, David, Peter, and others. They that have the greatest measure of grace, they get as much to do with it ; strong corruption, strong temptation, and strong trials to grapple with : and the more talents that a man doth receive, the more hath he to account for, as to the improvement of them ; for " to whom much is given, of them much shall be required."

2*dly*, Instead of despising others that are not come your length, study to be helpful and serviceable unto them. The vessels of cups are ordinarily filled out of the flagons ; so study to impart and communicate of your grace, of your faith, love, hope, knowledge, and other graces, unto those that are weak in grace. The strong children in a family are helpful to the young and weak. Thus it is in the natural body, the strong member is helpful unto the weak and infirm ; so ought

it to be in the mystical body of Christ. And when
you see any fall through weakness, do not triumph
over them ; but " strengthen the weak hands, and confirm the feeble knees ; say to them that are of a fearful heart, Be strong ; restore such an one with a spirit
of meakness."

3dly, Whatever grace you have received, be not
strong or confident therein, like Peter ; but be strong
in the grace that is in Christ Jesus, and let the life you
live be by faith in the Son of God.   Grace received
will soon give way in a day of trial and temptation.
An innocent Adam, left with the stock in his hand,
soon turned bankrupt, and ruined all his posterity.
And therefore, I say, do not trust to the life or grace
you have in hand, but in the grace and life you have
in your head Jesus Christ, the glorious Manager and
Steward of his Father's house.   Still remember, that
all the vessels hang upon him ; and therefore let all the
weight lie where God has laid it.

3. A word of advice unto vessels of all sizes, whether
they be vessels of cups, or vessels of flagons.

1st, Adore the riches of divine grace and mercy, that
put a difference between you and others, for naturally
you were as bad as others.

2dly, Let every one possess his vessel in sanctification and honour.   Do not debase or defile the vessel
of thy soul or body, by prostituting it unto the service
of sin, Satan, or any abominable lust.   You was once
lying in the miry clay of nature, but God has washed,
justified, and sanctified you ; and therefore study to
keep yourself clean and holy in heart, life, and in all
manner of conversation.   If you defile yourselves with
sin, the Manager of the house will be fair to cast you
into a furnace of affliction, or, like Jonah, to plunge
you into deep waters, till you acknowledge, " Mine
own iniquities correct me, and my backslidings do reprove me."

3dly, When you find any defilement of sin cleaving
to you (which you will never miss while in the body),

flee to the fountain opened for sin and for uncleanness in the house of David. Be often bathing thy soul in the blood of Jesus, which cleanseth from all sin.

4*thly*, Come to the fountain for supply under all wants, that you may obtain mercy, and find grace to help in time of need. " Out of his fulness do all we receive, and grace for grace." Let thy vessel just lie under the flowing of this blessed fountain, that it may never be found empty when the midnight cry is made, " Behold the Bridegroom cometh, go ye forth to meet him."

Lastly, Pray for a plentiful outpouring of the Spirit, according to the promise, Is. xliv. 3. " I will pour floods upon the dry ground," that so all the empty vessels of the land, that are destitute of the waters of God's grace, may be filled ; and those that are hanging upon the first Adam, and under the curse of the law, may, by the power of grace, change their holding, and hang upon the nail that God has fastened in a sure place.

I am the Lord thy God—thou shalt have no other gods before me.

SOLOMON says, " Where the word of a king is, there is power ;" what power then must there be, where the word of God is, who is the King of kings, and Lord of lords! Pray, Sir, notice and consider what is said, ver. 1. " God spake all these words." This is enough to make heaven and earth to listen with the most profound silence and adoration. Is. i. 2. " Hear, O heavens, and give ear, O earth, for the Lord hath spoken. The mighty God the Lord hath spoken." And when he speaks, he " calls the earth from the rising of the sun to the going down thereof :" to listen, and therefore, " O earth, earth, earth, hear the word of the Lord. God spake all these words." This is like the sounding of a trumpet before the king's proclamation. God spake all the words of this Bible in a mediate way, by the mouths of his holy prophets and apostles ; but here God himself is the immediate speaker : surely it must be some matter of vast moment, and of the highest im-

portance, when God himself is the preacher. Well,
what are the words God spake in such an immediate
manner ; *Answ.* All these words from the 2d verse of
this chapter to the close of ver. 17. And, Sirs, I would
have you to remember, that all these words are spoken
as directly to you, and to every soul hearing me, as ever
they were unto Israel ; and you and I are to reckon our
selves no less concerned now to hear and regard them,
than if we had been standing at the foot of Sinai among
the children of Israel, when the heavenly trumpet
sounded, and the voice of God was uttered with such
awful majesty as made Moses and all Israel fall a quak-
ing and trembling ; for all these words are directed
unto us, as much as they were unto them. And therefore do not shift them, as though they were spoken
only to Israel, or as if they were spoken to others, and
not to you. No, no ; to thee, man, to thee, woman,
God now speaks all these words in this Bible ; and
therefore hear and listen, with particular application of
them to thy own soul, as if God were calling thee out
of heaven, by name and sirname. Two of these ten
words I design to explain, namely these, taken in their
connection, " I am the Lord thy God—Thou shalt
have no other gods before me."

Where two things are considerable. 1. A great and
gracious promise, even the leading promise of the covenant, " I am the Lord thy God." 2. A great and
gracious law or commandment, founded upon the covenant promise and grant ; a law, the obligation whereof the very light of nature cannot shake off ; " Thou
shalt have no other gods before me."

1. We have a great promise or new covenant-grant ;
" I am the Lord thy God." The greatest word ever
God spake since the fall of Adam ! for here he not
only speaks forth his own glory and transcendent being,
but he speaks over himself unto us as our God. Here
is a promise, yea, something more than a promise. A
promise is commonly expressed with respect to the time
to come, concerning something God hath a mind to do

hereafter; but here God speaks in the present time, " I am the Lord thy God;" i. e. now while I am speaking, from this moment I become your God ; and from this time forward you may claim me as such, and hold me to it, by this my grant that I make of myself unto you. God's covenant of promise is not a thing past, or a thing to come only ; but a thing present, " I am the Lord thy God." Faith never wants a foundation ; no, it is always invariably the same : and if our faith did bear a just proportion unto the ground of faith in the covenant, we would not be up and down in our believing ; no, we would be always believing, and that with the fullest assurance of faith. There is a twofold title by which God describes himself here in this covenant-grant ; the one is essential and the other relative. (1.) The essential title is JEHOVAH ; the force of which is opened, Rev. i. 4. " He that is, that was, and is to come." And it implies his self-existence, that he hath his being of himself, independent of all other beings ; and that he giveth being to all other beings whatever, in heaven above, or in earth beneath. The Jews think this name so sacred that they judge it unlawful to pronounce it. It is a name common to each person of the glorious Trinity, Father, Son, and Holy Ghost, who are one God. Christ is called JE-HOVAH frequently in the Scripture, as well as the Father, Jer. xxiii. 6. " This is his name whereby he shall be called, JEHOVAH, our righteousness." And we have very good ground to think that it was JEHOVAH, in the person of the eternal Son, that spake all these words from the top of Sinai, unto Israel. (2.) Another title whereby he here describes himself is relative ; 'thy God.' This is it that sweetens the name of JEHOVAH unto us ; he is JEHOVAH our God. The terror of his amazing and infinite greatness were enough to affright and astonish all mankind ; but when he says, " I am thy God, even thy own God ;" not an avenging God, to execute the penalty of the broken law upon thee, but a " God with thee, a God on thy side," to pity, pardon, and defend thee, a " God gracious and merciful, abundant in goodness and in truth ;" this, O this ! renders his name JEHOVAH amiable and desirable.

2. In the words we have a law or commandment, suited unto, and founded upon, this covenant grant ; "Thou shalt have no other gods before me." This, as many of the rest of the commandments are, is delivered in negative terms, prohibiting and forbidding, " the denying, or not worshipping and glorifying the true God, as God and our God; and the giving of that worship and glory to any other which is due to him alone." And this law, or commandment, as the generality of the other commandments, is delivered in negative terms, because of the perpetual propensity of our natures, since the fall, to depart from the living God through an evil heart of unbelief. But although the command be delivered in negative terms, yet the contrary positive duty is manifestly included in it, or under it ; namely, "to know and acknowledge God to be the only true God, and our God ; and to worship and glorify him accordingly," as is well expressed in our Catechism. As for these words, " Before me," or "before my face," as it may be read : this expression plainly teaches us, that an omniscient and all-seeing God, before whom all things are open and naked, and who "sets our most secret sins in the light of his countenance," taketh notice of, and is much displeased with, the sin of having any other God ; and consequently is well pleased with the sinner who knows and acknowledges him as the only true God, and his own God, according to the gift of the covenant, which is the foundation of our claim to him.

And O that I could make all this company, and the whole world of mankind, if I had access, to understand what a glorious and rich treasure they have among their hands when they hear these words repeated, or repeat them themselves, " I am the Lord thy God." "Thou shalt have no other gods before me." Alas! there are many have these words by rote, who never

consider what is in them : just like a company of people travelling the highway where an immense treasure
lies under their feet ; they pass and repass it, but miss
the treasure, because they never dig into the field ; so
people read and repeat these words, and lose God
and eternal life, that lie hid in them, because they do
not advert to what they are saying or reading.

But O Sirs, let me beseech and intreat you, for
your souls' sake, to pause a little, and consider what is
in these words, " I am the Lord thy God." " Thou
shalt have no other gods before me." You and I, by
the breach and violation of the first covenant, in our
father Adam, lost our God ; and ever since, every man
and woman is " without God in the world," and being
without God, we are without hope, without help, without grace, light, life, strength, or any thing that is good.
When we lost our God, we lost all, and lost it to all
intents and purposes. Well, but, Sirs, I tell you glad
tidings of the greatest joy that ever mankind heard
since the fall of Adam ; here you have your God,
whom you lost by the first covenant, coming back again
to you in a new covenant, a covenant of grace, and
saying to every one of you, " I am the Lord thy God :"
he becomes our God, not upon the footing of works,
but of free grace. And because the sinner, through
a sense of guilt and wrath, might be ready to scare and
say, O I cannot think that God is speaking to me,
when he says, " I am the Lord thy God !" I doubt, may
the sinner say, if I be warranted to claim him as my
God, who have forfeited all claim and title to him.
In answer unto this, consider, that a royal law is issued
out, yea, the very law of nature, written at first upon
Adam's heart, is repeated and adapted unto the dispensation of the covenant of grace, binding and oblig-
ing every one, to whom these presents are intimated,
to take him as their God in Christ, upon the footing
of this new covenant. And it is remarkable, how Infinite Wisdom outwits the policy of hell, and " turns
the counsel thereof into foolishness." Satan ruins man

by tempting him to break the law, and so to affront God in his authority and sovereignty. Well, but God takes the very first commandment of that law which Adam broke, and brings it in under a new covenant, the sum of which is this, " I am the Lord thy God :" and so makes that very law subservient to man's recovery, and his greatest warrant to lay claim to JEHOVAH as his God. So that you see, this first commandment in this situation, connected with the preface, is just big and pregnant with amazing grace and love.

Remarks concerning the great covenant of promise, I am the Lord thy God.

1. I remark, that this, as all the other promises, is in Christ : my meaning is, that it goes upon a ransom found, and a satisfaction paid, unto justice by Christ our glorious Surety. Sirs, be aware of imagining, that an absolute God, or a God out of Christ, utters this promise : no, no ; an absolute God is a consuming fire unto guilty sinners, and he could never speak in such a dialect to any of the sinful rebellious race of Adam, in a consistency with the honour of his holiness, justice, and sovereignty, which were offended and affronted in the violation of his royal law. Unless the Son of God had promised, as our Surety, to pay the infinite ramsom that justice demanded, none of Adam's posterity had ever heard any thing but the terrible thun-ders of his wrath and justice pursuing them for sin So that this covenant grant or promise, as well as the other declarations of the grace and love of God in the word to perishing sinners, must needs go upon the foot-ing of the blood and satisfaction of Jesus: 2 Cor. v. 19. " God was in Christ, reconciling the world unto himself, not imputing their trespasses unto them ; and hath committed unto us the word of reconciliation." And therefore, Sirs, whenever you read or hear a word of grace from God, think upon Christ, in and through whom only God is a God of peace ; and let your soul say, " O thanks be unto God for his unspeakable gift !"

2. It is more than probable, that it was God in the person of his eternal Son, that uttered all these words at mount Sinai; and this promise in particular, whereby the law was ushered in. Here was a parliament, or general assembly of angels, called at mount Sinai; and Christ the great Angel of the covenant was the president, or great Lord-speaker. This I gather from Psalm lxviii. ver. 17 and 18. compared. Ver. 17. it is said, " The chariots of God are twenty thousand, even thousands of angels: the Lord is among them as in Sinai, in the holy place." Well, what Lord was it that was among them at Sinai? " Even that same Lord," ver. 18. "who ascended up on high, and led captivity captive, and received gifts for men," &c. See also to the same purpose, Acts vii. 37, 38, compared. Ver. 37. " A prophet shall the Lord your God raise up unto you, of your brethren, like unto me; him shall ye hear." Christ is that great prophet. But then notice what follows, ver. 38. " This is he that was in the church in the wilderness, with the angel which spake to him" (viz. unto Moses and the children of Israel) "in the mount Sinai, and with our fathers." So that it was Christ the Son of God that spake all these words in mount Sinai, saying, " I am the Lord thy God, which have brought thee out of the land of Egypt, out of the house of bondage." " Thou shalt have no other gods before me," &c. And by the way, this furnishes us with a notable confutation of the Arians, who deny Christ to be a supreme, self-existent, and independent God. Who did ever doubt, that it was the supreme God, the self-existent God, that spake all these words, and delivered the law with such awful solemnity at mount Sinai! Yet, from what I was saying, it appears, that it was none other than Christ the eternal Son.

3. I remark, that this covenant grant and promise is the same upon the matter with the promise God had made unto Abraham several hundreds of years before. Now, God's promise to Abraham was, " I will be thy God, and the God of thy seed:" and here he meets

with his seed at Sinai, and repeats what he had said to
their fathers, Abraham, Isaac, and Jacob, saying, " I
am the Lord thy God ;" *i. e.* I am the very same promising God that spake unto Abraham, and what I said
unto him, I say it over again unto you his posterity, and
give the same ground for your faith that he had ; as I
was his God, so " I am the Lord thy God." God does
not come and go upon his promise, he is not yea and
nay : he does not make a promise one day, and retract
it another ; no, it is always yea and amen. He does not
speak of the promise made to Abraham as a thing out of
date after so many years ; no, It is as fresh and green
with me as the first day I made it, " I am still the
Lord thy God." The promise is renewed in their own
persons immediately by God, and they have as good a
foundation laid by this means, as ever Abraham had,
who believed without staggering.

4. These words, " I am the Lord thy God," contain
the leading promise of the covenant of grace ; and
there is more in them than heart can conceive, or
tongue express ; for here is an infinite God, Father,
Son, and Holy Ghost, making over himself in two or
three words to man upon earth. O what can he give
more than himself! and what will he not give when he
gives himself! Rom. viii. 32. " He that spared not his
own Son, but delivered him up for us all, how will he
not with him also freely give us all things ?"

5. This promise is so framed by Infinite Wisdom, as
to point to every individual person in the camp of Israel. It is not ye collectively, but thou in the singular, as if he spake to every individual person in the
camp, and every man was to look to it as pointing at
him in particular ; like a well drawn picture, it looked
every man in the camp straight in the face. And not
only did this promise point to every man and woman
there present at mount Sinai, when the law was delivered, but it looked forward to all succeeding generations, and every man and woman that should spring of
them ; for this "promise was to them, and to their seed."

So that no sooner did any of the posterity of Abraham come into the world, but God said to him, as much as to the men that were at the foot of Sinai, " I am the Lord thy God." And no sooner did one of the Gentile nations join himself to the commonwealth of Israel, but immediately he found the God of Israel saying to him, " I am the Lord thy God : " and in this respect, this promise was a door of faith open unto the Gentiles, even before the coming of Christ. And when Christ came in the flesh, and by his death and resurrection, and publication of the everlasting gospel unto the Gentile world, broke down the partition-wall betwixt them and the Jews, this promise, as well as the law subjoined thereunto, extended itself, not only to the Jews and their seed, but to the Gentiles, who were " afar off, and to as many as the Lord our God shall call" by the sound of the gospel-trumpet. So that now, under the New Testament, this promise becomes a ground of faith unto us, as well as unto them ; and we have the same interest in it that they had. But, to clear this, I shall add,

6. A sixth remark, namely, that this promise may be considered in a threefold situation ; either as it is in the heart of God, or as it is in the word of God, or as in the hand of faith.

1st, As it is in the heart of God, or in his counsel or decree. And when viewed in this situation, it is peculiar only to his chosen people, whom he has " loved with an everlasting love" before the foundations of the world. But as it is in God's heart, it is not an object of faith unto any of Adam's posterity ; no, not to the elect themselves, because they do not know that they are among the number of the elect till they be actually believers : no man can say, at the first instant, in a way of believing, " The Lord is my God," upon the ground of electing love. So that the promise in this situation, being all one with the decree, must be laid aside as an object of faith at the first instance.

2dly, The promise may be viewed as situate in the

word, as it is published and proclaimed to the visible church, " to whom belong the adoption, and the giving of the law, and the promises." View it in this situation, it is a ground of faith to every one that hears it. God said to every man in the camp of Israel, and he says to every man and woman in the visible church, " I am the Lord thy God, " and " Thou shalt have no other gods before me." And the man or woman that does not know and acknowledge God as his God in Christ, upon the ground of the promise, considered in this situation, (in the word,) as it is held forth in common to all as the object and ground of faith, at once rebels against the authority of God in the command, and gives the lie to his faithfulness engaged in the promise. And, therefore, " Let us fear, lest a promise being left us of entering into his rest, any of us should come short of it ; for unto us is this gospel preached, as well as unto them," Heb. iv. 1, 2.

3dly, This promise is also to be considered as in the hand of faith, or as it is applied and professed in a way of believing. And, in this situation, it is only peculiar to a believer to have the Lord as his God ; because it is only he that has a saving interest ; it is he only whose " soul hath said unto the Lord, Thou art my Lord," upon a covenant-ground.

Important things implied in the Covenant Promise, " I am the Lord thy God."

1. THE infinite God, Father, Son, and Holy Ghost, makes over himself by covenant as the soul's portion and inheritance for ever. And O what a vast, large, and glorious inheritance is this ! O Sirs, when God says, " I am the Lord thy God, " he says more than if he had said, Heaven is thine, earth is thine, the glories of both are thine ! There is something in this promise, that " eye hath not seen, nor ear heard, neither hath it entered into the heart of man to conceive," &c. No wonder though David cried out upon the views of the Lord's being the portion of his cup,

Psalm xvi. 6. " The lines are fallen unto me in pleasant places, yea, I have a goodly heritage." O it is a
surprising armful the soul has, when by faith it grasps
an infinite God in this little word, " I am the Lord
thy God !"

2. When he says, " I am the Lord thy God," he in
effect says, All that I have I make it over unto you.
And O when he makes a grant of himself, what else
will he withhold!   " He that spared not his own
Son, but delivered him up for us all, how will he not
with him also freely give us all things ?" Rom. viii. 32.
Has he life ? Yea, he is the fountain of life.   Well, in
this promise he gives life unto thee.   " Because I live,
ye shall live also."   Has he light in himself? Yea,
" God is light, and with him is no darkness at all."
Well, " he shall be thy everlasting light, and thy God
thy glory."   Has he love ? Yea, " God is love."
Well, he who says he is ' thy God,' " will shed abroad
his love upon thy heart by the Holy Ghost, and circumcise thy heart to love him."   Has he honour ?
Yea, " his work is honourable and glorious."   Well,
thou shalt be preferred ; if thou take him as thy God,
thou shalt have a " place among them that stand by"
about his throne.   Has he riches ? Yea, " honour and
riches are with me."   Well, " he will fill all thy
treasures" with gold better than the gold of Ophir.
Has he " rivers of pleasures, and fulness of joy in his
presence, and at his right hand ?"   Well, " the times
of refreshing shall come forth from his presence" into
thy soul.

3. When he says, " I am the Lord thy God," he engages that all the attributes and perfections of his glorious nature shall jointly conspire and be forthcoming
for thy good. O Sirs, immediately upon the breach of
the first covenant, all the attributes of God put on an air
of wrath and vengeance against man ; hence Adam, after he had sinned, falls a trembling, and flees in among
the thickets of Paradise to hide himself. But O! the
divine attributes, as they shine in the face of our Im-

manuel, and are displayed through his blood and satisfaction, appears with an air of grace, love, and pity,
inviting sinners to come and shelter themselves under
them, from the wrath and curse due to them for sin. So
that when God says, " I am the Lord thy God," it is
upon the matter as if he should say, O impotent and
helpless sinner, come under my shadow, take me as thy
own God, and my power shall be employed to help
and protect thee.   O foolish and bewildered sinner, my
wisdom shall be thine, to direct and instruct thee.   O
polluted sinner, who hast " lien among the pots," my
holiness shall sanctify thee, and " make thee like the
wings of a dove," &c.   O guilty sinner, my mercy shall
pardon thee ; yea, my justice shall acquit thee, on the
score of the ransom that I have found : my goodness
shall supply all thy need, and my truth and faithfulness is pledged to accomplish all the promises unto
thee : my omniscient eye shall " run to and fro, through
the whole earth, to show myself strong on thy behalf :"
my providence shall be employed to manage all things
for thy good and advantage : " I will ride in the heavens for thy help, and in mine excellency on the skies."
    4. " I am the Lord thy God ;" i. e.   Whatever I
the infinite and eternal God can do for thy advantage,
it shall not be wanting.   And O what cannot the arm
of omnipotency do ! " he doth great things, yea, wonders without number." What wonders has God wrought
for his children and people, in all ages of the world ?
It was he that saved Noah by water from perishing
in the flood.   It was he that made a lane for Israel
through the deeps, as if it had been dry land.   It was
he that dissolved the flinty rock into floods of water,
suspended the fury of the devouring flames, and stopped
the course of the sun. " His hand is not shortened, that
it cannot save."   Now, whatever that omnipotent arm,
that " stretched out the heavens, and laid the foundations of the earth, can do for thy salvation, it shall
not be wanting.   All this, and infinitely more than I
can name, is wrapped up in the bosom of this covenant-

grant, which is here laid as the foundation and ground of our faith, " I am the Lord thy God."

Important remarks upon the precept, " Thou shalt have no other gods before me."

1. I REMARK, that as the promise, " I am the Lord thy God," is given forth by a God in Christ ; so the precept in this situation must needs come from the same fountain. This law or commandment must be viewed as in the hand of a Mediator, and not of an absolute God. The reason is plain, because the command obliges us to have him as our God, to love and trust him as our own God, which a sinner cannot do, but only as he is in Christ. Here the command stands under a covenant of grace, as is evident from the preface. Indeed, if that glorious preface or covenant-grant, " I am the Lord thy God," had not gone before the command, we might have taken it as coming from an absolute God ; but, taking the precept in connection with the preface, we must needs take up the law here as in the hand of a reconciled God in Christ, and as coming from that glorious fountain. And therefore let us say, with the church, " The Lord is our judge, the Lord is our lawgiver, the Lord is our king, and he will save us."

2. This commandment of the law, " Thou shalt have no other gods before me," narrows and extends its obligation upon the children of men, in a suitableness to the revelation that he makes of himself. When God reveals himself only by the works of creation and providence, as he doth to the heathen world, then this commandment obliges us to know and acknowledge him as a God, Creator, and Preserver ; but when he superadds to this revelation of himself as a reconciled God, a redeeming God in Christ, then the law superadds a new obligation, namely, to know and acknowledge him as such, and to claim him as the God of salvation ; a saving, pitying, pardoning God.

3. As the promise, " I am the Lord thy God," is the leading and fundamental blessing promised in the

covenant of grace, which draws all other blessings along
with it; so this precept, Thou shalt have the Lord
JEHOVAH as thy God, is the leading and fundamental
duty of the law, which sweetly and powerfully constrains the soul to obey all the other commands of it.
The reason of this is plain : when a person is determined to know and acknowledge God as his own God
in Christ, it binds and obliges him inevitably not to
bow down to images, or to give that worship and glory
to any other, which is due to him alone ; he will be
concerned to sanctify the name of God, and his holy
Sabbath, and in a word, to have a respect unto all his
commandments. Hence it is that faith in Christ Jesus
(which is just the first commandment in other words)
is so much inculcated in the scriptures, particularly of
the New Testament; yea, we are expressly told, that
" without faith it is impossible to please God ;" and "he
that cometh unto God, must believe that he is, and
that he is a rewarder of them that diligently seek him."

4. That the command and promise are of equal extent; so that every man that is bound to obey the
command, or to have a God in Christ as his own God,
is concerned in this promise, " I am the Lord thy
God ;" or, in other words, he is as much obliged to believe the promise with application, as he is obliged to
obey the command. The reason of this is plain, because a believing the promise with application, is the
very thing that the first command requires of us ; and
the promise is the very ground and foundation of that
faith that is required in the command ; and the foundation of faith must be as extensive as the command
of believing, unless we would say, that God commands
men to believe, without giving them a foundation to
believe upon : so that, if I be obliged to have the Lord
as my God, then it is lawful, yea, plain duty for me
viewing the covenant-grant, to say to the Lord, " Thou
art my Lord."

5. As the promise is indefinite, " I am the Lord thy
God," without mentioning any, or including any, but

pointing to every man in particular ; so the precept is indefinite, " Thou shalt have no other gods before me," without mentioning any particular person to whom it extends. And I think it is observable, that both the promise and precept are in the singular number, as if God spoke to every individual. And I do think that Infinite Wisdom has so ordered it of design, that no man might neglect the promise, that thinks himself bound to obey the precept. The legal heart of man is ready to fall in with this command of the law, and own its obligation ; while, in the meantime, it rejects the promise, as a thing it has no concern in. What more ordinary, than to hear some, especially under awakenings of conscience by the law, say, O it is a sad truth indeed, that I am a debtor to the law, and obliged to obey it ! but as for the promise of God, " I am the Lord thy God," I have no interest or concern in it. But, Sirs, whatever you may imagine, I tell you, that by this way you are separating what God has joined ; he has joined the command and the promise together, therefore let not your unbelieving hearts or legal spirits put them asunder ; for you can never obey the first command without closing with this promise, " I am the Lord thy God."

What the precept, " Thou shalt have no other gods before me," obliges us to believe.

1. This commandment obliges us to believe that God is, which is the first and fundamental truth both of natural and revealed religion ; and except you be established in the faith of this, you believe nothing to purpose. We cannot open our eyes, or look upon any of the creatures of God, whether in the heavens above, or in the earth beneath, but this truth must shine into our minds with such a glaring evidence, that one would think there were no need of a command to oblige us to believe it.

2. This command obliges us to believe, that he is such a God as he has revealed himself to be in his word

and in his works. It binds us to believe all the displays that he has given of his eternal power and Godhead, in his works of creation and providence ; but especially us, who enjoy the revelation of his word, to believe every thing that he has revealed of himself there ; as, that he is a Spirit, infinite, eternal, unchangeable, &c. ; that he is but one God in three persons, Father, Son, and Holy Ghost, the same in substance, equal in power and glory ; that from eternity he decreed all things that come to pass in time ; that he is the great Creator that made all things of nothing, by the word of his power, in the space of six days, and all very good ; that by his providence he preserves and governs all his creatures, and all their actions ; and that this great God in the "fulness of time, was manifested in the flesh," in the person of his eternal Son, and became a Redeemer and Saviour of lost sinners ; that he was "made under the law, to redeem them that were under the law, that we might receive the adoption of sons ;" and in a word, every other thing that God has revealed of himself.

3. This commandment requires us to believe and be persuaded, that this glorious God is the chief good of the rational soul ; that as his glory is to be our ultimate end, so our chief happiness lies in the enjoyment of him alone ; "Thou shalt have no other gods before me ;" *i. e.* Thou shalt place thy chief happiness in the enjoyment of me, who "am the Lord thy God." So that, when God commands us to have him as our God, he commands us to be happy for ever in himself, and to say with David, "Whom have I in heaven but thee ? and there is none in all the earth that I desire besides thee."

4. This command requires us to assent unto every word God speaks, as a truth of infallible verity, and unto the truth of this promise in particular ; that he speaks the truth in his heart, when he says, "I am the Lord thy God." And therefore, not to believe that it is as God says in this promise, is to call God a liar ;

it is an impeaching of his veracity in the promise, and a contempt of his authority interposed in the command. From whence it appears that an unbeliever breaks the very first command of the law of nature.

5. This command requires us, not only to believe the truth of the promise in general, but to believe it with particular application of it, each one of us unto ourselves. It is not a fulfilling of the contents of this command, to believe that he was the God of Israel, or the God of the visible church, or the God of the elect, or of all that believe in him, for all this do the devils and reprobates believe; but we must believe, know, and acknowledge that he is *our* God; and every one for himself must say, in faith, with Israel, " He is my God, I will prepare him an habitation." The first command requires of us a faith exactly corresponding unto the promise: now, the promise is to every one in particular, " I am the Lord thy God;" and the command runs parallel with it, pointing out every man in particular, " Thou shalt have no other gods before me:" and therefore it is a particular applying faith that is here required and called for. Perhaps this may appear somewhat surprising to those who never considered it, that by the first commandment, they are obliged to believe that the Lord is their God by covenant grant and promise. They believe that he is their Creator, and Preserver, and Benefactor; but they never thought he was their God by covenant-grant, or that they were bound to believe it with application, till once they found themselves so and so qualified. To take down this fortress of unbelief, I would only have you consider,

1*st*, If ever there was a time since you had a being, and had the law of God intimated unto you, wherein you was free from the obligation of the first command of the moral law, as it here stands connected with the covenant or the promise? No, surely. And if so, there was never a time wherein you was not obliged to believe, know, and acknowledge the Lord as your

God, upon the ground of the covenant-grant : and all
the time you have neglected to do so, you have been
living in disobedience to the first command ; and while
the first command is not obeyed, which is the foundation of all the rest, not one of them can be obeyed.
And I only leave it to yourselves to be considered,
whether you may lawfully live in disobedience to the
first command of the law of the great God, or suspend
your obedience thereunto, till you find qualifications
in yourselves, upon which you think you may lay claim
to him in a way of sense.   This is not to ground your
faith upon the veracity of God in his promise, but to
seek a ground for your faith within you.

2dly, However surprising this way of teaching may
appear from the first commandment, yet it is nothing
else than what you are taught in your lesser, received,
and approven Catechisms.   The first commandment
requires us to know and acknowledge the Lord as
God, and our God : and to worship and glorify him
accordingly.

3dly, I find God requiring faith of sinners, and of
notorious backsliders, in the same terms as is here called for, Jer. iii. 4. compared with ver. 1.   If we notice
the 1st verse, and the 2d following, we shall find that
God is there dealing with a company of people who
had made defection into idolatry ; and he charges
them with a perfidious and treacherous dealing with
him, under the notion of an adulteress that had forsak-
en the guide of her youth, and prostitute herself unto
other lovers.   However, infinite love opens up its bowels of pity, sends out a sound of grace and love to them,
saying, in the close of ver. 1, " Though thou hast
played the harlot with many lovers ; yet return again
to me, saith the Lord."   Well, what is the return
sovereign grace expects from them after such a discovery of his readiness to receive them ? See it, ver. 4,
" Wilt thou not from this time cry unto me, My Father, thou art the guide of my youth ?" i. e. Wilt
thou not from this time obey the first commandment

of my law, and know and acknowledge me, and me only, as thy God and Father in Christ?

4thly, I find that whenever a sinful people begins to act faith, their faith, even the first receptive by faith, is expressed in words which bear a plain obedience unto what is required in the first commandment; as in the case of these, Jer. iii. Whenever the call of the word is carried home by the efficacy of the Spirit upon their hearts, they cry out, ver. 22, "Behold, we come unto thee, for thou art the Lord our God;" whereby they acknowledge him as their God, even their *own* God. So Zech. xiii. 9. And I find that the saints of God in scripture, when in the exercise of faith, still yielding obedience to this first command of the law, and coming in with their appropriating *my*, Psalm xvi. 2. "O my soul, thou hast said unto the Lord, Thou art my Lord." With what pleasure does David obey his command, Psalm xviii. 1, 2. where eight or nine times he repeats his claim, acknowledging God as God, and his own God? And unbelieving Thomas, so soon as he gets his foot upon the neck of his unbelief, obeys this command, making a solemn acknowledgment of Christ, "My Lord, and my God."

Unto all this I shall only add, to prevent mistakes, that when the first commandment requires us to know and acknowledge God as our God, it is not to be understood, as if this were done by a saying it with the mouth only; no, no, "With the heart man believeth unto righteousness." We read of some that "remembered God as their rock, and the high God as their Redeemer: *but* they flattered him with their mouth, and they lied unto him with their tongues, for their heart was not right with him:" they did not acknowledge him as their God, with their hearts, acquiescing in him as their chief good and only portion; and therefore God rejects all their profession of kindness. Let us then embrace and acknowledge him as our God, with our hearts, lips, and lives, worshipping, glorifying, and serving him, as our God, all the days of our appointed time.

Soul quickening observations from these words, "I am the Lord thy God—thou shalt have no other gods before me."

1. SEE hence the necessity, excellency, and warrant-ableness of the great duty of believing, which we ministers are so much pressing upon you who are hearers. It must needs be the most necessary and excellent duty which God enjoins in the first precept of his law, and which he has laid as the very spring and foundation of obedience to all the other precepts, namely, to receive him, and to acknowledge him as our own God in Christ, and him alone ; and to rest in him, and upon him, as our upmaking and everlasting all. Hence, John vi. 28, 29. when the Jews were fond to know what they should do to work the work of God, he directs them to faith in himself ; because this was the first thing that the law required as it stood under a covenant of grace : " This is the work of God," (his work in a way of eminence ; the very first and fundamental work, and the spring and soul of all obedience,) " that ye believe on him whom he hath sent." For this reason, true obedience to the law is called " the obedience of faith :" and we are told, Heb. xi. 6, that " without faith it is impossible to please God ;" and, " Whatsoever is not of faith, is sin," Rom. xiv. 23 ; because, until this first command of the law be obeyed, till we receive, embrace, and acknowledge the Lord as our God in Christ, we do nothing at all in obedience to God's law, but break it every moment of our life. Again, as I said, we see here also the warrantableness of believing in Christ, and of embracing the promise, It is as warrantable for a lost sinner to embrace the promise, and to receive Christ by virtue of the promise, as to do any other thing that the law requires. Will any man doubt his warrant to honour and reverence the name of God, to honour his father and mother, to sanctify the Sabbath ? &c. As little reason has he to doubt his warrant by faith to lay claim to this glorious grant of sovereign grace through Christ, " I am the

Lord thy God :" seeing this is the very thing that is
required in this command, " Thou shalt have no other
gods before me." And as this command is a noble warrant for believing, so it is a warrant of universal extent : none who own the obligation of the moral law,
can shift the obligation of its very first command.
This view of matters, if taken up in the light of
the Spirit, serves to overthrow one of the principal
strong-holds of unbelief ; and at the same time discovers a ground of believing with boldness, without any
manner of presumption. The unbelieving deceitful
heart turns us away from the living God, by telling
us, that we are not warranted to believe in Christ,
and that it is arrogancy and presumption for us to intermeddle with the promise. But so far is this surmise
from being truth, that unless you believe in Christ, or,
which is all one, except you acknowledge a God in
Christ as your God, you make God a liar, who says,
" I am the Lord thy God ;" and rebel against his authority interposed in his first commandment, " Thou
shalt have no other gods before me."

2. See hence a solid ground for the assurance of
faith. Why, it has the noblest ground in the world
to go upon, namely, the infallible word of a God of
truth, saying, " I am the Lord thy God ;" and the best
warrant in the world, namely, the first commandment
of the law, requiring us to know and acknowledge
him as our God. The first command requires a persuasion of the promise, with application or appropriation of it to the soul in particular : and what is that
but the assurance of faith ? And no doubt the law requires every duty, and particularly this in its perfection ; the consideration of which may make every
one of us, yea, even the best believer upon earth, to
cry out with the poor man in the gospel, " Lord, I believe, help thou mine unbelief:" and, with the disciples,
" Lord, increase our faith."

3. See hence the proper bottom of true Christian
morality, and an excellent test whereby to distinguish

betwixt gospel and legal preaching. You see here, upon what foundation God himself inculcates the duties of the moral law: he first discovers himself as a reconciled God, a promising God in Christ, saying, " I am the Lord thy God :" and, upon this ground, urges the duties of the law. Now, the order of doctrine observed by God himself, ought certainly to be observed by us in our inculcating any duty of the law upon our hearers ; and if this method be not observed, it is certainly legal. Neither do I think that it is enough, when we are pressing any duty of the law, to come in with a direction or advice at the end, telling that all is to be done in the strength of Christ ; we see here that God begins his sermon of morality to Israel, from mount Sinai, with a revelation of himself as the Lord God gracious and merciful through Christ, " I am the Lord thy God ;" and lays this as the foundation of obedience to the following precepts. And I do think, that we who are ministers, when we inculcate the duties of the law upon people, we ought always to keep the grace of the new covenant in their eye ; for unless obedience to the law be influenced with this view, it cannot be the obedience of faith, and consequently cannot be acceptable : " Without faith it is impossible to please God." It is observable, that God, in the promulgation of the law to Israel, frequently intermixes the grace of the new covenant with the precepts of the law, and every now and then casts it up in their view, that he was the Lord their God in Christ. So in the second command, " Thou shalt not make unto thee any graven image, &c. : for I the Lord thy God am a jealous God, &c. showing mercy unto thousands of them that love me and keep my commandments." So in the third commandment, " Thou shalt not take the name of the Lord thy God in vain," &c. So in the fourth, " The seventh day is the Sabbath of the Lord thy God," &c. So likewise in the fifth, " Honour thy father and thy mother : that thy days may be long upon the land which the Lord thy God giveth thee." Thus, I say, he makes gospel-grace, like a thread of gold, to run through the duties of the law, whereby the whole law is sweetened and beautified, his yoke made easy, and his burden light.

Upon the other hand, there is an error, I fear too common among some. Whenever they hear a minister pressing duty, immediately they conclude him to be a legal preacher, without ever considering upon what ground he doth it; for if he press the duties of the law upon the ground of covenanted grace, he acts according to his commission, and keeps the order and method that God has laid; but if this method be not followed, if the duties of the law be urged as the foundation of our claim to the privileges of the gospel, or without keeping Christ and the grace of the gospel in the eye of the sinner, as the foundation of duty, you may indeed conclude, that it is legal. Although what the man says may be truth, abstractly considered, yet the truth is not delivered in its due order and connection; and therefore has a tendency to mislead the hearer, at least to lead him into perplexing exercises.

4. See hence the truth of what the apostle asserts concerning God, 1 John iv. 16, "God is love." Why, the promise here is a promise of love. What more can infinite love say than what is here said, " I am the Lord thy God?" What can he give more than himself? And as the promise is a promise of love, so the precept is a precept of love, "Thou shalt have no other gods before me." He first makes a free grant and gift of himself to us in his covenant, and then concludes us under a law of love, whereby he makes it the first and fundamental duty of obedience to him, that we shall know and acknowledge him as our own God; or in other words, that we should be happy for ever in the enjoyment of him. The most consummate happiness of the rational creature lies in what God here commands, viz. in having him, and none other, as our God. O how excellent is his loving kindness! surely

" God is love," it is the regnant perfection of his nature.   And O how reasonable is it that we should love
the Lord our God with all the heart, soul, strength,
and mind !   And O how unreasonable is the enmity
of the heart against God ! Do we thus requite a God
of love ?   Well may the Lord say to us, as he did to
Israel, " O my people, what have I done unto thee,
and wherein have I wearied thee ? testify against me."
    5. See hence what it is that makes the yoke of obe-
dience easy, and the burden thereof light to a believer.   Whence is it that the believer delights in the
law after the inward man ? why doth he rejoice to
work righteousness ?   Why, he remembers God in his
ways : he remembers that the Lawgiver is none other
than " the Lord his God and Redeemer :" and therefore he keeps all his commandments with pleasure :
therefore he " runs, and doth not weary : walks, and
doth not faint."   He views God, not as an enemy,
not as an avenging Judge, but as his own God in
Christ: he views him in Immanuel, as a God with him,
not a God against him : and this is like oil to his chariot wheels, which makes him run without wearying.
On the other hand, we may see here, what it is that
makes the duties of the law an insupportable yoke and
burden to hypocrites and Christless professors, who tire
in the duties of obedience before they be well set out :
why, they do not begin their obedience where God
begins his law, or they do not set their obedience upon the same foundation of gospel-grace that God has
set his law upon : they do not begin with acting faith
on the covenant, or with receiving a God in Christ
as their God by virtue of the covenant grant and promise : and if folk do not begin here where God begins, their blossoms cannot miss to wither and come
to nought.
    6. See hence the errors of those who imagine, that
it was a covenant of works which God entered into
with Israel at mount Sinai.   Indeed, if the promise
had followed after the commandments of the law ;

and if God had said, Keep these commandments, and, upon your so doing, I will be the Lord your God ; in this case it had been a pure covenant of works, whether perfect or sincere obedience had been the condition, it is all one ; still the reward would have been in a way of pactional debt, as in the first covenant. But, as you heard, the order of the covenant of works, or the connection betwixt the precept and promise, as it was laid in that covenant, is now inverted : for now God first promises, in a way of sovereign grace, to be the Lord our God and Redeemer, which is the substance and sum of the new covenant ; and having made such a grant of grace, to be received by faith, without, or before any works of obedience can be performed by us, he immediately subjoins the law of nature in ten words, showing us " what is good, and what the Lord our God requires of us," not as a condition of his own gracious grant, but as a testimony of our love and gratitude to him, who promises, of his free and sovereign grace, to be the Lord our God. So that, I say, it was God's covenant of grace that was promulgate at mount Sinai, and the law was added to it because of transgression, and graffed upon it as a rule of obedience. And whatever covenants or engagements to duty we read of, whether national or personal, still they went upon the foundation of grace laid in God's covenant of grace ; and in so far as Israel, or any else, go off from this foundation in their engagements to duty, in so far they pervert the design of the promise and law annexed to it, and turn back to a covenant of works.

Strong consolation to believers flowing from the promise, " I am the Lord thy God."

THAT you may see what strong consolation is here, I pray you consider, that this promise, " I am the Lord thy God," it draws all the blessings of heaven and eternity with it. There is not one promise from the beginning of Genesis to the end of the Revelation, which

thou mayest not confidently claim as thine own, if thou
nast obeyed the command of God, in laying hold of
God as thy God, thy only God, by virtue of this glorious grant of sovereign grace, " I am the Lord thy
God."

It is impossible that I can tell you the ten thousandth part of that grace and glory that lies in the
womb of this promise, " I am the Lord thy God ;"
an infinite God, who is an infinite good, is in it : " Who
can by searching find out God? who can find out the
Almighty unto perfection?"   New scenes of his infinite glory will be opening to saints and angels through
eternity in heaven.   O then, how immense is the
treasure that is here secured to thee, Oh believer, in
these two or three words, " I am the Lord thy God !"
Well mayest thou sing, " The lines are fallen unto me
in pleasant places."   He that gave himself unto the
death for thy redemption in the person of the Son, and
gives himself as JEHOVAH, Father, Son, and Holy Ghost,
by covenant gift and grant ; how will he not with this
freely give thee all things ?   Canst thou doubt of his
liberality as to other things, when he does not withhold his infinitely glorious self?   Canst thou doubt of
his fulfilling any other promise of the covenant, when
thou hast set to the seal of faith to this, with application of it to thy soul, " I am the Lord thy God."

I might here, for the believer's consolation, and the
encouragement of his faith, show how this covenant-
promise draws all the rest of the promises in its train,
they being inseparably connected therewith.   To instance only in a few, instead of many, " I am the Lord
thy God :" therefore " I will give thee an heart to
know me."   " I am the Lord thy God :" therefore " I
will sprinkle thee with clean water, and thou shalt be
clean : from all thy filthiness, and from all thine idols
will I cleanse thee."   " I am the Lord thy God ;"
therefore " I will be merciful to thy unrighteousness,
and thy sins and iniquities will I remember no more."
" I am the Lord thy God ;" therefore " I will put my

Spirit within thee, and cause thee to walk in my statutes, and thou shalt keep my judgments, and do them."
And so of all the other promises of the covenant; they
are all " yea and amen in him," who is " the Lord thy
God." He who is so kind and good, as to make over
himself to thee as thy God, will infallibly make out and
make good every promise ; and thou mayest trust him
with assured confidence, that he will do it, because he hath
said, " I am the Lord thy God." O let not the frequent
repetition of these words make them unsavoury: for there
is more than ten thousand millions of heavens of glory
in them to the soul that views them with the eye of
faith in the light of the Spirit.

I might further add, for the believer's comfort, that
this promise, " I am the Lord thy God," draws along
with it the sweetest and most endearing offices and relations that can be imagined. To instance in a few.

1. He who is thy God, is thy sun to enlighten, direct,
warm, and fructify thy soul with his benign and gracious influences, Psal. lxxxiv. 11. The day-spring from
on high hath begun to visit thee, the day-star hath
arisen in thy heart ; and though clouds may overcast
thy sky, yet the Sun of righteousness will break through
them, and return with the refreshing visits of everlasting kindness : for " his goings forth are prepared," or
secured, " as the morning." " Unto you that fear my
name, shall the Sun of righteousness arise with healing in his wings ; and ye shall go forth and grow up
as calves of the stall," Mal. iv. 2.

2. The Lord thy God is a shield to protect and defend thee against all the attacks of thy temporal or spiritual enemies. When sin, Satan, and the world, come
in like a flood, the Spirit of the Lord shall lift up a
standard against them. He is " the strength of the
poor, the strength of the needy in their distress, a refuge
from the storm, a shadow from the heat, when the
blast of the terrible ones is as a storm against the wall."
Thy God is "the shield of thy help, and the sword of thy
excellency ; he rides in the heaven for thy help, and
in his excellency on the skies."

3. Thy God is thy reward : " Fear not," says the Lord to Abraham, " I am thy shield and thy exceeding great reward," Gen. xv. 1. He is not only thy rewarder, but he himself is thy reward. And thy God being thy reward, it must be exceeding great, great beyond all expression or imagination ; it is exceeding great beyond what eye ever saw, or ear heard, or hath entered into the heart of man to conceive. Sure such a reward cannot be of debt, but of grace only. It is the reward, not of our service or obedience, but the reward of the obedience and death of our glorious Surety. He is the righteous new Heir, and we are " heirs of God, and joint heirs with Jesus Christ."

4. Thy God, believer, is thy friend. There is a covenant of friendship implied in my text, " I am the Lord thy God." It is said of Abraham that he was " the friend of God ;" and the friendship is mutual. Whatever kind offices ever one friend performed to another, these doth thy God perform unto thee. Thy God as a friend sympathises with thee in all thy afflictions, Is. lxiii. 9 ; supplies thy needs, Phil. iv. 19 ; imparts his secrets to thee, the secrets of his covenant, and mysteries of his kingdom, which he hides from the rest of the world, Matth. xiii. 11 ; promises to bear thee company through fire and water, life and death, Is. xliii. 2. As a friend, he will pay you kindly visits, and meet you more than half way when you come to visit him : " Thou meetest him that rejoiceth, and worketh righteousness, those that remember thee in thy ways."

5. Thy God, believer, is thy Father : 2 Cor. vi. 16, 17. " I will be their God, and they shall be my people." And, ver. 18, it is added, " I will be a father unto you, and ye shall be my sons and daughters, saith the Lord Almighty. Behold, what manner of love is this, that we should be called the sons of God !" Let men and angels wonder at it, that we who are sprung of hell, should be dignified with a name among the general assembly and church of the first-born. Thy

God is thy Father ; and, as a tender-hearted father,
his eye is upon thee for good, his ear is open unto thy
cry, his heart follows thee wherever thou goest, his
hand is ready to help thee and hold thee up, his Spirit,
in and by the word, to counsel and comfort thee, his
house of many mansions prepared and ready to receive
thee, whenever thou art dislodged from the earthly
house of this tabernacle.

6. Thy God is thy husband : Is. liv. 5. " Thy Maker
is thine husband, the Lord of hosts is his name ; and
thy Redeemer the holy One of Israel." Thy name
before him is Hephzibah and Beulah ; he rejoices over
thee, as the bridegroom rejoiceth over his bride. There
is a complication of interests betwixt him and thee ;
and thy concerns are so much his, that whatever action
the law has against thee, he is bound by virtue of his
relation to thee as a husband, to cover and defend
thee against all deadly.

7. Thy God, believer, is thy very life, yea, the
strength of thy life ; Psal. xxvii. 1. " The Lord is the
strength of my life, of whom shall I be afraid ?" Thy
God lives ; and " because he lives, thou shalt live also.
The Lord liveth, and blessed be my rock : and let the
God of my salvation be exalted." Thus you see by
these little hints, what this promise, " I am the Lord
thy God," draws after it for the consolation of the believer, who has by faith laid hold of it, and so obeyed
the first command. O Sirs, faith's views of the grace
wrapped up in this promise, would make us all to join
issue with David, Psal. xxxi. 19. " O how great is thy
goodness, which thou hast laid up for them that fear
thee ; which thou hast wrought for them that trust in
thee, before the sons of men.

*Exhortations and Directions to Sinners in general concerning Obedi-
ence to the First Commandment of the Moral Law.*

LET all in general be exhorted to obey and keep the
first commandment, by taking hold of this covenant-
grant," I am the Lord thy God;"which is all one, as if

I should exhort you to believe in Christ, or receive
and rest upon him alone, &c. When a sinner believes in Christ, what does he else but receive God
in Christ, as his God, by virtue of the covenant of
grace, placing his only rest and happiness through
eternity in the enjoyment of him alone? And is not
this the very thing required in the first commandment,
or a having no other gods before him? The gospel,
holding forth the object of faith, and the command
requiring the obedience of faith, has been one and
the same in all ages of the world, however differ-
ently expressed and dispensed. We generally look upon the law of God, delivered to Israel at mount Sinai,
as binding and obligatory upon us ; and no doubt it is
the rule of obedience to all mankind unto the end of
the world, who shall read or hear of it. And I am so
far from thinking, or teaching, that the obligation of
the holy law is dissolved by the grace of the gospel,
that I think it plain, from the connection Infinite Wisdom has laid betwixt them here, it is simply impossible
any man can share of the grace of the gospel, but in
a way of obedience to the very first commandment of
the law, as already explained. And therefore my exhortation to every one hearing me is, to yield obedience to this first commandment of the law ; lay claim
by faith unto a God in Christ as your God, by virtue
of the covenant, where he says, " I am the Lord thy
God ;" and see that you " have no other gods before
him." Do not think that I exhort you to this, as
though I supposed you had any strength or power of
your own to obey; no, we are naturally without strength,
wholly impotent to do any thing spiritually good : but
when I exhort you to obey this commandment, I exhort
you to obey it in a dependence upon the grace of him
who commands you to have him as your own God,
and who engages himself by covenant to be our God,
and so to be the author and finisher of our faith.

Now, to quicken your compliance, to excite your
obedience, consider these few particulars, which I shall
not much enlarge upon.

1. Consider, that, by the breach of the first covenant, you and I have forfeited all claim and title to the Lord as our God. Indeed he never ceased to be our sovereign Lord-Creator; in no state can this relation to God be dissolved; this relation stands even in the state of the damned. But, I say, by the violation of the holy law, we have lost our covenant-relation to God, as our God, our Father, our friend, our portion; and having lost our God, we have lost our life, peace, comfort, and happiness for ever; and not only so, but are under his wrath and curse, and so are liable to all miseries in soul and body through time and eternity. Now, by hearkening unto this exhortation, all this unspeakable loss is repaired. Here you have God coming in a new and better covenant, even in a covenant of grace, saying, "I am the Lord thy God;" yea, requiring thee, by his sovereign authority, to take him again as thy own God, and thy only God, upon the footing of this new grant of grace. O what sinner is it, that considers his own eternal interest, but will comply with this command, in knowing and acknowledging the Lord as his God! Who would not take back the forfeiture upon such an easy ground!

2. Consider who it is that says, "I am the Lord thy God:" who it is that issues out this command, "Thou shalt have no other gods before me." It is he "whose name alone is JEHOVAH, the most high over all the earth;" he who doth whatever pleases him in the armies of heaven, and among the inhabitants of the earth; he who humbles himself when he beholds things in heaven, cherubims and seraphims, angels and archangels. O what astonishing grace and condescension is it in this God, to come to a sinful worm of the fallen family of Adam, saying, "I am the Lord thy God!" O shall we not fall in with the design of such condescending grace, and say, We will have no other gods before him! "This God is our God for ever and ever!" If we do not, we reject the counsel of God against ourselves, and despise the riches of his grace.

3. Consider, that this is the very first duty of natural and revealed religion, to know and acknowledge God as the only true God, and our God. The light of nature teaches us to own him as our creating God, upon the ground of that revelation he makes of himself to us in the works of creation and providence. Revealed religion teaches us to own him as our God in Christ, upon the ground of his own promise and grant, " I am the Lord thy God." So that, till this command be obeyed, a man is an atheist, an idolater, without God in the world, and is an utter stranger both to natural and revealed religion. Woe, woe, woe to the man or woman that is in such a case; thou art condemned already, and the wrath of God abideth on thee, because thou rejectest JEHOVAH in the person of the Son as thy God and Redeemer ; and upon the matter, sayest, I will have other gods before him, I will not have him as the Lord my God.

4. Consider, thou can perform no duty of the law acceptably until thou obey this command, and close with this covenant-grant, as was cleared already. All thy acts of obedience to the other commandments, they are but splendid sins, an abomination to God, till this covenant-grant be received, in obedience to the first precept of his law. The soul of all obedience is wanting, till a man begin here ; hence all his works are but dead works.

5. Consider, how willing he is to be thy God, even thine ' own God,' O sinner. If he were not willing, would he ever speak in such a dialect to thee as here, saying, " I am the Lord thy God ?" Would he ever lay thee under such a command of love, as to say, " Thou shalt have no other gods before me ?" thou shalt know and acknowledge me as thy own God and portion, as thy only hope and happiness in time and through eternity ? O do not suspect his candour and ingenuity ; for " the Strength of Israel will not lie ;" he hates it in others, and therefore it is impossible he can be guilty of it himself. We would reckon that

man a blasphemer, who, with his mouth, should utter
such words as these, It is not as God says, he is not
the Lord my God : and yet this blasphemy every unbelieving sinner is guilty of: he makes God a liar, and
denies that God speaks the truth in his heart, when he
says to him, " I am the Lord thy God ;" and, at the
same time, rebels against his authority, requiring him
to make faith's application of this covenant-grant to his
own soul.

6. Consider, there is an absolute necessity that thou
lay hold on this covenant-grant in obedience to this
command. Why, there is no living, and no safe dying,
without God. Without God, thou art without hope
in the world : without God, thou, and all thou hast in
the world, are cursed ; cursed in thy basket and store,
in the house and field, in thy outgoings and incomings.
Without God you cannot die, without dying the second
death, as well as the first : " They that are far from
thee shall perish. What wilt thou do," O sinner, " in
the day of visitation," who livest in disobedience to
this command, and refusest the grace contained in this
covenant-grant? " to whom wilt thou flee for help ?
and where wilt thou leave thy glory ?" How will you
look God in the face, when arraigned before his awful
tribunal ? What a knell will it give to thy heart, when
thou hearest this, as the first and leading article of thy
indictment, There is the man who would not know
and acknowledge me as his God and Redeemer! me,
who stretched out my arms of grace to embrace him,
and whose bowels sent out a sound after him, saying,
" I am the Lord thy God : Thou shalt have no other
gods before me !" he preferred self and the world to
me, and therefore now " I will laugh at his calamity,
and mock when his fear is come" upon him. O
" consider this, ye that forget God, lest he tear you
in pieces, and there be none to deliver" out of his
hand.

7. Consider what advantage will redound to thy soul

by obeying this command with an eye to the covenant-promise. Thou art made up for ever ; all salvation, as you heard, is wrapped up in this one word, " I am the Lord thy God." And in the faith of it thou mayest go through the valley of the shadow of death, without fearing any evil ; for thy God is with thee, he will never leave thee, nor forsake thee.*

Objections of carnal reason to the promise, " I am the Lord thy God," stated and answered.

Object. 1. May one say, I have lost all claim and title to the Lord as my God, by violating the holy law ; and I think I hear God saying to me with a frown, " How shall I put thee among the children," who hast forfeited thy relation to me ? and therefore I dare not own and acknowledge him as the Lord my God. *Answ.* It is indeed true, that you and I, and all mankind, have lost our title and relation to him as our God by the first Adam, and the breach of the first covenant ; and since the fall of Adam, God never said to any sinner upon a law-ground, " I am the Lord thy God ;" no, when a sinner looks at that airth, his hope and strength perishes for ever from the Lord.   But, O Sirs,

* The ten commandments are founded on these words of the preface, " I am the Lord thy God, which have brought thee out of the land of Egypt, out of the house of bondage." The inestimable privilege here exhibited, is made the foundation of the duty required.—We may hence learn the great difference, between performing duties, in the way of the covenant of works and in that of the covenant of grace. According to the first covenant, sinners perform duties, in order that these may entitle them to life ; but according to the second, saints perform them because they already have a title to life : According to the former, unregenerate men do them in their own strength ; but according to the latter, regenerate persons perform them in the strength of grace derived from the second Adam. The motives to obedience under the covenant of works, are the slavish fear of hell, and the servile hope of heaven ; whereas the motives to duty, in the covenant of grace, are love and gratitude to God, not only as the Creator and Preserver, but as the God and Redeemer of his people.—*Colquhoun on Law and Gospel.*

here is a new covenant, a new gift or grant that God makes of himself, which does not go upon the ground of our obedience to the law as its condition, but upon the ground of sovereign grace, reigning through the righteousness of God-man : here, I say, is a new claim of right presented to the guilty sinner, " I am the Lord thy God ; I will be unto them a Father, and they shall be my sons and daughters, saith the Lord Almighty." These and the like absolute and indefinite promises are universally dispensed to all and every one as the ground of faith. And lest any sinner, through a sense of guilt, should scare to lay hold upon this new claim of right, here is the warrant subjoined and annexed to the claim, " Thou shalt have no other gods before me."

Object. 2. I am afraid lest God be not saying this to me in particular, " I am the Lord thy God ;" and therefore dare not lay hold of it. I fear lest he be not requiring me in particular, by this commandment, to know and acknowledge him as my God. *Answ.* It is by these and the like groundless surmises and insinuations, that an evil heart of unbelief turns us away from the living God, and from taking hold of his covenant. But pray, tell me, in good earnest, do you think to dispute away the binding obligation of the very first commandment of the law of God ? for, as was said, at the same time that you refuse to take hold of this covenant-grant, you disobey the first and leading precept of the law. Why, will you own the obligation of the other commandments of the law, and reject this ? I suppose there are none of you but will readily acknowledge, that you in particular are bound to honour your parents, not to kill, steal, commit adultery, &c. You may with as good reason say or think, that these other precepts do not bind you in particular, as imagine that you are not particularly bound by the first to know and acknowledge a God in Christ as your God. Why so much prejudiced against the first and chief commandment of God beyond all

others? What account can be rendered for it, that men
should thrust away from them the first commandment
of the very law of nature, when grafted into the gospel
covenant, and made so subservient to their eternal salvation? I know of no solid reason that can be given
for it, but that of the apostle, " The god of this world
hath blinded the minds of them which believe not."

Object. 3. I cannot refuse that the command, " Thou
shalt have no other gods before me," is binding upon
me in particular ; but I can never think that it is to
me in particular that God is saying " I am the Lord
thy God." *Answ.* Who authorized you, or any of
Adam's race, to put asunder what God has joined? I
am sure it is not by God's warrant that this is done ;
and therefore you may easily divine that it is from
something worse.   It is the great plot of Satan to
break that connection which God has laid betwixt
the gospel and the law ; for he knows very well
that if the gospel be separate from the law, or the
law from the gospel, in the matter of practice, not one
of the commandments of the law can be obeyed to
purpose.   And this first command in particular, if it
be disjoined from the gospel-promise laid in the preface, " I am the Lord thy God," it can no more be
obeyed by a sinner, than if he were commanded to
pull the sun or moon out of the firmament.   Pray
consider, while you own the obligation of the precept,
and meanwhile refuse your interest or concern with
the preface, you acknowledge your obligation to obedience, and yet at the same time cast away the foundation upon which your obedience is to stand ; thus you
build without a foundation, and how can that building
stand ?   It will fall, and great will be the fall of it.
And therefore, in the name of God, I proclaim that
this promise, " I am the Lord thy God," is to you, and
your seed, and to all that are afar off.   Did not God
speak to every individual in the camp, when he uttered
these words, "I am the Lord thy God;" as well as when
he added, " Thou shalt have no other gods before me?"

The same is he saying to you, and me, and every one of us ; and therefore let us not cast away our own mercy; to us, as well as unto them, " belong the adoption, and the covenants, and giving of the law, and the promises."

Obj. 4. What if all that is intended in these words, " I am the Lord thy God," be only either an assertion of divine sovereignty, or of an external federal relation to Israel as the seed and posterity of Abraham, and the only visible church ? And if so, where is there a foundation in them for me to believe in him as the Lord my God ? *Answ.* I am far from excluding any of these things the objection mentions as comprehended in these words, " I am the Lord thy God :" and I grant that if no more were included in them, I do not see, how they could be a foundation of special and saving faith to me, or any else. But that it is otherwise, will not readily be denied by any, if they consider what it is God requires of us in the first command, as inseparably connected with the preface. Pray consider it a little. Is this all that God calls for by the first precept of his law, to know and acknowledge him as our sovereign Lord-Creator, or that he is a God to the visible church by external federal relation ? No doubt, these are truths indispensably to be believed: but there is more required, namely, to believe that he is the Lord our God in Christ, and to worship and glorify him accordingly. The external federal relation that God bears to the visible church, becomes special when this promise is applied by a saving faith ; hence this is the common argument wherewith Israel is urged to believe and repent through all the Old Testament; particularly, Psal. lxxxi. 9—11. And whenever saving faith was acted, whereby their turn unto him was influenced, they commonly fasten upon, and apply this fundamental promise in my text, Jer. iii. 22. So that, I say, there is more in these words, " I am the Lord thy God," than a bare assertion of divine sovereignty, or of his covenant-relation to Israel as a visible church;

there is in them a glorious new-covenant grant or gift that God makes of himself to us in Christ as our God, to be applied by a saving faith : and when such a faith is acted upon it, the native echo of the soul unto it is, " This God is my God ;" I believe it, because he himself hath said it, and said it not to others only, but to me in particular ; " I will say, It is my people ; and they shall say, The Lord is my God." It is true indeed, no man can speak this dialect of faith without the Holy Spirit ; but to say that there is not sufficient ground for a particular applicatory faith in the bare word or promise of God, abstractly considered, is to apologise for the unbelief of the hearers of the gospel, and to run into the error of the enthusiasts, who suspend the duty of believing, not upon the word of God, but upon the work and light of the Spirit within.

Object. 5. If this promise be made to every one in the visible church, how shall the veracity of the Promiser be salved, or vindicated, seeing there are many who come short of it, many to whom he never becomes their God in a special covenant-relation.

Unto this objection I might answer, by way of retortion, How is it that the unbeliever makes God a liar, if the promise be not made to him in particular ? for if the promise, and the faithfulness of the Promiser, be not to him, he cannot be blamed for not believing, or not setting to his seal to a promise never made to him. Can he be condemned for not intermeddling with a thing that does not belong to him ? Again, I ask, How was it that God, in a consistency with his faithfulness, made unbelieving Israel to know his breach of promise, Num. xiv. 34. after he had made a grant or gift of the land of Canaan to them, and promised to bring them into it, while yet they never were allowed to enter it, but dropt their carcasses in the wilderness, God having sworn that they should not enter into his rest ? The faithfulness of God, in breaking his promise that he had made to that generation is salved by landing the blame upon their own unbelief; they believed not his word, they trusted not in his salvation, they gave more credit to the false lying report of the wicked spies, than to the word and promise of him for whom it is impossible to lie ; and because they made God a liar, therefore his promise made to them turned to be of no effect unto them.   In like manner, a promise is left us of entering into a spiritual and eternal rest ; but meantime most have reason to fear lest God make them to know his breach of promise, by excluding them out of that promised rest, because of their unbelief.   The faithfulness of God is not in the least impeached hereby, because the unbeliever calls his faithfulness in question, and rejects his promise, as a thing not worthy of regard.   Can a man be charged with unfaithfulness, in not bestowing himself and his estate upon a woman to whom he has made a promise of marriage, if the woman to whom it was made refuse his offer and promise ?   The faithfulness of the bankers of Scotland is engaged in particular to the bearer of their note; but if the bearer shall tear the note, or throw it away as a piece useless paper, their veracity is nowise impeached, though they never pay that man the sum contained in the note ; so here.

Object. 6. If I could find the marks and evidences of saving grace once wrought in my soul, then indeed I could acknowledge and believe the Lord is my God; but till then I dare not, neither do I think it my duty. *Answ.* I do own that none can warrantably draw this conclusion that they are in a state of grace, within the bond of the covenant, or savingly interested in the Lord as their God, till they have examined the matter at the bar of the word, and upon trial have found such marks of grace as warrant them to draw such a conclusion.   But this is not the question now under consideration.   The question at present is, Whether it be lawful and warrantable for a poor sinner, who is so far from finding any works of grace or gracious qualifications in himself, that he can see nothing but sin and misery, feels himself to be an heir of hell and wrath;

whether, I say, it be his duty, upon the footing of this covenant grant and promise, " I am the Lord thy God," to know, believe, and acknowledge the Lord as his God? And if this be the question, which it must be, it is all one as if it were asked, whether it be the immediate duty of such a person to obey the first command of the moral law as it stands under a covenant of grace? or, Whether a person is to forbear obedience to the first command in the law of God, till he find gracious qualifications wrought in his soul. To affirm which, were upon the matter to say, that the first commandment of the law does not enjoin the first duty of religion, but that something is to be done before we do the thing that God requires of us in the first place as the foundation of all other acts of obedience ; and that is, to know and believe that God in Christ is our God, by virtue of a covenant of grace contained in these words, " I am the Lord thy God." Such strange absurdities we inevitably run ourselves into, when we keep not in the cleanly path of faith chalked out to us in the word.

Object. 7. We fear that this way of teaching lead us in to a presumptuous confidence ; and therefore we are afraid to meddle with it. *Answ.* God teaches no man to presume when he requires him to have no other gods before him. Your approven Catechism does not teach you to presume, when it tells you, that God in this commandment requires you to know and acknowledge him as God, and as your God ; and that because he is the Lord, and our God, therefore we are bound to keep all his commandments. But besides, the man who in a presumptuous way lays claim to the Lord as his God, he either lays claim to him out of Christ, or he does it not upon the footing of the faithfulness of God engaged in the covenant ; or else, while he says with his mouth that the Lord is his God, he hath other gods before him : in which case, God says to the man, " What hast thou to do to make mention of my covenant ? seeing thou" hast other gods before me in thy heart, and thus thou " hatest instruction, and castest my counsel behind thy back."

Object. 8. God is angry, he carries toward me as an enemy, he smites by the word and rod : how then shall I adventure to say he is the Lord my God ? *Answ.* It is true God was angry ; but his anger or vindictive wrath having spent itself upon our glorious Surety, we may now say, with the church, Is. xii. 1. " His anger is turned away, and he comforteth us. Behold God is my salvation : I will trust, and not be afraid." Having smelt a sweet savour in the sacrifice of the death of Christ, the deluge of wrath is recalled, and a proclamation issued out, " Fury is not in me : I am the Lord thy God : Thou shalt have no other gods before me." O Sirs, this is not the language of anger and wrath, but the language of love, mercy, and of infinite bowels of pity and good-will toward man upon earth. As for the appearance of anger in his dispensations, no man can know either love or hatred, by all that is before him : the only way to judge of the love of his heart, is to read it in and by his words of grace ; for these, and not his external dispensations, are the exact portraiture of his deep and infinite heart. It is true indeed, we are told that " God is angry with the wicked every day :" but what is his grand and fundamental quarrel with them ? It is this, that though he has said, " I am the Lord thy God and Redeemer ;" though he has given such a glorious proof of this as to give his only begotten Son, and to give him up to the death for our redemption ; though he has engaged his faithfulness to us in a new covenant ; yet they will not know and acknowledge the Lord as God, and as their God, but will have some other gods before him. To conclude, the design of all the threatenings of the word, and of all the angry-like dispensations of his providence, is, that we may flee from his wrath, and may not rush upon the thick bosses of his buckler, but may turn to him as our God in Christ, and live, Ezek. xxxiii. 11.

Object. 9. What if it was only to the elect or believers in the camp of Israel that God spake, when he said, " I am the Lord thy God ?" If so, they cannot be a foundation of faith to all. *Answ.* This objection still breaks the connection God has made betwixt the promise and the precept, which must not be. I believe no man will adventure to say, that the command, " Thou shalt have no other gods before me," was only to the elect or believers; but to the elect and reprobate, believers and unbelievers. The whole law was given to every man, no man exemed: now, did God tie them all to obedience by his command, and yet at the same time take away the foundation of obedience, which lies in the promise? No, the one must run parallel with the other ; the promise in its exhibition must be as extensive as the obligation of the command ; the object of faith must be presented to all whose duty it is to believe ; the promise is among things revealed as well as the precept, and therefore do equally belong unto us. " What God has joined let no man separate." It is true, these words, "I am the Lord thy God," considered as in his mind, purpose, and decree, belonged only to the elect; but considered as uttered or spoken indefinitely, they cease to be a decree with respect unto us; we are to look upon them as a promise tendered to us as the ground of our faith ; and so they have a respect to every one commanded to have him as his own God.

The Divinity and Gracious Work of the Holy Spirit.

1. THE Spirit of the Lord, as to his essence, is the same God with the Father and the Son. There is but one God, and three persons in the Godhead, the Father, Son, and Holy Ghost; and these three are one God, the same in substance, equal in power and glory. We are not to imagine any superiority or inferiority among the persons of the Godhead, seeing they are one and the same most simple and undivided being.

2. As to the order of his existence, according to

the revelation of the word, he is the third person of the adorable Trinity, and proceeds from the Father and the Son, in an ineffable and inconceivable manner. All that we have revealed concerning the manner of the existence of these three divine persons of the Godhead, is, that the Father begat the Son, the Son is begotten of the Father, and the Holy Ghost proceedeth from the Father and the Son : but as to the generation of the Son, or the procession of the Holy Ghost, who can declare it ? God has drawn a vail over it, and it is dangerous for us, in this state of mortality, curiously to pry into this mystery ; and they who have adventured to go further than the revelation of the word leads them, have always run themselves into the bogs of Arian, Sabellian, or Socinian errors.

3. As to his office in the great work of salvation, he applies to us the redemption purchased by Christ ; in order to which he receives the things of Christ, that he may show them to us. All the blessings of a Redeemer's purchase, all the goods of his testament, both heritable and moveable, the whole estate of eternal life, and every thing that pertains to it, are lodged in his hand, that he may, according to his commission from the Father and Son, apply them, and make them effectual to the heirs of promise. And according to the various parts of his work, in applying the purchased salvation, he gets several names in scripture ; as,

1st, He is sometimes called a *reprover:* John xvi. 8. " When he is come, he will reprove the world of sin." And his reproofs are so sharp and piercing, that they are compared to keen arrows, and a sharp two-edged sword, piercing to the dividing asunder of soul and spirit.

2dly, He is sometimes called a *comforter :* " I will send the Comforter, and he shall teach you all things." He is so called, because he comforts them that mourn in Zion ; he gives the oil of joy for mourning, and the garments of praise for a heavy spirit." His consolations are so strong that they make the lips of them that are asleep to sing.

3dly, He is sometimes called an *advocate ;* the word rendered a *comforter*, signifies also an *advocate*. He pleads the cause of Christ in the world, against all that dare to speak against him ; he pleads his cause in the hearts of his people, against all the false surmises that Satan and an unbelieving heart are ready to suggest to his prejudice : and he acts the part of an advocate, by enabling us to plead and pray with groans which cannot be uttered.

4thly, He is sometimes called a *witness* : John xv. 26. " He shall testify of me." The Spirit bears witness of Christ, partly by external revelation, partly by internal manifestation ; hence called "the Spirit of wisdom and revelation in the knowledge of Christ." He bears witness of the sonship of believers; he " bears witness with our spirits, that we are the children of God :" he is in them a spirit of adoption, enabling them to cry, " Abba, Father."

5thly, He is sometimes called a *remembrancer* : John xiv. 26. " He shall bring to your remembrance whatsoever I have spoken unto you." Our memories are like leaking vessels, let all the good words of Christ slip from us ; but the Spirit will not let them slip : no, he keeps them for our use, and brings to remembrance with a fresh relish and savour in time of need : and in that case the believer finds such a sweetness in the word, that he cannot but say with Jeremiah, " Thy words were found by me, and I did eat them, and they were unto me the joy and rejoicing of mine heart."

6thly, He is sometimes called a *teacher* : " He shall teach you all things," John xiv. 26. He teaches so, as no man ever taught ; he is an interpreter among a thousand ; all the commentaries in the world are not able to give such a view of a word of scripture, as the Spirit of the Lord will do, when he opens it up in his own light ; he makes the heart of the rash to understand wisdom.

7thly, He is sometimes called a *guide :* " When the

Spirit of truth is come, he shall guide you into all truth." He saves the members of Christ from such damnable errors, as strike at the foundation of religion and Christianity ; none of his teaching shall be given up to strong delusions, to believe lies.

4. The Spirit of the Lord, as to his qualities or properties, we are told in scripture, is,

1*st*, A *renewing Spirit :* hence we read of " the washing of regeneration, and the renewing of the Holy Ghost." All the powers of the soul, and the image of God in them, are dislocate and defaced, the whole foundations are out of course ; but the spirit of the Lord, in a work of regeneration, repairs the image of God, and sets every thing again in its proper place and order.

2*dly*, He is a *sanctifying Spirit*, wherefore called " the Spirit of holiness." He draws lineaments of the divine holiness upon us, and enables us more and more to die unto sin, and to live unto righteousness ; he takes the beauty of Christ and puts it upon us, whereby we are made comely.

3*dly*, He is a *Spirit of glory :* " The Spirit of glory and of God resteth upon you," says the apostle Peter. He makes the King's daughter all glorious within, and so fits the soul for being brought to glory, " makes us meet to be partakers of the inheritance of the saints in light."

4*thly*, He is a *Spirit of power ;* he gives power to the faint, makes the feeble as David. When the Spirit of the Lord was with Samson, he slew the Philistines heaps upon heaps ; but when the Lord departed, the locks wherein his strength lay were cut.

5*thly*, He is a *Spirit of love.* Wherever he comes, he makes the heart to burn with love to God in Christ, so as the soul cannot but say, with David, " Whom have I in heaven but thee ?" The man loves his ordinances, and the place where his honour dwells : he loves his people, and all that bear his image : " My delight is with the saints, the excellent ones of the earth."

6*thly*, He is a *Spirit of a sound mind*, for he gives a sound judgment and understanding of the things of God ; hence it is, that one of the Lord's babes or little ones will have a more clear and sound uptaking of the things of God, than all the learned rabbies and plodding politicians in the world, that excel in human wisdom and literature.

I shall only add, 5. That the actings and operations of the Spirit of the Lord are set forth to us in scripture under different metaphors ; as,

1*st*, He is sometimes resembled to *fire*, therefore called a *Spirit of burning*, Is. iv. 4. He consumes and burns up the dross of sin and corruption. As the sparks of fire fly upward, so he makes the soul to seek those things that are above.

2*dly*, He is sometimes resembled to *water :* Isa. xliv. 3. " I will pour water upon him that is thirsty, and floods upon the dry ground." By his influences, the soul is so fructified, that it becomes as a tree planted by the rivers of waters, bringing forth fruit in season ; " I will be as the dew unto Israel, and he shall grow as the lily."

3*dly*, He is sometimes resembled to *wind :* Cant. iv. 16. "Awake, O north wind, and come, thou south, blow upon my garden." John iii. 8. " The wind bloweth where it listeth, and thou hearest the sound thereof, but canst not tell whence it cometh, and whither it goeth." When this wind filleth the sails of the affections, with what speed and liveliness does the believer move in his voyage to the haven of glory, his everlasting rest !

4*thly*, He is sometimes resembled in his operations to *oil :* " We have an unction from the holy One, and we know all things." We read of the anointing of the Spirit ; " God, thy God, hath anointed thee with the oil of gladness above thy fellows." And by this oil the countenance of the believer is made to shine, the joints of his soul are suppled, so that he runs and does not weary, walks and does not faint.

Evidences of Christ Manifested to the Soul by the Holy Spirit.

1. If ever the Spirit of the Lord lifted up the standard effectually over you, he has laid siege to thy heart,
and the strongholds of iniquity have been battered
and shaken by the thundering ordinance of the law.
Ordinarily before the Spirit of the Lord lift up the
standard of peace, he displays the standard of war in
and against the soul, whereby it is roused and awakened out of the lethargy of carnal peace and security ;
the lying refuges, in which the man was trusting, are
shaken and overturned.   By nature the strong man of
sin keeps the house ; for Satan, the god of this world,
" while he keeps the house, the goods are at ease,"
and the man is carried away with the flood in a pleasant dream, crying, " Peace, peace, while sudden
destruction is at the door."   But, I say, ordinarily
the Spirit of the Lord comes as a Spirit of bondage
unto fear ; taking some of the thunderbolts from
mount Sinai, he darts them in upon the heart, whereby the sinner's carnal peace is broken and disturbed,
the high imaginations of a righteousness by the law,
and of peace with God upon that footing, are cast to the
ground. This we see exemplified in the apostle Paul,
he " was alive without the law ; but when the commandment came," when the law was set home in its
spirituality, " sin revived, (says he,) and I died ;" q. d.
All my vain confidences of righteousness by the law
fell down ; I found myself stripped of my fig-leaf cov-
erings.   Try by this, Has the Spirit of the Lord shut
you up to the faith ; straitened you so with law-terrors,
that you saw no relief in heaven nor in earth, but by fleeing into Christ, who is the last refuge that ever a guilty
sinner will run to ?

2. If ever the Spirit of the Lord effectually lifted
up the standard, so as to drive back the enemy, the
everlasting doors have opened at his summons, and
there has been a surrender of the heart and soul to
the Lord.   Have you been made to lie down at

the foot of adorable sovereignty, like a poor sup-
plicant, crying with Paul, " Lord, what wilt thou
have me to do?" or with the jailor, " What shall I do to
be saved?" Lord, will the soul say, I put a blank in
thy hand, I am content to fall in with any method of
salvation that thou wilt prescribe. I have hitherto
been building castles in the air, expecting salvation
in a way of my own devising; but I find the bed too
short for me to stretch myself upon, the covering too
narrow to wrap my naked soul in. I see myself upon
the point of everlasting ruin, and of falling an eternal
sacrifice to avenging justice. O show me a city of
refuge. O lead me to the place where thou causest
thy flock to rest. O how shall I have peace with
God? for I see it is hard for me to kick against
the pricks. There is no prospering, by hardening
myself against him ; and therefore I yield to his summons, and surrender myself wholly unto him, to be
saved in the way that he thinks fit.

3. If the Spirit of the Lord has lifted up the standard effectually in thy heart, thy soul has been filled
with a silent wondering at the first sight of the sinner,
I mean, at the first view of the glory and excellency of
Christ; so that you could not but own with the spouse,
that he *is* indeed " white and ruddy, the chiefest among
ten thouand ;" or, as in the margin, " the standard-
bearer among ten thousand," Cant. v. 10. The name of
Christ, Is. ix. 6, would readily ring like sweet melody
in thy heart and soul, " Unto us a child is born, unto
us a son is given, and his name shall be called Wonderful." Usually at the first appearance of Christ to the
soul, after it has been wading through the clouds and
darkness of mount Sinai, there is something of an ecstasy
of admiration seizes the poor creature. He wonders
at the person of Christ, when he sees him to be Immanuel, God-man : " Without controversy, great is
the mystery of godliness, God manifested in the flesh."
He wonders at his love and loveliness; he wonders
at the beauty of holiness that shines in him ; he won-

ders at the everlasting righteousness he has brought in ;
he wonders at the victories that he has won, and at
the " redness of his apparel," Is. lxiii. 1, 2. In a word,
the soul wonders at the bright constellation of divine
and human excellencies that centre and meet in him.
If it be thus with thee, poor soul, it is an evidence,
that the Spirit of the Lord has lift up the standard in
thy heart.

4. If the Spirit of the Lord has lift up the standard
in and over thee, the iron sinew of thy will has been
bended in the day of the Mediator's power : Psal. cx. 3.
" Thy people shall be willing in the day of thy armies."
The language of our hearts by nature is, " We will
not have this man to reign over us. As for the word
of the Lord that thou hast spoken, we will not do it."
But O, whenever the Spirit of the Lord lifts up the
standard, there is such a sweet irresistible power comes
along with the discovery, that the heart, which was
like an adamant, is melted like wax in the midst of
the bowels ; it becomes pliable unto the promissory,
preceptive, and providential will of God. As for his
promissory will, when the Spirit of the Lord lifts up
the standard, the soul sweetly yields to that ; when
God says, " I will be their God, I will be to them a
Father, I will take away the heart of stone, I will put
my spirit within them," &c. the soul sweetly falls in
with every clause of the covenant, saying amen to
every part of it. As for his preceptive will, when the
Spirit of the Lord lifts up the standard, the soul falls
in with that also, according to the promise, Ezek. xxxvi.
27. " I will cause them to walk in my statutes, to
keep my judgments, and do them." Although the
man formerly did cast away God's bonds, saying with
proud Pharaoh, " Who is the Lord, that I should
obey him ?" yet now he is content to have the yoke
of Christ's law wreathed about his neck, and written
upon the tables of his heart. He has frequently that
prayer of David's in his mouth, " O that my ways
were directed to keep thy statutes ! Let my heart be

found in thy statutes, that I be not ashamed." As for his providential will, the heart yields to that also, saying, " Here am I, let him do to me as seemeth him good. The Lord giveth, and the Lord taketh away ; blessed be the name of the Lord." Under favourable providences he is ready to bless the Lord, saying, " What am I or my father's house, that I am brought hitherto ?" Under frowning dispensations he is ready to say, " I will bear the indignation of the Lord, be- cause I have sinned against him. I was dumb with silence, I opened not my mouth, because thou, Lord, didst it."

5. If the Spirit of the Lord has lifted up the stan- dard in and over thee effectually, thou hast been deter- mined to lift up the standard of war against all Christ's enemies : and the war between thee and them will be, like that between Amalek and Israel, irreconcileable ; the war will be turned to a rooted hatred of sin, and all the works thereof ; for there can be no agreement between God and Belial, between the works of the Spirit of the Lord, and the works of the prince of the power of the air : Psal. cxxxix. 21, 22. " Do not I hate them, O Lord, that hate thee ? And am not I griev- ed with those that rise up against thee ? I hate them with perfect hatred." And whenever Satan or the world would tempt thee to prove false to thy stan- dard, or to yield to their solicitations ; thou wilt be ready to start back, and say with Joseph, " How shall I do this great wickedness, and sin against God ? Depart from me, all ye evil doers ; for I will keep the commandments of my God."

6. For trial, I ask this question, Whether hast thou on the livery of the soldier who fights under the stand- ard which the Spirit of God lifts up? I remember it is said of Christ, the standard-bearer among ten thousand, that he is *white and ruddy.* The same may be said in some respects concerning all that war under his colours ; they are *ruddy,* in respect of justification ; *white,* in re- spect of sanctification. (1.) I say, they are *ruddy,* in

respect of justification, because Christ's vesture which was dipped in blood is upon them, " They have washed their garments in the blood of the Lamb." This was the best robe that was put upon the prodigal, when-ever he entered his father's threshold. So then I ask, Have you put on the red livery of imputed righteous-ness? has the blood of Christ cleansed you from all sin? The soldiers of Christ submit to the righteousness of Christ. Yea, this is one of the mottoes of the stand-ard which you have, Jer. xxiii. 6. " This is his name whereby he shall be called, the Lord our righteous-ness ;" and all the soldiers they get their name from this motto and livery. And whenever you fall under challenges for sin from the law, conscience, justice, or the world, you will find no ease or relief on this side the blood and righteousness of Christ ; no healing till the Sun of righteousness arise with it under his wings. (2.) Christ's soldiers, as they are ruddy in respect of justification, so they are *white* in respect of sanctifi-cation. I remember we are told, Rev. xix. 14. " that the armies which are in heaven follow the Lamb, rid-ing upon white horses, clothed in fine linen, white and clean." And in the day of his armies, his volun-teers are said to " shine with the beauty of holiness," Psal. cx. 3. Holiness to the Lord is the motto of the standard, and holiness to the Lord is the beautiful livery wherewith they are all adorned. This is not to be understood, as if they were perfect in holiness in this life ; no, the saints are only " fair like the moon," which hath a great many spots : but then, holiness in its per-fection is that which every saint is breathing after, saying with Paul, " I forget those things which are behind, and reach forth unto those things which are before," &c. ; and it is a grief of heart to them that they cannot be more holy. This makes them groan under the remains of sin, saying with Paul, " Wretched man that I am," &c.

7. If you be really under the standard lifted up by the Spirit of the Lord, you may know it by this, when ever

you are at any time worsted by sin, you will not be a volunteer, but a captive to it.   When sin overcomes the
believer, he reckons himself in captivity and bondage
as Paul did; " I find a law in my members warring
against the law of my mind and bringing me into
captivity to the law of sin, which is in my members."
You know, a loyal subject and faithful soldier may be
taken captive by a foreign enemy : but then there is a
great odds between the man, though in the enemy's
hand, and another that deserts his king and his colours,
and goes over to the enemy's side.   Now, the case with
the believer is, that though he sin, yet he does not go
over to the enemy's side: no sin besets him, betrays
him, surpriseth him ; and while he is taken captive by
it, he wearies of its drudgery, and never reckons himself at liberty, till he be brought back again to his
Captain, his colours, and company.   When he is in
company with sin and sinners, he is ready to say, " Woe
is me, that I sojourn in Mesech, that I dwell in the
tents of Kedar."   I will never be at liberty, till the
fetters of ignorance, unbelief, vanity, and carnality,
be quite shaken off.   O to be wholly rid of this evil
heart of unbelief, which turns me away from the living God! O that the very remains of sin were ruined
in me, and to be without the reach of sin, and all temptations and occasions of it ! So much for trial.

Comfort to distressed Believers

PERHAPS one may be saying, Alas! Satan has broke
in upon me with a flood of temptations, and the flood
is so strong, that I am like to be carried off my feet.
I am assaulted with temptations to blasphemous errors,
self-murder, and what not ; yea, to such evils, as I am
ashamed to let any of the world know of.   Well, poor
soul, is this thy case ? I tell thee for thy comfort, a
God of truth has said it, that his Spirit shall lift up
the standard, and drive back the enemy that comes in
like a flood upon thee : " And has he said it, and will
he not do it ? has he spoken it, and shall it not come

to pass?" Take this promise in the text, in the hand of faith, hold it up to the enemy, and this word of truth shall be thy shield and buckler. This was the way that Christ dealt with the enemy, when he came in upon him like a flood, Mat. iv. he lift up the banner of the word, the shield of God's faithfulness, saying, "Thus and thus it is written;" and thereby the enemy was driven back, and put to the worst. Follow the example of thy great General ; tell the enemy, " It is written, the Spirit of the Lord shall lift up the standard against thee: It is written, The seed of the woman shall bruise the head of the serpent, and tread thee under his feet:" and therefore I will believe and hope, believe and wait, till the Lord, according to his promise, come in for my relief. And if thou do so, depend upon it, the enemy will soon lose heart, and the strength of his temptations will fall.

Perhaps another may be saying, Alas! there is a flood of darkness broke in upon my soul, that I know not where I am, or what I am doing ; though once in a-day I thought the Lord manifested himself to me, yet now " the Lord hath forsaken me, and my God hath forgotten me ; the Comforter that should relieve my soul, is far from me ; and I, whither shall I cause my sorrow to go?" I answer, This is no strange case, for the children of light, to walk in darkness, yea, in such darkness that they can see no light ; but be assured, that " unto the upright light shall arise in darkness." And therefore " trust in the name of the Lord, stay thyself upon thy God ; his goings forth are prepared as the morning ; he that shall come will come, and will not tarry." When the Spirit of the Lord displays his standard, reveals the glory of Christ, he will make light, even the light of the knowledge of his glory, to shine through every corner of thy soul.

Perhaps another may be saying, There is a whole flood of challenges that fill my bosom ;. I am indeed in darkness, the Lord is hiding ; but that is not all, it is my own sins that hath done it, and God is saying to

me, "This is thy wickedness, because it is bitter. Hast
thou not procured this unto thyself? Thine own iniquities separate between thee and thy God." I answer,
All this may be true; and if true, thou hast indeed
cause to mourn and weep in secret places; but yet I
would not have thee to mourn like them that have no
hope, but turn unto a God in Christ, reconciling the
world to himself, not imputing their trespasses to them;
run into the blood of sprinkling, the fountain opened
to the house of David, that washes from sin and uncleanness. The Spirit of the Lord has displayed the
banner of his everlasting righteousness, and brought it
near in the gospel offer and promise, that so the guilty
sinner and discouraged believer, may come in under it,
and find ground of hope and courage under all challenges, saying as the apostle does, Rom. viii. " Who
can lay any thing to the charge of God's elect?" &c.
Improve the promise of pardon, " I, even I am he that
blotteth out thy transgressions for mine own name's
sake." Improve the name of a reconciled God, " The
Lord pardoning iniquity." Pray with David, " Pardon
mine iniquity, for it is very great."

Alas! may another say, indwelling sin and corruption breaks in upon me like a flood, I have whole
swarms of hellish abominations within me. Well, here
is comfort, "When the enemy shall come in like a flood,
the Spirit of the Lord shall lift up a standard against
him." A discovery of Christ in the light of the Spirit,
wastes, weakens, and withers the body of sin. And
therefore, O plead, and believe the promise, for the
Spirit is promised for this very end, Ezek. xxxvi. 25
—27. The Spirit takes the holiness of the head, and
applies it to the members, whereby sin is weakened,
and holiness is advanced. Has not the Lord said,
" Sin shall not have dominion over you : I will subdue
their iniquities?" Art thou oppressed with remaining
ignorance ? Well, the Spirit of the Lord shall lift up
the standard ; for he is a " Spirit of wisdom and revelation ;" he is the anointing, whereby we are made to

know all things. Art thou oppressed with unbelief, like a flood carrying thee away from the living God? Well, here is comfort, the Spirit of the Lord shall lift up the standard against it; for he is a Spirit of faith, and he testifies of Christ, as "the Author and Finisher of faith," and will "fulfil in thee all the good pleasure of his goodness, and the work of faith with power." Art thou oppressed with remaining enmity against God, discovering itself in the works of the flesh? Well, the Spirit of the Lord shall lift up the standard; for he is a Spirit of love, his banner is a banner of love, his peculiar work and province is to shed abroad the love of God upon the heart; and when he discovers the love and loveliness of our glorious Redeemer, enmity is driven back: nothing so much kills enmity, as the discovery of the love of God in Christ. O! says another, the vanity and carnality of my spirit comes in like a flood upon me; I no sooner set myself to any spiritual work, but the world and the concerns thereof, come in like a flood, and divert my thoughts from the things of eternal concern. Well, here is comfort, the Spirit of the Lord shall lift up the standard; for he is a Spirit of power, whereby we overcome the world. He it is that gives wings to the soul, whereby it mounts up, like the eagle, above things visible and corporeal, where Christ is at the right hand of God. O! says another, I have so many errors in my heart, that I fear my heart fall in with the errors of the day, and so I be carried away with the flood. "Blessed is the man that feareth always;" but do not fear with a fear of distrust, for the Spirit of the Lord will lift up the standard of truth, and he is given to lead his people into all truth; he is the Spirit of a sound mind, to enable believers to distinguish between light and darkness, between truth and error; he it is that causeth the wayfaring man, though a fool, to walk in the way of truth, without erring. O! says another, grace is so weak, and corruption so strong, that I fear any little spark of grace that is in me be carried away, and ruin-

ed by the flood. I answer, Be encouraged, the Spirit
of the Lord will carry on his own work, and lift a
standard in its defence; "he will not break the bruised
reed, nor quench the smoking flax, till he hath brought
forth judgment unto victory." O! says another, I can
find no quiet or rest for the workings of Satan and
corruption together, they are making perpetual inroads
upon me by night and by day. *Answ.* Poor soul, here
is comfort, the Spirit of the Lord shall lift up the
standard, he will testify of Christ, and then thou shalt
have rest in him, as " under the shadow of a great rock
in a weary land." Is. xi. 10. Christ is there set up by
the Spirit of the Lord, "as an ensign to the nations;"
and then immediately it is added, "Unto him shall the
Gentiles seek, and his rest shall be glorious." You
have another sweet promise to this purpose, Is. lxiii.
14. "As a beast goeth down into the valley, the Spirit
of the Lord causeth him to rest." It is the work of
the Spirit, to show to the weary soul the place where
Christ causeth his flock to rest at noon.

Another perhaps may be saying, There is a terrible
flood breaking in upon me, and that is a flood of divine terrors. I may say with David, Psal. lxxvii. "I
remembered God, and was troubled." With God is
terrible majesty indeed, and his terrors set themselves
in array against me. *Answ.* Here is comfort, the Spirit
of the Lord shall lift up the standard, and drive away
these terrors; for he is the Comforter, and Christ has
promised to send him in this capacity; "I will send
the Comforter, which is the Holy Ghost; and when
he comes, thy heart shall rejoice, and thy joy shall no
man take from thee. We have not received the Spirit
of bondage again to fear, but we have received the
Spirit of adoption, whereby we cry, Abba, Father."
And it is his usual way, after he has wounded and
broken, to bind up and heal, to make the bones which
he hath broken to rejoice.

May another say, The fear of death breaks in upon
me like a flood, the king of terrors keeps me in per-

petual bondage, I am not able to look upon his grim countenance. *Answ.* The Spirit of the Lord shall lift up the standard, he shall discover the glory of Christ, and then thou shalt be put in case to say, " O death, where is thy sting? Yea, though I walk through the valley of the shadow of death, I will fear no evil." Christ is the plague of death, and the destruction of the grave ; he has wrung the keys of hell and death out of the devil's hand : and therefore " lift up thy head, for the day of thy redemption draweth near."

Royal proclamation from heaven to rebel sinners.

1*st,* Be it known to all men, and the sons of men, it is given out from the royal standard of Heaven, even a proclamation of liberty and freedom to all the slaves and vassals of hell.   Christ the great Captain of salvation, he has broken up the devil's prison, broken the gates of brass, and cut asunder the bars of iron ; and he calls to the prisoners to *come forth ;* to them that sit in darkness, *show yourselves ;* the Son of God by his proclamation makes you free, and therefore be ye free indeed.   Whosoever they be that will come in under the standard of Heaven, shall be free from the guilt of sin, that it shall not condemn them ; from the dominion of sin, that it shall not reign over them ; from the pollution of sin, that it shall not separate between God and them : they shall be free from the law as a covenant, and from its sentence of death ; from Satan, the roaring lion, that he shall not be able to devour them.

2*dly,* From the royal standard of Heaven it is given out, and we proclaim peace to you who are rebels, and have been in arms against God: Is. xxvii. 4, 5. "Fury is not in me : who would set the briars and thorns against me in battle ? I would go through them, I would burn them together.   But let them take hold of my strength, and be at peace with me, and they shall make peace with me."   The royal Prince of peace sends us out as ambassadors in his name, " pray-

ing you in Christ's stead as though God did beseech
you by us, that you be reconciled to God." We proclaim " peace, peace to them that are afar off, and to
them that are near." O rebels, lay down your rebellious arms, surrender yourselves to the great King,
whose name is " the Lord of hosts."

3dly, From the royal standard of Heaven we issue
forth a proclamation of pardon to condemned criminals,
lying under sentence of death.   See a surprising proclamation of pardon, Is. xliii. 25, which you may read.
The very name of the glorious General is, " The Lord
pardoning iniquity. O let the wicked forsake his
way, and the unrighteous man his thoughts : and let
him return unto the Lord, and he will have mercy
upon him, and to our God, for he will abundantly
pardon," or multiply to pardon ; you shall have a free
discharge of all the debt you owe to divine justice ;
the handwriting against you, which is contrary to you,
shall be cancelled.

4thy, From this royal standard a proclamation of
health comes forth to the diseased.   Are there any maim-
ed or lame, halt or withered creatures here, who are unfit
for service, cannot creep or walk in the Lord's way ?
We call you in the name of the great General, and
tell you, that there is room for you ; that moment you
come in under the standard, though *lame,* you *shall
leap like an hart.*   Perhaps you think yourselves very
unfit for war, after you have been so lamed by sin
and Satan ; but we tell you good news, when you come
in under this standard, " the bones which were broken
shall be made to rejoice."

5thly, From this royal standard we issue a proclamation of great riches to the poor.   O Sirs, here is
gold tried in the fire, gold better than the gold of
Ophir, lying scattered about the tents of the great
King, whose name is the " Lord of hosts.   Riches and
honour are with me ; yea durable riches and righteousness :" and " we preach among you Gentiles the unsearchable riches of Christ."

6thly, A proclamation of "bread to the hungry, and drink to the thirsty ; fat things full of marrow, wines on the lees well refined.   Wisdom hath builded her house, she hath hewn out her seven pillars.   She hath killed her beasts, she hath mingled her wine ; she hath also furnished her table.   She hath sent forth her maidens, she crieth upon the highest places of the city, Come, eat of my bread, and drink of the wine which I have mingled," Prov. ix. at the beginning.   Again, we issue forth a proclamation of marriage with the Son of God to them that have " played the harlot with many lovers ;" a proclamation of life, to you that are " dead in trespasses and sin ; O hear the voice of the Son of God, for they that hear shall live."   Thus you see what glorious encouragement the great General, whose standard we lift up in the everlasting gospel, gives to lost sinners, to come and list themselves in his service.

How God in Christ is a God of love.

1. God in Christ is a reconciled God, a God of peace, that has received the atonement : 2 Cor. v. 19. " God was in Christ, reconciling the world unto himself." Rom. v. 10. " When we were enemies, we were reconciled to God by the death of his Son."   He both finds the ransom, and accepts of the ransom that he has found ; and having accepted of the ransom, of the Surety, he proclaims himself to be " the God of peace, that brought again from the dead our Lord Jesus Christ."   Oh Sirs! does not this say that God is love ? what greater evidence of it could God give, than to provide a ransom, and to receive it, than to cry, " Deliver them from going down to the pit, for I have found a ransom ?"

2. God in Christ is a promising God ; and does not this say that he is a God of love?   God abstractly considered is a threatening God, a revenging God ; but, in Christ, a promising God ; and we find, 2 Cor. i. 20. that all the promises of God are in Christ, and

"in him yea and amen." Whenever you meet with
any promise in the Bible, of grace or of glory, of
peace or of pardon, or be what it will, you would still
take it up as a promise of a God in Christ : Christ
having fulfilled the condition of the promise of eternal
life, by his obedience and death, the promises are given
out to us, through him, as the immediate ground and
foundation of our faith, with an intimation and adver-
tisement, "The promise is unto you, and to your seed,
and to all that are afar off, even as many as the Lord
our God shall call." Sirs, if any man should present
to you a bond, bill, or security, for a vast sum of money
which would enrich you for all your days, you would
look upon it as a great and indisputable evidence of
his love to you. Well, this is the very case between
God and you : through Christ, he is a promising God ;
he comes in a gospel-dispensation, saying, "I will put
my Spirit within you: I will be merciful to their unrighteousness, and their sins and their iniquities will I
remember no more," &c. These promises are presented to you as the ground of your faith : and that very
moment you take hold of them in a way of believing,
you come to be possessed of them, and all the benefits
of his purchase, according to that, Is. lv. 3. "Hear,
and your soul shall live, (it is the hearing of faith
that is intended) ; and I will make (or establish) an
everlasting covenant with you, even the sure mercies
of David." Oh Sirs ! does not this say that "God is
love ?"

3. God in Christ is a God sitting upon a throne of
grace : and does not this say, that "God is love ?"
God has a threefold throne,—a throne of glory, a
throne of justice, and a throne of grace. The first of
these, his throne of glory, is so bright, that it dazzles
the eyes of angels, and they cover their faces with their
wings when they approach it. The second, viz. his
throne of justice, is clothed with red vengeance ; and
it is so terrible, that the most holy saints tremble when
they behold it. "If thou, Lord, shouldst mark iniqui-

ties, O Lord, who shall stand? In thy sight shall no
man living be justified." And because we were not
able to stand here, he has erected another throne,
namely, a throne of grace, from whence he issues out
acts of grace and mercy to guilty sinners ; and so soon
as he is seen sitting upon this throne, he is taken up
as a God of love ; and thereupon the poor sinner, that
was trembling at the thoughts of being cited before
the throne of justice, flees for his life to the throne of
grace, saying with the apostle, Heb. iv. 16. " Let us
therefore come boldly unto the throne of grace, that
we may obtain mercy, and find grace to help in time
of need."

4. God in Christ is a God matching with us, and
betrothing us unto himself in loving kindness ; and
does not this say, that he is a God of love? There is
a twofold match that the great and infinite JEHOVAH
has made with Adam's family. (1.) He matches with
our nature by a personal union in the person of his
eternal Son ; he marries our nature ; and thus he becomes sib to the whole family of Adam, an honour
that the angelic family was never dignified with ; for
" he takes not on him the nature of angels, but the
seed of Abraham." Oh Sirs! what shall I tell you?
strange and surprising news indeed, " God is manifested in the flesh !" The great God becomes sib to us
in Christ; for he is clothed with our nature ; he is become bone of our bone, and flesh of our flesh ; and
what is the language of this, but that of the angels at
his birth, " Glad tidings of great joy, good-will and
peace towards men upon earth ?" (2.) Another match
he makes with us, is, by taking us actually under the
bond of a marriage-relation. The match is proposed
to all in the call and offer of the gospel ; but you know
the bare proposal of marriage does not make marriage,
till once the consent of the bride be obtained ; and
that moment the soul gives its assent and consent unto
the proposal made in the gospel, he betroths that soul
to himself in loving-kindness and in mercy, in right-

eousness and in judgment; and the Lord rejoices over that soul, as a bridegroom rejoices over the bride, saying to it, "Thy Maker is thine husband, the Lord of hosts is his name," Is. liv. 5. And, Oh Sirs! does not this say, that "God is love?" Because the distance between him and us was too great (abstractly considered), therefore he first comes on a level with us, by taking on our nature, that so the inequality of the persons might be no stop: he becomes our husband, and we his spouse and bride.

5. God in Christ is a God with us, on our side, our friend, and takes part with us against all deadly or danger: and does not this say that "God is love," as he is in Christ? Oh Sirs! God out of Christ is a God against us; hence he is said to be "angry with the wicked every day;" he whets his glittering sword, and his hand takes hold on judgment, to render vengeance unto every transgressor of his holy law. But, Oh! God in Christ is not a God against us, but a God with us, or a God for us; the name Immanuel imports, "God with us." And every one that takes a God in Christ for their God, they may say, upon warrantable grounds, with the church, Psal. xlvi. 7. "The Lord of hosts is with us, the God of Jacob is our refuge." And they may say it upon a covenant ground, for God in Christ has said, Is. xliii. 2. "When thou passest through the waters, I will be with thee; and through the rivers, they shall not overflow thee. I will never leave thee, nor forsake thee."

6. God in Christ is a pardoning God: and does not this declare him to be a God of love? "I, even I, am he that blotteth out thy transgressions for mine own sake, and will not remember thy sins. I will be merciful to their unrighteousness," &c.

7. God in Christ is a pitying God; he pities Christless and unbelieving sinners, and is loath at his very heart to give up with them: Hos. xi. 8. "How shall I give thee up, Ephraim? how shall I deliver thee, Israel? how shall I make thee as Admah? how shall I set thee

as Zeboim? Mine heart is turned within me, my repentings are kindled together." And Oh! how great
is his pity to the soul that believes in him! His pity
to them is like the pity of a father to his son : Psal.
ciii. 13. " Like as a father pitieth his children, so the
Lord pitieth them that fear him." It is like the pity
of a fond mother to a sucking child : Is. xlix. 15.
" Can a woman forget her sucking child, that she
should not have compassion on the son of her womb?
yea, they may forget, yet will I not forget thee."

8. God in Christ is a God of infinite bounty and
liberality, and a prayer-hearing God ; (I cast things
together, that I may not be tedious). Oh Sirs! his
heart is free, and his hand is full and open ; open
hearted, open handed : " If any man lack wisdom, let
him ask of God, that giveth to all men liberally, and
upbraideth not." Such is his bounty and liberality,
that it is nothing but ask and have with him : " Ask,
and it shall be given you ; seek, and ye shall find ;
knock, and it shall be opened unto you," Matth. vii.
7. When we have asked great things of him, he
quarrels us as if we had asked nothing : he does not
deal with a scrimp or a sparing hand : no, no ; " Ask,
and ye shall receive, (says he,) that your joy may be
full." Yea, such is his bounty, that he is ready to do
for us exceeding abundantly above what we can either
ask or think ; yea, such is his bounty, that he prevents
us with the blessings of his goodness : his goodness and
mercy is like the rain and dew, that do not wait for
the sons of men : Is. lxv. 24. " And it shall come to
pass, that, before they call, I will answer, and while
they are yet speaking, I will hear."

9. God in Christ is an inciting God, an entreating
God, to sinners : and does not this say, that he is a
God of love ? He invites us to come to him for all
needful grace : Is. lv. 1. " Ho, every one that thirsteth, come ye to the waters, and he that hath no money ;
come ye, buy and eat ; yea, come, buy wine and milk
without money and without price." He is an entreat-

ing God in Christ: 2 Cor. v. 20. " We are ambassadors for Christ, as though God did beseech you by us:
we pray you in Christ's stead, be ye reconciled to God."
He complains of the backwardness of sinners to come
to him : " Ye will not come to me, that ye might
have life." He expostulates with them on this account;
" O my people, what have I done unto thee, and
wherein have I wearied thee? testify against me." He
waits for an answer ; he will not take a repulse, " Behold, I stand at the door, and knock." And he stands
knocking till his locks are wet. Oh! does not all
this say, that God in Christ is love ?

10. God in Christ is our God (to crown all). He
makes a grant of himself in the covenant as such, " I
will be their God :" and he allows us to claim him by
faith as our God, upon this very grant he makes of
himself to us in Christ, Zech. xiii. 9. " I will say, It
is my people; and they shall say, The Lord is my
God." And Oh! happy that soul that is enabled to
give faith's echo to this covenant grant, and say,
" This God is my God for ever and ever ; and he shall
be my Guide even unto death." In a word, God in
Christ is our Father; for it is only God in Christ that
says, " I will be unto them a Father, and they shall be
unto me sons and daughters." He hath taught us to
say, " Our Father which art in heaven." And he is
displeased with us, when we are shy with him, through
unbelief, to call him by this endearing title : Jer. iii.
4. " Wilt thou not from this time cry unto me, My
Father, and not turn away from me?" Oh! what but
the infinite bowels of love could speak in such a style
and dialect! Now, from all this I think the truth of
the doctrine is abundantly evident, that God in Christ
is a God of love.

Excellent properties of the love of God.

1. His love is a free love : Hos. xiv. 4. " I will
heal their backsliding, I will love them freely." This
love is free in its first fountain, viewing it, I mean, as

it lies in the heart of God. What made him to set
his love on any of Adam's posterity, and to choose them
from eternity? The cause of it is not to be found in
the creature, but in himself; only his own sovereign
will and grace is the cause of it; for he " predestinated us unto the adoption of children by Jesus
Christ to himself, according to the good pleasure of his
will," Eph. i. 5. " He hath saved us and called us with
an holy calling, not according to our works, but according to his own purpose and grace which was given
us in Christ Jesus, before the world began," 2 Tim. i.
9. And then again, this love is free, not only in its
first fountain, but free in the offer, revelation and manifestation of it in the word ; and the love of God, as it
is in the word of grace, is a common love, common to
all the hearers of the gospel, in regard it comes to
every man's door, and offers itself unto him : " Ho,
every one that thirsteth, come. Whosoever will, let
him come," &c. " Unto you, O men, I call, and my
voice is to the sons of men." And then it is a free
love, in regard of the application of it to the elect soul
in a day of power ; the love of God is manifested in
the word of grace taken by the Holy Ghost, and shed
abroad upon the sinner's heart, and that without regard
to any good qualification or work of righteousness in
us. In a word, this love of a God of love, it is free,
in opposition to merit. That which conciliates love
among men, is either beauty, strength, wisdom, riches,
or some such qualification or inducement; but no such
thing is to be found in any of Adam's posterity ;
" When thou wast in thy blood, I said unto thee, Live;
and thy time was a time of love." Instead of beauty,
nothing but deformity ; instead of strength, nothing
but weakness ; instead of riches, nothing but poverty,
And as it is free in opposition to merit, so it is free in
opposition to any constraint or force. Love is a thing
that cannot be forced ; no, it is voluntary, and of its
own accord. God's love is only owing to the freedom
of his own will, Eph. i. 9.

2. The love of this God of love, it is a strong and invincible love. Before his love could reach us in the application of it, it had mountains to level : but, " behold, he cometh, leaping upon the mountains, and skipping upon the hills." There were deep seas and floods in the way of his love, but many waters could not quench it, neither were all floods able to drown it: it runs through every difficulty, it encounters every impediment in its way. The infinite distance between God and a creature, was a bar in the way of this love: but he conquers this impediment : for " God is manifested in the flesh." The moral distance between a filthy guilty sinner is an impediment in the way of this love : but he breaks this bar also; for the son of God is not only manifested in the flesh, but " made in the likeness of sinful flesh, yea, made sin for us." The curse of the law was a bar in the way : but this bar he breaks; for Christ was " made a curse for us, that we might be redeemed from the curse of the law." Sin in its guilt, and filth, and power, lay in the way of his love : but love breaks through this, and " finishes transgression, and makes an end of sin." Ignominy and disgrace lay in its way, grief and sorrow : but this love conquers that : for he was content to endure the cross, and love *despises the shame* of it; he is content out of love, to become " a man of sorrows and acquainted with grief." And then, when this love comes to the sinner, in order to conversion, it finds him dead, " dead in trespasses and sins :" the man has perhaps lain 20, 30, 40, or 60 years in the grave of sin, so that lo he stinketh : Oh, what an object is he! he is an object of loathing instead of love : but yet this love of a God of love conquers this impediment also : for " when we were dead in sins, for the great love wherewith he loved us, he quickened us." And then, after this love has actually griped the soul in effectual calling, how many provocations gets it by the whoredoms of heart and life-departing from the Lord? and yet such is the invincible nature of this love that it over-

comes all, and abideth firm unto the end; hence is that of the apostle, Rom. viii. 35, 37. " Who shall separate us from the love of Christ ? shall tribulation, or distress, or persecution, or famine, or nakedness, or peril, or sword. Nay, in all these things we are more than conquerors, through him that loved us." It is because his love is invincible, that we are more than conquerors though him that loved us : because his love is strong as death, therefore death shall not se parate ; because it is strong as hell, therefore neither hell nor devils shall be able to make a separation.

3. The love of this God of love, it is an incomparable, yea, a superlative love. Let us but view here how much a God in Christ loves them who trust under the shadow of his wings, because of the excellency of his loving-kindness. (1.) He loves them more than he loves all other men : Is. xliii. 3, 4. " I will give men for thee, and people for thy life." (2.) He loves believers more than he loves angels. Angels are his servants, believers are his sons ; angels are his subjects, believers are his bride. (3.) He loves them more than he loves the whole world. The world consists of heaven and earth. As for the earth, he did not value that, for the love he had to his people : when the devil proffered him all the kingdoms of the world, and the glory of them, he contemns them all, out of love he had to them. As for heaven, he left the glory of the higher house, to dwell with men upon earth. Yea, I shall add, (4.) The love of an incarnate Deity is greater to his people than to himself. He loved their life and safety more than his own ; for he laid down his life for his friends, that they might not die : he prayed more for them than he did for himself, as you may see, John xvii. throughout. In a word, out of love he bore to us, he parted with these things that are reckoned most valuable among men. Men make a great account of their good name ; but, out of love to us he became a " reproach of men." Men make a great account of their riches ; but " though he was rich, yet

for our sakes he became poor." Men make a great
account of their life; "skin for skin, yea, all that a
man hath will he give for his life;" but Christ parted
with this, " He loved me, and gave himself for me."
Men do or should make a great account of their souls;
and yet, out of love to us, he made his soul an offering, "My soul is exceeding sorrowful even unto death."
Men, I mean holy men, saints, they make a greater
account of the love of God than of their life, " Thy
love is better than life," says David ; and yet Christ
was content to lose the sense of that for a while, out
of love to us ; and it was withdrawn from him, to
that degree, that he cried out on the cross, " My God,
my God. why hast thou forsaken me ?"

Exhortations to believe the Gospel and trust in a God of love.

1. Is it so that "God is love?"   Is God in Christ a
God of love : Oh ! then, Sirs, believe the report of the
gospel : Oh ! receive it as a faithful saying, and worthy
of all acceptation, that God in Christ is love : and do
not receive it upon my testimony, but receive it upon
the testimony or the record of the three that bear record
in heaven, the Father, the Word, and the Spirit: a Trinity of persons is witnessing and declaring to you, that
" God is love ;" and therefore set to your seal that
God is true of what he says of himself: and, Sirs, remember, that if you do not, you make God a liar, because
you receive not the record that God has given of himself.

2. My exhortation is, not only to believe this truth
concerning God, but, Oh ! eat it (as Jeremiah did),
and let it be " the joy and rejoicing of your heart."
Eat it, say you ; what is that? how can we eat it ?   I
answer, The way to eat it, is to apply and bring it
home to your own souls.   Oh Sirs, there is meikle
feeding for faith in this little word, " God is love."
Oh ! may faith say, is God love ? then surely he will
make me welcome to his table : he is a God of infinite
bounty and liberality in Christ, and he will give that
which is good ; a God of love he will give grace and

glory, and no good thing will he withhold from his people.

3. Is God in Christ a God of love? yea, love itself? Oh! then, put your trust in him. This is the use the Spirit of God would have you to make of this doctrine, Psal. xxxvi. 7. (a sweet and remarkable word), "How excellent is thy loving-kindness, O God! therefore the children of men put their trust under the shadow of thy wings." Oh sinners! the wings of a God of love are spread out to you, and his bowels are sending out a sound after you in this glorious gospel; and his hand is stretched out to you in this gospel, saying, "Behold me, behold me." Oh! do not run away from him as an enemy, but trust him as a friend that bears good-will towards you. What is it, O man, that a God of love in Christ is not ready to grant unto thee? Wants thou garments to cover the shame of thy nakedness? a God of love is ready to grant thee this. Perhaps thou hast some thoughts of coming to a communion-table; but thou art afraid lest thou be found naked in his presence, and the Master of the feast say unto thee, "Friend, how camest thou in hither, not having a wedding-garment?" Is this thy case? O put your trust in a God of love through Christ, and he will clothe you with the garments of salvation, and with the robes of righteousness. Wants thou a pardon for sin? art thou a broken bankrupt, that owes thousands of talents to the law and justice of God? Art thou crying, "Mine iniquities are gone over mine head; as an heavy burden, they are too heavy for me." Well, a God of love is a pardoning God; and therefore trust him for the pardon of thy sins; for he says, "I, even I, am he that blotteth out thy transgressions for mine own sake, and will not remember thy sins." Oh! may you say, I am a poor captive, I am in chains, under the fetters of captivity to my spiritual enemies; the bonds of iniquity are wreathed about my soul. Well, a God of love proclaims "liberty to the captives, and the opening of the prison to them that are bound;"

and therefore, O trust him, and he will make thee to share of the glorious liberty of his own children ; he will make thy chains and fetters to fall off from thee. Art thou a black and ugly sinner, by lying among the pots, black like the Ethiopian, spotted like the leopard? Well, put thy trust under the wings of a God of love ; for he says, "though thou hast lien among the pots, I will make thee as the wings of a dove covered with silver, and her feathers with yellow gold. I will sprinkle clean water upon you, and ye shall be clean." Art thou a diseased sinner, full of bruises and putrefying sores ! Well, put thy trust in a God of love in Christ ; for his name is JEHOVAH ROPHI, " I am the Lord that healeth thee." Art thou a poor wandering bewildered sinner, that hast lost thy way to heaven, and hast gone astray like a lost sheep ? Well, come put your trust in a God of love : for he has "pity on the ignorant, and on them that are out of the way :" a God of love in Christ has said, that he will " lead the blind," &c. and that he will make " the way-faring man, though a fool, to walk without erring." Art thou a treacherous dealer, thou hast gone a-whoring after other lovers, prostrated thyself unto every vile lust? Well, come yet and put thy trust under the wings of a God of love ; for his voice unto you is, Jer. iii. 1. " Though thou hast played the harlot with many lovers, yet return again to me." He is crying from the top of the high places this day, " Return, O backsliding Israel ; for I am married unto thee. For I will heal thy backslidings, and love thee freely, and receive thee graciously." So then, I say, whoever thou art, or whatever thou art, I invite and call you to trust under the wings of a God of love, because of the excellency of his loving-kindness. And for motives, consider,

1*st*, That you cannot do a God of love a greater pleasure. Would you please God to-day, or oblige his very heart? Well, trust him as a God of love ; for " he taketh pleasure in them that fear him, in those that hope in his mercy," or that trust in him as a God of love.

2dly, Would you be fed, yea, feasted, this day at a communion-table, with the fatness of God's house, with fat things full of marrow?   Oh! then, here is the way to it? put your trust in a God of love, come in under his wings: Psal. xxxvii. 3. "Trust in the Lord, and do good; so shalt thou dwell in the land, and verily thou shalt be fed." You see you have not only his promise, that you shall be fed, but his promise supported and ratified with a strong asseveration, "Verily thou shalt be fed." Would you be fed with the blessings of heaven, the blessings of a well-ordered covenant, the sure mercies of David! Oh! then, trust in a God of love; for "blessed are all they that trust in him," Psal. lxxxiv. 12.   Would you have languishing grace revived, brought into a thriving and blooming condition? Oh! then, trust in a God of love, Jer. xvii. 7, 8. "Blessed is the man that trusteth in the Lord, and whose hope the Lord is.   For he shall be as a tree planted by the waters, and that spreadeth out her roots by the river, and shall not see when heat cometh, but, her leaf shall be green, and shall not be careful in the year of drought, neither shall cease from yielding fruit." Would you be filled with peace? then trust in a God of love: Is. xxvi. 3. "Thou wilt keep him in perfect peace, whose mind is stayed on thee; because he trusteth in thee." Would you be filled with the joys of God's salvation? then trust in a God of love: Psal. xiii. 5. "I have trusted in thy mercy, my heart shall rejoice in thy salvation." In a word, not to insist, trust in a God of love, and you shall never perish: "none perish that trust in him:" you shall never be confounded nor dismayed: and he will never forsake you: "Thou, Lord, hast not forsaken them that seek thee, and trust in thee." You shall have all needful preparation for a communion-table; for the preparation of the heart, and answer of the tongue, comes from him. So then, I say, trust in a God of love. I think it is enough to engage you all to trust

him, to repeat the text, and to say, " God is love."
If any of you apprehend a man to be your enemy, in
that case you will have no trust to put in him ; but if
you be once persuaded he loves you, and wants only
an opportunity to do you all the service he can, in that
case you will trust him with assured confidence. Well,
Sirs, we tell you, that God is not only a friend, bearing
good-will to you, but he is love, love itself ; love is the
imperial or commanding attribute of his nature : O how
excellent is his loving-kindness ! therefore let the sons
of men, let sinners and saints, put their trust under
the shadow of his wings

4. A fourth exhortation from the text is this. Is
it so, that a God in Christ is a God of love ? Oh !
then, Sirs, ware your love on a God of love, and render him love for love. " This is the first and great
commandment" of the moral law, and the sum of the
first table of the law, Mat. xxii. 37, 38. " Thou shalt
love the Lord thy God with all thy heart, and with all
thy soul, and with all thy strength, and with all thy
mind." Here is the most reasonable and just command that ever was. What can be more reasonable
than to love him, who is not only lovely, but love itself, and whose love runs out towards us in such a
surprising and astonishing way ? Sure I am, it is your
reasonable service, to love him with all thy heart, soul,
strength, and mind. And, Sirs, this is a command
which I am sure needs be no pain to obey ; for when
God commands you to love him, he commands you to
make yourselves happy ; for the very happiness of the
rational soul lies in the outgoings of God's love to you,
and the outgoings of your love and affections towards
him. Oh Sirs ! love to a God of love is the fulfilment
of the law ; you perform all duties, and exercise all
graces at once, when you get your hearts drawn out
in love to a God in Christ. What is faith, but love
trusting and confiding in the beloved object ? What
is hope, but love expecting and longing after the enjoyment of him ? What is patience, but love bearing

and suffering what a God of love lays on? What is humility, but love lying at the feet of a God of love? What is heavenly-mindedness, but love soaring, as upon eagles' wings, after a God of love? What is zeal, but love inflamed with desire to serve a God of love? What are all good works, but love displaying itself in actions of obedience to the commands of a God of love? What is it to communicate? It is just to show forth the dying love of a God of love. What is it to pray, but to offer up our desires to a God of love? What is it to praise, but to give vent unto the heart in the commendation of a God of love? So that, I say, when you love a God of love, you, as it were, do all things at once. And then to engage and encourage your love, in the very command itself, he presents himself unto thee as thy God, " Thou shalt love the Lord thy God." Thus he ushers in the commandment of the moral law, with, " I am the Lord thy God, which have brought thee out of the house of bondage." He is thy God, not only by creation, as he is the God of all living; but he is thy God in covenant, thy God in Christ : and when he says, " I am thy God," he in effect says, All that I am, all that I have, all that I can do, I make over to you in an everlasting covenant, which shall never be broken. Oh Sirs! shall not all this kindle a flame of love in your bosoms to a God of love?

In what Unbelief doth consist.

1. A DENYING of the truth of the gospel ; a looking upon the word of God, contained in the scriptures, as a fiction, or " cunningly devised fable." I am very jealous, there are unbelievers of this stamp among these who are called by the name of Christians ; men pretending to be great masters of reason, who, because their weak and depraved minds cannnot grasp the unsearchable mysteries of our holy religion, do therefore turn infidel, and reject the whole as an incredible paradox. This very thing upon which they stumble,

proves it to be of a divine original. The unsearchable wisdom that appears in every one of the works of God, proves them to be indeed his works, and not the works of any created being. And shall it be imagined, that there is less wisdom in his words than in his works, when they are the more immediate product and picture of his infinite understanding, which can never be searched out? Here, if any where, we may expect the " deep things of God ; the wisdom of God in a mystery, which none of the princes of this world knew."

2. A doubting or wavering uncertainty of mind about the truths of the gospel, will amount to this crime of unbelief pointed at in my text. There are some who, though they do not go the length of denying flatly that the Bible is the word of God, or that the gospel is of a divine original, yet they are in a hover and suspense about it ; like the worshippers of Baal, they halt between two opinions, they neither believe nor disbelieve it; but are like the scales of an even balance, ready to turn either to this or the other side. Such are unbelievers, in Christ's reckoning ; for " he that is not with me (says he) is against me."

3. When though a person may be convinced in his mind, by rational arguments, that the Bible is the word of God, that the gospel is of a divine extract, yet does not fall in with the great design of the scriptures, by receiving Christ, and resting upon him alone for salvation, as he is there presented and discovered. We have the design of the whole word of God expressed in one verse, John xx. 31. " These things are written, that ye might believe that Jesus is the Christ the Son of God, and that believing ye might have life through his name." And therefore when Christ is not received as the promised Messiah, the Saviour of the world, and actually improved for these ends and uses for which he is revealed and exhibited in the word ; particularly for " wisdom, righteousness, sanctification, and redemption ;" in this case, I say, a person

falls under the heavy charge of unbelief, and is condemned already. This last is the unbelief which I
take to be principally pointed at in my text, and is
most frequent and prevalent among the hearers of the
gospel. So much for the nature of unbelief.

The Causes of Unbelief.

1. THE devil has a great hand in it. Faith is the
great engine whereby his kingdom and interest is over-
thrown in the world ; and therefore he studies, by
might and main, to keep the sinner under the power
of unbelief: for which end, he uses a great many wiles
and stratagems. His first and principal care is, to
hush the house, and keep it in peace and quiet. In
order to this, ·he persuades the man that his state is
good enough ; that, though he be a sinner, yet his sins
are but small and venial ; and that it cannot consist
with the justice of God to pursue such small sins with
eternal punishment. If, notwithstanding of these surmises, the man's conscience cannot be satisfied, but it
begins to awaken, challenge, and smite him ; he studies
to lay him asleep again, with the prospect of general
and absolute mercy. If again this lying refuge be
beat down by the hail of divine terrors, he betakes
himself to another artifice ; he conceals and hides the
attribute of mercy, presenting God to the soul as an
implacable and inexorable Judge, who will by no means
acquit the guilty ; and thus, by hiding the remedy, he
studies to drive the sinner to despair. And indeed the
devil is much more skilled in representing the justice
than the mercy of God to a sinner's view, being an
utter stranger to the last, but well acquainted with the
first from his sad experience. But whatever views he
gives of God to the sinner, whether in his justice or
mercy, his design is still to carry the soul off from
Christ, and the mercy of God running in the channel
of his satisfactory blood. By presenting absolute
mercy, he encourages the sinner to go on in sin, hoping
to be saved, though he never be sanctified by the

Spirit of Christ. When he presents the justice of God
he studies to drive the sinner to a hopeless despair of
salvation by his atoning blood; and thereupon the sinner either with Judas runs to a halter for ease, or puts
on a desperate resolution, that if he be damned, he
shall be damned for something; and so takes a full
swing in gratifying his lusts, crying with these, Jer. ii.
25. " There is no hope. No, for we have loved strangers, and after them will we go." If, notwithstanding
of the utmost arts and efforts of hell, the remedy be
discovered to the sinner, viz. Christ, as the alone foundation God hath laid in Zion: then the enemy has another
stratagem at hand to discourage the poor sinner from
making use of Christ; he persuades the man that he
is not fit enough for Christ; he must be so humble,
so holy, so penitent, and have this and the other qualification, before he adventure to come to Christ, O if
I were sanctified, mortified, self-denied, washed, then
Christ would make me welcome. This is nothing but
an artifice of hell, for the ruin of souls, persuading
sinners that they must bring money and price with
them to Christ; that they must have such and such
things before they come to Christ, which are only to
be got by an actual union with him by faith. Thus,
I say, the devil has a great hand in unbelief, it being
the very strength of his kingdom ; and so long as he
keeps this hold in safety, he is very easy what shapes
of morality, civility, or profession, a man may cast
himself into; for he knows well, that he who believes
not, shall be damned, let him do else whatever he
pleases.

2. Ignorance is another great cause of unbelief.
" My people (says the Lord) are destroyed for lack of
knowledge." Ignorance of God, in his holiness, justice, and other adorable excellencies : ignorance of
the law of God in its purity, extent, and spirituality ;
ignorance of sin in its exceeding sinfulness ; ignorance
of the great mystery of godliness, the union of the two
natures in the person of our wonderful IMMANUEL ;

ignorance of his substitution in the room of sinners, and of that everlasting and law-magnifying righteousness he has brought in by his obedience unto the death ; ignorance of the free access sinners have unto Christ, and his whole salvation, in and by a confirmed testament or promise, which is put in their hands, and left to them, Heb. iv. 1. that they may use and claim the benefit of it in a way of believing : I say, the god of this world he "blinds the minds of them which believe not," that they may not know these things which belong to their eternal peace ; he is afraid, "lest the light of the glorious gospel of Christ, who is the image of God, should shine into their hearts." I am persuaded, did sinners but know how near Christ, and his purchased salvation, are brought to them by the gospel, there would not be so many unbelievers among us. People generally look on Christ, and eternal life in him, as things that are far out of their reach ; and thereupon they turn careless and easy about them, having no hope of ever attaining them, being things too high and great for them. But, O Sirs, this is only a vail or mist cast before your eyes, by the great enemy of your salvation, that you may not see your own mercy ; for were your eyes opened, you would see Christ, and all the blessings of his purchase, brought, as it were, within the very reach of your hand. The manna is lying round your tent-doors, and you have no more ado but to gather and use it, Is. xlvi. 13. Rom. x. 7, 8. John vi. 32.

3. Pride is another great cause of unbelief. This is just the poison of the old serpent, who being lifted up with pride, fell into condemnation. By pride he ruined all mankind at first, "Ye shall be as gods ;" and by pride he still keeps us under his power : hence we read of high and towering imaginations in the heart of man, which exalt themselves against the knowledge of Christ. There is a pride in the heart of man, by nature, which stands directly opposite to the way of salvation by grace : God is willing to give life but

we will needs merit and deserve it: God will have all
to be of grace, that boasting may be excluded ; but
we will have all in a way of debt, that we may have
whereof to glory. What, says the proud heart, will
ever God give, or shall I take, eternal life for nothing?
No, I will not have it, unless God will accept some
equivalent, some service or work for it. " Will the
Lord be pleased with thousands of rams?" &c. The
pride of the heart will set a man a-work, to do or suffer any thing for life and salvation, rather than believe
in Christ, and be saved in a way of grace ; as we see
in the case of the poor deluded Papists. They will
rather quit their kingdoms and thrones, put themselves
into monasteries, lie on hair, live on alms, tire themselves by saying the book of Psalms over once every
twenty-four hours ; and for that end break their sleep,
by rising twice or thrice a night, saying so many prayers to the virgin Mary, and to this and the other saint ;
they will whip themselves, tear their bodies, go into
penances and long pilgrimages ; all this, and much
more, will they do, for pardon and salvation, rather
than take God's method, which is to receive eternal
life, as the free gift of God, through Jesus Christ our
Lord. Whence comes all this stir, but only from the
pride of our hearts, which will stoop to any thing of
our own devising, though never so base and mean,
rather than stoop to be saved in a way of grace?
That is a strange instance of the pride of the heart,
which we have, Rom. x. 3. where it is said of the
proud self-righteous Jews, " they went about to establish their own righteousness, and would not submit unto
the righteousness of God." O strange! shall a poor
naked beggar, that has not a rag to cover him, reckon
it submission or humility in him to accept of a robe?
Shall a condemned malefactor reckon it submission to
receive the king's pardon? the captive to accept of
liberty? or a man mortally wounded to accept of a
healing balm? Yet this is the very case with us,
through the pride of our hearts we will not submit to

the righteousness of God, but will needs establish a
righteousness of our own. Nature, though assisted
by external revelation, can never think of another way
of salvation than that of the first Adam, viz. by doing
and working. To be saved and justified by the doing
and dying of another, is a mystery which flesh and blood
cannot receive, till the strength of natural pride be
broken by the almighty power of God. Men naturally will wear no other garment than that which, like
the spider, they spin out of their own bowels. But
what says God, Is. lix. 6. "Their webs shall not become garments, neither shall they cover themselves
with their works." Man will needs enter into life
and glory, by the door of the law, which God has condemned and barred against all mankind since the fall ;
"for by the works of the law shall no flesh living be
justified." Sirs, allow me to tell you, that God never
designed to bring man to life by the law, or the works
thereof; no, the law of works was only intended as a
scaffold, by which he meant to rear up a house of mercy, in which he designed to harbour a company of
broken dyvours and bankrupts, that they might live
upon his charity and grace for ever : and immediately
upon the entry of sin, the scaffold of the law as a covenant was taken down, and broken in pieces, O! what
devilish pride is it in us, to attempt the rebuilding of
the scaffold, that we may climb up to heaven by it,
rather than enter the threshold of the house of mercy,
which God has resolved "shall be built up for ever !"
Psal. lxxxix. 1. Sirs, allow me to tell you, however
high you may climb heaven-ward upon the scaffold of
the law, in your own conceit, and in the esteem of
others ; yet you shall be cast into hell, like Capernaum.
Your house being built upon the sand, it will fall, and
great will be the fall thereof. "The day of the Lord
of hosts shall be upon every one that is proud and lofty ; and the loftiness of man shall be bowed down, and
the haughtiness of men shall be made low : and the
Lord alone shall be exalted," Is. ii. 12, 17.

4. A pretended humility and self-denial is another
great bar in the way of believing to many. They
thrust away Christ and the mercy of God from them,
under a pretence that they are not fit for it. O!
says the man, I am such a hell-deserving sinner, my
sins are so great, that I dare not think of coming to
Christ ; he was never intended for the like of me,
This carries a fair show of humility and self-denial,
while it is only a devil of pride, transforming himself
into an angel of light. You say you are not worthy
of the mercy of God. I answer, It is very true : but
then you would consider, that mercy could not be
mercy, if you were worthy of it ; it would be merit,
and not mercy : grace would not be grace, but debt, if
you could deserve it. This way of thinking or speaking is quite subversive of a covenant of grace, where
Christ, and all the blessings of his purchase, are made
over to us, in the form of a testamentary deed, or free
gift and legacy. " I will be their God, and they shall
be my people : I will take away the stony heart ; I will
sprinkle them with clean water," &c. In these, and
the like absolute and unlimited promises, the grace and
favour of God in a Redeemer comes to every man's
door, be who or what he will ; and by these great and
precious promises, we must receive Christ, and apply
him in a suitableness to our soul's need, or perish for
ever. And to refuse Christ, and his salvation tendered
in the word of grace, under this pretext, that we are
great sinners, is all one, as if a traitor should refuse his
prince's pardon, because he has been in arms against
him; or as if one should refuse to accept of a free discharge, because he is a bankrupt, drowned in debt.

5. A secret jealousy, as if God were not in good earnest with us, when he offers Christ and his salvation to
us in the gospel. I am afraid that this lies at bottom
with many ; they do not really believe, that God is
willing to bestow his Christ, and salvation through
him, upon them, though he be every day calling, commanding, beseeching, and entreating them to embrace

him.   But, Sirs, what else is this, but to charge God
with treachery and disingenuity, as if he said one thing
in his word, and intended another in his heart ?   God
says, " He is not willing that you should perish ;" yea,
he swears by his life, that he has no pleasure in your
death, but rather that you turn unto him, through a
Redeemer, and live : and yet, to think or say that he
is not in good earnest, what else is this, but to make
God a liar, yea, to charge him with perjury ?   And
what an insufferable affront is this unto a God of truth,
for whom it is impossible to lie ?   We cannot offer a
greater indignity unto a man than to call him a liar ;
yea, if we but insinuate a jealousy of his veracity and
ingenuity, it is enough to exasperate and enrage his
spirits ; for " jealousy (says Solomon) is the rage of a
man :" and how then shall we imagine that God will
sit with it ?   O Sirs! be persuaded that God speaks
the truth in his heart ; his words of grace and truth in
the scripture, are the sweet picture of his thoughts.
And therefore beware of harbouring the least jealousy
in your hearts, as if he were not in good earnest when
he offers his Christ to you, and commands you to receive him, and his whole salvation.

6. People their finding peace and ease in some one
thing or other on this side Christ, is another great cause
of unbelief.   Perhaps the man has had some challenges
and wakenings ; thereupon he falls to his prayers, vows,
promises, and resolutions to be a better man in time
coming, and better servant to God ; upon this he finds
quiet and ease, and there he rests, without ever coming
to the blood of the Lamb.   But, Sirs, as sure as God
lives, this is but a refuge of lies, a hiding place which
the hail shall sweep away.   Do not mistake me ; I am
not dissuading you from duties, but only persuading
you not to rest in your duties ; let duties be as waggons
to carry your souls to Christ, who is " the end of the
law," and of all the duties it enjoins ; for when you rest
in them as a righteousness or ground of acceptance before God, they become a bar in the way of your coming

to Christ, and they prove soul damning and ruining things, instead of being the causes or means of salvation. And therefore go a little further than these; do not make a plaster of them to heal the wound of conscience ; for if your healing do not come from under the wings of the Sun of righteousness, the wound will fester, and prove deadly in the issue. Let him only be the well-spring of your comfort, who is the "consolation of Israel," and in whom all our well-springs are. We read of the brook Cherith, which supplied the prophet Elijah with water for a time ; but at length the brook dried up, and he had perished, unless God had brought him to a spring of water. Just so is it with many : they lie for a long time by the brooks of their own duties; and finding some sort of ease and comfort there, conscience is pacified, and they rejoice, because they think God will pity and save them, while they have done as well as they can. But depend on it, these brooks will dry up, and your souls will starve and perish for ever, if you do not, by faith, come to the fountain opened in the house of David, and draw water out of this well of salvation. O come, Sirs, to this open and overflowing fountain : " Whosoever will, let him come, and drink of the waters of life freely :" here you shall find water in the time of the greatest drought, Is. xli. 17. "When the poor and needy seek water," in duties, ordinances, and created comforts, " and there is none, and their tongue faileth for thirst, I the Lord will hear them, I the God of Israel will not forsake them." Jer. xvii. 7, 8. " Blessed is the man that trusteth in the Lord, and whose hope the Lord is. For he shall be as a tree planted by the waters, and that spreadeth out her roots by the river, and shall not see when heat cometh ; but her leaf shall be green ; and shall not be careful in the year of drought, neither shall cease from yielding fruit." So then, beware of resting on this side of Christ.

In what Courts the Unbeliever is condemned already.

1. Then, He is already condemned in the court of the law as a covenant, by which he is seeking to be justified and saved : Rom. iii. 19. " Now we know, that what things soever the law saith, it saith to them who are under the law: that every mouth may be stopped, and all the world may become guilty before God." Every unbeliever is upon a law-bottom, he is seeking salvation and righteousness by the works of the law, by some good thing or other, which he apprehends to be in him, or done by him, or which he hopes to do. But I may say to you, who are of this law-spirit, as Christ said to the self-righteous Pharisees, John v. 45, " There is one that accuseth you, even Moses, in whom ye trust;" where, by Moses, we must understand the law of Moses. The same say I to you, The law accuseth and condemneth, it is denouncing its heavy anathemas against you, while you cleave to it as a covenant: "As many as are of the works of the law, are under the curse; for it is written, Cursed is every one that continueth not in all things which are written in the book of the law to do them." While you are out of Christ, cleaving to the law as a husband, it lays you under the curse for every and the least failure in obedience. O Sirs, the vengeance of Heaven lies upon you while you are under the power of unbelief ; you are cursed in your basket and store, in soul and body, and all that belongs to you : and the curse not being causeless, it shall come ; yea, it cleaves to you, and will cleave to you for ever, unless by faith you flee to him who " hath redeemed us from the curse of the law. being made a curse for us."

2. The unbeliever is already condemned in the gospel-court. Now, do not mistake this way of speaking, as if when I speak of the gospel-court, I meant as if the gospel, strictly considered, condemned any man : the gospel, like its glorious Author, comes not into the world to condemn the world, but that the world, through

it, might be saved. Neither do I mean, as if there
were new precepts and penalties in the gospel, considered in a strict sense, which were never found in the
book or court of the law. This is an assertion which
has laid the foundation for a train of damnable and
soul-ruining errors ; as of the Antinomian error, in dis-
carding the whole moral law as a rule of obedience
under the gospel ; the Baxterian error, of an evangelical
righteousness different from the imputed righteousness
of Christ ; the Pelagian and Arminian error, of a sufficient grace given to every man that hears the gospel,
to believe and repent by his own power. But when I
speak of the unbeliever's being condemned in the court
of the gospel, my meaning is, that the sentence passed
against him in the court of the law, is aggreged and
heightened by his contempt of gospel-grace. All
I intend by it is comprised in that awful word, Heb.
ii. 3. " How shall we escape, if we neglect so great a
salvation ?" or that, Heb. x, 28, 29. " He that despised Moses' law, died without mercy, under two or three
witnesses ; of how much sorer punishment, suppose
ye, shall he be thought worthy, who hath trodden under foot the Son of God, and hath counted the blood
of the covenant, wherewith he was sanctified, an unholy thing ?"

3. The unbeliever is condemned already in the court
of his own conscience. Conscience is God's deputy
and vicegerent, and, in the name and authority of the
God of heaven, it keeps a court in every man's breast,
and either approves or condemns, accuseth or excus-
eth, according to the views and uptakings that it hath
of the holy law of God. When the law is only known
by conscience in the letter of it, it condemns only for
sins which lie against the letter of the law ; but when
conscience comes to be irradiated and instructed by
the Spirit of God, in the spirituality and extent of the
law, then it condemns even for these spiritual wickednesses that are of a more refined nature, and which
lodge in the high places of the soul ; of which kind is

the sin of unbelief. A natural conscience, even though assisted by external revelation, will smite a man for a thousand sins, before it gives him one check for his unbelief. This seems to be the peculiar province of the Spirit of God, to "convince the world of sin, because they believe not in Christ," John xvi. 8, 9. And O! when once conscience, by the direction of the Spirit, begins to smite for this sin of unbelief, there is no sin in the world that appears in such a formidable hue; and there is no sin that the worm of conscience will gnaw a man so much for in hell through eternity, than that he had a Saviour in his offer, and yet refused him. In a word, let a man be never so moral and sober, let him have never so much seeming peace and quiet, yet he still carries an evil conscience in his breast, till by faith he come to get "his heart sprinkled from an evil conscience by the blood of sprinkling," Heb. x. 22.

4. The unbeliever is already condemned in the court of the church; or, may I call it, in the ministerial court. Ministers, by virtue of the commission they have received from their great Lord and Master, must "go and preach the gospel to every creature," and having acted according to their commission, they must, in the same authority, declare, that he who believes this gospel, shall be saved; he who believeth not, shall be damned. Indeed, this ministerial sentence is but little regarded by a profane and secure world, who are ready to say or think, that our words are but wind. But whether sinners hear or forbear, we must, by our commission, declare to the righteous or believer, "it shall be well with him:" but "woe unto the wicked, it shall be ill with him; for the reward of his hands shall be given him." And when this ministerial sentence, whether doctrinal or judicial, is faithfully pronounced, whatever men may think of it, it is ratified in heaven: Mat. xvi. 19. "Whatsoever ye shall bind on earth, shall be bound in heaven; and whatsoever ye shall loose on earth, shall be loosed in heaven."

5. The unbeliever is condemned in the court of the great God. It is true, every one of these courts I have mentioned is his; he sits as supreme Judge in each of them : but they are only his inferior courts ; and while the sinner's sentence is in dependence before them, there is still access for an appeal by faith unto a throne of grace, or mercy-seat. But when once a man comes to be personally sisted before the bar of God at death or judgment, no further appeal can be admitted : the man then goes out of mercy's reach ; he that made him will have no mercy upon him; the things that belonged to his peace, are then for ever hid from his eyes. O that an unbelieving world may lay this to heart in time, before their case become absolutely hopeless and helpless : " Consider this, ye that forget God, lest he tear you in pieces, when there is none to deliver."

Why the unbeliever is condemned already.

1. THE unbeliever is condemned already, because, by his unbelief he has offered the highest indignity to a Trinity of persons in the glorious Godhead, that a creature is capable of. He despises the love of the Father, who out of his good-will and kindness to a lost world, "gave his only-begotten Son." He gives him to be incarnate ; he gives him unto death ; and gives him and his whole purchase in the revelation of the gospel, " that whosoever believeth in him, should not perish, but have everlasting life. But now the unbeliever he despises all the riches of this grace and love, and practically says, that the unspeakable gift of God is not worthy to be taken up at his foot. And as he despises the love of the Father, so he tramples upon the blood of the Son, as if it were an unholy thing. He says upon the matter, that Christ shed his blood in vain ; hence unbelievers are said to " crucify the Son of God afresh ;" they re-act the bloody tragedy that was once acted upon Mount Calvary ; and, upon the same account, the unbelieving communicant is said to be " guilty of

the body and blood of the Lord." Again, the unbelieving sinner, he sins against the Holy Ghost. I do
not mean that every unbeliever is guilty of the unpardonable sin, for then we needed not preach the gospel
to them. But I mean, that every unbeliever, in rejecting Christ, he runs directly cross to the work and office
of the Spirit, in the economy of redemption. It is the
office of the Spirit to " convince the world of sin, because they believe not in Christ; " but the man is so
far from owning this, that he practically denies unbelief
to be any sin at all. It is the office of the Spirit to
" convince of righteousness," i. e. of the necessity and
excellency of the righteouness of Christ for justification : but the unbeliever, he goes about to establish a
righteousness of his own, and will not submit to this
righteousness of God. It is the office of the Spirit to
glorify Christ, to " take of the things of Christ, and
show them unto us :" But the unbeliever upon the
matter says, " There is no form nor comeliness in him
why he should be desired." Thus, I say, the unbeliever
affronts a whole Trinity, Father, Son, and Holy Ghost ;
and therefore he is condemned already.

2. The unbeliever is condemned already, because he
has injured all the glorious attributes and perfections
of the divine nature. He rebels against awful and
adorable majesty and sovereignty. The authority of
God is in a peculiar manner interposed in the command
of believing; God speaks of this command as if he had
never given another command to the sons of men, 1
John iii. 23. " This is his commandment, that we should
believe on the name of his Son Jesus Christ." Now, the
unbeliever, he flies in the face of all this authority,
saying, with proud Pharaoh, " Who is the Lord, that
I should obey him?" Let the Almighty depart from
me ; for I desire not the knowledge of his ways. Again,
the man makes a mock of the master-piece of Infinite Wisdom, as though it were nothing but arrant folly. The
device of salvation through a Redeemer, is "the wisdom
of God in a mystery;" it is "hidden wisdom :" but the

unbeliever, with the Greeks, calls it " foolishness ;" and
with the Athenians, looks on it as a mere babbling,
when it is brought out in a gospel-revelation.   The
unbeliever, he also spurns against the bowels of infinite and amazing love ; yea, as it were, runs a spear into
the bowels of a compassionate God, which are sending
out a sound after him, " O turn ye, turn ye ; why will
ye die ?   As I live, I have no pleasure in your death."
He dares and challenges Omnipotency to do its worst,
while he refuses to take sanctuary in Christ, and to
turn in to the strong hold, where he may be sheltered
from the storm, wind, and tempest of divine vengeance.
He laughs at the shaking of God's spear, and the
whetting of his glittering sword.   He gives the lie
also to the veracity of God, 1 John v. 10.   " He that
believeth not God, hath made him a liar :" not as if
he could do so indeed ; for God will be true, and every
man a liar : but the unbeliever does what he can to
make God a liar.   This is the language of his sin, God
is a liar, he is not to be trusted, there is no truth in
his words.   Which is blasphemy in the highest degree.
Thus, I say, the unbelieving sinner, he injures God
in all his glorious excellencies.   And is it any wonder
then though he be condemned already ?

3. Another ground of this awful sentence is, because
the man counteracts and runs directly cross to the
most glorious designs that ever God had in view ; I
mean, his designs in the work of redemption through
Christ.   I shall only clear this in two or three instances.   (1.) God's design in redemption was the illustration and manifestation of his own glorious excellencies,
which were sullied or obscured by the sin of man :
but the unbeliever, as was showed just now, does his
uttermost to darken and affront every one of them.
(2.) God's design is, that in all things Christ should
have the pre-eminence ; that he should have " a name
above every name, that at the name of Jesus every
knee should bow."   But now the unbeliever, like the
devil, being lifted up with pride, refuses to bow, or
submit to that name, JEHOVAH-TSIDKENU, " the Lord

our righteousness," Jer. xxiii. 6. Rom. 10. 3. He refuses to own or bow unto that royal name written upon his thigh and vesture, Rev. xix. 16. The KING OF KINGS, AND LORD OF LORDS. He joins in a confederacy with those who refuse to stoop unto his royal sceptre, saying, " Let us break his bands asunder, and cast away his cords from us," Psal. ii. 3. (3.) God's design in redemption is, that grace only should reign, and that all ground of boasting and gloriation should be cut off from man for ever, so as he that glorieth may glory only in the Lord. But now the unbeliever's language is, Not grace but self shall reign. He chooses rather to be damned for ever, than submit to grace's government, " reigning through righteousness unto eternal life, by Jesus Christ our Lord." What, says the man, will not " God be pleased with thousands of rams ?" &c. If God will give him life for some equivalent, some good thing wrought in him or by him, he is content ; but to take it for nothing as the gift of free grace, through Jesus Christ our Lord, this is too low a bargain for his proud heart to stoop to. And for this pride of his heart, which makes him to run cross unto God's glorious designs in redemption, he is condemned already.

4. He is condemned already, because his sin (I mean his unbelief) is of a more criminal nature, in God's reckoning, than any other sin that can be named or thought upon. The sin of Adam, in eating the forbidden fruit, was a most aggravated crime. For a creature newly dropt out of his Creator's fingers, a creature dignified with the lively image of God upon him, exalted unto sovereignty over this lower world, having all things put under his feet; I say, for such a creature, upon a slender temptation, to turn his back on God, and cast himself into the devil's arms, to ruin himself and the whole tribe of mankind at one blow ; this, no doubt, was a most crying sin. But yet the sin of unbelief far surpasses it : for our first parents they sinned only against God as a Creator ; but the unbeliever sins against him as a

Redeemer, consequently he sins against more love than they could sin against, before the revelation of Christ. Again, unbelief is more criminal than the sin of the Jews in crucifying of the Lord of glory ; they crucified him when vailed and disguised under the form of a servant ; but the unbeliever crucifies him upon his throne, when the evidences of his being the true Messiah are completed by his resurrection from the dead, Rom. i. 4. It would be a crime of a far more capital nature, to maltreat a king sitting on the throne, with all his nobles about him, than to maltreat him when under a disguise, sitting upon the dunghill with a company of beggars about him : yet the former is the case with the unbeliever. Again, unbelief is worse than the sin of Sodom, which provoked God to rain hell out of heaven upon its inhabitants. Christ tells us that Sodom and Gomorrah will have a cold hell in comparison of these who have had the offers of a Saviour in the gospel, and yet have rejected him, Mat. xi. 24, " It shall be more tolerable for Sodom and Gomorrah in the day of judgment, than for" Chorazin, Bethsaida, Capernaum, and other cities where Christ had preached. Again, all the sins of the blinded nations are not comparable to the sin of unbelief. We have a black roll of their sins, Rom. i. toward the close : but yet Christ speaks of them as no sins, in comparison of the sin of those who remain in unbelief under the drop of the gospel ; " If I had not come, and spoken unto them, they had not had sin ; but now they have no cloak for their sin." Witchcraft is a very monstrous sin ; for a man or woman to enter into compact with the devil, and give themselves, soul and body, to be his for ever ; and yet the unbeliever he does the same upon the matter : for he is in league with hell, and with death is he at an agreement. I remember, the rebellion of Saul against the express command of God, ordering him utterly to destroy the Amalekites, is compared to the sin of witchcraft, 1 Sam. xv. 23. Now, the unbeliever (as was said) he

rebels against the greatest command that was ever issued out from the throne of the Majesty on high.   I
shall only add, that unbelief is a sin attended with ag-
gravations which are not to be found in the sin of
devils.   The devil never rejected a Saviour, as the
unbeliever does ; for " he took not on him the nature
of angels, but the seed of Abraham."   Some think,
that the devil, and his angels who joined him, were
cast out of heaven for refusing to be subject to God
in man's nature, when intimation of this design was
made in heaven.   No doubt he would have been well
enough pleased to subject himself to God, manifesting
himself in the nature of angels ; but to be subject to
God manifested in the flesh, he looked upon it as a
disparagement.   But the unbeliever he rejects God
appearing in his own nature, saying, " We will not
have this man to rule over us."   Is it any wonder
then, though the unbeliever be condemned already ?

5. He is condemned already, because unbelief is
the spring and ringleader of all other sins.   Every sin
is a turning away from the living God : and whence
comes this, but from an evil heart of unbelief? Heb.
iii. 12.   The name of the sin of unbelief may be Gad,
for a troop doth follow it.   Why are men proud ? why
are their hearts lifted up within them, as if they were
rich, and increased with goods, and stood in need of
nothing ?   Why, the reason is, they do not believe the
verdict of the Spirit of God concerning them, that they
are indeed wretched and miserable, and poor, and blind,
and naked. Why are men covetous? why have they the
world set in their hearts, but because they do not believe that Christ is a better good than this world, and
the things of it ?   Why are men uncharitable to the
poor, but because they do not believe that what is
given to the poor is lent to the Lord, and that he will
pay it again ?   Why are men secure in a way of sin,
crying, Peace, peace, but because they do not believe
that wrath and destruction from the Lord is pursuing
them ?   Why is the blessed Bible so much slighted

and neglected by many, like an almanack out of date, but because they do not believe it to be the word of God, or that eternal life is to be found therein? Why do people generally hear us, who are ministers, preaching the everlasting gospel, with such raving hearts and careless ears, but because they do not believe that we are ambassadors for Christ, and that God doth beseech them by us to be reconciled unto him? Why do many live in the neglect of prayer? Why are they so formal, heartless, and careless in prayer, but because they do not believe God to be the hearer of prayer? Why are there so many hypocrites, contenting themselves with a show of religion, but because they do not believe there is a reality in religion, and that God searches the heart, and tries the reins? Why do men remain under the power of natural enmity, but because they do not believe that God is love, 1 John iv. 16. and that through the ransom he hath found, he bears a hearty goodwill toward them? Ezek. xxxiii. 11. Whence comes that flood of profanity, which, like Jordan, has over-run all banks and bounds in our day, such as, cursing, swearing, cheating, lying, Sabbath-breaking, thefts, robberies, forgeries, and the like abominations! Why, the plain reason is, they do not believe there is a God, or that ever they shall stand before his tribunal to answer for the deeds done in the body. The plain language of the heart of unbelief is, "The Lord doth not see, neither doth the God of Jacob regard;" and therefore they give themselves loose reins in a way of sin.

To conclude this head, unbelief is the principal pillar of the devil's kingdom in the world, and in the soul of man. Let this pillar be but broken, and all his strong holds go to ruin. Faith is the radical grace, which gives life and spirit to all the other graces; it is the spring of all true gospel-obedience, therefore called "the obedience of faith:" so, in like manner, unbelief is the radical sin, which gives life and spirit unto all vicious habits and acts of disobedience in the life and conversation. Faith is a shield that beats back the fiery darts of Satan ; so unbelief is a shield that beats back all the good motions of the Spirit of God. Faith is the victory whereby we overcome the world ; unbelief is the victory whereby the world overcomes us. After all, is it any wonder though such a severe sentence pass against the unbelieving sinner, as that in my text, " He that believeth not, is condemned already ?"

Marks of Sinners yet under the Sentence of Condemnation.

1*st*, You who never yet saw yourselves to be condemned in the court of the law and conscience for sin, and particularly for the sin of unbelief, you are surely under sentence of death to this day ; for the first work of the Spirit, when he comes to liberate a poor soul from condemnation, is to " convince the world of sin ; of sin, because they believe not on him," John xvi. 8, 9.

2*dly*, You whose minds are so blinded with ignorance and prejudice against Christ, that you can see no form or comeliness in him, notwithstanding of the bright displays of his glory that are made to us in the word. " If our gospel be hid, it is hid to them that are lost : in whom the god of this world hath blinded the minds of them which believe not, lest the light of the glorious gospel of Christ, who is the image of God, should shine unto them," 2 Cor. iv. 3, 4.

3*dly*, You who are yet wedded to the law as a covenant, and are seeking life and righteousness by that first husband, you are to this moment under the sentence of death ; for " as many as are of the works of the law, are under the curse." If you never knew what it is to be dead to the law by the body of Christ, to have as little hope of life and salvation by the law and its works, as though you had never done any one duty commanded by the law in your whole life, you are yet married to the law as a husband, consequently under the law's sentence. Yea, I will adventure to say,

that the legalist, or self-righteous person, is a step farther off from heaven and eternal life, than the grossest
of sinners; for "publicans and harlots (says Christ)
shall enter into the kingdom of heaven before you."

4*thly*, You who cast off the obligation of the law as
a rule of obedience, under a pretended hope of being
saved by grace, without the works of the law. All
practical Antinomians, who are following the swing of
their own lusts, are under the power of unbelief, and,
consequently, condemned already. Away with lying,
swearing, drinking, whoring believers. Will you pretend to be the people of a holy God, the members of a
holy Jesus, the federates of a holy covenant, the heirs
of an undefiled inheritance, and yet wallow in your
sins, or yet retain any known iniquity in your hearts?
No, no. To such, not I, but God himself saith, "What
hast thou to do to declare my statutes, or that thou
shouldst take my covenant in thy mouth? seeing thou
hatest instruction, and castest my words behind thee."
O Sirs, they that are dead to the law as a covenant,
they are so far from casting off its obligation as a rule
of duty, that they bind it about them as an ornament,
choosing it for a light to their feet, and a lamp to their
paths. We are not without law to God, when under
the law to Christ. The law is so dear and sweet to
a true believer, that it is his meditation day and night.
"O how love I thy law!" says David: as if he had
said, I love it so well, that I cannot tell how well I love
it: "My soul breaketh for the longing that it hath unto
thy judgments at all times," Psalm cxix. 20.

Serious advices and directions to Unbelievers.

Is it so that every unbeliever is a condemned criminal before God? O then, Sirs, be concerned at your
hearts to get rid of that dismal sentence you are under.
What can be matter of concern, if this be not? I come,
in the name of God, to tell you that, this is not impossible; yea, I dare go further, and tell you, that if
you will but "hear, your souls shall live," and not

die under that condemnatory sentence which is gone
forth against you. I dare promise you not only a re-
prieve, but a remission ; for thus saith the great Judge,
as a reconciled God in Christ, to the poor trembling
pannel, standing condemned before the bar of his holy
law, " I, even I, am he that blotteth out thy transgressions for mine own sake, and will not remember thy
sins," Is. xliii. 25. Here is an act of grace passed at
a throne of grace, sealed with the blood of the Lamb,
published and proclaimed in the tops of the high places,
that none may pretend ignorance, and that every condemned sinner may take the benefit thereof, and come
in upon the King's royal indemnity, granted upon the
satisfaction made to justice by his eternal Son. O
then, Sirs, " Hear, and your souls shall live, and he
will make an everlasting covenant with you, even the
sure mercies of David," Is. lv. 3. "O earth, earth,
earth, hear this word of the Lord."

I come not to tell you, how you may be rich, great,
and honourable in the world ; these things are but
trifles to people in your circumstances. Should you
come to a condemned man, and talk to him of riches,
honours, crowns, robes, sceptres, kingdoms : Alas!
would he be ready to say, what is all that to me ? I
am a poor man going into another world within a few
hours ; if you can tell me how I may save my life, or
how I may get rid of my sentence, chains, prison, you
will say something to the purpose. This is the very
case with thee, O sinner ; for " by the offence of one,
judgment is come upon all men to condemnation."
And therefore, O poor criminal, listen, lend me a believing ear for a few moments, and I will tell thee how
infallibly thou shalt make thy escape.

Quest. O, may the poor criminal say, how is that ?
I answer, I have no advice to give thee but one ; it is
an old advice, a new advice, and the only advice that
can be given while the world stands ; it is the very
same which Paul and Silas gave to a poor pannel,
trembling at God's bar, crying, " What must I do to

be saved?" The plain advice they gave him, I give this day to you, Acts xvi. 31. "Believe on the Lord Jesus Christ, and thou shalt be saved;" agreeable to which are the words of Christ himself, in the first part of the verse where my text lies, "He that believeth on the Son of God, is not condemned;" and ver. 16. "Whosoever believeth in him, shall not perish, but have everlasting life."

Quest. You advise us to believe in Christ; but pray tell us, what is it to believe in him? You have the answer in your Catechism: To believe, is to "receive Christ, and to rest upon him alone for salvation, as he is offered to us in the gospel;" or, in other words, it is to trust and credit him, as the Saviour of sinners, with the salvation of thy lost soul, upon the warrant of his own call and command in the word. Christ's business and occupation is to save that which was lost. Now, you all know what it is to trust a man in his trade and occupation; you who have some business at law know what it is to trust your advocates with your most valuable concerns, and the whole management of your cause depending before the judges. Well, in like manner, to believe, is, upon the credit of God's testimony concerning Christ in the word, to trust him, as the Saviour of sinners, with the salvation of thy own soul in particular. This, I say, is the business, the office, and occupation of Christ, to save sinners; and he is so fond of employment in his trade of saving, that he says, "Come to me who will, I will in no wise cast out." And therefore trust in him in his occupation; put thy condemned soul in the hand of the sinner's Saviour, for that is to believe in him and on him. O what a happy suitable meeting is it, when the sinner and the Saviour of sinners thus meet together! Some have a notion, when we bid them believe, we bid them do some great thing as the condition of salvation. But this is a mistake. Believing is a resting from works in point of salvation, and a resting on Christ alone for salvation from sin, and all the effects of it.   It is to receive a salvation already completed and prepared to your hand, and brought near to you in the word of grace.   But I must not stand further in describing faith at present.

Quest. What influence (may you say) will our be lieving have upon our being delivered from this condemnatory sentence we are under?   *Answ.* Much every way.   For,

1. That moment thou believest, thou becomest a member of Christ, as a new covenant head.   While under the power of unbelief, thou art a member of the first Adam, and consequently under Adam's covenant, which is a cursing and condemning covenant to all who are under it, "judgment being come upon all men to condemnation," through Adam's breach of it; but in believing, thou becomest a member of Christ the second Adam, the head of the new covenant, the covenant of grace and promise, which contains nothing but blessings to the soul that takes hold of it, Rom. viii. 1. "There is therefore now no condemnation to them which are in Christ Jesus."   It is not said, there is nothing culpable or condemnable in the believer; but there is no condemnation to him; he is no more liable to the penalties of Adam's covenant, Christ, his glorious Surety, having endured these in his room and stead; and it were inconsistent with justice, to demand payment of the same debt, both from the cautioner and principal debtor.

2. To clear this yet further, the poor soul in believing is married unto a new husband, even Christ; and being under his roof, the covert of his blood and righteousness, the condemning law can have no action against it, this new and better husband having made his spouse free indeed, by the imputation of his law-magnifying righteousness: Rom. vii. 4.   "Ye are dead to the law by the body of Christ (or by the offering of his body on the cross), that ye should be married to another, even to him who is raised from the dead."   He that does that for us, which the law could

not do, through the corruption of nature ; particularly, "condemns sin in the flesh, that the righteousness of the law might be fulfilled in us. Christ is the end of the law for righteousness to every one that believeth." And if the law have its end, and be fulfilled in the believer, by virtue of his union and marriage with the Son of God, how can he be liable to condemnation, or any law penalties ?

3. That moment the condemned sinner believes in Christ, he is entered heir of a new family, a member of a new corporation : he is come, not to Mount Sinai, but to Mount Zion : not to the earthly Jerusalem, which is in bondage, but to the heavenly Jerusalem, which is free. He is " no more a stranger and foreigner, but a fellow-citizen with the saints, and of the household of God." He comes in among the " general assembly, and church of the first-born." He becomes an " heir of God, and a joint-heir with Jesus Christ ;" and the inheritance is settled upon him by a charter, which contains no irritant clauses. No, no ; having "taken hold of God's covenant by faith, he hath a name and a place within the walls of God's house, even an everlasting name, that shall not be cut off;" and therefore must needs be free from the condemnatory sentence he lay under before he believed.

4. That moment you believe, your cause is carried into a new court; I mean, from a tribunal of justice to a mercy-seat, where all the acts and interlocutors that pass are acts of grace and mercy, acts of pardon and acceptance in the beloved. No sentences of condemnation pass in the court of grace : no; this is inconsistent with the nature of the court. O let every guilty sinner, who finds himself condemned in the court of the law, and of conscience, carry his cause, by a solemn appeal, unto this court : for the court is open to all comers, and the Lord merciful and gracious, who sits upon this throne of grace, receives all appeals that are made to him, and will in no wise cast out the sinner, or cast his appeal over bar. O, there-

fore, " let us come with boldness unto a throne of grace, that we may obtain mercy, and find grace to help us in time of need."

Quest. But (may you say) if matters stand thus with a believer, that he cannot fall under the sentence of the law, cannot come into condemnation, then he may live as he lists. Does not this doctrine open a wide door for licentiousness and profanity ? for if once a man be a believer, according to this doctrine, he has nothing to fear, and so may do what he will. Were it not better for ministers to forbear doctrines that are liable to such abuse ? I answer,

1. The whole counsel of God must be revealed, and not one hoof of divine truth must be suppressed, though a whole reprobate world should break their necks on it, by wresting it to their own destruction. The gospel will be the savour of death unto some ; Christ crucified will be a stone of stumbling, and a rock of offence. But shall we, because of this, forbear to preach Christ, and his gospel ? God forbid ; we must not starve God's children, out of fear lest dogs snatch at it to their own perdition.

2. I own, that a carnal gospeller, who has some swimming notions of the grace of God in his head, may abuse the doctrine of the believer's freedom from condemnation, by virtue of his union with Christ ; but the grace of God in the heart teaches the very reverse of this, namely, to "deny all ungodliness and worldly lusts, and to live soberly, righteously, and godly, in this present world."

3. Though the believer be delivered from the law as a covenant, and its condemnatory sentence, through Christ, yet it does not in the least pave a way to licentiousness ; because at the same time that he is assoilzied and acquitted from his obligation to the law as a covenant, he comes under stronger and more powerful ties than ever to yield obedience to it as a rule of duty.

The believer under the strongest bonds to obey the law as a rule of life.

1*st,* He is still under the bond of the royal authority of the great God, both as a Creator and Redeemer. The authority and obligation of the divine law can never be dissolved, while God is God, and the creature a creature.

2*dly,* He is under the bond of interest, to obey the divine law. It is true, his obedience does not give him the title to the reward of glory; it is only his union with Christ, the heir of all things, that gives him this; but yet his own personal obedience is evidential and declarative of his title through Christ. And is it not much for the believer's interest, to have his claim to glory and everlasting life cleared up and made evident to his own soul? In this sense I understand that word, Rev. xxii. 14. " Blessed are they that do his commandments, that they may have right to the tree of life, and may enter in through the gates into the city."

3*dly,* He is still under the bond of fear : Jer. xxxii. 40. " I will put my fear in their hearts, that they shall not depart from me." This is not a slavish fear of hell and vindictive wrath, for that is inconsistent with his freedom from condemnation ; but it is a filial fear of God as a Father, flowing from an affectionate regard unto his authority, interposed in the commands of the law. Though they be not afraid of being cast into hell ; yet they " fear him who is able to cast soul and body into hell." Though they have no reason to fear him as a revenging and condemning Judge ; yet they have much reason to fear him as a fatherly Judge, lest he " visit their transgressions with the rod, and their iniquity with stripes ;" for, pass who will unpunished, they shall not pass ; " You only have I known of all the families of the earth ; therefore I will punish you for all your iniquities."

4*thly,* He is under the bond of love. He studies to love the Lord his God with all his heart, soul,

strength, and mind ; and this love of God in Christ,
like a strong cord, draws him on in the way of obedience, " I drew them with the cords of love ;" " The
love of Christ constraineth us," says Paul.   This love
laid in the believer's heart has such a force and power
with it, " that many waters cannot quench it, neither
are all floods able to drown it," Cant. viii. 7. Rom. viii.
35. 39.

5thly, He is under the bond of gratitude ; being
bought with a price, he studies to glorify God in soul
and body, which are his.   Christ having delivered
him from the hand of his enemies, he serves the Lord
without fear, in holiness and righteousness, all the days
of his life.   The believer, when delivered from the
hand of the condemning law, he says to Christ, as the
men of Israel did to Gideon, Judg. viii. 22.   " Rule
thou over us ; for thou hast delivered us from the
hand of our enemies."   Suppose a king should not
only pardon a rebel, but restore him his forfeited inheritance, advance him to the highest places of honour about the throne ; yea, make him his son, his heir,
and set him upon the throne with himself ; would not
that man be under a far greater obligation to serve
and obey the king, than if he had never received such
singular favours at his hand ?   There is no bond of
obedience like the bond of gratitude to an ingenuous
spirit.

6thly, He is under the bond of a renewed nature.
The man is made a partaker of the divine nature,
whereby the life of God, the love of God, and the law
of God, is laid in his very heart ; and this is a mighty
bond to obedience : Heb. viii. 10. " I will put my
laws into their mind, and write them in their hearts."
It is engraven there with the finger of the Holy Ghost :
his heart is cast into a divine mould, moulded into the
will of God, his will of grace, his will of precept, and
his will of providence ; so that he " delights in the
law of God, after the inward man.   The law of his
God is in his heart," and therefore " none of his steps
shall slide."

Lastly, The inhabitation of the Holy Ghost is another efficacious bond to obedience ; Ezek. xxxvi. 27. " I will put my Spirit within you, and cause you to walk in my statutes ; and ye shall keep my judgments, and do them." This law of the Spirit of life, which is in Christ Jesus, makes them " free from the law of sin and death." And being " led by the Spirit, they do not fulfil the lusts of the flesh." To conclude, that very grace of God which frees them from the law as a covenant, binds them to it as a rule, Tit. ii. 11, 12.

These are some gospel-bonds of obedience : and you who never knew what it is to have your souls under the sweet influence of these, but only obey the law with a view to purchase a title to heaven, or to redeem your souls from hell and wrath, I, in the name of God, pronounce the heavy doom of my text against you, " He that believeth not, is condemned already."*

Gracious visits of Christ, or gradual advances of the day-spring from on high.

1. THEN, there was the early visit that he made us in his eternal purpose from the ancient years of eternity, before ever the world was made : Mic. v. 2. " But thou, Beth-lehem Ephratah, though thou be little among the thousands of Judah, yet out of thee shall he come forth unto me, that is to be ruler in Is-

---

* Although true believers be not under the law as a covenant of works, to be thereby justified or condemned ; yet it is of great use to them as well as to others, in that, as a rule of life, informing them of the will of God and their duty, it directs and binds them to walk accordingly.—*Confession of Faith, chap.* 19.

While they have no concern with the covenant-law, in the matter of their justification ; they have a most lively concern with it, according to all its extent and spirituality, as a rule of life or righteousness, in the matter of their sanctification.—It is therefore to Christ that they are under the law ; while he takes the moral law, in its supernatural state, or as divested of its covenant form, for the rule of spiritual government in his mediatory kingdom.—*Gib's Sacred Contemplations.*

rael : whose goings forth have been from of old, from everlasting." Which last words may either denote the eternal generation of the Son ; he was begotten of his Father from eternity, being the same eternal, independent, self-existent God with him; or it may point out his eternal destination by the Father to be the Redeemer and Saviour of lost sinners ; agreeable unto which is that of Christ, Prov. viii. 23. " I was set up from everlasting, from the beginning, or ever the earth was." This was, as it were, his first motion toward us, though, as yet, at a great and inconceivable distance. O Sirs, wonder at this wonderful grace and love of God, that paid us a visit when he saw us in our blood, and before we had any other being, save in his own decree! " When I saw thee in thy blood, I said unto thee, Live."

2. There is a visit that he made us in our first parents after the fall, when he told them, that " the seed of the woman should bruise the head of the serpent." This was, as it were, the first peep of day-light on a lost world of mankind. As I was saying just now, no sooner had man sinned, but a dark and dismal night of wrath from the Lord of hosts did overspread our horizon, which struck our first parents with such horror, that they endeavoured to hide themselves among the bushes of Paradise : even while they are every moment expecting to be stricken through with the barbed arrows of divine vengeance and wrath, the Messiah is revealed and promised, and light and deliverance appears with him. And all the prophecies, types, promises, and ceremonies of the Old Testament dispensation, were nothing else but the gradual advances of the Sun of righteousness toward our horizon. But yet all this time the Sun is not actually arisen in our view, though after the break of day, in the first promise, the light did shine more and more brightly till the sun did actually arise. And therefore,

3. There is the visit of the day-spring from on high, in his actual incarnation or manifestation in our nature.

This was, I say, the rising of the sun in the open view of the world, which, how glorious it was, we are told by those that saw it, John i. 14. " The Word was made flesh, and dwelt among us (and we beheld his glory, the glory as of the only begotten of the Father) full of grace and truth." The angels, these morning stars, they sing together, and proclaim the tidings of his arrival, as a matter of joy and triumph, Luke ii. 10. We " bring you good tidings of great joy, which shall be to all people. For unto you is born this day, in the city of David, a Saviour, which is Christ the Lord." And thereupon they break forth with an anthem of praise, saying, " Glory to God in the highest, and on earth peace, good-will towards men." O how did this Sun of righteousness rejoice to run his race of humiliation in this lower world, having his divine glory obscured with a vail of flesh, lest his dazzling glory should have overwhelmed us ! The beams of divine glory were ever and anon breaking through the vail of flesh, in his doctrine, in his miracles, in his birth, life, death, resurrection, and ascension ; which I have not now time to insist upon. Only, I would have you to remember, that by this one visit, which he made us in our nature, which continued for the space of about three and thirty years, he fulfilled the law, satisfied divine justice, finished transgression, made an end of sin, brought in everlasting righteousness, confirmed the covenant, overthrew principalities and powers, destroyed death, opened up the way to the holy of holies, laid a bridge of communication between heaven and earth, by which God might come to man without prejudice to his justice, and man might come unto God without being consumed or overwhelmed.

4. Another visit is the day-spring of a gospel-revelation : when the glad tidings of salvation come first to be published, and " life and immortality brought to light," Mat. iv. 15, 16. to a people or nation. O what a sweet spring of day was it, when, after the resurrection of Christ, the apostles, and other ministers,

as the heralds of the great Messiah, began to proclaim
pardon, peace, and salvation through his blood, first to
the Jews, and afterwards to the Gentile nations! how
did the dark mists of Jewish rites, types, and ceremonies, and of Gentile idolatry and abominations,
evanish before the bright rays of the Sun of righteousness conveyed in the dispensation of the gospel!
and what multitudes of converts were added unto the
church, compared, for their innumerable number, unto
the drops of the dew from the womb of the morning!
And what a sweet spring of day was there in our own
land, when the gospel came at first to be preached to
our forefathers, who were lying under a dark night of
Pagan idolatry! And when after that a dark night
of Popish blindness and idolatry had overspread us
again, what a sweet day-spring from on high did visit
us in our reformation! and what a pleasant edge of
life and zeal for God and his glory was there to be
found upon the spirits of our nobles, gentry, and com-
mons, which discovered itself in their frequent renewing of their solemn covenants, to stand by, and maintain a work of reformation against the emissaries of
hell and Rome! and how signally did the Lord countenance that work by the downpouring of his Spirit,
and the remarkable success of the gospel in the conversion of many souls! So then, I say, the preaching
of the gospel in a land, or among a people, is a sweet
visit of the day-spring from on high.

5. The day of conversion is another visit of the
day-spring from on high; when "God who commanded the light to shine out of darkness, shines into
the heart, to give the light of the knowledge of the
glory of God, in the face of Jesus Christ." O how
sweet and surprising a visit is this! and what a sweet
day does then break and spring up in the soul! It
is such a visit as brings light, and such a light as turns
the shadow of death into a pleasant morning. It is a
light that not only shines upon the man, but shines
into his heart, irradiating all the powers of his soul,

and translating him from darkness to a marvellous
light. It is "the light of the knowledge of the glory
of God." The Spirit now begins to rend the face of
the covering that was upon the soul, so that the beams
of divine glory, which shined externally in a gospel
dispensation, do now break in upon the soul, changing
him from glory to glory; the Spirit now glorifies
Christ by taking the things of Christ, and showing
them unto the soul. And all this is in the face or person of Christ. The man who before could see no form
or comeliness in him why he should be desired, he
now sees him to be "fairer than the children of men,
the brightness of his Father's glory, and the express
image of his person," and his heart rises at every word
or doctrine, that has the least tendency to disparage
his divine glory. O Sirs, has the day-spring from on
high thus visited you? If so, then I may safely say,
as Christ did to Zaccheus, "This day is salvation come
to thy house," to thy heart, to thy soul.

6. There is the day-spring of a renewed manifestation of Christ, after a dark night of desertion. Perhaps the poor believer has been walking in darkness,
and could see no light; clouds and darkness were
round about him; God was hiding, Satan harassing
him with his fiery darts, iniquities prevailing, trouble
and distress surrounding him on every hand, and the
poor soul brought to that pinch, as to be crying out,
"O that it were with me as in months past! I am
cast out of his sight; his mercy is clean gone, he hath
forgotten to be gracious;" like Zion, "the Lord hath
forsaken me, and my Lord hath forgotten me."
However, at length, the day breaks, the Sun of righteousness arises, breaks through all interposing clouds,
giving such a challenge of grace as that, Is. xl. 27.
"Why sayest thou, O Jacob, and speakest, O Israel,
My way is hid from the Lord, and my judgment is
passed over from my God?" and he takes the poor
soul all in his arms and bosom, saying to it, as he did
to Ephraim, "thou art my dear son, thou art my

pleasant child, I remember thee still, my bowels are troubled for thee, I will surely have mercy upon thee; and with everlasting kindness am I now returned to thee, though for a small moment I had forsaken thee." O what a sweet visit is this, and what a sweet day breaks upon the soul! How is unbelief, jealousy, despondency, and false surmises of God put out of countenance! And heartily does the soul beast itself for its rash and hasty conclusions of the Lord's love and faithfulness, saying, "so foolish was I, and ignorant: I was as a beast before thee." O now, now, the day is again broken, and I see that "his anger endureth but a moment; in his favour is life: weeping may endure for a night, but joy cometh in the morning." Such a visit of the day-spring from on high had the spouse, Cant. iii. 1—4. and Cant. ii. 8.

7. I might tell you, that there is a sweet day-spring visit that Christ makes to his people at death and the last judgment: John xiv. 3. "I go *away, but* I will come again, and receive you unto myself, that where I am, there ye may be also." This is the day-spring and of eternal glory, which shall never suffer an eclipse, and which shall never end in a night of desertion, or affliction, or death. Lift up thy head, believer, for this day of complete redemption is drawing near; the day of complete redemption to thy soul is coming at death, and complete redemption to thy soul and body is a-coming: for "when Christ who is thy life shall appear, then shalt thou also appear with him in glory;" thou shalt then sing, and say, "Lo this is our God, we have waited for him, we will be glad and rejoice in his salvation."

What sort of a day Christ's visits bring to a lost world.

1. IT is a day of power: Psal. cx. 3. "Thy people shall be willing in the day of thy power." When he comes to visit the soul with efficacious grace, the bars of death are broken, the gates of brass are opened, the everlasting doors are lifted up, the foundations of

Satan's usurped kingdom are shaken, and the soul
translated out of darkness into the kingdom of his
dear Son ; hence we read of the revealing of God's
arm, Is. liii. 1. It is a day wherein Christ comes "travelling in the greatness of his strength," showing himself " mighty to save."

2. Christ's visits make a day of salvation to spring
from on high on the soul ; hence when Christ pays a
visit to Zaccheus, he tells him, " This day is salvation
come to thy house." Salvation follows the Saviour's
visits in his train ; salvation from the curse of the law,
the stroke of justice ; salvation from the power of sin,
the guilt of sin, the filth of sin ; salvation from " the
wrath that is to come." And when this day springs
from on high on the soul, the poor creature cannot
but say and sing, " He that is our God, is the God of
salvation ; and unto God the Lord belong the issues
from death. Salvation to our God which sitteth upon
the throne, and unto the Lamb, for ever."

3. Christ's visit brings a day of espousals with it ;
Jer. ii. 2. " Thus saith the Lord, I remember thee,
the kindness of thy youth, and the love of thine espousals.' Song iii. 11. " Go forth, O ye daughters
of Zion, and behold king Solomon with the crown
wherewith his mother crowned him in the day of his
espousals, and in the day of the gladness of his heart."
Whenever Christ approaches, and manifests his glory
to the soul, he appears as a bridegroom presenting the
marriage-contract of the covenant in his hand, saying
as the servant of Abraham to Rebekah, " Wilt thou
go with this man ?" Whereupon the soul immediately
yields itself, with heart and hand, saying, " I am the
Lord's. Whither thou goest I will go; and where thou
lodgest, I will lodge. Neither death, nor life, nor things
present, nor things to come, shall separate " me from
this better husband, " who is raised from the dead."

3. Christ's visit makes a day of liberty to spring up.
The poor creature was under the hardest bondage and
captivity, shut up in the prison of sin, shut up under

the law's curse, shut up in the very gall of bitterness ; but, O ! whenever Christ comes, he cries to the prisoners to come forth, to them that sit in dark, Show yourselves. He "proclaims liberty to the captives, and the opening of the prison to them that are bound." O Sirs, there is no liberty like that which comes with Christ's visit ; "whom the Son makes free, they are free indeed ;" hence called "the glorious liberty of the sons of God." Freedom from sin, from Satan, from the world, from unbelief, the reign of natural enmity. Christ's visit brings a year of release, a jubilee with it ; "the acceptable year of the Lord, the day of the redeemed of the Lord."

5. Christ's visit makes a day of rest to spring up to the soul. It is a Sabbath, a day of rest : for then it is that the soul enters into his rest by believing. The poor creature was wearying itself in the greatness of its way, toiling and working at the oar of the duties of the law, in order to get life and righteousness ; it was going under the weight of sin, as a burden too heavy for it to bear, going under the arrows of the Almighty, that were drinking up his spirits : but, O ! when the day springs from on high, it cries with David, " Return unto thy rest, O my soul, for the Lord hath dealt bountifully with thee." At the first sight of Christ the soul cries out, as the Lord said of Zion, " This is my rest for ever : here will I dwell, for my soul desires it, and likes it well."

6. Christ's visit from on high brings a day of love along with it : Ezek. xvi. " Thy time was a time of love," viz. when I visited thee. It is a time of love on Christ's side ; for then it is that he gives vent unto electing and redeeming love, and says to the soul, " I have loved thee with an everlasting love, and with loving-kindness have I drawn thee." His love to the poor soul was like a fire pent up in his breast, seeking a vent and longing for a vent ; but, O ! when the day springs from on high, the love of God runs out like a *river*, from " the throne of God and of the Lamb."

And then it is a day of love on the believer's side also ; the love of God being shed abroad in his heart by the Holy Ghost, it makes his heart to burn within him ; so that he loves the Lord with all his heart, soul, strength, and mind. " Many waters cannot quench love, neither are all floods able to drown it : if a man would give all the substance of his house" to draw it away from Christ "it would utterly be contemned. Who shall separate us from the love of Christ ?" &c.

7. It is a day of grace ; for then it is that "grace reigns through righteousness," in a triumphant manner. The essence of grace lies in the freedom and liberality of love, without regard unto merit, or without any manner of constraint. O how doth the freedom of grace shine with a peculiar lustre and majesty in the day of Christ's visit to the soul ! The soul that before saw God sitting on a throne of justice, expecting every moment a sentence of condemnation from him, now sees him in Christ sitting on a throne of grace, stretching out a sceptre of grace, calling the sinner to come and receive grace and mercy to help it in time of need. O how liberal is a God of grace in Christ, when the day springs from on high ! He gives himself, he gives his Son, he gives his Spirit, he gives grace, he gives glory, he gives all the sure mercies of David, and all without money or price.

8. Christ's visit is a day of wonder ; for then the man sees him whose name is " Wonderful, Counsellor, The mighty God, The everlasting Father, The Prince of peace." The man, he enters into a new world, " a new heaven, and a new earth wherein dwelleth righteousness." The man, when he looks back to his former state of darkness, deadness, distance, he cannot miss to be surprised at the wonderful alteration of affairs with him ; hence in the day of Christ's visit in the morning of conversion, the man is said to be " translated into a marvellous light." The man wonders at Christ, as though he had never heard of him before ; he wonders at the great mystery of godliness,

" God manifested in the flesh." He wonders at the
love of God in Christ, " O the height, the depth, the
breadth, and length of the love of God, which passeth
knowledge !" He wonders at the freedom, fulness,
stability of a new covenant. He wonders to see Christ,
the head of the covenant, and all the promises of it
" yea and amen in him." In a word, he wonders at
every thing ; and he wonders where his eyes were,
that he never saw these things before.

9. It is an everlasting day that springs from on
high, when Christ first visits the soul, a day that shall
never end. Indeed the light of he day may sometimes be sadly obscured, insomuch that, to the believer's sense, he may be under a dark night, and see
no light ; but, O ! whenever the sun arises, he shall
never set again : no, no ; " the Lord shall be thy everl-
lasting light, and thy God thy glory."

Beams of divine glory to be seen in the day spring from on high.

1. COME and see a beam of adorable sovereignty
in him ; for he is the most high God, and there is no
God greater than he, no God above him. Gen. xxii.
16, 17. there the angel speaks to Abraham out of
heaven, and that angel was Christ, as the apostle tells
us, Heb. vi. He makes an oath to Abraham, saying,
" In blessing I will bless thee. By myself, (says he,)
have I sworn." And if you ask the apostle, why he
did swear by himself? he will tell you, Heb. vi. 13.
that " when God made promise to Abraham, because
he could swear by no greater, he sware by himself."

2. Come and see a beam of eternity in this day-
spring ; for he is " the everlasting Father," or the Father of eternity, Is. ix. 6. " I am Alpha and Omega,
the beginning and the ending, the first and the last.
Before Abraham was, I am." He was in the beginning, John i. 1. " In the beginning was the Word,
and the Word was with God, and the Word was God."

3. Come and see a beam of unchangeableness in
this morning star, Heb. i. 10, 11, 12. compared with

Psal. cii. 25. Who reads that word, Psal. cii. "Of old hast thou laid the foundation of the earth, and the heavens are the work of thy hands," but immediately would understand it of the one only living, true, and unchangeable God? It is impossible to understand it of any other than of God himself. We see it expressly applied to Christ, Heb. i. 10, 11, 12.

4. Come and see a beam of adorable wisdom in this day-spring, viz. in an incarnate God, 1 Cor. i. 24. Christ is there called " the wisdom of God, yea, the wisdom of God in a mystery, the hidden wisdom of God ; all the treasures of wisdom and knowledge are hid in him." Never did the wisdom of God display itself after such a manner, as it hath done in Christ, in bringing these two natures of God and man, which were at an infinite distance, into a personal union one with another. O sirs, a sight of this great wonder would make you and me to join issue with the apostle, and say, " O the depth of the riches both of the wisdom and knowledge of God ! how unsearchable are his judgments, and his ways past finding out !"

5. Come and see a ray of glorious and amazing power springing up in the day-spring of his incarnation. Hence Christ is called not only *the wisdom of God*, but *the power of God.* The power of God is manifested in the creation of the world, by a word speaking ; it is manifested in the government of the world, and turning the great wheels of providence with an unerring steadiness : but never did God make such a discovery of his power as he did in Christ, when he brought infinite and finite, God and man, to centre in the person of our Immanuel. O sirs, lift up the eye of faith, and see Omnipotency exerting itself in *the man of God's right hand*, whom he hath *made strong for himself.* See him treading down the strength of hell, turning the battle to the gate, spoiling principalities and powers, destroying death by death, laying the foundation of a happy eternity, in the death and blood of his eternal Son.

6. Come and see a ray of divine holiness springing out from an incarnate Deity. Isaiah, when he saw his glory, he saw the angels covering their faces with their wings, that they might not be blinded and dazzled with the beauty of divine holiness, crying one to another, " Holy, holy, holy is the Lord of hosts ; the whole earth is full of his glory." Holiness did shine in his perfect obedience to the holy law, whereby he not only fulfilled it, but *magnified it*, and *made it honourable*. Holiness did shine in his death, wherein he gave such a discovery of his hatred of sin, that he would *finish* it, and *make an end of* it, even at the expense of his blood.

7. Come and see a ray of awful and tremendous justice shining forth in the dayspring of his incarnation. Was there ever such an act of justice put forth, as that of bruising his own Son ? Sin was found in him by imputation : " It pleased the Lord to bruise him :" he cried, " Awake, O sword, against the man that is my fellow; smite the shepherd." O sirs, come and see justice satisfied, and judgment executed on the Son of God as our surety, and this laid as the foundation of a throne of grace, that so he might be just, when he is the justifier of them that believe in Jesus.

8. Come and see a bright ray of divine mercy and love breaking forth in the day-spring of his incarnation ; the sounding of his bowels, the beating of his blessed heart. O sirs, what is Christ, but just the love of God wrapped up in flesh and blood ! 1 John iv. 9, 10. Here is the highest flight that ever the love of God took ; and higher it cannot mount. It is observed by some divines, that the other attributes of God are able to do more than they have done : infinite power can make more worlds, infinite wisdom devise greater things than ever yet appeared unto man ; but as for the love of God, it hath stretched itself to the uttermost ; it can go no further : what could he do more for us than to give his Son, the Son of his love,

to give him unto the death? and how will he not
with him freely give us all things? "O the height,
the depth, the breadth, and the length of the love of
Christ, which passeth knowledge!"

9. Come and see a glorious ray of divine faithfulness in this day-spring of a God manifested in the flesh.
God made a promise to our first parents in paradise,
that "the seed of the woman should bruise the head
of the serpent;" that is, that God should be incarnate,
and, in our nature, overturn the devil's kingdom and
government. This was the hardest promise that ever
God made, and the most difficult to accomplish.
Well, but he has done it : what was said in a way of
prophecy under the Old Testament, is now to us a
piece of glorious history, as a thing already done. O
it is done, it is done ; "God is manifested in the
flesh :" and so that first promise is fulfilled ; and it is
"a faithful saying, worthy of all acceptation." Now,
I say, seeing this promise is fulfilled, all the rest
are easy ; and we may have no manner of doubt about
them, especially considering that they are all "yea
and amen in him ;" they are all sworn to him as the
great covenant head : "Once have I sworn, I will
not lie unto David."

Pleasant sights, in the light of the Day-spring from on high.

1. COME and see the council of peace opened, and
what was transacted among the persons of the glorious
Trinity. We are all naturally fond of secrets, to know
what is in the hearts of others ; and to know what
God was doing, and what were his thoughts before the
world was made. Well, sirs, the day-spring from on
high brings this to light ; Christ has opened the book,
and loosed the seven seals of it, which none else in
heaven or earth were able to do. The Father, Son,
and Holy Ghost, were from eternity contriving a way
how sinners might be saved, in a consistency with justice and the law. Come and see the Father undertaking to send and uphold his Son in the great service

of redemption ; the Son undertaking to do his Father's will, by fulfilling the law, and satisfying justice by his death ; and the Holy Ghost undertaking the application of the whole to an elect world, in the fulness of time.

2. Come and see the temple of God opened, for the day-spring from on high discovers this also ; for the temple of God is opened now under the New Testament, a far more beautiful temple than ever Solomon's was, though it was the wonder of this lower world. But O here is a temple that is the wonder of heaven and earth, it draws all the spectators in the higher and lower house to behold it ; and, sirs, what shall I tell you, " God is in his holy temple, honour and majesty are before his face, strength and beauty are in his holy place." God dwelt in the temple of Solomon typically ; but here in the temple of the human nature he dwells really, yea, the fulness of the Godhead dwells bodily here ; and every one that sees him in this temple, sees the brightness of the Father's glory, and the express image of his person.

3. The day-spring from on high is broken ; and therefore come and see the way opened to the holiest by the blood of Jesus, even a new and living way consecrated for us. O sirs, the door of access to God was immediately condemned and shut up upon the entry of sin : but by the day-spring from on high we may see it opened again, and our way to the Father patent, and every step of the way sprinkled with the blood of the Lamb, and God crying to you to come forward to him " with boldness, " yea to " draw near with a true heart, in full assurance of faith."

4. Come and see the Red sea divided, Jordan dried up, that the Israel of God may have a safe and easy passage to the promised land of glory. O sirs, there was a Red sea of wrath, a deep Jordan of death, and of the law's curse, between us and glory, but Christ has drunk of the brook in the way, yea, he has drunk it dry by his obedience unto the death.

5. Come and see the pure river of water of life, proceeding out of the throne of God and of the Lamb. The spring of day has discovered this also, a river of pardoning, justifying, sanctifying, comforting, establishing, strengthening, and sin-killing grace, proceeding out of a throne of grace, and a voice coming out of the throne, saying, " Whosoever will, let him come, and drink of the water of life freely." " Ho, every one that thirsteth, come ye to the waters, and he that hath no money ; come ye, buy and eat, yea, come buy wine and milk, without money and without price."

6. Come and see the tree of life that grows in the upper Paradise, which bears twelve manner of fruits, and whose leaves are for the healing of the nations. O sirs, here is a sight worthy to be seen ! Indeed Christ himself, that blessed branch that springs from on high, as the text may be rendered ; the boughs of the tree are so loaden with fruit, that they bow down from heaven to earth, that we may sit down under its shadow, and taste of the sweetness of these fruits.

7. Come and see the royal law of God, which was violate and broken in the first Adam, again magnified and made honourable by Christ the second Adam, and its Lord well pleased for his righteousness' sake ; come and see this righteousness of the law fulfilled in us who believe, Christ being " the end of the law for righteousness to every one that believeth." O sirs, is not this a wonder to see God fulfilling his own law as a surety for the broken sinner, and imputing his righteousness unto us for justification ? yet this the day-spring brings to light.

8. Come and see the round sum that our Cautioner paid unto justice ; not indeed a sum of silver and gold, but the precious blood of our Lord Jesus Christ, as of a lamb without spot ; blood which is the blood of God, blood of more value than heaven and earth, blood sufficient to ransom ten thousand worlds, as to its internal value ; blood crying for better things than the blood of Abel.

9. Come and see the new covenant confirmed and established: the day-spring discovers this also. Adam's covenant was broken, and we are all lying under the curse of it by nature; but lo here a far better covenant, even a covenant of grace, whereof Christ is the surety, having sealed it with his blood, and appended new visible seals to it under the New Testament, baptism and the Lord's supper, the last of which we are this day about to celebrate.' Come and see the fulness, freedom, comely order, stability, and perpetuity of this covenant, and how it stands fast in Christ.

10. Come and see the head of the old serpent bruised, by his bruising the heel of the woman's seed; " For this purpose the Son of God was manifested, that he might destroy the works of the devil." He spoiled principalities and powers, and triumphed over them in his cross. So that, believer, thou mayest take courage, for thou hast only a routed, broken, and shattered enemy to grapple with.

11. Come and see death, that last enemy, destroyed by the death of a Redeemer; for he has destroyed death, as well as him that had the power of it. The day-spring from on high lets us see light even in the valley of the shadow of death, so as we need not fear any evil from it; but on the contrary, that we may rejoice over it as a slain and disarmed enemy, saying, ".O death, where is thy sting? O grave, where is thy victory?" Yea, the day-spring from on high lets us see through the grave, and the sweet morning of the resurrection on the other side of it; so that we may sing and say with Job, Our " Redeemer lives; and therefore though worms destroy our bodies, yet in our flesh shall we see God."

12. Come and see a complete discharge of the . debt that we were owing to justice in the resurrection of our glorious Surety. This also may be read by the light of this day-spring from on high. As Christ died for our offences, or for the punishment of our debt, so he rose again for our justification, or to declare that he had

brought in everlasting righteousness, on the account of which we are discharged of the debt, and accepted as righteous in the sight of God. O sirs, Christ rose from the dead in the capacity of a Surety and Representative ; and therefore we are said to rise in him, and with him, Col. iii. 1. Eph. ii. 6. Our Surety, he did not steal out of prison, or break it, no, but " he was taken from prison and from judgment ;" the prison-door was opened by an express order from the court of heaven; and therefore upon the third day, early in the morning, a messenger was despatched from the throne of justice to roll away the stone from the door of the sepulchre. O sirs, the lively view of this mystery of love and grace, in the resurrection of Christ, would make us all to take up that sweet doxology, 1 Pet. i. 3. " Blessed be the God and Father of our Lord Jesus Christ, the Father of mercies, which according to his abundant mercy hath begotten us again unto a lively hope, by the resurrection of Jesus Christ from the dead."

13. Come and see an angry and inexorable Deity looking out to us as a God of peace in the light of this day-spring from on high. And how can he be but a God of peace, seeing he has brought again from the dead our Lord Jesus Christ ? If he were not a God of peace, would he ever have testified his acceptance of the satisfaction at the hand of our Surety at such a rate ? No surely. And therefore when we look up to a risen Christ, sitting in our nature at the right hand of God, we may warrantably conclude, that " though he was angry, yet his anger is turned away. Behold, God is our salvation : we will trust and not be afraid : for the Lord Jehovah is our strength and our song, he also is become our salvation," Is. xiii. 1, 2.

14. As an evidence that he is a God of peace, a reconciled God in Christ, come and see him making for all people in the mount of the gospel, " a feast of fat things, a feast of wines on the lees, of fat things full of marrow, of wines on the lees well refined." O sirs,

the day-spring from on high discovers a well-covered table of the blessings of heaven, of all the sure mercies of David, presented and ready for our entertainment, with a frank invitation and call unto every one, to come and eat of this bread, and drink of the wine that he has mingled. And, O sirs, we tell you in the name of God, that you have as good a right to take and eat, to receive and apply Christ and his whole fulness, as held out in the dispensation of the gospel, as ever you had to a meal of meat when it was set before you. And therefore, " Eat, O friends, drink, yea, drink abundantly, O beloved."

15. Come and see that life that was lost, forfeited by the fall of the first Adam, recovered and lying ready for us in the hand of the second Adam. Christ, as the second Adam, he stept into the room of the first Adam, and fulfilled every point and article of the covenant of works, which required perfect obedience as the condition of life. And therefore life now belongs to him; and accordingly this life is in the Son. God has given unto him eternal life, John xvii. 2. 1 John v. 11. He is the new heir of eternal life, and of all the promises that belong to it. O sirs, is not this good news, that our Goel, our kind kinsman, has bought back the mortgaged and forfeited inheritance?

16. Come and see our Kinsman and elder Brother assigning and making over himself and his right to eternal life unto us in a new testament, or new and better covenant. " God hath given eternal life unto us" in his word of grace and promise, 1 John v. 11. This testament, this promise, this grant, this offer of life, is made to every man and woman that hears the gospel, or reads the Bible, with an express command to " search the testament," that therein he may find " eternal life :" and we had need to "fear, lest, a promise being left us of entering into his rest, any of us should come short of it." O sirs, be not like fools, having a price put in their hands, yet have no wisdom to improve it.

17. Come and see to read, and subscribe all these as the record of a glorious Trinity ; for the day-spring from on high discovers this also. The " Three that bear record in heaven, the Father, the Word, and the Spirit," they attest all this in the capacity of habile witnesses ; they have deponed upon the truth of every thing I have been saying ; particularly on the truth of this, " that God hath given to us eternal life : and this life is in his Son." And therefore come and see to set to your seal, " that God is true ;" for if you do not, you make God a " liar" by unbelief ; for which crime you are " condemned already "

Object. 1. These are indeed sweet discoveries that are made by the day-spring from on high ; but O, say you, how shall we come by a sight of them ? *Answ.* You must open your eyes, that the light of day may enter in to you. Let the day-light shine never so bright, or whatsoever beautiful desireable objects may be round about a man, yet he cannot see while his eyes are shut ; and therefore you must needs open your eyes, if you would see the day-spring from on high and the discoveries that it makes.

Object. 2. You bid me open mine eyes, but, alas ! I want a visive faculty, and you may as well bid a man that is stone blind open his eyes, as speak after that manner to me ; for I was born blind, and therefore cannot see. *Answ.* 1. We would think you brought a good length, if you were but sensible really of your spiritual or soul blindness ; for the most part that we have to deal with, they are just like the Pharisees, who said unto Christ, " Are we blind also ?" They think they see well enough, while indeed they are stark blind like moles in the things of God. (2.) Remember that it is not we, but God himself, that bids you who are blind look up and see this day-spring from on high : Is. xlii. 1. " Behold my servant whom I up-hold. Look unto me, and be ye saved." And there-fore, in obedience unto him who commands, attempt, and mint, and essay to open your eyes, and see these

glorious things, which the day-spring from on high
discovers ; for it is in this way that he recovers sight
to the blind.   He that bids you look and see, he also
counsels you to buy of him eye-salve that you may see.
(3.) Follow the example of blind Bartimeus.   Christ
is coming this way to-day, for his way is in his sanctuary : and while you hear the sound of his retinue
or attendants on this occasion, lift up your voice to
him and say, " Jesus, thou son of David, have mercy on
me, and let me receive my sight :" only ask in faith,
nothing doubting of his ability and willingness to do
it ; for it is his promise to open blind eyes, to make
the lame to leap like a hart, and the tongue of the
dumb to sing.

Objections to the entertainments of Christ's visits, answered.

Object. 1. You bid me entertain his gospel visit :
but, alas ! I am aye thinking, that his visit is to others,
and not to me.   I answer, That is just the art and
subterfuge of unbelief; under a pretended modesty it
will not receive Christ's visits, as if his visits were for
others, and not for the soul in particular.   But, sirs,
allow me to tell you, that though unbelief may carry a
blush of pretended humility in its countenance, yet it is
nothing but devilish pride at the root or bottom.   But
whatever may be the surmise of unbelief, yet I can
assure you in the name of God, that his visit in the
gospel-dispensation is to thee, man, to thee, woman, as
particularly as if thou wert named by name and sirname ; he stands at every individual man's door, and
knocks, saying, " Open to me, and I will come in ;"
and to you is the voice of wisdom directed, even to
the " sons of men."   And therefore, take it home and
apply it to yourself in particular, with as great assurance as though you heard a voice out of heaven calling
you by name and sirname.

Object. 2. I would fain receive his visit, but I think
I see great mountains between him and me, he is

behind the mountain, and I am far off from him, and
he is far away from me. *Answ.* Jesus Christ is not
so far off, as every unbelieving heart would suggest;
for, behold he standeth behind our wall, waiting to
see if we will rue upon him and receive his visit.
Thou sayest thou art afar off, but his voice is even
unto such, Is. lvii. 19. " I create the fruit of the lips ;
peace, peace to him that is far off, and to him that is
near." "The promise is unto you, and to your children,
and to all that are afar off," says Peter to his hearers,
Acts ii. 39, and the same say I unto you. You say
there are mountains between him and you ; but " behold he cometh leaping upon the mountains, and skip-
ing upon the hills." If thou wilt but give him entertainment, he will make all mountains as a plain at his
presence ; " Jordan is driven back ; the mountains
skip away like rams, and the little hills like lambs."

Object. 3. My sins are so great, that he will never
visit me. *Answ.* See him visiting the greatest of sinners with the offers of his love and grace, Is. i. 18.
" Come now, and let us reason together, saith the
Lord ; though your sins be as scarlet, they shall be as
white as snow ; though they be red like crimson, they
shall be as wool."

Object. 4. I am a condemned sinner, under sentence
of death from the holy law ; therefore his visits cannot
be to me. *Answ.* He comes to visit you and me, because we are condemned to die. His visit that he
made in his incarnation, was, " to them that were
under the law, to redeem them that we might receive
the adoption of sons." And if you will receive his visit
in the gospel, the sentence of condemnation shall that
moment be taken off you ; for " he that believeth on
the Son of God, is not condemned ; yea, there is no
condemnation to them which are in Christ Jesus."

Object. 5. I am vile, filthy, and polluted ; therefore
his visit is not to me. *Answ.* " Though thou hast lien
among the pots he will make thee as the wings of a
dove, covered with silver, and her feathers with yellow

gold." He is saying to thee this day, " Wilt thou be made clean ? I will sprinkle clean water upon thee, and thou shalt be clean ; from all thy filthiness, and from all thine idols will I cleanse thee."

Object. 6. I have refused his visits in the gospel so often, that I am afraid he is gone, he is departed, and will never come again. *Answ.* Jer. iii. 1. " Though thou hast played the harlot with many lovers ; yet return again unto me, saith the Lord." He calls backsliders to return, and he will *heal their backslidings.*

Object. 7. I do not know if I be among the elect that were given to Christ ; and, if so, his visit is not to me. *Answ.* His visits and offers of grace in the gospel are to sinners, to " men, and to the sons of men ;" and if thou find thy name there, thou hast no reason to exclude thyself. You begin at the wrong end of things, when you meddle with the decrees of God, which are secret things, and belong to the Lord. Look ye to things that are revealed in the word first, and that is the way to win to the knowledge of the secret designs of his heart ; and, for your encouragement to take this way, I never yet heard it miscarry. They who take God at his word, and hold him at his word, they find themselves among the number of the elect ; whereas they that will needs begin first to search God's secret decree, and die in this way of doing, they find themselves among the number of reprobates in the end. And therefore meddle you first with things that are revealed, search the Scriptures, consult the oracles of the word, read your name there, and see whether or not Christ be speaking to you, and visiting you there : and thus you shall know that love lies in his heart to you.

Object. 8. You bid me receive Christ's visits ; but alas! how can I do it? I have no entertainment for him. *Answ.* He brings entertainment with him. When his visit is received, he comes and he sups with us, and causes us to sup with him. If you think that you have any entertainment but what he brings with him, I have little hope of you indeed.

Object. 9. I am a poor hard-hearted sinner, my heart is like a piece of the nether millstone. *Answ.* Entertain his visit; for " he takes away the stony heart, and gives the heart of flesh."

Object. 10. I am so impotent, that I cannot open to him when he comes; how can I receive his visit, when the key of the heart hangs only at his own girdle? *Answ.* He comes to visit thee because thou art impotent, to give thee strength; and he has said, that he will " give power to the faint, and increase strength to them that have no might:" only put the work in his hand, and he will work all thy works in thee and for thee.

Advantages of gracious visits of the day-spring from on high.

1. His visits by his Spirit's influences and communications of his grace and love, whether in conversion, or in renewed manifestations, bring life with them unto the dead sinner, or languishing saint and believer. And O how can it be otherwise! for he is the Lord and Prince of life; he is " the resurrection and the life, the way, the truth, and the life." Whenever he comes near unto the dead sinner, the Spirit of life enters into him, though he were as dead as the dry bones that were scattered about the grave's mouth. And whenever he comes near unto the languishing believer, he revives as the corn, when a warm shower of the rain of heaven falls upon it. The fields laugh, the bread of corn, that was withered, pricks up its head, and looks pleasant, with a shower of rain, and a warm blink of the sun. Just the same effect has a visit of the day-spring from on high on the soul; " I will be as the dew unto Israel:" and what then? " He shall grow as the lily, and cast forth his roots as Lebanon. They that dwell under his shadow shall return, they shall revive

as the corn, and grow as the vine, the scent thereof shall be as the wine of Lebanon," Hos. xiv. 5, 7.

2. A visit of this day-spring from on high brings riches and wealth along with it; and no wonder, for he is "the heir of all things." " In him are hid all the treasures of wisdom and knowledge;" unsearchable riches are with him. And when he visits the soul with his salvation, he does as the wise men of the east did to him, when they came and saw him in his swaddling clothes, they made a present of gold to him; and he makes a present of gold when he visits the soul, far better than the gold of Ophir; yea, he says to the soul, as he said to his Father in his prayer, John xvii. "All mine are thine;" all that I have is thine; I am thine, and all that follow me; all the treasures of my grace and glory, I assign them, and make them over unto thee. O! is not such a visit valuable?

3. Christ's visit brings honour along with it: "Riches and honour are with me." "Ever since thou wast precious in my sight, thou hast been honourable." When this day-spring visits the soul, he sets the soul on high; "he raiseth up the poor *soul* out of the dust, and lifteth the needy out of the dunghill: that he may set him with princes, even with the princes of his people," Psal. cxiii. 7, 8. It is nothing else but a visit of this day-spring, that makes the believer "more excellent than his neighbour."

4. His visits bring alacrity, joy, and cheerfulness along with them. When this day-star arises in the heart of a sinner, that has been wading through the blackness and darkness of a law tempest, O what a strange alteration doth he make in the soul! The poor thing that was expecting every moment to drop into hell, begins to rejoice in the hope of the glory of God. David, Psal. cxvi. 3. he is crying out through the terrors of the law and of conscience, and the melancholy apprehensions of vindictive wrath, " The sorrows of death compassed me, and the pains of hell gat hold upon me; I found trouble and sorrow:" how-

ever the day-spring from on high arises on his soul,
in the following part of the psalm, and thereupon he
alters his note, and chants and sings to the praises of
the Lord, saying, " I was brought low, and he helped
me. What shall I render unto the Lord, for all his
benefits towards me ? I will take the cup of salvation,
and call upon the name of the Lord."

5. A visit of the day-spring brings strength with it to
the weak and weary soul. " He giveth power to the
faint, and increaseth strength to them that have no
might." O ! whenever he comes he makes the feeble
as David, and as the angel of God before him. The
man who had no might becomes strong for work, saying, " Lord, what wilt thou have me to do ?" strong
for war, the arms of his hands are " made strong through
the mighty God of Jacob ;" strong for enduring trials
and afflictions, saying, " Though he should kill me,
yet will I trust in him." " Who shall separate me from
the love of Christ ?" In a word, the man that was
sinking through despondency, by the prevailing of
unbelief, becomes "strong in faith, giving glory to
God."

6. A visit of the day-spring from on high makes the
timorous and faint-hearted soul courageous, and bold
as a lion. The poor thing that durst not look God in
the face, through a sense of guilt, but was like the timorous dove, hiding himself in the clefts of the rock,
when a visit comes, it lifts up its face with a holy and
humble boldness : " Having, brethren, boldness to enter into the holiest by the blood of Jesus." It comes
with boldness to a throne of grace, for " grace and
mercy to help in time of need." And then the man
gets boldness toward all his accusers, so that he dare
look the law and conscience, the devil and the world,
in the face, saying, " Who can lay any thing to my
charge ? It is God that justifieth : who is he that
condemneth ? It is Christ that died, yea rather that is
risen again, who is even at the right hand of God,
who also maketh intercession for me." He gets such

boldness, by the visit of the day-spring from on high, that he can now "go to the altar of God, to God *his* exceeding joy." He is not afraid to go to a communion-table, lest he eat and drink damnation to his soul ; no, he sees it to be a cup of salvation : and therefore eats and drinks with a merry heart, knowing his right to the children's bread. He gets such boldness and courage when the visit comes, when the day-spring arises, that he dare look death, the king of terrors, in the face, with a holy courage and bravery, saying with David, Psal. xxiii. 4. " Yea, though I walk through the valley of the shadow of death, I will fear no evil : for thou art with me, thy rod and thy staff they comfort me." Thus you see some of the great advantages that do accompany and attend a visit of the day-spring from on high.

What in Christ our Faith should fix upon that he may visit us.

1. TAKE a view of his name, and let faith and hope fasten upon that : Is. l. 10. " Let him that walketh in darkness, and sees no light, trust in the name of the Lord, and stay upon his God." O sirs, every name of his is like ointment poured forth. Will you but think little upon that name " Immanuel, God with us," and see if your faith and hope can fasten upon that for a visit of the day-spring from on high to your souls : he is not only God-man in our nature, but he is " God with us ;" that is, he is not in Christ a God against us, but a God for us, a God with us, a God on our side, he is on our side to take part with us against all deadly : Psal. cix. 31. " He standeth at the right hand of the poor to save him from those that would condemn his soul." He takes part with the sinner, to save him from his own wrath, the curse and condemnation of his own law, to save him from Satan and the world, and death and hell ; he is aye with us a reconciled God, a pitying, pardoning, saving God in Christ. And therefore, say, I trust, that he who is " Immanuel, God with us," will even pay me a visit from on high.

2. Let faith and hope for a visit fasten upon his word of grace and promise. O, may not the soul say, has he not said, "Wherever I cause my name to be remembered, I will come unto you and bless you. Lo, I am with you, unto the end of the world." Has he not promised his presence and countenance to his own ordinances? Has he not promised to "pour water upon him that is thirsty, and floods upon the dry ground?" Has he not said, "I will be as the dew unto Israel, that his goings forth are prepared as the morning, and that he will come unto us as the rain : as the latter and former rain unto the earth, that the second day he will revive us, and the third day he will raise us up, and we shall live in his sight?" O has he said it, and will he not do it? has he spoken, and shall it not come to pass? Yea, he will, for "faithful is he that hath promised."

Object. But the promise is not mine, I have no claim to it. *Answ.* The promise is to every one that hears it ; and if you will but set to the seal of faith that God is true, it is yours in possession ; and if you believe the promise, you have the thing promised.

3. Ground your faith for a visit of the day-spring from on high, upon the visits that he has already made to you. O, may faith say, did the day-spring from on high, rejoice from eternity "in the habitable parts of the earth, and were his delights with the sons of men," before ever the foundations of the world were laid? O has he made such an amazing stoop, as to be manifested in the flesh? Is he become my brother, bone of my bone, and flesh of my flesh? Has he showed such good-will towards men, as to be made in the likeness of sinful flesh? And does he visit me in a gospel-dispensation and word of grace, with the offers of his grace and love, and eternal life through him? Doth he stand at my door and knock, saying, "Open unto me, and I will come in?" Yet shall I doubt of his love to me? shall I doubt whether he will come and sup with me, and I with him? Yea, surely he will

do it; for he that hath done the greater, he will also do the lesser.

4. Let faith fasten upon the suretyship of Christ, or his substitution in our room and stead. He gave bond, may faith say, to his Father, for the payment of my debt, and accordingly has paid it to the uttermost farthing; he has paid my debt to the precept of the law by his perfect obedience, he has paid what I owed to the penalty of the law and justice by his death on the cross; and so he has blotted out the hand-writing that was against me: he was "made sin for *me*, that *I* might be made the righteousness of God in him; *he* was made a curse, that *I* might inherit the blessing;' he has made way for his visit to my soul in a way of love by the complete satisfaction of justice; and now his name is "the Lord our righteousness." And why then should I doubt but that the day-spring from on high shall pay me a visit of love?

5. Let faith fasten upon the relation that he bears to us in all his saving offices. He is "our Lord Jesus Christ; to us *this* son is given, to us *this* child is born;" he was not born for himself but for us; and whatever he is as Mediator, that he is unto us. O he is the Saviour of sinners; and will not the sinner's Saviour pay the sinner a visit, that is looking and longing for a visit from him? He is a prophet, a teacher of the will of God; and will not the master pay the scholars a visit? He is a Priest ordained for men, and a merciful and faithful high Priest, a high Priest touched with the feeling of our infirmities; and may not I then call for a visit from him? He is an Advocate for the transgressor; and will not the Advocate visit his client? He is our King; and will not the King pay a visit to the subject? will he not rule and subdue his enemies in my heart? He is our Shepherd; and will not the Shepherd of Israel visit his flock? Yea, he will; for "he carries the lambs in his bosom, and gently leads those that are with young." He is our Physician that came to heal the diseased, his name is *Jehovah-Rophi;*

and will not the Physician pay a visit to his patient?
Thus, I say, let faith fix on the relation that he bears
to us in his person and offices.

6. Let faith and hope for a visit of love fix on the
excellency of his loving-kindness manifested in Christ,
and displayed in the word of grace. O sirs, " God is
love," love is the regnant attribute of his nature ; and
his whole design in sending of his Son, and in a gospel
dispensation, is to persuade us of his love. Now, let
faith fix on this, and persuade itself, that he will come,
and will not tarry. See this laid as a ground of faith
and hope, Psal. xxxvi. 6. " How excellent is thy loving-
kindness, O God! therefore the children of men put
their trust under the shadow of thy wings."

A *serious word to Sinners.*

I WOULD cry to all mankind, if my voice could reach
them, to come and get their losses repaired by the Son
of God, who " restores that which he took not away."
Do not say, " I am rich, and increased with goods, and
stand in need of nothing ;" for I can assure you, that
he who is infinitely wise, and knows you better than
you do yourselves, declares, that you are " poor, miserable, wretched, blind, and naked," through the robbery that sin hath committed.—Say you, I cannot get
time to come, because of worldly business. But let
me tell you, that your worldly business is but mere
trifles in comparison with this ; therefore make all other
business but by-business in comparison with this one
thing needful.—Says another, I will get time enough
afterwards. I will tell you, delays are dangerous ;
what know you, man, what a day may bring forth?
Death may come, and then you are gone for ever
through eternity.—Says another, I am afraid the time
is gone already, and that he will not make a reparation
of my losses. No, sirs, I will tell you, that while there
is life there is hope, and the Son of God is at the back
of your heart, crying, " Behold, I stand at the door
and knock; if any man (out of hell) hear my voice,

and open to me, I will come in to him, and will sup
with him, and he with me."—But O, say you, I fear
my losses are irreparable. I will tell you, poor sinner,
as broken a ship has come to land, as we use to say ;
as great sinners as you, have got a reparation of their
losses, and a full pardon to the boot. What think you
of Manasseh, and Mary Magdalene, and Paul? The
same hand that repaired their losses is ready to repair
yours ; " his hand is not shortened, that it cannot save,"
&c.—Says another, What if I be not among the number of the elect? I answer, You have nothing ado
with election ; for " secret things belong unto the
Lord, but that which is revealed unto us and our children." Election does not belong directly and immediately to the business of believing, but only things revealed; and if revealed things belong unto us, then
put in your claim ; for " the promise is to you and your
seed."—Say you, I am impotent, and cannot come.
I answer, That was one of the losses Christ came to
restore ; " he gives strength to the weak, and to them
that have no might he increaseth strength."—Say you,
My will is an iron sinew, it will not answer. *Answ.*
He that restores that which he took not away, offers to
restore your good heart and your will. " Thy people
shall be willing in the day of thy power," Ezek. xxvi.
26. " I will take away the heart of stone, and give the
heart of flesh."—Says another, I would fain come to
get my losses repaired, but I think when I come to
him he boasts me away. Do not think so ; for he says,
" Whosoever will come to me I will in no wise cast
out." When he frowns upon you, and calls you a dog,
be as the Syrophenician woman, do not give over, and
you shall prevail, " Truth, Lord, I am a dog, yet the
dogs eat of the crumbs that fall from the master's table :" the Lord repaired her losses, and granted her all
the desires of her heart.

A view of the good of God's chosen people.

1. I SAY, will you take a view of his love and kind

ness towards you " before time," and let that engage
you to cry, What is man that thou takest knowledge
of him, and of me in particular? (1.) Then I say,
Let us run back to the ancient years of eternity,
and see how the kindness and love of God to man did
appear then; " when God looked upon you in your
blood, he said unto you, Live, and your time was a
time of love." Oh! is it not wonderful to see electing
love passing by the fallen angels, and resting upon
such a poor pitiful creature as fallen sinful man? And
when he passed by kings and princes, noble and wise,
and rich, and many thousands that the world would
think would have been the objects of his love, he passed
by them, and pitched upon thee, a poor creature that no
body regards. Oh! is not thy soul saying, " What am
I that God hath taken such knowledge of me? that he
should have loved me with an everlasting love? that
he should have chosen me before the foundations of
the world? and predestinated me to the adoption of
children, by Jesus Christ to himself?" (2.) The decree of electing love being passed, a method must be
found out for thy salvation, consistent with the honour
of the law and justice of God: and therefore, as if
man, and the son of man, had been some great creature,
and thou in particular, believer, a council of the Trinity
must be called to advise the matter; and thus the
plan of thy salvation was laid.—Oh, says the eternal
Father, my love is set upon a remnant of Adam's family,
and I have proposed to save them, and to bring them
to glory: but oh, how shall I put them among
the children? I see that they will violate my law, and
become liable to my wrath and justice, and my love
to them cannot vent in a prejudice unto justice: and
therefore, O Son of my eternal love, I set thee up, and
ordain thee to assume their nature in the fulness of
time; a body for this end have I prepared for thee,
that thou mayest, as their Surety and Redeemer, fulfil my law in their room, and satisfy my justice, by the
sacrifice of thy death: and I hereupon promise, that

I will stand by thee in the work; mine arm shall strengthen thee; I will raise thee from the dead, and set thee on my right hand; and I will give them as a seed to serve thee, thou shalt be their Head, their Husband, their Advocate, and Mediator, and thou shalt reign over them as a peculiar kingdom, for ever and for ever.——I agree with my whole heart to the overture, says the eternal Son; " Lo, I come; in the volume of thy book it is written of me : I delight to do thy will, O my God ;" yea, this law of redemption is within my heart; it is seated in the midst of my bowels. ——Agrees to it, says the Holy Ghost : I will form his human nature, by my overshadowing power, in the womb of the virgin : I will sanctify his human nature, and make it a fit residence for the fulness of the Godhead to dwell in, that out of that fulness, they may receive grace for grace : I will take of the things that are his, and show them unto them; and carry on the work of sanctification in them, till they be brought unto glory.——Thus, I say, the plan and method of thy salvation was laid, believer, in eternity, before the foundation of the world was laid. O then, shall not the consideration of all this make us cry, " Lord, what is man that thou takest knowledge of him ? or the son of man, that thou makest account of him ?"

2. Let us come down from eternity to time, and see what work is made, in the execution of this glorious project of free grace and love towards man. This world being created, as a theatre upon which the glorious scene was to be acted; man is brought forth into the stage; a covenant of works transacted between God and him by the breach of which man is plunged into an abyss of misery and sin. But no sooner is he fallen, but the eternal purpose and project of infinite love and wisdom begins to break forth; and so the scene of grace begins to be acted. When man is trembling at the apprehensions of being stricken through with the flaming sword of justice, a promise of relief and deliverance breaks out from under the dark cloud

of wrath, " That the seed of the woman should bruise the head of the serpent." An angry and offended God on a sudden becomes IMMANUEL, God with us, to avenge the quarrel upon the old serpent, for the hurt he had done his viceroy and representative in this lower world. This grace contained in the first promise is gradually opened in promises, types, and prophecies, during the Old Testament economy ; until, according to the concert in the council of peace, and declared resolution in paradise, the great and renowned champion, the Son of God, actually takes the field : and having put on the coat of the human nature that his Father had provided for him, he works wonders in it for that petty creature man, that he might bring about his salvation. What did he? say you. *Answ.* Oh! What did he not, that was necessary to break up the way, and clear the passage to glory and eternal life, for man ? Why, in so many words (for I cannot insist on particulars), by his obedience to the death, He finishes transgression, and makes an end of sin ; he makes reconciliation for iniquity : he brings in an everlasting righteousness. He confirms a new covenant with many : he makes the sacrifice and oblation to cease, and unhinges the Mosaic economy ; he reveals the .counsel of God anent redemption ; opens up the mystery of salvation in his doctrine ; confirms it from heaven by a multitude of miracles; he magnifies the law and makes it honourable ; he spoils principalities and powers, and triumphs over them in his cross; through death he destroys death, and him that had the power of death ; he wrests the keys of death out of the devil's hand, and takes them into his own custody, that he might make it a passage to glory, instead of being a passage to hell : he dies for our offences, and rises again for our justification ; he ascends up into heaven with a shout of triumph and victory ; and sits down on the right hand of the Majesty on high, as the public Head and Representative of his friends on earth, and to " appear in the presence of God for them." A little after he is set down upon the throne, he pours down his Spirit like the rushing of a mighty wind, upon his disciples at Pentecost ; and gives gifts unto men ; gives some apostles, some prophets, some evangelists, some pastors, some teachers ; and sends them abroad with a power of working miracles, and of speaking all langua- ges ; to proclaim the glory of his finished salvation to every creature under heaven : That whosoever believed in him might not perish, but have everlasting life. And oh ! may not a reflex view of all this work about *man* make us cry, " Lord, what is man that thou takest know- ledge of him ? or what the son of man that thou makest so great account of him ?"

Well, is that all ? No ; for he doth yet more for man in time. Having finished the salvation of man in a way of purchase, his voice is unto men, and the sons of men ; he proclaims his salvation unto the ends of the earth, and causes the joyful sound of the gospel- trumpet to be heard to the world's end. And oh ! what wonders doth he work here to make way for the salvation of poor man ! A throne of grace is reared, to which man may have recourse with boldness, " that he may obtain grace, and find mercy to help him in every time of need. Acts of grace are emitted from this throne, indemnities, promises, and proclamations of grace : " Ho, every one that thirsteth, come ye to the waters : and he that hath no money, let him come," &c. Heralds are sent abroad to proclaim the grace of God through Christ to man, and to lift up their voice in the tops of the high places ; a word of reconciliation is committed unto them : and they as ambassadors for Christ, pray men and the sons of men, to be reconciled unto God : because Christ was made sin for us, that we might be made the righteous- ness of God through him. The great store-houses of grace are opened ; his righteousness and salvation brought near to every one's door in a dispensed gospel, with a voice from heaven, Come and welcome to Christ and all his fulness. He stands with outstretched arms

of redeeming love, crying, "Behold me, behold me!
O how would I gather you, as a hen gathers her
chickens under her wings!" O what is man that he
is thus mindful of him! But then what work is he at
with man after all this, in order to the effectual application of the purchased and exhibited salvation! The
hammer of the law must be applied, in order to break
the rocky heart in pieces; the fallow ground must be
plowed up, to prepare it for the reception of the incorruptible seed of gospel truth; the strong holds of Satan
must be pulled down; the high imaginations of the heart
levelled: Satan and proud self must be dethroned. The
sinner is dead, buried, and stinking in the grave of sin;
the stone must be rolled away from the sepulchre, and
wonders must be showed unto the dead, the spirit of life
must breathe upon the dry bones: the sinner is blind,
and he must have his eyes opened; he is a prisoner, and
his chains of captivity must be loosed; the obstinate
iron sinew of his will must be bended by the almighty
power of God, and "he persuaded and enabled to embrace Christ, and salvation through him, as he is freely
offered in the gospel." The sinner being thus translated
from death to life, from darkness to God's marvellous
light, in effectual calling, O what work doth the Lord
make about the poor inconsiderable creature! how
doth he heap favours and privileges, one after another,
upon him! He betrothes the poor forlorn creature to
himself, as if it had been a chaste virgin, makes it the
bride, the Lamb's wife, and says to it, Now, "thy
Maker is thine Husband, the Lord of Hosts is his
name," &c. He takes away the filthy rags, and clothes
it with change of raiment, even the white linen of his
own everlasting righteousness, and makes it to sing
that song, Is. lxi. 10. "I will greatly rejoice in the
Lord, my soul shall be joyful in my God; for he hath
clothed me with the garments of salvation, he hath
covered me with the robe of righteousness, as a bridegroom decketh himself with ornaments, and as a bride
adorneth herself with her jewels." He takes the bur-

den of all the debt it owed unto justice upon himself, and stands between it and all charges that law and justice had against it, enabling it to say, Who can lay any thing to my charge? it is God that justifieth, who is he that condemneth? it is Christ that died, yea, rather that is risen again, who is even at the right hand of God, who also maketh intercession for us: he becomes an everlasting Father to the poor creature, and puts it among the children, making it an heir of God, and a joint heir with himself, and says to it, Wilt thou not from this time cry unto me, My Father, &c. He puts the beauty of his own holiness upon the soul, and makes it like " the king's daughter, all glorious within," like the embroideries of needle-work; he maketh it " like the wings of a dove, covered with silver, and her feathers with yellow gold:" he visits the soul frequently, and manifests himself to it, so as he does not manifest himself to the world; he waters it with the dew of his Spirit, like the vineyard of red wine; he breathes on it by his Spirit, makes the north and south wind to awake, come and blow on it, whereby the graces of the Spirit, like so many spices, are made to send forth a pleasant smell; he bears it company through fire and water, and never leaves it: he makes the man to dwell in the secret of his presence and under his shadow, and as the mountains are round about Jerusalem, so his attributes pitch their tents on every hand of it for its defence; he plants a guard of angels about his bride, for her honour and safety, as a lifeguard, Heb. i. ult. and in a word, he keeps it by his power through faith unto salvation; makes goodness and mercy to follow it; and at last divides Jordan and brings it home, under a guard of angels, to the promised land of glory, and presents it before his Father " without spot or wrinkle, or any such thing." And upon a review of all this that he doth before time, and in time, may we not justly cry out in a rapture of admiration, " Lord, what is man!"

3. If we follow the Lord's way with men, from an

eternity past, through time, to an eternity to come, we
shall see just cause to cry, " What is man?"—but here
a vail lies between us and that glory and happiness that
God has ordained and designed for man in the world
to come.   And the things there ordained for man are
so great, that "eye hath not seen, nor ear heard, neither have entered into the heart of man to conceive,
the things which God hath prepared for them that love
him," 1 Cor. ii. 9.   What thinkest thou, believer, of
being "for ever with the Lord," and of having " places
among them that stand by," and beholding the glory
of God and of the Lamb? what thinkest thou of coming in person to " Mount Zion, the city of the living
God, the heavenly Jerusalem " above, described Rev.
xxi. whose wall is of jasper, and the city itself of
pure gold, like unto transparent glass ; where there is
no need of the sun or moon, or of these ordinances,
word and sacraments, and ministers, because the glory
of the Lord doth lighten it, and the Lamb is the light
thereof? what thinkest thou, believer, of coming to
the general assembly, and church of the first-born,
which are written in heaven? what thinkest thou of
joining an "innumerable company of angels, and the
spirits of just men made perfect, who sing a new song,
crying, " Salvation to our God, and to the Lamb, for
ever and ever."   Rev. vii. 10. " Worthy is the Lamb
that was slain, to receive power, and riches, and wisdom, and strength, and honour, and glory, and blessing?" what thinkest thou of coming to God the judge
of all, as thy God and Father? what thinkest thou of
coming to Jesus the mediator of the new covenant:
and of seeing him no more darkly as through a glass,
but face to face, seeing him as he is, and beholding
the glory that his Father hath given him?" what thinkest thou of sitting down at the table that shall never
be drawn, and of eating and drinking with him, and
the ransomed company, in the kingdom of heaven?
Mat. xxvi. 29. " I will not drink henceforth," said he,
at the institution of the supper, before he died, " of

the fruit of the vine, until that day when I drink it new with you in my Father's kingdom." What thinkest thou of these new scenes of glory, wisdom, power, holiness, justice, mercy, grace, and love, and faithfulness that will be opening through eternity, in the immediate vision of God, and in the works of creation, providence, and redemption ; every one of which will fill thy soul with a new rapture of wonder and praise ? what thinkest thou of sitting down with Christ victoriously upon his throne, as he also overcame, and is set down with his Father upon his throne ? what thinkest thou of possessing these thrones in glory, that became vacant by the apostasy of the angels that fell ? what thinkest thou of ruling the nations with a rod of iron ? of binding their kings with chains, and their nobles with fetters of iron ? yet this honour have all the saints, 1 Cor. vi. 2. " Do ye not know, that the saints shall judge the world ?" ver. 3. " Know ye not that we shall judge angels ?" what thinkest thou of eating of the hidden manna, and the fruits of that tree which grows in the midst of the paradise of God ; which beareth twelve manner of fruits every month, and whose leaves are for the healing of the nations ? what thinkest thou of entering into these ivory palaces of glory, with joy and triumph, on every side, the house of many mansions, the house of Christ's Father, " whose builder and maker is God ?" thou shalt be satisfied then, to the full, with the fatness of his house, and drink of the rivers of his pleasures. What thinkest thou of becoming a pillar in the temple of God, where thou shalt go no more out, and having Christ's name, his Father's name, and the name of the city of our God written on thee for ever ? what thinkest thou of being for ever freed and delivered of all these burdens under which thou groanest ? of all these fiery darts whereby thou art now harassed ? of all these oppressions, fears, and challenges ? of all these tears, sorrows, and afflictions, which make thee to go through the world, with a bowed down back, hanging thy harp upon the willows ? what thinkest thou of these eternal things, that are shortly to be possessed ? of an eternal God, an eternal life, an eternal light, eternal love, eternal rest, eternal vision and fruition, eternal likeness and conformity to the Lord, that are abiding thee ? what thinkest thou of the "crown of glory that fadeth not away ?" what thinkest thou of a kingdom that shall never be moved : an inheritance that is incorruptible, and undefiled, and that fadeth not away ? what thinkest thou of having these twilight blinks of glory through the vail, turned into an eternal day of glory ? for there the Sun of righteousness shall never set, never, never be eclipsed.   O sirs, all this, and ten thousand, thousand, thousand times more than I can tell you, is prepared for you on the other side of death ; and after all, have we not reason to sing and say, as in the text, "Lord, what is man that thou takest knowledge of him ? or what the son of man, that thou makest such account of him ?"

Isaiah xlii. 21. *explained.* " *The Lord is well pleased for his righteousness sake ; he will magnify the law and make it honourable.*

WHERE we may notice, 1. The great and glorious party here spoken of, and that is *the Lord,* or as in the original, *Jehovah* the righteous Judge, the offended Lord and Lawgiver, to whose wrath all mankind are obnoxious and liable, through the breach and violation of the first covenant.

2. Something asserted concerning him, which may arrest the attention of all mankind, and fill their hearts with joy, and their mouths with praises, and that is, that he is well pleased.   Whenever man had sinned, the anger and wrath of God was kindled against him, and his fury was breaking out like fire, and nothing remained for poor man, but a fearful looking for of wrath, and fiery indignation, to consume him and all his posterity, as a company of traitors and rebels ; but here is a surprising declaration, that though he was angry, yet his anger is turned away, his frowns are turned into smiles ; "the Lord Jehovah is well pleased."   Again,

3. We have the cause and ground of this surprising declaration. Why, what is the cause of his being well pleased? It is "for his righteousness sake;" not for the sake of any ransom, atonement, or satisfaction, that the sinner could make, for no man can by any means redeem his own or his brother's soul, nor give unto God a ransom for it. The redemption of the soul is precious, and ceaseth for ever as to him; but it is "for his righteousness sake," who finished transgression, and made an end of sin, who makes reconciliation for iniquity, and so brings in an everlasting righteousness; and without it he cannot look with pleasure on any of Adam's race; while Christ becomes the end of the law for righteousness, he fulfils the precept, and undergoes the penalty of it, whereupon the Lord declares himself to be "well pleased for his righteousness sake."

4. We have the reason why the Lord Jehovah sustains the righteousness of the Surety in the room of the sinner, or why he is so "well pleased for his righteousness sake;" why "he shall magnify the law and make it honourable," the holy law of God given unto man in innocency as a covenant or an eternal rule of righteousness, was violate and broken, and the authority of the great Lawgiver affronted and contemned by man's disobedience: but Christ as our Surety, he is made of a woman, and made under the law; and by bringing in everlasting righteousness, he not only fulfilled the law, both in its precept and penalty, but he magnifies it and makes it honourable; he adds a new lustre and glory unto the law, which it never had before, through the dignity of his person who obeys it.

Some read the latter clause of the verse thus, "He shall magnify the law, and make (him) honourable:" and so the meaning is this: 1. Christ shall not only repair the honour of the law, but restore honour to God the great Lawgiver; and, indeed, never was there such a revenue of glory and honour brought in to the crown of heaven, as by the obedience and satisfaction of

Christ : "Now (says Christ) is the son of man glorified, and God is glorified in him." Through Christ, God can save sinners, and give vent to his love, grace, and mercy, upon terms that are honourable to his law, justice, holiness, severity, and other perfections, that were lesed and injured by the sin of man. Or, 2. "He shall magnify the law and make him (*i. e.* Christ) honourable ;" and so the latter clause of the verse is a promise of the Father unto the Son, that, upon his repairing the honour of the law by his humiliation, he would make him honourable by a glorious exaltation, he would give him a name above every name.

Observations concerning the Law of God which man has transgressed.

1. KNOW, that the *law* here principally intended is the moral law of the ten commandments, at first engraven upon the hearts of our first parents at their creation, and afterwards because that edition or copy of it was much obliterated and defaced by the fall, published to Israel from the mouth of God upon mount Sinai, and written upon tables of stone, and laid up in the ark for the use of Israel. This, I say, is the law here intended. The ceremonial and judicial law were things peculiar unto the Jews, or commonwealth of Israel; but the moral law had a being so soon as man was created, and is binding upon all nations. For the breach of this law man was condemned, and all his posterity laid under the curse ; and therefore this must be the law which Christ, as our Surety, came to magnify and make honourable. And concerning it, I offer,

1*st*, That the moral law is nothing else but a transcript of the original holiness and purity of God's nature. God's essential holiness and righteousness was too bright and dazzling a pattern for man, even in a state of innocency ; and therefore he transcribes a copy of it, and pictures it out upon the heart of man, that he might make it the rule of his obedience in heart and in life, requiring him to be holy as he is holy.

2dly, The law being a copy or emanation of God's holiness and righteousness, it must be dearer to him than heaven and earth, or the whole frame of nature. Hence is that of Christ, Mat. v. 17, 18. " Think not that I am come to destroy the law and the prophets ; I am not come to destroy, but to fulfil.   Verily I say unto you, Till heaven and earth pass, one jot or tittle shall in no ways pass from the law, till all be fulfilled." Sirs, whatever mean or low thoughts we may have of the law, through the blindness of our minds, yet I can assure you, that it is such a sacred thing with God, that he will sooner unhinge the frame of nature, and reduce it to its original nothing, than suffer it to be trampled upon by sinners, without showing a suitable resentment.

3dly, This law was given to our first parents under the form of a covenant : a promise of life being made to them, upon condition of their yielding a perfect obedience ; and a threatening of death added, in case of disobedience, " In the day thou eatest, thou shalt surely die."   In this covenant Adam stood as the public head and representative of all his posterity : had he continued in his obedience to the law of that covenant, eternal life had been conferred on him, and all his posterity, by virtue of the promise of God ; the sum and substance of that covenant being, as the apostle tells us, " the man who doeth these things shall live by them."

4thly, Man being left to the freedom of his own will, through the flattering hisses of the old serpent, did break the law of God, and so forfeited his title to life by virtue of that covenant ; and brought himself, and all his posterity, under the curse or penalty of death temporal, spiritual, and eternal, Rom. v. 12. " By one man sin entered into the world, and death by sin ; and so death passed upon all men, for that all have sinned."

5thly, The law being broken and violated by sin, the honour of the law, and the authority of God, the

great Lawgiver, are, as it were, laid in the dust, and
trampled under foot, by the rebellious and disobedient
sinner. When man sinned, he, upon the matter, denied that the law was holy, just, and good : and, at the
same time, disowned God for a sovereign, saying, with
proud Pharaoh, " Who is the Lord, that I should obey
him ? I myself am lord, and will come no more unto
thee." In a word, every sin, every transgression of
the law, is a breaking God's bands, and a casting his
cords from us, and a saying practically, " Let the Almighty depart from us, for we desire not the knowledge
of his ways." And what an insufferable affront and indignity is this, for worm man to offer unto the " high
and lofty One that inhabits eternity ?" and what a
wonder is it, that " indignation and wrath, tribulation
and anguish," does not pursue every sinner through
eternity?

6thly, The law being violated, and the Lawgiver
affronted, in such a way as has been hinted, the salvation of sinners by the law, and the works of it, becomes
utterly impossible, unless the honour of the law, and
of the great Lawgiver, be repaired and restored some
how or other. It is among the irreversible decrees of
heaven, that " in his sight no flesh living shall be justified," unless the holiness of the law be vindicated by
a perfect obedience to its precepts, and a complete satisfaction be given unto justice for the injuries done to
the honour of the great Lord and Lawgiver : without
this, " he will by no means acquit the guilty." Thus
matters stood with Adam before the first promise of
Christ, and thus matters stand with all his posterity,
until we fly to him, who is " the end of the law for
righteousness to every one that believeth."

How Christ magnifies the law and makes it honourable.

Now, for clearing this matter, I would have you to
consider, that the moral law comes under a twofold
consideration ; it may be considered as a covenant, and
as a rule of life. As a covenant, promising the reward

of life eternal to every one that yields a perfect obedience to its commandments, and threatening death
eternal to every one that fails in the performance of this
condition : or it may be considered as a rule of obedience, simply prescribing the duty which the rational
creature owes unto God, its great Creator, and Preserver, and Benefactor, without any promise of life or
threatening of death annexed to it, which gives it its
covenant form. Now, Christ magnified the law, and
made it honourable, under both these views and
considerations.

First, As a covenant, he magnifies it, and makes it
honourable ; and this he did, by fulfilling all its demands. As I hinted already, there were three things
which the law insists upon from fallen man, by virtue
of the covenant-transaction between God and Adam in
a state of innocency. 1. Holiness of nature. 2. Righteousness of life. 3. Satisfaction for sin and disobedience : None of which we are in the least capable to
afford ; but every one of them is completely afforded
in Christ.

1. I say, the law, as a covenant, demands of us a
perfect holiness and rectitude in our very natures. This
God gave unto Adam in innocency ; for he made him
upright after his own image. This uprightness and
integrity of nature was quite lost by the fall ; we are
" conceived in sin, and shapen in iniquity : the whole
head is sick, and the whole heart faint : from the sole
of the foot, even unto the head, there is nothing but
wounds, and bruises, and putrifying sores." Hence
we are " by nature the children of wrath :" so that the
law cannot find a holy, pure, and innocent nature,
among any sprung of Adam by natural generation.
But this demand of the law is fulfilled in Christ, the
second Adam, as the public head and representative of
his spiritual seed ; for " he was conceived by the power
of the Holy Ghost, in the womb of the virgin, and
born of her without sin :" Luke i. 35. ' That holy
thing, which shall be born of thee." That holy thing

that is, that innocent human nature which shall be born of thee. Heb. vii. 26. He is "holy, harmless, undefiled, separate from sinners." The law requires of every son of Adam, that he should have a nature as upright and holy as that which he received from God, the great Lawgiver, at his creation. This is absolutely impossible for us to give, but it is found in Christ; for in him the human nature is also restored unto its integrity and perfection; and every believer being in him, as their public head and representative, they are in the reckoning of the law born holy in Christ, the second Adam, even as they were created holy in the first Adam. Hence believers are said to be complete in him, Col. ii. 10. They have a complete holiness of nature in him. This, according to the demand of the law, is continued in Christ: for the law not only demands that our nature should be holy, but that we should persevere and continue in this condition. Now, this demand of the law is fully answered in Christ; for in him our nature continues to be perfectly holy for ever, however unholy it may be in us personally or abstractly considered : and God looking upon our nature, as it is in him, not as it is in us, sees us altogether fair and perfect in holiness in him, not in the least marred : according to what we have, Cant. iv. 7. " Thou art all fair, my love, there is no spot in thee." And thus, this first demand of the law is fulfilled in Christ, as to the perfect holiness of our nature.

2. The law not only demands a perfect holiness of nature, but also a perfect and sinless obedience of life. The language of the law, as a covenant unto all the sons of Adam, is, " He that doth these things shall live by them. If thou wilt enter into life, keep the commandments." We must "continue in all things which are written in the book of the law to do them." But now this demand of the law cannot be answered or fulfilled by us ; for ' no mere man since the fall is able perfectly to keep the commandments of God, but doth daily break them in thought, word, and deed :' Our

nature, as you were hearing, being wholly corrupted, every thought and imagination is evil only and continually. Now, although this active, perfect obedience by the law, cannot be yielded by any of mankind, descending from Adam by natural generation, yet it hath its demand from Christ our glorious Surety, Head, and Representative. The law required of us, that our obedience should be universal, perfect, and constant: these are all to be found in the obedience our Surety yielded unto it. For,

(1.) His obedience to the law as our Surety is universal; all things written in the book of the law must be obeyed: if there be the least failure of obedience as to any one jot, or any the least of its commandments, it lays the man under the curse. Now, I say, Christ did every thing that the law required; he fulfilled all righteousness; he did "no violence, neither was guile found in his mouth."

(2.) His obedience to the law was every way perfect as to the manner. The law required that we not only do every thing that it requires, but that we love the Lord, and serve him, with all the heart, and with all the soul, and with all the strength, and with all the mind, and our neighbour as ourselves." Oh! who among all Adam's race can obey and love the Lord after this manner? Well, but this is done in Christ: love to God and man shined to its perfection in him, and in the whole course of his obedience.

(3.) His obedience was constant, and continued unto the very end. Thus the law required that we should not only do all things, but "continue in all things which are written in the book of the law to do them." Man "being in honour continueth not;" and in the best state, in his best frames, cannot continue in such an universal and perfect obedience, as the law requires, for one moment; but Christ our glorious Surety, continued in an universal and perfect obedience, to the very end; from his birth to the grave; from his womb to the tomb. Hence we are told, Philip. ii. 8. That

he was "obedient to death;" and John xvii. That
he finished the work which the Father gave him to do.
Thus you see the law is magnified and made honourable, as to this demand of righteousness of life, in
Christ our glorious Surety; and this is what divines
commonly call his active obedience.

3 Another thing that the law demands of fallen man,
is a complete satisfaction unto justice, in consequence
of the penalty or sentence of the law; " In the day
thou eatest thereof thou shalt surely die." The veracity and faithfulness of God was engaged in this
threatening, and justice stood upon its execution, insomuch that without death, or shedding of blood, there
could be no remission of sin. Now, supposing that
the threatening of death temporal, spiritual, and eternal, had been executed upon Adam and his posterity
for ever, the law and justice of God would have been
glorified in our ruin; but yet it could never have been
said that the law and justice of God were satisfied, far
less could they have been magnified and made honourable : but by the death and sufferings of the Son of
God in our room and stead, the penalty of the law is
so fulfilled, and the justice of God so fully satisfied,
that the Lord Jehovah declares himself " well pleased
for his righteousness sake," the law being thereby
" magnified and made honourable." It was the man
who is God's fellow, and who thinks " it not robbery
to be equal with God," who became a curse and a
sacrifice for us. The best blood of the whole creation
goes for the satisfaction of law and justice. And thus
you see how all the demands of the law are satisfied to
the full in Christ : and thus he magnifies the law to
the full as a covenant.

Secondly, Christ magnifies the law, not only as a
covenant, but likewise as a rule of life, and this he doth
several ways.

1. By writing a fair copy of obedience to it, in his
own example, for the imitation of all his followers.
Christ calls the law, as a rule of obedience, his yoke,

" Take my yoke upon you ; and to make the yoke
easy to his friends, he first wears it, and smoothes it
himself, that it might not gall their necks ; hence we
are told, that he has left " us an example that we should
follow his steps ;" and we are so to walk even as he
walked, to follow him, and to run our race looking
unto him, as our glorious Pattern of obedience. We
must be holy, " as he that hath called us is holy,"

2. By explaining it in its utmost extent, for as David tells us, " it is exceeding broad." The Jewish
doctors, in order to establish a righteousness of their
own, they pared off the spirituality of the law, and confined the meaning of it to the bare letter ; but Christ,
in his sermon upon the mount, vindicates the law from
these narrow and corrupt glosses, and lays it open in
its extent and spirituality, showing, that the law of
God not only concerned the external man, or overt acts
of the life, but reached the heart, and the innermost
recesses of the soul, as you see, Mat. v. where he tells
them, that rash anger was murder in the eye of the
holy law, and that a lascivious look towards a woman
was heart-adultery, and the like.

3. By establishing the obligation of it as a rule of
obedience unto all his followers. Although indeed he
dissolves the obligation of it as a covenant to all believers, so as they are neither to be justified nor condemned by it, yet he establishes it, I say, as a rule of
duty even to believers, as well as others, " Think not
that I am come to destroy the law or the prophets, nay,
I am not come to destroy, but to fulfil it," Math. v.
17. Rom. iii. at the close, " Do we then make void the
law through faith ? God forbid : yea we establish the
law." The law is now delivered to us in the hand of
a Mediator ; it has lost nothing of its original authority
as coming from a God-creator, but this law of the
Creator receives an additional authority, as being issued
to us through a God-redeemer.

4. By writing it upon the heart of all his followers,
by the finger of his eternal Spirit, according to that

promise, Jer. xxxi. 33. "I will put my law in their inward parts, and write it in their hearts, and will be their God, and they shall be my people." Whenever a soul is called effectually by the word and Spirit of Christ, he, that moment, inlays a principle of holiness, or conformity to the law, in its heart; hence are these breathings of soul after obedience to it that we find so frequent among the saints; "Let my heart be found in thy statutes: O that my ways were directed to keep thy statutes: Hold up my goings in thy paths, that my footsteps slip not."

5. By enforcing obedience to the law among all his followers, by stronger motives than the law itself, abstractly considered, could afford. Death, hell, and ruin are the principal motives that the law makes use of in exacting obedience from fallen men: In the day that thou eatest thereof, thou shalt surely die: The soul that sinneth it shall die: Indignation and wrath, tribulation and anguish, upon every soul of man that doeth evil. But now Christ in the gospel does not drag but draws the soul sweetly into the ways of obedience, by the consideration of redeeming love; he draws them with the "cords of a man, and with the bands of love: The love of Christ constrains me (says Paul:) If ye love me, keep my commandments." He sets them at liberty from wrath, and the curse, and then calls them "to serve him without fear, in holiness and righteousness, all the days of their life:" and so he makes his yoke easy, and his burden light.

6. By actuating them in their obedience to the law by his own Spirit, according to that promise of the covenant, Ezek. xxxvi. 27. "I will put my Spirit within you, and cause you to walk in my statutes, and ye shall keep my judgments, and do them." Hereby they are made to study holiness "in all manner of conversation, and the light of their obedience and holiness in their walk shines forth, so as others seeing their good works, are made to "glorify their Father which is in heaven."

Thus you see how Christ magnifies the law and makes it honourable, as a covenant, fulfilling the righteousness of it in his own person, as our Surety, and as a rule of obedience in the hearts and lives of his followers.*

How to know whether the Righteousness of the Law be fulfilled in us.

1*st*, I ASK, has the law slain you, and put you out of conceit of your own righteousness? Paul, before his conversion, was a mighty man for the law, and he thought himself alive because of his obedience to the law, and his zeal for it, being " touching the law blame-less:" But Oh! when the commandment came, in its spirituality, sin revived and he died ; he saw that, not-withstanding all his pretended obedience to the law, and his zeal for it he was but a dead man ; and then, what

* To be under the law to God, is, without question, to be under the law of God; whatever it may be judged to import more, it can import no less : therefore to be under the law to Christ, is to be under the law of Christ. This text gives a plain and decisive answer to the question, How the believer is under the law of God ? namely, as he is under the law to Christ.—He who hath believed on Jesus Christ, though he be freed from the curse of the law, is not freed from the command and obedience of the law, but tied thereunto by a new obligation, and a new command from Christ, which new com-mand from Christ importeth help to obey the command.—*Notes on the Marrow.*

The authority and obligation of the law of nature, which is the same as the law of the ten commandments, being founded in the nature of God, the Almighty Creator and Sovereign Ruler of men, are *necessary, immutable, and eternal.* They were the same before that law received the form of a covenant of works that they are after it has received this form, and that they are and will continue to be, after it has dropped this form. It is divested of its covenant form to all who are ritually united to the last Adam, who have communion with him in his righteousness, and who are instated in the covenant of grace. But though it is to them wholly denuded of its covenant form, yet it has lost nothing of its original authority and obligation. Now that it is taken in under the covenant of grace, and made the instrument of government, in the spiritual kingdom of Christ, it re-tains all the authority over believers that as a covenant of works it has over unregenerate sinners. It is given to believers as a rule to *direct* them, and as an authoritative law to *bind* them to holy obedi-ence.—*Colquhoun's Law and Gospel.*

things were gain to him, these he counted loss, and
particularly he saw that his own righteousness was but
dung and loss. Oh! says he, "I through the law
am dead to the law," and to all righteousness by the
works of the law. Now try yourselves by this; has
the law come with such power upon thy conscience,
as to break all these rotten planks of the covenant
of works to pieces, on which you was swimming for
your life?

2dly, I ask you, where have you set down your stand
for eternity, and for an awful tribunal? I am sure, if
the righteousness of the law be fulfilled in you through
faith in Christ, you have set it down only upon the
foundation of the law-magnifying righteousness of
Christ, saying with the church, "Surely in the Lord
only have I righteousness;" and in this only will ye
be confident, as the ground of your acceptance here,
and of your through-bearing before the bar of the great
God. When you look to the holy law, and your own
personal obedience to it, you will be ready to cry,
Away with it, it is but as filthy rags; if thou, Lord,
shouldst mark iniquities, O Lord, who shall stand?
But when you look to the law, as magnified and made
honourable by Christ, you will be ready to say, In
this, and in this alone, will I be confident; in him will
I be justified, and in him alone will I glory, as the Lord
my righteousness. And whenever the law or conscience
charges you with the debt of obedience to it, as the
condition of life, you will be ready to say, I indeed
own myself a debtor to thee in point of obedience, as
a rule, but in point of righteousness and justification,
I owe thee nothing at all; no, I am dead to the law,
through my better Husband, who has in my name
magnified and made it honourable, and therefore to
him thou must go for payment of that debt.

3dly, If you be under the covering of that righteousness which magnifies the law, I am sure you will
put all the honour you can upon the law as a rule of
obedience, and your gratitude to him who fulfilled the

law for you as a covenant, will be as oil to your chariot wheels in running the ways of his commandments. Your hearts will be so enlarged in love and gratitude, that his commandments will not be grievous to you ; no, but you will " delight in the law of the Lord, after the inward man." His yoke will be easy, and his burden will be light to you.

You to whom the way of holy obedience is a burden, and who are never in your element but when you are " fulfilling the lusts of the flesh," by lying, swearing, drinking, Sabbath-breaking, do not imagine that ever you have come in under this law-magnifying righteousness : Why ? because the law, as a rule, is none of your delight.

4thly, You will be concerned to magnify him, who magnified the law as your Surety. The high praises of the Redeemer will be much in your mouth : you will think and speak honourably of him, upon all occasions, like these who are clad with the white livery of his righteousness. In mount Zion they cry, " Worthy is the Lamb that was slain. Salvation to our God, and to the Lamb, for ever and ever." Oh, men are blessed in him with a perfect righteousness, and therefore let all nations and generations call him blessed, Psal. lxxii. at the close.

5thly, You will be on all occasions improving the righteousness of Christ by faith, for all the ends and uses of it which I mentioned, when discoursing of the excellency of this righteousness. You will improve it as a ransom unto justice, to deliver you from going down to the pit ; you will improve it as a laver, to wash you from sin and from uncleanness ; as a spiritual banquet, on which you will feed your hungry souls, for it is meat indeed and drink indeed ; as a robe to cover your nakedness, and the best robe whereby to appear in the presence of God ; as a shade to defend you from the scorching heat of the fiery law, or an awakened conscience ; as a refuge to shelter you when pursued by avenging justice ; as a ladder by which you will ascend unto communion with God, here and hereafter; and as the only title and foundation of your claim to eternal life. Thus, I say, you will be constantly improving the righteousness of Christ by faith, for some of these ends and uses; and in this sense we may understand that word of the apostle, Rom. i. "The righteousness of God revealed from faith to faith." It is that which faith fastens upon at first for justification, and it is that which faith is continually afterwards applying for some good use or other, in the soul's progress in the way to glory.

6*thly*, If the righteousness of the law be fulfilled in you, through the righteousness brought in by the Messiah, you will have many an inward battle with sinful and legal self. The apostle Paul, who gloried in the righteousness of Christ, and preached the mystery of justification to others, more than ever any mere man did, yet we find he has many an intestine combat with self, Rom. vii. 23. "But I see another law in my members warring against the law of my mind, and bringing me into captivity to the law of sin which is in my members: O wretched man that I am, who shall deliver me? You, who say that ye submit and trust to the righteousness of Christ, as the only ground of your justification and acceptance, and yet have no struggle with this home-bred enemy, and are not laid in the dust before the Lord because of its prevalency, I dread, whatever orthodox heads you may have, yet your hearts are not soundly settled upon the foundation of the law-magnifying righteousness of Christ; and my reason for it is, because in every believer there is, through the remains of indwelling corruption, such a strong bias towards the law as a covenant, and towards sin, as gives him continual matter of exercise, insomuch that his heart is just like a field of battle where two armies meet, and contend for the victory one against another? "What will you see in the Shulamite? as it were the company of two armies?" the flesh lusting against the spirit, and the spirit against the flesh, and these are contrary, the one to the other. The motions of sin which a man finds in his members are continual matter of humiliation to him, and set him a-work to mortify the deeds of the body, to crucify the flesh, with the affections and lusts thereof; and the strong bias that he finds in his soul towards the law as a covenant fills him with fears and jealousies, lest he never yet in reality submitted to the righteousness of Christ, which sets him a-work to examine and prove himself, whether he has ever yet won Christ, and is found in him, having that "righteousness which is through the faith of Jesus Christ." You that never knew any thing of this, and the like exercise of spirit in your souls, I dread that you are yet strangers to a real closing with the righteousness which is brought in by the great Messiah.

7thly, When conscience is bleeding through some wound that you have got from an arrow of law-terror, or when the guilt of sin is staring you in the face, and an angry and frowning God, whither do you fly, or run for ease and relief? As for the desperate sinner, he drowns the voice of conscience with diversions and recreations. They will, like Saul, sometimes take up the timbrel and harp; or, like Cain, when God and conscience were crying for vengeance against him for the blood of his brother Abel, he goes into the land of Nod, and diverts himself with building cities and houses. As for the hypocrite he wraps himself up in his profession, and feigned graces, and there he finds ease. As for the legalist, when he is wounded with the terrors of God, being married to the law, he runs to the duties and works of the law, and studies to please God, and satisfy the cries of his conscience with these. But as for the believer, the whole creation cannot give him ease, till, by a renewed act of faith, he get in under the shadow of that everlasting righteousness, by which the law is magnified and made honourable, until he see God well pleased for this righteousness' sake, and sensibly smiling on his soul again through this righteousness; this, and nothing but this, can yield comfort. And Oh! when he sees God smiling on him through this righteousness, this puts gladness in his heart more than when corn, wine, and oil, did abound. Try yourselves by this.

In a word, if the righteousness of the law be fulfilled in you through the righteousness of the Messiah, the life you live in the world will be by faith in the Son of God, and ye will not reckon so much that ye live, but that Christ liveth in you. Many a flight will thy soul be taking to him upon the wings of faith and love, as the Lord thy righteousness. Whenever you look towards the majesty of God, and view his unspotted holiness and unbiassed justice; whenever thou looks upon the fiery law, or hears a thunder-clap from mount Sinai; whenever thou looks into another world, or an awful tribunal; whenever thou looks to the depravation of thy nature, and the innumerable evils that compass thee about; whenever thou looks to the melancholy aspect of providence, thy soul will aye be taking the other flight by faith unto Christ, as thy Surety and Redeemer; and the viewing the law magnified, and justice satisfied, and God reconciled in the person and undertaking of Christ; and whenever thou looks to him, thou wilt find thy spirit lightened and eased, and be ready to say with David, " Return unto thy rest, O my soul; for the Lord hath dealt bountifully with thee."

The spiritual marriage between Christ and his people illustrated.

1*st*, GOD the Father, from all eternity, had a purpose of marriage betwixt his own beloved Son, and a select company of the fallen race and posterity of Adam; hence Christ tells us, Mat. xxii. 2. " The kingdom of heaven is like unto a certain King who made a marriage for his son." The marriage was made in the purpose of God from eternity, and the bride was given unto the Bridegroom before ever she had a being, " Thine they were, and thou gavest them me," John xvii. 8. Psal. ii. " I shall give thee the heathen for thine inheritance, and the uttermost parts of the earth for thy possession." And that they were given him in a design of marriage, is plain from what the Lord says to, and concerning the church of the Gentiles, by the spirit of prophecy, long before their being called by the gospel, Is. liv. 1, 5. "Sing, O barren, thou that didst not bear; for more are the children of the desolate, than the children of the married wife." And ver. 5. " Thy Maker is thine Husband, the Lord of hosts is his name.

2dly, This proposal of marriage with a bride of Adam's family was graciously received and entertained by the Son of God before the world was made, Prov. viii. 3. He rejoiced in the habitable parts of the earth, and his delights were with the sons of men.—" I delight to do thy will, O my God," says he, Psal. xl. 8. *q. d.* I consent to, and am heartily willing and content; a bargain be it; let it be registrated in the volume of thy book; *i. e.* Let it be entered into the records of heaven, and an extract thereof be given out in the scriptures of truth unto sinners of mankind, that they may have their thoughts about it.

3dly, So much was the heart of the Bridegroom set upon the match, that he undertook to remove all impediments that lay in the way: and indeed the impediments were so great and insuperable, that nothing but almighty power, inspired with infinite and amazing love, could remove them: and yet they are all rolled away by the wisdom and power of the Bridegroom.

The *first* impediment was the inequality of the parties as to their nature. We may easily suppose that the question would be put upon the first proposal of the marriage, How shall God and man, the Creator and the creature, be ever brought unto a conjugal relation? The distance of natures is infinite, and therefore there can be no marriage. Well, (says the Son of God, the brightness of the Father's glory, and the express image of his person,) [he takes care to remove that,] I will assume the human nature unto a personal union; I will become the seed of the woman, the seed of Abraham;

Immanuel, God with them, and so that natural impediment shall be moved : I will come upon a level with
the bride, and so I will be a help meet for her.

(2.) There is another impediment arises from the
law : O, says the Law, I have an action against the
supposed bride. She was once married unto me, and 1
promised her the inheritance of life, upon the condition
of her fulfilling perfect obedience to my commands :
but she disobeyed, and played the harlot, and she is
under the curse ; and therefore there can be no marriage. Well but (says the Bridegroom,) I will remove
this impediment also ; I will be made a curse for her,
and so redeem her from the curse : I will cancel the
hand-writing that is against her, and contrary to her.

(3.) Well but (says Justice,) I stand upon a complete satisfaction ; for without death, and the shedding
of blood, there can be no remission of sin. Well (says
the Bridegroom,) I will die for the bride, and in her
room and stead : the sword of justice shall be soaked
in my blood instead of her's : my life shall be a ransom
for her's ; I will be wounded for her iniquities, and
bruised for her transgressions ; I will be made sin for
her.

(4.) There is another impediment yet that must be
removed ; The bride hates the Bridegroom ; she is
wholly averse from the match : and what will be done
in this case ? Well (says the Bridegroom,) I will undertake to gain her affection. Psal. cx. 3. " Thy people
shall be willing in the day of thy power." I will draw
with the cords of a man, and with the bands of love ;
and then her affections shall be gained, and she shall
call me *Ishi.*

(5.) Another great impediment in the way of the
marriage is, that the bride is a lawful captive to sin and
Satan ; Now (says Satan,) shall the lawful captive be
delivered ; both law and justice have put her in my
power : and therefore I will not part with my prisoner.
Well but (says the blessed Bridegroom,) it is true, Satan, thou hast law and justice on thy side : but I will

fulfil the law, and satisfy justice; and, in so doing, thy head shall be bruised, and the lawful captive shall be delivered, and the prey shall be taken from the terrible. I will redeem her by purchase and by power. And accordingly he spoiled principalities and powers, and took the bride by main force out of the devil's prison, saying to the prisoners, " Go ye forth," &c.

From what is said, it appears, that the heart of the Bridegroom is exceedingly set upon the match, with desire he desired to be baptized with his own blood, that he might finish her redemption ; and having completed her redemption, he longs for the day of espousals, when he gains the love and affection of the bride. So much was the heart of the Bridegroom set upon the match, that when he saw the bride in danger of perishing, he flew, as it were, from his Father's bosom, left all the glories of heaven behind him, and travelled through the armies of hell and earth, yea, encountered the legions of his Father's wrath, in order to accomplish her deliverance. Hence is that of the church, Is. lxiii. 1. " Who is this that cometh from Edom ? with dyed garments from Bozrah ? this that is glorious in his apparel, travelling in the greatness of his strength ? I that speak in righteousness." And ver. 3. " I have trodden the winepress alone, and of the people there was none with me."

4thly, A fourth premise is, That the covenant of grace is the contract of marriage, the plan of which was agreed upon in the council of peace, betwixt the Father and the Son, from all eternity : Psal. lxxxix. 3. " I have made a covenant with my chosen, I have sworn unto David my servant." It was originally made with the Bridegroom, as the Head, Husband, and Representative of the bride, wherein he undertakes, that the grace of God shall reign and be glorified through his own righteousness, to her eternal life and salvation. As Surety of the covenant, he undertakes to fulfil the condition of it, by his own obedience unto death, to buy his bride from the hands of justice, by paying a ransom of his own blood for her, and to buy, at the same time, all the blessings and goods of the covenant for her use; and that, by the power of his word and Spirit, he will make her to take hold of his covenant, bring her within the bond of it, and make an effectual application thereof in due time, according to the order of the covenant; and that he will betroth her unto himself for ever, in righteousness, and in judgment, and in loving-kindness, and in mercies; yea, that he will betroth her unto himself in faithfulness, and that she shall know the Lord, Hos. ii. 19, 20.

5thly, In the day of his espousals all this is fulfilled. The Bridegroom presents himself to the bride in his divine and human glories, fulness, and excellencies; he makes the "light of the knowledge of the glory of God," in his own person, to shine in her heart; wherewith she is made to see him, and fall so much in love with him, that she cannot but cry out, "O! he is infinitely fairer than the sons of men, he is as the apple-tree among the trees of the wood, the chiefest among ten thousand, white and ruddy, his countenance is as Lebanon, excellent as the cedars; his mouth is most sweet, yea, he is altogether lovely. O! this is my Beloved, this is my Friend: if I had ten thousand hearts and hands to give he should have them all. I am well pleased with his person; well pleased with the contract he has made, and signed with his blood; well pleased with all the promises, which I see to be yea and amen in him; well pleased with his law: I will follow him whithersoever he goes." And in this way the marriage is concluded and agreed upon, "I will make an everlasting covenant with them, even the sure mercies of David," Is. lv. 3. Jer. xxxii. 40. I will make (or establish) an everlasting covenant with them, that I will not turn away from them to do them good, but I will put my fear in their hearts, that they shall not depart from me. I will never leave thee nor forsake thee."

Important questions which those, who desire to match with Christ, are ready to put, answered.

Quest. 1. WILL you tell us, what is the Bridegroom's name, if you can tell? *Answ.* That is not easily answered, for it is a part of Agur's confession of faith, Prov. xxx. 4. "Who hath ascended up into heaven, or descended. What is his name, and what is his Son's name, if thou canst tell?" And when Manoah asked the angel what was his name? (that he might do him honour), He (viz. Christ the angel of the covenant) answers, "Why askest thou thus after my name, seeing it is secret?" or, as in the margin, seeing it is Wonderful. Such a secret is his name, that no man can call him Lord, but by the Holy Ghost; you may read his name in your Bibles, and still his name will be a secret, till the Spirit of the Lord open it unto you by glorifying his person in your eyes, and then, and never till then, will you cry out, O! his name is like ointment poured forth; O! he has a name above every name that can be named, whether in this world or that which is to come. Every knee must bow unto this name, and every tongue must acknowledge, that Jesus Christ is Lord, to the praise and glory of God the Father.

I will just tell you of a few of the scriptural names of the Bridegroom. And, O! look up to him for a glimpse of his glory in them.

His name is Jesus. Matth. i. 21. Now what think ye of that name? for the sound of salvation is in it: "Thou shalt call his name Jesus, for he shall save his people from their sins." O lost sinner, roll the name of the Bridegroom as a sweet morsel under thy tongue. His name is Christ, or the renowned Messiah, the Anointed One of God. Grace was poured into his lips, for God, even his Father, anointed him with the oil of gladness above all his fellows. His name is the Lord; for he is Lord of all; Lord of Lords. He is God's first-born, whom he hath made higher than the kings of the earth;

yea, all the kings of the earth must do homage unto him, some time or other ; and no wonder, for by him " kings reign and princes decree justice." What is his name ? His name is Immanuel, God-man, or God with us, to stand in our quarrel ; to take our part against the old serpent ; and accordingly he has bruised his head, and through death has destroyed him that had the power of death.

See a whole cluster of the names of the Bridegroom together, Is. ix. 6. Where the bride, the Lamb's wife, glorying in her beloved consort, cries out, in a holy triumph, " Unto us a child is born, unto us a son is given, and the government shall be upon his shoulder, and his name shall be called Wonderful, Counsellor, the mighty God, the everlasting Father, the Prince of peace."

1*st*, His name is a great, glorious, and renowned name, a name above every name, Philip. ii. 9—11. " God hath highly exalted him, and given him a name which is above every name, that at the name of Jesus every knee should bow, of things in heaven, and things in earth, and things under the earth. And that every tongue should confess, that Jesus Christ is Lord, to the glory of God the Father." So Eph. i. 20, 21, 22. God " hath set him at his own right hand in the heavenly places, and exalted him far above all principality, and power, and might, and dominion, and every name that is named, not only in this world, but also in that which is to come."

2*dly*, His name is a savoury name ; Cant. i. 3. " Because of the savour of thy good ointment, thy name is as ointment poured forth, therefore do the virgins love thee." Oh Sirs ! there is such an odoriferous perfume in the name of Christ, that when once a poor soul gets a scent of it, it can never forget it, and the very remembrance of it is a feast and banquet to the soul, Is. xxvi. 8, 9. " Yea, in the way of thy judgments, O Lord, have we waited for thee ; the desire of our soul is to thy name, and to the remembrance of thee. With my soul have I desired thee in the night: yea, with my spirit within me, will I seek thee early."

3dly, His name is a medicinal name. If faith be but acted upon his name, it makes the bones that were broken to rejoice; makes the blind to see; the deaf to hear; the lame man to leap like an hart, and the tongue of the dumb to sing, Acts iii. ·6, 7, 16. So Acts iv. 12, &c.

4thly, His name is a sheltering and hiding name: when storms are blowing, whether from heaven, earth, or hell, Prov. xviii. 11. "The name of the Lord is a strong tower, the righteous fly into it and are safe." It is not only a tower, but a strong and impregnable tower, and the gates of hell shall never prevail against that soul that has fled for refuge unto it.

5thly, His name is an attractive name, it draws the heart and soul to him : it is by the sound of this name that the gathering of the people is unto him as the blessed Shiloh. What is it that makes the gospel the power of God unto salvation? Why, it is just the displays of the glory of his renowned name, " If I be lifted up from the earth (says Christ), I will draw all men unto me."

6thly, His name is an enlightening name to the poor soul that is walking in darkness; hence Is. l. at the close, " He that walketh in darkness, and hath no light, let him trust in the name of the Lord," &c. plainly intimating, that a glance of the name of Christ, by the eye of faith, will make light to spring out of darkness to the soul, under the darkest clouds of desertion : and no wonder, for he is the " light of the world, the true light, the Sun of righteousness."

7thly, His name is a quickening and enlivening name : By the name of Jesus the dead are raised unto life ; and no wonder, for this is one of his names. " The Life," John xiv. 6. and xi. 25. " The Resurrection and the Life." Let but a languishing saint, when he is crying, with the eunuch, Is. lvi. " I am a dry tree," let him but hear the name of the Lord Jesus, let him but get a glimpse of the glory of his person, he will be ready to cry with the apostle, Col. iii. 3. "I am dead, but my life is hid with Christ in God." Or with Paul, Gal. ii. 20. " I am crucified with Christ ; nevertheless I live ; yet not I, but Christ that liveth in me : and the life which I now live in the flesh, I live by the faith of the Son of God, who loved me, and gave himself for me."

8thly, His name is a prevalent name in heaven, insomuch that, if this name be set in the front of our prayers and petitions, they will prevail and obtain a hearing, and a gracious answer and return, John xiv. 13. "And whatsoever ye shall ask in my name, that will I do," &c. This name perfumes our prayers like incense.

9thly, It is a worthy name, James (ii. 7.) speaking of the rich man with the gold ring and gay clothing, tells us, they blaspheme that worthy name by the which ye are called ; the triumphant company in heaven know it to be so, for they warble forth the praises of his name, saying, " Worthy is the Lamb that was slain," Rev. v.

10thly, It is a durable and everlasting name, Psal. lxxii. at the close, " His name shall endure for ever, his name shall be continued as long as the sun ; for men shall be blessed in him, and all nations shall call him blessed ; and therefore blessed be his glorious name for ever, and let the whole earth be filled with his glory." This name will make sweet melody in heaven, through all eternity.

Now, Sirs, what think ye of the Bridegroom, when you hear of his name ? will you match with him ? will you marry him ? if thy heart can say, "O, if I had ten thousand hearts and hands, I would give them all to him." Well, if this be the language of thy heart, it is a done bargain ; he is thy Bridegroom, and thou art his bride, the Lamb's wife.

Quest. 2. Oh I would hear more about him ! Will you tell me what is the Bridegroom's pedigree and parentage? of whom is he descended? *Answ.* I can tell you some things anent his genealogy : " He is of the seed of David according to the flesh," he is the offspring of ancient kings, as you may see from his genealogy, Matth. i. and Luke iii. If you ask anent his divine pedigree, he "is the only begotten of the Father, and the brightness of his glory, and the express image of his person." But as to the manner of his generation, who can declare it! this is a secret, and secret things belong unto the Lord. Only from this hint you may see the Bridegroom is so honourably descended, that it is a wonder he should match with any of the fallen tribe of Adam.

Quest. 3. What is the Bridegroom's personal worth and excellency ? *Answ.* There is such a divine glory in his person, that the lustre of it darkens the sun in the firmament, that it appears to be as sackcloth and darkness. Such glory is in his person, as dazzles the eyes of angels to behold him, Is. vi. They cover their faces with their wings, crying, one to another, " Holy, holy, holy Lord of hosts," &c. All the perfections of the Deity shine with a meridian lustre and glory in the person of our glorious Bridegroom. The fulness of the Godhead dwells in him bodily. He is " in the form of God, and thinks it not robbery to be equal with God." So glorious is the person of the Bridegroom, that he captivates every eye and heart that beholds him, and imparts his glory, in some measure, to every soul that looks on him by the eye of faith, 2 Cor. iii. 18. " But we all, with open face beholding as in a glass the glory of the Lord, are changed into the same image, from glory to glory," &c. The bride, by looking on the glory of the Bridegroom, is made like the " king's daughter, all glorious within, and to look forth, as the morning, fair as the moon, clear as the sun, and terrible as an army with banners : O go forth, ye daughters of Zion," and behold his glory.

Quest. 4. What are the endowments and qualifications of the Bridegroom ? *Answ.* His qualifications are so rare and singular, that tongue cannot tell them, nor heart conceive them. Only, to commend him to your esteem, love, and affections, there are these few quali- fications that may recommend him to any rational soul.

1. " For beauty he is white and ruddy, the chiefest among ten thousand, his countenance is as Lebanon, excellent as the cedars, fairer than the children of men, and altogether lovely."

2. For wisdom, all the " treasures of wisdom and knowledge are hid in him :" he is wise in heart, and mighty in counsel. So wise, that he has outwitted all the power and policy of hell and earth : although his enemies dig counsel as deep as hell, yet hell and de- struction being naked before him, he just takes the wise in their own craftiness, and the counsel of the froward he carrieth headlong ; and he imparts wisdom unto the simple bride, making her wise unto salvation, ac- quainted with the mysteries of the kingdom, which are hid from the wise and prudent of the world.

3. For riches, the Bridegroom that offers to match with you is immensely rich ; he is a man of substance indeed, and he causes those that love him to inherit substance ; his riches are unsearchable, Eph. iii. 8. his riches are durable, Prov. viii. 18.

4. For honour, he is renowned in heaven and earth, having a name above every name that can be named ; Prov. viii. 18. " Honour and riches are with me." Honour and majesty are before his face ; and he makes all that believe on him honourable, Is. xliii. 2. " Ever since thou wast precious in my sight, thou hast been honourable," &c.

5. For strength he is the man of God's right hand, whom he has made strong for himself. The strength of omnipotence is in him, for he is the mighty God, Is. ix. 6. and the Almighty, Rev. i. 8. He came from Edom and from Bozrah, " travelling in the greatness of his strength, showing himself mighty to save."

6. For authority, he has power over all flesh, " that he may give eternal life to as many as the Father hath

given him. All power is his in heaven and in earth; things in heaven, and things in earth, and things under the earth, yea, every knee must bow unto him, and every tongue must confess, that Jesus Christ is Lord, to the glory of God the Father."

7. For meekness and lowliness he is incomparable, and proposes himself as the great pattern of it for our imitation, Matth. xi. 29. " Learn of me, for I am meek and lowly."

8. For constancy in his love, in his promises, and in all his amiable excellencies, he is Christ Jesus, " the same to-day, yesterday, and for ever." His name is " I AM; he rests in his love, and changes not, therefore the sons of Jacob are not consumed." His promises are not like the promises of men, yea to-day, and nay to-morrow; no, but " all the promises of God are in him yea and amen ; one jot or tittle of what he says shall never pass away ; the mountains shall depart, and the hills be removed ; but my kindness shall not depart from thee, neither shall the covenant of my peace be removed, saith the Lord, that hath mercy upon thee." These are some, and but a small part, of the qualifications of the blessed Bridegroom : " Go forth then, ye daughters of Zion, and behold him."

Where Christ the Bridegroom is most readily to be met with.

You call us to go out and meet the Bridegroom. Where may we meet him ? Oh ! may some poor soul say, That I knew where I might find him. Oh ! tell me where he feedeth, and where he maketh his flocks to rest at noon. *Answ.* Although the Bridegroom, as to his human nature, be in heaven, and in this respect the heavens are to "receive him until the times of restitution of all things ;" yet he is to be found any where upon earth as to his divine, spiritual, gracious presence, by these that are really seeking after fellowship and communion with him by faith, in the ways and means of his own appointment : and this is what he has promised

to his church, " Lo, I am with you alway, even unto
the end of the world. In all places where I record my
name, I will come unto thee, and I will bless thee.
Where two or three are gathered together in my name,
there am I in the midst of them." So that I say, there is
as real communion and fellowship to be had with Christ
now, though ascended, as ever his disciples had when
he was going out and in among them, in a state of humiliation here upon earth ; hence says the apostle John
concerning Christ, after he was gone away to heaven,
1 John i. 3. "Truly our fellowship is with the Father,
and with his Son Jesus Christ."

But Oh, say you, Will you tell me more particularly
where I may meet him and find him ? *Answ.* He is
so fond of a meeting with sinners, that he is sometimes,
yea, many times, found of them that seek him not, as
in the case of Paul going a black errand to Damascus,
and poor Zaccheus upon the sycamore tree, seeking
only to satisfy his curiosity : and if so, much more will
he be found of them that seek him in the ways of his
appointment; for he has said, he meeteth him that
rejoiceth and worketh righteousness, those that remember him in his ways.

Quest. What are these ways and means of his appointment where I may meet the Bridegroom, and have fellowship with him?

Answ. He is sometimes found in the mount of secret
meditation, " While I was musing, the fire burned,"says
David. Many a sweet interview have the souls of believers with Christ in meditation, Psal. lxiii. 6. "When
I remember thee upon my bed, and meditate upon
thee in the night watches—ver. 5. My soul shall be
satisfied as with marrow and fatness." He is to be
met with in secret prayer, " Then shall ye find me,
when ye seek me, and search after me with all your
hearts." In this duty Jacob found the Lord, and
wrestled for the blessing till break of day, and like a
prince prevailed, Hos. xii. 3, 4. " He took his brother by
the heel in the womb, and by his strength he had power

with God : Yea, he had power over the angel and prevailed : he wept and made supplication unto him :
He found him at Bethel," &c. compared with Gen.
xxxii. 24, 26. " And Jacob was left alone ; and there
wrestled a man with him, until the breaking of the day.
And when he saw that he prevailed not against him,
he touched the hollow of his thigh ; and the hollow
of Jacob's thigh was out of joint, as he wrestled with
him. And he said, Let me go, for the day breaketh ;
and he said, I will not let thee go, except thou bless
me." He is to be met with in the duty of personal,
family, or public fasting and humiliation, " But to
this man will I look, who is poor and of a contrite
spirit, and trembleth at my word." He is to be met
with in the duty of Christian conference and fellowship, when they that " feared the Lord spake often one
to another, the Lord hearkened and heard." He is
to be met with in reading and searching the Scriptures,
John v. 39. " Search the Scriptures, for in them ye think
ye have eternal life, and they are they which testify of
me." While the Ethiopian eunuch was reading his
Bible, the Lord met him in the ministry of Philip, insomuch that he " went on his way rejoicing." Many
a sweet glimpse of the glory of the Bridegroom has the
Bride, while she is looking after him, through the glass
of the revelation, 2 Cor. iii. last, " We all with open
face, beholding as in a glass the glory of the Lord, are
changed into the same image, from glory to glory, even
as by the Spirit of the Lord." He is especially to be
found in the gates of Zion, the public ordinances of his
worship, where his people attend upon him in their
assemblies, for prayer, for praise, for preaching and
hearing the gospel, and for the celebration of the
sacraments of baptism and the Lord's supper in a solemn manner ; " the Lord loves these gates of Zion
more than all the dwellings of Jacob." These are the
streets and broad ways where the spouse sought him,
Cant. iii. It is true she missed him for a while, but at
length, she met the Bridegroom, and was in case to

say, " I found him whom my soul loveth, I held him
and would not let him go." David saw his power and
glory in his sanctuary; hence Psal. lxxxiv. he declares
how amiable his tabernacles were unto him; " A day
(says he) in thy courts is better than a thousand; I
had rather be a door-keeper in the house of my God,
than to dwell in the tents of wickedness."

He is especially to be met with in the breaking of
bread, at a communion table: for " the cup which we
bless, it is the communion of the blood of Christ; and
the bread which we break, it is the communion of the
body of Christ." Here the blessed Bridegroom is to
be seen in his dyed garments; for, out of love to his
bride he trode " the wine-press alone, when of the people there were none with him." If that question be
put to him, " Why art thou red in thine apparel, as
one that treadeth the wine fat?" He may well answer,
It is no wonder my apparel be red, for I was " wounded for thine iniquities, and bruised for thy transgressions."

Sure marks of our being Christ's true Bride.

1st, THE true bride of Christ has the Bridegroom in
great admiration; her esteem of him is such, that she
just admires every thing in him and about him. She
admires his personal glory as IMMANUEL; she wonders
that ever the second Person of the glorious Godhead
should ever have passed by the angelic nature, and
joined himself in a personal union to the human nature,
out of love to her, that he might be a help meet for
her. Hence that word of the apostle is much in her
mouth and heart, 1 Tim. i. 3. " Without controversy,
great is the mystery of godliness," God was manifest
in the flesh. Oh, he is just a Nonsuch! " as the apple tree among the trees of the wood. The chiefest among ten thousand." And when the bride
thinks of the love he bore to her before the world
was made; and how, in the fulness of time, he came
and spent his blood for her redemption; how in time

he drew her with the cords of love, conquered her enmity by shedding abroad his love upon her heart ; she
is just swallowed up with admiration, and is ready to
cry out, " O, what am I or my house, that thou hast
brought me hitherto ! Is this the manner of men, O
Lord God ? O, what hath God wrought ! O the
height, the depth, the breadth, and the length of his
love ! It passeth all knowledge."

2dly, The true bride of Christ knows the voice of
the Bridegroom, and is much delighted with the words
of his mouth, " My sheep hear my voice," John x.
You see, Cant. ii. 8. how her heart flighters at the first
opening of his lips, " It is the voice of my beloved :"
It is sweeter to me than the melody of angels or archangels. Every word of the Bridegroom creates admiration in her heart, and she remembers them with delight and pleasure, Cant. ii. 10. " My Beloved spake,
and said unto me, Rise up, my dove, my love, my fair
one, and come away." Such words make her heart to
glow and burn within her. O, says Job, " I have esteemed the words of his mouth more than my necessary food ;" and O, says David, " the law of thy mouth
is better unto me than thousands of gold and silver,
more to be desired are they than gold, yea, than much
fine gold, yea, sweeter also than honey, and the honey
comb." O, says Jeremiah, " thy words were found,
and I did eat them, and thy word was unto me the joy
and rejoicing of mine heart."

3dly, Not only every word, but every thought of the
Bridegroom, is a banquet unto the soul of the bride,
" How precious also are thy thoughts unto me, O God.
My meditation of him shall be sweet : I will be glad in
the Lord." So David, Psal. civ. 34. and Psal. lxxiii.
6. " When I remember thee upon my bed, and meditate on thee in the night watches ;" ver. 5. " My soul
shall be satisfied as with marrow and fatness." Many
a sweet interview has the bride with Christ upon the
mount of meditation, which strangers do not intermeddle with.

4*thly*, The true bride of Christ hates all his rivals. She is dead to the law her first husband, and is ready to say, " I, through the law, am dead to the law." She is dead to sin, and crucifies the flesh, with the affections and lusts, though as dear as a right hand, or a right eye. She is dead to the world, and counts all its profits, pleasures, and honours, nothing but a mass of vanity. " I am crucified to the world, and the world to me." Thus, I say, the true bride of Christ hates all Christ's rivals; " I count all things but loss for the excellency of the knowledge of Christ, and do count them but dung," &c. Yea, she is ready to part with all relations whatever for him, father, mother, wife, children, let them all go for him ; yea, if her life comes in competition with Christ, she will be ready to say, " I am ready not to be bound only, but to die," for the glory of the Bridegroom ; " They loved not their lives unto the death," for the love that they bore unto the Lord Jesus.

5*thly*, The bride of Christ has much trust and confidence to put in the Bridegroom, and by trusting in him is kept in perfect peace, and is filled with joy and peace in believing. She dares venture upon the greatest dangers, when called upon the credit of his word, " Fear not, for I am with thee ; be not dismayed, for I am thy God," &c. The very name of the Bridegroom is the ground of her trust, and is to her like a strong tower, where she flies and is safe. The language of the bride's confidence towards the Bridegroom is that, Psal. xxxvi. 7. " How excellent is thy loving-kindness, O God, therefore the children of men put their trust under the shadow of thy wings ;" and Psal. xxvii. 5. For " in the time of trouble he shall hide me in his pavilion ; in the secret of his tabernacle shall he hide me," &c.

6*thly*, The bride of Christ has a great regard for his commands, and is ready to follow him whithersoever he goes. The bridegroom says to the bride, " If ye love me, ye will keep all my commandments," John

xiv. 15. ; and ver. 21. " He that hath my commandments, and keepeth them, he it is that loveth me."
The wise virgins will keep themselves chaste for the
service of the Bridegroom, and will not defile themselves with " the corruption that is in the world
through lust." Hence is that, Rev. xiv. 4. speaking
of the hundred forty and four thousand, that stood
with the Lamb upon Mount Zion : " These are they
who were not defiled with women (*i. e.* with the errors,
idolatry, and abominations of Antichrist), for they are
virgins : These are they who follow the Lamb whithersoever he goeth."

7*thly*, The true bride of Jesus holds fast the testimony of Jesus in opposition to the devil, and the
world, and all errors and corruptions that are cast out
of hell in order to obscure his declarative glory, Rev.
xii. 17. There we are told, that the dragon " was
wroth with the woman and went to make war with the
remnant of her seed, which keep the commandments
of God, and have the testimony of Jesus Christ." And
if it be asked, What is the testimony of Jesus ? it is
answered, Rev. xix. 10. For " the testimony of Jesus
is the spirit of prophecy," *i. e.* the word of God, which
holy men of God spake as they were moved by the
Holy Ghost." Now, the true bride of Christ " con-
tends earnestly for this testimony or faith which was
once delivered unto the saints," and will receive no
doctrine, no practice, no decision, though it were of
the general assembly of angels, but what quadrates or
agrees with and is founded upon this testimony and
word of Jesus ; and this is what Christ hath given in
charge to his bride, the church, and every believer in
particular, Is. viii. 20. " To the law and to the testimony, if they speak not according to this word, it is
because there is no light in them."

8*thly*, The bride of Christ is very fond to bring
forth a seed to serve him ; and for this end she studies
to bring him to her mother's house, and the ordinances
of his appointment. It is only his presence in the

church that makes the word effectual for the conversion of sinners and the edification of saints ; and therefore they that are married to the Bridegroom are fond to see his power and glory in the sanctuary, that so it may be said of Zion, " This and that man was born in her," Psal. lxxxvii. 5. and " who hath begotten me these," Is. xlix. 21.

9*thly,* The bride of Christ longs sometimes for the consummation of the marriage at death, especially at the last judgment, when the collective body of Christ shall be made fully up, and when the Bridegroom shall present his bride to his Father, " not having spot or wrinkle, or any such thing," and when she shall shine forth as the sun in the kingdom of her Father." Paul had this in his eye, when he said, " There is laid up for me a crown of righteousness, which the Lord, the righteous judge, shall give me at that day, and not to me only, but unto all them also who love his appearing ;" and the church when she said, Cant. viii. last verse, " Make haste, my beloved, and be thou like to a roe, or to a young hart upon the mountains of spices."*

* A man may know his blessed estate in respect of time past, by a work, that is to say, with a word or promise made to it, and the Spirit revealing it, namely, the everlasting thoughts and election of God towards him. " Them that love God, who are called according to his purpose," notwithstanding all their miseries and sins, yet they love him, and therefore must be called according to his purpose, for so the apostle raises up his thoughts.

In respect of time present, by it we know our present union to the Lord Jesus. 1 John 2. 4. " He that saith I know him, and keepeth not his commandments, is a liar."—It is heaven to cleave to him in every command, it is death to depart from him in any command.

In respect of the state of glory for time to come ; we may know our blessed estate by a work, 1 Cor. 2. 9. " Eye hath not seen what the Lord hath prepared for them that love him." Psal. 31. 19. " O how great is thy goodness, which thou hast laid up for them that fear thee."

Shepard's Parable of the ten virgins.

Serious address to sinners to match with Christ the Bridegroom.

Now my call and exhortation unto all is, to give the assent and consent of faith unto the bargain. I, as a friend of the Bridegroom, have a commission to court for him, and to say to you, as Rebekah's friends said unto her, upon a proposal of marriage with Isaac, "Wilt thou go with this man?" the Man IMMANUEL, GOD-MAN; the Man of God's right hand; the Man whose name is the Branch, who builds the temple, and bears all the glory; the Man who hath all power in heaven, and on earth; who is KING OF KINGS AND LORD OF LORDS. O, will you sign the contract of the new covenant with the hand of faith, and say, "I am the Lord's, my Maker is and shall be my Husband, whose name is the Lord of hosts, and my Redeemer, the Holy One of Israel." O, what a happy day would it be to this assembly, if every individual soul would give Rebekah's answer to the proposal, with the same affection and resolution, "I will go with the man. I will follow him whithersoever he goes; his God shall be my God, his Father shall be my Father, where he dwells there will I dwell; neither death nor life, nor things present, nor things to come, shall ever separate between him and me." Now, because it is Christ's way not to drag with violence, but to draw his bride to him with the cords of a man, and the bands of love, therefore I shall essay to enforce the exhortation with a few motives or arguments.

Mot. 1. Shall be taken from the glory and excellency of the blessed Bridegroom. And here it is fit you remember what was said of him in the doctrinal part. As to his name, he has a "name above every name that can be named." As to his pedigree, who can declare his generation? As to his personal worth and excellency, his qualities are every way incomparable. Now, seeing such a Bridegroom offers to betroth you to himself, O let it be a bargain: give your consent unto him, that the everlasting knot may be cast between you and him.

Mot. 2. To engage you to match with the Bridegroom, O consider how fond he is of the match, how much his heart is set upon it. This will appear, if you consider,

1. That he had it upon his heart from all eternity, before the world was made : " I have loved thee with an everlasting love," Jer. xxxi. 3. Before we had any being, save in his own purpose, when he saw us in our blood, his time, even then, was a time of love, Ezek. xvi. ; and the accomplishing of that project of love was the joy of his heart, Prov. viii. 30. He rejoiced " in the habitable parts of the earth, and his delights were with the sons of men."

2. He was so fond of the match, that, though he be God's fellow, and thinks it not robbery to be equal with God, yet he consented voluntarily to become his Father's bond servant out of love to us. This is the import of that word, " Mine ear hast thou bored, Lo, I come ; I delight to do thy will, O my God ! yea, thy law is within my heart." As Jacob became Laban's servant for fourteen years, out of love he had to Rachel; so did Christ become his Father's servant in the great work of redemption, out of love he had to the bride, that his Father promised him out of Adam's family.

3. Because he was none of our kindred, therefore he became our Kinsman, by manifesting himself in the flesh, or taking part of our flesh, Heb. ii. 14. John i. 14. " The Word was made flesh ;" he became as one of us, that so the natural distance being removed, the marriage might be accomplished.

4. Because the bride was a bond slave to law and justice, and could not be redeemed but with a ransom of infinite value ; therefore the Bridegroom dies for the bride, and redeems her, not with silver and gold, but with his own precious blood : he gave his life a ransom for many.

5. Because she was a prisoner unto Satan, and a lawful captive unto her greatest enemy, who was ready to devour her ; therefore he comes in the quality of a victorious and renowned conqueror, and travels in the greatness of his strength, spoils principalities and powers, makes a show of them openly, and " through death destroys him that had the power of death," setting the captives of the mighty at liberty.

6. Because the bride was as black as hell, by lying among the pots ; therefore he undertakes to wash and cleanse her, and to put his own beauty upon her, whereby she should be as the wings of a dove, covered with yellow gold.

7. Because the bride was naked, the devil having run away with her beautiful ornament of original righteousness ; therefore the Bridegroom undertakes to clothe her with white raiment, so as the shame of her nakedness might not appear : the Bridegroom is made of God to her, " righteousness and sanctification," &c.

8. So fond is the Bridegroom of the match, that he despatches his heralds to make open proclamation of his purpose of marriage to her, and he gives it us ministers in our commission, to insist upon it, and not to take a refusal ; 2 Cor. v. 20. " Now then we are ambassadors for Christ, as though God did beseech you by us, we pray you in Christ's stead be ye reconciled to God," by embracing his beloved Son, and consenting to him as your Head, Husband, and Bridegroom.

9. So fond is he, that he waits for a good answer from the bride ; he waits, that he may be gracious, and he exalts himself, that he may show mercy ; he stands at the door and knocks, till his head is filled with dew, and his locks with the drops of the night.

10. He is grieved at the heart when he gets a refusal. How did he weep over Jerusalem, saying, O, " If thou hadst known, even thou, at least in this thy day, the things which belong unto thy peace ! How shall I give thee up Ephraim ! How shall I deliver

Israel? Mine heart is turned within me, my repentings are kindled together."

11. How glad is his heart when the consent of the bride is gained? He is so glad, that he calls heaven and earth to rejoice with him : for there is joy in heaven when but one sinner is converted : O then the cry is given, Rev. xix. 5. " Let us be glad and rejoice, and give honour to him, for the marriage of the Lamb is come, and his bride hath made herself ready." The joy of that day is expressed by the joyful solemnity of a king's coronation, Cant. iv. last, " Go forth, O ye daughters of Zion, and behold king Solomon, with the crown wherewith his mother crowned him in the day of his espousals, and in the day of the gladness of his heart."

Now, is Christ so fond of a match with you, and will you be cool, careless, and averse? especially, if you consider by way of

Mot. 3. The vast disparity and disproportion between you and him. Never was there such an inequality in marriage between parties as here ; and yet his love and kindness towards the bride makes him come over all inequality. O let heaven and earth, angels and men, stand amazed! He who is the Lord, the Creator of all the ends of the earth, offers to match with his own creature, the work of his own hand, Is. liv. 6. " Thy Maker is thine Husband." He who is the ANCIENT OF DAYS, the EVERLASTING FATHER, offers to match with a forlorn infant cast out into the open field. He who is the most noble Branch of heaven or earth, offers to match with a vile prostitute, who had played the harlot with many lovers, whose father was an Amorite, and her mother a Hittite. He who is the Heir of God, Heir of heaven, the Heir of all things, offers to match with the children of Satan, and heirs of hell. He who is the greatest beauty of heaven and earth, the brightness of the Father's glory, offers to match with a bride, black as the Ethiopian, and spotted like the leopard, who is full of wounds and bruises, and putrifying sores. O let heaven and earth stand amazed at the condescension of the Bridegroom, and the folly of sinners in refusing such a match!

Mot. 4. To win your hearts to the Bridegroom, consider how much it will turn out to your advantage, if you take on with him as your Husband. View this in these following things.

1. The Bridegroom will clear, and ease you of all your debts. As for temporal and worldly debts he has a thousand ways to rid you of these, if he see it for his glory, and your good : for the earth is his, and the fulness thereof, and he bids you cast all your cares upon him, for he careth for his bride ; he that paid a ransom for your souls, how will he not with that freely give you all things ? But as to the debts you owe to law and justice, which indeed of all are the greatest and heaviest, heavier than you can bear, the least farthing of which you could never have paid, either by an eternity of obedience, or an eternity of punishment, that moment you close with Christ, you are cleared and discharged ; the Bridegroom stands between you and all your creditors. You know the wife is not sueable at law while clothed with a husband, he answers for all. Just so when you close with Christ, the better Husband, who is raised from the dead, you become dead to the law, Rom. vii. 4. *i. e.* you have no more concern with the law, and the debts you owe to it as a covenant, either for obedience or punishment, than if they had never been ; insomuch that, with joy and triumph you may lift up your heads in the presence of all your creditors or accusers, and say, Who can lay any thing to my charge ? for it is Christ that died for my offences, and rose again for my justification and acquittance ; I am under his covering, I am with him in the bride-chamber, where law and justice have no action against me. O then, poor diver, broken, and bankrupt sinner go out and match with the Bridegroom, and that moment, " it is God that justifies you,"

saying, "I, even I am he that blotteth out your transgressions."

2. O Sirs, go out and meet the Bridegroom, and take on with him, and all your wants shall be supplied, be they never so great and many, Phil. iv. 19. " My God shall supply all your need, according to his riches in glory, by Christ Jesus." The Bridegroom, as you have heard, has unsearchable riches : all the treasures of wisdom and knowledge, of grace, and of glory, are in him ; and out of his fulness you shall receive grace for grace ; quickening grace, for he is the Resurrection and the Life ; enlightening grace, for he is the Sun of Righteousness, the bright and the morning Star ; strengthening grace, for he giveth power to the faint, and increaseth strength to them that have no might. In a word, he will give grace and glory, and no good thing will he withhold from the soul that consents to marry him.

3. The Bridegroom will heal all your soul maladies : for he is well skilled in physic ; he is the Physician of value, and there is no disease so obstinate, but he will cure it with a word speaking. Hast thou a hard heart? he will soften it, and turn it unto a heart of flesh. Hast thou a withered hand, that cannot work ? well, he strengthens the weak and withered hand. Hast thou lame feet that cannot walk ? well, he makes the lame to leap like an hart. Hast thou a blind eye ? or wast thou born blind ? well, he has eye-salve to make the blind to see clearly. In a word, the first moment the soul matches with Christ, he begins the cure, and against the day of consummation of the marriage, the bride will be fully ready, the good work will be perfected, and the bride will be presented without spot or wrinkle or any such thing.

4. O go out and meet the Bridegroom, and match with him, and he will bear all your burdens, let them be never so heavy : " Cast thy burden upon the Lord, and he shall sustain thee." Christ is the most sympathising Husband, that ever was : If he see his bride

or beloved spouse oppressed in spirit with any sort of trouble, be what it will, he is just afflicted in all her afflictions, and he will be with her in fire and in the waters, that the fire may not burn, nor the waters over-whelm her. See how he speaks to his beloved spouse in her tossings, Is. liv. 11. " O thou afflicted, tossed with tempest, and not comforted, behold, I will lay thy stones with fair colours, and thy foundations with sapphires."

5. O match with the Bridegroom, and he will subdue all thy enemies, and make thee a conqueror, yea, more than a conqueror over them. They that match and take on with Christ, must indeed lay their account to have the armies of he l upon their top : The old ser-pent casts out water like a flood against the woman, and the remnant of her seed, that keep the command-ments of God, and have the testimony of Jesus Christ." But be not discouraged, poor soul ; thy Bridegroom has already bruised the head of the old serpent, and, ere it be long, will also make thee to tread Satan under thy feet. He that stood between thee and avenging justice, will likewise stand with and for thee, in opposi-tion to all enemies whatever. Let men and devils curse the bride of Christ, he will bless her. Let her be excommunicate, or cast out of the church unto the devil's common, Christ will not affirm, but make void such sentences. In the ninth chapter of John we read of a poor man born blind, whose eyes Christ had open-ed upon the Sabbath day, by making a little clay, and putting it upon his eyes. The Jewish Sanhedrim met ; and, under a very religious pretence of zeal for the Sabbath day, they convene the man before them, who professed Christ, in as far as he knew him ; and thereupon they excommunicate him, and cast him out of the church, and held him as a heathen man and a publican. Well, was this sentence bound in heaven ? No ; so far from that, that ver. 35, when Christ heard they had cast him out (or excommunicated him, as in the margin), Christ seeks him out and finds him, and

manifests himself the more to him, as you may see ver. 35—38 : and in the 39th verse, he passes a heavy doom and sentence upon them that had cast him out : " For judgment I am come into this world, that they who see not might see, and that they who see (or imagine that they are the only men that see things, or know them in a better light), might be made blind." Thus Christ will take up and defend his bride, to the confusion of them that do her hurt.

6. O match with the blessed Bridegroom, and he will manage all your concerns for you, and that both in heaven above, and earth below; for he has "all power in heaven and in earth." Thy Bridegroom, be- liever, will agent all thy business·for thee on earth ; for all the wheels of providence, they are rolled in a subserviency unto his design of love towards his be- loved spouse and bride, Rom. viii. 28. Deut. xxxiii. " He rides upon the heavens in thy help, and in his excellency on the sky." And as for thy concerns in the high court of heaven, he is thy Agent and Advo- cate there, 1 John ii. 1, 2. " If any man sin, we have an Advocate with the Father," &c.

7. O match with Christ the Bridegroom, for he pro- vides his bride in a large jointure. Although she con- tracts nothing with him but debt, and want, and po- verty ; yet he, in a way of free grace and love, con- tracts all things with her. See the tenure of the contract, 1 Cor. iii. 21. " All things are yours, whether Paul, or Apollos, or Cephas, or the world, or life, or death, or things present, or things to come ; all are yours, for ye are Christ's, and Christ is God's." Oh ! how well is the spouse of Christ provided, by virtue of the contract of the new covenant ? He provides his bride of a crown, and " a crown of glory that fadeth not away." He provides her of " a kingdom that can- not be moved, an inheritance incorruptible, undefiled, and that fadeth not away." He provides her of " a city that hath foundations, whose builder and maker is God ;" and a jointure house " not made with hands,

eternal in the heavens." In a word, he contracts, that his own God and Father shall be her God and Father for ever. What more can the most enlarged heart desire? More " eye hath not seen, nor ear heard, neither hath it entered into the heart of man to conceive."

Song viii. *explained. Who is this that cometh up from the wilderness leaning upon her Beloved ?*

IN the words we may notice, 1. The designation given to this world, with ref rence to the church and people of God ; it is but a *wilderness*, or a weary land, through which they are travelling toward their own home.

2. We have the course they are steering while in the wilderness; they are not sitting still in it, or going further into it, as if it were their home ; no, they are coming up from the wilderness : their affections are set upon things that are above, and not upon things that are below : they have got a tasting of the grapes of Eshcol, they have got a view of the land afar off, and of the king in his beauty, which makes them disrelish this present world, and look and long, not for the things that are seen, but the things that are not seen, and which are eternal.

3. We have the spouse's posture as she comes up from the wilderness ; she is *leaning*. Hebreans observe that this is a word not elsewhere used in scripture ; the seventy interpreters translate it, " confirming, or strengthening" herself. It plainly supposes the spouse's weakness and impotency in herself to grapple with difficulties in her way through the wilderness, together with her dependence on the grace and furniture that was laid up for her in Christ ; and that she must needs fag and fail in her journey, without new supplies and communications of light, life, and strength from him in whom all fulness dwells.

4. We have the blessed show and prop on which she leans and rests her weary soul, in coming up from the wilderness ; it is " upon her beloved," that is, upon

Christ, whose love and loveliness had ravished her heart, and drawn out her cordial assent and consent to him as the Bridegroom of souls, who had betrothed her to himself in mercy, faithfulness, and loving-kindness. It is pleasant here to observe how the heart of God the Father, and the heart of the believer, jump and centre upon Christ: " This is my beloved Son (says God the Father), in whom I am well pleased ;" he is " my servant whom I uphold, mine elect in whom my soul delighteth." And O! says the believer, as he is the Father's beloved, so he is my beloved too: he is just the darling and delight of my soul : " Whom have I in heaven but thee? and there is none in all the earth that I desire besides thee."

5. We have the influence or impression that this pleasant sight has upon the daughters of Jerusalem, expressed in a way of question, " Who is this ?" This is not a question of ignorance, as though they wanted to be informed who the spouse was; but, (1.) It is a question of wonder. They are struck with a holy amazement at such intimacy and familiarity between parties that are at such infinite distance ; that " the high and lofty One who inhabits eternity," should admit dust and ashes, defiled with sin, " the abominable thing that his soul hates," into such friendship and fellowship. (2.) It is not a question of contempt, but of esteem. Although believers, who are the spouse of Christ, be in themselves despicable and polluted ; yet, by virtue of their relation to Christ, they are worthy of the highest esteem, being made beautiful through the comeliness that he puts upon her. (3.) It is a question of approbation and commendation. They hereby express their satisfaction with her practice, and the exercise of her faith in coming up from the wilderness leaning upon her beloved, as the safest course she could take for accomplishing her journey to the Canaan that is above, through the dens of lions and mountains of leopards. Observe, that it is, and will be, the pleasure and satisfaction of a gracious soul, to

see others thriving and prospering in the Lord's way, and in acquaintance with Christ, even though they themselves be outstripped and darkened thereby in the world's view.

Important Lessons from Song viii. 5.

1. SEE hence the paucity of true believers who are espoused to Christ. Why, the greatest number, instead of coming up from the wilderness, are going down the wilderness : " Wide is the gate, and broad is the way, that leadeth to destruction, and many there be which go in thereat." Oh what shoals of people are there in the world, " whose god is their belly, and who mind earthly things !" But how few are they who have their " affections set upon things above," and who are really pointing heavenwards ! " Strait is the gate, and narrow is the way which leadeth into life, and few there be that find it." The world perhaps may laugh at them who keep the narrow way of religion ; but behold the end of the day, " The triumphing of the wicked is short, for they shall lie down in sorrow :" but as for the righteous and the upright, mark him, for the end of that man is peace ; his " weeping endures but for a night, joy shall come in the morning.

2. See hence why believers are called " men of another spirit " than the rest of the world : it is said of Caleb and Joshua, that they were of another spirit ; and the apostle speaking of himself, and other believers, says, " We have not received the spirit of this world, but the Spirit which is of God ; that we might know the things that are freely given to us of God." Why, here is the ground of it, other men are of a mean sordid spirit, and are content with the wilderness, and fill their belly with the husks that they find in the wilderness ; but it is otherwise with the true believer, he comes up from the wilderness, he seeks and affects " those things which are above, where Christ sitteth on the right hand of God." The world generally have a mistaken notion of true greatness of spirit ; they fondly

imagine, that it lies in pushing their resentment against those that injure them, or in pushing their fortune, as they call it, in scrambling up the pinnacles of worldly honour, wisdom, riches, or preferment; whereas true greatness of spirit lies in a contempt of all these things, in comparison of things that lie beyond the wilderness; it lies in "looking not at the things which are seen, but at the things which are not seen." O sirs, we sink our souls below their original make and excellency, when we lie down, with the serpent to lick up the dust and vanity of this world : true greatness of spirit is, with the spouse of Christ, to soar above the world, to mount up with wings like eagles, to things calculated for the soul and its heavenly nature.

3. See hence the excellency of the Christian religion, which makes a discovery of things that lie beyond the wilderness of this world, and calls a man to come up from the wilderness in order to his being possessed of them. "Life and immortality are brought to light by the gospel." The heathen philosophers had indeed some foolish guesses about another world, a life to come; but how strangely were they in the dark about it! One of the best of them, when he was dying, told his friends, "that he was persuaded of a future state; but whether he was going to a state of happiness or misery, he did not know." But now the Christian religion brings life and immortality (I say) to light, and opens a way and passage to a happy eternity : it is like mount Pisgah, from which one may stand and discover the goodly land that lies on the other side of Jordan. David, Psal. xvi. when he wins up to the top of it, and gets a view of the glories of heaven and eternity, he cries out like a man in a transport, "My heart is glad, and my glory rejoiceth;" Why ? "Thou wilt shew me the path of life : in thy presence is fulness of joy, at thy right hand there are pleasures for evermore."

4. See hence a good reason why the saints express such longings to be away out of the body, "I desire

to be clothed upon with our house which is from
heaven :" why, it is no wonder ; for this world is but
a wilderness unto them : and how natural it is for a
traveller in a wilderness to wish and long to be at home
in his own country, and among his own kindred, where
their inheritance lies, even " an inheritance that is incorruptible, undefiled, and which fadeth not away ?"

5. See a good reason why the saints should possess
their souls in patience under all the trials of a present
life. Who is it, that, travelling through a wilderness,
does not lay his account with inconveniencies and difficulties ? But besides, believer, thou art coming up from
the wilderness, and ere long thou wilt come out of it,
and beyond it altogether. " In the world (says Christ)
ye shall have tribulation ;" but look beyond the wilderness to thy fellow travellers, whose journey is ended.
" What are those which are arrayed in white robes ?
and whence came they ?" Rev. vii. 13. You have the
answer in the verse following, " These are they which
came out of great tribulation, and have washed their
robes, and made them white in the blood of the Lamb.
Therefore are they before the throne of God, and serve
him day and night in his temple." Wait a little, believer, and thou shalt be there also ; and then thy present light afflictions, which are but for a moment, shall
resolve in " a far more and exceeding and eternal
weight of glory ; and God shall wipe away all tears
from thine eyes."

Interesting view of the influence and exercise of faith.

1. It is faith that gives the soul the first ken of
Christ, and of the way of salvation through him ; it is
the eye that first spies him out as the all-sufficient
Saviour provided by God the Father. When the poor
soul has been as it were beaten, battered, and tossed
among the waves and tempests of law terrors, and apprehensions of eternal wrath and vengeance, in which
case it has been as it were casting its most valuable
goods overboard, its own righteousness, morality, civil-

ity, its duties, abilities, legal attainments, and every thing else : now, while the soul is in this condition, every moment expecting to be swallowed up in the great deeps of the sea of God's wrath, faith as it were steps up to the top of the mast, and gets a view of Christ, and of salvation in him ; and thereupon the poor soul cries out, Oh there is Christ, let me get aboard of him ; Oh there is the Rock of ages, I will venture my all upon him ; Oh there is a stronghold and a refuge, I will flee in unto him ; Oh " this is my rest, here will I dwell, for my soul likes it well." Thus, I say, it is by faith that we first enter into a state of grace, peace, and righteousness ; according to that word of the apostle, Rom. v. 2. " We have access by faith into this grace wherein we stand." When the soul was surrounded with nothing but the black thoughts of despair and ruin, faith lands the soul in a safe harbour : therefore " he that hath believed " is said to have " entered into his rest," Heb. iv.

2. It is by faith that the union is made up between Christ and us. Indeed there is a radical union that we have with Christ before faith ; for he takes hold of us first by his Spirit, before we take hold of him by faith : but yet the union is made up on our part by faith, it is that which ties the marriage-knot. It is not love, but consent, that makes marriage between man and woman : so here it is the soul's coming off from the law, and all other husbands ; its coming off from its own righteousness, and submitting unto Christ as a Saviour, a Husband, and a Surety ; this is it that makes up the union, and this is done by faith. There are two things that marry Christ and the soul together, as is plain from Hos. ii. 19, 20. The first is on God's part ; he says to us in the covenant, and by his Spirit, " I will betroth thee unto me in faithfulness, and in loving kindness : there, I say, is God's part. But what is it on our part that makes the marriage ? It follows, " and thou shalt know the Lord," that is, thou shalt believe in him ; for this is the way that faith is very

commonly expressed by in the Old Testament, viz. by the knowledge of the Lord. It is faith that brings Christ unto the heart, and reveals him to the soul in all his glory and excellency.

3. As union, so our communion with Christ is by faith. There are two things requisite in order to our having fellowship with another ; the first is, to make the person real and present ; the second is, to have a familiar access with boldness unto him. Now, it is faith that doth both these. (1.) It is faith that makes God in Christ present unto the soul : for it " sees him who is invisible :" yea, it brings Christ and God in him, down from heaven unto the heart ; hence Christ is said to " dwell in our hearts by faith." It is not love that can make another person present ; it may indeed set the fancy a-work to frame the picture and image of the person beloved ; but it is only faith that can view God in Christ as present in and with the soul. And then, (2.) It is faith that gives us familiarity and boldness of access unto the Lord : Eph. iii. 12. " In whom we have boldness and access with confidence by the faith of him." And, 2 Cor. iii. 18. " Beholding him with open face," we come to him ; " with open face," that is, with confidence and boldness : Psal. xxxiv. 5. " They looked unto him, and were lightened :" and what follows ? " Their faces were not ashamed ;" that is, when they viewed Christ by faith, they had boldness of access unto God in him. The communion that we have with Christ, is frequently compared unto eating and drinking, John vi. because it is faith alone that fetches nourishment from Christ, and makes a person to find the sweetness that is in him, and draws virtue from him : and thus it has the most close and intimate union and communion with him, insomuch that he is one with the soul, and the soul one with him.

4. As faith brings us into union and communion with Christ, so faith brings the Spirit of God down into the heart. I own indeed, that, in the work of re-

generation and conversion, he is like the rain, that
" waits not for the sons of men ;" he comes unsent for
or unsought for ; " he is found of them that seek him
not ;" faith has no instrumentality there ; faith itself
is a part of the new creature, that is formed by the
hand of the Spirit.   But, I say, faith brings the Spirit
into the heart as a Spirit of sanctification, and of con
solation, Eph. i. 13. " In whom also, after that ye believed, ye were sealed with the Holy Spirit of promise."
Gal. iii. 14. we are said to " receive the promise of the
Holy Spirit through faith."   All the fulness of the Spirit
dwells in Christ, for the use of his mystical body ; now,
it is by faith that this fulness is received, even grace
for grace.

5. I might tell you further, that our standing in a
state of grace is by faith.   As we have access or entrance into a state of grace, so we have standing in
that state by faith, Rom. v. 2. 2 Cor. i. ult.   " By
faith ye stand."   1 Pet. i. 5. we are said to be " kept
by the power of God through faith unto salvation."
There you see, that faith is joined in commission with
the power of God to keep the believer.   Doth the
power of God keep you ? so doth faith.   God is not
shy of ascribing that to faith, which is peculiar only to
himself, because faith ascribes all to the power of God,
and gives him the honour of every thing that it doth :
hence we are said to be " kept by the power of God
through faith unto salvation."   When other graces,
such as love, repentance, &c. do fag and fail, and have
as it were their heels tript up, faith will stand its
ground : hence, Eph. vi. 16. there is a particular mark
of distinction put upon faith beyond all the other pieces
of armour ; "Above all, take the shield of faith."
When a man's head-piece is cracked, his sword, his
breastplate, and other armour is taken from him ; yet
his shield will do him good service, he will lie under it,
and thereby defend himself against all the strokes and
blows that are levelled at him.   Let the devil, corruption, and hell, rage and roar as they will, yet faith will

keep its gripe, and maintain its ground : let Satan cast his fiery darts, faith quenches them, Eph. vi. 16 : let indwelling sin roar and rage, faith will say, Let it rage, yet it shall never reign ; for God has said, that " sin shall not have dominion ;" yea, let God himself carry as an enemy, and set himself in battle-array against the soul; yet even then faith will look in his face, and say, " Though thou shouldst even kill me, yet will I trust in thee," Job xiii. 15. When other graces are fainting, and crying, " We know not what to do ;" faith will say, " Mine eyes are toward thee : I will look unto the Lord : I will wait for the God of my salvation : my God will hear me : Though I sit in darkness, the Lord will be a light unto me," &c. When other graces like poor faint-hearted things, stand as it were trembling, and crying, " Who shall deliver us ?" faith will lift up the head and cry, " Thanks be to God, which giveth *me* the victory, through our Lord Jesus Christ."

6. It is faith that fetches in peace and quiet to the soul in the midst of trouble, whether from without or from within. When nothing but storms from heaven, earth, and hell, are blowing on the soul, faith will cast out its anchor of hope, and keep the soul steady and quiet, saying with David, Psal. xlii. 11. " Why art thou cast down, O my soul ! and why art thou disquieted within me ? hope thou in God, for I shall yet praise him." To the same purpose is that famous text, Is. xxvi. 3. " Thou wilt keep him in perfect peace, whose mind is stayed on thee : because he trusteth on thee." And how is the mind stayed on the Lord but by faith ? Oh, says faith, let me have what tribulation I will "in the world, yet in Christ I shall have peace : This man shall be *my* peace, when the Assyrian comes into the land."

7. Faith not only brings peace, but joy unto the soul, amidst all other disturbances from without : hence we are said to be filled with joy, as well as peace in believing. And, 1 Pet. i. 8. " Whom having not seen, *we* love ; in whom though now *we* see him not, yet

believing we rejoice with joy unspeakable, and full of glory." The language of faith is, Psal. xlvi. at the beginning, " God is our refuge and strength : and therefore though the mountains should be removed, yet there is a river, the streams whereof do make glad the city of God."

8. It is by faith that we are recovered after falls in- to sin. Many a time the devil, the world, temptation and corruption, so far prevail against the believer, as to trip up his heels : " The righteous man he falleth seven times a day." Now, in such a case, what is it that recovers him? It is faith : " Though I fall I shall arise (says faith) ; for the Lord upholdeth me with his hand." Oh, sirs, if you let faith go, when you fall into sin, you cannot miss to fall into the bottom ; just like a man climbing up a ladder, if his foot slip, and he quit the gripe of his hand also, what can hin- der him from falling down to the ground ? When Christ foresaw that Peter would sin by denying him, what said he ? " I have prayed for thee that thy faith fail not." As if he had said, I plainly see that thou wilt deny me in the hour of temptation ; but I have prayed that thy faith may not fail, and this is the thing that will recover thee. Oh sirs, when you fall into any sin, study to renew the acts of faith on the Lord Jesus Christ ; according to that advice of the apostle, 1 John ii. 1, 2. " If any man sin, we have an Advocate with the Father." As if he had said, The only way for a fallen saint to recover himself, is by faith to go to Christ as the great Advocate and Propi- tiation.

9. I might tell you further, that faith is as it were the mother-grace, the radical grace, on which all the other graces of the Spirit do depend. If faith be lively, so will all the other graces be. If faith be languid and faint, so will all the other graces be. If faith be set a-work, it will work by love, that celestial fire will burn, the fountain of holy sorrow will flow ; " They shall look upon him whom they have pierced, and mourn ;"

the foot of obedience will be active to "run the way of God's commandments."

10. Faith carries the soul on high, above time and time's enjoyments; it "mounts up with wings as eagles." It carries the soul to mount Nebo and Pisgah, and gives the soul a view of the goodly mountain, even Lebanon; and then the believer is like the "woman clothed with the sun, having the moon under her feet."

To conclude, as it is by faith that you must live, so it is by faith you must die, and shoot the gulf comfortably. It is said of the worthies, Heb. xi. "All these died in faith." Faith as it were lays its head in Christ's bosom, and says, with a holy confidence, "Into thy hand, O Lord, I commend my spirit." Faith, leaning on the staff of the divine promise, can say with David, "Yea, though I walk through the valley of the shadow of death, I will fear no evil: for thou art with me thy rod and thy staff shall comfort me." Psal. xxiii. 4.

Answers to the question, What is it in Christ that Faith lives and leans upon in its passage through the wilderness of this world?

IN general, Christ is such a suitable good that there is no case the soul can be into in its wilderness-condition, but faith will always find something corresponding to its necessity in him. Is the soul in darkness? "He is the Son of righteousness, the bright and morning Star." Is the soul in danger? He is "a shield, a hiding place, and refuge." Is the soul in trouble? He is a rest to the weary, he is "the shadow of a great rock in a weary land;" he is bread to the hungry, drink to the thirsty soul. But more particularly, there are these things following in Christ, that faith lives upon in the wilderness, and which it finds like marrow and fatness to the soul.

1. Faith lives and leans upon the name of Christ; for "his name is a strong tower unto which the righteous flee, and are safe:" hence we are so frequently

exhorted to "trust in the name of the Lord." O he
has a great name, and a pleasant name, "a name above
every name, and at his name every knee shall bow."
Whenever a believer engages with work, he is to do it
in the name of the Lord : " Whatsoever ye do in
word or in deed, (says the apostle,) do it all in the name
of the Lord Jesus, to the glory of God by him." And
whenever we go a warfare against sin, Satan, or the
world, we are to do it in his name ; otherwise we can
never prosper. This was the way of the church :
" We will be joyful in thy salvation, and in the name
of our God we will set up our banners." Whenever
we go to God in prayer, we are to present our persons
and petitions in the name of Christ : " Whatsoever ye
ask the Father in my name, he will do it." Oh sirs,
the name of Christ works wonders, when it is managed in a way of believing. When the disciples or
apostles went forth and preached the gospel among the
nations, they went forth in the name of JESUS ; and
when they wrought miracles, they did it in the name
of JESUS CHRIST : Acts iii. " In the name of Jesus
Christ of Nazareth, rise up and walk," said Peter and
John to the cripple man ; and presently he arose.
God is so delighted with the name of Christ, that for
the sake of that name he will do any thing to us or for
us. And therefore let us live by faith, and lean upon
his name, as we come up out of the wilderness.

2. Faith lives upon the flesh of Christ, that is, upon
the human nature as it stands personally united unto
the divine : " My flesh is meat indeed." You know,
Israel in their travels through the wilderness to Canaan, which was a shadow or type of our travels
through this world unto glory, they lived upon the
manna that was rained from heaven upon the camp.
But, O sirs, that was but a shadow of the true bread
of life, an incarnate God, that we present to you in
this gospel, John vi. 32. " My Father giveth you the
true bread which is from heaven." And again, says
Christ, in that same chapter, " Except ye eat the flesh

of the Son of man, and drink his blood, ye have no life in you." This seems to be a hard saying to a blind carnal world, and they are ready to think or say, with these Jews, John vi. 52. " How can Christ give us his flesh to eat?" But whatever ye may think of it, the flesh of Christ or his human nature, as it stands united to the divine in the person of the Son, when taken up by faith in the light of the word and Spirit, is the sweetest meal and banquet to a believer in heaven or earth ; no meat or drink like it to a poor perishing soul : and a believer, in travelling through the wilderness, he is aye taking a look of an incarnate Deity ; and thus he is enlightened, strengthened, quickened, and comforted. O sirs, what think you of this food ? I am sure if ever ye tasted of it, you will be ready to say, it is like " wines on the lees well refined, and fat things full of marrow."

3. Faith lives in the wilderness, not only on the flesh of Christ, or the mysteries of his incarnation, but upon the blood of Christ ; by which I understand his satisfaction, which is frequently in Scripture expressed by his blood : " Behold the blood of the covenant ;" that is, the satisfaction or death of Christ, that whereby the covenant is confirmed. This is drink indeed to the believer, in passing through the wilderness ; let the believer get a draught of this red wine of the blood of the slain Lamb of God, he is able to go forth like a giant, or a strong man to encounter all the powers of hell. Rev. xii. 11. It is said of the saints in their wars with the devil, that " they overcame him by the blood of the Lamb," that is, by faith's improvement of the death and satisfaction of Christ. Let faith be but set a-work upon the death and blood of Christ, it can look God himself in the face with an undaunted boldness, without fear of danger, or without fear of being rejected : " Having, brethren, boldness to enter into the holiest by the blood of Jesus, let us draw near," &c. Let faith act on the blood of Christ, it can go to God in prayer, and ask any thing that lies within the com-

pass of the whole testament of Christ; for whatever is
in the testament, is the purchase of this blood. O,
will faith say, give me peace, give me pardon, give me
light, life, strength, grace, or glory, give me the Spirit;
for here is the blood of the Lamb that bought it. Let
faith be acted on this blood, and the man dare, with
courage, comfort, and joy, look death, eternity, and a
tribunal, in the face: Why? Because faith sees the
curse of the law abolished, death unstinged, the grave
vanquished, and a tribunal sprinkled by the blood of
Jesus. The gates of glory are opened to receive the
soul that is sprinkled by the hyssop of faith dipt in the
blood of the Lamb.

4. Faith lives in the wilderness upon the life of
Christ: "Because I live, ye shall live also. I live
(says Paul); yet not I, but Christ liveth in me;" and
then follows, "The life which I now live in the flesh,
I live by the faith of the Son of God." Faith's way is
to follow Christ from his birth to his cross, from his
cross to his grave, and from his grave to his life again;
and then it cries in a way of triumph, "He who was
dead is now alive, and lives for evermore: I know
that my Redeemer liveth;" and he lives as my head,
my representative, my husband, my advocate, my king,
my priest, my prophet, and my all and in all. O sirs,
the resurrection of Christ unto life, never to die any
more, is a sweet and pleasant banquet in the wilderness, by which we are begotten again unto a lively
hope of the inheritance that is incorruptible and undefiled."

5. Faith lives upon the advocacy and intercession of
Christ: "If any man sin we, have an Advocate with
the Father, Jesus Christ the righteous, who makes intercession for the transgressors." And O how sweetly
doth the soul feed here by faith: O, will the soul say,
I may be condemned by the world, or by the law, or
by conscience; yet I know that I shall carry the
day in the court of heaven, because my Advocate is
the Lamb in the midst of the throne: he never lost a

cause, he has the Father's ear : he has such interest and moyen in heaven, that all power in heaven is his, and his will is a law in the higher court. "Father, I will that those whom thou hast given me, be with me where I am," &c.

6. Faith lives upon the word of Christ as it comes up from the wilderness. Christ has passed his word in his testament, and he has it sealed with his blood, and he lives as the executor of his testament : and I know, will faith be ready to say, that the Spirit of Christ will take all that is in his testament, and show it unto me, and show it so as to make all the testament and latter-will effectual : and therefore "in his word do I hope ;" his promise is not yea and nay, but it is always "yea and amen in him." O when faith gets the word of promise, the confirmed testament of Christ in its hand, how will it go to God, and crave the fulfilling of the latter-will of his own Son, saying with David, "Remember the word upon which thou hast caused me to hope ?"

7. Faith lives and leans on the righteousness of Christ, particularly. in the matter of justification and acceptance ; it casts away all the works of the law like dung and loss, saying, " Surely in the Lord have I righteousness and strength."

8. Faith leans on the fulness of Christ, and says, "Out of his fulness do all we receive, and grace for grace :" My wants are great, I am just made up of wants ; but O what wants will not the all-fulness of the Godhead dwelling in Christ supply ? for he fills all in all. What is my poor empty vessel unto that ocean that is in him ? I will go with confidence, for that fulness is in him for my use ; for " he received gifts for men, even for the rebellious."

9. Faith lives on the offices of Christ, his general offices as Mediator and Redeemer, and his particular offices as Prophet, Priest, and King. Oh, will faith say, no man taketh an office upon him, but with a design to execute the duties of his office. Will any man

pretend to be a magistrate, a minister, an advocate, or judge, and yet live in the neglect, or refuse to discharge the duties of such an office? the world would look on him as very unfaithful : and shall we imagine such a thing of Christ, who is "faithful in all his house?" Oh, will faith say, he is a Mediator and Peace-maker ; and therefore I trust that he will make my peace with the offended Majesty of heaven. He is a Saviour and Redeemer ; and therefore I trust he will deliver me from the hands of all mine enemies ; he will save from sin, because it is his office to "finish transgression and make an end of it." He is a Prophet ; and therefore I will trust that he will teach me the good and perfect will of God, open the secrets of his covenant, the mysteries of his kingdom, unto me. He is a Priest, and the great High-priest of our profession now, under the New Testament ; and therefore he will, by the great sacrifice of atonement, purge away my sins, and make my person and duties acceptable unto God. He is a King, and therefore he will subdue my corruptions, and sanctify me throughout, in soul, body, and spirit. He is a Shepherd ; and therefore I trust he will feed me, and lead me in his pastures, and I shall not want. He is a Physician, his name is JEHOVAH ROPHI ; and therefore I trust he will heal all my diseases, he will open my blind eyes, he will cure the obstinacy of my will, the hardness of my heart, the carnality of my affections. He is the Captain of salvation, who "leads many sons unto glory ;" and therefore I trust he will fight all my battles, and make me a conqueror, &c. Thus, I say, faith comes up from the wilderness, leaning on the offices of Christ, general and particular. I shall only add,

10. That faith comes up from the wilderness, leaning upon the divine attributes, as they are manifested and displayed in Christ. God, absolutely considered, is the sinner's terror ; and every attribute of God taken up absolutely, or in a law-view, breathes nothing but wrath and ruin to the whole tribe of Adam in their

fallen estate : but God manifesting himself in the flesh, or in the nature of man, through his death and satisfaction every attribute of the divine nature presents itself as with a pleasant smile, inviting sinners to come to him as an object of trust ; and accordingly faith leans upon these attributes of God as the soul comes up from the wilderness. I shall only instance in these few.

1*st*, Art thou surrounded with troubles on every hand ? Art thou called to engage with work thou art not able to manage ? Well, here is the arm of Omnipotence stretched out, to "strengthen, help, and uphold," Is. xli. 10. And accordingly faith leans on the power of God, according to that command, Is. xxvi. 4. " Trust ye in the Lord for ever : for in the Lord JEHOVAH is everlasting strength." Paul leaned on the power of God, when he cried, " I can do all things through Christ strengthening me." So did the three children ; " Our God whom we trust is able to deliver us." So did Abraham ; he was " persuaded, that he who had promised was able also to perform," &c.

2*dly*, Art thou at any time brought to thy wits end, that thou knowest not what to do ? Well, in that case faith leans on the infinite wisdom or omniscience of a God in Christ : 2 Chron. xx. 12. " Neither know we what to do, but our eyes are upon thee. The Lord knows how to deliver the righteous." When the poor soul has been trying and searching itself, and, alas ! is afraid it be deceived by a treacherous heart ; in this case, faith will have recourse unto the omniscience of a God in Christ, and say, " Search me, O God, and try me, and see if there be any wicked way in me," &c. When the poor soul is afraid of the secret plots of Satan or of his confederates ; in this case faith leans upon an omniscient God in Christ ; who " discovers deep things out of darkness, and brings out to light the shadow of death."

3*dly*, Is the believer in the wilderness deserted by friends, or separated from them by banishment, impri-

sonment or the like, saying with the church, Psal. cii.
6, 7. " I am like a pelican of the wilderness : I am
like an owl of the desert : I watch, and am as a spar-
row alone upon the house-top ?" In this case faith
leans upon the immensity of a God in Christ, and is
ready to say, Though I be alone and forsaken by all
creatures, yet I cannot be parted or separated from my
God ; for a whole God, Father, Son, and Holy Ghost,
is every where present : " Do not I the Lord fill heaven and earth?" and " my way is not hid from the
Lord, and my judgment is not passed over from my
God :" and my fellowship and converse shall be with
him, when I cannot have fellowship with my friends
and familiars who are removed far from me.

4*thly*, O but, may the believer say, I am a vile polluted creature, defiled in heart slip, and life ; and
therefore the holiness of God is a terror to me, that I
dare not so much as look towards the place where his
honour dwells : " He is of purer eyes than that he can
behold iniquity." *Answ.* The very holiness of a God
in Christ, which thou makest use of to discourage thy
faith, is glorious matter of support and encouragement ;
for faith's way of arguing from God's holiness is this ;
God is infinitely pure and holy, and therefore he will
sanctify and purify me from iniquity ; he hates sin, and
punishes it, therefore he will destroy my lust ; for it is
not my person, but my sins and lusts, that are the objects of his hatred. If the rod come, why not ? for
thereby he will make me a " partaker of his holiness,"
and purge away my iniquity. It is mine iniquity, and
not me, that he will " visit with the rod, and my transgression with stripes ;" it is not me, but my sins, that
he designs to destroy. But,

5*thly*, Say you, Can faith lean upon the justice of
God ? *Answ.* Yes, it can : for though this attribute
be a rock of offence, to grind the wicked into powder ;
yet it is a rock of sweet repose and rest to the believer.
O, will faith say, Lord, I have indeed sinned, and de-
served thy wrath ; and if thou mark iniquity, I cannot

stand : but here is my relief, my Surety has done and suffered all that the law required ; " he was wounded for our transgressions, bruised for our iniquities," &c. ; and it is inconsistent with justice to punish the same transgression twice : hence faith concludes, with Paul, " There is therefore. now no condemnation : Who can lay any thing to the charge of God's elect ?" &c.

6thly, Faith sweetly leans upon the goodness, mercy, and love of God in Christ. Oh, will faith say, has God been so good, and gracious, and merciful, as to send his only begotten Son, &c. ; he has given him unto the death to be a curse, and to be made sin for me ; and will he not do every other thing ? " He that spared not his own Son, but gave him unto the death for us all, how will he not with him also freely give us all things ? Oh how excellent is this his loving-kindness! therefore the sons of men shall put their trust under the shadow of thy wings."

7thly, Faith leans on the truth and faithfulness of God in Christ. Oh, says faith, " faithfulness is the girdle of his loins;" he is so true to his word, that " heaven and earth shall pass away before one jot of his word fall to the ground ;" and therefore I will lean and rest myself here with assured confidence ; and though he may defer the accomplishment of his word, yet I will believe and wait, and will not make haste ; " The vision is for an appointed time, but at the end it shall speak, and not lie ; though it tarry I will wait for it, because it will surely come, it will not tarry."

How faith is to act upon a God in Christ.

1. LET faith view a God in Christ in a way of appropriation, as its own God. This we find has been the way of the saints in all ages and generations ; it still lays claim to God in Christ, with its appropriating *my*, &c. Psal. xvi. 2. " O, my soul, thou hast said unto the Lord, Thou art my Lord." And ver. 5. " The Lord is the portion of mine inheritance, and of my cup," &c.

And Psal. lxxiii. 26. "My flesh and my heart faileth: but God is the strength of my heart, and my portion for ever." And if you ask, Upon what ground doth faith go, in laying claim to a God in Christ as its own God? I answer, It goes upon the ground of his assuming our nature in the person of his eternal Son, and the covenant grant and promise through him; "I am the Lord thy God; I will be your God, and ye shall be my people." Faith sets to its amen unto the grant, and says, "This God is my God for ever;" and it shall be so, because he has said it; and, "Has he said it, and will he not do it? hath he spoken, and shall it not come to pass?"

2. Having fixed thy claim unto a God in Christ as thy own God, then proceed to take a view of all his attributes and perfections; for every one of them (as I showed before) is a pillar and strong rock, on which thy faith may lean with the greatest confidence and security, even "though the earth should be removed, though the mountains should be cast into the midst of the sea." O, will faith say, my God is a God of infinite power, and "doth whatever pleaseth him in the armies of heaven, and among the inhabitants of the earth;" and this power is through Christ engaged for my preservation, "He will hide me as in a pavilion in the evil day." My God in Christ is a God of infinite wisdom; and therefore he will lead me in the way I know not, and make me wise to salvation. He is a God of infinite justice; and therefore, having accepted a satisfaction for my sins in the Surety, he is "faithful and just in forgiving;" he will "blot out mine iniquities as a cloud," &c. He is a God of unspotted holiness; and therefore he will sanctify me according to his covenant; "I will sprinkle them with clean water," &c. He is a God of infinite bowels and mercy; and therefore he will pity and pardon me, and "hear me when I cry," &c. He is a God of infinite faithfulness, this is the girdle of his loins and reins; and therefore he will not suffer his promise to fall, "his covenant he will not

break," &c. Thus faith leans and rests on the divine
attributes as they are manifested in Christ.

3. Faith leans upon a God in Christ, as one that is
infinitely bountiful and liberal; and argues as the
apostle doth, Rom. viii. 32. " He that spared not his own
Son, but delivered him up for us all, how will he not
with him also freely give us all things ?"   Faith sees
that his treasures can never be diminished, far less can
they be spent or exhausted ; and O how heartsomely
doth faith lay claim to these treasures, when it hears
him saying, as James i. 5. " If any man lack wisdom,
let him ask of God that giveth to all men liberally, and
upbraideth not : and it shall be given him."

4. Faith views the providence of a God in Christ
as calculate and designed for the advancement of his
own glory, and levelled at the good of them that love
him ; and this quiets the soul amidst all the reelings and
shakings of this lower world.   " The Lord reigneth,
let the earth rejoice : let the multitude of isles be glad
thereof."

5. *Lastly,* Faith acting upon a God in Christ, will
see an eternity of happiness beyond time, in the immediate fruition and enjoyment of him ; hence is that
David, Psal. lxxiii. 26. " My flesh and my heart faileth : but God is the strength of my heart, and my portion for ever."

---

1 *John* iii. 8. *explained,*—" *For this purpose the Son of God was
manifested that he might destroy the works of the devil.*"

In these words we may notice, 1. The great champion who takes the field, and appears in the quarrel of
fallen man ; and he is no less a personage than the
Son of God. I remember the church, Is. lxiii. 1. when
he hears tell of a Saviour coming to rescue a lost world
of mankind sinners, she cries, " Who is this that
cometh from Edom, with dyed garments from Bozrah ?
this that is glorious in his apparel, travelling in the
greatness of his strength ?" Here you have a pointed
and positive answer to this inquiry ; it is none other

than the Son of God. But O! "who shall declare his generation?" or who can frame to pronounce his great and glorious name; for it is a "name above every name," a name "at which every knee must bow, and every tongue confess that he is the Lord," the Son of God. This is he who under the Old Testament was known sometimes by the name of the "seed of the woman, the seed of Abraham, the Shiloh, the man of God's right hand, Immanuel, the branch of righteousness, the plant of renown, the messenger of the covenant, the sun of righteousness, the ruler of Israel, whose goings forth are of old, from everlasting;" and who in the New Testament is called the "Lord Jesus Christ, the Son of man, the sent of God, the Mediator, the Redeemer" of lost sinners. O sirs, let "his name be as ointment poured forth" unto you; for "the virgins love him."

2. We have the grand enemy this renowned champion had in his eye, and that is the devil, the old serpent, the head of the apostate angels; he and his confederated spirits, who had commenced a rebellion against God, their great Lord and Creator, for which they were tumbled out of the glories of heaven, into the depths of hell, and laid under chains of darkness, in which they were reserved unto the judgment of the great day. Sirs, here is matter of surprise and wonder. Our guilty consciences would have been ready to tell us, upon hearing of the coming of the Son of God unto this lower world, that his errand would have been to be avenged upon rebel man, who had renounced his allegiance unto God, and joined against him in a covenant with hell, and in an agreement with death: we might have expected to have heard him saying, "Ah, I will ease me of these mine adversaries, and be avenged on mine enemies" of Adam's family. But O, to the eternal surprise of heaven and earth, he takes the field, not against fallen man, but against fallen angels, who had ruined man,

by drawing him into the same condemnation with themselves.

3. We may notice the way and manner how the Son of God takes the field against these enemies. He does not make his attacks upon him in a secret and clandestine manner, he does not lay a secret ambush or steal a dint of the enemy unawares; no, but he acts in an open and fair way, he is manifested. He proclaimed war against him in paradise, and gives the enemy four thousand years to prepare himself for battle, before he actually takes the field against him in person; so that the enemy cannot say he wanted warning, or was taken in a surprise. Every prophet raised up under the Old Testament was a herald sent before the renowned Captain of salvation, to give devils and men warning of his approach; they proclaimed the acceptable year of the Lord to lost man, but the day of vengeance upon fallen angels, and all the wicked world, who keep by them.

4. We have the stated ground and design of the war commenced against this enemy; it was to destroy his works: "For this purpose the Son of God was manifested, that he might destroy the works of the devil." The grand plot of hell was to ruin the works of God, to disturb the creation, to deface the image of God, and to set up his empire in these lower regions: being cast out of heaven, he would set up his throne upon earth, and reign without control as the god of this world. But now the purpose of the Son of God was to counteract the enemy, to sap and overturn the foundation of his usurped kingdom, and to set up and establish his own and his Father's authority among the sons of men: "For this purpose the Son of God was manifested, that he might destroy the works of the devil."

What those works of the devil are which the Son of God came to destroy.

THE grand and fundamental work of the devil is sin. This is, as it were his first born, and the beginning of

his strength, as you see from the former clause of the
verse ; " He that committeth sin, is of the devil ; for the
devil sinneth from the beginning." And then it follows, "For this purpose the Son of God was manifested,"
&c.   So that the main work of the devil is sin : this is
just the poison and venom of the old serpent.   The
flood that he casts out of his mouth, in order to destroy the church, represented under the notion of a woman, Rev. xii. 15. what else is it but a flood of sin ?
This is the main engine whereby the devil carries on
all his other hellish works and stratagems either against
God or man.   If it had not been for sin, the devil had
never got any power over men in the world ; so that
sin is the very seat and strength of his kingdom in the
world.   I remember it is said, that "justice and judgment are the habitation of God's throne ;" and I may
add, that iniquity and sin is the habitation of the devil's
throne and empire.   And here I might tell you of a
multitude of sins which are evidently the works of the
devil, if I were not afraid of entering upon a field large
and wide like the heavens.   Atheism is the work of
the devil ; he studies to persuade men that there is no
God to call them to an account, no judgment to come,
no hell or heaven.   Ignorance is a great work of the
devil ; he " blinds the minds of them that believe not,
lest the light of the glorious gospel of Christ should
shine into their hearts."   Hence his kingdom is called
a kingdom of darkness.   Unbelief is the work of the
devil, which is nothing else but a " making God a liar,"
a discrediting of a God of truth, speaking either in a
way of promise, precept, or threatening, in his word.
It was by unbelief that he ruined our first parents, he
brought them to doubt if God had said so and so.   And
when once a man begins to waver and question whether
this or that be a point of the truth of God, he is gone,
the enemy has him fair before the wind.   Enmity is
another work of the devil : " The carnal mind is enmity against God."   This is just the poison of the old
serpent, that has run through all the powers of the

soul. Pride is a work of the devil, yea, it is the very picture of the devil. Pride was his first sin ; and by telling them that they should be as gods, by eating the forbidden tree, " knowing good and evil," he ruined them and their posterity. This sin of pride has so much of the devil in it, that God cannot look near a proud man ; he "beholds the proud afar off." Hypocrisy and dissimulation either with God or man, that is another work of the devil. He himself dissembled the matter with our first parents, he transformed himself into an angel of light : and so doth every hypocrite, he appears to be what he really is not. Idolatry, superstition, charms, witchcraft, error, swearing, lying, Sabbath-breaking, murder, adultery, theft, covetousness, perjury, and all sin that I can possibly name, they are all the works of the devil, and they that commit them are of the devil.

But now, to illustrate this head yet a little further, I will tell you of some works of the devil brought about by sin, which are just the devil's sport and recreation. 1. The dishonour of God. 2. The disturbing of the creation. 3. The ruin of man. 4. The erection of his own kingdom of sin and darkness.

1. I say, the devil by sin designs the dishonour of God, every sin being a violation of his law, a contempt of his authority, a denial of his sovereignty, and affront to his justice and holiness, and a casting dirt upon all his perfections. Now, what a sport and pleasure is it unto that proud and rebellious spirit, when he can get men and women to join him after this manner in affronting God, and trampling upon his laws ? hence sinners are said to be in a covenant or confederacy with hell, to dishonour God

2. By sin he disturbs the creation, and disorders all the works of God in this lower world. You know, Gen. i. when God had made the heavens and the earth, and all the rest of the creatures, he pronounced them all good ; every thing was in its proper joint and lith, subservient unto the great ends of their creation ; not

a jar or groan to be heard among all the creatures of God. But now, Satan, by sin, disturbs and disorders the creation of God. Having tempted man to break his allegiance to God, he brings the curse of God upon the very ground, and all the inferior creatures that stood in subordination to man. Hence follows war between man and the inferior creatures; and the creatures that are subject to man, it is unwillingly that they serve him; they groan under it as a servitude, that they should be any way useful unto man, a rebel against their great Lord and Creator; hence is that of the apostle, Rom. viii. 20—22. It is just the pleasure and diversion of the devil to see that order, and beauty, and harmony, that God placed in the creation at first, disturbed.

3. By sin he brings about the ruin of poor souls, which is as great a pleasure and diversion to the wicked spirit, as it is for a lion to tear and devour his prey when he is hungry. To illustrate this to you, I will tell you of some things the devil does to you when he gets you to sin, which are just the work and sport of the devil.

1st. He takes away our sight. The god of this world blinds all his votaries by sin; so that, though the man is as it were just upon the mouth of hell, yet does he not know it. Like the Philistines, he puts out our eyes, and then makes a sport of us.

2dly, By sin he takes away our beauty. Man, before sin entered, shined with the beauties of holiness; but now by sin we are become hell-hued, black like the Ethiopian, by lying among the devil's pots; and this is the work and sport of hell.

3dly, He takes away our clothing, he leaves us stark naked. Man, before sin entered, was clothed with a robe of perfect law righteousness; but when through sin we fell into the hand of the devil, he stripped us of that ornament; hence Laodicea is said to be " wretched, miserable, blind, poor, and naked," without a rag to cover her.

4*thly*, He takes away our strength and ability for any good work; so that we are not sufficient to conceive a good thought, though it could purchase heaven. "When we were without strength, in due time Christ died for the ungodly."

5*thly*, He takes away our peace with God, and confidence towards him ; as you see in our first parents immediately after the fall, they fled from the presence of God as an enemy ; the Almighty became a terror to them, that they durst not look him in the face.

6*thly*, He takes away peace with conscience, God's deputy in the bosom. The devil has a continual hell in his breast, through his guilty conscience ; only it is some pleasure and ease to him to see men and women through sin feeling his own smart, and crying with Cain, " My sin is greater than can be forgiven."

7*thly*, He takes away our life ; for every sin is a thrust given to the life of the soul. And the devil, who murdered himself, and who is a murderer from the beginning, he just takes pleasure to set men and women a-work to murder both soul and body at once, every sin being a draught of the poison of the old serpent put in the man's hand.

8*thly*, He takes away our title to God and glory, and makes us children of wrath, and heirs of hell and the curse with himself. These are some things that the devil works by sin, which are just his pastime and recreation. To all which I add,

4. In the fourth place, that another work of the devil by sin is, to establish his own kingdom and empire in opposition unto God's government. And indeed, by the first sin, he drew all mankind under his dominion. He takes God's viceroy in this lower world (man. I mean), whom God had " made a little lower than the angels, and crowned with glory and dignity ;" he not only makes him his drudge and vassal, but he arms him against God his righteous Lord, and makes him say to the Almighty, Depart from us, for we desire not

the knowledge of thy ways." And thus you see what
are the works of the devil.

---

*Arguments proving that the Son of God destroys the works of
the devil*

THIS is evident from the whole current and tenor of
the Scriptures from the beginning to the end of them,
Gen. iii. 15. he was to bruise the serpent's head. No
sooner did he enter upon his mediatory work, Matth.
iv. but he enters the lists with this enemy, and foils
him with the sword of the Spirit. By his death he is
said to have " spoiled principalities and powers." He
threw him out of the souls and bodies of men when
upon earth ; and, by the preaching of the everlasting
gospel, his kingdom falls like the lightning from heaven. And, Rev. xii. we read of a war between Mi-
chael and his angels, and the devil and his angels.
But now this will be further cleared by the induction
of a few particulars.

1. Was it the plot of hell, to have God dishonoured
and affronted in all his attributes and perfections by the
sin of man? Well, Christ counteracts the devil in this;
for he brings a greater revenue of glory to the crown
of heaven by the work of redemption, than could ever
have accrued to it by all the service that men or angels
could have done to God through all eternity; hence
it was that the angels, immediately upon Christ's appearing in the world, cry, " Glory to God in the
highest." O the bright displays of the divine attributes, in him who is " the brightness of the Father's
glory !"

2. It was the work of the devil, to disgrace the holy
law of God, by breaking it himself, and teaching man
to break in upon it ; but the work of Christ is, to
" magnify the law, and to make it honourable." " Think
not (says Christ) that I am come to destroy the law :
I am not come to destroy, but to fulfil it." He himself fulfilled it as a covenant, and establishes it as a rule

to all his followers, and puts his Spirit within them, causing them to walk in his statutes, and to do them.

3. Was it the work of the devil, to disturb God's government in the world, and to cast all into disorder and confusion? Well, God the Father lays the government upon Christ's shoulders, he puts the reins of administration in his hands, on purpose that he may restore every thing into the order wherein he had set them at first: and at the end of the day, when he has done his work, it will be a " time of restitution of all things;" and the very creatures long for that happy day, Rom. viii. 19, &c.

4. Was it the devil's work, to establish his own kingdom of darkness in this lower world, by establishing error, ignorance, unbelief, atheism, pride, carnality, profanity, and all manner of sin and wickedness? Well, it is the work of Christ to pull down these pillars and strongholds of Satan's kingdom : Dan. ix. he shall " finish transgression and make an end of sin." And in the 5th verse of this chapter, where my text lies, " And ye know that he was manifested to take away our sins; and in him is no sin. His name is Jesus, because he saves his people from their sins."

5. Was it the devil's work, to break all fellowship and friendship betwixt God and man? Well, it is the work of Christ, to bring them into fellowship and friendship one with another; therefore he is called a Mediator, or a Peace-maker. His work is " to make reconciliation for iniquity : When we were enemies, we were reconciled to God by his death : God was in Christ reconciling the world unto himself." Yea, Christ himself becomes " a new and living way," by which God comes down unto us, and we come up unto God, and have " our fellowship with the Father, and with his Son Jesus Christ."

6. Was it the work of the devil, to bring man under the curse and condemnation of the law, that so he might be in the same condition with himself? Well, it is the work of Christ, to " redeem us from the curse of the

law, being made a curse for us." And they who believe in Christ, being wrapt up in his righteousness,
there is no condemnation to them, nothing can be laid
to their charge.

7. Was it the work of the devil, to deface the image
of God which he stamped upon man? It is the work
of Christ, to restore it; and for this end he manifests
himself in the glass of the gospel, that we, by beholding
of his glory, may be "changed into the same image,
from glory to glory."

But, not to insist upon particulars, Christ just "restored what he took not away," but what the devil
and sin took away. Satan spoils us of our light and
sight; Christ comes to "open the blind eyes, to give
light to them that sit in darkness, and in the region of
the shadow of death." Satan spoils us of our beauty,
and rubbed the hue of hell upon us; Christ takes them
that have "lain among the devil's pots," and makes
them "like the wings of a dove covered with silver,
and her feathers with yellow gold." Satan strips us
naked; Christ clothes the poor sinner with white raiment, with the garment of salvation, and the robe of
righteousness. Satan spoils us of our strength; but
Christ makes his strength sufficient for our weakness,
makes the feeble as David, so as to resist the devil
himself, and to put him to flight. Satan spoils us of our
peace with God, and peace with conscience; but
Christ restores both: "Being justified by faith, we
have peace with God through our Lord Jesus Christ.
Peace I leave with you, my peace I give unto you;
not as the world giveth give I unto you: and a
peace that passeth all understanding." Satan takes
away, through sin, our title to God and glory; but
Christ restores this again with advantage, and settles
our claim to God as our God, and to the inheritance
of glory, upon a better foundation than the claim that
the first Adam stood upon. In a word, the devil, and
his first born (sin), took away our spiritual life, and
leaves us "dead in trespasses and sins;" but Christ

restores life to the dead : " I am the resurrection and
the life ; and, He that believeth in me, out of his belly
shall flow rivers of living waters." And then he himself becomes the continual fountain of their life, and
their " life is hid with Christ in God." Thus then you
see, that it is a clear truth, that Christ the Son of God
destroys the works of the devil.

How Christ the Son of God destroys the works of the devil.

1. CHRIST destroys the works of the devil by the virtue of his blood. Now, when I speak of the blood or
death of Christ, I understand the whole of his satisfaction, including his perfect active obedience unto the
mandatory part of the law, as well as his suffering the
minatory part of it in his death. Now, I say, by the
death of Christ, in this extensive view, Satan and his
works are destroyed. This, of all others, unto our
sense and reason would appear to be the most impro-
bable ; and yet it was the best, and the only way how
it could be accomplished. The power of Satan, and
his whole destroying works, are founded in sin ; the
obligation of the sinner unto death, by virtue of the
curse of the law, was that which gave him all his
power to destroy and ruin lost sinners ; and therefore,
if that obligation be destroyed, Satan's power and all
his works of darkness must of course dissolve ; the
foundation being destroyed, all that is lying upon it
must fall to the ground. Now, this was done in the
death of Christ ; justice was satisfied, reconciliation
made for iniquity, the sinner redeemed from the curse,
he being made a curse for us ; and whenever the sinner by faith closes with Christ as crucified, or comes to
the blood of sprinkling, the sentence passes, Rom. viii.
1. " There is therefore now no condemnation to them
which are in Christ Jesus."

2. Christ destroys the works of the devil by the light
of his word. This is that weapon which is not carnal, but
mighty through God to the pulling down of strong holds,
to the casting down of imaginations, and every high

that exalteth itself against the knowledge of Christ."
When Christ sent out his disciples to preach the gospel through the cities of Israel, Satan's kingdom fell
down before it like lightning; and when Christ sent
out his apostles through the world, in order to overturn the kingdom of Satan, the weapon he put in their
hand was just the word of the gospel; " Go, teach all
nations ; go, preach the gospel unto every creature ;"
go, manifest the Son of God, and what he has done and
suffered for the redemption of sinners. And accordingly they went and preached the gospel of the kingdom ; and such was the power that accompanied it,
that the idolatries of the nations fell down apace before
it. It is very observable, that upon the very external
manifestation of the gospel, the gross works of the devil fell down. In the time of paganism and popery,
the devil used to appear and converse with men and
women in a familiar way, and they worshipped and
served him as though he had been a god ; but, upon
the entry of the gospel, he quitted that gross way of
doing, and betook himself to a more secret and subtle
way of ruining souls, by fostering them in security,
pride, enmity, unbelief, and such spiritual wickednesses.
And wherever the gospel comes with power, he is driven out of these high places also.

3. Christ destroys the works of the devil by the efficacy of his Spirit, whereby the virtue of his blood, and
evidence of the word is carried in upon the soul ; for
it is the Spirit that applies to us the redemption purchased by the blood of Christ, and manifested and
exhibited in his word. There could be no efficacy in
the word, in itself considered, for destroying the works
of the devil, without the concurring power of the Holy
Ghost, who upon this very account, is called a " Spirit
of power : not by might, nor by power of man, but by
my Spirit, saith the Lord of hosts." And O, when the
Spirit of the Lord comes along with the revelation and
dispensation of the word, then the devil's prisoners are
loosed, the captives of the mighty are delivered, and the

soul that was bound for many years with the devil's chains is raised up, and made "partaker of the glorious liberty of the sons of God."

4. Christ destroys the works of the devil by the prudence and wisdom of his government and administration, of which you have an account, Is. xi. 2—4, &c. Christ is given as a head of government unto his church, and the sceptre of power is put in his hand, a rod of strength, and a rod of iron, whereby he dashes his most powerful enemies in pieces as a potter's vessel ; he is "made head over all things unto the church, which is his body." And that he may be in a better capacity to manage the reins of government for the benefit of his mystical body, and the great ends of their salvation, "all the treasures of wisdom and knowledge are hid in him ;" so that his administration is unerring and infallible. Satan the old serpent, and his agents, they are continually plotting the ruin and overthrow of the interest of Christ in the world ; sometimes by fraud, and sometimes by force and violence, they endeavour to make the work to cease, and never more than at the present time ; but Christ, by the prudence, wisdom, and energy of his government, he counteracts all the deep laid plots of the gates of hell, so as they never have, nor never shall be able to prevail to the overthrow of his work and interest ; "He takes the wise in their own craftiness, and turns the counsel of the froward headlong." Thus you see how it is that Christ destroys the works of the devil.

Times and seasons when Christ destroys the works of the devil.

1. The day of Christ's death gave a notable blow, as I told you just now, unto the devil's kingdom ; for then he "spoiled principalities and powers, and made an open show of them" before God and the holy angels. Men and devils, to the world's view, were triumphing over Christ ; Christ at the same time was triumphing over them before the invisible world of spirits. The "hand-writing that was against us," and from

which the devil derived all his authority and power in this world, was torn and cancelled.

2. The day of Christ's resurrection gave a signal blow to the works of the devil ? for he "rose for our justification." The devil, the Jews and Romans, they thought they had obtained the victory over Christ, when they got him in the grave, and his stone sealed : but "he was taken from prison and from judgment;" by an order from Heaven, the stone was rolled away from the door of the sepulchre, and he comes forth carrying the spoils of death and hell in his hand, and carrying also the discharge of the debt of a whole elect world in his hand, &c.

3. The day of Christ's ascension into heaven was a notable destruction unto Satan and his works; for "when he ascended up on high, he led captivity captive;" he opened a passage between this world and heaven, through the territories of the prince of the power of the air, by which all his friends might follow him to glory. And O how did it torment the devil, when Christ went through the air in triumph with his "twenty thousand chariots of angels," every one crying, "God is gone up with a shout, the Lord with the sound of a trumpet : sing praises to God, sing praises ; sing praises unto our King, sing praises !"

4. In the day of Pentecost Christ gave another stroke to the devil and his works. When Christ newly sat down on his throne of glory, poured out his Spirit upon his apostles in an extraordinary manner, enabling them to work miracles, and to preach the gospel in all languages, that it might spread through all the known world ; how did Satan's kingdom begin to fall, when at one sermon three thousand souls were plucked out of his kingdom, and added to the church of Christ ! And from that time forward, how did the light of the gospel fly like lightning from one end of the world (as it were) to the other, insomuch, as the apostle observes, Rom. x. 18. "their sound (in a little time) went unto the ends of the earth !" And to this I may add, that

when at any time the renowned Captain of salvation " girds his sword upon his thigh, and rides prosperously " in his chariot of truth, " making the people to fall under him," convincing and converting sinners unto his knowledge and obedience, that is a time when Christ destroys the works of the devil, and pulls down his strongholds.

5. The day of a sinner's believing in Christ is a time when Satan's works are destroyed. It is the great design of hell, to slander God and his word among the children of men, as though he were not worthy of credit: thus he slandered him to our first parents; " Hath God said " so and so ? Now, when a sinner is brought to " set to his seal that God is true," and is made to give such credit unto the record of God that he ventures his eternal salvation upon the veracity of a God of truth; this, I say, is just a stab (as it were) given the devil's heart, who " abode not in the truth" of God himself, and cannot endure to see any poor sinners abiding in it. The same I may say with respect unto every renewed act of faith on Christ, upon the footing of the promise of a God of truth; hence we are told that it is by faith as a shield that we " quench the fiery darts of Satan."

6. Times of espousals, nearness betwixt God and a soul, are times of destroying the works of the devil. It was the great plot of hell, as you heard, to separate between God and man; and how doth it gall that enemy to the heart, when he sees himself defeated, and the poor soul, that was through his means put far off from God, brought so nigh unto him, that he is just taken up, and taken in to the " chariot of the wood of Lebanon," and made to " sit down under his shadow with great delight," having the banner of love displayed over it! Sirs, every new manifestation of the Son of God unto the soul gives a wound unto Satan's interest in the soul; it weakens unbelief, pride, carnality, hypocrisy, enmity, and the other branches of the body of sin and death.

7. When at any time an honourable testimony is
given to the Lord, to the doctrine, discipline, worship,
and government of his church, in a day of uncommon
defection and backsliding.   It is the great work of the
devil to sow the tares of error, and corruption, and ty-
ranny, and discord, and division, in a church ; and
when these evils are " coming in like a flood," the
Lord spirits any of his saints or servants to lift up the
banner, and to testify against these works of the devil,
and to dismantle them of their fair colours under which
they are carried on ; this, I say, torments the devil, and
those that live under his government, as you read, Rev.
xi.   And Christ's kingdom and interest in all ages of
the world, particularly in this church, has been maintained by a faithful witnessing for the Lord and his
way, in opposition to errors and corruptions, &c.

8. When a believer dies, and goes away to glory,
under a guard of angels, along that lane or road that
Christ opened when he ascended, to take possession of
these vacant thrones that the devil deserted, when he
" left his first habitation ;" what a vexation is it unto
that proud spirit to see the poor believer, whom he
tossed and tempted many a day in this lower world,
going up in a triumphant manner, to sit down on the
throne he himself once sat upon !

*Reasons why the Son of God is manifested to destroy the works of
the devil.*

1. CHRIST encounters this enemy, and destroys his
works, because it was his Father's will and pleasure ;
and he did always these things that pleased his Father,
rojoicing always before him.   " I delight to do thy
will, O my God : yea, thy law is within my heart.   I
lay down my life of myself ; this commandment have
I received of my Father."   The devil by his works
had affronted and dishonoured the God and Father of
our Lord Jesus Christ, and Christ rejoiced to resent his
Father's quarrel upon this enemy.

2. Christ destroys the works of the devil, because it

was for his own honour to engage in this expedition. There is a new revenue of glory accrues to the crown of Christ, as Mediator, by this undertaking. All the ransomed in glory, through eternity, will be celebrating the glory of his achievements, whereby "through death he destroyed him that had the power of death, that is, the devil." Hence the ransomed, Rev. v. 9, cry, " Worthy art thou to take the book, and to loose the seven seals thereof; for thou wast slain, and hast redeemed us to God by thy blood."

3. Christ destroys the works of the devil, out of the ancient and wonderful love that he did bear to man upon earth, particularly to that remnant of Adam's family which were given him by the Father from all eternity. It was the love of the Father that sent him, and it was the love of the Son that made him come to deliver us out of the paw of the roaring lion, when we were ready to be devoured of him. " He loved me (says Paul), and gave himself for me." And O the love of Christ in this matter, it passes all understanding.

4. Out of regard to his own law, which the devil by his works had dishonoured. The devil made it his business to abrogate and abolish the law of God from among the children of men, that it might not be the rule of their actions; and such is the devil's spite and malice against Heaven, that, if it were possible he would not leave the least print of it in the world : but now, Christ had such a regard for the honour of the law, that he would " magnify it, and make it honourable," both as a covenant and as a rule ; " I came not to destroy the law, but to fulfil it."

5. Christ destroys the works of the devil, that he may " still this enemy and avenger." When the devil had so far prevailed, as to deface the image of God upon man, to bring him under the curse, and to draw him into a confederacy against God with himself, he thought that he had carried the day, and that now man, and all this lower world, was his own; and he was no

doubt saying like proud Pharaoh, " Now will I divide the spoil ;" I will tear, and devour, and rage as I have a mind. But how is this enemy stilled, silenced, and confounded, when he sees all his game spoiled, and his kingdom ruined, his head bruised, by the child born, and the Son given to us, whose name is " Wonderful, Counsellor, The mighty God, The everlasting Father, The Prince of peace !"

6. He destroys the works of the devil, for the illustration and manifestation of all the divine perfections. The wisdom of God is manifested in outwitting all the policy of hell, and " taking the wise in their own craftiness, and turning his counsel headlong :" the power of God in " spoiling principalities and powers," and in bringing life out of death, and light out of darkness, salvation out of misery, and " glory to God in the highest " out of that which had the greatest tendency to dishonour him : the holiness of God, in expressing the greatest hatred and indignation against sin, as the abominable thing which his soul hates : his justice, in the execution of the penalty of the law upon the Surety, and justifying the ungodly upon the footing of a better righteousness than ever Adam had before he fell : the goodness, love, and mercy of God in finding a ransom, that we might not go down to the pit : his truth and faithfulness, in taking care that the threatening of the law should be fulfilled in the sufferings of Christ, and in fulfilling that ancient promise of the seed of the woman his bruising the serpent's head, after the delay of four thousand years ; the accomplishment of which is a glorious security for his accomplishing every other promise of the word. Thus you see why the Son of God destroys the works of the devil.

Important remarks concerning the covenant of grace.

1. I REMARK, that the occasion of the covenant of grace, like that of God's covenant with Noah, was a deluge of wrath, which broke out upon Adam, and

all his family, for the breach and violation of the covenant of works. This is what is pointed at, Ezek. xvi.
4—8, where you see that that which gave occasion to
God's entering into a covenant of grace, is that miserable estate man had brought himself into by sin,
"When I passed by thee, and saw thee polluted in
thine own blood, behold, thy time was the time of love,
and I spread my skirt over thee, and covered thy nakedness : yea, I sware unto thee, and entered into a
covenant with thee, saith the Lord God, and thou be-
camest mine." Here it may readily be asked, What is
that state we are reduced unto by the breach of the
first covenant ? I answer, in short, it is a state of sin ;
original sin like a contagion, has overrun all men, and
the whole man from the crown of the head to the sole
of the foot. It is a state of alienation and estrangement from God ; we are "alienated from the very life
of God, through the ignorance that is in us ;" like the
prodigal, we have gone into a far country, and care not
for returning to our Father's house. Yea more, it is a
state of enmity and hostility against God ; "the carnal
mind is enmity against God," we are "enemies in our
minds by wicked works." It is a godless and hopeless
state ; therefore are we said to be "without God, and
without hope in the world." It is a state worse than
Egyptian darkness ; we are not simply in the dark, but
we are darkness itself : "Once ye were darkness." It
is a state of impotency and weakness ; "for when we
were yet without strength, in due time Christ died for
us." It is a state of bondage and captivity to sin, Satan, and the world ; we are led captive by these potent
enemies. It is a cursed and condemned state ; we are
"condemned already, and the wrath of God abideth
on us." It is a state of death ; we are dead spiritually,
under the power of sin, and lying upon the very borders of eternal death. Now, this is the condition we
are reduced unto by the fall ; upon which account we
may well take up that melancholy song, "The crown
is fallen from our head ; woe unto us that we have sin-

ned." However, infinite mercy and love takes occasion from this miserable and ruined estate of man, to enter into a new covenant, even a covenant of grace, in order to his deliverance.

2. I remark, that the rise and spring of this covenant of grace was not foreseen, faith or good works, or any thing else in the creature ; but only the free and surprising love of God : John iii. 16. "God so loved the world, that he gave his only begotten Son, that whosoever believeth in him, should not perish, but have everlasting life." Jer. xxxi. 3. " I have loved thee with an everlasting love : therefore with loving-kindness have I drawn thee." This love of God to lost sinners was altogether and absolutely free ; free in opposition to merit, free in opposition to constraint ; it hath no other cause but only the freedom of his own will, Eph. i. 4, 5. And as it is free, so it is superlatively great ; love that passeth knowledge ; love which hath a height and depth, a breadth and length, which can never be fathomed, or found out. It is distinguishing love ; it lighted upon men, when it passed by angels that fell ; it lighted upon some of Adam's family, when it passed by others.

3. I remark that this covenant of grace in the original make and constitution of it, was transacted with Christ as a new-covenant head, a public person, representing all the spiritual seed which the Lord had given him ; for, sirs, you would know, that since the fall of man, God never entered into any covenant with him directly and immediately, but only by the intervention of a Surety and Mediator. Hence in our Larger Cate chism, in answer to that question, ' With whom was the covenant of grace made ?' the answer is, that ' it was made with Christ, and with the elect in him as his seed.' Hence it is that we read of " grace given us in Christ, before the world began." In this covenant there are some things that relate particularly to Christ himself as Surety and Redeemer, and some things in it that relate to the members and seed of Christ. The

Father having promised sufficient furniture and through-bearing to his Son, both for the purpose and application of our redemption ; the Son, he not only undertakes to satisfy justice, to fulfil the law, to bruise the head of the old serpent, but also by his Spirit, which he would send into their hearts, to sprinkle them with clean water, to take away the stony heart, to enlighten them, to justify them, to adopt and sanctify them, and at last to present them " without spot or wrinkle, or any such thing." And when all this comes to be revealed and set forth in a gospel-dispensation, what is incumbent upon us, but to subscribe to this glorious transaction and plan of redemption, that was laid by Infinite Wisdom ? Thus, I say, the covenant of grace was originally transacted with Christ, and with us in him, and through him. And they who either in print or pulpit, ridicule or exclaim against this, as a new scheme of doctrine, they do not ridicule us, but the doctrine asserted by the church of Scotland in her standards ; which, as it is founded upon the word, so we are bound by solemn covenant to cleave unto it.

4. I remark, that the revelation of this covenant of grace transacted with Christ before the world began, was made very early to our first parents in Paradise, immediately after the fall : Gen. iii. 15. " The seed of the woman shall bruise the head of the serpent." Here it was that the grand secret which lay in the breast of God, did first break forth. When our first parents were waiting, with a trembling heart, every moment for the execution of the sentence of the broken covenant of works; behold glad tidings of great joy are issued out from a throne of grace, namely, that in the fulness of time, the Son of God was to take on the seed of the woman, and bruise the serpent's head, to destroy the devil and his works, and redeem man from that gulf of misery into which he was plunged. This was the covenant of grace. And it is remarkable, that in its first edition, it came forth in a promise of Christ; this was enlarged and explained to Abraham, Moses,

David, and yet more fully opened after the Babylonish captivity, by Jeremiah, Ezekiel, and other prophets, till Christ himself actually came, in whom all the Old Testament types, prophecies, and promises, received their full accomplishment. And having by his death " confirmed the covenant with many," the covenant of grace, after his resurrection and exaltation, came forth in its last and best edition ; namely, in the form of a testament, having the two great sacraments of baptism and the Lord's supper appended to it, as full and incontested evidences of its being confirmed by his death. This glorious charter is now passed the seal, and therefore faith may make use of it with boldness.

5. I remark, that this covenant of grace, or testament of our Lord Jesus Christ, may be viewed and considered in its dispensation or exhibition. God, in his infinite wisdom, for reaching the great end and design of a covenant of grace, has appointed ordinances, the word, sacraments, and prayer, and other proper means, by which the benefits of his death, and blessings of his covenant, may come to be actually applied to us ; he has authorised ministers to dispense word and sacraments, that by these, as through conduit pipes, his grace and fulness may be communicated to us. And here it would be remembered, that the covenant of grace in the dispensation and exhibition of it, comes to every man's door ; it is presented as the ground and foundation of faith in common to all the hearers of the gospel, elect and reprobate. We call all and every one to take hold of God's covenant, and tell them, " To you is the word of this salvation sent : The promise (or covenant) is unto you, and to your children, and to all that are afar off, even as many as the Lord our God shall call."

6. I remark, that this covenant of grace may be considered in the application and execution of it. And this is either initial, progressive, or consummate. (1.) I say, there is the initial application, or the soul's first entry into the bond of the covenant ; or rather, the

Spirit of the great new covenant Head taking hold of the poor soul, and the soul at the same moment taking hold of the covenant by faith, receives it as a good and sufficient security for that life and happiness, which was lost by the sin of the first Adam. This is in Scripture called the day of espousals, wherein the soul does as it were sign and subscribe the marriage contract, saying, " I am the Lord's." (2.) There is the further improvement of this covenant of grace, for the soul's daily supply in a way of believing, whereby it is made to " grow in grace, and in the knowledge of our Lord Jesus Christ." This is called a " drawing water with joy out of the wells of salvation." The believer, finding himself under this and the other want, improves the promises of the covenant, as they are suited and adapted to his case. And thus the work of sanctification is daily advanced : " they shall go from strength to strength." (3.) There is the full execution of the designs of this covenant, when the soul is brought to glory, and " presented faultless before the presence of God, without spot or wrinkle, or any such thing." " When Christ, who is our life, shall appear, then shall we also appear with him in glory." At that day, the covenant and all the concerns of it, is fully executed and performed, even the day of Jesus Christ : Phil. i. 6, " Being confident of this very thing, that he which hath begun a good work in you, will perform it until the day of Jesus Christ."

Faith fixed upon the Covenant of Grace, the best support in times of trouble.

1*st*, THEN, perhaps, poor believer, a storm of vindictive wrath in appearance may blow from heaven, which will startle thy conscience to that degree, that thou shalt be made to cry, through a sense of guilt, and the impressions of God's anger on thy soul, " The arrows of the Almighty are within me, the poison whereof drinketh up my spirit : the terrors of God do set themselves in array against me." Well, if that

happen to be thy case, as I know not but it may, look
to the rainbow of the covenant about the throne, and
there you shall see the faithfulness of God engaged,
that vindictive wrath shall never touch thee. Read
for this, Is. liv. 7, 8, 9, 10. There you see the oath
of God is passed that the deluge of vindictive anger
shall no more return to destroy thee : and what more
wouldst thou have ? will unbelief dare to charge God
with perjury ?

2dly, Perhaps, believer, a storm of trouble from the
world may blow upon thee, times of public calamity
may come, days of persecution for righteousness' sake ;
or if that fail, a storm of personal trial may be abiding
thee, trouble in thy name, in thy estate, in thy family,
or relations ; the storm may blow so hard as to sweep
away all that is dear to thee in the world.   Well, say
you, what shall I do in that case ?   Why, my advice
to you is, to cast the eye of faith upon the bow of the
covenant, and there thou shalt find what will cheer and
keep up thy heart ; there thou shalt find thy covenanted God in Christ promiseth his sympathy in all
thy troubles : Is. lxiii. 9, " In all their affliction he is
afflicted."   Psal. ciii. 13, " Like as a father pitieth his
children : so the Lord pitieth them that fear him."
There you shall find him engaged to go through the
fire and water with thee : Is. xliii. 2, " When thou
passest through the waters, I will be with thee ; and
through the rivers, they shall not overflow thee : when
thou walkest through the fire, thou shalt not be burnt ;
neither shall the flame kindle upon thee."   There you will
find him engaging himself by covenant to carry thy head
above : Is. xli. 10, " Fear thou not, for I am with thee :
—I will help thee, yea, I will uphold thee with the right
hand of my righteousness."   There thou shalt find him
engaged to bring thee safely through all thy troubles ;
" Many are the afflictions of the righteous : but the
Lord delivereth him out of them all."   Thou shalt
find that " thy light afflictions, which are but for a

moment, shall work for thee a far more exceeding and eternal weight of glory."

3dly, Perhaps a storm from hell may be abiding thee, " principalities and powers, and the rulers of the darkness of this world ;" the armed legions of the bottomless pit, like the bulls of Bashan, may ere long be goring at thee. Well, in this case look to the throne of grace, and to the bow of the covenant that surrounds it, and thou shalt find what may, and will relieve thee ; you will find that Christ has, according to the first article of the covenant, " bruised the head of that serpent, spoiled principalities and powers, triumphed over them, and made a show of them openly on his cross ;" he has " destroyed death, and him that had the power of death." There thou wilt find him engaged to stand by thee as thy leader and commander, to make thee tread Satan under thy feet shortly : and by faith acted upon this covenant, thou art assured of the victory, yea, that thou art a conqueror, and " more than a conqueror, through him that loved thee."

4thly, Perhaps, believer, thou may in a little find the strong man of indwelling sin, like Samson after his locks were cut, recover strength, and begin to rage in thy soul, insomuch that thou shalt be made to cry with the apostle, " Wretched man that I am, who shall deliver me from the body of this death !" Well, in that case look to the throne of grace, and the bow of the covenant, and thou shalt find God engaging himself to give grace and mercy, to help thee in this time of need : Rom. vi. 14, he has said, " Sin shall not have dominion over you." Micah vii. 19, " I will subdue their iniquities." Ezek. xxxvi. 25, " From all their filthiness, and from all their idols will I cleanse them." Is. lix. 19, " When the enemy shall come in like a flood, the Spirit of the Lord shall lift up a standard against him."

5thly, Perhaps in a little, Satan and corruption together may give thee a trip, and lay thee on thy back, and as it were tread thee in a mire, so that thy own

clothes shall abhor thee ; and what shall be done in
that case ?   Well, even in that case look up to the
throne, and behold the exalted Prince that gives repentance and remission of sin, that he may lift thee up
again, and by the blood of his covenant, bring thee
out of the pit, wherein there is no water.   Take a view
of the bow of the covenant, and thou wilt find written
upon the arch of this bow, that "though thou hast lien
among the pots, he will make thee as the wings of a
dove covered with silver, and her feathers with yellow
gold."   Listen to his voice that sits upon the throne
and thou wilt hear him saying, "Though thou hast
played the harlot with many lovers ; yet return again
to me, saith the Lord."

6thly, Perhaps a black and melancholy night of desertion may overtake thee in thy way ; God may hide,
and thou be brought to cry with the church, " The
Lord hath forsaken me, and my Lord hath forgotten
me."   Well, though thou "walk in darkness, and see
no light, yet trust in the name of the Lord, and stay
thyself upon him," by virtue of the covenant, as thy
God ; for here he is engaged, that he will be "thy
God for ever," that he will "never leave thee nor forsake thee," as to his real presence ; and that " though
weeping may endure for a night, yet joy cometh in
the morning.   For a small moment have I forsaken
thee, but with great mercies will I gather thee.   In a
little wrath I hid my face from thee, for a moment ;
but with everlasting kindness will I have mercy on thee,
saith the Lord thy Redeemer."

7thly, Perhaps you may fall under the melancholy
fears and apprehensions, that thou shalt be so left of
God, as to prove an apostate in the end.   Well, look
up to the bow of the covenant about the throne, and
thou wilt find security against that also : Phil. i. 6.
" He which hath begun the good work in thee, will
perform it until the day of Jesus Christ.   The righteous shall hold on his way, and he that hath clean
hands shall wax stronger and stronger."   Grace and

glory are connected by the covenant so inseparably, that they can never be divorced: Psal. lxxxiv. 11, " The Lord will give grace and glory."

8*thly*, Perhaps thou may in a little fall under a melancholy deadness and indisposition of heart; the spices of the garden, that seem now to be sending out their smell, may wither, and thou may be crying, I am a dry tree. Well, in that case, look up to the throne of grace, and thy glorious Head sitting on the throne, and thou wilt see thy life in him : "Our life is hid with Christ in God. Because I live, ye shall live also. After two days, will he revive us, in the third day he will raise us up, and we shall live in his sight. I will be as the dew unto Israel, and they shall revive as the corn," Hos. vi. and xiv.

9*thly*, Perhaps the terrors of death may shortly take hold on thee, poor believer; the dark curtains of the grave, and the shadows of the land of forgetfulness may begin to stretch themselves upon thee : O! what shall be done in that case? I answer, even in that case look up and take hold of the bow of the covenant surrounding the throne ; as David did, when his latter end was approaching, " Although my house be not so with God ; yet he hath made with me an everlasting covenant, ordered in all things and sure : for this is all my salvation, and all my desire." The same holy man, Psal. xxxiii. viewing the covenant, and God engaged to be with him in death, cries out, ver. 4, "Yea, though I walk through the valley of the shadow of death, I will fear no evil: for thou art with me, thy rod and thy staff they comfort me." See a sweet promise of the covenant to this purpose, Hos. xiii. 14, " I will ransom them from the power of the grave : I will redeem them from death : O death, I will be thy plagues ; O grave, I will be thy destruction."

A view of some of the great Blessings to be had by taking hold of the Covenant of Grace.

1. WOULD you have JEHOVAH, Father, Son, and Holy Ghost, to be thy God, even thy own God, to be " the strength of thy heart and thy portion for ever ?" Well, come within the rainbow, by taking hold of God's covenant, or trusting in the word of a promising God in Christ, and it shall be so ; for this is the leading article of the covenant, " I am the Lord thy God. I will be their God. I am thy shield, and thy exceeding great reward." O sirs, you lost your claim to God by the first covenant ; and while in a state of nature, under a covenant of works, you are " without God in the world :" but here is a God in Christ coming back again in a new covenant, a covenant of grace and peace. O take him at his word, and take him in his word ; for " faithful is he that hath promised." Let thy soul say to the Lord, upon the covenant ground and grant, " This God is my God for ever and ever ; and he shall be thy God even unto death," because he has said it in his covenant. But, say you, must I not first close with Christ before I can claim the Lord as my God ? I answer, To close with Christ is nothing else but to take a God in Christ as thy own God, by virtue of the covenant of grace and promise, wherein his faithfulness is more deeply engaged than ever it was in God's covenant with Noah, whereof the rainbow is a perpetual and standing sign. But O, say you, I am afraid it would be presumption for me to claim a God in Christ for my God, upon the covenant-grant, " I will be their God." I answer, It is so far from being presumption, that it is rebellion against the authority of the great God interposed in the very first command of the moral law, not to know and acknowledge him, and trust in him as God, and as thy own God : and till thou take him as thy God in Christ, thou art living in open rebellion against the authority of Heaven : and wilt thou adventure to be a rebel against God to avoid the

danger of presumption, and so rush upon the thick bosses of Heaven's buckler? O that I could persuade you
to obey the first command of the moral law, as it stands
in a subserviency to the covenant of grace, contained
in the preface to the ten commandments, which teaches
us to believe that he is the Lord our God and Redeemer, upon the ground of his own faithfulness pledged
in these words, "I am the Lord thy God." O sirs, if
you can but find in your hearts through grace to obey
the first command in the law, you will find it easy to
obey the rest; and if you can but find in your heart
through grace to believe this first, and leading promise
of the covenant of grace, "I am the Lord thy God,"
you will find it easy to lay claim by faith to all the
subsequent promises of the covenant; for it would be
remembered, that the first promise of the covenant, and
the first command of the moral law, are inseparably
linked together.

2dly, Take hold of the covenant, and come within
the arch of this blessed bow that goes round about the
throne, and there thou shalt find a sealed pardon of sin,
an indemnity, an act of oblivion for all thy sins, though
they be innumerable as the stars, and great and heinous
like the lofty mountains: Heb. viii. 12, "I will be
merciful to their unrighteousness, and their sins and
their iniquities will I remember no more." So Jer.
xxxi. 34. View him that sits upon the throne within
the rainbow, and thou wilt hear him saying, "I, even
I, am he that blotteth out thy transgressions for mine
own sake, and will not remember thy sins." O condemned sinner, trust a God in Christ for this, by virtue of his covenant, or by virtue of his promise; for
"the Strength of Israel will not lie nor repent."

3dly, Thou art by nature an alien, a stranger, a foreigner, a child of hell; wouldst thou fain come back
again to God's family, and have a God in Christ as
thy Father? Well, view the rainbow, come within
the circuit of it, and there thou shalt have this: "I
will be a Father unto you, and ye shall be my sons and

daughters, saith the Lord Almighty.   But as many as
received him, (by virtue of this covenant-grant,) to
them gave he power to become the sons of God, even
to them that believe on his name, John i. 12.

4thly, Wants thou a principle of spiritual life, who
art by nature dead in trespasses and sins?   Well,
believe in the Son of God, by virtue of the covenant,
and thou shalt have it; for, says Christ, John xi. 25,
" He that believeth in me, though he were dead, yet
shall he live."   Wouldst thou have thy spiritual life
more abundant? new quickenings under the languish-
ings of grace?   Well, this is within the rainbow of
the covenant : " Thy life is hid with Christ in God ;"
and he has said, that " thou shalt revive as the corn,
and grow as the vine."

Again, wants thou to have thy heart sprinkled from
an evil conscience?   Here it is to be had, Ezek. xxxvi.
25, " I will sprinkle clean water upon you, and ye shall
be clean : from all your filthiness, and from all your
idols will I cleanse you."

Would you have the power of sin broken in thy
soul?   Take hold of God's covenant, or believe in
Christ by virtue of the covenant, and thou shalt have
this also : Mic. vii. 19, " I will subdue their iniquities."
Rom. vi. 14, " Sin shall not have dominion over you :
for ye are not under the law, but under grace."

Wouldst thou have thy stony heart softened and
turned into a heart of flesh ?   This also lies within the
rainbow of the covenant : Ezek. xxxvi. 26, " A new
heart also will I give you, and a new spirit will I put
within you, and I will take away the stony heart out of
your flesh, and I will give you an heart of flesh."

Would you have the Spirit of God within you as the
Spirit of wisdom and revelation, as a quickening, guiding, and sanctifying Spirit? Well, this is within the
covenant also : Ezek. xxxvi. 27, " I will put my
Spirit within you, and cause you to walk in my statutes, and ye shall keep my judgments, and do them."

Would you have protection against all enemies and

dangers? This also is to be had within the circuit of this rainbow. The man Christ, who sits upon the throne, "is a hiding-place from the wind, and a covert from the tempest."

Wouldst thou have strength to encounter thy enemy, strength to grapple with difficulties, and to manage thy work and warfare? This is within the rainbow of the covenant: Zech. x. 12. "And I will strengthen them in the Lord, and they shall walk up and down in his name, saith the Lord." Is. xli. 10, "I will strengthen them, yea, I will help them, yea, I will uphold them with the right hand of my righteousness."

Lastly, Would you have grace to keep in the Lord's way to the end, till the good work be perfected? Well, this is in the covenant: "The righteous shall hold on his way, and he that hath clean hands shall wax stronger and stronger. He which hath begun the good work in you, will perform it until the day of Jesus Christ." All these and innumerable other blessings, lie within the circuit of this rainbow, which goes round about the throne of grace.

Impediments, in the way of sinners taking hold of God's Covenant of Grace, removed.

1. THE law of God. O, says the sinner, I am condemned already by God's law, and how then shall I look towards God's covenant, or take hold of it for my safety against the deluge of wrath? *Answ.* If thou had not broken the divine law, thou wouldst not stand in need of the grace of God's covenant. The law is so far from being against the promise in the business of salvation, that, that moment thou takest hold of Christ by virtue of the covenant or promise, the righteousness of the law is fulfilled in thee; "for Christ is the end of the law for righteousness to every one that believeth Christ was made under the law to redeem them that were under the law."

2dly, But O, says the sinner, the justice of God is against me, the thoughts of incensed justice make my heart to tremble within me. *Answ.* The throne of grace that is surrounded with the bow of the covenant, is founded upon justice satisfied, and judgment executed upon the Surety ; and that moment thou comest within the bow of the covenant, justice becomes thy friend, assoilzing thee on the ground of Christ's satisfaction : for " God has set forth Christ to be a propitiation, through faith in his blood, to show forth his righteousness for the remission of sins ; that he might be just and the justifier of him which believeth in Jesus."

3dly, The holiness of God sometimes scares the sinner to look toward the throne of grace, or covenant of grace. But, sirs, I tell you, that, that moment you come within the bow of the covenant, you are made partakers of his holiness ; and the holiness of God being laid in pawn for the outmaking of the promise, stands up for its own interest in the sinner's behalf. And besides, by the blood of Jesus, the filth of sin is covered from the eyes of unspotted holiness, as well as the guilt of it hid from the eye of incensed justice.

4thly, The sinner is ready to be scared from taking hold of God's covenant, and his faithfulness engaged therein on the account of the decrees of God. O, will the sinner say, it is true, if I were among the number of the elect, I might meddle with God's covenant ; but, alas! I think I am none of these, and therefore I need not think of taking hold of Christ by virtue of his covenant. But, sirs, let me tell you, that " secret things belong unto the Lord, but those things which are revealed belong unto us and to our children." Let God's decrees alone ; you have no more business with them in the matter of believing, than you have to trouble yourself with what they are doing in Mexico or Peru. Meddle you with the things that are revealed, for these are the things that " belong to us and to our children." Now, what are the things that are revealed ? Christ is revealed, the covenant and the promises are revealed as the ground of faith, the command of God enjoining you to believe is revealed, God's good will to man upon earth is revealed : these are the things that belong to you, and therefore meddle you with these. And let not the devil and your own ill heart together brangle and confound you, by telling you, that you do not know if you be elected ; for that moment you come within the bow of God's covenant, you may know your election, and that God hath loved you with an everlasting love ; and no other way you can possibly know it.   But besides all this, let me tell you, that God's promise registrated in his word, is but an extract of the eternal thought and purpose of his heart : so that by believing his promise, immediately you may know that you are "the called according to his purpose."

But, may the sinner say, that though there be no bar on God's part, yet there are many bars and impediments on my part.   I shall endeavour to roll away these also, by answering the following objections of unbelief.

Object. 1. I am a poor unworthy creature, I dare not think of meddling with God's covenant.   *Answ.* It is a bastard devilish humility, that keeps you from believing ; for the more unworthy you are of the grace and favour of God, the more fit you are for receiving the grace of God at a throne of grace, by virtue of the covenant of grace.   Grace is only calculated for the unworthy sinner, and not for these that think themselves worthy of it.

Object. 2. My sins are like the great mountains, and I fear the grace of God will never level them.   *Answ.* Take hold of God's covenant, and you shall find these mountains removed, and cast into the midst of the sea : Is. i. 18, "Come now, and let us reason together, saith the Lord : though your sins be as scarlet, they shall be as white as snow ; though they be red like crimson, they shall be as wool."

Object. 3. I want a law work, I am not weary and heavy laden, and therefore am not fit to take hold of God's covenant. *Answ.* If thou think to make a law-work and humiliation a price in your hand to recommend you to Christ, and fit you for him; I tell you that instead of fitting yourself for Christ, you are building up a wall between Christ and you, that you shall never win over. If you see an absolute need of Christ, that you are undone without him, do not stand to seek more law-work; for that moment you close with Christ, by virtue of the covenant of grace, the law has gotten its end, Christ being "the end of the law to every one that believeth." It is the weary and heavy laden that are called; but that is not to exclude others, who cannot find that disposition in themselves; and they are mentioned in particular in the call, because they are most ready to exclude themselves from having any concern in Christ or his covenant.

Object. 4. I am afraid to take hold of God's covenant in case I turn away from his commandments, and so render myself unworthy of a covenant relation to him. *Answ.* If you really take hold of his covenant, the grace of his covenant will keep you in the way of his commandments: Jer. xxxii. 40, " I will make an everlasting covenant with them, that I will not turn away from them to do them good: but I will put my fear in their hearts, that they shall not depart from me."

Object. 5. I am afraid to take hold of God's covenant, in case that I never be able to bear the cross: I will faint in the day of adversity, for my strength is small. *Answ.* Do not fear that, for he that sits on the throne has said in his covenant, " when thou passest through the waters he will be with thee; and through the rivers, they shall not overflow thee: when thou walkest through the fire, thou shalt not be burnt; neither shall the flame kindle upon thee." His presence shall go with thee to the hottest furnace, and unto the deep waters of Mara: and if so, there is no fear: but thy head shall be carried above.

Object. 6. I have formerly minted to take hold of God's covenant; but I have played the harlot with many lovers since that. *Answ.* Renew thy grips of the covenant; for the grace of God's covenant, the rainbow about the throne, is still pointing thee out as it were by name : Jer. iii. 1, " Though thou hast played the harlot with many lovers ; yet return again to me, saith the Lord."

Object. 7. But 1 have acted as a rebel against Heaven, I have been waging war against God, and will ever he allow me to meddle with his covenant, or come within the verge of this rainbow? For answer, see Psal. lxviii. 18, where we are told concerning him that sits upon the throne of grace within the rainbow, " He received gifts for men ; yea, even for the rebellious, that the Lord God might dwell among us," See also, Is. lv. 7, " Let the wicked forsake his way, and the unrighteous man his thoughts : and let him return unto the Lord, and he will have mercy upon him, and to our God, for he will abundantly pardon."

Object. 8. I want power to take hold of the covenant, I want power to believe in Christ by virtue of the covenant. *Answ.* He that sits upon the throne, with the rainbow about it, he is saying, " I will give power to the faint, and increase strength to them that have no might;" yea, he has said that he will " make thee willing by the day of his power :" and if he has given thee the will to believe, there is no fear for the want of power ; for he that works the will by his covenant, he has engaged to work the do also ; he " works in us, both to will and to do of his good pleasure."

Object. 9. You are aye speaking of the bow of the covenant, but I would fain see it ; I have seen the natural bow, but the rainbow of the covenant is invisible. *Answ.* It is strange not to see it, when you have it in your hand ; the Old and New Testament is the rainbow that I am speaking of; the rainbow is at this

moment shining upon you in a preached gospel. O
remember that awful word, 2 Cor. iv. 3, 4, "If our
gospel be hid, it is hid to them that are lost ; in whom
the god of this world hath blinded the minds of them
which believe not, lest the light of the glorious gospel
of Christ, who is the image of God, should shine unto
them."

Object. 10. I am afraid I be one of those from whom
this rainbow is hid, and so am lost for ever. *Answ.*
If thou dost not see it, I ask, Art thou longing to see
it ?   If so, I can tell you for good news, thou shalt see
it ere long : "for he satisfieth the longing soul, and
filleth the hungry soul with goodness ;" and then he
that sits on the throne has said, that he will "open the
blind eyes, and turn thee from darkness, that thou shalt
behold the glory of the Lord, and the excellency of
our God."

Thus I have endeavoured to roll away all the impediments I can think upon, that you may be encouraged
to come within the bow that is about the throne of
grace.   What are you resolved to do ?   Will you come
within the bow of God's covenant or not ?   I would
fain expostulate the matter with you.   What will you
do in the day of death, if you come not within this rainbow ?   What will you do in the day of reckoning, when
standing before the bar of God ?   Whither will you
flee, when rocks and mountains refuse to fall on you,
to hide you from the face of the Lamb ?   O sirs, there is
no shunning the deluge of divine wrath, but by taking
hold of the covenant, and of the faithfulness of God
engaged therein ;   the whole creation cannot help you,
if you do it not, but you must lie under the fiery mountains of God's wrath for ever ;   for "he that believeth
not is condemned already ;   and the wrath of God abideth on him."*

---

*"Come unto me," says Christ, "all ye that labour and are heavy
laden, and I will give you rest."   Dost thou think that the faithful
High Priest in heaven will break his word, or that he hath promised
what he cannot perform ?   Trust thy cause in his hands ; he hath

What sort of life springs out of the Tree of Life mentioned,
Rev. xxii. 2.

1. THERE is a life of justification, in opposition to legal death.   Every man by nature he is dead in the eye of the law? just like a malefactor under sentence of death ; though he be not actually execute, yet we reckon him a dead man, because he is dead in the eye of the law, the judge having passed sentence against him, and the day of his execution approaching.   This is it which every sinner who is out of Christ is under ; he is under the law as a covenant, and therefore a dead man in law ; the law hath already condemned him, for the law says to every sinner, "The soul that sinneth shall die." Now, so soon as ever the poor sinner comes under the shadow of the tree of life, or by faith tastes of the fruit of this tree, this sentence of the law is repealed, and cancelled by virtue of the imputation of the everlasting righteousness of the Son of God as our Surety ; so that the man begins to live even before God as the right-eous Judge and Lawgiver, he being vested with that righteousness, whereby the law is magnified and made honourable.   God allows the poor soul to count and reckon upon this, Rom. vi. 11, " As Christ died and rose again ; so likewise reckon ye yourselves to be dead indeed unto sin ; but alive unto God through Jesus Christ."   The believer, by virtue of the righteousness of Christ, is so much alive unto God, that he dare say with the apostle, " Who shall lay any thing to the charge of God's elect ?   It is God that justifieth : who is he that condemneth ?" &c.

saved thousands and millions, a number that no man can number, and dost thou think he cannot save thee ?   What is thy case, O soul ?   Art thou more vile than Manasseh, a worse backslider than Solomon, a fiercer persecutor than Saul, or one in whom there are more devils than were in Mary Magdalen ?   If thou art more vile than these were, yet do not despair, whilst the atoning High Priest says, " Come now, and let us reason together ; though thy sins be as scarlet, they shall be as white as snow ; though they be red like crimson, they shall be as wool."—*Allen's Spirit. Mag.*

2. In Christ the blessed tree of life there is to be found a life of sanctification or of holiness. This is the fruit and consequent of the former. A legal death inevitably brings on a spiritual death under the power of sin, for " the strength of sin is the law." The law slays us and puts out our spiritual life, because of the violation of it. And, on the other hand, a life of justification, it inevitably brings with it a life of sanctification or holiness, which lies in the soul's freedom from the dominion and filth of sin : so that the man now having an inward principle of life, he begins to yield obedience to the law, not as a covenant, seeking life by it, but as a rule of obedience, that he may " show forth the praises of him who hath called him out of darkness into his marvellous light." And this life of sanctification he has from Christ the tree of life ; " I am like a green fir-tree (says he); from me is thy fruit found. Abide in me and I in you ; so shall ye bring forth much fruit." All the fruits of righteousness and holiness are by Jesus Christ.

3. By this tree of life we live a life of consolation or comfort, for he is " the consolation of Israel : With joy shall ye draw water out of the wells of salvation." The spouse " sat down under his shadow with great delight, and his fruit was sweet to her taste." By eating the fruit of this tree, David declares his soul was " satisfied as with marrow and fatness ;" so that he blessed God with joyful lips. Whenever the poor soul tastes of the fruit of this tree, an air of heavenly joy appears in the countenance ; the man lays aside his sackcloth, and girds himself with gladness, and is filled with a " joy unspeakable and full of glory." This life of consolation is just up or down, according to the fruit or lively exercise of faith, or according to the coming or going of the Lord ; whenever Christ appears, the soul revives and laughs like the fields after a pleasant shower and warm blink.

4. There is a life of glory grows out of the tree of life ; for " this is the record that God hath given to us

eternal life : and this life is in his Son.   And he that
hath the Son hath life ; and he that believeth in the
Son of God hath everlasting life ;" he hath the arles,
and the security of it here, and he shall have the full
possession of it in heaven for ever hereafter.   Thus
you see what life springs out of the tree of life.

*What is signified by the tree of life being on each side of the river,
as mentioned* Rev. xxii. 2.

1. THAT a living Redeemer, though he be in heaven
exalted " at the right hand of the Majesty on high," and
though the heavens are to contain him till his second
coming ; yet still he is to be found by his people upon
earth ; yea, he is in every part of his church ; for here
the tree of life is " in the midst of the street, and on
each side of the river ;" that is, wherever believers (the
true church of God) are, or whatever be their situation,
while in a militant state, Christ is aye to be found ; the
boughs of the tree stretch themselves out to them where-
ever they are, though it were to the " uttermost wings
of the earth," as the expression is, Is. xxiv. 16. O what
unspeakable comfort is it, that wherever the body
is, there the glorious head of the body is ! " Lo, I am
with you alway, even unto the end of the world. And,
In all places where I record my name, I will come unto
you, and I will bless you. And, Where two or three are
gathered together in my name, there am I in the midst
of them."

2. The expression takes in, that Christ is the centre
and as it were the very heart of his church and people ;
for he is here said to be in the midst of the city : as the
heart is in the midst of the body, so Christ is in the
midst of his church. " God is in the midst of her : she
shall not be moved : God shall help her, and that right
early," Psal. xlvi. 5. Christ is the centre of the church's
life : " Our life is hid with Christ in God :" he holds our
souls in life.   He is the centre of light, as the sun in
the firmament is to this lower world : " I am the light

of the world." He is the centre of comfort ; therefore
called " the consolation of Israel :" he gives the oil of joy
for mourning. He is the centre of love and desire, " the
desire of all nations : The desire of our soul is to thy
name, and to the remembrance of thee." The centre of
faith ; every one of the inhabitants of the city of God
have their eyes fixed upon him ; they " look unto him,
and are saved : Our eyes are towards the Lord our
God." He is the centre of union ; they all " hold him
as the head, from which the whole body, as by joints
and bands, having nourishment ministered, and knit
together, increase with the increase of God." There
is a great cry for peace, peace, and many politic endeavours to keep the peace and unity of the church,
but it is impossible that we can be one, unless it be in
the Lord. He is the centre of doctrine ; " to him
bear all the prophets witness ;" and to him bear all the
apostles witness ; and every truth of the word points
unto him ; there is not a word in the Bible but it points
toward Christ, as the needle in the compass points to
the pole-star. He is the centre of worship ; the prayers
and praises of all believers terminate in him ; they all
cry, " Worthy is the Lamb that was slain."

3dly, Christ, the tree of life, being in the midst of
the street, says, that Christ is a common and public
good unto the church, that he is set up for the benefit of all the inhabitants. This tree of life doth not
grow in a corner or in any inclosed place, where only
some particular persons may enter, but in the public
street, in the market place, where every body has free
access to him. It is remarkable to the same purpose,
what the spouse says concerning Christ, Cant. ii. 3,
she doth not say, that her beloved was as the apple
tree among the trees of the garden, which is an inclo-
sure ; but, he is " the apple-tree among the trees of
the wood," which every passenger may pluck, and eat,
and use with freedom. As every man in the camp of
Israel had the privilege of looking to the brazen serpent that was set up in the camp ; so every man within

the visible church has equal access unto Christ the tree of life, for he is " in the midst of the street of it." O sirs, do not doubt of your warrant to come to Christ, since he is in the midst of our streets accessible from all quarters of the city. Christ is equally tendered unto all in a preached gospel ; he is every man's penny-worth, who will but take him, apply him, and lay claim to him. As every subject in Britain may say of our present sovereign, He is my king, because he is set as a public good to the whole body-politic ; 'and as every soldier of an army may say of the principal commander, He is my general, in a way of application, and have recourse to him as such ; and as every soldier may lay claim to the physician of a regiment, and say, He is my physician, because of the relation he stands under to the whole company : so Christ being the common Saviour of sinners, the prophet, priest, and king of his church by office, every one may, in a way of particular application, claim the benefit of him in his saving offices, and say, in a way of believing, He is my Saviour, my prophet, priest, and king, for he is " a son given, and child born, unto us ; he is made of God unto us wisdom, righteousness, sanctification, and redemption ;" and whatever he is as Mediator, that he is unto us ; he is " in the midst of the street of the city."

4*thly*, It implies, that they who would find Christ must seek him in the streets and broad ways of gospel-ordinances ; for here the tree of life is said to be in the midst of the street, in the public ordinances of the church, such as preaching of the word, and administration of sacraments. O sirs, it is " in his temple that every one is made to speak of his glory," Psal. xxix. 9. It is there he causes his name to be recorded ; and there it is he has promised to come to his people and bless them, Exod. xx. 24. And therefore, they that turn their back on public ordinances, they are out of the way of coming to the tree of life. I own indeed, that the Lord will sometimes meet with a sinner going on

in the broad way to destruction, as he did with Paul going to Damascus ; but when he does so, he steps out
of his ordinary road of convincing, converting, and
healing souls, in his sanctuary.   We read of one (Paul)
converted on the way to Damascus, but we read of
three thousand added unto the church, when attending
upon the word preached by Peter, Acts ii. 41.   So I
say, they who would find Christ the tree of life, must
come unto the streets and broad ways of ordinances,
as the spouse did.   Many a sweet meeting have believers with the Lord there ; I hope some here can seal
it from their experience.

    5thly, The expression implies, that Christ is to be
met with, not only in public ordinances of the church,
but that sweet fellowship with him is to be had also
in the more private and secret retirements of the Lord's
people ; for here the tree of life is not only in the street,
but on each side of the river, through all parts of the
city.   When employed in family prayer, in secret
prayer, secret meditation, private or secret reading of
the word, Christian converse, and the like ; many a
sweet communion with the Lord does the believer enjoy in these.   O, says David, " When I remember
thee upon my bed, and meditate on thee in the night
watches, my soul shall be satisfied as with marrow and
fatness."   The hearts of the disciples going to Em-
maus, were made to burn while they talked together
by the way.

    6thly, It implies, that the influences of the Spirit are
absolutely necessary, in order to the sweetening of ordinances, and conveying the fruit of a Redeemer's purchase to them in the use of ordinances : for here the
pure river of the water of life, it intermingles itself in
the streets of the city, with the spreading boughs and
branches of the tree.   Unless the river of the Spirit's
influences come along with word and sacrament, taking
the things of Christ, and showing them unto us, we shall
find them to be but dry breasts and miscarrying
wombs ; and therefore there is need of a continual

dependence on the Lord for the concurring influences of the Spirit of life : " Paul may plant, and Apollos may water ; but God giveth the increase." And therefore pray that the river of the water of life may run down from the throne of God, and of the Lamb, in the streets of the city of God, and that the tree of life may be seen on each side, on every hand, bearing his twelve manner of fruits.

7thly, It is implied here, that Christ is the ornament of his church and people ; for the tree of life is here spoken of as the ornament of the city in the midst of its streets.   Christ is " the glory of his people Israel ; and in him shall all the seed of Israel be justified, and shall glory."   He reflects a beauty and glory on the church collectively considered ; his presence in the streets of it makes her " beautiful as Tirzah, comely as Jerusalem, fair as the moon, clear as the sun, and terrible as an army with banners."   And he is the beauty and ornament of every particular believer in the church ; every one of them is beautiful through the comeliness that he puts upon them ; it is by his merits upon them, and his Spirit within them, that they become like the King's daughter, " all glorious within, their clothing being of wrought gold."   He it is that makes them " like the wings of a dove covered with silver, and her feathers with yellow gold."

8thly, It is implied here, that the whole city, and every one of its inhabitants, dwell or abide under the shadow of the tree ; for the tree is on every side, and in the midst of the street.   I remember the spouse, speaking of this tree of life, she says, " I sat down under his shadow with great delight," viz. the shadow of his blood and everlasting righteousness, under the shadow of his faithfulness engaged in his promise, under the shadow of his providence.   O happy they, who by faith sit down under this shadowy tree.   This is the place where Christ makes his flock to rest in the noon of temptation, affliction, desertion, and tribulation.

Motives to come to the tree of life, Rev. xxii. 2.

1. CONSIDER what life is to be had by coming to this tree of life ; a life of justification, sanctification, consolation, and of eternal glory ; a divine life, a royal life, a heavenly life, a growing life, an immortal life ; all which I spoke to in the doctrinal part.

2. Consider what an excellent defence thou shalt find under the shadow of this tree. Here thou shalt find a defence, (1.) Against the wrath of an angry God, who is a consuming fire. Our Jesus, he saveth from the wrath to come. God declares fury is not in him against any soul that will come under the shadow of his righteousness. (2.) Here thou wilt find shelter against the rage of Satan. The devil must take away the life of the tree of life, he must cut him down again, and pluck off his leaves, before he can win at the soul that is under his shadow. (3.) From the fury of men ; he says, John xvi. 33, " In me ye shall have peace. In the world ye shall have tribulation : but be of good cheer, I have overcome the world."

3. Consider the excellent qualities of the fruit of the tree of life. (1.) It is pleasant fruit, sweet to the taste, Cant. ii. 3. None of the trees of Paradise yielded fruit like that which grows in the midst of the New Testament Paradise. (2.) It is profitable fruit ; it " cheereth the heart of God and man." God smelt a sweet savour in his death, and " he is well pleased for his righteousness' sake :" and it cheers the heart of the believer who eats of it, puts more gladness in his heart, than the wicked can have in the greatest abundance of their corn and wine. (3.) It is plentiful fruit. Come and eat thy fill even to satiety ; nothing will be missed, the tree is loaden. (4.) There is variety of fruits in this tree. Some fruit trees they bear plenty of one kind of fruits ; but here is the excellency of this tree, that it has twelve manner of fruits, fruits of all sorts, adapted to the necessity of the soul. (5.) The fruits of the tree of life are

permanent and perennial, always continuing; for it brings forth fruit every month, every season. (6.) It is nourishing fruit. By the fruit of this tree, the soul is made to grow, and "go from strength to strength, until it appear before the Lord in Zion."

4. Take a view of the leaves of the tree, and let this invite you to come to it in a way of believing. They are for the healing of the nations. What is thy disease, O sinner? Be what it will, thou shalt find a leaf of this tree for thy healing (1.) Art thou a blind sinner? Well, here is a leaf of the tree suited unto thy disease, Psal. cxlvi. 8, "The Lord openeth the eyes of the blind." Rev. iii. 18, "I counsel thee to buy of me eye-salve, that thou mayest see." (2.) Art thou deaf, that thou cannot hear the voice of God in his word or rod? Well, here is a leaf of the tree of life for healing thy disease, Is. xxxv. 5, "The ears of the deaf shall be unstopped." John v. 25, "The hour is coming, and now is, when the dead shall hear the voice of the son of God : and they that hear shall live." (3.) Art thou a lame sinner, that cannot walk in the Lord's way? Here is a leaf for thee, Is. xxxv. 6, "Then shall the lame leap as an hart :" then, viz. when the gospel shall be preached among the nations for their healing. (4.) Art thou a dumb sinner, that thou cannot speak a word in the matters of God, cannot pray nor praise? Well, here is a leaf for thy disease, Is. xxxv. 6, "The tongue of the dumb shall sing." Art thou a hard-hearted sinner? is this thy disease, that thou finds thy heart like an adamant in thy breast? Well, there is a leaf for thee, Ezek. xxxvi. 26, "A new heart will I give you, and a new spirit will I put within you, and I will take away the stony heart out of your flesh, and I will give you an heart of flesh." Hast thou a foul polluted conscience in thy breast, that is defiled with the guilt of sin? Well, here is a leaf for thee, Ezek. xxxvi. 25, "I will sprinkle clean water upon you, and ye shall be clean : from all your filthiness, and from all your idols will I cleanse you." Zech.

xiii. 1, " In that day there shall be a fountain opened
to the house of David, and to the inhabitants of Jerusalem, for sin and for uncleanness," 1 John i. 7,
" The blood of Jesus Christ his Son cleanseth us from
all sin." Is prevailing corruption, atheism, unbelief,
enmity, thy disease? Well, here is a leaf for thee,
Mic. vii. 19, " I will subdue your iniquities." Rom.
vi. 14, " Sin shall not have dominion over you : for ye
are not under the law, but under grace." Is thy soul
like the mountains of Gilboa, dry, withered like the
ground for want of rain? Here is a leaf for thee, Is.
xliv. 3, " I will pour water upon him that is thirsty,
and floods upon the dry ground." Art thou troubled
with a restlessness of spirit, that thou cannot find rest
in any thing? Here is a leaf for thee, Is. xi. 10, " To
him shall the Gentiles seek, and his rest shall be glorious." Matth. xi. 28, " Come unto me, all ye that labour, and are heavy laden, and I will give you rest."
Art thou troubled with a fainting of thy spirit in the
Lord's way? Well, here is a leaf for thee, Is. xl. 29,
"He giveth power to the faint; and to them that
have no might, he increaseth strength." Thus you
see that in the tree of life there is a leaf for every
disease.

5. Consider, that as the tree of life is calculate to
thy necessity, so it is ordained for thy use, and for the
use of every sinner that will make use of it by faith,
John iii. 14, 15, 16. He is given to us : Is. ix. 6,
" Unto us a Son is given." Whatever he is as Mediator,
that he is unto us. Is he a saviour? it is to them that
are lost. Is he a prophet? it is to teach the ignorant.
Is he a priest? a priest is ordained for men. Is he a
king? it is that he may conquer and captivate, rule
and govern us. Is he a physician? it is that he may
heal the diseased. Is he a shepherd? it is that he
may feed us in his pasture. Is he a door? it is that
we may enter by him unto God. Is he a foundation?
it is that we may build upon him. Is he meat? it is
that we may feed on him. Is he drink? it is for the

poor soul that is in want of salvation, as a thirsty man is in want of water. Thus whatever he is as Mediator, that he is unto us ; "he is made of God unto us wisdom, righteousness, sanctification, and redemption."

6. Consider, that this tree is accessible ; for he is in the midst of the street. And though he be highly exalted, and lifted up above the heavens, yet his boughs stoop and bend down to the very ground, that the hand of faith may reach his fruits and leaves, Rom. x. 6—8. Yea, not only doth he bend his boughs, to make his fruit and his leaves accessible ; but he shakes and drops his fruit to you in the valley of vision, and makes it to fall about our tent-doors, just as he did the manna about the tents of Israel. O then put forth the hand of faith and gather.

7. You are not only invited, but commanded to eat the fruit, and apply the leaves of the tree by faith. This is the very work of God which he requires of you, " This is his commandment, that we should believe on the name of his Son Jesus Christ." There is a call that every one that hears of Christ should make use of him ; and if ye do not comply, ye disobey the great God, in the greatest command that ever he issued out to men ; it is not left optional ; no, concluded you are under a law to take the fruits of this tree.

8. You will die except you eat of the fruit of the tree of life : John viii. 24, " If ye believe not that I am he, ye shall die in your sins," and so perish for ever : "He that believeth not is condemned already." Stand to your hazard then. But if you believe, ye shall be saved : " Whosoever believeth in him shall not perish, but have everlasting life." The fruits and leaves of this tree of life are an antidote against the hurt we sustained by our first parents eating of the forbidden fruit, whereby they and all their posterity were ruined.

Explanation of these words Isaiah ii. 3, " *For out of Zion shall go forth the law.*"

FROM the beginning of this chapter and downwards, we have a prophecy concerning the glorious kingdom of grace, to be erected by the Messiah, under the New Testament dispensation. Where two or three things may be noticed. (1.) By what name the prophet speaks of the New Testament church; he calls it " the mountain of the Lord's house." This is that mountain upon which the Lord promises to " make unto all people a feast of fat things, a feast of wines on the lees," Is. xxv. 6. Under the Old Testament, the mountain of the house of the Lord was restricted to Jerusalem, the church of God was mostly pent up within the narrow boundaries of Jerusalem, and Judea; but under the New Testament, the mountain of the Lord's house is to be found, wherever God is worshipped, the gospel preached, and the mystery of salvation through a Redeemer opened. (2.) We have an account of the ingathering of the Gentile nations, into the bosom of the church under the New Testament; "all nations shall flow unto it." The kingdom of Christ shall no longer be confined to the nation of the Jews, the natural posterity of Abraham; no, the partition wall shall be broken down, and " from the uttermost wings of the earth songs shall be heard, even glory to the righteous." This flowing in of the nations into the bosom of the church, points out both the great multitude of converts, and their cheerful submission unto the obedience of Christ; they shall be innumerable like the drops of water in a river: and as the water of a river flows into the sea, so should the gathering of the nations be unto the blessed Shiloh; they shall come in like troops of volunteers under the banner of Christ: " Thy people shall be willing in the day of thy power," or in the day of thy armies, Psal. cx. 3. (3.) We have the encouragement which the New

Testament converts give to their friends and neighbours to come along with them, and partake of the blessings of Christianity, and share of the advantages of the Messiah's administration ; "many people shall go and say, Come ye, and let us go up to the mountain of the Lord, to the house of the God of Jacob," &c. They that know Christ, and who have obtained grace and salvation through him, are fond that others should share with them ; saying with the woman of Samaria to her fellow-citizens, "Come see a man which told me all things that ever I did : is not this the Christ?" They would have all the world the better of him, could they get their desire. Now follows an account of the great mean or instrument whereby all this should be effected, how the kingdom of Christ under the New Testament should be erected, "The law shall go out of Zion, and the word of the Lord from Jerusalem." The last part of the verse is exegetic or explicatory of the first, the word of the Lord that goes out of Jerusalem being the same thing with the law that goeth out of Zion : and it is this I am to insist upon at present. Where notice,

1. The designation given to the gospel ; it is expressed here under the notion of a law. It is generally agreed among all orthodox interpreters, that by the law here is to be understood the gospel. And it is not without good reason that they make this to be the meaning ; for it is not a law coming out of Sinai, but out of Zion ; it is a law which is the great instrument of gathering the nations in to the bosom of the church : "All nations shall flow unto it, for the law shall go out of Zion." And this is not effected by the law of commandments, but by the gospel only. Indeed the law of commandments is the instrument of conviction, and was added because of transgression ; but it is the gospel that is the great instrument of conversion, Rom. x. 17, "Faith cometh by hearing, and hearing by the word of God, even the gospel of our salvation." This is the rod of Christ's strength, which he sends out of Zion, and by swaying of which he brings in armies of volunteers,

like " the drops of dew from the womb of the morning."
Neither is this the only place where the gospel is called
by the name of a law; we find Paul, the great apostle
of the Gentiles, using the same form of speech, Rom.
iii. 27, " Where is boasting ? It is excluded.   By what
law ? of works ? Nay ; but by the law of faith."

  2. In the words we may notice the royal seat from
whence this law is issued ; it cometh forth from Zion.
Zion was the usual name whereby the Old Testament
church was called : " The Lord hath chosen Zion : he
hath desired it for his habitation.   This is my rest for
ever : here will I dwell, for I have desired it.   Out of
Zion the perfection of beauty, God hath shined."   And
the then church was called Zion, from the mount upon
which the temple was built : thither the tribes of Israel,
went up to worship the God of Israel, who dwelt between the cherubims.   And we find this name of Zion
transferred from the Old to the New Testament church,
Heb. ii. 22, " Ye are come unto mount Zion, the city
of the living God."   The reason of which is, because
the New Testament church was graffed, as it were
into the root of the Old Testament church : all the Old
Testament economy being nothing else but a prepara-
tive to the glorious displays of the grace, mercy, and
love of God, which were to be made to a lost world,
upon the coming of the great Messiah : and adorable
Providence so ordered it, that at Zion or Jerusalem,
where the Old Testament church expired upon the
resurrection of Christ from the dead, there the gospel
Zion, or the New Testament church was first founded,
with the solemnity of the downpouring of the Spirit
in a visible manner upon the day of Pentecost, and the
conversion of the three thousand by Peter's sermon,
Acts ii. where people of different nations were gathered,
such as Parthians, Medes, Elamites, dwellers in Mo-
sopotamia, and Judea, and Cappadocia, in Pontus,
and Asia, Phrygia, Pamphylia, Egypt, Lybia, Cyrene,
strangers of Rome, Jews and proselytes, Cretes and
Arabians ; I say, people gathered out of all these na-

tions to Zion or Jerusalem were the hearers of the first
gospel sermon; and their hearts being touched with
the efficacy thereof, no doubt they would immediately
spread and propagate it upon their return to their
several countries; and thus " the law went out of Zion,
and the word of the Lord from Jerusalem." Further, I
find in Scripture an opposition stated between mount
Sinai and mount Zion, Gal. iv. 24, and Heb. xii. 22.
Mount Sinai, where the law of commandments was
delivered, was a place of terrible blackness, and darkness, and tempest; but mount Zion, whence the gospel law is issued, is a place of joy, comfort, and light,
a vision of peace.   Upon mount Sinai, God appeared
in his terrible majesty; but from mount Zion, he appears as a God of peace, grace, and love.   Mount
Sinai and its law-covenant gendereth into bondage;
but mount Zion or Jerusalem, which is from above, is
free, and her children are the children of the free
woman.   God came down upon mount Sinai only for
a season, and then utterly forsook it; but mount
Zion, spiritually considered, is his fixed residence,
" Here still I'll stay."   In a word, the law of works
cometh forth from Sinai; but the law of faith, the law
of grace and love, cometh forth out of Zion.

3. We have the egress of this law from Zion; it
goeth forth, like a proclamation issued out by royal
authority unto his subjects, that none may pretend ignorance; it goeth forth like the waters of the sanctuary, which issued out from under the threshold of
the temple, and did run into the desert of the Gentile nations, making every thing to live whether it
cometh.

What the Gospel is.

1. THAT the word gospel properly signifies any
good speech or joyful message : and fitly it is applied
unto the gospel, because it brings the most joyful message unto lost sinners that ever was heard.   " Behold,"

said the angels unto the shepherds, " we bring you good
tidings of great joy, which shall be to all people.   For
unto you is born this day, in the city of David, a Saviour, which is Christ the Lord."   On the same account also it is called " the joyful sound," Psal. lxxxix.
15, 16, and " O blessed are the people that know this
joyful sound : they shall walk, O Lord, in the light of
thy countenance.   In thy name shall they rejoice all
the day : and in thy righteousness shall they be exalted."   The gospel brings a sound of liberty to captives,
of pardon to condemned criminals, of peace to rebels,
a sound of life to the dead, and salvation to them that
lie on the borders of hell and condemnation.

2. You would know that the gospel strictly taken is
a word of promise.   The first gospel that ever was
preached to our first parents, when a dismal cloud of
wrath was hanging over their heads in Paradise after
the fall, was in a promise, Gen. iii. 15, " The seed of
the woman shall bruise the head of the serpent."
The gospel preached unto Abraham, what was it but
a promise of Christ?   " In thy seed shall all the
nations of the earth be blessed," Gal. iii. 8.   And I
think it observable, that the same thing which the
apostle calls the gospel, ver. 8. he calls the promise,
and the covenant, ver. 17, 18, 19.   So that the gospel,
strictly taken, is a word of promise : so Heb. iv. 1, 2,
compared what the apostle calls " a promise of
entering into God's rest," in the 1st verse, he calls
" the gospel" in the 2d verse.   And a God of love and
grace dispenses his grace in a promise, for our encouragement to take hold of it in a way of believing ; for
there is nothing wherein the faithfulness of God is so
much engaged as in a promise, the very design of
which is to be believed.

3. We are carefully to distinguish between the gospel, and the dispensation of the gospel ; for although
the gospel strictly taken be a word of promise, yet
there are many other things that belong to the gospel
dispensation.   For instance, the whole law of God,

considered both as a covenant and as a rule, falls in under the dispensation of the gospel; the law as a covenant is a school-master to lead us to Christ, by convincing us of sin and misery; the law as a rule comes in to show us what is good, and what the Lord our God requires of us, not for justification, but in point of love and gratitude, even, " to do justly, to love mercy, and to walk humbly with our God;" and every man that really by faith closes with the promise, or law of grace, will infallibly approve of the law of commandments, as holy, just, and good: and thus it is for a light to his feet and a lamp to his paths. All gospel-institutions, such as the word, sacraments, and prayer, and other means of God's appointment, belong to the dispensation of the gospel, being as so many golden pipes, by which the golden oil of the grace of God in the promise is conveyed to the city of God. All the histories, prophecies, and types of the word, what are they but an opening and explication of the promise? Every thing in the word, from the beginning to the end of it, is, some way or other, subservient to the exhibition or application of the promise unto us.

4. Since the coming of Christ in the flesh, and the erection of a New Testament church, the gospel is much more clearly preached than it was under the old dispensation. Under the Old Testament, the glorious mysteries of redeeming love lay under a veil of dark prophecies, types, ceremonies, and the like: but now " life and immortality is brought to light;" the mystery which was hid from ages and generations, is made manifest unto the saints; the fountains of the great depth of the love, wisdom, and knowledge of God in Christ, are broken up, and set forth in the purest light. Thus much for a general view of the gospel.

Excellent properties of the Law of Grace coming out of Zion.

1. THEN, it is a life-giving law to them that are legally and spiritually dead. Since the fall of Adam
the law of commandments never gave life to any of
his posterity ; no, the law of works is weak through the
corruption of nature, to do any thing for fallen man.
Instead of giving life, it claps on the sentence of death
upon us for every and the least sinful thought, word, or
action. The apostle plainly insinuates, that neither
life, righteousness, or any good, can come to a sinner
by any commanding law whatever, Gal. iii. 21, " If
there had been a law given, which could have given life,
verily righteousness should have been by the law."
But, sirs, I bring you glad tidings of great joy, which
may make the heart of a sinner to flighter in his breast ;
although the law coming out of Sinai, or the law of
commandments, cannot give life or righteousness, yet
here is a law of grace coming out of Zion, that gives
both ; and if thou wilt but give this law a fair hearing,
life will come in with it to thy dead soul, Is. lv. 3,
" Hear, and your soul shall live, and I will make an
everlasting covenant with you, even the sure mercies
of David." And what is it that the lost sinner is to
hear ? You see how earnest the Lord is for sinners to
listen, three times in a breath he calls them, ver. 2, 3,
to arrest their attention, " Hearken diligently," and
then a second time, " Incline your ear," and a third
time it is repeated, with a promise of life, if they will
give him a hearing, " Hear, and your soul shall live."
Well, surely something of moment is to be said after
all this solemnity, ver. 4, you have an act of sovereign
grace, making a grant of Christ to lost sinners, and it
is (besides all the former solemnities) ushered in with
a Behold, as a note of attention and admiration, " Behold, I have given him for a witness to the people, for
a leader and commander to the people." There is the
law of grace coming out of Zion, and " whoever

believes it shall not perish, but have everlasting life."
O let the lost sinner entertain and welcome it, for " it
is a faithful saying, and worthy of all acceptation."
See the law giving life proclaimed by the apostle
John, under the notion of the record of God, 1 John
v. 11, " This is the record, that God hath given to us
eternal life : and this life is in his Son." O sirs, set to
the seal that God is true, apply this grant of eternal
life through Christ to your own souls in particular, hold
God at his word, for he will not go back ; " his gifts
are without repentance."

But O, may you say, that God has given eternal life
to the elect, and to believers, I believe to be a truth ;
but he has not given eternal life to the like of me, for I
am none of these. I answer, Many a one shall go to hell
who set to their seal to this as a truth, that God has
given eternal life to the elect, and to believers ; and
therefore that cannot be the thing intended by the Spirit
of God in that record : no, the meaning must be, that
God has in his indefinite promise, by an act of sovereign grace, made a grant of eternal life to sinners, lost
and undone sinners of Adam's family ; and this is issued out of Zion, that every one may take the benefit
of it, by setting to the seal that God is true and faithful, not to others only, but true to his own soul in particular ; that he has given or granted eternal life to me
in and through his Son Jesus Christ, in whose
hand eternal life lies, ready to be given out to every
one that takes hold of it, by virtue of the law of grace,
or covenant of grace and promise. O sirs, take the
benefit of this grant of sovereign grace, since no less
than your life, yea, the eternal life of your souls lies at
the stake : " Skin for skin, yea, all that a man hath
will he give for his life." And if the life of the body
be so valuable, that a man will risk all that he hath in
a world to preserve it, how much more valuable is the
life of the immortal soul ? O think, and think again,
upon that awful word of Christ, " What is a man profited if he shall gain the whole world and lose his own

soul ? or what shall a man give in exchange for his
soul ?" Matth. xvi. 26.   For the Lord's sake then, take
the benefit of this law, giving life to your poor souls,
which must inevitably perish through eternity if you
do not.

2. This law coming out of Zion is a law of love.
The gospel it is just the warm breath of a God of love.
Love is the imperial attribute of his nature ; and to
make way for its manifestation, in a consistency with
the honour of justice, God spared not his own Son, but
gave him to the death for us all : O "herein is love,
not that we loved God, but that he loved us, and sent
his Son to be the propitiation for our sins.   The gospel is
the proclamation of this love of God, in giving Christ
and all things freely with him : John iii. 16, " God so
loved the world that he gave his only begotten Son,
that whosoever believeth in him should not perish, but
have everlasting life."   Every word of the gospel
smells rank of the love of God to lost sinners.   Here we
may see his wings of love spread out to cover and hide
them from avenging wrath and justice, the arms of
love stretched out to embrace them, the hand of love
held out to help them, the eyes of love beholding them
with infinite compassion, the bowels of love sending
out a sound after them, crying, " Turn ye, turn ye,
why will ye die ?   As I live, I have no pleasure in the
death of the wicked, but rather that they turn unto me
and live."

3. The law coming out of Zion is a righteous law,
or a law of righteousness to the guilty sinner, who is
far from righteousness.   Sirs, you and I are fond
enough by nature to seek righteousness by the law of
works, though it be a thing utterly impracticable for
any sinner, that has but once broken a command of
that law, to attain it.   We read indeed that the Jews
attempted it, " they went about to establish a righteousness by the law, and would not submit unto the
righteousness of God."   Well, but did they make it
out ? No ; see what the apostle says, Rom. ix. 31, 32,

" Israel, which followed after the law of righteousness
hath not attained to the law of righteousness. Wherefore ? Because they sought it, not by faith, but as
it were by the works of the law ; and by the works of
the law shall no flesh living be justified." But, sirs,
though you can never attain righteousness by the law
of works, yet here is a law by which righteousness may
be attained, yea, a righteousness which will answer the
law of works in all the commands, demands, and penalties of it : Rom. viii. 3, 4, " What the law could not
do, in that it was weak through the flesh, God sending
his own Son, in the likeness of sinful flesh, and for sin
condemned sin in the flesh : that the righteousness of the
law might be fulfilled in us, who walk not after the
flesh but after the Spirit." The gospel, which is the
law coming out of Zion, reveals the righteousness of
Christ, for the sake of which God is well pleased, because it magnifies the law of works, and makes it honourable. It not only reveals this righteousness, but
brings it near to the sinner, who is far from having
any righteousness of his own : Is. xlvi. 12, 13, " Hearken unto me, ye stout-hearted, that are far from righteousness : I bring near my righteousness." Sirs,
the devil and an unbelieving heart, will persuade you,
that Christ and his righteousness are quite out of your
reach, and that it is needless for you to look after it ;
Christ is in heaven, and how shall I be the better of
him ? But, for the sake of your immortal souls, beware of this way of thinking, for it brings in a secret
despair into the heart, that makes men hang down their
hands, and turns them quite careless and indifferent
about Christ, his righteousness, and salvation. See
what the apostle says, to you and me, Rom. x. 6—8.
He had told, ver. 5, what the law of works says, " The
man which doeth those things, shall live by them ;"
but then he tells what the gospel says, which he calls
" the righteousness of faith, because therein the righteousness of God is revealed from faith to faith," from
the faith of God revealing to the faith of man receiv-

ing. Well, what says the gospel, or the law giving righteousness? It "speaketh on this wise, Say not in thine heart, Who shall ascend into heaven? (that is, to bring Christ down from above,) or Who shall descend into the deep? (that is, to bring up Christ again from the dead.) But what saith it? The word is nigh thee, even in thy mouth, and in thy heart: that is the word of faith, which we preach." What can be nearer to a man, than the word that is in his mouth, or the thought that is in his heart? Yet so near doth Christ, and his righteousness, and salvation, come to every man that hears the gospel; for if when we are speaking of it, or thinking of it, our souls would but believe it, Christ and his righteousness becomes our own for ever. And therefore, you that would have a righteousness to answer the charge of the law of works, a righteousness that will bear you through when you come to the tribunal of God, O take hold of the law of faith coming out of Zion; " for therein is revealed the righteousness of God," Christ is therein given and offered as " the Lord our righteousness. He was made sin for us, who knew no sin; that we might be made the righteousness of God in him."

4. The law which comes out of Zion, is an indemnifying law, Heb. viii. 12, Is. xliii. 25. The very name of him whose law it is, is " The Lord, merciful, and gracious, pardoning iniquity, transgression, and sin," that is, all sorts of sins, great and small ; and whatever be their number or quality, it is his glory and prerogative to forgive. It is true " he will by no means clear the guilty," without a satisfaction to justice ; but the satisfaction is made, the ransom is found, and he is just in pardoning as well as in condemning ; he is just in pardoning the sinner that believes, as well as just in condemning the sinner that believes not. Yea, for your encouragement to take the benefit of God's indemnity that comes out of Zion, I tell you, that the justice of God is more glorified in pardoning the sinner through Christ, than in punishing and exacting

the debt from the sinner in his own person : for when justice falls upon the sinner, and exacts the debt of him, it will be taking satisfaction of the criminal for ever, and yet will never be satisfied ; but when he assoils a sinner through the blood of Jesus, as mercy is magnified, so justice is satisfied to the full.   Hence is that of the apostle, Rom. iii. 25, 26, "Whom God hath set forth to be a propitiation, through faith in his blood, to declare his righteousness for the remission of sins that are past, through the forbearance of God ; to declare, I say, at this time his righteousness: that he might be just, and the justifier of him which believeth in Jesus."

5. The law coming out of Zion is a law of peace, or a law enacting peace, and proclaiming peace to the sinner, who has been waging war against heaven : "I create the fruit of the lips ; peace, peace to him that is far off, and to him that is near."   Indeed an absolute God appearing from a tribunal of justice, proclaims red war against every sinner, every transgressor of his law ; "he is angry with the wicked every day," yea, so angry that he declares "there is no peace to the wicked ; he will wound the head of his enemies, and the hairy scalp of him that goes on in his trespasses." But the same God appearing from mount Zion, from a mercy-seat sprinkled with the blood of Jesus, proclaims peace to the greatest sinner on this side of hell ; he holds out the sceptre of peace to them, inviting them to touch it, and "take hold of his strength, that they may make peace with him, and they shall have peace with him."   See a word to this purpose, 2 Cor. v. 19, 20, "God was in Christ reconciling the world unto himself, not imputing their trespasses unto them ; and hath committed unto us the word of reconciliation. Now then we are ambassadors for Christ, as though God did beseech you by us : we pray you in Christ's stead be ye reconciled to God."   O then, rebels, take the benefit of the law coming out of Zion ; and he who "ascended up on high, and led captivity captive, and

received gifts for men, even for the rebellious," will give grace even unto you. "Let the wicked forsake his way, and the unrighteous man his thoughts;" and let him turn by faith to a God in Christ, "and he will have mercy upon him, and to our God, for he will abundantly pardon."

6. This law coming out of Zion is a law of liberty to the sinner, who is a lawful captive to the law and justice of God, and under bondage to sin and Satan; Christ having satisfied justice, grace steps up to the throne, and issues out her warrant for sinners to go free. By this law coming out of Zion, it is enacted that the sinner should come forth, and he that sits in darkness is allowed to show himself as a freeman in the eyes of the whole world. I say, this law is a law of liberty, not of sin, but of liberty from sin, from the guilt, filth, and power of it. "Sin shall not have dominion over you," is one of the royal statutes of the court of grace. O "prisoners, come forth," accept of liberty, upon the law issuing out of Zion. How deservedly shall ye lie in chains through eternity with the devils if ye do not?

7. The law coming out of Zion is an easy law, no hard task imposed on you as the condition of life. It does not require you to do and live, as the law of works doth; it does not require you to spin a righteousness out of your own bowels, but to receive a righteousness wrought out by a Surety, and made ready to your hand; it does not require you to purchase salvation to yourselves, but to receive a salvation already purchased by Christ; it does not bind you to obey the law, in order to obtain a title to life, but it presents you with a title to life, through him who is the righteous Heir, even Jesus Christ. Here then is a law that needs not be grievous, a yoke that is easy, a burden that is light indeed; yea, this law of faith, it makes the law of works easy and light, because it affords righteousness to fulfil it as a covenant, and strength to obey it as a rule. So that, I say, it is an easy law that comes out

of Zion, it is a law of rest to the weary ; " Come unto me all ye that are weary, and heavy laden, and I will give you rest :" and whenever a poor soul by faith takes the benefit of this law of grace, immediately he enters into rest, Heb. iv. 3.

8. This law coming out of Zion is a dignifying and nobilitating law ; whoever takes the benefit of it, that moment he becomes " a son of God, an heir of God, and a joint heir with Jesus Christ ; he has a name given him better than of sons and daughters, even an everlasting name that shall never be cut off." You, and I, as we are descendants from the first Adam, are base-born heirs of hell, children of wrath and condemnation ; but here is a law, which, if improved and received by faith, doth, by an act of grace, translate you out of the family of hell into the family of heaven. " To as many as received him, to them gave he power to become the sons of God, even to them that believe on his name." O then take the benefit of the law of grace.

9. It is a law of adorable sovereignty. Never did the sovereignty and royal majesty of Heaven shine with such a lustre and beauty in the law issued from Sinai, as it doth in this law of grace, which comes out of Zion. Indeed the sovereignty of justice, equity, and holiness, shined and doth shine in the commandments of that law which was published at mount Sinai ; but in this law which comes out of Zion, the sovereignty of grace, love, and mercy shines, and the justice, holiness, power, and wisdom, and other attributes of the divine nature which were displayed in the law of works, appear as so many pillars supporting the fabric of grace, and the acts of grace, which are published in the gospel.

10. This law coming out of Zion is a sure, firm, and irrepealable law, which can never be disannulled ; it is " of grace that it may be sure to all the seed ;" it is surer, than the laws of the Medes and Persians, surer than any bond or charter that ever was framed by the

wisdom of man. The worm and moth will eat all your
charters to your earthly inheritances ; but the gospel-
covenant, which is the law of grace, is a charter, that
cannot change for ever, it is " established in the very
heavens ; yea, heaven and earth shall pass away, but
one jot or tittle of it shall never fall to the ground.
The mountains shall depart, and the hills be removed,
but my kindness shall not depart from thee, neither
shall the covenant of my peace be removed, saith the
Lord, that hath mercy on thee."

11. The law coming out of Zion is a law that lies
open to every man that hears or reads it ; I mean,
every man has liberty to take the benefit of it.   You
know every man in Britain has the benefit of the laws
of the kingdom, or of the acts of parliament, or proclamations of the king.   Acts xix. 38, says the
town-clerk of Ephesus to the people that were risen in
a mob at the instigation of Demetrius, " If Demetrius
and the craftsmen which are with him, have a matter
against any man, the law is open :" so say I, as the laws
of the kingdom are open to rich and poor, to claim the
benefit of them in the proper courts of the kingdom ;
so the law of grace, the covenant of promise, is open to
all that live within the visible church, the kingdom of
Christ."   " O blessed are the people that know this
joyful sound," so as to take the advantage of it ; " the
promise is unto you, and to all that are afar off."   We
that are ministers intimate and proclaim the gospel, the
law of grace, that every creature may take the benefit
of it ; that which was once spoken in the ear, or round-
ed in secret into the ears of the disciples, do we now
proclaim, as " upon the house tops, or in the high
places of Zion : Unto you, O men, do we call, and our
voice is to the sons of men.   O ! Let us fear, lest a
promise being left us, any of us should seem to come
short of it."

Difference between the Law and the Gospel.

1. THEN, the law of commandments coming out of Sinai is a thing known (though not in its uttermost latitude and extent) by the light of nature ; as is clear, Rom. ii. 14, 15, where the apostle tells us, that " the Gentiles which had not the law, do by nature the things contained in the law, these having not the law, are a law unto themselves : which show the work of the law written in their hearts," &c. The writings of Seneca, Plato, Confucius, and other heathen moralists, are incontested evidences of the truth of this. But now the gospel, or the law of grace, which cometh out of Zion, is a thing only known by supernatural revelation from on high. Search all the volumes of the heathen philosophers, from one end to the other, you shall never find them in the least hint of an incarnate Deity, or of the glorious mystery of salvation through a crucified Christ. Indeed they discovered God as a creating God, and as a governing God, as a commanding and threatening God ; but they never discovered him as a promising God in Christ ; no, no, this is only owing to the discovery that God has made of himself in the gospel. Yea, the mystery of salvation through Christ is so much out of the ken of natural reason, that even after it is revealed externally in the dispensation of the word, yet such is the ignorance and depravation of nature, and the strong bent that it hath toward the law, that it cannot know, and cannot receive it, till a beam of supernatural light shine into the heart : hence Christ tells his disciples, " Unto you it is given to know the mysteries of the kingdom of heaven, but to others it is not given." The light of natural reason is so far from receiving the gospel revelation, that it spurns at it, and opposes it with might and main : " How can this man give us his flesh to eat ?" said the Jews to Christ. The gospel preached by Paul, was " a stumbling-block to the Jews, foolishness and vain babbling to the

Greeks and wise Athenians." Hence comes the difficulty of believing in Christ to the saving of the soul.
The strong bias and current of nature must be altered,
and reason (which sits king in the soul) deposed from
its sovereignty, and lie down as a servant at the feet of
sovereign grace reigning through the imputed righteousness of the Son of God : and you know the change
of government and administration in a kingdom is not
effected commonly without a mighty struggle between
parties contending for the sovereignty ; hence comes
the " confused noise of the warrior, and garments rolled
in blood :" self-reason, self-will, self-righteousness, and
self-confidence, study to maintain their claim to the
government of the heart against grace ; and this makes
as it were the company of two armies, between whom
the war is continued, till death sound the retreat.

2. The office of the law of works coming out of Sinai
is to discover sin and guilt ; " it was added because of
transgressions," says the apostle. " By the law is the
knowledge of sin, and sin by the commandment appears to be exceeding sinful ;" and at the bar of the
law, " the whole world is found guilty before God ; no
flesh living can be justified," if God deal with us according to the terms and tenor of the law. But now the
office and province of the gospel coming out of Zion
is to discover Christ, as " the Lord our righteousness,
and the end of the law for righteousness to every one
that believeth." The gospel tells us, that " Christ has
finished transgression, and made an end of sin, brought
in an everlasting righteousness ; that he was made sin
for us, who knew no sin, that we might be made the
righteousness of God in him." The gospel shows how
the righteousness of the law may be fulfilled in us,
namely, by God's imputation and faith's acceptance of
the righteousness of God revealed for this end in the
gospel.

3. The law of works is a cursing and condemning
word to the guilty sinner, " Cursed is every one that
continueth not in all things which are written in the

book of the law to do them ;" it cries, " Woe, woe, woe to the inhabitants of the earth :" nothing but clouds of wrath and vengeance are to be seen by a guilty sinner when he looks towards Sinai ; "indignation and wrath, tribulation and anguish unto every soul of man that doth evil." But now the gospel is a word of blessing, it presents Christ the blessed seed of Abraham, and cries, " Men shall be blessed in him, and all generations shall call him blessed." The law is a word of wrath, but the gospel comes with the olive branch of peace ; the law displays the red flag of war, but the gospel casts out the white flag of reconciliation, saying, " God was in Christ, reconciling the world unto himself," sending out a word of reconciliation ; and, "O how beautiful are the feet of them that preach the gospel of peace, and bring glad tidings of good things '"

4. The law coming out of Sinai is a slaying and killing word to the sinner. Paul had the experience of this at his first conversion ; it was a keen arrow dipped in law-vengeance, that struck him to the ground in his way going to Damascus, and made him cry, " Lord, what wilt thou have me to do ?" Hence it is that he thus expresses himself, Rom. vii. 9, 10, " I was alive without the law once : but when the commandment came, sin revived, and I died. And the commandment which was ordained to life, I found to be unto death." But now the gospel or the law coming out of Zion, is a word of life ; the first sound of the gospel, when it reaches the heart, is like life from the dead to the poor soul that was lying in the regions and shadow of death ; by it we are " begotten unto a lively hope of eternal life, to an inheritance incorruptible, and undefiled, and that fadeth not away." It is with a view to the preaching and publication of the gospel in the power of it, that Christ says, John v. 25, " The hour is coming, and now is, when the dead shall hear the voice of the Son of God : and they that hear shall live :" hence the gospel is " the power of God unto salvation," it contains " the words of eternal life." " Go (says the

Lord to the apostles, when he is dismissing them from the prison into which they were shut up by the persecuting Jews), Go, stand and preach in the temple to the people, all the words of this life; that is, go preach the gospel, publish my law of grace unto lost sinners, maugre all the malice and power of your enemies, Acts v. 20.

5. The law of works coming out of Sinai, is a word of bondage; but the gospel coming forth from Zion, is a word of freedom and liberty. This the apostle illustrates at great length, Gal. iv. from ver. 22, and downward, where he compares these that are under the law unto Hagar and Ishmael her son; these who are of the gospel, or children of the promise, unto Sarah and her son Isaac, ver. 24, " Which things are an allegory; for these are the two covenants, the one from the mount Sinai, which gendereth to bondage, which is Agar." And, ver. 25, 26, " This Agar is mount Sinai in Arabia, and answereth to Jerusalem which now is, and is in bondage with her children. But Jerusalem which is above, is free, which is the mother of us all." And ver. 28, " Now we, brethren, as Isaac was, are the children of promise." And, ver. 30, " Cast out the bond-woman and her son : for the son of the bond-woman shall not be heir with the son of the free-woman." From all which it appears, that the law is a word of bondage, and they that cleave unto it are in bondage to sin, to Satan, to the curse and wrath of God; but the gospel is a word of liberty, and they who do by faith receive and entertain the joyful sound of it, are not the children of the bond-woman, but of the free, being freed from the law as a covenant, freed from its curse, from the dominion of sin, and the power of Satan, and advanced into the glorious liberty of the children of God. It is very remarkable, that Ishmael, the son of the bond-woman, is cast out of the family, even after he had done many things in obedience to his father Abraham; all his services he had done in the family would not give him a title to the inheritance;

works abstractly considered, through the depravation of nature, irritates and fortifies corruption. But now the gospel or law coming out of Zion enters into the heart, and through the power of the eternal Spirit, wastes, weakens, and kills it in the very source and fountain; for " we through the Spirit do mortify the deeds of the body." And how do we receive the Spirit? " Not by the works of the law, but by the hearing of faith." I own indeed, that the law which urges obedience and doing, may have so much influence upon those who are under it, as to smooth and polish their outward conversation; but yet it leaves the heart and will obstinate against its spiritual commands; the iron sinew is never bowed by any power that the law hath, corruption keeps the throne in the heart: but gospel-grace enters the strong-holds of iniquity, casts down the high imaginations that advance themselves against the knowledge of Christ, and brings every thought unto his obedience. Moses, we read, entered the border and outskirts of Canaan, such as the country of Sihon king of the Amorites, and Og king of Bashan, but never pierced into the heart of the country to subdue the Canaanites; this was left for Joshua, a type of our JESUS: just so is it here, the most the law can do to them that are under it, is only to restrain sin in the conversation, to reform the life; it may bring a man to serve in the oldness of the letter, while sin still keeps the throne in the heart; hence either pride or hypocrisy, or raging despair, remains with the legalist; it is only the gospel or the law coming out of Zion, that is " the power of God unto salvation."

9. The law of works coming out of Sinai, is a word of precept, or a commanding word; but the law coming out of Zion is a promising word. By the gospel God shows what he is to do for us and to us of his sovereign grace; by the law he shows what we are to do for him in point of duty, " He hath showed thee, O man, what is good; and what doth the Lord require of thee, but to do justly, and to love mercy, and to

walk humbly with thy God?" By the gospel God shows what we may expect from him; and by the law he shows what he expects from us, in a way of duty and gratitude. The gospel is the boundary of faith or things to be believed; the law is the boundary of practice, or things to be done by us. In a word, all precepts whatsoever belong to the law; but all promises, offers, and revelations of grace, belong to the gospel.

10. The law of works enjoins duty, but gives no strength to discharge it; the law does not furnish the bankrupt with ary new stock wherewith to fall a-trading, but supposes us to have the stock and strength that God gave us at our creation; it abates nothing, remits nothing of its demands upon the account of our weakness, but requires as much service of the sick and weak sinner as if he were sound and strong; it admits of no composition or allowance to the insolvent debtor. But now the law coming out of Zion considers the sinner as bankrupt; and therefore presents him with an "everlasting righteousness," wherewith to answer the law as a covenant : it considers him as wholly impotent for any duty; and therefore leads him out of himself to Christ, as the "strength of the poor and needy; it gives power to the faint, and increases strength to them that have no might;" it teaches the soul to say, Though I be not sufficient to think a good thought, or to do any duty of the law, yet "I can do all things through Christ strengthening me." The gospel-law coming out of Zion considers the man as poor; and therefore presents him with "gold tried in the fire, to enrich him :" it considers him as naked; and therefore presents him with "white raiment :" as blind; and provides him with "eye-salve, that he may see :" it considers him as starving for want; and therefore invites him to "eat that which is good, and to delight himself in the abundance of fatness :" as bewildered; and therefore shows him "the new and living way" to glory, crying, "This is the way, walk ye in it."

Agreement between the Law and the Gospel.

THEY sweetly stand together in their proper place ;
the law is not against the gospel, nor the gospel against
the law ; no, there is a pleasant harmony, which will
appear, if we consider, that by the gospel, the law
reaches its end, " Christ is the end of the law for righteousness to every one that believeth." In the gospel
we see the law fulfilled as a covenant, and settled as a
rule of obedience. I say, it is fulfilled as a covenant by
the righteousness revealed in the gospel ; yea, not only
fulfilled, but " magnified and made honourable," a new
and superadded glory reflected upon it, by Christ the
Son of God, his being " made under the law, to
redeem us who were under the law."   And then
by the gospel it is also settled as a rule of obedience, Rom. iii. 31, " Do we make void the law through
faith ?   God forbid : yea, we establish the law."   The
gospel brings to light new motives and arguments to
obedience, which the law itself, abstractly considered,
could never afford, namely, arguments drawn from the
consideration of redeeming grace and love, which have
a more constraining power to obedience with an ingenuous spirit, than all the curses and penalties that the
law denounces against these who do not continue in
obedience thereto.

Again, the harmony of the law and gospel appears
in this, that the law paves the way to the entertainment
of gospel-grace ; for it is " a schoolmaster to lead us
unto Christ, that we may be justified by faith."   The
law is a lance in the hand of the chirurgeon to open the
ulcer of sin and corruption within us ; the gospel as a
medicinal balsam drains and gradually heals it, when
applied in a way of believing : the law is a plough to
till up the fallow-ground of the heart of man ; the gospel is the good seed cast into the furrows, which being
impregnate by the dew of heaven, makes it spring up
to everlasting life : the law is as a hammer to break

the rock in pieces; the gospel dissolves it with the warm fire of the love of God shed abroad in the heart by the holy Ghost. Thus the law is subservient to the great design of the gospel.

Again, what the law teaches preceptively, the gospel teaches effectively; the law enjoins the duty, the gospel furnishes with grace to obey it; there is no duty the law requires, but there is suitable furniture in the gospel-promise to discharge it. Doth the law require us to "know the Lord," which is the first precept in the moral law? Well, here is suitable grace provided in the gospel, " I will give them an heart to know me that I am the Lord." Doth the law require us to "trust in him at all times?" Well, the gospel promise is suited unto this, " They shall trust in the name of the Lord." Zeph. iii. 12. Doth it require of us to "love the Lord our God with all our heart, soul, strength, and mind?" Here is gospel grace to effect it, " I will circumcise their hearts to love the Lord their God." Doth it crave obedience, saying, " Walk before me, and be thou perfect?" Well, the grace of the gospel says, " I will put my Spirit within you, and cause you to walk in my statutes, and ye shall keep my judgments and do them." Doth the law enjoin us to "sanctify the Lord in our hearts, and make him our fear and our dread?" The grace of the promise exactly suits that, " I will put my fear in their hearts, and they shall not depart from me." Doth the law require us to " call on the name of the Lord, to worship and serve him?" The gospel promises, that "the spirit of grace and supplication shall be poured out, to help our infirmities, and to teach us to pray, and praise," and perform other acts of worship. Does the law enjoin us to repent, and turn from the evil of our ways? The gospel promises the heart of flesh in place of the heart of stone; and tells us, that "God sent his Son to bless us, in turning away every one of us from our iniquities." Thus you see that what the law teaches preceptively, the gospel teaches effectively.

Again, I might tell you that the harmony between the law and the gospel appears in this, that the law discovers the sinner's duty, and the gospel discovers the object of duty; the law enjoins faith, the gospel lifts up Christ the object of faith : " As Moses lifted up the serpent in the wilderness, even so is the Son of man lifted up," viz. upon the gospel pole ; " that whosoever believeth in him, should not perish, but have everlasting life." The law enjoins the sinner to love God with all the heart ; but it is the gospel only that presents God in such a view, as to become an object of love to a guilty sinner, namely, as he is a reconciled God and Father in Christ ; for viewing God absolutely, as he is presented in the glass of the holy law, he is an object of terror instead of love. The law enjoins us to turn from sin under the pain of eternal wrath and vengeance ; the gospel shows the sinner a refuge unto which he is to turn, " Turn ye to your stronghold, ye prisoners of hope." The law enjoins mourning for sin, " Rend your hearts and not your garments ;" the gospel presents a crucified Christ, wounded for our transgressions, bruised for our iniquities, whom when the sinner views by faith, he " mourns, as one doth for an only son, and is in bitterness, as one is in bitterness for a first-born." The law requires us to worship the Lord our God ; the gospel discovers both the object and the way of worship ; I say, the gospel discovers the object of worship, namely a God in Christ, and the way to the holiest opened by the blood of Jesus.

To conclude, the law by its terror sweeps away the refuge of lies ; the gospel discovers a new foundation of hope and help, saying, " Behold, I lay in Zion for a foundation, a stone, a tried stone, a precious corner-stone, a sure foundation : and he that believeth on him, shall not be confounded." The law saps the foundation of sand, and overturns the tower that the sinner was building in order to reach heaven by it ; the gospel discovers the rock of ages, upon which the sinner may build his house, against which the gates of hell shall never prevail. The law, when viewed spiritually, drives the sinner out of himself, by discovering his emptiness, poverty, and misery; the gospel draws and invites him out of himself, by discovering the all-fulness of a Redeemer to supply his wants, though never so great. The law lets the man see that he has no money nor price; the gospel shows, that though he has no money nor price, yet he may come and buy gold tried in the fire, white raiment, and eye-salve. The law lets the sinner see that he is shut up in a it, wherein there is no water; the gospel shows how the sinner, by the blood of God's covenant, may come forth out of the pit, and opens a fountain of living water, where he may draw and drink with joy. The law leads us to Christ for righteousness; the gospel sends us to the law as a rule of obedience, as a light to our feet and a lamp to our paths. Thus the whole life and work of a Christian is a continual traffic from the law to the gospel, and from the gospel back again to the law as a rule.

How to know whether we be under the Law Covenant, or the Gospel Covenant.

1. If the law never slew you, you are yet under it, and married to it as a husband: Gal. ii. 19, " I through the law, am dead to the law." Rom. vii. 9, " I was alive without the law once; but when the commandment came, sin revived, and I died." Every man naturally sits mounted upon the throne of his own imaginary righteousness; he imagines himself to be alive, and that he is capable to do well enough, by his own endeavours after life; but when the law of God comes in its spirituality, it shakes the foundation of his refuge of lies, just as the earthquake shook the foundation of the prison at the jailor's conversion, making the poor man to cry out, " O what shall I do to be saved?" Try yourselves then by this. Has God brought you to the foot of Sinai, making the thunders of his law to awaken you out of your security? Has he given you

such a view of he law in its extent and spirituality, that you became quite dead to all conceit of righteousness by any doing or obedience of your own, saying, "All my righteousness is as filthy rags?" If you were never yet brought to this pass, I fear you are yet strangers to the law of grace issuing out of Zion, and that you are yet under the law of works as a covenant.

2. You who do not know what it is to watch, and pray, and wrestle against the legal bias of your hearts, it is a sign that you are yet cleaving to mount Sinai law. As every man by nature is seeking righteousness by the law of works : so believers themselves, while they have any thing of the old Adam in them, will find a strong bias in their hearts to return to that husband ; he finds it a matter of the utmost difficulty to keep his treacherous legal heart from resting on his duties, frames, graces, attainments, as a ground of acceptance before God ; and a sense of this makes him mourn before the Lord as much, if not more, than for his other failings and infirmities. And therefore you who know nothing of this natural bent of your hearts towards the law as a covenant; and you who do not know what it is to watch and pray, and wrestle against this bias of your hearts ; it says, that you are yet within the confines of mount Sinai, not as yet come to mount Zion.

3. When you are under any distress or trouble of conscience, what airth do ye run to for comfort and relief? what is it that affords you ease ? The man that is married to the law, he runs to his husband for relief. I mean, he plies the oar of his own obedience, he heals his wound with a plaster of vows, tears, penances, and endeavours after amendment. But, sirs, you that heal the wounds of conscience with such a plaster, you are yet at mount Sinai, which gendereth to bondage. The true believer, who is "come to mount Zion," when an arrow from mount Sinai smites and wounds him, he does not run to Sinai, but "to mount Zion, to the blood of sprinkling, that speaketh better things

than the blood of Abel." No balm but that of Gilead
will heal his wound ; he cannot find ease, but only
under the wings of the Sun of righteousness.

4. Ye who can be troubled for gross sins and out-
breakings, but were never affected with, or afflicted for
the guilt of Adam's sin, the corruption of your nature,
the heinous nature of the sin of unbelief, I suspect you
never saw the law in its spirituality ; and consequently
are not dead to it as a covenant. There are two things
that are more heavy to a believer, who is " come to
mount Zion," than any other thing whatsoever, viz.
original sin and the sin of unbelief ; these, Oh these,
are the things that make him many times go with a
bowed-down back, crying, " Wretched man that I am,
who shall deliver me from this body of sin and death !"

5. What is it that sets you a-work in the mortification of sin ? for the legalist may set himself to mortify
sin, as well as the true believer ; but here lies the odds,
they are acted from different principles. The legalist
mortifies sin, and opposes it merely out of self-love,
that he may be kept out of hell, or procure a title to
heaven : but the true believer is principally acted from
a principle of love to Christ, he looks on him whom he
has pierced, and this fires him with resentment, so that
he studies to avenge Christ's quarrel by piercing the
heart of his most beloved lusts and idols ; the man has
a love to Christ, a desire to glorify God, and to maintain fellowship and communion with him ; these are
the principal things that constrain him to duty, and restrain
him from sin. And therefore turn inward, and see
whether self-love, or love to Christ, have the principal
influence in your obedience. I do not deny but a desire after the enjoyment of God in glory, and the eternal happiness of the soul, may and actually do influence
the soul to obedience in a secondary way ; but beyond
doubt the love of Christ, and the glory of God, is the
ultimate and principal spring of obedience.

6. If you do not see so much weakness and corruption, so much deadness and distraction, attending your

best duties, as to convince you of the absolute need of the blood of Jesus, and of his merit and mediation, to render both you and them acceptable to God, it is an evidence, that you are not yet come off from mount Sinai law as a covenant. The poor believer, when he has win to the greatest enlargement in duty, and to the best frame that he can desire, yet he will be ready to cry out, " If thou, Lord, shouldst mark iniquities; O Lord, who shall stand?" He sees himself to be an " unprofitable servant," and that " his goodness extends not to the Lord."

7. If you be more concerned to bulk well in the externals of religion, than in an acquaintance with the inward power of it, it is an evidence that you are yet upon a law-bottom, like these who cry, " Will the Lord be pleased with thousands of rams, or with ten thousands of rivers of oil ? shall I give my first-born for my transgression, the fruit of my body for the sin of my soul ? Wherefore have we fasted, and prayed, and thou takest no knowledge ?" But the believer, who is come to mount Zion, although he will not neglect the external duties of religion, yet his particular concern is to grow in internal holiness, and conformity of heart and life to the Son of God, " to have the same mind in him, which was also in Christ Jesus ;" he longs to know more of " the power of his resurrection," of the virtue of his sin-killing blood, and the efficacy of his Spirit, lifting him up after " things that are above, where Christ is at the right hand of God ;" and if he can win at this, he is the less careful about the flourishes of a profession, which is all that the hypocrite and legalist aims at, although in the meantime he will " flourish like the palm-tree, and grow like the cedars in Lebanon."

8. You who have your hearts filled with enmity and prejudice against the children of grace, the heirs of the promise, and cannot endure strict and holy walking with God, but are ready to envy those who you think outshine you, and have your hearts filled with inward rancour and prejudice against them, or perhaps mock

and persecute them, either with heart, tongue, or hand, it is an evidence that you are yet in the confines of Sinai, among the children of the bond-woman : Gal. iv. 29, " But as then he that was born after the flesh persecuted him that was born after the Spirit, even so it is now." A persecuting spirit or a spirit of rancour and envy against those whom we think more holy than ourselves, and whom we fancy darken us, is a plain evidence of a legal spirit. They that are of a true gospel-spirit, are ready to love the society of saints, whom they think excel themselves; and the more holy they are, the better they love them ; the more of the image of God is on them, or in them, the more desirable will they be unto them.

9. If you be come off from mount Sinai to mount Zion, from the law to the gospel covenant, then those things which once in a day you accounted gain, will be but loss in your reckoning. So soon as Paul was brought off from the law, to be a partaker of gospel-grace, " what things were gain to him those he counted loss for Christ," Phil. iii. 7. What these things are the legalist accounts gain, which the believer reckons loss for Christ, you have an account of, Phil. iii. 4—6, which you may read and consider at your leisure.

All boasting excluded by the Law of Faith.

1. THIS appears from gospel declarations or testimonies : Eph. ii. 8, " By grace are ye saved, through faith ; and that not of yourselves : it is the gift of God :" ver. 9, " Not of works, lest any man should boast," &c. Where you see that self is stripped of every thing that might afford matter of boasting, and the whole glory of our salvation ascribed unto grace, and to grace only. What is the first gospel lesson that Christ the great gospel-prophet teaches his scholars ? It is just this, " If any man will be my disciple, let him deny himself;" that is, he must renounce his own wisdom, his own righteousness, holiness, and every

thing on which he laid the stress of his salvation, or the ground of his hope, and be content to lie down at the foot of sovereign grace, as " wretched, miserable, poor, blind, and naked," to receive all in a way of free grace.   This lesson the apostle Paul learned well, Phil. iii. 7, 8, " What things were gain to me, those I count- ed loss for Christ.   Yea, doubtless, and I count all things but loss for the excellency of the knowledge of Christ Jesus my Lord," &c.   We find him every where renouncing self, and giving the glory of all unto free grace; whatever he was, he owed it not to himself, but unto grace, " By grace I am what I am ;" whatever he did, he gives the glory of it to grace, " Not I, but the grace of God in me."

2. This is evident from gospel-interrogations or ques- tions, which are of such a nature as to stop the mouth of all flesh from boasting.   You have two or three of them in the very words of my text, " Where is boasting ? It is excluded.   By what law ? of works ?   Nay, but by the law of faith."   You have the like train of silenc- ing questions, 1 Cor. iv. 7, " Who maketh thee to differ from another ? and what hast thou that thou didst not receive ? now if thou didst receive it, why dost thou glory as if thou hadst not received it ?"   It is a vain spirit that glories in borrowed robes.

3. This is evident from the gospel way of reckoning. It is a strange way the apostle directs us to, Rom. vi. 11, " Reckon ye yourselves to be dead indeed unto sin ; but alive unto God through Jesus Christ."   A believer must never reckon upon what he is, has, or has done ; but he must reckon upon what he is, hath, or has done in his glorious Head and Surety : when he looks to himself, he reckons that he is a dead man, dead in law, " condemned already," under sentence of death, and spiritually dead under the power of sin ; but, on the other hand, he must reckon himself " alive unto God, through Jesus Christ."   Thus the apostle reck- ons, and teaches us to reckon also, Col. iii. 3, " Ye are dead, but your life is hid with Christ in God ;   so

Gal. ii. 20, " I am crucified with Christ : nevertheless I live ; yet not I, but Christ liveth in me." As if he had said, I live ; what is this I am saying ? I have mistaken my reckoning, I am reckoning wrong when I say that I live ; for it is " not I that live, but Christ that liveth in me." So let us see how they reckon upon the head of righteousness. Paul was " touching the law blameless," before his conversion ; and after his conversion, " he knew nothing by himself," or he knew nothing wherein his conscience condemned him ; but does he look on this as the ground of his acceptance before God ? No, " I know nothing by myself, yet am I not hereby justified :" he reckons all his righteousness before and after his conversion, but σκυ̂ϛαλα, dog's meat, the vilest of things, " that he might be found in Christ, not having his own righteousness, which is of the law, but that which is through the faith of Christ," &c. See the gospel reckoning on the score of righteousness, Is. xlv. 24, " Surely, shall one say, In the Lord (not in myself) have I righteousness."— Again, how do they reckon upon the point of strength ? O, says Paul, " I am not sufficient of myself to think any thing as of myself: but my sufficiency is of the Lord ;" but though I be not sufficient for any thing in and of myself, yet " I can do all things through Christ strengthening me. Surely, in the Lord, shall one say, have I righteousness and strength." Christ is the fountain of their strength, and they reckon themselves strong, not in their own, but " in the power of his might." Thus you see that the whole tendency of the gospel-way of reckoning is always to carry the creature out of itself, that it may not glory in itself, but in the Lord and in his free grace.

4. Let us take a view of gospel doctrines, and we shall find they are all levelled for this glorious end of sinking self, and exalting the freedom of the grace of God through Christ in the salvation of sinners ; there we are taught that man has ruined himself, but his recovery is only by grace, Hos. xiii. 9, " O Israel, thou

hast destroyed thyself, but in me is thine help." " Where
is boasting then ?   It is excluded by the law of faith."
In the gospel we have the doctrine of regeneration
or effectual calling. Well, what interest has the man in his
own regeneration ? Even as little as the infant has in its
formation in its mother's belly, John i. 13. " We are
born, not of blood, nor of the will of the flesh, nor of the
will of man, but of God."   Grace, and not self, must
have the glory of that.   Again, there is the doctrine of
justification ; how admirably is that laid for abasing
self, and all our works of righteousness, that grace may
have the glory. " We are justified freely by his grace,
through the redemption that is in Jesus Christ." Then
there is the doctrine of our adoption and sonship : Do
we put ourselves among the children ?   No, it is grace
that does it ; it is " he that gives us power, right, or
privilege to become the sons of God.   Behold what
manner of love is this, that the Father hath bestowed
upon us that we should be called the sons of God."
Then for the doctrine of sanctification : Do we wash
and cleanse ourselves ?   No, it is grace that does it, it
is " the beauty of the Lord our God ; we are beautiful
through the comeliness he puts upon us."   And for the
doctrine of perseverance, or standing in a state of grace :
Do we keep ourselves in that state ? No, not we ; but
it is " he that keeps us by his power through faith unto
salvation."   In a word, the whole of the gospel doctrine
is aye levelled for this end to beat down self, " that he
who glorieth, may glory in the Lord."

5. Let us consider the tendency of gospel parables.
Christ was a parabolical preacher, he commonly taught
by similitudes, many of which, if not all, if duly considered, are always to lead sinners out of themselves.
To instance only in two or three.   We read, Luke xv.
of the parable of the prodigal son : what is the scope
of it but to let sinners see they are a set of poor bankrupts that have squandered away all the stock they
received in the first Adam, that so they may have recourse to the mercy and grace of God in Christ ?   We

read of the parable of the Pharisee and publican, how
the one boasted of his good deeds, and the other stood
afar off trembling under a sense of sin, looking to the
mercy of God in Christ, and " he went home to his
house justified rather than the other." Again, we have
the parable of the wise and foolish virgins ; what is the
design in that, but that sinners may not rest themselves
satisfied with any thing of their own, be it a profession
or any seeming grace in themselves, but that they may
go to the market of grace to buy that oil, which is in
the dwellings of the wise, which alone will make acceptable at the coming of the great Bridegroom ? Again,
to add one more, we have the parable of the wise merchant ; the scope of which is to lead sinners out of
themselves, for they must sell all, that they may buy
the pearl, *i. e.* they must renounce themselves, and all
their good qualifications, and betake themselves to the
free grace of God in Christ.

6. I might clear this by the tenor of the gospel
covenant and promises, the new covenant by which we
are saved. What sort of a covenant is it ? It is a
covenant of grace, *i. e.* a covenant calculate for abasing
self, and exalting the freedom of the grace of God in
the sinner's salvation. The covenant itself is not a
covenant of our making, but of God's making. Indeed
we read of covenants made by men in Scripture, Psal.
l. 5, " Those that have made a covenant with me by
sacrifice." Israel entered into covenant with the Lord.
But these covenants that are made by us, are only engagements unto duty in the strength of that grace that
is promised in the covenant of grace, which is not of
our making, but of God's making : " I will make with
you an everlasting covenant : I have made a covenant with my chosen : I will make an everlasting covenant with you, even the sure mercies of David," and
the like. Again, self is ready to creep in, and to make
terms and conditions, and qualifications of our own, to
interest us in this covenant and the blessings thereof :
but this covenant is so framed by Infinite Wisdom, as

to exclude all these, that no man may boast; for the promises of it are so framed, as every thing is freely bestowed without regard either to any good or ill in the creature; it runs in the form of a testamentary deed or gift, than which nothing can be conceived more free; " I will be their God; I will be merciful to their unrighteousness: I will see their ways, and heal them;" *i. e.* I will do this and that of my own sovereign grace, without regarding the creature's qualifications. This will further appear,

7. If we consider the tenor of gospel calls and invitations to receive Christ, and to take hold of God's covenant of grace. Is the invitation or call to them that are so and so qualified? Is it to the righteous or holy? No, " I came not to call the righteous, but sinners to repentance." Is it to them that have money or price to recommend them? No, Is. lv. 1, " Ho every one that thirsteth, come ye to the waters and he that hath no money; come ye, buy and eat, yea, come, buy wine and milk without money, and without price." Is it to them that have their stock to the fore? No, it is to those that are dyvours and bankrupts: " Thou art wretched, miserable, poor, and naked; therefore I counsel thee to buy of me gold tried in the fire:" it is to the blind, the maim, the halt, the wretched; and, in a word, it is to every creature under heaven, if it be on this side of hell.

Faith exalting the freeness of Grace in Salvation.

1. Faith is a mere receiving or taking grace; so we find it expressed in John i. 12, Col. ii. 6, Rev. xxii. 17. This constitutes the very soul and essence of faith, to take or receive all, but give nothing. All other graces of the Spirit give something unto God. Love gives him a warm and glowing heart, repentance a melting and bleeding heart, obedience a working hand, patience a broad back for bearing burdens, fear a trembling heart: but as for faith, it is of such a beggarly nature

that it does not come to give, but to get, or take all
from the Lord : hence it is called an opening of the
mouth to be filled." The whole of our salvation, as
it lieth in a covenant of grace, from first to last, is a
mere gift of sovereign grace : " I will give grace and
glory, and my Son for a covenant to the people," and
in him the new heart and new spirit, peace and pardon,
and all "the sure mercies of David." Now what
grace could be so fit for the purpose of God in the salvation of sinners by this covenant as faith, which is a
mere recipient? You know a liberal giver wants only
a receiver. Now, such a thing is faith, it just receives
or takes in what God gives in his bounty to man in the
covenant of grace. I think it is remarkable what is
said of Lydia, when she believed at the hearing of
Paul's sermon, Acts xvi. 14, " God opened her heart
to attend unto the things which were spoken of Paul ;"
in the original it is, " God opened her heart to take
them to her," viz. the things which Paul spake, God
opened her heart to take them in, or to receive them,
Acts xxvi. 18, " That they may receive remission of
sins, and inheritance among them which are sanctified
by faith that is in me." Now, if faith be nothing else
but a receiving, " where is boasting ? It is excluded
by the grace of faith," as well as the gospel, which is
the law of faith.

2. As faith is a mere receiver, so it will receive nothing but what comes out of the hand of free grace.
If you offer any thing to faith in a way of debt, or as
a reward due to itself, it will shake its hands from holding any such bribe, and cry, Away with any thing that
savours of debt, it is none of mine. Faith will trade
at no market but that of grace, where no money passeth, and where no price or bartering is in fashion ;
hence it is said to " buy without money and without
price," Is. lv. 1. Hence it is that faith and works are
opposed to one another in Scripture, particularly Rom.
iv. 5, " To him that worketh not, but believeth on him
that justifieth the ungodly," &c. Works claim privi-

leges in a way of debt, but faith on the score of grace,
and refuses to have them another way ; yea, so averse
is faith from the merit of works, that it refuses to be
reckoned among the category of acts of obedience
in the matter of justification, so that it excludes its
own act; for it is not by the act, but the object of
faith that we are justified : " Where is boasting then ?
Surely it is excluded by the law and grace of faith."

3. This will further appear, if we consider, that faith
will receive nothing but as it lies in a word of grace, a
promise, a covenant, or offer of grace.   This is the
very genius of faith, that it intermeddles with the blessings and privileges which it receives, only on the warrant of God's word of grace, wherein he has gifted or
granted them unto us, as it is well worded in our Confession ; faith receives and applies Christ and his salvation, by virtue of a covenant of grace.   And herein
lies one main difference between presumption and saving faith, that presumptuous faith gripes at the gift of
grace, but not by virtue of a covenant of grace ; it will
take nothing without the command of God as its warrant, or his promise as its encouragement ; and having
these two in its eye, it is sure it cannot be guilty of
vicious intromission.   Let faith once fix on the promise
of God, and let it see God commanding it to receive
the promise, and thing promised, then it will triumph
and say, " God hath spoken in his holiness, I will rejoice ; Gilead is mine," God is mine, Christ is mine,
the Spirit is mine, peace is mine, pardon and glory are
mine, because " God hath spoken in his holiness ; and
this is all my salvation."   Thus, I say, faith goes upon the ground of the promise, it knows no other law
but the law of faith ; and therefore it must needs exclude boasting, and be calculate only for the advancing
the freedom of grace.

4. This will yet further appear, if we consider that
faith has no will of its own, but only the will of sovereign grace.   As it is said of the marigold, that it opens
and shuts with the sun, and turns itself round with it,

holding an exact correspondence therewith : so does
the grace of faith hold an exact correspondence with
God's will of grace in the word, or covenant of grace.
As the human nature of Christ united unto the divine,
did not act as a distinct person, and had not a will of its
own separate from the divine, but was wholly resolved
into the will of the divine nature; so faith has no will but
God's will of grace; God's will of grace is the will of
faith, and faith is the echo of the will of grace intimated
in the word.   Says grace, " I will be their God, I am
the Lord thy God ;"   Amen, says faith, and that is
my will too.   " I will heal their backslidings," says
grace : Even so be it, that is my will too, says faith.
" I will sprinkle them and cleanse them from all their
filthiness, and from all their idols :" Amen, says faith,
that is my will too.   " This is the will of a God of
grace, even our sanctification ;" O, says faith, that is
just what I will too.   Thus you see that it is calculated
merely for advancing God's will of grace, consequently
for excluding boasting.

5. Faith will address no throne but a throne of grace.
Bring faith to a throne of justice, it " stands afar off,
smites on the breast," and cries, " If thou Lord
shouldst mark iniquities : O Lord who shall stand ?"
and therefore, " God have mercy on me a sinner; for
in thy sight no living can be justified." Faith has no
work or business at a throne of justice. But bring
faith within view of a throne of grace which has justice satisfied, and judgment executed on the Son of
God for its basis and foundation, and then it will
gather spirits and courage, saying, Heb. iv. 16, " Let
us come boldly unto the throne of grace, that we may
obtain mercy, and find grace to help in time of need."
Heb. x. 19, 20, &c. " Having, brethren, boldness to
enter into the holiest by the blood of Jesus, by a new
and living way, &c. let us draw near with a true heart,
in full assurance of faith." Now, seeing it does not
deal with a tribunal of justice, but only with a mercy-

seat, it follows that faith excludes boasting in the creature, and is levelled for the exaltation of grace only.

6. Faith will have no praise or glory to itself, but
gives all the glory to grace, and to grace alone.   We
are told, that God will not give his glory to another ;
and yet we find him giving his glory to the grace of
faith.   Sometimes we find him giving it the glory of
his omnipotence, " To him that believeth all things are
possible ;" and faith will speak like a little omnipotent,
" I can do all things."   Sometimes we find him giving
it the glory of the forgiving and pardoning of sin, which
is his alone prerogative ; we " receive the remission of
sins through faith in his blood."   The cleansing of the
heart is God's prerogative, and yet it is ascribed unto
faith, Acts xv. 9, " Purifying their hearts by faith."
Now, why, think you, will God set his own crown upon the
head of the grace of faith, which he will not do to men
or angels, or any creature whatsoever ?   Why, the plain
reason is, because faith is such an honest self-denied
kind of thing, that it will have no glory to itself, but
turns all back again upon the grace of God, saying,
" Not unto us, not unto us, but unto thy name be the
glory."   Whatever a man does by faith, he will be far
from boasting in himself, or grace received ; it pays
the rent of praise full tale unto the grace of God alone,
without keeping back the least mite, as Ananias and
Sapphira did, and as all hypocrites commonly do.   It is
true, will faith say, " I can do all things;" but it is
" through Christ strengthening me."   It is true, 1 have
a perfect righteousness ; but it is " in the Lord surely
that I have righteousness ; in him will I be justified,
and in him will I glory."   It is true, I purify the heart ;
but it is by the Spirit and blood of Jesus that I do it.
I have forgiveness ; but it is in his blood.   I have a
title to a reward of glory ; but not as a reward of my
labour, but as the travel of Christ's soul ; the reward
is a debt due to him and not to me.   I am an heir of
God ; but it is by being a joint heir with Christ.

Motives to renounce the Law of Works and to take the benefit of the Law of Faith.

MOTIVE 1. Shall be drawn from the consideration of the evil and danger of cleaving to mount Sinai law for righteousness.   And this will appear, if you consider,

1. That, since the fall of Adam, the mount Sinai law never brought righteousness or life to any of his posterity ; no, no, "the law is weak through the flesh," says the apostle, Rom. viii. 3, : it is strong to condemn the sinner ; but, through the corruption of nature, and our weakness to obey, it is become weak and insufficient to give life to us.   The apostle tells us, Gal. iii. 21, that "if there had been a law given which could have given life, verily righteousness should have been by the law :" where he plainly supposes, that no commanding law since the fall can possibly give life or righteousness to man ; yea, so far is the law of commandments incapable to give life, that it sends the whole family of Adam to hell together, "Cursed is every one that continueth not in all things which are written in the book of the law to do them."

2dly, This law of works or commandments requires and exacts of you what is impossible as a term or condition of life, and that is a perfect or sinless obedience. No mere man since the fall is able perfectly to keep the commandments of God ; and yet this law will not abate one ace ; it "requires brick but gives no straw ;" it requires obedience, but gives no strength ; yea, it exacts as much service and obedience of a sick man as though he were perfectly sound, of fallen man as though he were in his primitive integrity.   It is a common foolish notion of many ignorant people, that if they yield sincere obedi-ence, and do as well as they can in obedience to the commandments of God, God will accept of that in room of that perfect righteousness which the law re-quired in innocence.   But beware of hazarding your souls upon such a damnable delusion ? for the law of

God must have not only a sincere, but perfect and sinless obedience, or nothing ; if you do not continue in
all things written in the book of the law to do them,
the curse of the law takes place.   Indeed sincere obedience is admitted as a return of gratitude to God upon the soul's closing with, and submitting to, the perfect righteousness of Christ, but not as a ground of
acceptance before God either in part or whole : and if
you but imagine in your heart, that your own imperfect
obedience, though never so sincere, will be a ground of
acceptance, or a title to life, either in part or whole,
you " become a debtor to do the whole law," Gal. v. 3.

3dly, So long as you cleave to the law as a covenant, there is a hand-writing standing against you before God uncancelled, the justice of God hath a bond
over your head : " The sin of Judah is written before
him as with a pen of iron, and the point of a diamond."
This hand-writing is never cancelled till you believe in
Christ, and submit unto his righteousness ; no, no, you
are " condemned already, and the wrath of God abideth
on you."   But that moment you quit the law as a covenant, and take the benefit of the gospel, or law of grace,
the Surety of the better testament comes in betwixt
you and all obligations the law has upon you ; and then
" there is no more condemnation."   Who can lay any
thing to your charge ?

4thly, While you are within the confines of mount
Sinai law, a lowering cloud pregnate with wrath hangs
over your head, which will infallibly dissolve in a tempest of wrath to the everlasting ruin of your souls, unless you make your escape to mount Zion and take the
benefit of the law of grace : " Snares, fire and brimstone, and a horrible tempest, this shall be the portion
of your cup."   Perhaps you may be crying, Peace,
peace ; but what will that avail, seeing God says otherwise, " There is no peace, saith my God, unto the
wicked ?"

5thly, It is no wonder though God have a controversy with you, while you cleave unto the law of works ;

for while you do so, you are running directly cross to
God in the greatest design ever he had in hand, which
is the glorious work of redemption through Jesus Christ:
Gal. ii. 21, " If righteousness come by the law,
then Christ died in vain." The opening up "a new
and living way to the holiest by the blood of Jesus," is
the chief of the ways of God, the very master-piece of
Infinite Wisdom : but now, while you cleave to the law,
and seek righteousness by it, you are running counter
to God's design of grace, doing what in you lies to condemn and shut up that " new and living way which
God has opened, and to frustrate the design of the incarnation and death of the eternal Son of God : Gal.
v. 4, " Christ is become of no effect unto you whosoever of you are justified by the law ; ye are fallen from
grace."

   6thly, To cleave to mount Sinai-law, in point of
righteousness, is the greatest folly and madness in the
world ; why, because the law of works, or the law-covenant, is broken, and can serve you in no stead for salvation ; yea the breach of it was intended by Infinite
Wisdom as an inlet unto the law of faith, or the gospel
method of salvation by Christ, and his everlasting righteousness. I was hinting formerly, that since the fall
of man, the law was never given, that man might stay
in it as a ground of hope, but that by it he might be
carried beyond the law to Christ, who is " the end of
the law for righteousness." And now I shall adventure
to say more, That when God gave the law to Adam
in innocence in the form of a covenant, he never designed that man's happiness should stand upon that
footing ; no, the covenant of works was only designed as
a scaffold for rearing up a more glorious building of
grace and mercy, which God has said " shall be built
up for ever," Psal. lxxxix. 2. Now what strange madness is it for a man to keep by the scaffold, when the
fabric for which it was erected is complete and finished !
O sirs, " Wisdom hath builded her house, she hath
hewn out her seven pillars ;" her house is finished,

provided and accommodated with every thing needful
for the sinner's salvation.   Why then will you stay
longer upon the broken scaffold of the law, as though
by it you could make your way to heaven ?   Christ is
the only bridge of communication betwixt God and
man : no Mediator but he, "no coming to the Father
but by him."   O then do not adventure to pass the
gulf upon the broken shreds and planks of your own
lame righteousness by the works of the law, lest you
go to the bottom : " As many as are of the works of the
law, are under the curse," Gal. iii. 10.   O will you
choose rather to risk the salvation of your souls for
ever, than venture on the obedience and satisfaction of
Christ, the alone " foundation God hath laid in Zion ?"
For the Lord's sake then take care what you do.

Mot. 2.   To persuade you to quit the law of works,
the mount Sinai law, as a covenant, and to fall in with
the law of faith, I mean to take the benefit of the glorious gospel, and the promises thereof, will you but consider what advantageous discoveries the gospel makes
to the miserable sinner ; it discovers and presents to
him whatever he needs or wants in that miserable situation he is reduced to by the fall.

1. O sinner, thou wants a ransom unto justice, that
thou mayest not go down to the pit.   Well, here it is,
Christ is that ransom ; " He gave himself a ransom for
many ;" and he is set forth in the gospel, " as a propitiation through faith in his blood."   Tell me, sirs, you
that cleave to the law of works, can the law afford you
this ?   No, by no means, Rom. viii. 3.   All your doings will not do the business, yea, though you were but
guilty of one sinful thought in your whole life, that
one flaw in your obedience renders the law weak to
save you, and is like a dead fly, which makes all your
obedience to stink ; and will ever such a stinking obedience be a ransom for a soul ?   Nothing can be a ransom for a guilty soul but blood : " Without the shedding of blood there is no remission of sin :" Blood,
blood is the demand of justice, either the blood of the

sinner or of the Surety, and no less blood than the blood of an infinite person can be admitted. Now, the gospel, I say, discovers and presents this ransoming and atoning blood, whereby all the demands of justice are answered to the full.

2dly, Art thou in a starving condition, like to drop down for want of soul-food, like the poor prodigal, who in a far country, was perishing for want, attempting to fill thy belly with husks of carnal comforts, or of legal duties, but still finds thy soul empty? Well, the gospel casts up a banqueting house, where thou mayest "eat that which is good, and delight thyself with abundance of fatness," Is. lv. 2. To this purpose is that, Is. xxv. 6, "In this mountain," viz. mount Zion, or the gospel church, "shall the Lord of hosts make unto all people a feast of fat things, a feast of wines on the lees, of fat things full of marrow, of wines on the lees well refined. Wisdom hath not only builded her house, but she hath mingled her wine, killed her fatlings, and made all things ready." Christ the bread of life is ready for the starving sinner; no more but to take and eat, to receive and apply him, and his whole fulness. O then take the benefit of the law of faith; fall in with the gospel call and invitation.

3dly, O sinner, there is a loathsome disease that cleaves fast unto thee, thou art "full of wounds, bruises, and putrifying sores, from the crown of the head even to the sole of the foot, which have not been bound up, nor mollified with ointment." Well, the gospel tells thee that there is "balm in Gilead, and a physician there," whose name is JEHOVAH-ROPHI, "I am the Lord that healeth thee." O sirs, Christ is the sinner's Saviour, the sinner's physician; and every sinner has as good right to come to him, as such, as ever a wounded or sick man in a regiment had to call for the help of the physician or chirurgeon of that regiment; the very office of a physician obliges him to serve the sick. Now, Christ being a physician by office, warrants the lost sinner to come to him with his dying diseased soul;

and, beyond peradventure, whoever comes to him, he will not, not, not cast him out.

4thly, O sinner, thou art polluted and defiled "among the pots," spotted like the leopard, black like the Ethiopian. Well, the gospel discovers "a fountain opened to the house of David, and to the inhabitants of Jerusalem, for sin, and for uncleanness." O come and wash in this fountain, in the Jordan of a Redeemer's blood; and "though ye have lien among the pots, ye shall be like the wings of a dove." Do not say ye have no right to come to the fountain, for ye have God's command to wash, to "make you clean," Is. i. 16. He has promised to "sprinkle with clean water," Ezek. xxxvi. 25.

5thly, The gospel, or law of faith, presents thee with a robe to cover the "shame of thy nakedness," even the best robe that heaven can afford : Rev. iii. 18, " I counsel thee to buy of me white raiment, that thou mayest be clothed, and that the shame of thy nakedness do not appear." Suppose you were stripped naked going from door to door, seeking a rag to cover you, if one should present you with clothes, and put them upon you, would you not reckon yourself obliged to that person ? Well, this is the case ; thy soul is naked before God; but here is " a robe of righteousness, and a garment of salvation," presented in the gospel, to cover thee, " Hearken unto me, ye that are stout-hearted, and far from righteousness. I bring near my righteousness : it shall not be far off." The law of works is a bed too short, a covering too narrow for a sinner. Thy righteousness by the law is as filthy rags, and, instead of a covering, does but deform and defile the soul; but here is a clothing, bright like the sun, Rev. xii. 1. and every one that puts it on by faith, " shall shine as the sun in the kingdom of their Father." Our first parents, whenever they found themselves naked, fell a-work to sew fig leaves together for aprons to cover their shame, until God provided them coats of skins, probably skins of the beasts offered in sacrifice,

thereby teaching them, that their soul-nakedness was
to be covered with the righteousness of Christ, our
great atoning sacrifice : I say, whenever these coats of
skins were provided for them, they threw away their
fig leaves as useless. This is the very case with the
sinner ; so soon as he falls under a conviction of his
spiritual nakedness before God, he studies to sew together an apron of his own works. The whore, Prov.
vii. 14, pleads, that she " had peace-offerings with her ;
this day (says she), have I paid my vows ;" and with
this apron she imagined to cover the filthiness of her
adultery. But, alas ! this will not do ; for God says,
" Their webs shall not become garments, neither shall
they cover themselves with their works," Is. lix. 6.
Therefore, for the Lord's sake, cast away these fig
leaves, as useless, as dung and loss, seeing ye are now
called to accept of the white raiment of God's providing.
Say with Paul, when Christ was discovered to him, " I
count all but loss and dung, that I may be found in
him." Paul in this case is just like a man swimming for
his life upon a broken plank ; so soon as ever he comes
to a vessel that will carry him ashore, he quits his
plank, and betakes himself to the whole and sound vessel ; and so reckons himself in safety.

    6thly, The gospel discovers or presents thee with a
cooling, refreshing shadow, to defend thee from the
heat of divine wrath. Perhaps some of you have been
at the foot of Sinai, or at present are scorched with
the flashes of divine wrath, cast out from that burning
mountain. Well, here is mount Zion, take the benefit
of the gospel, and thou shalt find the "shadow of a
great rock," where the flames of vindictive wrath cannot reach thee : Cant. ii. 3, " I sat down," says the
spouse, " under his shadow with great delight," &c.
When the children of Israel travelled through the burning sands of Arabia, they had no shelter from the scorching heat but a miraculous cloud, with which God
overshadowed the camp, for the space of forty years.
I have read of some, who travelling through these sandy

deserts, have dropped down dead with the heat of the sun : so that this cloud that covered the camp of Israel, was of absolute necessity to them, otherwise they could never have subsisted there, especially for such a long tract of time; it was not their thin tents that would defend them. This cloud typified the righteousness of Christ revealed in the gospel ; this is the only covering under which a guilty sinner can be preserved from the " devouring fires and everlasting burnings" of divine wrath. It is not any thing done by you that will defend you, unless you get under "the shadow of this great rock in the weary land." The cloud that screened Israel from the beams of the sun was itself exposed to the burning heat ; so Christ exposed himself to the wrath of his Father that he might be a lasting and perpetual shadow to protect us from it. As Israel did, for the space of forty years, travel under the shadow of the cloud ; so while we are travellers in this weary land, we must be journeying under the shadow of Christ, and his everlasting righteousness. If any of the children of Israel went out from the shadow of the cloud, they were in danger of being burnt up with excessive heat ; so, if at any time a believer, through a remaining legal spirit, and an evil heart of unbelief, depart from Christ, seeking relief from the law, he is in danger of being scorched with mount Sinai flames, and never shall he find rest till by faith he return to the place where Christ "maketh his flocks to rest at noon."

7thly, The gospel discovers a city of refuge for the poor sinner, who is pursued by the law and justice of God. We read of cities of refuge under the law, that were a common good to the children of Israel, Num. xxxv. 15, 23, 24. If a man had killed his neighbour but by mere accident, without any design, yet he must not stay at his own house, expecting safety there, but he must with all speed flee to the city of refuge, as the ordinance of God for his safety. This was a faint type and shadow of Christ, the blessed refuge and hope set before us in the gospel. The sinner being guilty

of death, and the sword of justice being drawn and fur-
bished, in order to be bathed in his blood, God cries to
him from heaven to flee for his life to Christ, " Turn
ye to your stronghold, ye prisoners of hope.   Turn ye,
turn ye : why will ye die, O house of Israel ?"   And
as the manslayer when within, the gates of the city of
refuge, could freely confer and talk with the avenger
without fear of danger : so a God of vengeance and a
guilty sinner may have sweet fellowship with one another in Christ ; for " by this better hope we draw nigh
unto God." Heb. vii. 19.   If the manslayer, during the
life of the high priest, had come without the walls of
the city of refuge, the avenger of blood might warrantably kill him : so if the best and holiest of saints should
go forth out of Christ, and from under the covering of
his blood and righteousness, imagining themselves to
be in safety under the shelter of their own inherent
holiness, God's revenging justice might warrantably
cut them off ; and therefore it is your wisdom to abide
in Christ, 1 John ii. 28. " Little children, abide in him."
Let us, with Paul, be concerned to be for ever found
in him.

  8thly, The gospel discovers a blessed stair, or ladder,
by which we, who have fallen by our iniquities, may climb
up to heaven, and have access to the holy of holies.   If
it were possible that a lost sinner could fly to heaven
upon the wings of his own works, or get up thither by
the broken ladder of the law of works, what need was
there that God should provide such an expensive one,
as that of the incarnation, obedience, and death of his
own eternal Son ?   When Jacob, Gen. xxviii. was travelling to Padan-aram, in a dream he saw a ladder, the
foot of which stood upon earth, while the top of it
reached the heavens.   By this ladder was signified the
person of Christ, as Emmanuel, God-man, who, as to
his human nature, stood upon earth, and, as to his divine nature, is above the height of the highest heavens,
and likewise the office of Christ as Mediator, who joins
heaven and earth together in a blessed amity and con-

cord.   The foot of this ladder stood in Bethel, " the house of God,' in the church.   Christ revealed and exhibited in the gospel, is the lowest step of the ladder, and comes near to every man, that he may set the foot of faith upon it, in order to his climbing up to glory. This ladder is " the gate of heaven : I am the door ; by me if any man enter in, he shall be saved.   I am the way, and the truth, and the life : there is no way of coming unto the Father but by me."   By faith in his atoning blood we enter into the holy of holies.   At the death of Christ the vail was rent from the top to the bottom, and the way to the holiest laid open, that we, through the human nature of the Son of God, (which was rent in twain by justice,) might enter with boldness.

9thly, The gospel discovers a rich mine or treasure, by which ye may be made up for ever, even " the unsearchable riches of Christ."   If I should tell this company, that there is such a treasure of gold or silver hid in the highway betwixt this and the next town, and that every man might go and take as much of it as he had a mind, O what a strange run would there be among this multitude !   But sirs, though I cannot tell you of earthly riches, yet I can tell you of a field where far better riches are to be found, even gold tried in the fire, better than the gold of Ophir, riches that do not rot in the grave ; and the field is not far off, you have it in the Old and New Testament, which is among your hands, you have it in this gospel that you are hearing ; Christ and all the fulness of the Godhead, Christ and everlasting life in him, is there.   O search the Scriptures, &c.   Prov. ii. 4, 5, " He that seeketh it as silver, and searcheth for it, as for a hid treasure, shall understand the fear of the Lord, and find the knowledge of God." Thus you see what glorious and advantageous discoveries are made to sinners by the gospel, (the law of faith) ; and therefore, for the Lord's sake take the benefit thereof.

Mot. 3. To engage you to take the benefit of the

law of faith, by believing in Christ, pray consider, that
the moral law, or law of commandments, upon the revelation of Christ in the gospel, binds and obliges you
so to do.   I do not say that the law of works reveals
Christ; no, not one word of Christ is to be found in the whole
law abstractly considered : but this I say, that whenever the gospel reveals Christ, the law wills, requires,
and commands the sinner, under the severest penalty,
to close with him.   Will not the law lead to its end,
and require the sinner to betake himself to him who is
" the end of the law for righteousness," upon the revelation of him by the gospel?   Yea surely, "This is his commandment, that you believe on the name of his Son
Jesus Christ ;" and, " he that believeth not is condemned already."   But, say you, that is a command of
the gospel, not of the law.   I answer, It is a command
of the law, yea, the very first commandment of the
moral law, " Thou shalt have no other gods before me ;"
i. e. thou shalt believe and trust in me as thy God and
Redeemer, and in none other, for life and salvation.
So that although the moral law abstractly considered does
not reveal Chrirt, or speak one word of him ; yet considered in the concrete, or as it stands connected with, and subservient unto, the gospel-revelation, it enjoins, it requires, and commands us to take the benefit of Christ
and his righteousness.   And therefore, if ye do not
take the benefit of the law of faith, you break and violate even the law of works, by which ye are seeking
righteousness and salvation.   You desire to work the
work of God ; well, " this is the work of God, that
ye believe on him whom he hath sent."   And do what
ye will in obedience to the law of works, it will all be
rejected, like the " offering of swine's blood," except
ye obey this commandment of the law of works, which
is to take the benefit of the law of faith, or to " believe
on the name of the Son of God."

Mot. 4. Consider that there is a double vengeance
attending them that do not take the benefit of the law
of faith ; and no wonder, since (as you have heard)

they despise a double law, viz. of works and of faith, at once ; every and the least transgression even of the law of works infers wrath and vengeance, death and damnation, against the sinner. See how the apostle argues upon this head, Heb. x. 28, 29, " He that despised Moses' law died without mercy," &c. Now, all this the man is guilty of, who does not by faith fall in with the revelation of the law of faith, he " crucifies the Son of God afresh," re-acts and approves the tragedy acted on mount Calvary, he " tramples the blood of the covenant under foot, and does despite unto the Spirit of grace," who revealed the law of faith ; and therefore a double vengeance must be abiding you, if you do not receive the law of faith. O unbelieving sinner, " consider this, lest he tear you in pieces, when none shall be able to deliver you out of his hand." But I do not incline to end with terrors : and therefore,

Mot. 5. Consider, that moment you take the benefit of the law of faith (the gospel coming forth from Zion), you are acquitted and discharged of all that ever the law of works could demand of you. The law of works craved only a single debt of Adam in innocency, viz. the debt of obedience ; but it hath a double charge upon the sinner, not only of obedience unto its precept, but also it craves that its penalty be endured ; and of this double debt you are not capable to pay the least farthing. Though you were to live to Methuselah's days, you could never obey one precept of the law, as it is the law of works being utterly destitute of that principle from which, and of the end to which, all acts of obedience to the law must be performed ; for the holy law does not look so much to the matter of the action, as to the principle and end thereof ; so that our best actions, instead of being acts of obedience to the law, are but splendid sins before God the great Lawgiver; and therefore the debt of obedience to the precept you can never pay, while you cleave to the law as a covenant. And as you are not capable to pay the debt of

obedience, so neither are you in your own person capable to pay the debt of punishment or satisfaction,
though you were to lie in hell-fire through an endless
eternity. The reason is, because justice requires an
infinite satisfaction for an infinite offence ; and can the
punishment of a finite creature ever amount to an infinite satisfaction ? Thus you are insolvent debtors to
justice, by virtue of the precept and penalty of the law
of works. But now, I say, whenever you take the benefit
of the law of faith, or believe in Christ as he is offered and
gifted in the promise of the gospel, you are that moment
assoilzied and acquitted from both these debts, and all
charges that the law of works hath against you ; you
are no more concerned with it either in point of justification or condemnation. "There is therefore now no
condemnation to them which are in Jesus Christ :
Who can lay any thing to the charge of God's elect ?"
Perhaps indeed the devil may set home the law as a
covenant upon the believer in Christ, craving the debt
both of obedience and punishment for sin ; but the believer, under the lively exercise of faith, has a ready
answer to these charges. As for the debt of obedience,
may the believer say, my Surety paid it by his spotless
obedience, " he magnified the law and made it honourable, and JEHOVAH is well pleased for his righteousness
sake," and through him the righteousness of the law is
fulfilled in me ; so that although now, by strength derived from him, I resolve to honour and obey the law
as a rule of obedience, from a principle of love and
gratitude to my blessed Husband and Redeemer, yet
as a covenant I owe it nothing : will I ever dishonour
my glorious Surety so far, as to offer my own grace and
holiness or obedience in the room of his everlasting
law-biding righteousness ? No, no ; I am " dead to
the law by the body of Christ, being married to another, even to him who is raised from the dead, that I
may bring forth fruit unto God." And then, as for
the debt of punishment and satisfaction, I owe the law
of works nothing either ; why its penalty was endured

by my Kinsman and Redeemer, "he finished it upon the cross, he was wounded for mine iniquities, the just suffered for the unjust," his blood answers for my offences, and his resurrection is my discharge for justification ; " It is Christ that died, yea, rather, that is risen again, who is even at the right hand of God, who also maketh intercession for me ;" and therefore "who is he that condemneth," seeing upon this ground God does justify ? It is remarkable, that the apostle puts a note of distinction on the resurrection of Christ, saying, "Yea rather, that is risen again," because the resurrection of Christ from the dead is an invincible proof of the full payment of the debt which he as our Surety undertook to pay. If he had not made full payment, the prison of the grave had never been opened, and he dismissed, or "taken from prison and from judgment," Is. liii. 8. O sirs, I bring you glad tidings of great joy, our brother Joseph, our elder brother Jesus, his head is lifted up out of prison by a glorious resurrection and exaltation ; and therefore let all the seed of Israel rejoice, for he having lifted up the head as a public person and representative, our heads are lifted up in him, and with him : Eph. ii. 5, 6, " Even when we were dead in sins, he hath quickened us together with Christ (by grace ye are saved,) and hath raised us up together, and made us sit together in heavenly places in Christ Jesus." And therefore, O come and let us all return unto a God of peace, who hath raised up Jesus Christ our Lord from the dead : " he hath torn him, and he will heal us : he hath smitten him, and he will bind us up : after two days he revived us," who were dead in law, " in the third day he raised us up " in him ; and therefore let us say in a way of believing, " We shall live in his sight : Because Christ lives, we shall live also." Sure I am, if we had but the lively uptaking of this mystery of a risen Christ, we would be ready to join the apostle in his doxology, 1 Pet. i. 3, " Blessed be the God and Father of our Lord Jesus Christ, which according to his abundant mercy, hath begotten us

again unto a lively hope, by the resurrection of Jesus
Christ from the dead."

Mot. 6. By taking the benefit of the law of faith
coming out of Zion, the law of commandments coming
out of Sinai will be an easy yoke, and a light burden
to you. The covenant of works was such " a yoke of
bondage, that neither we nor our fathers were able to
bear it ;" this is spoken, Acts xv. 10, of the legal dispensation of the covenant of grace under the Old Testament, by types, ceremonies, and sacrifices, &c.
But if even the legal dispensation of the covenant
of grace was an unsupportable yoke, what must
the covenant of works be ? But now, I say, by
faith's improvement of the gospel-law of grace, that
heavy yoke is now become a light and easy burden. The reason is, whenever a sinner believes in
Christ, by virtue of the gospel, or covenant of grace,
the righteousness of the law, as a covenant, is fulfilled
in him, and he gets strength from Christ to obey the
law as a rule. " Surely in the Lord, shall one say,
have I righteousness and strength :" and faith falling
on this fund of righteousness and strength, cries with the
Psalmist, Psal. lxxi. 16, "I will go in the strength of the
Lord God, making mention of his righteousness, even
of his only." Now the man rejoices to work righteousness, remembering the Lord and his ways, his steps are
enlarged under him, and his feet become as hinds' feet
in the way of the Lord ; so that he " runs and does
not weary, he walks and does not faint :" the man finding himself redeemed and delivered from the hands of
his enemies, he "serves the Lord without fear
(without a servile or slavish fear,) in holiness and
righteousness, all the days of his life :" with Paul he
" delights in the law of the Lord, after the inward
man ;" consenting unto it, that it is " holy, just, and
good ; esteems it the good, and acceptable, and perfect will of God ;" makes it " a lamp unto his feet, and
a light unto his paths ;" and so he " goes on from
strength to strength, until he appear before the Lord

in Zion. Thus I have endeavoured to deal with you as a rational creatures, and to draw with the bands of a man, to take the benefit of the law of faith coming forth from mount Zion ; look to the Lord, that he may, by the power of his Spirit, concur and make it effectual to persuade and enable you thereto

Faith as it fortifies the soul against the fear of evils.

First, I offer a view of it in its scriptural names. Sometimes it is called a trusting in the Lord : "What time I am afraid I will trust in thee : Though he should kill me, yet will I trust in him." Sometimes it is called a looking to the Lord, "They looked to him, and were lightened. Look unto me, and be ye saved, all ye ends of the earth. Let us run our race, looking unto Jesus." Sometimes a staying ourselves on the Lord : Is. xxvi. 3, "Thou wilt keep him in perfect peace, whose mind is stayed on thee," &c. Sometimes a casting of our burden on him : Psal. lv. 22, "Cast thy burden upon the Lord, and he will sustain thee," &c. Sometimes it is called a fleeing to him as a refuge, as the manslayer fled to the city of refuge when pursued for his life : Psal. cxliii. 9, "Deliver me, O Lord, from mine enemies : I flee unto thee for help." Faith is a fleeing in under the wings of Christ's mediation and interecssion, as the birds under the wings of the dam.

Secondly, I would give you some of the ingredients of that faith which fortifies the soul against the fear of evil.

1. Then, it has in it a knowledge and uptaking of a God in Christ, revealing himself as reconciled, and making over himself to us in a well-ordered covenant: for it is only a God in Christ that can be the object of our faith and love ; and "they that thus know his name, will put their trust in him."

2. It has in it a firm and fixed persuasion of the truth and certainty of the whole revelation of His mind

and will in the word, and particularly of his promises as yea and amen in Christ. Hence Abraham's faith (Rom. iv.) is described by a persuasion; he was "also fully persuaded that what he had promised, he was able also to perform." And it is said (Heb. xi. 13,) of the Old Testament worthies, who died in faith, "They saw the promises afar off, and were persuaded of them."

3. It has in it an application of the promises to the soul itself in particular; so that it not only looks on it as true in general, but true to me. The man finds the promise indefinitely indorsed to every man to whom it is intimate, Acts ii. 39, "The promise is unto you, and to your seed, and to all that are afar off," &c. attended with this declaration and promise, that "whoever believes sets to the seal that God is true;" and that "whosoever believeth shall not perish:" therefore the man takes it home to himself in particular, as a security for all the grace that is contained in it, saying, "I believe that through the grace of the Lord Jesus Christ I shall be saved: God hath spoken in his holiness, I will rejoice:" and "In this will I be confident."

4. It has in it a persuasion of the power, love, and faithfulness of the Promiser. A persuasion of his power to do as he has said; as Abraham, Rom. iv. he was "persuaded that what he had promised, he was able also to perform." A persuasion of his love; "How excellent is thy loving-kindness, O God!" &c. A persuasion of his veracity and faithfulness, that "he is not a man, that he should lie, neither the son of man that he should repent."

5. It has in it a renouncing of all other refuges, as entirely insufficient to shelter the soul against these evils wherewith it is surrounded: Hos. xiv. 3, "Ashur shall not save us," &c. Jer. iii. 23, "In vain is salvation hoped for from the hills, or multitude of mountains."

6. An expection of help and safety from a God in Christ, against all these evils that the man is pursued with: Psal. lxii. 5, 6, "My soul, wait thou only upon

God ; for my expectation is from him. He only is my rock and my salvation ; he is my defence ; I shall not be moved." Psal. cxlii. 4, 5, " I looked on my right hand, and beheld, but there was no man that would know me ; refuge failed me ; no man cared for my soul. I cried unto thee, O Lord, I said, Thou art my refuge, and my portion in the land of the living."

7. This faith has a leaving of ourselves and all our cares and concerns upon him, to be disposed of accord- to his will and pleasure. The man is content to take what lot God in his providence shall see fit to carve out for him : 1 Sam. xv. 25, 26, " The king said unto Zadok, Carry back the ark of God into the city : if I shall find favour in the eyes of the Lord, he will bring me again, and shew me both it, and his habita- tion. But if he thus say, I have no delight in thee : behold. here am I, let him do to me as seemeth good unto him."

Thirdly, I will give you a few of the concomitants of this faith which guards the soul against intimidat- ing fears in a time of danger.

1. Then, it is accompanied with a blessed quietness and tranquillity of soul, amidst all the dangers of a pre- sent life. Hence says the Lord to his people, Is. xxx. 15, " In quietness and in confidence shall be your strength." The man having run in under the wings of Shiloh, the perfections of a God in Christ, he cries with David, " I will both lay me down in peace, and sleep : for thou, Lord, makest me to dwell in safety," Psal. iv. last.

2. It is accompanied with a waiting upon the Lord, in a way of duty, for his gracious presence either in grace or providence : " He that believeth, does not make haste. The vision is for an appointed time ; though it tarry, wait for it," &c. Mic. vii. 7, " I will look unto the Lord ; I will wait for the God of my sal- vation," &c. Psal. cxxx. "My soul waiteth for the Lord, like them that wait for the morning," &c.

3. It is aye accompanied with prayer, earnest prayer,

at a throne of grace.   Faith having got the promise in
its arms, it runs straight to a throne of grace with it,
to sue for the promised blessing, Psal. lxii. 8, "Trust
in him at all times; ye people, pour out your heart before him." Prayer is just the breath of faith; and to
pray, and not to believe, is to beat the air; and to believe, and not to pray, is nothing but a presumptuous
confidence, that will never bear a man through in the
evil day.

4. It is accompanied with a holy obedience or regard
unto all God's commandments : Psal. cxix. 166, "I
have hoped for thy salvation, and done thy commandments.
Show me thy faith by thy works," Jam. ii. 18.   Let us
never pretend to believe the promise, if we do not
keep his. commandments : Psal. l. 16, 17, "Unto the
wicked God saith, What hast thou to do to take my
covenant in thy mouth? seeing thou hatest instruction," &c.

5. It is frequently accompanied with a soul-ravishing
joy in the Lord : Is. xii. 2, "Behold, God is my salvation : I will trust and not be afraid :" and then it
follows, "With joy shall ye draw water out of the wells
of salvation." Psal. lxiv. 10, "The righteous shall
be glad in the Lord, and shall trust in him; and all
the upright in heart shall glory." 1 Pet. i. 8,
"Whom having not seen, we love; in whom, though
now we see him not, yet believing we rejoice with joy
unspeakable, and full of glory." Hab. iii. 17, 18,
19, &c.

The boldness and courage of Faith in the Christian warfare.

THIS appears, first, from that serenity wherewith it
possesses the soul amidst these evils and dangers that
threaten it with utter ruin : Psal. xxxii. 6, 7, "Surely
in the floods of great waters, they shall not come nigh
unto him.   Thou art my hiding-place, thou shalt preserve me from trouble : thou shalt compass me about
with songs of deliverance." Psal. xxvii. 3, 5, "Though

a host should encamp against me, my heart shall not
fear: though war should rise against me, in this
will I be confident. For in the time of trouble he
shall hide me in his pavilion : in the secret of his tabernacle shall he hide me, he shall set me up upon a
rock." The man through faith, like Noah, sings in
the very midst of the waves, without fear of being swallowed up.

2. The courage of faith appears in the hard work and
service that it will venture on when the Lord calls.
O, says faith, when it hears God saying, " Whom shall
I send, and who will go for us ? Here am I, send me:
I can do all things through Christ strengthening me :"
he has promised to bear my charges, and therefore " I
will go in his strength," &c.

3. From the enemies and dangers that it will look in
the face without being daunted. The three children,
when the wrath of the king was like the roaring of a
lion against them, threatening them with a burning
fiery furnace seven times heated, their faith enabled
them to a holy and indifferent boldness : " We are not
careful to answer thee, O king, in this matter ; the God
whom we serve will deliver us."

4. The courage of faith appears in the bold and dar-
ing challenges that it can give to all enemies and accusers. O, says Paul, Rom. viii. 32, 33, " Who can lay
any thing to the charge of God's elect ?" The challenge is universal in respect of all accusers, in respect
of all accusations, and in respect of all the accused ;
" Who can lay any thing ?" &c. And then you have
another challenge of faith in the close of that
chapter, " Who shall separate us from the love of God?
shall tribulation, or distress, or famine, or nakedness, or
peril ?" &c.

5. From the weapons which it wields, which no
other hand but the hand of faith can manage. The
" sword of the Spirit, which is the word of God," that
is the weapon which faith deals with. With this weapon, Christ the Captain of salvation teaches us to fight

by his own example, Matth. iv. " Thus and thus it is written." And it is the truth and faithfulness of God in his word, that is the shield and buckler whereby faith encounters its enemies.

6. From the battles it has fought, and the victories it has gained over the stoutest and strongest enemies. " This is the victory whereby we overcome the world, even our faith." It resists the devil, and makes him to flee like a coward : it presents the blood of the Lamb, and bears witness to the truth of the word, and so it defeats the old serpent, Rev. xii. 11, " They overcame him by the blood of the Lamb, and by the word of their testimony." It treads upon death as a vanquished enemy, " O death, where is thy sting ? O grave, where is thy victory ?" Thus faith puts to flight the armies of the aliens.

7. From the heavy burdens it will venture to bear upon its back without fear of sinking under the load. The cross of Christ is a burden that frightens the world to look to him, or own him ; but faith takes it up, and takes it on, and cries, O the world is mistaken ; for " his yoke is easy, and his burden is light ;" and his commandments are not grievous. " Our light afflictions, which are but for a moment, they work for us a far more exceeding and eternal weight of glory."

8. From the hard and difficult passes that faith will open. When the way seems impassable, it sees the breaker going up before it : and therefore, though heaven, earth, and hell, stood in the way, it will clear the road of all difficulties. Pihahiroth and Baalzephon, impassable mountains on every hand, the Red sea before, and an enraged powerful enemy behind ; can there be any door of help ? Yes, says faith, only " stand still and see the salvation of God ;" and thereupon the waters divide, and a lane is made through the depths of the sea for Israel. If we have faith as a grain of mustard seed, we may say to this, and that, and the other mountain, " Be thou removed," and it shall be done.

9. The courage of faith appears from the great exploits that it hath performed ; for which I refer you to Heb. xi. *per totum,* particularly ver. 33—35. And does not this say, that it is a bold and courageous grace?

10. From the trophies of victory and triumph that it wears. It takes up the trophies of Christ's victory over sin, Satan, hell, and death ; and cries, " I will be joyful in thy salvation, and in the name of our God we will set up our banner." O, will faith say, there lies the head of the old serpent bruised by the seed of the woman : there lies the curse of the law, that hand-writing that was against us, torn by the nails of his cross ; "He hath redeemed us from the curse of the law, being made a curse for us :" there stands the world, and its good and bad things, as a mass of mere vanity, overcome by Christ ; and therefore I will tread upon them as " dung and loss, that I may win Christ," who is all in all : there lies death and the grave, slain by the death of Jesus ; and therefore I will play on the den of this lion and cockatrice, for it cannot hurt me. Thus it appears that faith is a courageous grace, that fears no evil.

In what Capacity and upon what Business " God is gone up."

1. God is gone up with a shout, as our forerunner, to open the way to glory, and to make a report of what was done in the days of his humiliation upon this earth : Heb. vi. 20, " Whither the forerunner is for us entered, even Jesus who is made an high priest for ever after the order of Melchizedeck." As a forerunner he rids the way, that we may follow him by faith into the holiest, and may follow him at death without fear of that last enemy, Rev. i. 17. And as a forerunner he goes before to tell tidings that the law is fulfilled, justice satisfied, and every thing agreed upon in the council of peace for the redemption of lost sinners actually accomplished. " I have finished the work which

thou gavest me to do," John xvii. " Shout for joy
then, all ye that are upright in heart."

2. He has gone up as a victorious general, to receive
a triumph after the battle. When man sinned, he fell
under the power of Satan the god of this world, and he
was carrying all Adam's posterity away, as so many
prisoners in chains ; and when that question was put,
" Shall the lawful captive be delivered, shall the prey
be taken from the terrible ?" angels and men were concluding that it was impossible, because not only was
the enemy powerful, but he had the justice and faithfulness of God engaged in the penalty of the broken
covenant of works on his side. Well, but, says the
glorious Redeemer, Emmanuel, the Son of God,
" Even the lawful captive shall be delivered, the prey
shall be taken from the terrible ;" and I will do it in a
consistency with the law, and to the honour of God's
holiness, justice, and sovereignty, and other perfections.
Accordingly he takes and bruises the head of the serpent in the satisfaction of justice ; " he comes from
Edom with dyed garments, like one that treadeth in
the wine fat ;" and after the victory he goes up to heaven with a shout, leading captivity captive ; and now
he has made all his and our enemies his footstool : and
may not this make all the redeemed to shout with the
voice of triumph ?

3. He is gone up as a bridegroom, to prepare a lodging for his bride, and to make suitable provision for
her against the day of the consummation of the marriage : John xiv. 2, 3, " In my Father's house are
many mansions :—I go to prepare a place for you.
And if I go and prepare a place for you, I will
come again and receive you unto myself, that where
I am there ye may be also." Hast thou been determined, poor soul, to give heart and hand to this better
Husband, saying, " I am the Lord's, I will be for him,
and not for another ?" Well, here is good news,
" God is gone up with a shout, the Lord with the
sound of a trumpet ;" and he is gone to make ready

thy lodging and room in heaven, against the time when thou shalt follow him.   Perhaps thou dwells in a crazy house of clay now, that is aye drooping, and thou art afraid every day it fall down about thy ears ; but up, thy heart, the day of thy redemption draweth nigh, ere long the Bridegroom himself will come and fetch thee home to himself, and " thou shalt enter the King's palace with gladness, and rejoicings, and mirth on every side ; and thou shalt be brought unto the King in raiment of needle-work, and presented unto him without spot or wrinkle," &c.

4. God is gone up with a shout in our nature, as " the great high priest of our profession :" Heb. iv. 14, " Having a great high priest, that is passed into the heavens, Jesus the son of God, let us hold fast our profession." And, chap. ix. 12, " Neither by the blood of goats and calves, but by his own blood, he entered in once into the holy place, having obtained eternal redemption for us." Heb. x. 21, 22. It was the ground of Israel's confidence towards God, when their priest went into the holy of holies, with the names of all the tribes of Israel on his breast-plate, and was accepted of God ; so it is the ground of our confidence and boldness, that our Jesus is passed into the heavens, " Having an high priest over the house of God, let us draw near with a true heart," &c.

5. God is gone up in our nature as " an advocate with the Father :" 1 John ii. 1, " If any man sin we have an advocate with the Father, Jesus Christ the righteous." There is a special emphasis in that word, " we have an advocate :" the meaning is, he is constitute and appointed to appear in our cause, and negotiate in our affairs. O ! lift up thy head, believer, do not doubt of the success of his negotiations ; for his interest is so great in the court, that never any man's cause was lost in his hands ; the Father always hears him : Heb. vii. 25, " Wherefore he is able to save unto the uttermost all that come unto God through him, because he ever liveth to make intercession."

6. God is gone up as our exalted King. He is set down upon the throne, in the midst of the throne, and upon the right hand of the Majesty on high, and " he shall rule the house of David for ever, and of his kingdom there shall be no end." Men are combining together for the ruin of his kingdom at this day, violating his laws, changing the order of his house, beating their fellow-servants ; but let all the children of Zion be joyful in their King, for he will make all these crooks of his administration even before the day be ended ; the reins being in his hand, he will ride upon the corruptions of men, and the "wrath of man shall praise him, and the remainder of his wrath he will restrain."

7. He is gone up to mount Zion above, as the great Shepherd, to look after his sheep that are wandering in the wilderness. Although Christ, as to his human nature, be out of our sight, yet he is not so far off as to lose sight of us. Sirs, if your eyes were but strengthened, as Stephen's, to look through these heavens over your heads, you would see Jesus sitting at the right hand of God. And is it to be supposed that he does not see his poor people upon earth, and know how it fares with them ? " He that formed the eye, doth he not see ?" Yea, he stands upon mount Zion above, and he has his eyes fixed upon every little sheep and lamb of his pasture ; he tells all their wanderings ; he is putting all their tears into his bottle ; and there is not a sigh or a groan, that goes from the heart of any of his oppressed ones through the land at this day, but it goes to his very heart ; and in a short time he will call the under shepherds, that are beating and abusing his flock, to an account for their management ; and in the meantime, however harshly they may be dealt with by others, yet " he will feed his flock like a shepherd, he will gather the lambs with his arms, he will carry them in his bosom, and gently lead those that are with young."

8. He is gone up as our glorious Representative, to take possession of the inheritance of eternal life, until

his fellow-heirs, all believers whom he represents, follow him. Hence we are said to "sit together with him in heavenly places," Eph. ii. It is a very strange expression, " we sit in heavenly places with him," even while we are sitting upon the dunghill of this world, because he sits in heaven as our representative. There is a kind of mutual representation between Christ in heaven, and believers here upon earth. Christ in heaven represents us there ; for " he appears in the presence of God for us ;" and we, on the other hand, are his representatives here upon earth. The life of the believer in this world should just, as it were, picture forth the life of a living Christ in glory ; hence the life of Jesus is said to be manifested in us : so that no man who looks on our walk and way in the world, but should presently know that Christ is living in heaven ; " the life also of Jesus is manifested in us." Now, considering all these things, is it any wonder that Christ's going up to heaven in our nature, be attended with a shout of joy and triumph, among all the redeemed in the church militant or triumphant ?

Motives to praise and glorify God.

1. THIS is the end and design of our very being ; it is the chief end of man, that we should be to the glory of him that made us ; and God will levy glory to himself upon us one way or another ; and therefore let us study the end of our being, by being active to advance his glory in our day.

2. This is the end of our effectual calling and new creation in Jesus Christ. " This people have I formed for myself, that they should show forth my praise. Ye are a chosen generation, a royal priesthood," &c. 1 Pet. ii. 9.

3. This is the end of our redemption by Christ : " ye are not your own, but ye are bought with a price : therefore glorify God with your bodies and spirits, which are his."

5. This is the work wherein all the creatures round about you are employed. "All his works praise him ;" and therefore let his saints bless him," saying, as David, Psal. ciii. "Bless the Lord, O my soul : and all that is within me, bless his holy name."

Quest. How shall we praise him in an active way, whom the very wrath of man shall praise ?

Answ. 1. By believing in the name of his Son, and setting to the seal that the record of God is true. Thus Abraham believed God, by not staggering at the promise through unbelief : for he was strong in the faith, and thereby gave glory to God."

2. By being obedient unto his commands, and having a well ordered conversation ; for fruitful professors are the glory of Christ, and the ornament of his garden : " They shall be called the trees of righteousness, the planting of the Lord, in whom he will be glorified." Psal. l. 23, " Whoso offer th praise glorifieth me ; and to him that ordereth his conversation aright, will I show the salvation of God."

3. By a steady adherence to him, his cause and interest, the rights of his crown and kingdom, when the wrath of man would rob us of them ; hence we are called at such a time to "contend earnestly for the faith delivered to the saints," and to stand fast in the liberties wherewith Christ hath made us free ;" and when we willingly walk after the commandments of men, and quit his cause, we cast a reflection upon him, as if neither he, nor his truths or cause, were worthy the contending for.

4. By a cheerful suffering for him, whenever he shall call us to it, saying, with Paul, " I am ready not to be bound only, but also to die at Jerusalem, for the name of Jesus." Sirs, we must lose our lives sometime or other, and we can never lose them more honourably than by dying for the name of Christ. This is the Christian's bed of honour, and if any man lose his life for Christ, he shall find it ; it will come again to him

with advantage, both at death and the resurrection of the body.

What the name of God is, and that his name is in Gen. xxiii. 21.

1. THEN, the name of God is just God himself : Psal. xx. 1, " The name of the God of Jacob defend thee ;" *i. e.* the God of Jacob himself be thy defence : Psal. cxv. 1, " Not unto us, not unto us, but unto thy name be the glory ;" that is, unto thee be the glory. The word name is frequently in Scripture put for the thing or being designed by it, as Acts i. 15, it is said, " The number of the names were an hundred and twenty ;" that is, the number of the persons. So here, says God, My name, that is, my very being and essence, is in him. And that it is so indeed, is evident beyond all contradiction from John xiv. 11, " I am in the Father and the Father in me." John xiv. 7, " If ye had known me, ye should have known my Father also : and from henceforth ye know him, and have seen him." Unto which Philip replies, ver. 8, " Lord, show us the Father, and it sufficeth us." Christ answers, ver. 9 " Have I been so long a time with you, and yet hast thou not known me, Philip ? he that hath seen me hath seen the Father, and how sayest thou, Show us the Father ?" So that you see God himself is in Christ, 2 Cor. v. 19, " God was in Christ reconciling the world to himself." And if you would know who Christ is, and what he is, the apostle will tell you that he is just God himself manifested in the flesh, 1 Tim. iii. last. Oh ! sirs, pause here, stand still and wonder at this strange thing that God has wrought in the earth ; the divine and human nature linked together in a personal union in our glorious Immanuel. So then the meaning of the words, My name is in him, is all one as if he had said, I am in him, my nature, my being and essence is in him ; and therefore, whenever you look on him, behold me in him ; for he is " in the form of God, and

thinks it no robbery to be equal with God." Sirs, be aware of the mistaken and blasphemous notions of Christ that some, particularly the blasphemous Arians and Socinians, would give you, as though he were a different being, and of a distinct and inferior nature from his Father; for he and the Father are one, the same in substance, equal in power and glory. "There are three that bear record in heaven, the Father, the Word, and the Spirit; and these three are one." So then, I say, the name of God in Christ, is just God himself; and this will further appear from what is to follow. Therefore,

2. God's name is his titles that are peculiar to himself; and these we find in Scripture are every where ascribed unto Christ, the Angel of the covenant. To mention in a few; his name is JEHOVAH. This is a name peculiar unto the self-existent, supreme, and independent God, who hath his being of himself, without depending upon another, even "him who is, and was, and is to come. Thy name alone is JEHOVAH, most high over all the earth." This great name we find frequently ascribed unto Christ, with some additional epithets. To encourage your faith, he is sometimes designed JEHOVAH ZABAOTH, "the Lord of hosts," to show his absolute authority, that he has all power in heaven and in earth, and the armies of both under his command. Sometimes he is called JEHOVAH ROPHI, because he heals the broken in heart, and binds up all their wounds. Sometimes JEHOVAH TSIDKENU, "the Lord our righteousness," because he brings in an everlasting righteousness for the justification of condemned sinners. Sometimes JEHOVAH SHAMMAH, "the Lord is there," because he is with his people always, unto the end of the world. Sometimes JEHOVAH JIREH, "the Lord will see or provide," because when the poor and needy seek water, he will hear, help, and supply. Sometimes JEHOVAH NISSI, because he gives a banner unto them that fear him, that it may be displayed because of truth.

3. God's name is his word; for by it he makes his mind known unto the children of men. And this name of his is in Christ: hence he is called, in a way of eminence, "the Word of God," John i. 1, 2, 3, 14. Rev. xix. 13, "His name is called, The Word of God." Hence, when the word of God, or the precious truths of the gospel are held, Christ reckons his name held. Rev. ii. 13, says the Lord to the church of Pergamos, "I know thy works, that thou holdest fast my name, and hast not denied my faith." Thou holdest fast my name, that is, thou retains the gospel in its purity. The whole word of God, and all the truths of it, are in Christ; he is the great Oracle of heaven that reveals them: Rev. v. no man was found able to open the book with the seven seals, till the Lion of the tribe of Judah did it. All the commands of the law of God, are issued unto us in and through him; hence says the Lord here to Israel, "Beware of him, and obey his voice." He is constitute the King and Lawgiver of the church, and whatever laws do not bear the stamp of his authority, and are touched with his royal sceptre, they should have no regard paid to them in the church of God. And as all the laws, so all the promises of God, are in him, and in him they are "yea and amen;" they are just the articles of his latter will and testament. He is the marrow and substance of the whole revelation, and of all the truths thereof, they meet in him as their centre; hence we read of "knowing the truth as it is in Jesus." And whatever doctrines or sermons do not hang upon and quadrate with this foundation, God hath laid in Zion, they are but hay and stubble that are to be burned; the sweetness of every truth lies in the connection that it bears unto him, and in its being a vehicle to convey the grace that is in Christ unto our souls. So that, I say, this name of God is in Christ.

4. God's works are his name: Psal. viii. 1. David there viewing the glory of God, as it is expressed in his works, cries, "How excellent is thy name in all the

earth !" Now, this name of his is in Christ. Is his name
the Creator of all things, that stretched out the heavens, and laid the foundations of the earth ? Why, this
name of his is in Christ : John i. 3, "Without him was not
any thing made that was made." Psal. xxxiii. 6, " By
the word of the Lord," viz. of Christ, as the context
clears, " were the heavens made : and all the host of
them by the breath of his mouth." Is the name of
God, the glorious Preserver and Governor of all things?
Why, this name is in Christ : Heb. i. 3, " He upholdeth all things by the word of his power ;" and Col. i.
16, 17, there we see both the works of creation and
providence ascribed unto him, " By him were all things
created that are in heaven, and that are in earth, visible
and invisible, whether they be thrones, or dominions ;
or principalities or powers : all things were created by
him and for him. And he is before all things, and by
him all things consist."

5. God's name is his worship : Exod. xx. 24, " In
all places where I record my name, there will I come
unto you, and will bless you." This is a glory that he
will not give to another ; it is idolatry to make any
thing or person in heaven or in earth the object of worship and adoration, but God alone, Is. xlii. 8, Matth.
iv. 10. And therefore we find that when divine worship is offered unto angels, they reject it as a thing not
due to them, Rev. xix. 10, and xxii. 9. And when it
was offered unto Paul and Barnabas, they reject it with
horror and indignation, Acts xiv. 14, 15. But though
this crown of glory, this name, the object of worship,
cannot fit any created head, yet it suits the head of our
Immanuel : John v. 23, " This is the will of him that
sent me, that all men should honour the Son, even as
they honour the Father." Accordingly, the church,
Psal. xlv. is commanded to adore him, " He is thy
Lord, and worship thou him :" the powers of the
earth are commanded to " kiss the Son (that is, to
worship him) lest he be angry, and they perish from
the way :" yea all the angels in heaven are commanded

to worship him, Heb. i. 6, " When he bringeth in his first-begotten into the world, he saith, Let all the angels of God worship him ;" and accordingly we find all the ransomed in glory paying the tribute of worship unto him equally with the eternal Father, Rev. v. " Worthy is the Lamb that was slain, to receive power, and riches, and wisdom, and strength, and honour, and glory, and blessing.   Salvation to our God which sitteth upon the throne, and unto the Lamb for ever and ever."

6. His perfections and excellencies are his name ; and these are really and originally in Christ, as they are in the Father. To instance in a few. God's wisdom is his name ; " Wise in heart and mighty in counsel."   And this is in Christ : "Christ the wisdom of God : In him are hid all the treasures of wisdom and knowledge."   His power is his name : " The Lord God almighty."   This name is in Christ : "Christ the power of God ; and, The Almighty," Rev. xix.   Hence called "the arm of the Lord, and the man of God's right hand, whom he has made strong for himself."   By the power of God in him he "spoiled principalities and powers."   The holiness of God is his name, frequently called "the holy One of Israel."   And this attribute shines so brightly in our Immanuel, in the eyes of the angels, that they fall down with covered faces before his throne, crying, " Holy, holy, holy is the Lord God of hosts, the whole earth is full of his glory."   The justice of God is his name : " The Lord is a rock ; and his work is perfect: a God of truth, and without iniquity, just and right is he."   And this name of his is in Christ, in its greatest lustre : it shines more eminently in him than in all the torments of the damned in hell.   Never did the justice of God appear in such a lustre, as when he cried, " Awake, O sword, against the man that is my fellow :" he has fulfilled the command, and borne the penalty of the law as our surety, and so has obtained that name of " Jesus Christ the righteous ; and the Lord is well pleased for his righteousness' sake."   The love of God

is his name; for God is love.   But it is in Christ that
he is so to sinners : John iii. 16. " God so loved the
world that he gave his only begotten Son, that whosoever believeth in him might not perish, but have everlasting life."   The mercy of God is his name, Exod.
xxxiv. 6.   But it is through Christ that his mercy vents
towards us sinners of Adam's family : hence, Cant. v.
" his belly " or bowels are said to be as " bright ivory
overlaid with sapphires."   His grace is his name, Exod.
xxxiv. 6, " The Lord, the Lord God merciful and
gracious."   But it is only through Christ that his grace
reigns towards unworthy sinners, Rom. v. at the close,
" That grace might reign through righteousness unto
eternal life, by Jesus Christ our Lord."   His name is
" the Lord pardoning iniquity, transgression, and sin."
This name is in him, as you see in the context ; and,
when he was here in a state of humiliation, he acted
frequently as one that had power to forgive sin : " Go
in peace, thy sins are forgiven thee."   His name is his
truth ; " a God of truth, and without iniquity."   Our
Immanuel wears this name ; hence called the truth itself, John xiv. 6, " I am the way, and the truth, and
the life ; the Amen, the faithful and true Witness."   I
might tell you of many other names that are peculiar
unto God, every one of which is in Christ.   His name
is the everlasting God, Is. xl. at the close.   " From everlasting to everlasting thou art God."   You may see this
name of God in Christ, Rev. i. " The Alpha and Omega, the beginning and the ending, which is, and which
was, and which is to come."   His name is the unchangeable God, without any " variableness or shadow of turning."   See this name in Christ, Heb. xiii. 8, " Jesus Christ,
the same yesterday, and to-day, and for ever."   His
name is the omniscient God, that searcheth the hearts,
and trieth the reins."   See this name in Christ, John
ii. at the close, " He needs not that any should testify
of man ; for he knows what is man."   Rev. i.   " His
eyes are as a flame of fire ;" he searches the heart, and
tries the reins, and knoweth all the works of the church.

His name is "the God of salvation. Our God is the
God of our salvation." And this name is in Christ:
hence, old Simeon, when he gets him in his arms,
blesses God and cries, "Now lettest thou thy servant
depart in peace; for mine eyes have seen thy salvation."

The excellency of the name of God as in Christ.

1. THEN, his name in Christ is a glorious name.
His essential glory, instead of being darkened, is illumi-
nate by being set in Christ, for Christ is " God manifested in the flesh;" plainly implying, that God out of Christ
is an unknown God to sinners, but God in Christ is a
God whose glory is manifested or displayed to our
view. Never did the glory of God shine so as in Christ·
hence he is called "the brightness of his Father's glory,
and the express image of his person." So that, I say,
the name of God in Christ is a glorious name : Psal.
lxxii. at the close, " Now blessed be his glorious name;
and let the whole earth be filled with his glory." His
name is the glory of the church militant, for "in him
shall all the seed of Israel be justified, and shall glory;"
and the glory of the church triumphant, for " the Lord
God, and the Lamb, are the light" of the place.

2. This name that is in Christ is a transcendant and
incomparable name, "a name above every name that
can be named, whether in this world, or in that which
is to come, Eph. i. at the close. His name is more excellent than the names of all the great powers of the
earth ; for " who among the sons of the mighty can be
compared unto him?" This is one of his royal titles,
" The Prince of the kings of the earth, the King of
kings, and Lord of lords." His name transcends the
name of the angels in heaven ; Heb. i. 4. "being made
so much better than the angels, as he hath by inheritance obtained a more excellent name than they."

3. The name of God in Christ is a most powerful name.
Such power or authority is in this name, that " every

knee must bow, and every tongue must confess, that Jesus Christ is the Lord, to the praise and glory of his eternal Father," Phil. ii. 9—11. Such power or strength there is in this name, that devils were cast out, the dead were raised, the eyes of the blind, and the ears of the deaf, were opened, and all manner of diseases were healed by the power or virtue of this name, in the infancy of Christianity; as we read in the histories of the Acts of the apostles. Such power is there in the name of a God in Christ, that when prayers and petitions are put up to heaven with this name upon them, they prevail and obtain any thing : " Whatsoever ye shall ask the Father in my name, I will give it," John xiv. 13, 14, Mark vii. 26, &c.

4. His name in Christ is a most helpful and saving name, " Our help is in the name of the Lord, who made the heavens and the earth." If a poor soul can but, by the eye of faith, read the name of God in Christ, immediately he reads his own salvation in it : Is. xlv. 22. " Look unto me and be ye saved :" Why, how comes this about?   " For I am God, and there is none else." It takes every burden off the back to see this name in Christ; Psal. xxxiv. 5, " They looked unto him and were lightened ;" and no wonder, for whenever God's name is taken up as in Christ, it is seen to be " the God of peace." God in Christ is a " God reconciling the world to himself, not imputing their trespasses unto them."

5. His name in Christ is a wonderful and a secret name : " His name shall be called Wonderful ;" and why wonderful, but because the " child born unto us, and the son given unto us," is called " The mighty God, The everlasting Father ?" It is so wonderful and mysterious, that it is just a secret which the world cannot conceive aright of, and cannot frame to pronounce it : God in a crucified Christ is " to the Jews a stumbling-block, and to the Greeks foolishness." And even they that have it manifested to them in a saving way, it is such a secret and wonderful name, that they are ready to cry

with Agur, " What is his name, and what is his Son's
name, if thou canst tell ?" Prov. xxx. 4.

6. His name in Christ is a sweet and a savoury name;
it is like " ointment poured forth" to a poor soul that
takes it up in a way of believing. And the reason of
this is, because whenever a sinner is enabled to read
the name of God in Christ, he sees him to be his own
God: as we see in Thomas, whenever he took him up
in a proper light, he immediately cries out, " My Lord,
and my God :" according to that of Christ, " I ascend
unto my Father, and your Father, and to my God and
your God."

7. It is a holy and reverend name : " Holy and reverend is his name :" and they that know it, will sanctify it in their hearts, and make him their fear, and their
dread. So holy is this name, that it sanctifies the soul
that knows it, and kills indwelling corruption ; and no
wonder, for he finishes transgression, and makes an
end of sin.

8. It is a dreadful and terrible name to all the devils,
the wicked and unbelieving world. The devils fall a
trembling at the name of a God in Christ ; his work is
to " bruise the head of the serpent, to spoil principalities
and powers." And this name, however despised and
rejected by the wicked now, yet the day comes, when,
at the sight of him, they will cry to the rocks and
mountains to cover them.

9. It is a durable and everlasting name : " His name
shall endure for ever, his name shall last like the sun,"
As his name is from everlasting, so will it be " to everlasting God."

*Marks by which we may know whether Christ hath manifested his
Father's name to us, as he says, John xxvii. 6.*

1. If so, then his name will have a sweet savour and
relish in your very souls, so that you will eat it, and it
will be to you " the joy and rejoicing of your hearts :
Because of the savour of thy good ointments, thy name

is as ointment poured forth, therefore do the virgins love thee." Oh sirs! how goes the name of Christ away with you? You that are contented with dry sapless harangues of morality, and the airy flourishes of human rhetoric, pleased with sermons wherein scarce any thing of the name of Christ is to be found; you never yet had his name or his Father's name manifested to you, ye are strangers to it; for to them that know his name, that sermon, that ordinance, that communion, where the name of Christ is not recorded with honour, it is unsavoury, to them tasteless like the white of an egg, in which there is no relish.

2. You will frequently think on his name with pleasure, and roll it as a sweet morsel under your tongue. Oh! says David, "My meditations of him are sweet, and I will be glad in the Lord: When I remember thee upon my bed, and meditate on thee in the nightwatches, my soul shall be satisfied as with marrow and with fatness." It is given as a character of the saints, especially in an evil day, that "they feared the Lord, and thought upon his name," Mal. iii. 16, and Is. xxvi. 8, "In the way of thy judgments, O Lord, have we waited for thee; the desire of our soul is to thy name, and to the remembrance of thee."

3. You will be often speaking to the commendation of his name, and of his Father's name that is in him. Oh! will the soul say, that I had a tongue like a trumpet, that could sound through all the corners of the universe, to proclaim the glory and excellency of his name; "Now blessed be his glorious name for ever and ever; and let the whole earth be filled with his glory." And you will be ready sometimes to call in the whole powers of your soul to bless his holy name, and to summon angels that excel in strength, and all his ministers that do his pleasure, and all his works in all places of his dominions, to help you to celebrate the glory of his worthy name.

4. If you be acquainted with the name of God as it is in Christ, you will make much use of that name in all

your addresses to God, and you will lay the only stress
of your acceptance upon that name; when you offer
up either prayers or praises to God, you will set the
name of Christ before you, and the name of God in
him, as that which will bear you through, and render
you accepted; Eph. i. 6, "He hath made us accepted
in the Beloved." Heb. x. 19—22, you see there that
it is in the name of our great New Testament high
priest, that we are to "draw near with full assurance of
faith." See Heb. iv. at the close. Now, try yourselves
by this, whether you be acquainted with the name of
God in Christ; when you go about any duty, whether
it be praying, praising, communicating, or whatever it
be, you will do all in the name of the Lord Jesus, to
the glory of God through him.

5. If you be acquainted with the name of God as it
is in Christ, you will be ready to bow at or in the name
of Jesus, and you will put equal honour upon him as
upon his Father : " For this is the will of him that sent
him, that all men should honour the Son, even as they
honour the Father ; and to him every knee must bow,
and every tongue shall confess that Jesus Christ is
Lord, to the glory of God the Father." Sirs, you
entertain mistaken notions of the Deity, if you think
that it is a slight put upon the Father to give the same
divine worship and homage to him as to the Father, for
God the Father is glad when every knee bows unto
Christ. And therefore try yourselves by this. God
the Father says, " Kiss the Son ; hear him : He is thy
Lord, and worship thou him." Now, do you obey
this command, do you trust in his name, do you glory
in his name, and obey and honour the name of God in
him.

6. You will be very tender of his name, you will sanctify it in your hearts, and make it your fear and your
dread ; you will be tender of his honour, when you
hear his name profaned, Psal. xlii. 10, " It is a sword
within my bones, while they say daily unto me, Where
is thy God ?" tender of his laws, afraid of sin yourselves,

and grieved when you see his laws broken by others; tender of his Spirit, afraid of grieving it ; tender of his members and ministers that have his name upon them; tender of his house, and the concerns thereof will be dearer to you than the concerns of your own houses ; " The zeal of thine house hath eaten me up," says David ; more concerned to see these thieves and robbers spoiling the house of God, than if you saw your own house rifled before your eyes.

Answers to the question, For what should we trust in the name of God as in Christ?

1. TRUST him with the government of the world in this dark and cloudy day in which the nations are shaking and staggering like a drunken man ; for his Father has lodged the reins of the world's government in his hand ; and if his Father has committed that trust to him, you have no reason to fear, though heaven and earth were mingling ; for all power in heaven and earth being in his hand, he will bring all to good account.

2. Trust him with the government of his church, for " he rules in Jacob, he is King in Zion ;" by his Father's appointment, the government is upon his shoulders. His Father has hung upon him all the glory of his house, as upon a " nail fastened in a sure place." The offspring and the issue hang upon him ; the vessels of the smallest quantity, even from the vessels of cups, to the vessels of flagons. The servants of the house may misplace the vessels, disorder the house ; but no fear, he will bring all to rights in his own time and way ; though before he do this he may come in such an awful manner as to make all the house to tremble ; yet trust him, for he is faithful in all his house ; he has founded it upon a rock, and the gates of hell shall not prevail, so as to destroy it.

3. Trust him with all your temporal cares and concerns. Perhaps you are ready to be filled with anxiety

of mind in the present posture of affairs, and to say, Oh! what shall come of me and mine, if the Lord shall, for the sins of these lands, order the bloody sword that is raging abroad, to pass over and visit us? Why, trust him even in that case? "For this man shall be the peace when the Assyrian shall come into our land." This man shall be "a hiding-place from the storm, a covert from the tempest, and as the shadow of a great rock in a weary land." The name of God in him is "a strong tower; the righteous fly unto it, and are safe." Oh! sirs, trust him for your provision and protection, for he has said his people shall "dwell on high, the place of their defence shall be the munitions of rocks; your bread shall be given you, and your water shall be sure." Psal. xxxvii. 3, "Trust in the Lord, and do good, so shalt thou dwell in the land, and verily thou shalt be fed."

4. Trust him for all your spiritual and eternal concerns, for all that he is "made of God unto us; for he received gifts for men," and he will not betray his trust. More particularly,

1. Trust him for wisdom and counsel in every difficult case; trust him for instruction in the knowledge of the great mysteries of the kingdom, and secrets of the covenant. "He opens the book, and looses the seven seals thereof." When you come into dark paths, where ye know not your way, trust him that he will lead the blind in the way they know not, for he is "given for a leader and a commander to the people."

2dly, Trust him for peace and reconciliation, and for acceptance to your person and services through his everlasting righteousness; for "he hath brought in everlasting righteousness, he has magnified the law, and made it honourable, and the Lord is well pleased for his righteousness' sake."

3dly, Trust him for a supply of all your wants, supplies of light, supplies of life, supplies of strength and grace; for "all we out of his fulness do receive grace for grace; and when the poor and needy seek water, and there is none, and when their tongue faileth for thirst, I the Lord will hear them, I the God of Jacob will not reject them."

4thly, Trust him for freedom from the temptations and fiery darts of the devil, for his Father's name is in him, which is the terror of hell, he has "spoiled principalities and powers," and has said, that "the God of peace shall bruise Satan under your feet shortly."

5thly, Trust him for a safe through-bearing at death, for "he was dead, and is alive, and lives for evermore, and hath the keys of hell and death;" and he has said, "I will ransom them from the power of the grave, I will redeem them from death."

Thus, I say, seeing his Father's name is in him, let him be the object of your trust in every case. And to encourage your trust in him, consider,

1. That it is for this end that his Father's name is in him as Mediator, that he may be the object of your trust. Oh sirs! God had been an eternal object of terror instead of trust, if he had not manifested himself to us in Christ as "the Lord God merciful and gracious," &c.

2. That it is the design of the whole scriptures, and of the whole of a gospel dispensation, to bring sinners to trust him, and saints to trust him better, and more firmly: John xx. at the close, "These things are written, that ye might believe in the Son of God, and believing," or trusting, "ye might have life through his name."

3. It is the command of God that you trust in his name. It is not a thing optional, whether you do it or not as you please: no, you are concluded under the command of God to make him the object of your trust, even for your eternal salvation, 1 John iii. 23, "This is his commandment, that ye believe in the name of the only begotten Son of God," &c. And remember that this commandment is fenced with an aw-

ful penalty, that if you do it not, you are "condemned already," &c.

4. Consider, that he himself, as well as his Father, requires your trust and confidence in his name: Is. xlv. 22, "Look unto me," or trust in me, "all ye ends of the earth;" for my Father's name is in me, "I am God, and there is none else." And Oh! when a sinner trusts him, he is well-pleased, for "he taketh pleasure in them that fear him, in those that hope in his mercy," &c.

5. Consider the advantage that shall accrue to you by trusting him that has his Father's name in him.

1. Stability in a shaking and trying day. When many on every hand of you are carried away with the wind of error, temptation, affliction, reproach, and persecution; yet by trusting in this name, ye shall be as "mount Zion, which cannot be removed for ever:" your faith and hope, like an "anchor sure and steadfast entering within the vail," will keep you firm in all storms that may blow, either from heaven, earth, or hell.

2dly, Ye shall have the advantage of much inward peace when the world is reeling about you: "He shall not be afraid of evil tidings: his heart is fixed, trusting in the Lord." Is. xxvi. 3, "Thou wilt keep him in perfect peace, whose mind is stayed on thee: because he trusteth in thee."

3dly, Not only peace, but joy, is the fruit of trusting in this name which is set in Christ: "I have trusted in thy mercy, I have rejoiced in thy salvation. In whom, though now we see him not, yet believing, we rejoice with joy unspeakable and full of glory."

4thly, Ye shall be kept alive in famine, if you trust in this name. Sirs, there is a famine of the word of the Lord in many corners of this land, many of the Lord's remnant put sore to it for want of their ordinary meals: set a wandering for the bread of life through violent intrusions, and otherwise: well, in this case look to, and trust in the name of a God in Christ, and ye shall not want; he will lead you to the place where he causes his flocks to rest at noon. See a sweet promise to this purpose, Jer. xvii. 7. 8. Psal. xxxvii. 2.

What there is in the Name of God in Christ that is matter of Joy.

1. THERE is light in this name; he is "the Sun of righteousness, the light of the world, the day-spring from on high." Whenever he is revealed to a land, by the dispensation of the gospel, light arises there : " The people which sat in darkness, saw great light : and to them which sat in the region and shadow of death, light springs up," Matth. iv. 16. And whenever his name is savingly manifested to a soul, there is a divine light diffused through all the nooks and corners of the heart, insomuch that the man that moment is called out of darkness unto God's marvellous light ;" and Oh ! but this light is sweet, and "it is a pleasant thing for the eyes to behold the sun." Oh, sirs ! cry, cry, that this name may be manifested unto you, so as it is not manifested unto the world, and let your cries to heaven be accompanied with a diligent attendance on his word read and preached, "as unto a light shining in a dark place, until the day dawn, and the day-star arise in your hearts ; and wait for it, as they that wait for the morning, I say, more than they that wait for the morning ; for whenever this name is displayed in its glory to the soul, it will make your heart to rejoice with the light that is in it ; then " the time of the singing of birds is come."

2. There is life in this name, and this affords matter of joy and gloriation in it : John i. 4, " In him was life, and the life was the light of men." Yea, this is one of his famous titles, " the resurrection and the life, the way, the truth, and the life : This is the record of God, that God hath given to us eternal life : and this life is in his Son," 1 John v. 11, and in the last verse of the chapter save one, " We are in him that is true, even in his Son Jesus Christ. This is the true God, and eternal life ; and he that hath the Son hath life."

The name of God as in Christ, it works wonders among the dead; let but this name be manifested to a poor soul dead in trespasses and sins, immediately it is quickened, the spirit of life enters into it. Oh! sirs, how comes it about that there lie such a multitude of dead souls like dry bones in the valley of vision, notwithstanding of a clear dispensation of the gospel? Why, the matter is, though the name of Christ, and of God in him, be externally manifested or revealed, yet they never to this day took up the name of God in the light of the Spirit, or by faith of the Spirit's operation; and therefore it is, that they that are dead remain dead still, and they that are filthy remain filthy still. But though the unbelieving ignorant world should never know this name, yet there is life in it to them that know it; a life of justification to the soul that is condemned by the law; a life of sanctification to them that are perishing under the power and pollution of sin; a life of consolation to them who through pressures of divine terrors are laid in the lowest pit, in darkness, and in the deeps; a life of eternal glory to them that should have died the second death, and been "punished with everlasting destruction from the presence of the Lord, and the glory of his power."

3. There is peace in the name of Christ, and of God in him. God in Christ is a God of peace, committing to us a word of reconciliation; hence one of the famous titles of Christ is "The Prince of peace:" he is our peace with God, for he "makes peace by the blood of his cross: When we were enemies, we were reconciled to God by the death of his Son." He makes peace with conscience, by sprinkling his blood upon it; let but the name of Christ be manifested to a soul distracted with the terrors of a guilty conscience, immediately the storm is hushed into a pleasant calm. And by the manifestation of this name peace is made up between man and man; the name of Christ displayed in its power makes the "wolf to dwell with the lamb, and the leopard to dwell peaceably with the kid." What is

it that creates such divisions among us at this day? the church is rent, the state is rent, judicatories are rent, congregations are rent, families are rent, the hearts of ministers rent from their people, and the hearts of the people rent from their ministers, town councils and corporations rent, and run into different parties : why, the name and glory of a God in Christ, which is the centre of peace and love, is departed ; little of Christ, or of his cause and interest, is before our eyes, "every one minding his own things, but few the things of Christ:" and I despair ever to see either our kirk or state divisions settled, till the name and glory of Christ, and his cause and interest, come to be greater in our eyes than any private views or interests of our own.

4. Redemption and remission of sin is in his name; hence called the Redeemer : Is. lix. 20. "The Redeemer shall come to Zion." We are said to " have redemption in his blood, even the forgiveness of sin." He is the Lord ; "pardoning iniquity, transgression, and sin." Whenever he manifests his name savingly unto a poor soul, crying, " Mine iniquities are gone over my head, as a burden too heavy for me to bear ;" the poor soul can read pardon of its sin, and sing with David, Psal. ciii. " Bless the Lord, O my soul : and all that is within me, bless his holy name. Who pardoneth all thine iniquities : and who redeems thy life from destruction."

5. There is not only remission of sin, but a law-magnifying and justifying righteousness in his name : Jer. xxiii. 6. " In his days Judah shall be saved, and Israel shall dwell in safety : and this is his name whereby he shall be called, The Lord our righteousness." And, oh ! whenever this name of his is read with the application of faith, saying, as Is. xlv. 24, " In the Lord have I righteousness ;" the man begins to rejoice and glory in his name, saying, as Is. xli. 10, " He hath clothed me with the garments of salvation, and covered me with the robe of righteousness." The poor con-

demned sinner, that was trembling before the bar of his own conscience, begins to lift up his head and say, Who can lay any thing to my charge? It is God that justifieth : who is he that condemneth?" Christ is the end of the law, and through him the righteousness of the law is fulfilled ; for he was "made sin for us, who knew no sin, that we might be made the righteousness of God in him."

6. Health or healing is in his name : Exod. xv. 26, "I am the Lord that healeth thee, JEHOVAH ROPHI." Mal. iv. 2, "Unto you that fear my name, shall the Sun of righteousness arise with healing in his wings." By this name the eyes of the blind were opened, the ears of the deaf unstopped, the lame man made to leap like a hart, and the tongue of the dumb to sing. Let this name be but whispered into the heart by the Spirit, or let it be but called upon by faith in prayer, it will make the bones which were broken to rejoice. All foul maladies and diseases evanish before it. "He sent forth his word," which is in his name, "and healed them."

7. There is shelter in a stormy day in his name : "The name of the Lord is a strong tower." When storms and tempests are blowing, the believer, when he gets this name over his head, he can sing and say, "In the floods of great waters they shall not come near unto me, for the Lord is my refuge, and my strength, and a very present help in time of trouble ; therefore I will not be afraid," Psal. xlvi. This name is the "strength of the poor, and the strength of the needy in his distress, a refuge from the storm, a shadow from the heat, when the blast of the terrible ones is as a storm against the wall. I will lay me down in peace, and sleep, for thou, Lord, makest me to dwell in safety. I will not be afraid of ten thousands of the people, who set themselves against me round about."

8. There is honour and preferment in his name ; Psal. xci. 14, "I will set him on high, because he hath known my name." Whenever this name is manifested

to a soul, it gets a name and a place within God's house, better than of sons and daughters among men ; and hence it is, that the " righteous is more excellent than his neighbour : Ever since thou wast precious in my sight thou hast been honourable," Is. xliii. 4. In a word, not to multiply particulars here, salvation is in the name of our God in Christ : " Our God is the God of salvation ; and unto God the Lord do belong the issues from death." And whenever a poor soul by faith reads the name of God in Christ, it is capable to read its own salvation, and to sing, as Is. xii. 2, 3, " Behold God is my salvation : I will trust and not be afraid : for the Lord JEHOVAH is my strength and my song, he also is become my salvation. And there- fore with joy will I draw water out of the wells of sal- vation." Thus you see what matter of joy and gloria- tion there is in the name of God as it is displayed in Christ ; and therefore let us rejoice in this name, and glory in it all the day long.

Cases of Conscience, concerning Glorying in the name of God in Christ, resolved.

1. You bid me rejoice and glory in the name of a God in Christ; but alas! how can this be, for the name of God is just my terror : " When I remember God I am troubled?" I answer, I own indeed his law name, or his absolute name, is enough to terrify the strongest believer, or the saint of the highest magnitude, while any thing either of the guilt or filth of sin hangs about him : but it is absolutely impossible that his name in Christ can be a terror, but rather a comfort unto any sinner on this side of hell. Can the name " merciful or gracious," can the name, "Lord pardoning iniquity, the God of salvation," be a terror ? No, it cannot be. So that when thou sayest thou art troubled at the re- membrance of the name of God, it is plain thou art reading his absolute name, or his name not in Christ, but out of Christ : and therefore look again toward his

holy temple, and view him upon the mercy-seat between the cherubims, and thou shalt see his name to be, "The consolation of Israel."

2. How can I glory in his name, for alas! I fear I do not know this name of a God in Christ, "I am more brutish than any man, I have not the understanding of a man; I have not learned this wisdom, nor have I the knowledge of the holy?" *Answ.* If this be really the exercise of thy soul, it is an evidence thou hast been at the school of Christ, for self-denial is the first lesson, that he teaches all his scholars. Whenever the name of Christ is revealed unto a soul, its own name, its own knowledge, attainments, righteousness, strength, and all evanish, and go as clean out of the man's sight, as the twinkling stars in the firmament when the sun arises; self hides its head when Christ is formed. And therefore if this sense of ignorance of the name of Christ be accompanied with an earnest desire and longing of soul to be better acquainted with this name, it is a sign thou knowest it, and shalt "follow on to know it," and that his goings forth to thy soul shall be prepared as the morning. And therefore, I say, rejoice and glory in this name.

3. "I am plagued all the day long, and chastened every morning, deep calleth unto deep" with me, and therefore I cannot rejoice in this name, for through continued affliction "my harp is turned to mourning, and my organ unto the voice of them that weep." *Answ.* If by this affliction the Lord is "purging away thy dross," and making thee a partaker of his holiness, thou hast reason to rejoice and glory in his name, for these light afflictions will soon be at an end, and they will "work for thee a far more exceeding and eternal weight of glory." Do but view the name of God in Christ, and it will lighten thy heart under all the burdens of affliction that lie upon thy back, "They looked unto him and were lightened." Job, when the waters of affliction were rolling in upon him on every hand, he views this name, and comforts himself with it, being

enabled thereby to see a scene of glory opening upon
the other side of death, chap. xix. 25, " I know that my
Redeemer liveth, and that he shall stand at the latter
day upon the earth," &c.

4. You tell me to rejoice in this name, when reproach
has broken my heart, my name is torn, my reputation
sunk and covered with calumny. *Answ.* The name of
Christ was covered with calumny when he was in this
world, called "a blasphemer, a wine-bibber, a friend of
publicans and sinners ;" yea, he was branded with being
in league with " Beelzebub the prince of devils ;" and
can any thing worse be said of thy name? And therefore
bear it patiently, and rejoice : for as the name of Christ
outshined all the clouds of calumny, so shall thine, if
thou be a member of Christ, and reproached for well-
doing : " If ye be reproached for the name of Christ,
happy are ye ; for the Spirit of glory, and of God resteth upon you.'

5. I carry such a burden of sin upon me, I have so
many wants, so many plagues, so many maladies, hanging about me, that I cannot get up my heart. *Answ.*
Do but read the name of God as it is in Christ, and thou
shalt find redress of all grievances, ease under all burdens,
and healing of all plagues. Is it not matter of joy and
triumph under a sense of guilt, that his name is " the
Lord pardoning iniquity ?" Is it not relief under burdens, that he bids you " cast your burdens on him, and
he will sustain you ?" Is it not matter of joy under
all wants, that "all fulness is in him" for thy supply ;
and under all the plagues of thy heart, that his name
is " the Lord that healeth thee ; that there is balm in
Gilead, and a physician there ?" It is the way of faith
to reckon upon, and to rejoice in what the soul hath in
Christ ; under deadness, to rejoice that its " life is hid
with Christ in God ;" under self-emptiness and poverty to rejoice in his unsearchable riches ;" under a
sense of guilt, to rejoice in his resurrection from the
dead as its discharge ; under inability to pray, to re-

joice in his intercession. And therefore, I say, learn still to glory in the name of a God in Christ.

6. I cannot get the Lord served as I would be at when I set about duty, my wicked heart turns aside like a deceitful bow, I drive heavily like the chariots of Pharaoh. *Answ.* Do you know what is the cause of your driving so heavily ? You turn away your eyes from the name of God as it is set in Christ, and then indeed it is no wonder though your heart turn away from the living God. Do but view this name, and you shall be set upon the high places of Jacob, and thy soul shall, ere thou art aware, be made like chariots of Amminadib.

7. I do not know if ever I believed in this name, how then shall I glory and rejoice in it ? *Answ.* If thou really never yet believed in this name, believe in it now, without any longer delay, for it is manifested to be believed in. God has set forth his name in Christ as an object of faith and trust unto all the world : and rejoice, Oh sinner ! that thou hast this name to fly to as a refuge ; for it is glad tidings to men, and the sons of men, that God's name and our name are mingled together in our great Immanuel, and " they that know this name, will put their trust in it." And whereas you say you do not know if ever you believed in this name, I only ask you, Is not this name precious to thy soul ? Well, that is given as an evidence and mark of faith ; for " to you that believe, he is precious." Dost not thou love him, and all that bear his image ? This is another mark of faith ; for "faith worketh by love ;" and by this " we know that we are passed from death unto life, because we love the brethren."

8. This is a lowering day, storms are brewing, and the clouds are raking ; God seems to be upon his march with the weapons of wrath in his hand ; he is making the earth to tremble and shake with the noise of wars abroad, and divisions at home ; and this is a time of rejoicing ? *Answ.* It is all true you say ; but is there no comfort in that case, in the name of the Lord ? Yes,

there is. Let seas roar, let the nations shake, let heaven and earth blend into confusion, the name of a God in Christ is the "river that makes glad the city of God;" and therefore, I say, still "let the children of Zion be joyful in their King. The Lord sitteth upon the floods; the Lord sitteth King for ever; and therefore let the earth rejoice, and let the multitude of the isles be glad."

9. Jacob is brought low, the ark of God is in a great measure taken, the hedges are broken down, violence is done to God's heritage, wolves in sheep's clothing have got in to the spoiling of the tender vines; the authority of Christ, and the sacred liberties of his crown, trode under foot, which makes me to "weep, and hang my harp upon the willows;" how then shall I rejoice and glory in this name? *Answ.* Indeed these things have a very melancholy aspect, and we have reason to join trembling with our mirth, because of these sins that have provoked the Lord to smite and cover the daughter of Zion with a cloud. But yet there still remains ground of triumph and gloriation in the name of a God in Christ, because by this name all Zion's enemies shall be confounded; the terror of it will at length make Zion's proud enemies and oppressors, whether they be men in civil or ecclesiastical authority, to enter into the rock, and to-hide themselves in the dust, for fear of the Lord, and for the glory of his majesty. This name cuts off the spirits of princes, and is terrible to the kings of the earth, that invade or trample upon his authority. It is the eternal joy and comfort of all the true children of Zion, however oppressed and borne down, Zion shall yet be built up by the mighty God, when he appears in his glory, and in his majesty; and therefore there is still ground of glorying in his name.

By the downcasting of Zion, he is but making way for her upbuilding; and though she may be "afflicted, tossed with tempests, and not comforted," yet he will "lay her stones with fair colours, and her foundations with sapphires;" and though all should go to all, the

Lord will take care of his remnant of mourners. " I will gather them unto me that are sorrowful for the solemn assemblies, to whom the reproach of it is a burden."

Cries of the Angel of the Covenant unto the children of men.

1. ONE general cry he gives unto all men is, that " All have sinned, and come short of the glory of God ; " or that which he uttered to the old world, that " All flesh have corrupted their ways, they are altogether become filthy ; there is none that doeth good, no not one." He is crying to all mankind since the fall, as in Jer. ii. 12, 13, " Be astonished, O ye heavens, at this, and be horribly afraid, be ye very desolate, saith the Lord. For my people have committed two great evils ; they have forsaken me," &c. O sirs ! hear this cry of the Angel of the covenant, and consider it, that all mankind since the fall of Adam, and therefore you in particular, are far from God ; that though God "made you upright," yet you have "found out many inventions ;" that though God " planted you a noble vine, wholly a right seed," yet ye are become " the degenerate plant of a strange vine : The whole head is sick, and the whole heart faint ; from the sole of the foot even unto the crown of the head, there is nothing but wounds, and bruises, and putrefying sores." Oh sinners ! hear what the Angel is saying, and lay to heart the corruption of your nature, till ye be made to acknowledge with David, " I was conceived in sin, and brought forth in iniquity. Behold, I am vile, what shall I answer thee ?" It is for want of a right uptaking of natural corruption and depravation, that the gospel has so little success, and that Christ is so little valued and prized ; for " the whole need not a physician, but they that are sick."

2. The angel of the covenant, Jesus Christ, is crying unto every Christless sinner, that death and the curse of God is pursuing him on the account of sin. You know

the curse or penalty of the law is, " In the day that thou eatest thereof thou shalt surely die; The soul that sinneth shall die:" and accordingly "by one man sin entered into the world, and death by sin ; and so death passed upon all men, in that all have sinned :" and therefore, "Cursed is every one that continueth not in all things which are written in the book of the law to do them." Oh sirs ! for the Lord's sake think upon it, for he that speaks from heaven is telling you, that the vengeance of an infinite God is pursuing you on the account of sin ; you are "condemned already, and the wrath of God abideth on you ; and therefore you are cursed in your basket and store, in the city and field, in your outgoings and incomings ; cursed in your soul and body ; cursed in time and through eternity. And therefore I warn you, that "in the hand of the Lord there is a cup, and the wine is red, it is full of mixture, and all the wicked of the earth shall wring out the dregs thereof, and drink them."

3. Another cry I think the Angel of the covenant is giving, is that, Rom. viii. 22, " The whole creation groaneth, and travaileth in pain together until now." Whenever man sinned, the curse of God not only lighted upon him, but spread itself over the creation. The inferior creatures felt the dint of the curse of God, and were subjected unto bondage by the sin of man ; yea, the very earth under our feet lies groaning under the weight of it, " Cursed is the ground for thy sake ;" insomuch, that if it were not for the patience and long-suffering of the great Creator, the earth would very soon do with men and women as it did with Korah, Dathan, and Abiram, swallow them up.

4. The Angel of God is crying to all men, that death and the grave will shortly devour and swallow them up : " Dust thou art and unto dust shalt thou return." See to this purpose, Is. xl. 6—8, " The voice said, Cry. And he said, What shall I cry ? All flesh is grass," &c. And therefore sirs, in the name of the Angel of God, I warn you to make ready for death ;

for that grim messenger of the Lord of hosts is every day making his approaches toward you, and will hew down these carcases of yours, that you are now pampering and feeding ; they will be a pleasant feast for the worms.

5. Another cry is, that as " it is appointed for all men once to die, so after death the judgment." Sirs, think upon it now ; no sooner hath death dislodged you from these tabernacles of clay, and the eyes of your bodies shut, but that very moment you will find your souls sisted before the awful tribunal of an infinite God, in order to have your eternal state determined. Oh sirs ! " prepare to meet your God," for a meeting with him you must have ere it be long. There is another sort of a scene to open upon the back of death, than you now see with your bodily eyes, or yet with the eyes of depraved reason, though assisted with revelation. And if you die out of Christ, your hearts will be stricken with a horrible surprise at the first sight of the awful and infinite majesty of God, as a vindictive Judge and implacable enemy. Oh ! " who knows the power of his wrath ? according to his fear, so is his wrath." Desolation and destruction will overtake the sinner as a whirlwind.

6. Another cry the uncreated angel of the covenant is uttering by the voice of his dispensations, is that which you have, Matth. iii. 10, " And now also the axe is laid unto the root of the trees ; therefore every tree which bringeth not forth good fruit, shall be hewn down and cast into the fire." Sirs, the awful dispensations of God, and his providential appearances, seem to have this language, that he is taking the axe of his indignation in his hand, to hew down the generation of his wrath ; especially those who have had a long standing under the means of grace, and yet have continued barren. "Cut it down, why cumbereth it the ground ?" Oh sirs ! God will soon or syne avenge him of his enemies, who through unbelief and contempt of the glorious gospel,

have affronted him and his Anointed; he will send forth his armies and destroy these rebels. "Bring forth those mine enemies which would not that I should reign over them, and slay them before me." He may bear long, but he will not bear always: no, no, "my Spirit shall not always strive with men upon earth." Oh! if a fire be once kindled in his anger, it will consume the earth with its increase, it will set on fire the foundations of the mountains, and burn to the lowest hell. And Oh! "who can dwell with devouring fire? who can dwell with everlasting burnings?"

7. Another cry he is uttering, is that, Prov. i. 20—23, "Wisdom crieth without, she uttereth her voice in the streets. How long, ye simple ones, will ye love simplicity?" &c. He is crying to all men every where to repent, as Is. lv. 7, "Let the wicked forsake his way, and the unrighteous man his thoughts," &c. Ezek. xxxiii. 7, "Turn ye, turn ye; why will ye die, O house of Israel? for as I live, saith the Lord God, I have no pleasure in the death of sinners," &c. Oh sirs, the Angel that has his Father's name is crying to you to flee from the wrath that is to come, for "there is yet hope in Israel concerning you;" if you will flee to him, he will hide and deliver you from the wrath of God, the rage of men and devils; and therefore "turn ye to your strong-holds, ye prisoners of hope."

Special cries of the Angel of the Covenant from mount Zion.

1. HE is crying to the condemned sinner to come to him, and he shall have a free pardon of all his sins: Is. i. 18, "Come, and let us reason together, saith the Lord: though your sins be as scarlet and crimson, I will make them white as snow and as wool." Is. xliii. 25, "I, even I am he that blotteth out thy transgressions for mine own name's sake."

2. He is crying to the rebels to submit, and they shall have peace: Is. xxvii. 4, 5, "Fury is not in me: who would set the briers and thorns against me in bat-

tle? I would go through them, I would burn them together. But let him take hold of my strength that he may make peace with me, and he shall make peace with me. We are ambassadors for Christ, as though God did beseech you by us : we pray you in Christ's stead, be ye reconciled to God."

3. He is crying to captives to accept of liberty, and he will make them free indeed : "The lawful captive shall be delivered," &c. Liberty from sin, from Satan, and the world, &c.

4. He is crying to the wounded and diseased soul to come unto him and be healed, for his name is JEHO-VAH ROPHI. There is healing in his wings for every disease, &c.

5. He is crying to the weary and burdened soul to come unto him for rest, Matth. xi. at the close. Psal. lv. 22, "Cast thy burden upon the Lord, and he will sustain thee," &c.

6. He is crying to the ignorant to come to him for instruction, for he hath pity on the ignorant, that are groaning under a sense of ignorance : " Come hither, ye children, and I will teach you the fear of the Lord. He is made of God unto us wisdom," &c.

7. He is crying to naked souls that have not a rag to cover them, to come to him for clothing for the garments of salvation and the robes of righteousness. " Hearken unto me, ye that are stout-hearted, and far from righteousness. Behold I bring near my righteousness : it shall not be far off, and my salvation shall not tarry," &c.

8. He is crying to the hungry and starving soul to "come, eat of his bread :" Is. xxv. 6, " A feast of fat things, a feast of wines on the lees, of fat things full of marrow, of wines on the lees well-refined." Is. lv. 1. Prov. viii. at the beginning. Prov. ix. at the beginning.

9. He is crying to the sinner that is bewildered, and cannot find the way to life and happiness, that he is given for a " leader and commander," and that he " leads the blind in a way they know not," &c.

10. He is crying to the base-born sinner, to come unto him, and he will give them the adoption of children, a place in God's family that shall never be cut off: John i. 12, " But as many as received him, to them gave he power to become the sons of God." Gal. iv. 4, 5, He was "made of a woman, made under the law, to redeem them that were under the law, that we might receive the adoption of sons."

11. He is crying to the sinner that is in a compact and confederacy with hell, to break his covenant with hell, and his agreement with death, and take hold of his covenant of grace and peace : Is. lv. 3, " Incline your ear and come unto me ; hear, and your soul shall live, and I will make an everlasting covenant with you, even the sure mercies of David.'

12. He is crying to the sinner that is upon the very borders of hell and eternity, to believe in him, to look unto him, and be saved.

Now, sirs, for the Lord's sake hear the voice of the Angel ; for ye see, if ye do not hear, he will not pardon your transgressions, for his Father's name is in him. Oh ! " how shall ye escape, if ye turn away from him that speaketh from heaven ?"

What it is to obey the voice of the Angel of the Covenant.

Answ. 1. It implies a knowledge and uptaking of Christ and of his voice : " My sheep (says Christ) they know my voice." There is something of a divine light, life, and power, in the voice of Christ, that the soul is made to feel to its experience, whereby it can distinguish between his voice, and the voice of a stranger : " It is the voice of my beloved," says the spouse ; " I know it to be his, and not another's."

2. It implies a diligent attention of mind unto what the Lord speaks, either by his word or his providence. " Speak, Lord (will the soul say,) for thy servant heareth." This is what the Lord requires of us, Is. lv. 2, 3, " Hearken diligently unto me.—Incline your ear :

—hear, and your souls shall live." While Lydia hearkened diligently unto the voice of the Angel in the ministry of Paul, the Lord opened her heart. Sirs, do you know what it is to have your minds and hearts so arrested in hearing of the word, that your ear and mind is as it were tied to the minister's mouth in hearing? Alas! there are many hearers whose minds are in the ends of the earth when hearing of the word of the kingdom.

3. It implies a belief and persuasion of what the Angel speaks to be the voice of God. It is said of the Thessalonians, that they "received the word, not as the word of men, but as it is indeed the word of God." The man he looks above and beyond the earthen vessel through which the word is conveyed, and hears God himself, whose voice is full of majesty and power. Sirs, as long as the devil can persuade you, that your ministers are only speaking their own thoughts and conceptions, he is easy how much or how frequently you hear the word, for he knows well, that until you hear the word preached as the voice of Christ, your hearing will do no service unto your souls, or no hurt unto his kingdom. You know that while Samuel did mistake the voice of the Lord, as if it had been the voice of Eli, he ran the wrong way; so while men come and hear the word preached, and fancy that it is only the voice or word of a man like themselves, they will run the wrong way; it will never have any impression upon heart or life, to turn them from sin unto God: but whenever the voice of Christ is taken up in the word of providence, they run directly to the Lord himself, saying, as Israel did, Jer. iii. "Behold we come unto thee, for thou art the Lord our God. In vain is salvation expected from the hills, and from the multitude of mountains: in the Lord God alone is the salvation of his people."

4. It implies application of the word to a man himself in particular. O! says the man, it is to me that this word of threatening, this word of promise or command, is directed, and the Lord is pointing out me

in particular by it, as though he were calling me by name and sirname. There are some hearers that have a dexterity of applying the word unto others; Oh, will they say, the minister met with such a one, he fell foul upon such a man or party : but though their own idol be touched they take no notice of that ; or when a Saviour is revealed and offered, they imagine that this is only to the elect or to believers. But, sirs, they that obey the voice of Christ, they take him up as directing his word unto them ; and therefore they bring it home to their own souls in particular, as though they heard Christ saying, as Nathan did unto David, " Thou art the man."

5. It implies an esteem and approbation of what the Angel speaks : " Good is the will of the Lord." The man's will bends and stoops unto the will of the Lord, when intimate to him, either by his word or by his providence, and he loves and approves it as " worthy of all acceptation." " O how love I thy law! it is my meditation all the day. I esteem all thy precepts concerning all things to be right." He esteems the word of promise, and rolls it like a sweet morsel under his tongue, saying, " It is sweeter to me than honey from the honeycomb :" he esteems the word of command, and cries, " I delight in the law of the Lord after the inward man ;" he would have it written in his heart, and hid in his inner parts.

6. It implies a regulating of heart and life according to the voice of Christ in his word. The man is not simply a hearer, but a doer of the word. " He that doth the will of God, shall know of the doctrine, whether it be of God, or whether I speak of myself." There are many hearers of the gospel, who gather up more of the manna of the word than they make good use of ; they have it in their heads and memories, but it never either enters into their heart or practice ; and so it turns to the worms and vermin of pride and hypocrisy, and so lands in their destruction, not in their edification. But they

that hear the voice of Christ in his word by faith, they study to reduce all into practice ; hence it is, that the light of the word within them shines out in their walk, so as others " seeing their good works are made to glorify their Father which is in heaven."

The awful consequences of not obeying Christ's voice to men.

(1.) SIN will get the full power and ascendant over you ; you will be given up to the empire and reign of your own lusts, than which there cannot be a greater judgment on this side of hell : Psal. lxxxi. 11. " My people would not hearken to my voice : and Israel would none of me.   Wherefore I gave them up unto their own hearts' lusts : and they walked after their own counsels."   And what will the man stick at that is given up to the counsels of a deceitful and desperately wicked heart, where the seed of all sin is lodged.

(2.) When the voice of the angel is not regarded, he claps up sinners under a judicial hardness of heart, so as all means for recovery shall prove utterly ineffectual. God strikes Pharaoh and the Egyptians with hardness of heart, because they would not hearken unto the command of the Angel, requiring them to let Israel go. God says concerning the sinner that is disobedient to the voice of Christ, " He is joined to his idols, let him alone."   My Spirit shall let him alone, and cease to strive with him.   My ministers, let him alone, or else go and preach him dead and lifeless, and senseless, Is. vi.   Conscience, let him alone, and cease to be a re-reprover.   Rod and affliction let him alone, allow him peace and prosperity in his way until he and I meet together upon the back of death.   O how dismal is the case of the sinner when it comes to this with it ! " I would have purged them, and they would not be purged, therefore they shall not be purged from their filthiness any more, till I have caused my fury to rest upon them.

(3.) The curse of God mingles itself with every

thing in a man's lot, that will not obey the voice of the Angel that has the name of God in him. If the man have fulness and prosperity, the curse of God follows him there, so that his bread is baken, and his drink mingled with a curse, Deut. xxviii. 15, Mal. ii. 2, &c. If trouble and affliction be upon the man, the curse of God is in that cup also ; his temporal troubles are but the beginnings of sorrows, the prelibation and foretastes of the cup of trembling that he shall drink through eternity ; they are but like some drops of rain to the full shower upon the wicked ; God is determined to rain snares, fire and brimstone, this shall be the portion of their cup.

(4.) Public desolation, and down-hewing of churches and nations, frequently follows upon disobedience to the voice of the Angel. " Be instructed, O Jerusalem, lest I make thee desolate, a land not inhabited." Jerusalem and the temple, where are they now ? what is become of the once famous church and nation of the Jews, God's peculiar people ? Their land has spued them out, and the songs of the temple are turned into melancholy howlings. Why, what is the meaning of the heat of God's long continued anger against his ancient people for the space of seventeen hundred years ? Why, the Angel here spoken of, " Came unto his own, and his own received him not ; he would have gathered them, as a hen doth her chickens under her wings, and they would not ;" and therefore, "behold their house and land is left unto them desolate."

In a word, to shut up this consideration according to the instructions that we have received from our great Lord, I proclaim from this high place of the city of God, " Woe unto the wicked, it shall be ill with him : for the reward of his hands shall be given him," Is. iii. 11. Perhaps you may think our words are but wind ; but remember that they will be a heavy wind to you ere all be done. It is not our word, but the word of God proclaimed by us, " Woe unto the wicked, it shall be ill with him."

(1.) It will be ill with you in the day of personal or public distress, when an angry and revenging God will meet you in the face, whatever hand you turn to: " Whither will ye fly from his presence ?"

(2.) It will be ill with you in the day of death, when that grim messenger of the Lord of hosts is coming with that heavy message, " This day thy soul shall be taken from thee." Oh! what a comfortless creature is a Christless sinner in the day of death, when his riches, honours, profits, pleasures, lands, houses, relations, and all things that he adored, are bidding him a final farewell!

(3.) It shall go ill with you after death. When you begin to look into that awful and eternal world, what horror and confusion will seize you, when, instead of angels to carry you unto Abraham's bosom, you shall meet legions of devils to hurry you down to the lake that burns with fire and brimstone!

(4.) It shall be ill with the wicked who refuse to hear the voice of Christ now, at the resurrection and the last judgment. You that refuse him a hearing now, you will hear him at that day, saying, " Bring forth these mine enemies who would not that I should reign over them, and slay them before me ;" he will then " tear in pieces, when there is none to deliver."

(5.) It shall be ill with the wicked after the last judgment, through all eternity, when " the wicked shall be turned into hell, with all the nations that forget God :" there the smoke of your burning shall go up for ever and ever, and you shall there through eternity be crying with Dives, for a drop of water to cool the tip of your tongue, and it shall not be allowed. Oh! consider these things, ye that forget God, ye that stop the ear, and pull away the shoulder from the voice and cries of the Angel ; let the terrors of God persuade you to consider what you are doing, before it be too late.

The power that accompanies Christ's voice to elect souls.

1. It has a killing power coming along with it, especially his voice from mount Sinai: " When the commandment came (says Paul,) sin revived, and I died." The man was so full of himself, and of his own righteousness, that he thought himself alive without the law ; touching the law he imagined himself to be blameless ; like Laodicea he fancied himself " rich and increased with goods and so stood in need of nothing ;" but whenever he heard the voice of Christ, he is struck to the ground, and all his fine airy imaginations about his own righteousness by the law falls to the ground ; he sees himself to be a dead man, and " what things were gain to him before, these he counts loss and dung now." Did you ever find this self-killing power of the voice of Christ from mount Sinai ? for if proud self was never battered down by the hammer of the law, which breaks the rock in pieces, you never yet heard the voice of Christ. You know before ever Israel cried for a mediator between God and them, they got such a hearing of the voice of the Angel, as made the whole camp of six hundred thousand to fall a-quaking: " The law is our schoolmaster to lead us unto Christ, that we may be justified by faith ;" not that the law in itself reveals Christ, but prepares the soul for the revelation of him in the gospel. I do not limit adorable sovereignty in his way of working ; but so much of law work is necessary, as to shake the soul out of all its lying refuges, and created confidences, that it may betake itself unto Christ, and to him alone, for righteousness and life.

2. The voice of Christ, where it has been heard in a saving manner, it has had a quickening power : John v. 25, "The hour is coming, and now is, when the dead shall hear the voice of the Son of God : and they that hear shall live. Are not my words spirit and life?" says the Angel with the name of God in him, John vi.

"The spirit of life which is in Christ Jesus," comes in and with the word of the gospel, which reveals Christ unto the soul, and "makes it free from the law of sin and death," Rom. viii. 2. The law considered as a covenant is a law of sin and death to the poor soul while under it. It is a law of sin, because "the strength of sin is the law ;" sin has the dominion over the man, and is in its full power, while he is cleaving to the law as a husband ; sin has dominion over him, because he is not under grace, but under the law. And then the law considered as a covenant, is not only the law of sin, but of death, because it binds over the man to undergo the penalty, however he may work and weary himself in the greatness of his way, to make out a title to life by his obedience and works, yet he being weak to yield that obedience that the law requires, which must be every way perfect, it becomes a law of death to him, the penalty takes place upon him, "The soul that sinneth shall die." But now the law or power of that Spirit of life, which is in the word or voice of Christ, makes a man free from this law of sin and death ; it makes a man fly from the law as a covenant, unto him who is "The end of the law for righteousness to every one that believeth ;" and then the man becomes a living man : he reckons that he is "dead indeed unto sin, but alive unto God through Jesus Christ," and cries with David, "I shall not die, but live, and discover the works of the Lord," and the wonders of his grace, and love through Christ unto my soul. "I live ; yet not I, but Christ that liveth in me," &c. Alas ! may some poor soul say, I find so much deadness in my heart, that I am afraid I never heard the quickening voice of Christ to this day. *Answ.* It is just the fruit of the voice of Christ to discover, that thou hast no life, no strength, no righteousness, no goodness in thyself, but to see, though thou be legally and spiritually dead in thyself, yet your life is in the Son, it is hid with Christ in God. Oh ! say you, if my life were hid there, all would be right ; but I cannot think that I can be so dead and lifeless, and yet have my life hid in Christ. *Answ.* Can thou say before God, that thy life so much bound up in Christ, that thou seest such an absolute need of Christ, that thou can neither live nor die without him ? I see myself so unrighteous and guilty before God, that if I get not him for the Lord my righteousness, I am a dead man, a dead woman, through eternity ? If this be the case, "surely in the Lord hast thou righteousness and strength ;" and therefore thou " shalt not die, but live ;" the voice of the Angel has quickened thy soul to fly to him.

3. The voice of Christ has an enlightening power with it, for " the entrance of his word gives light." The word of the Lord is powerful, " enlightening the eyes." At the same time that Christ unstops the deaf ear, so as to hear his voice, he opens the blind eyes of the sinner also, to behold his glory and the glory of God in him. We are told, Rev. i. that John, whenever he heard the voice of Christ, saying, "I am Alpha and Omega, the first and the last," he immediately turned to hear the voice of him that spake unto him, and he saw one like unto the Son of man, clothed with a garment down to the foot. When Christ spoke unto Paul in his way going to Damascus, he at the same time revealed himself unto him : " It pleased God to reveal his Son in me." And therefore try yourselves by this, Have you ever seen an incarnate God ? has " the light of the knowledge of his glory in the face of Jesus Christ, shined into your hearts ?" Oh ! say you, how shall I know if ever that divine light did enter with the voice of Christ into my soul ? I answer, You may know it by this, that whenever this light is withheld, you will be troubled : Psal. xxx. 7, " Thou didst hide thy face, and I was troubled. I go mourning without the sun." Your aim and design in reading, hearing, praying, and any other duty, will be to get a new beam of that light of life : Psal. xxvii. 4, " One thing have I desired of the Lord, that will I seek after, that I may behold the beauty of the Lord, and inquire after

him in his temple." And you will wait for it " as they that wait for the morning, yea, more than they that wait for the morning." And when it comes from his countenance, your hearts will be glad, and more glad than when corn, wine, and oil, doth abound.

4. The voice of Christ has a soul-turning and converting power in it. This is the ordinary way the efficacy and power of Christ in the gospel is expressed, Psal. xix. 7. It converts the soul, or it turns the sinner from darkness unto light, from the power of Satan unto the living God. Whenever the Lord's voice is carried in upon the heart of backsliding Israel; whenever he says, " Return, thou backsliding Israel," immediately they turn to him, saying, " Behold we turn unto thee, for thou art the Lord our God." The whole soul gets a turn by the power of the voice of Christ. The understanding is turned from darkness to light, from ignorance to a saving uptaking of the things of God. The will is turned from enmity to a voluntary subjection to the Lord : Psal. cx. 3, " Thy people shall be willing in the day of thy power." The heart is turned from its rockiness and obstinacy to a blessed yielding to the will of God, therefore called a heart of flesh. The conscience is turned from its former security and searedness, to act as God's deputy, and to rebuke for every swerving from the holy law. The affections, such as the love, delight, desire, and joy of the soul, are turned from following after vanity, to centre in Christ, and God in him, as the only object of delight and joy, so as the man does not any longer set his affection on things below, but on things above. In short, the man is turned from calling God a liar, to set to his seal that God is true. And with this turn of the heart and soul, there is a turn of all the members of the body, and of the whole conversation. The eyes that were full of adultery, and fed themselves with beholding vanity, now delight in reading the word of God, and in beholding of his works. The ears that were delighted with hearing idle stories and profane songs, are now delighted in

hearing the word of God. The tongue that was set on fire of hell, and that talked of vanity, is now employed in prayer and praise, and in commending Christ, and speaking things that are good for the use of edifying. The feet that were swift to run the devil's errands, are now employed in carrying the man to the house of God, to the ordinances of his appointment, where his soul may get edification and nourishment. Thus, I say, the voice of the Angel Christ has a turning and converting power in it.

5. The voice of Christ has a sanctifying and sin-killing power: Psal. cvii. 20, " He sent forth his word and healed them." The dominion of sin is broken by the power of the voice of Christ; for this is the end of every manifestation of the Son of God, in the flesh, in the word or Spirit, to "destroy the works of the devil," and particularly to destroy the reign of sin, which is the first-born of the devil.

Object. Alas! if this be so, I am afraid I never yet heard the voice of Christ in me ; for I never found unbelief, enmity, carnality, pride, and other evils, so much prevail against me, as since I began to lay things to heart.

Answ. The very feeling of these heart-plagues, or a sense of them, is the fruit of the light or power of the word or voice of Christ in the heart. It is the work of the Spirit and voice of Christ to " convince of sin, and to pierce to the dividing asunder of joints and marrow," and to humble and meeken the soul so, as that it may give employment unto Christ the great Physician. See how Paul groans under the remains of a body of sin, Rom. vii. 24, " O wretched man that I am, who shall deliver me from the body of this death !"

6. If the power of the Angel's voice has reached thy heart, thou hast been awed with the majesty, and charmed with the melody of it.

1. You have been awed with the majesty of his voice ; and no wonder, for the name of God is in him, and the voice of the Angel, is the voice of God, and therefore

his voice must be full of divine majesty, and this brings the awe and fear of God into the heart: hence believers are sometimes described to be such as tremble at his word and tremble at his dispensations : " My flesh trembleth because of thee, and I am afraid of thy judgments." Alas ! the generality of gospel-hearers in our day, are no more moved, either with the voice of Christ in his word, or yet in his rod, than the smith's anvil is with the beating of the hammer ; so that we may take up Isaiah's complaint, Is. xxvi. 11, " Lord, when thy hand is lifted up, they will not see, they will not behold the majesty of the Lord ; but they shall see." It is otherwise with these that have effectually heard the voice of Christ ; they are, I say, awed with the majesty of his voice.

2dly, They are not only awed with the majesty, but charmed with the melody of his voice. His voice is the voice of the charmer, Psal. lviii. It has such a charming captivating quality, that the dead live when they hear it ; the lips of them that are asleep begin to speak, the lame leap like a hart, and the tongues of the dumb begin to sing. I may appeal to the experience of all that know the voice of Christ, for the truth of this. Hence it is that his sheep hear his voice, and at the hearing of it they follow him. If they hear him inviting them to follow him in prayer, meditation, christian conference, or in any ordinance of his worship, saying, " Come with me from Lebanon, my sister, my spouse," immediately their soul echoes, " Behold, I come, for one day in thy courts is better than a thousand : I had rather be a door-keeper in the house of my God, than dwell in the tents of sin." If they hear his voice calling them to go into the fire or water for him, they will be ready to say with Paul, " I am ready not to be bound only, but to die for the name of the Lord Jesus." If they hear him calling them to any piece of work, they will be ready to say, Lord, command what thou wilt, only give strength to obey : " I will run the way of thy commandments, when thou hast enlarged my heart.

I will go in the strength of the Lord, making mention
of thy righteousness, even of thine only." If they hear
his voice inviting them to come away to glory to him
through death, they will be ready to say with David
" Though I walk through the valley of the shadow of
death, I will fear no evil : for thou art with me, thy
rod and thy staff shall uphold me :" or with Paul, " To
me to live is Christ, and to die is gain. I desire to be
dissolved, and to be with Christ, which is best of all."

Object. If this be a mark of them that have heard
and felt the power of the voice of Christ, I am afraid
of myself, for the thoughts of death are a terror to me.

Answ. Death, or the dissolution of nature, is indeed
a terror unto nature ; and I own, that the best of the
saints shrink at it, under this consideration : but will
you answer me this question, Does not the thoughts of
being with the Lord, and of seeing him as he is, and
the thoughts of perfect freedom from a weary body of
sin and death, and of being perfectly like unto him in
holiness, sometimes sweeten the thoughts of death, and
reconcile thy heart unto it ? If so, it is an evidence
that thou hast heard the voice of Christ, and that ere
it be long thou shalt be among that ransomed company,
who are singing his praises in the higher house.

A fourfold ability and sufficiency in Christ to save lost sinners.

1. THERE is an ability of merit for the obtaining of
pardon and acceptance through his obedience unto
death. As was already showed, there are two things
the sinner wants in order to restore him to the favour
of God, and to his title to eternal life, that was forfeited
by his breach of the covenant of works : (1.) Pardon of
sin ; and (2.) A perfect law righteousness. Now both
these are to be found in Christ. As to the first, viz.
pardon, why this we have in him, for he hath finished
transgression and made an end of sin, Dan. ix. 24.
As to its condemning power, " he is the Lamb of
God which taketh away the sin of the world," John. i.

29. "We have redemption in his blood, the forgiveness of sins according to the riches of his grace," Eph. i. 7. Hence the apostle John declareth, chap. i. 7, "The blood of Jesus Christ his Son cleanseth us from all sin;" and it is upon the ground of the satisfaction of Jesus that God declares himself to be the "Lord pardoning iniquity, transgression, and sin," Deut. xxxiv. 7, and promises to be merciful to our unrighteousness, Heb. viii. 12. As to the second, viz. a perfect law righteous-ness, this is to be had to the full in Christ, for he is "the end of the law for righteousness unto every one that believeth," Rom. x. 4. "He is made sin for us, who knew no sin, that we might be made the righteousness of God in him," 2 Cor. v. 21. "The righteousness of the law is fulfilled in us," Rom. viii. 4. This is that best robe that is put upon the poor prodigal when he comes home, Luke xv. 22, "whereby the shame of his nakedness is covered;" this is the wedding garment that fits for communion with God, and entitles the soul unto that "inheritance incorruptible, undefiled, and that fadeth not away," 1 Pet. i. 4. So that there is in Christ a fulness of merit for justification.

2. There is in Christ a fulness of wisdom for the soul's instruction and direction in all cases; "for in him are hid all the treasures of wisdom and knowledge," Col. ii. 3. By his Spirit of wisdom and understanding he gives unto fools and babes the knowledge of the "deep things of God, which are hid from the wise and pru-dent of the world," Matt. xi. 25, compared with 1 Cor. ii. 10. And by his skill and wisdom he directs and guides his poor people through all the dark and diffi-cult steps in their way, until he bring them to glory, and so accomplish that promise, "I will bring the blind by a way that they knew not, I will lead them in paths that they have not known; I will make darkness light before them, and crooked things straight," Is. xliii. 16.

3. There is in him a fulness of strength and ability to bear up the poor soul under all work and warfare that it is called to engage with. Sometimes the poor

believer, looking to the poor weak fund of grace within him, is ready to succumb, and cry out, Alas! such and such work as the Lord carves out for me will be marred in my hand, I am not sufficient to think, to will, to do. But here, believer, lies an all-sufficient fund of ability, " Thy God hath commanded thy strength," Psal. lxviii. 28. " Then mayest thou be strong in the Lord, and in the power of his might," Eph. vi. 10. " He gives power to the faint, and he increaseth strength to them that have no might," Is. xl. 29. Sometimes again the poor weak believer is ready to faint, because of the many and mighty enemies he has to grapple with; Alas! (will he say) I have no might to subdue this or the other strong lust and corruption ; it will master me; one day or other I shall fall into the hand of the enemy; Satan supports the power of indwelling sin, so that I have not only flesh and blood, but principalities and powers, spiritual wickednesses in high places to contend with, Eph. vi. 12. I know not what to do. Well, poor believer, here lies the glory of thy strength, Psal. lxxxix. 17, even in Christ who has already, in his own person, destroyed sin and Satan, and who has also said, that he will subdue thine iniquities, Mic. vii. 19, " Sin shall not have dominion over you," Rom. vi. 14. And as for Satan, " the God of peace will shortly bruise him under thy feet," Rom. xvi. 20, and meantime his grace shall be sufficient for thee, 1 Cor. xii. 9.

4. There is in him an all-sufficient stock of grace for the supply of all thy wants; for " it hath pleased the Father, that in him should all fulness dwell," Col. i. 19. " that out of his fulness all we might receive grace for grace," John i. 16. The grace that is in him, as Mediator, is not in him for himself, but for us poor needy sinners, 1 Cor. i. 30, " He is made of God unto us wisdom, and righteousness, and sanctification, and redemption." " He received gifts for men," Psal. lxviii. 18, that men might be " blessed in him with all spiritual blessings in heavenly things," Eph. i. 3, and therefore men, and the sons of men, are invited to come to him

and get their own, for he and all that he is, or has, as Mediator, is for us. Oh then, "Come, come, come, and take of the water of life freely," Rev. xxii. 17.

Objections to believing in Christ answered.

Object. 1. 'I am afraid it be presumption in me to believe in and apply Christ.

Answ. It can never be presumption to obey an express and positive command of God. Is it presumption to pray? Is it presumption to read the word? Is it presumption to hear the word? Is it presumption to sanctify God's name? and is it presumption to remember the Sabbath? You do not reckon it presumption to do any of these, because ye are commanded of God; as little can it be presumption to "believe in Christ, seeing this is his commandment," 1 John iii. 21.

Object. 2. 'I am such a great sinner, that I am afraid it is not I that is commanded to believe.'

Answ. The command of believing is to all without exception, great sinners, and sinners of a lesser size, Is. i. 8, "Come now, and let us reason together, saith the Lord: Though your sins be as scarlet, they shall be as white as snow; though they be red like crimson, they shall be as wool:" If the command of believing were not to every one, then unbelief would not be their sin; for "where there is no law, there is no transgression," Rom. v. 13. But unbelief is a sin of the deepest dye, and makes every sin else unpardonable, by rejecting the only remedy.

Object. 3. 'You tell us, That we are commanded to believe: and yet at the same time tell us that we want power to believe; that it is the work of God, John vi. 29, and that exceeding great and mighty power of God, that raised Christ from the dead, that must make us to believe,' Eph. i. 19, 20.

Answ. It is very true, ye cannot believe; "No man can come to Christ, except the Father draw him,"

John vi. 44, and yet ye are commanded to believe, not by us, but by that God that commands "things that are not as though they were," Rom. iv. 17, and he commands you, impotent sinners, "dead in sin, to believe in the name of his Son ;" that from a sense of your own impotency, you may turn the work upon himself, as "the Author and Finisher of faith," Heb. xii. 2, and his command is the vehicle of power : As when he commanded the man with the withered hand, "Stretch forth thine hand," Matth. xii. 13, the poor man minted to obey, and in the mint of obedience he got power to stretch out his hand as he was commanded : so, after his example, do ye. Mint at the duty depending on the power of him who commands you to believe, that he may "fulfil in you all the good pleasure of his goodness, and the work of faith with power," 2 Thess. i. 14.

Object. 4. 'But all my labours will be in vain if I be not elected ; for it is only they that are ordained to eternal life that will believe,' Acts xiii. 48.

Answ. It is true the election shall obtain, Rom. xi. 7, though others be hardened ; but let me tell you, in the matter of believing, you have no more concern with the secret counsels of God, than you have in buying or selling, eating or drinking, or such like common actions of life. If any man should say, I will not open my shop door, because I do not know if God has decreed that I should sell any wares ; or I do not know if God has ordained that any man should buy them : Or, if a man should say, I will neither eat nor drink, because God has fixed the term of my life ; I am sure I shall live as long as God has ordained, whatever I do, &c. : Or, I may cast myself down a precipice, or attempt to walk upon the waters, because I shall not perish till God's appointed time come : I say, would you not reckon that man mad, or distracted, that would argue at that rate ? Follow commanded duty: believe in the Son of God ; and then you shall know your election of God.

The Old Testament Tabernacle a type of the New Testament Church.

1. The tabernacle was God's lodging and habitation in the camp of Israel, a symbol of God's gracious presence among them : hence Balaam, when he viewed the camp and tents of Israel, and the tabernacle of God in the midst of the camp, he cries, " How goodly are thy tents, O Jacob, and thy tabernacles, O Israel ! The Lord his God is with him, and the shout of a king is in the midst of him." Moses had his tent, Aaron had his, every commander and soldier had his tent, and the tabernacle was the tent or habitation of the great God. In this respect the church is called a tabernacle, because she is God's lodging or habitation upon earth; with this view Christ the wisdom of God says, Prov. viii. that " he rejoiced from eternity in the habitable parts of the earth, and his delights were with the sons of men." The symbols of his presence are in his church, and there he holds communication and fellowship with his people ; Psal. lxxvi. 1, 2, " In Judah is God known ; his name is great in Israel. In Salem is his tabernacle, and his dwelling-place in Zion." Psal. cxxxii. 13, 14, " The Lord hath chosen Zion, he hath desired it for his habitation. This is my rest, here will I dwell, for I have desired it."

2. The divine oracles, the law and the testimony, were preserved and kept in the tabernacle, and from thence they were given out for the use of Israel : so to the church pertains the oracles of God, his revealed mind and will in the scriptures of truth is committed to her trust : " He showeth his word unto Jacob, and his testimonies unto Israel : he hath not dealt so with every nation." Every jot and tittle of the revealed will of God in his word, is to be maintained and preserved pure and entire by the church, without any diminution or alteration, and that under an awful certification, Rev. xxii. 18, 19 ; hence we are commanded to

"contend earnestly for the faith once delivered to the saints." And whenever any error in doctrine, corruption in worship, or iniquity in practice, is broached in the church, presently it is to be brought unto the standard and touchstone of the word, in order to its being condemned as dissonant thereunto : Is. viii. "To the law and to the testimony : if they speak not according to this word, it is because there is no light in them." Hence heretics, who maintain doctrines repugnant unto the word of God, after two or three admonitions, are to be cast out of the church and delivered over to Satan.

3. The tabernacle was the place of worship. In the courts of the tabernacle Israel were to stand and do homage unto the great God, the God of Israel ; and every one was to worship there, according to God's appointment, and not according to their own fancy. So the church of Christ is the place where he will be worshipped and sanctified of all that are about him. The ordinances of divine institution, particularly public ordinances of preaching and hearing of prayer, and praises, are the courts of the great King, where he will have his people to attend him with their offerings, and to pay him their tribute : Is. lvi. 7, "I will bring them to my holy mountain, and make them joyful in my house of prayer; their burnt-offerings and their sacrifices shall be accepted upon mine altar ; for mine house shall be called an house of prayer for all people."

4. The pattern of the tabernacle was given by God unto Moses in the mount, together with all the laws, statutes, and regulations thereof. Moses was not left at liberty to order one pin of the tabernacle otherwise than according to the pattern. So the model of the church, with a perfect system of laws, by which she is to be governed, is given of God in the mount of divine revelation. And for any man to assert that the government of the church of Christ is ambulatory and uncertain, or that he has left no orders how to manage in the election of officers to his New Testament church,

is upon the matter to impeach the Scriptures of truth, with imperfection ; or to affirm, that God has less regard to his church now under the New Testament, than he had about the management of that little portable thing called the tabernacle of old.

5. No man was to intrude himself into the service of the tabernacle, or to " take this honour unto himself, but he that was called of God, as was Aaron." If any man had usurped the priesthood, besides these whom the Lord called, all Israel would have been ready to stone him to death. And what an awful indication of divine wrath was it against Korah, Dathan, and Abiram, when, for usurping the priesthood, among other things, the Lord made the earth to open its mouth, and swallow them up alive. All Israel, by God's appointment, were ordered to make a secession from them, lest the anger of God should fall upon them also. In like manner, under the New Testament church, no man is to intrude himself into the sacred offices of the church, without he be qualified and called of God unto that work. These who enter into the fold of the church, and assume the name and notion of shepherds, without entering by the door of a lawful and regular call, are branded with the infamous character of thieves and robbers by Christ, John x. Men in our day are become so polite, that they think these hard names to be given to any man ; but scripture styles and characters will stand firm, and be in request, when all the pretended politeness and eloquence of men will be buried in the dust of oblivion.

6. The greatest and most sacred thing in the tabernacle was the ark and mercy-seat, with the cherubims covering it with their wings and looking down continually unto it. This pointed out the sacred mystery of the incarnation, obedience, and death of Christ, by which the law is magnified and made honourable, and through whom God declares himself to be a merciful and reconciled God. These sacred mysteries, typified in the tabernacle, are now opened in the promulgation

of the gospel : hence, Rev. xi. it is said, "The temple of God was opened, and the ark of his testament was seen." It is the great business of ministers of the gospel, now under the New Testament, to disclose or open the ark of the covenant of grace, to preach Christ, and the manifold wisdom of God through him, in the salvation of lost sinners ; "which things the cherubims, or angels, desire to look into."

7. The ark was a portable or moveable kind of a tent, and was carried about by God's appointment, from one place to another, and never had a fixed abode, until it came to mount Zion, and was set in its proper place in the temple. In like manner the church of God, while in this world, is not fixed to any particular nation ; he lifts it from one nation to another, as best serves his glorious ends in gathering in his elect, until the mystical body of Christ is completed ; and then the church militant will be transported to the church triumphant in glory.

Other things might be added. The manna was in the ark ; so the bread of life is in the church. Aaron's rod was in the ark ; so ecclesiastical authority is only to be administered in the church, and by the officers and judges of God's ordination. The candlesticks and the lamps were in the ark ; so in the church the light of the Lord shines, therefore called a valley of vision. Thus you see on what account the church of Christ is called a tabernacle.

Notable years of the Redeemed, and the glorious things done in them.

First, THERE is the year of redemption by ordination or purpose. And this is such an ancient year, that it never had a beginning, the glorious frame and plan of our redemption being laid in the heart of God from eternity, before ever the foundations of the world were laid : with respect to this year, Christ is called "a Lamb slain from the foundation of the world." If it be asked, What were the principal occurrences of this year?

Answ. 1. This year electing and everlasting love lighted upon the redeemed, when he saw them in his own decree lying in their blood : Ezek. xvi. 6, " And when I passed by thee, and saw thee polluted in thine own blood, I said unto thee, when thou wast in thy blood, Live : yea, I said unto thee, when thou wast in thy blood, Live." And ver. 8, " When I passed by thee, and looked upon thee, behold, thy time was the time of love."   O is not this a great matter, a wonderful occurrence, that from the ancient years of eternity God passed by the fallen angels, and pitched his love upon a company of poor sinners of Adam's family ; who were like the new-born infant, cast out into the open field, wallowing in its native blood and filth, without hope, without help, without strength, beauty, or any thing else to commend them unto him ! Oh let heaven and earth wonder at that strange word, Jer. xxxi. 3, " I have loved thee with an everlasting love : therefore with loving kindness have I drawn thee," from the ancient years of eternity.

2. This year of everlasting love, the grand council of peace was called in heaven among the persons of the adorable Trinity ; where the affair under consideration was, how Satan's usurped kingdom in this world might be sapped and overturned ; and in order to this, how sinners of Adam's family might be saved, in a consistency with the honour of the divine law and justice, sovereignty and other attributes.   A question which would have nonplussed a general assembly of angels, and put them to an everlasting stand.   " How shall I put them among the children ?" is a query which we must leave unto God himself, and his infinite wisdom and grace, only to answer.

3. This year the happy overture was made, and agreed to in the council of peace, that the second person of the glorious and adorable Trinity, the only begotten Son of God, should, in the fulness of time, as-

sume the nature of man, take his place in law, and
act the part of a Saviour for lost sinners, and, by his
obedience unto the death, fulfil the law, satisfy justice,
finish transgression, make an end of sin, and do every
thing requisite, for their salvation, and the ruin of Satan's kingdom.   That this was agreed, and gone into,
appears from what we have, Psal. xl. 6—8, " Burnt-
offering, and sin-offering, hast thou not required.   Then
said I, Lo, I come: in the volume of the book it is
written of me : I delight to do thy will, O my God :
yea, thy law," this law of redemption, " is within my
heart."   O how did the heart of our glorious Immanuel leap in his breast when the overture was made !
" Lo, I come," &c.   With what pleasure doth he speak
of it, Prov. viii. 23, " I was set up from everlasting,
from the beginning, or ever the earth was ! I rejoiced
in the habitable parts of the earth, and my delights were
with the sons of men !"

4. In this year it was agreed upon, and finally ended,
that the eternal Son, God coequal with the Father,
should come under a new covenant relation to his own
Father, and that he, as head of the new covenant, should
have the right to eternal life, and all the blessings of
the covenant subservient thereunto, settled in his own
person ; that so having the right in his person, he
might give it unto as many as the Father had given
him.   It was with a view to this new-covenant right
with his own Father, that it was prophesied of him,
Psal. lxxxix. 26, " He shall cry unto me, Thou art my
Father, my God, and the Rock of my salvation."   And
upon this new-covenant conveyance, he tells his disciples, when he was about to ascend into glory, " I ascend
unto my Father, and your Father, and to my God, and
your God."

5. It was agreed upon this year, that the whole
power and strength of the eternal Father, yea, the whole
power of the glorious Trinity, should be forthcoming
to our glorious Redeemer, for his support and through-
bearing in his glorious undertaking of man's redemp-

tion : " He is my servant whom I uphold, saith the
Lord.   With him my hand shall be established : mine
arm also shall strengthen him," Psal. lxxxix. 21.
Therefore Christ is called " the man of God's right
hand."   As also it was agreed, that the fulness of the
Godhead should dwell in him bodily ; that he should
receive the spirit above measure, to fit, furnish, and
qualify him for his undertaking : " I will put my Spirit
upon him, and he shall bring forth judgment unto the
Gentiles."

6. This year it was agreed, that "the pleasure of
the Lord should prosper in his hand," that he should
be successful in his undertaking, maugre all the opposition that either hell or earth should be capable to raise
against him ; for this end he engaged that his hand
should be upon the man of his right hand, whom he
had made strong for himself; that he would make his
enemies his footstool, and strike through kings in the
day of his wrath, and plague all these that hated him.
Many other things I might name, as transacted in this
year of our redemption by ordination ; but if I should
insist here, I might anticipate all that was transacted
in the following years, because whatever occurred in
them was fixed upon and determined this first year of
redemption.   And therefore I proceed to a

Second year of the redeemed, and that is, the year
of our redemption by purchase or impetration ; under
which period I comprehend the whole time that the
Son of God sojourned in this lower world in our nature, till he ascended again into glory.   This was the
acceptable year of the Lord, which the Old Testament saints so much longed for ; this was the day
which Abraham saw afar off, and was glad when he
saw it.   If it be asked, What were the transactions of this
year ?   I answer, Great things were done this year,
yea, wonderful without number.   I shall only instance
in a few.

1. This year the great God was incarnate : " The
Word was made flesh, and dwelt among us."   Sirs,

what think you of this piece of strange news, were your souls never affected with it? Whatever you may think of it, yet Paul, the great apostle of the Gentiles, rehearses it as a matter of the highest wonder, 1 Tim. iii. 16, " Without controversy, great is the mystery of godliness, God manifested in the flesh." And heaven thought it a matter of so great moment, that so soon as ever this year commenced, a messenger was despatched from the throne of glory, to notify it unto the shepherds, saying, Luke ii. 10, " I bring you good tidings of great joy, for unto you is born this day in the city of David, a Saviour, which is Christ the Lord." And immediately a multitude of the heavenly host begin their song of praise, crying, "Glory to God in the highest, and on earth peace, good-will towards men." The morning stars sang together, and shouted for joy, crying, " Glory to God in the highest," when the foundation-stone of our redemption was laid. O sirs, let heaven and earth, angels and men, wonder at what God hath done for us! The great Creator became a creature, the Ancient of days became an infant, and made of a woman ; here is a mystery of wisdom, grace, and love, that may make us cry, " O the depth of the riches, both of the wisdom and knowledge of God! how unsearchable are his judgments, and his ways past finding out!"

2. This year the great Lawgiver, whose will is a law to angels and men, voluntarily subjected himself to his own law, and that in the room and stead of rebels who had violate his law, and contemned his authority : Gal. iv. 4, 5, " In the fulness of time God sent forth his Son, made of a woman, made under the law, to redeem them that were under the law, that we might receive the adoption of sons." O sirs, had ever the law such a subject! No, no ; here is the Creator made under the law given to the creature ; hence it was, that his obedience to the law reflected a glory and honour upon the law, which it never had before, and which the obedience of men and angels, though never so perfect,

could not have done : Is. xlii. 21, " The Lord is well pleased for his righteousness' sake, for he shall magnify the law and make it honourable."

3. This year God blessed for ever was made a curse ; and he who is of purer eyes than that he can behold iniquity, was made sin : Gal. iii. 13, " He hath redeemed us from the curse of the law, being made a curse for us." And, 2 Cor. v. 21, " He was made sin for us who knew no sin ; that we might be made the righteousness of God in him." O were not these strange and remarkable events ! " Shall it not be said in Jacob and Israel, What hath God wrought !"

4. This year everlasting righteousness was brought in for the justification of ungodly sinners. Sirs, immediately upon Adam's fall, by the breach of the first covenant, sin entered into the world ; and that moment that sin entered into the world, righteousness went quite out of the world, so that there was none righteous, no not one. But this year Christ the Son of God brought it in again into the world by his obedience unto the death ; " What the law could not do, in that it was weak through the flesh, God sending his own Son, in the likeness of sinful flesh, for sin condemned sin in the flesh : that the righteousness of the law might be fulfilled in us, who walk not after the flesh, but after the Spirit."

5. This year God actually laid the foundation of a throne of grace, in justice and judgment, and of the house of mercy, which shall be built up for ever. God intended to rear up a new house of mercy for miserable sinners upon the ruins of the broken covenant of works ; and Christ himself is the first stone of the building : Is. xxviii. 16, " Behold, I lay in Zion for a foundation, a stone, a tried stone, a precious corner-stone ; and he that believeth on him shall not be confounded." Indeed this stone was rejected by the Jewish builders, but God has made it the chief stone of the corner ; and another foundation no man can lay : " This is the Lord's doing, and it is wondrous in our eyes."

6. This year the vail of the temple was rent from the top to the bottom, and the way to the holiest was opened by the blood of Jesus. Immediately upon the fall of man, the door of access to God and glory was shut, and bolted against Adam and all his posterity; this was signified by the cherubims, with the flaming sword, turning every way to guard our access unto the tree of life. But by the blood of Jesus, a new and living way is opened, which is consecrated for us; and by this new way we have entered with boldness. "I am the door (says Christ): by me if any man enter in, he shall be saved, and shall go in and out, and find pasture."

7. This year sin was finished and transgression ended in a way of satisfaction, insomuch that the uttermost farthing of debt, that we owed unto divine justice for sin, was paid down in the red gold of a Redeemer's blood. This Christ testified in his dying words; he cried out, It is finished; and thereupon bowed the head and gave up the ghost. And upon Christ uttering of that word, sin was condemned in the flesh of the Son of God, and the hand-writing that was against us, even our debt-bond unto justice, was cancelled and torn, he having nailed it to his cross.

8. This year the covenant of grace, or the testament of Christ was confirmed and made sure by his blood: Dan. ix. 27, "He shall confirm the covenant with many." The testament is now of force since the Testator's death, as the apostle argues, Heb. ix. The death and blood of Jesus has given such a validity unto his latter will contained in this blessed Bible, that we may pursue for the goods of the testament with boldness at a throne of grace, and do it with full assurance of faith.

9. This year the sacrifice and oblation was made to cease, the Mosaic economy was unhinged: all the shadows of the Jewish ceremonies did flee away, Christ the substance of them all being come. Not to insist upon particulars: This year the Prince of life was in-

carcerate for our debt, died and came under the power of death for a time. This year he was "justified in the Spirit, taken from prison and from judgment," and fully discharged of our debt, which he had undertaken to pay. This year he was "declared to be the Son of God with power, according to the spirit of holiness, by his resurrection from the dead." This year God was declared to be a God of peace, by the resurrection of Christ from the dead : and this year the foundation of a lively hope was laid for us, even the hope of " an inheritance that is incorruptible, undefiled, and that fadeth not away." This year a whole elect world was raised from the dead in their glorious representative ; he having drunk of the brook in the way, immediately he lifted up the head in his resurrection, and our heads were lifted up in him. This year God went up with a shout, (I mean God in our nature,) yea, God with the sound of a trumpet; and " when he ascended up on high, he led captivity captive, and received gifts for men, even for the rebellious, that the Lord God might dwell among them." O sirs, God is ascended in our nature, and sitting upon the throne of glory, swaying the sceptre of heaven ; and he is wearing our nature in glory, as a pledge that we shall follow him, for the human body was assumed for the sake of the mystical. Thus you see what great events happened in the year of our redemption by purchase. O let songs be heard from this end of the earth, at the hearing of this joyful sound, even glory to the righteous.

Thirdly, A third year of the redeemed, is the year of exhibited redemption ; by which I understand, the year of a gospel-dispensation among a people. This is sometimes called also a day in Scripture : "O that thou hadst known, in this thy day, the things that belong unto thy peace !" says the Lord to Jerusalem. If it be asked, What are the great transactions of this year? *Answ.* Great things are done for the redeemed this year also. Only before I proceed to particulars, I would have you to remember, that redemption in this situation of it, or considered in its revelation or exhibition, is a thing common to all the hearers of the gospel. Here we are to abstract from the secret decrees of election and reprobation, and to make open proclamation of redeeming grace and love in Christ to every creature under heaven ; we are to tell every man and woman sprung of Adam, this good news, "That God was in Christ, reconciling the world unto himself, not imputing their trespasses unto them ;" that "the promise is unto you, and to your seed, and to all that are afar off, and to as many as the Lord our God shall call" by the sound of the gospel. O sirs, "secret things belong unto the Lord, but things that are revealed belong unto us, and to our children :" and therefore let alone this secret of election or reprobation, as pertaining to God, do not invade his property, but hearken unto things revealed, things brought to light by the glorious gospel ; for this belongs unto you, and "to you is the word of this salvation sent," and therefore intermeddle with it with the greatest freedom by faith ; it is no presumption for us to claim what (God says) "belongs unto us, and to our children."

Now, this premised, I come to tell you of some great things that are done in this year of exhibited and revealed redemption, which you and I do at this moment enjoy, you in hearing, and I in preaching. The great things done in this period are so many, that I can only point at them.

1. Then, this year the people that sat in darkness are made to see great light, and to them that sat in the regions of the shadow of death, light is made to spring up. And O! is it not matter of praise, that this is the privilege of Scotland at this day ? The time was, when the gross darkness of Pagan and Popish error and idolatry did overspread our land : but the day-spring from on high hath visited us, and brought life and immortality to light ; the temple of God is opened, and the ark of his testament may be seen, the vail is rent, the face of the covering is destroyed, I mean, as

to the objective revelation, and the mysteries which were hid from ages and generations are now made manifest.

2. This year of exhibit redemption a throne of grace is reared, a court of grace erected, and liberty granted to every man that finds himself condemned in the court of conscience, in the court of the law or justice, to carry his cause by an appeal; which if he do, he is sure to find grace and mercy to help him in time of need. O sirs, know your own privilege. Art thou saying within thy breast, If God mark mine iniquity, according to the tenor of his holy law, I cannot stand? O, I am condemned already, and the wrath of God is pursuing me? Well, I tell you for certainty, the court of grace stands open to you, and if you will carry your cause there, though it be never so desperate, the cause is won; for all the acts and interlocutors of this court are acts of grace, acts of indemnity and oblivion, for the name of him that sits on the throne is "The Lord, the Lord God merciful and gracious, pardoning iniquity, transgression, and sin. I, even I am he that blotteth out thine iniquities for mine own sake, and will not remember thy sins."

3. This year the batteries of heaven are reared up against the gates of hell. Error, ignorance, unbelief, Atheism, pride, profanity, security, and the like evils; they are the strong-holds of the devil's kingdom, whereby he secures sinners in his service. Now, by the dispensation of the gospel, God's batteries are mounted against these, all the ordinances of the gospel, particularly the preaching of the word, is calculated for casting these strong-holds to the ground. 2 Cor. x. 4, "The weapons of our warfare are not carnal, but mighty through God, to the pulling down of strongholds," &c.

4. This year the fountains of the great deep of the love of God toward a lost and perishing world are broken up; I mean his love in sending of his only begotten Son upon the glorious errand of our redemption:

John iii. 16, "God so loved the world, that he gave
his only begotten Son, that whosoever believeth in him,
should not perish, but have everlasting life." What is
the great business of gospel ministers, but to represent
to sinners the excellency of this loving kindness, that
so the sons of men may put their trust under the shadow of his wings?

5. This year God reveals and brings near his righteousness and salvation, even to them who are stout-
hearted and far from righteousness; Is. xlvi. 12, 13,
" Hearken unto me, ye stout-hearted, that are far from
righteousness. I bring near my righteousness : it shall
not be far off, and my salvation shall not tarry ; behold,
I will place salvation in Zion for Israel my glory." O
sirs, we tell you it for good news this year, that "he
who knew no sin, was made sin for us, that we might
be made the righteousness of God in him ;" and that
he is become the "end of the law for righteousness to
every one that believeth."

6. This year the tree of life which grows in the midst
of the paradise of God shakes his fruit, which is for
the feeding, and his leaves, which are for the healing
of the nations. And O many a ripe cluster of fruit,
many a healing leaf of sound doctrine has been dropt
in this very place ; happy they who by the hand of
faith have gathered and applied them. You who have
not yet gathered, will you fall to work yet, gather and
glean in the field of our blessed Boaz, our Kinsman and
Redeemer, and you will find his fruits sweet to your
taste, and his words, if you eat them, to be the joy and
rejoicing of your heart.

7. This year Jacob's ladder is set up in Bethel, by
which we may scale heaven, and recover that glory
and happiness from which we fell by the sin of the first
Adam. The gospel shows unto us the path of life, a
stair by which we may ascend unto these regions of
bliss and glory that are above; and the lower part of
this ladder of communication stands at every man's
foot, inviting him, as it were, to take the benefit of it.

" I am (says Christ) the way, the truth, and the life. I am the door, by me if any man enter in, he shall be saved, and shall go in and out, and find pasture."

8. This year the pure river of water of life issues forth from the throne of God and of the Lamb, and runs in the very streets of the city of God, I mean of the visible church, and a voice comes forth from heaven, crying, " Whosoever will, let him come and take of the water of life freely. Ho, every one that thirsteth, come ye to the waters, and he that hath no money; come ye, buy and eat, yea come, buy wine and milk without money and without price."

9. This year the doors of God's banqueting house are opened, and the manna falls about the camp of the visible church. He " makes unto all people a feast of fat things, a feast of wines on the less, of fat things full of marrow, of wines on the lees well refined." This year that scripture is fulfilled, Prov. ix. 1—5.

10. This year the gates of the city of refuge are cast wide open, the ways and avenues to it are cleared, stumbling blocks are removed, and a cry made to self-destroying sinners, who are under the arrest of law and justice, " Turn ye to your strong-holds, ye prisoners of hope ;" flee for refuge unto the hope set before you. This year prison doors are opened, and a cry made to the prisoners to come forth, and to them that sit in darkness, " Show yourselves." This year a charter for heaven and eternal life is put in every man's hand, with an express command from God to every man to take the benefit thereof by faith, "Search the scriptures, for in them ye think to have everlasting life." This year the latter-will or testament of Christ is opened, that every man may, by virtue of the testament, claim the legacies thereof. O then " let us fear, lest a promise being left us of entering into his rest, any of us should come short of it." Thus you see some of the great things that are done this year.

Fourthly, Another notable year of the redeemed, is the year of applied redemption ; under which may be comprised and comprehended the whole period of time from the soul's conversion unto the day of death. This year, what was purposed by the Father, purchased by the Son, and exhibit in the gospel, is applied and made effectual. If it be asked, What great things are done for the redeemed this year? I answer,

1. Commonly in the beginning of this year, some thunder-claps are heard from mount Sinai, whereby the poor soul that was lying fast asleep within the sea mark of God's wrath, is awakened to perceive his danger. The poor vessel of mercy was under the power of sin and Satan, promising himself peace, though he walked after the imagination of his own heart, hiding himself from wrath in the refuge of general mercy, in the refuge of a profession of law-righteousness, or the like; but a storm of hail, I mean of terrors of the law, comes and sweeps away the refuge of lies, it blows away his fig-leaf covering; and thereupon the man, who before thought himself sure of salvation, begins to cry out with the jailer, "Men and brethren, what shall I do to be saved?" The man finds himself to be dead in law, condemned already, yea, to be not only legally but spiritually dead, under the power of sin and Satan, and his bonds to be so strong, that neither he nor the whole creation is able to loose them; and this fills him with such anxiety and trouble of spirit, that he is even at his wit's end, that he does not know what to do. O! whither shall I flee for help, where shall I leave my glory? O that I knew of a refuge in heaven or earth, to which I might run for shelter!

2. In the begining of this year the dead soul is raised up unto a new spiritual life: "You hath he quickened who were dead in trespasses and sins." The great Redeemer, who hath life in himself, and received it for men, yea, for the rebellious, he comes to the sinner's grave of sin, in which he was buried, and cries to him, as he did to Lazarus, "Come forth, O sinner;" and immediately the bars of spiritual death are broken, the bonds of death are loosed, and the law of the Spirit of life

which is in Christ Jesus enters into him, whereby he is
made free from the law of sin and death.

3. In the entry of this year, the Redeemer recovers
sight to the blind. The poor creature was so blinded
by Satan the god of this world, that though the light
of the Sun of righteousness had been shining upon
him, and about him in a gospel dispensation, yet he did
not behold it, the enemy had done with him as the
Philistines did with Samson, put out his eyes ; but now
the glorious Redeemer with his eye-salve touches the
eyes of the understanding, whereby the blind eyes are
opened ; God, who commanded the light to shine out
of darkness, shines into his heart, and gives him the
light of the knowledge of the glory of God in the face
of Jesus Christ, he is translated out of darkness into a
marvellous and surprising light. And now he begins
to see things in another view ; and the first sight that he
gets of Christ, he is even surprised and overjoyed at the
sight, crying, O ! " this is my rest for ever ; here will
I dwell, for I have desired it." I have been seeking
rest, but could not find it, but now I have found it,
" To him shall the Gentiles seek, and his rest shall be
glorious." Once in a day I could see no form nor
comeliness in him, why he should be desired ; but now
I see him to be " white and ruddy, the chiefest among
ten thousand."

4. In the beginning of this year, the man is entered
into the kingdom of heaven, even upon this earth, he
enters into the new heaven and the new earth, the kingdom of God is reared up in the soul, and sin and self are
dethroned. The glorious Redeemer, who is the Lord
of hosts, by the power of his eternal Spirit, he makes
his entry at the everlasting gates of the soul, saying,
This soul is mine ; it was given me by my Father, I
redeemed it with the price of my blood ; and therefore
sin, and Satan, and self, resign your government, and
render up this soul and all its powers and faculties unto me ; and he binds the strong man, spoils him of
his goods ; the batteries of the gospel, and ordinances

thereof, are so well managed, in the hand of the Spirit, that the strong-holds of Satan, and the high and tower- ing imaginations of the soul, they fall down at the feet of the glorious Redeemer, and every thought of the heart becomes a captive unto the obedience of the great Captain of salvation, and the soul becomes a vo- lunteer in the service of Christ.

5. In the beginning of this year, the prodigal stray- ing son is brought home again; that wonderful ques- tion is answered, How shall I put thee among the children, who had wandered away into a far country? and the Father and all the family rejoice and make merry at his return; and no sooner doth he enter his Father's threshold, but his filthy rags are cast away, and he is clothed with the best robe of the Son of God, whereby he is made to look like his Father's son. Which leads me also to tell you, that this year the righteousness of the law is so fulfilled in the guilty sinner, that was standing condemned at the bar of God and conscience, that now there is no condemna- tion for him; yea, he can lift up his head with courage and say, " Who is he that condemneth? It is God that justifieth; it is Christ that died, yea, rather that is risen again," &c.

6. Again, this year King Solomon is both crowned and married; a match is made up and concluded between the Prince of life and heir of hell. In the former year the purpose of marriage was proclaimed, saying, I will betroth thee unto me in righteousness, mercy, faith- fulness, and loving-kindness, yea, I will betroth thee unto me for ever; and this year the bride gives her con- sent unto the bargain, saying, " I am the Lord's :" and that day that the bride gives her consent, the Bride- groom reckons it his coronation day: " Go forth, O ye daughters of Zion, and behold King Solomon with the crown wherewith his mother crowned him, in the day of his espousals, and in the day of the gladness of his heart."

7. This year the poor soul finds the pearl of great

price in the field of the word, whereby it is made up and enriched for ever. It discovers a mine of unsearchable riches of grace, riches of wisdom, riches of righteousness, riches of glory, and claims all as its own upon the grant made thereof in the word, or in the record of God, in which he gives us that eternal life, which is in his Son. This year the soul sets to its seal that God is true, acquiescing in it as a faithful saying, and worthy of all acceptation, that Christ Jesus came into the world to save sinners. This year the soul enters into the holiest by the blood of Jesus; enters upon a state of fellowship and communion with God, in his light, in his life, in his love, and is put in a capacity to say, " Verily our fellowship is with the Father, and with his Son Jesus Christ." This year the vessel of mercy is plucked as a brand out of the fire, and hung upon the nail fastened in a sure place, from whence all the powers of hell shall not be able to pull it down again ; for "neither death, nor life, nor angels, nor principalities, nor powers, nor things present, nor things to come, shall be able to separate us from the love of God which is in Christ Jesus our Lord. This year the foundation of a new and spiritual temple is laid for God to dwell in : " Know ye not that ye are the temple of God, and that the Spirit of God dwelleth in you ?" This year the branch of the old Adam is cut off, and grafted into the true vine, the plant of renown, and these who were limbs of Satan, are made members of Christ, and to hold that new head, from which the whole body by joints and bands having nourishment ministered, and knit together, increaseth with the increase of God. Thus you see what great things are done in the very beginning of this year of applied redemption.

I might here also tell you, that in the progress of this year, the Redeemer doth many great things for the redeemed. The great work of the remaining part of this year, is to advance, and carry on the good work of sanctification or holiness in their souls, whereby they are more and more ripened for the year of everlasting

life and glory. For which end he trysts them with a
variety of dispensations, both as to the outward and
the inward man ; sometimes with health, sometimes
with sickness ; sometimes with prosperity, sometimes
with adversity ; sometimes he smiles, sometimes he
smites ; sometimes the candle of the Lord shines on
their heads, and they behold the glory of the Lord,
sometimes they go mourning without the sun, crying,
" O that I knew where I might find him !" sometimes
he pinches them with hunger, and thirst, at other times
he anoints their heads with oil, and makes their cup to
run over ; sometimes they ride upon the high places of
Jacob, at other times they drive heavily like the chariots of Pharaoh ; sometimes they are plunged in a ditch
of sin, so that their own clothes do abhor them, at
other times he takes them up from among the pots,
and makes them to shine like the wings of a dove
covered with silver, and her feathers with yellow gold :
and this way the remaining part of the year is spent :
by all which variety of dispensations, he is still advancing the soul in grace and holiness, till it be ripe for
glory ; according to his promise, " All things shall
work together for good to them that love God, to
them who are the called according to his purpose."
And so much for the fourth year of applied redemption.   I come now to

The *fifth* and *last* year, and that is the year of consummate and perfected redemption.   This is an everlasting year, which never, never ends.   All the former
years are already come with respect to every believer ;
but this year is not yet come, but is fast a-coming,
" Behold I come quickly," says the Lord : and therefore I may say, Lift up thy head, believer, for the year
or day of thy redemption draweth nigh.   Now, this
year of perfected redemption has a twofold period, the
one at death, and the other at the resurrection, or the
day of Christ's second coming.

If it be asked, *first*, What is done for the ransomed
of the Lord at death ?

Answ. 1. In the beginning of this year, Jordan is divided, the waters thereof file off on every hand, that the redeemed of the Lord may have a safe passage to the promised land of glory. Poor believer, thou hast many a weary thought about thy passage, lest the waters of the Jordan of death swallow thee up ; but do not fear, the moment thou sets thy foot within the brink of this river, thou wilt see the ark of God before thee, and multitudes of thy fellow-travellers on the other side, and nothing but dry ground between thee and them, where there is no manner of danger.

2. In the very beginning of this year Christ comes, according to his promise, John xiv. 2, 3, to receive his ransomed ones to glory, that where he is, they may be also. And when he comes, he comes with the keys of hell and death in his hand, saying, Fear not, for I was dead, and I am alive, and I live for evermore ; I am the Lord and Master of death, I open the grave, and shut it at my pleasure ; I have ransomed thee from the power of the grave, I have redeemed thee from death ; I have plagued death, I have destroyed the grave ; and therefore do not fear.

3. In the very beginning of this year the believer flits from his house of clay, into "a house not made with hands, eternal in the heavens." Perhaps, believer, thou pays a dear house-meal for thy lodging in this tabernacle of clay, " We that are in this tabernacle do groan, being burdened ;" but up the heart, thou shalt have a better lodging ere it be long, where all the rent thou wilt pay for thy quarters, will be to sing hallelujahs of praise to the glorious Redeemer, and to join in that heavenly choir, " Salvation to him that sits on the throne, and to the Lamb for ever and ever."

4. In the very beginning of this year, the believer goes to his bed to rest him till he awakes in the morning of the resurrection. The poor man has toiled himself all the day, and perhaps his day has been sixty, seventy, or a hundred years long; but at length he falls asleep in Jesus : may be like Job, wearisome days

and nights were appointed to him, he could not get rest upon his other beds, his couch could not ease, or comfort him ; but this year he enters into peace, he rests in his bed, sleeps on a soft pillow, sleeps in Jesus, lays his head down upon the warm bosom of Jesus, where he sleeps sound without disturbance from hell or earth, till that voice come from heaven, " Awake and sing, ye that sleep in the dust."

5. In the very beginning of this year, the believer is gathered unto his own people, even unto the general assembly and church of the first-born. It is said of Jacob, when he died, " he drew up his feet in his bed, and was gathered unto his people :" a strange expression ! Jacob, when he died, was in the midst of his children and family, and a goodly family he had about him, children and grandchildren ; he was dying in honour, and in favour and respect with the king of Egypt; one would think that he was but departing from his people ; but it is called a gathering unto his people, because death brought him to far better company, even " to the spirits of just men made perfect, and the general assembly of the first-born." All the company above are the first-born, because every one is an heir, not one of them misses the inheritance. In so many words, not to insist on particulars : in the beginning of this year the believer drops the body of sin, which made him to go with a bowed down back, and is made perfect in holiness, presented without spot or wrinkle, or any such thing. This year the believer drops mortality, and enters upon immortality, comes to the possession of that life everlasting, which shall run parallel with the life of God. This year the believer leaves the wilderness of this world behind him, bids it adieu for ever, and comes to his own country, the " inheritance of the saints in light ;" he was a stranger and a pilgrim, but now he comes to his own home. This year his warfare with sin, Satan, and the world is ended, and he comes off the field like a victorious conqueror, with the palm of victory in his hand,

singing that song, " Thanks be to God, that giveth me the victory, through Jesus Christ our Lord." In the beginning of this year he ends his race, and comes at the mark and prize of the high calling of God ; he comes even to the end of his faith and hope, the salvation of his soul, in the full and immediate enjoyment of God for evermore. This year distance and darkness ends, and everlasting light begins, no more clouds of desertion to overcast his sky through eternity, now the Lord shall be his everlasting light, and his God his glory ; the Lord God and the Lamb are the light of that place. This year the believer quits the by-table of ordinances, word, and sacraments in the church militant, and sits down at the high table with Abraham, Isaac, and Jacob ; yea, he drinks of the fruit of the vine new with Christ in the kingdom of heaven. In a word, this year all the believer's sobs, and tears, and sorrows end, and he begins his songs and triumphs : " The ransomed of the Lord shall come to Zion with songs, and everlasting joy upon their heads : they shall obtain joy and gladness, and sorrow and sighing shall flee away."

But then, *secondly*, for the other period of this year, viz. the resurrection, great things are done by the Redeemer for his ransomed and redeemed ones ; take these few among many others.

1. This year the Redeemer translates the seat of his empire from the highest heavens to these clouds that are above our heads : " Behold he cometh with clouds, and every eye shall see him." O with what royal splendour and magnificence will he appear when he descends from heaven with a shout, with the voice of the archangel, and the trump of God, when his white throne will be surrounded with ten thousand times ten thousand, and thousands of thousands ! This year the visible frame of nature is to be unhinged, and this earth, which has been a theatre of so much sin, is to be burnt : " The day of the Lord cometh, wherein the heavens shall pass away with a great noise, and the elements

shall melt with fervent heat, the earth also, and the works that are therein, shall be burnt up," 2 Pet. iii. 10. And ver. 12, " Looking for and hastening unto the coming of the day of God, wherein the heavens being on fire shall be dissolved, and the elements shall melt with fervent heat." Oh with what awful solemnity will the second coming of the great Redeemer be attended! This year God is to send out his reapers to reap the field of this world, I mean, the holy angels : and they will reap so clean, that they will not leave one soul that ever sprung of Adam behind them ; no, no, they will be all gathered together to the tribunal.

2. This year death and the grave are to render the prey which they have devoured ; the sea will give up its dead, and the earth will give up its dead. Thy head, believer, this year is to be lifted up out of the prison of the grave ; God will open his cabinet, and bring forth his jewels in the view of men and angels ; every one of them shining like the sun in the kingdom of their Father ; insomuch that Christ will be admired in his very saints and members : when they are purged from the dross of sin and mortality, they will shine like the brightness of the firmament, and like the stars for ever and ever; our vile bodies shall be made like unto Christ's glorious body. This year this mortal is to put on immortality, and death shall be swallowed up in victory. This year Christ's scattered jewels and members will all be gathered together unto him; he will call to the earth, from the rising of the sun to the going down thereof, saying, " Gather my saints together unto me, those that have made a covenant with me by sacrifice." And O what a bright constellation will they make, when they shall be all seen standing at the right hand of Christ in white raiment, with the triple crown of glory joy, and righteousness upon their heads, being an innumerable company which no man can number !

3. This year the upright are to have dominion over the wicked. The tables will be turned, and the scene

of this world will be quite altered, and turned upside down; the wicked proud, who refused or disdained to set the poor believer with the dogs of their flocks, will be standing at the bar like a company of trembling pannels waiting for their sentence, when the poor believer that was contemned by them will be sitting upon the bench with Christ as his assessor, applauding him in all his judicial proceedings. " Know ye not that the saints shall judge the world ? yea, Know ye not that the saints shall judge angels ?" Then shall that scripture receive its full accomplishment, Psal. cxlix. 5—9.

4. This year Christ will confess his redeemed ones before his Father, and before his angels, who confessed and owned him before men, saying, " Lo, I and the children whom thou hast given me." And not only will he acknowledge, but he will acquit them of all the charges and accusations that were laid against them by the devil and the world, their sins shall be " blotted out, when this time of refreshing shall come from the presence of the Lord."

5. This year the marriage of the Lamb is to be consummate with the most triumphant solemnity, so as the very arches of heaven will echo and resound, while the redeemed are crying one to another, " Let us be glad and rejoice, for the marriage of the Lamb is come, and his bride hath made herself ready." Then shall that word receive its full accomplishment, Psal. xlv. 14, 15, " She shall be brought unto the King in raiment of needle-work : the virgins her companions that follow her shall be brought unto thee. With gladness and rejoicing shall they be brought : they shall enter into the King's palace," and take possession of these thrones that were prepared for them before the foundation of the world, and so they shall spend this endless year in following the Lamb, and singing, " Salvation to our God that sits upon the throne, and to the Lamb for ever and ever." Thus I have given you an account of the long year of the redeemed, which is

from everlasting to everlasting its several periods, and some hints of the transactions of each period; but the ten thousandth part cannot be told of what has been done, and is yet to be done in them, for the redeemed of the Lord.

The great question whether the year of applied Redemption be yet come to us, with several exhortations, &c.

O SIRS, what year is it with you yet? You are all under the year of revealed and published redemption, but that will not prove you to be among the redeemed of the Lord. The great question is, Whether the year of applied redemption be come to you, yea or not? You heard what things are commonly done in the year of applied redemption; try whether they be done upon your souls in particular. Has the hail-storm from mount Sinai swept away the refuge of lies? Has the water so overflowed your hiding place, that you was shut up to the faith? you found no place in heaven or in earth to hide you in, but in him who is "a hiding-place from the wind, and a covert from the tempest, as rivers of water in a dry place, as the shadow of a great rock in a weary land?"—This year the dead are raised unto life; and therefore I ask, Has the Spirit of life which is in Christ Jesus entered into thy soul? If so, then thou wilt not find thy life in thy hand, as the hypocrite, but thou wilt find thy life to be in thy head, and be ready to say, I am dead, and my life is hid with Christ in God. Again, this year the blind eyes are opened; and therefore I ask, Hast thou received thy sight? Can you say with the poor man, "How he opened mine eyes I know not; but this I know, once I was blind, but now I see?" I see such form and comeliness in Christ, that he is in mine eye "more glorious and excellent than all the mountains of prey." Again, this year the kingdom of God is reared up in the soul; and therefore I ask, Who bears the principal sway within? Who sits on the throne of thy heart?

Christ, or any of his rivals? If Christ have the throne, you will treat self, sin, the world, and every thing that would rival him, as usurpers and enemies; saying with David, " Do not I hate them that hate thee? and am not I grieved with those that rise up against thee?" Again, you heard that this year the prodigal son is brought home to his Father's house from the far country where he was starving; and therefore I ask, Have you yet broken your Father's bread? have you in and by the word tasted that the Lord is gracious? have you been made to say, " Thy word was found by me, and I did eat it, and it was to me the joy and rejoicing of my heart?" If so, then the year of thy redemption is come. Again, this year the guilty condemned criminal is vested with a law-biding righteousness; and therefore I ask, Have you laid aside your filthy rags, and put on your elder brother's robe? I mean, have you renounced your own righteousness as dung and loss, and submitted to the righteousness of God, saying, " In the Lord have I righteousness and strength, in him will I be justified, and will glory?"—Again, this year King Solomon is crowned and married; and therefore I ask, Hast thou by faith gone forth from sin, self, and the world, and beheld him with the crown upon his head? Did his matchless glory captivate thy heart, so that thou wast made to say, " I am the Lord's, and I will henceforth be called by his name?" Art thou resolved that from this time forth, through grace thou wilt keep the bed of thy heart and soul for him, and that he shall lie as a bundle of myrrh between thy breasts?—Again, this year the poor bankrupt beggared sinner finds the pearl of great price; and therefore I ask, if you have acted as the wise merchant, selling all, that you may cleave to him as your only riches, saying with Paul, " Yea doubtless, I count all things but loss, for the excellency of the knowledge of Christ Jesus my Lord?" Do you esteem him, and the riches of grace that are in him? for " to you that believe he is precious."—Again, this year the soul seals the re-

cord of God; and therefore I ask, How do you hold
your claim to eternal life? Is God's grant of it, through
Christ in the covenant of grace and promise, your only
charter? Can you rejoice in the hope of the glory of
God, grounded on the bare word of God, as one that
findeth great spoils, saying, "This is all my salvation?
God hath spoken in his holiness, I will rejoice?"—
Again, this year the soul enters into the holiest upon a
state of fellowship and communion with God; and
therefore I ask, With whom is your fellowship? Is it
with the Father, and his Son Jesus Christ? If so, you
will have no fellowship with the unfruitful works of
darkness, you will be afraid of the least appearance of
sin, or temptation to it, lest it separate between you
and your God.—Again, this year the vessel of mercy
that was like a brand in the fire, is pluckt out, and
hung upon the nail fastened in a sure place; and therefore I ask, Where and on whom hangs the main stress
of thy salvation from sin, Satan, hell, and wrath? Dost
thou lay the weight where God has laid it, even upon
the foundation God has laid in Zion?—Again, this year
the foundation of a new temple is laid for God to dwell
in; and therefore I ask, art thou concerned to keep
the temple pure from every thing that has a tendency
to defile it? "The temple of God is holy; and if any
man defile the temple of God, him shall God destroy."
You will study to be holy in soul, body, and in all manner of conversation. Now, I say, try by these, or the
like questions, whether or not the year of applied redemption be come.

And if so, then I have a word of exhortation
to offer you. Is the year of thy redemption come?
Then,

1. Be exhorted to remember the year of thy redemption, both the year in which it was purchased, and the
year in which it was applied by he power of the eternal Spirit. The children of Israel are frequently commanded to remember the year and day in which God
brought them forth out of the land of Egypt, Deut.

xvi. 1, "Observe the month of Abib, and keep the pass-over unto the Lord thy God : for in the month of Abib the Lord thy God brought thee forth out of the land of Egypt." Were they obliged to remember their typical and temporal redemption? and shall not we much more remember the time of our spiritual and real redemption? It is indeed a time that is to be remembered through all generations of God's Israel.

2. Now, upon a thanksgiving day, celebrate the praises of your great Redeemer, who had the year of your redemption so much at his heart: Jer. xxxi. 11 —13, " The Lord redeemed Jacob, and ransomed him from the hands of them that were stronger than he : therefore come and let us sing in the heights of Zion." I remember it is said, Is. xxiv. 16, " From the ut-termost parts of the earth have we heard songs, even glory to the righteous ;" that is, unto Christ Jesus the righteous. It is, as I conceive, a promise of an echo that should be heard among the Gentile nations upon the publication of the year of redemption among them ; echo of praise should be heard rebounding to heaven upon the utterance of this joyful sound, which you have been hearing this day, and the days bygone. O there-fore let songs be heard among you from this wing of the earth, glory, glory, glory to Christ Jesus the right-eous. Glory to him, who though he be the mighty God, yet was made of a woman, took on him my na-ture, that he might become my kinsman, and have the right of my redemption. Glory to him, who though he be the great Lawgiver, was made under the law, that I might not sink under the curse and condemnation of it for ever. Glory to him who laid the foundation of the house of mercy, which shall be built up for ever, and has brought me within the walls thereof, and given me a name and place there, even an everlasting name that shall not be cut off. Glory to him that has rent the vail of the temple from top to bottom, so that I see now there is no impediment on God's part to hinder my access unto God and glory. Glory to that right-

eous one who is become the Lord my righteousness. having magnified the law and made it honourable, and the Lord is well pleased for his righteousness' sake. Glory to him that has finished transgression, and made an end of sin ; and it is so much ended, that it shall never have power to condemn me ; he " condemned sin in the flesh : and therefore there is no condemnation to them that are in Christ Jesus." Glory to the great Redeemer, that has confirmed the covenant, and made it sure with his own blood, so that the mountains shall depart, and the hills be removed, but his covenant of peace shall never depart. Glory to him that entered the territories of death, the king of terrors, and came forth again like a renowned conqueror, carrying the keys of hell and death in his hand. Glory to him that has quenched the flames of wrath with his own blood, that would have consumed me for ever, and that through him God is a God of peace, and he is declared to be so by the resurrection of Christ Jesus from the dead ; so that I can now take up that song, Is. xii. 1, 2, " Though thou wast angry with me, yet thine anger is turned away, and thou hast comforted me. The Lord is become my salvation," &c. O glory to the righteous one, who as he was delivered for my offences, so he is risen again for my justification, and I am discharged of my debt in him ; he being justified, I am acquitted, and can say, " Who can lay any thing to my charge ?" O glory to Christ Jesus the righteous, that because he lives, I shall live also : and " though worms shall destroy this body, yet in my flesh shall I see God." O glory to him that is ascended to heaven as my forerunner, and to be an advocate for me with his Father and my Father, with his God and my God, and I look for him to come the second time without sin to my everlasting salvation. Thus, I say, let these or the like songs be sent up as an echo of praise from the uttermost parts of the earth. And to quicken you unto this exercise, consider,

1st, It is commanded and required of you, as a due

debt for his kindness to you, " Rejoice in the Lord, ye
righteous : and shout for joy, all ye that are upright in
heart."

2dly, It is commended as a suitable and agreeable
exercise ; " Praise is comely for the upright :" Psal.
xcii. 1, 2, " It is a good thing to give thanks unto the
Lord, and to sing praises unto thy name, O Most High ;
to show forth thy loving-kindness in the morning, and
thy faithfulness every night."

3dly, This is the very design of your formation, especially as one of the redeemed of the Lord : "This
people have I formed for myself, that they may show
forth my praise."

4hly, The more you sing his praises, the more occasion you shall have to sing : the thankful beggar is best
served ; and the thankful believer shall be made fat,
and have his mouth more and more filled with the good
of God's chosen.

5thly, This will be your occupation for ever in the
land of praise that is above, to sing the praises of the
great Redeemer, as you see, Rev. v. 9, 10. And
therefore you should even be lisping out the song of
praise in a strange land.

6thly, It is for the honour of your Redeemer, that
you celebrate his praises : " Whoso offereth praise
glorifieth me," says the Lord, Psal. l. 23. This is all
the revenue that he receives either from the church
militant or triumphant, Psal. lxv. 1, " Praise waiteth
for thee, O God, in Zion." And sure if you be among
the number of the redeemed, you will not deny or
withhold the Redeemer's tribute.

Quest. How shall we praise him ?

Answ. 1. O praise him by believing in him and on
him. Abraham, the father of the faithful, glorified
him by believing, so should all the seed of Abraham ;
" He staggered not at the promise through unbelief;
but was strong in the faith, giving glory to God." It
is for the honour of your Redeemer that you give credit to his word of promise, and that you trust and cre-

dit him with all your concerns, in time and through
eternity.

2. Praise him by thinking much upon him : " While
I was musing, the fire burned ; then spake I with my
lips." When the heart indites a good matter concerning him, the tongue will be as the pen of a ready writer.
O, says David, " My meditation of him shall be sweet,
and I will be glad in the Lord." And let your thoughts
of him be high and raised thoughts, saying, " Whom
have I in heaven but thee ? and there is none in all the
earth that I desire besides thee."

3. O praise your Redeemer, by commending him
unto others, and by studying to make his name to be
remembered for ever. This was the practice of the
spouse and bride of Christ, Psal. xlv. 17, and Cant. v.
10. You can do him no greater honour, than to make
the favour of him known in all places, and in all com-
panies, where you have occasion to appear.

4. O praise him by a single regard unto his preceptive, and a holy submission unto his providential will.
When he manifests his commanding will, be ready to
run his errands, and do whatsoever he commands you ;
and when he brings you under affliction, lay yourselves
at his feet, and say, " Here am I, let him do to me as
he sees meet."

5. Praise him by a steadfast and resolute owning him
and his truths, his ways, his ordinances, his worship, in
this day of blasphemy against him, contending earnestly
for the faith delivered to the saints ; and in your sphere,
testify against every thing that has a tendency to bring
a reflection upon his glory.

6. Praise him by inviting others to join with you in
celebrating his praise. O, will the soul say, I am under such a burden of obligations to him, that I would
even invite the whole creation, angels and men, sun,
moon, and stars, to join issue with me, in helping me
to lift up his great and glorious name : " O magnify
the Lord with me, and let us exalt his name together."

This was frequently David's practice, Psal. ciii. 20—22, and Psal. cxlviii. throughout to the end.

I conclude at present with a word of exhortation unto all in general.   O sirs, what shall I tell you, the year of jubilee, the year of release and redemption, is come ; and I tell you that it is even come to you; to every soul hearing me I proclaim the acceptable year of the Lord, as well as the day of vengeance from our God against all that will not embrace it.   We come in the name of the Lord of hosts to proclaim a purchased redemption to every one of you ; " That God was in Christ reconciling the world unto himself, not imputing their trespasses unto them."   O let this joyful sound be received, let this acceptable year of the Lord be accepted of you by faith, and let your soul say, " O blessed be he that cometh in the name of the Lord to save us."

I told you in the doctrinal part what great and glorious things are done for sinners in the year of exhibit or revealed redemption ; O improve the day, the year of your merciful visitation.

1. In this year light is arisen to you who were sitting under Pagan, Popish, and Prelatical darkness, even the light of a gospel-revelation.   And therefore let me exhort and beseech you to beware of continuing under the power of darkness, beware of continuing ignorant and blind, as to the knowledge of that Redeemer, that life and immortality that is brought to light by the gospel ; for ignorance of God, where the gospel-light shines, will be punished with a double vengeance ; Christ will come, " in flaming fire, to take vengeance on all them that know not God, and obey not the gospel."

2. I was telling you that this year of exhibit redemption the throne of grace is set up among a people, and proclamations of grace issued forth from it to the wretched, miserable, blind, and poor, and naked.   And therefore, O let me beseech you to come to this throne of grace, " that ye may obtain mercy, and find grace

to help you in time of need." And let not a sense of sin and unworthiness keep you back; for a throne of grace is not made for the worthy, but for the unworthy, it is made for beggars, for bankrupts, for these that are undone, and the throne of grace has its standing by liberality.

3. This year God is planting his batteries against the high imaginations of the heart, and summons rebels to surrender their hearts unto him. And therefore open the gates, saying, " Lift up your heads, O ye gates, and be ye lift up, ye everlasting doors, and the King of glory shall come in."

4. This year Jacob's ladder is set up that reaches to heaven. And therefore let every man try if he can scale heaven by it, in order to recover that glory and happiness which we all lost, by the sin of the first Adam.

5. This year the fountain of the great deeps of the love of God in Christ are broken up, good-will toward man upon earth is proclaimed. And therefore let every man cast himself into the arms of a God of love and mercy : " How excellent is thy loving-kindness, O God! therefore the sons of men shall put their trust under the shadow of thy wings."

6. This year God reveals, and brings near his righteousness to you who are guilty criminals ; in this year the righteousness is revealed, offered, presented to you. And therefore take the benefit of it, submit to it, put it on, that you may stand in judgment.

7. This year the fruits and leaves of the tree of life are scattered and shaken in our valley of vision. And therefore gather, apply, and eat, that you may be filled and healed ; O taste of the bunches of the grapes of the true vine, and your souls shall live ; O apply the healing leaves of his promises, that you may partake of the good promised.

8. This year the pure river of water of life runs from under the throne of God, it runs even in our streets and broad ways. And therefore " whosoever will, let

him come and drink :" O poor dying sinner, taste but
of this water, and it shall be in thee "a well of water
springing up unto everlasting life."

9. This year the manna of heaven is rained down,
God's banqueting house is opened, he is making to
you a feast of fat things.   And therefore, O starving
sinner, come, and take, and eat and drink abundantly;
for there is bread enough here, and to spare : and as
every man and woman in the camp had a right to gather the manna, so has every soul a right to take Christ
and to eat his flesh, and drink his blood, by an applying
faith to make use of him for wisdom, righteousness,
sanctification, and redemption.

10. This year the city of refuge is standing open,
that every sinner that has slain his soul by sin may
flee in for shelter from avenging wrath.   And therefore, O turn in to your strong-hold, for you are prisoners of hope ; you have as good a right to flee to
Christ for shelter, as ever the manslayer had to run to
the city of refuge : and, let me tell you, all refuge will
fail you but this only ; none of the other cities of Israel, nor yet the man's own home, could be a shelter to
him ; so here.

11. *Lastly*, This year Christ's testament and latter-
will is opened, and opened to all the hearers of the
gospel, and every man allowed and required to put in
for his share of the legacies, yea, to claim the whole
legacies of the testament.   And therefore, O let us
enter, "lest a promise being left us of entering into his
rest, any of us should seem to come short of it ;"   O
set to your seal to the testament by believing, which
Christ has sealed with the blood of his heart; and let
not unbelief or Satan cheat you out of your souls, when
you have such a good charter for your salvation, and
the command of God to use it, and lay hold on it,
John v. 39, "Search the scriptures, for in them ye
think ye have eternal life, and they are they which testify of me."

Gospel Consolation to the Redeemed.

1 THY kind Kinsman, the avenger of thy blood, he will surely pay thy debt, and stand between thee and all the charges that either law, or conscience, or justice, or the devil, or the world has against thee. Would he ever avenge thy blood upon Satan, and yet suffer thee to sink under the charge of the law of justice? No, no; " he stands at the right hand of the poor, to save him from them that would condemn his soul." And therefore thou mayest lift up thy head with joy and boldness, saying, "Who can lay any thing to my charge? It is God that justifieth; who is he that condemneth? It is Christ that died," &c. Yea, at the same time that he spoiled principalities and powers on the cross, he tore the hand-writing that was against thee, nailing it to his cross.

2. Here is comfort against remaining corruption and indwelling sin. Perhaps thou art crying, " O wretched man that I am!" Well, here is help at hand; he that has avenged thy blood on Satan, by bruising his head, he will never suffer his work to stand long in thy soul; no, no; down they must go, all his strong-holds shall go to ruin. Art thou pestered with the prevalency of unbelief, aye turning thee away from the living God? Well, the Redeemer's vengeance will destroy that, for it is one of the works of the devil; he is " the Author and Finisher of faith;" and therefore he must answer his name and fulfil in thee the whole good pleasure of his goodness, and the work of faith with power." Art thou pestered with remaining enmity? Well, this is a work of the devil, to fill the mind of man with enmity and prejudice against God, who is love; and therefore the day of vengeance is in his heart against that also: he has already slain the enmity on God's part by his blood, and he will slay the enmity on thy part more and more by his Spirit; and as he carries on the work of faith, he will also carry on the work of love; for faith

worketh by love ; and the Spirit of faith is also a spirit
of love. Art thou groaning under remaining ignorance,
that thou cannot win to more knowledge of Christ, and
of God in him, more knowledge of his will ?   Well,
this is a work of the devil, his kingdom is a kingdom of
darkness ; and the Redeemer's vengeance shall be upon it also ; for he is " the true light, that lighteth every
man that cometh into the world ;" and as he has already begun to shine into thy heart by the light of the
knowledge of his glory ; so thou shalt find his goings
forth prepared as the morning, and thy path shall be
" as the shining light, which shineth more and more
unto the perfect day."   Art thou burdened with the
legality of thy spirit, a strong inclination to rest on the
works of righteousness done by thee, rather than upon
Christ and his righteousness, the alone foundation that
God hath laid in Zion ?   Well, here is comfort, this
work of the devil shall be destroyed more and more
by the Avenger of thy blood. " The secret of the Lord
is with them that fear him, and to them will he show
his covenant." He will more and more wean thy heart
from the way of works, and reconcile thee more and
more unto the way of grace through Jesus Christ ; for
he has said, " That grace shall reign through righteousness unto eternal life, by Jesus Christ our Lord."   In
a word, not to multiply particulars, whatever sin or
lust usurps the throne of Christ in thy heart, down it
shall go, the Redeemer's vengeance shall be upon it as
a work of the devil ; for he has said, " I will subdue
their iniquities.   From all idols will I cleanse them.
Sin shall not have dominion over you : for ye are not
under the law, but under grace."

3. Is Christ the Avenger of thy blood upon Satan ?
Then surely he will not suffer that enemy continually
to harass thee with his fiery darts ; no, he will still this
enemy and avenger ; he will either rebuke the tempter,
or else his grace shall be sufficient for thee, and his
strength shall be so perfected in thy weakness, that,
through thy God assisting thee, thou shalt leap over

his walls, and break his bows of steel in pieces; yea, his faithfulness is engaged that he " will not suffer thee to be tempted above what thou art able to bear, but with the temptation will provide a way to escape, that thou mayest be able to bear it."

4. Art thou covered with the dark clouds of desertion, crying, " O that I knew where I might find him ?" Here is comfort, he that has avenged thy blood upon Satan, he will not himself keep thee long in torment with his own absence; "he will not contend for ever, neither will he be always wroth; lest the spirit should fail before him, and the soul which he has made. Weeping may endure for a night, but joy cometh in the morning. For a small moment have I forsaken thee, but with great mercies will I gather thee. In a little wrath I hid my face from thee, for a moment; but with everlasting kindness will I have mercy on thee, saith the Lord thy Redeemer."

5. Here is comfort against the fears of apostacy, or falling away to the reproach of religion, and the ruin of thy soul for ever. He that has avenged thy blood and pulled thee out of the paw of that enemy, he will not quit thee; all his saints are in his hand; he keeps them by his power through faith unto salvation, and no man, no devil, shall be able to pluck thee out of his hand. And therefore thou may sing and say, " Though I fall, I shall arise; for the Lord upholdeth me with his hand."

6. Here is comfort, he that has avenged thy blood, he will supply thy wants, both outward and inward. Would he ever do so much for thee, and then suffer thee to starve? No, no; " My God shall supply all your need, according to his riches in glory by Christ Jesus." Thy Kinsman is full handed, he doth not want, and thou shall want nothing that is good for thee.

7. The Avenger of thy blood will take care of thee in public reelings; when the mountains are removed, and the waters roar, he sitteth upon the floods, and he will make all things work together for thy good.

8. The Avenger of thy blood will pity and sympathize with thee in all thy afflictions.

9. He will strengthen thee for the work he calls thee to, whatever weakness be in thee, for " he giveth power to the faint."

10. *Lastly,* The Avenger of thy blood, he will make thee victorious over death, the last enemy : " Death shall be swallowed up in victory." He has made the grave a bed of rest, a passage to thy Father's house and kingdom, and he himself will carry thee through Jordan ; and therefore thou mayest say in faith, " This God is our God for ever and ever ; and he will be our guide even unto death.'

Exhortations to Sinners to accept of the Liberty proclaimed in the Gospel ; with Answers to Objections.

O SIRS, the devil has made prisoners of the whole family of Adam ; because we rebelled against the words of God, and contemned the counsel of the Most High, therefore we are made to sit in the darkness and the shadow of death, bound and manacled by the god of this world, with the cords of our own iniquity as with fetters of iron : but I bring you glad tidings of great joy, our Goel, our Redeemer and Avenger, he has broken up the devil's prison, he has broke the gates of brass, and cut the bars of iron in sunder : and he comes and cries to his prisoners to come forth, to them that sit in darkness, Show yourselves. And therefore we, as the heralds of this great King which has the armies which are in heaven following him, and whose name is written upon his thigh and vesture, " The KING of kings, and LORD of lords ;" I say, we as heralds sent forth in his name, proclaim the year of jubilee unto you, the year of release and freedom from your bondage and captivity unto this enemy. The Son of God makes you free, and therefore be ye free indeed : he " proclaims liberty to the captives, and the opening of the prison to them that are bound ;" liberty

from the guilt of sin, that it may not condemn ; liberty
from the power of sin, that it may not reign in your
mortal bodies ; liberty from the filth and defilement of
sin, that it may not obstruct fellowship between God
and you ; liberty from the law as a covenant, that it
shall not have power to condemn you ; liberty from
the power of death and the grave, that it may not sting
you, or have the victory over you ; liberty from this
present evil world, that it may not insnare you ; liberty
from all your enemies, that you may serve the Lord
without fear, in holiness and righteousness all the days
of your lives.   O sirs, I proclaim this acceptable year
of liberty and release from captivity to all these enemies unto you.   O, for the Lord's sake, accept of the
liberty that your Kinsman and Avenger of your blood
proclaims to you his kinsfolk.

    This exhortation and call to accept of liberty from
the power of darkness, from the dominion of Satan the
prince of darkness, has such a charm with it to every
rational and thinking person, that one would think
there needed no motives or arguments to persuade
people to fall in with it.   Folk that are in hard temporal bondage and thraldom will purchase their liberty
with the most valuable things they have in the world ;
and they who are in possession of their liberty, will spend
not only their estates and substance, but their very
blood in the maintenance and defence thereof; folk will
quit their lives rather than give up even their temporal
liberty.   Who doubts but if a company of men were shut
up in a prison by their powerful enemy, who designs their
death, if one more powerful should come and vanquish him,
and break up the prison doors, and call the prisoners
to go free ; I say, who doubts but, in that case, every
prisoner would make his escape, every one would run
out of prison faster than another ?   But, sirs, although this liberty that our Kinsman proclaims unto
us be infinitely more valuable than all the temporal
liberties of the world ; yet sad experience lets us know,
that the greater part of the hearers of the gospel, to

whom the Lord's jubilee and year of freedom is proclaimed, they choose rather to be the devil's bond-men, and to continue under the bonds of iniquity that he has wreathed about them, than to accept of this glorious liberty that I am speaking of; Satan has so bewitched and intoxicated them with sin, that they lie still in the devil's fetters, as if their bondage were perfect freedom and liberty, and never reckon themselves at liberty, unless they be " walking according to the course of the world, according to the prince of the power of the air, the spirit that now worketh in the children of disobedience." And therefore I say, though one would think men needed no motive to persuade them to accept of liberty ; yet such is the backwardness of the heart of man, through the power that Satan and sin has upon them, that we must not only proclaim liberty to them, but we must use arguments to persuade them to it : and therefore allow me, in the name of our kind Friend and Avenger, to bespeak you in a rational way ; for we are dealing with men and women that must be " drawn with the cords of love, and the bands of a man." O that God by his Spirit may both persuade and enable you to comply with the call.

Motive 1. Will you consider the evil and danger of that bondage and captivity you are under. It is the most comfortless captivity ; no comfort in the pit of sin, which is the devil's prison, therefore called "a pit wherein there is no water," Zech. ix. 11. Indeed Satan, he promises pleasure, profit, and comfort in the way of sin, and in his service ; but, alas ! it is but like the crackling of thorns under a pot, or like a glass of sweet poison, which so soon as it is swallowed down, it is like the gall of asps in the bowels : " There is no peace, saith my God, to the wicked." The bondage thou art under, O sinner, it is a wearisome bondage ; sinners are said to " weary themselves to commit iniquity." Many a wearisome day has the sinner in the devil's service ; he leads them about, as it were in a chain, and makes them to drudge in gratifying this,

and that, and the other lust. It is a disgraceful bondage to be the devil's drudge, who is himself " reserved
in chains under darkness, unto the judgment of the
great day." Oh who would choose to serve, and to
be servant unto that chained roaring lion ! It is the
most cruel bondage that ever was ; this enemy and
avenger, he handles poor creatures that are under
his power, in the most barbarous manner, torturing
both soul and body ; you have an emblem of his cruelty,
in that poor man, Mark v. 2, 5, and Luke viii. 27. It
is a terrible bondage, there they are said to dwell in
darkness, and in the regions of the shadow of death,
where there is nothing but horror and terror, a terror
to themselves, and to others round about them. O sirs,
who would not accept of liberty from such a captivity
and bondage ?

Mot. 2. By way of motive, will you consider what
kind of freedom and liberty the Son of God, the
Avenger of our blood, offers and presents you with ; it
is a liberty never enough to be wondered at, that ever
the Son of God should have taken our nature, a nature inferior to that of angels, in order to his having
the right of redemption as our Kinsman and Avenger,
who had violate the law, trampled upon the authority
of his Father ; that he should come from Edom and
Bozrah, dying his garments with his own blood, and
the blood of his enemies in order to our release. Oh,
may we not cry out with admiration, as the church
doth in the first verse, " Who is this that cometh !"
O who would ever have thought that he would have undertaken such an expedition on our behalf ! And then
will you consider, that this liberty we proclaim to you,
it was purchased with a great sum, as that captain said,
Acts xxii. 28, " With a great sum obtained I this freedom." It cost our Kinsman dear, not silver and gold,
but the very blood of his heart. It is the most real
freedom ; it is not an imaginary thing ; no, " If the
Son make you free, you shall be free indeed." It is a
glorious freedom ; you shall be preferred unto the glo-

rious liberty of the children of God, you shall be fellow-heirs with the general assembly of the first-born,
who are all heirs of God, joint-heirs with Christ. And
your liberty shall not last for a day, a year, or an age,
but it shall last for ever ; you shall have a final discharge
and manumission, neither sin nor Satan shall any more
have dominion over you, if you will accept of this liberty that our Kinsman and Avenger of our blood offers
and proclaims to you. Indeed Satan and sin may
tempt you, and endeavour to reduce you under your
former slavery, but they shall never be able, no man,
no devil, shall ever be able to pluck you out of the
hands of our Kinsman ; you shall be kept by the power
of God through faith unto salvation. O sirs, shall not
such a liberty be greedily accepted ? Unto all I shall
only add, that although the Son of God paid dear for
this liberty that he proclaims to you, yet you have it for
nothing ; no terms, no hard condition required of you,
only accept of freedom, and you shall be free indeed :
no money, no price, only go forth.

Mot. 3. Consider, sirs, that the devil he has no law-
right to detain you in his captivity ; he lost his right
when justice was satisfied by the blood of our Kinsman. What right has the jailor to keep a person in
prison when the judge is satisfied by a friend, and the
debt completely paid to the creditor ? So that it is
wrongous imprisonment, especially after the King's
proclamation of liberty is issued out. But I will tell
you more, the devil as he has no right, so he has no
power to detain you prisoners or captives against your
own will. Indeed the devil has blinded the understanding, and so perverted the will, that they are volunteers in his service, they willingly walk after his
commandment ; but the devil can force no man's will ;
if once you were but willing, heartily willing, to be liberate
from Satan's bondage, the business were done. O sirs,
put your wills in the hand of our Kinsman, that according to his promise, he may make you willing in the
day of his power. But O what encouragement is it

to you to accept of freedom, that the devil has neither
right nor power to detain you his prisoners contrary to
your own will.

Mot. 4. By accepting of this liberty, you will make
glad the heart of Christ, and make our Kinsman to see
the travail of his soul.   He travailed in soul in order to
obtain our freedom from the power of sin and Satan;
yea, he travailed till his soul was exceeding sorrowful
even unto death : O will you be so unkind after all his
hard and sore travail, as to deny him that satisfaction
which he desires so much, namely, to see you fairly
freed from the hands of Satan ?   And, on the other
hand, it will affront him, it will grieve him to the heart,
if you remain in your chains under the power of Satan,
refusing to be delivered from the power of that enemy,
after he has invaded his kingdom, and destroyed him
through his own death.   O how did he weep over Jerusalem, who refused the relief and freedom that he
proclaimed to them in the days of his flesh ! he said
with tears, "O that thou, even thou, in this thy day,
hadst known the things which belong unto thy peace !
He would have gathered them as the hen gathers her
brood under her wings, but they would not."

Mot. 5. You will gratify the devil, if you reject this
offered liberty, and give him an occasion of insulting
over our glorious Redeemer, as if his bondage were better than Christ's liberty that he has been at so much
cost to purchase.   And O, can you find in your hearts
to furnish that enemy with an opportunity of upbraid-
ing our glorious Redeemer ?   But, on the other hand,
if you accept of this liberty and freedom which Christ
offers you, it will gall the enemy at the very heart ; for,
as I was saying in the doctrinal part, it is a day of
galling vengeance unto Satan, when he sees a poor
creature going out of his prison, and going into Christ's
side.   So then, would you do the devil a disservice, (I
am sure you owe him nothing,) then accept of the freedom and liberty which our glorious Avenger purchased

with his blood, and proclaims to every one of you in this glorious gospel.

To all which I shall only add, that if you do not, your ruin is of yourselves, and your blood shall be upon your own head. O how just will your condemnation be, who had liberty in your offer, and yet choosed rather to continue in the devil's chains! Surely your bonds cannot miss to be made stronger, and your condemnation shall be more just than that of the devil himself; for the devil never had liberty offered him, otherwise he would accept of it with all his heart; but for sinners under the drop of the gospel, they had life, liberty, and salvation proclaimed to them, and yet preferred death to life, bondage to liberty, damnation to salvation.

Object. You press us to accept of liberty from Satan's bondage; but what if Christ never designed or decreed that liberty for me, if I be not among the elect, I shall never get free of my bondage. *Answ.* This objection is just one of the wiles that the devil makes use of to dissuade sinners from attempting to get free of his service and dominion; it is a mere sophism, and when it is rightly considered, it is as weak as water: for it is just all one as if a company of prisoners lying under sentence of death, when their prison-doors are opened, their jailor bound neck and heel, and the king's proclamation intimate to the prisoners to come forth; I say, it is just as if the prisoners in this case should begin to say, Though the prison be opened, and the king's proclamation read in our hearing; yet we do not know if the king has an intention or design in his heart, that we should take the advantage and make our escape, we do not know if he intends that we should lie continual prisoners; and therefore we will just lie still where we are. Who would not reckon the prisoners a company of madmen who would argue at such a rate? Why, how is the king's mind to be known, but by his overt act or proclamation? So here the devil tells you, that you need not accept of liberty from sin and Satan,

because you do not know if Christ has designed this
liberty for you.   Why, how shall you ever know the
mind of Christ but by his word, his proclamation of
grace, which is the very picture of his thoughts and
designs ? O sirs, look aye into the heart of God, and the
designs of God by his words of grace, his acts of grace,
his proclamations of grace ; and if you do, you shall
find nothing but grace and love, and mercy in his heart
to you : but if you will take the devil's way, and look
to God's heart and secret thoughts, without looking to
his words, and believing what he speaks to you, there is
no help for it, you shall perish with the devil.

   Object. You bid us accept of freedom from Satan's bondage ; but alas ! our bands are so strong
that we have no power to shake them off, or accept of
this liberty. *Answ.* The question between Christ and
you is not, Are you able to quit the devil's bondage
and slavery ?   But the question is, Are you willing ?
And if you be but willing to be made free, all the devils in hell cannot detain you.

   Object. There indeed lies the stress of the matter, my
will has got such a woeful cast, that I cannot get it
bended toward this offered freedom. *Answ.* If the
iron sinew of the obstinate will be too strong for thee
to bend, put it in the hand of Christ thy blessed Kinsman, that he may do the work for thee, " Thy people
shall be willing in the day of thy power."   And
O it is a sweet evidence of a soul already made willing,
that he is groaning under the sense of the backwardness of his heart to yield to the call of Christ.   And for
your encouragement to put your obstinate will in his
hand, you have him bound by promise to do the work,
even to take away the stony heart, and to give the heart
of flesh, that is, to master the enmity and obstinacy of
the heart and will against him : O plead the promise,
believe the promise, put him to his word, and pursue
him upon his word before a throne and court of grace ;
for he never said nay to a person that took this method.
And then it is the pleasure of Christ to take vengeance

upon Satan, by driving out the devil's poison of enmity and obstinacy from the heart of the sinner. And therefore let the words of my text be a ground of faith to you as to this matter, "For the day of vengeance is in mine heart, and the year of my redeemed is come."

Trusting in Christ explained and exhorted to.

1. It necessarily supposes a deep and hearty concern about salvation or deliverance from that thraldom, bondage and misery that we are brought under by Satan and his first-born sin. O sirs, you who never yet saw yourselves to be the devil's prisoners, under the power of the guilt and filth of sin by virtue of a broken law, and who were never brought under a deep and hearty concern how to make your escape, crying, with the jailor, "What shall I do to be saved?" whatever may be your pretensions of trusting in Christ, they are but all hypocritical and notional; for "the law is our schoolmaster to lead us unto Christ, that we may be justified by faith."

2. This trust has in it a cordial approbation of the person and undertakings of our blessed Kinsman and Redeemer, in order to our freedom and delivery from this bondage to sin and Satan, and approbation of it as a method worthy every way of Infinite Wisdom, and of all others most suited and adapted to the glory of God, and safety of the sinner. Whenever a sinner is awakened, and hath his eyes opened to take up his lost and ruined condition, these two questions very naturally cast up, viz. how shall God be glorified? and how shall ever I be saved in a consistency with his glory? Now, when Christ is discovered, and the method of salvation through him opened to the soul's view, it is made to see these questions sweetly answered in him, it sees how Christ restores glory to God and to all his attributes, and salvation to the lost ruined sinner: "Mercy and truth are met together, righteousness and peace kiss

each other," in this method of salvation ; and this draws out the soul's cordial approbation of this glorious device, saying, O " this is my rest, for my soul desires it, and likes it well."

3. It has in it a renouncing of all other ways and means of relief, saying with these, Jer. iii. 23, " In vain is salvation expected from the hills and multitude of mountains ; in the Lord alone is the salvation of his people." And Hos. xiv. 3, " Ashur shall not save us, we will not ride upon horses, neither will we say any more to the work of our hands, Ye are gods." Phil. iii. 3, " For we are the circumcision, which worship God in the spirit, who rejoice in Christ Jesus, having no confidence in the flesh." O sirs, Christ is never the first course or method that a sinner takes for salvation, no, no, he is aye the last shift ; many a way will the man try before he land in Christ. While in a state of profanity, living in a manifest contempt of the law, the man, he ordinarily trusts to the general mercy of God, imagining with some, that it is enough to bring them to heaven, if they have as much time in a dying hour, as to cry, God have mercy upon my soul. When the man is brought, through a spirit of conviction, to see that this will not do, he then runs to the way of works by the law, and tries what he can do for his own salvation, by his reformation, his prayers, tears, vows, penances, and the like. When the man has wearied himself in pursuit of salvation in this way, and finds the law so holy, so spiritual and extensive, that it is impossible for him to obey it perfectly, then he will join Christ and the law together, I mean Christ, and his law-works, and thinks with himself, Now I cannot scale heaven, or make out salvation by my own obedience, it is so defective ; but wherein I am deficient in obedience to it, I will rely upon Christ's righteousness to supply my defects. Thus he takes the new cloth of Christ's righteousness to patch up his own filthy rags. And here it is that many a man stays, without going a step fur-

ther, seeking salvation by Christ and the law together, which is the thing the apostle calls a " seeking righteousness, not directly, but, as it were, by the works of the law." But when a sinner is brought really to trust in the Lord Jesus, he receives him, and rests upon him alone as he is offered in the gospel, disclaiming his own righteousness as filthy rags, saying with the apostle, " What things were gain to me, those I counted loss for Christ, yea, doubtless, I count all things but loss, for the excellency of the knowledge of Christ Jesus my Lord."

4. This trusting in Christ carries in it a satisfaction with the warrant that God affords in his word for intermeddling with Christ and his salvation. It is a very ordinary case with these that are awakened to a due concern about salvation, to have this language in their mouths, O it is true, Christ is a suitable and sufficient Saviour, able to save to the uttermost ; but, alas ! I do not know if I have a right or warrant to intermeddle with him. I am afraid I am guilty of presumption. Now, when a man believes in Christ, or trusts in him for salvation from sin and Satan, hell and wrath, he looks to the word, and .there he sees that Christ is held out as the ordinance of God for the salvation of sinners of mankind ; that this Son is given to us, born to us; there he finds the word of grace and salvation indorsed and directed to all and every creature, that " the promise is even to us and our children, and to all that are afar off, and to as many as the Lord our God shall call" by the joyful sound ; there he finds God commanding and requiring every man to " believe in the name of his Son Jesus Christ, to look unto him and be saved." And upon these and the like grounds the man is persuaded that he has sufficient warrant to receive Christ, and rest the salvation of his soul upon him without danger of presumption ; and upon this he ventures his salvation upon him. O sirs, take care that you set the foot of faith upon a sicker ground ; and I do not know how our faith in

Christ can ever be well founded, without finding our warrant for it in the word; the word is the immediate ground of faith, and without it we could never believe, Psal. cxix. 49, " Remember the word, upon which thou hast caused thy servant to hope." Psal. cxxx. 5, " In his word do I hope."

5. Thus trusting in Christ, as our Avenger and Redeemer, has in it a firm and full persuasion of Christ's willingness and ability to rescue and deliver us from the hands of Satan and sin, and all our spiritual enemies; yea, a persuasion of his faithfulness, that, according to his promise, he will deliver. The poor soul is persuaded of his ability from the word, because there it finds the record of God concerning him, that he is " mighty to save, able to save to the uttermost all that come unto God through him." It is persuaded of his willingness, from the same record; because there he finds it said, " Come to me who will, I will in no wise cast out." O would he ever come upon such an expedition to avenge the quarrel of lost sinners, to "finish transgression and make an end of sin," if he were not willing to save a lost sinner that comes to him! It is persuaded of his faithfulness, that he will save according to his promise, because that he will pity and pardon, and heal and deliver, according to his promise, because it is impossible for God to lie. O " hath he said it, and will he not do it ?" yea, surely, " yet a little while, and he that shall come, will come, and will not tarry."

6. And more directly, When a person trusts this glorious Redeemer and Kinsman for salvation, he is not only persuaded in general of the power, goodness, and faithfulness, of the Lord Jesus; but he is persuaded of all this with particular application of him, and of salvation unto his own soul in particular; the man is confident, that whatever Christ has purchased with his blood, and whatever he has promised in the covenant, shall in due time be forthcoming to him, and he relies and rests on the security he finds in the word, in

the promise, or covenant of God, sealed with the blood of his blessed Kinsman ; he takes Christ as held out in his word of grace, and says, "This is all my salvation, God hath spoken in his holiness, I will rejoice ;" this is mine, and that is mine, and all is mine, because God hath spoken in his holiness ; I have his word for it, and that is enough : this faith is "the evidence of things not seen, the substance of things hoped for." And although God may see fit to defer the actual accomplishment of the promise, whereby his heart is made sick ; yet when he views the good things promised, faith reckons them its own, upon the security God has granted in the promise ; and therefore says with the church, Mic. vii. 7—9, "I will look unto the Lord : I will wait for the God of my salvation : my God will hear me. Though I sit in darkness, the Lord will be a light unto me ; he will bring me forth to the light, and I shall behold his righteousness." I do not say that this trust and confidence is aye alike strong in all believers, or yet in the self-same believer ; for sad experience makes it evident beyond all contradiction, that the believer's confidence of faith may be, and actually is, many times sadly shaken, through the prevalency of unbelief, the assaults of temptation, and providences seemingly running cross to the promise ; by reason of this, the poor believer has many doubts, many fears and staggerings, so that sometimes he is made to cry out, "Is his mercy clean gone? will he be favourable no more? doth his promise fail for evermore? One day I shall fall by the hand of Saul ;" and in his haste he is made to cry out, "All men are liars," the prophets of God not excepted. But these doubts, and fears, and staggerings, although they be in the believer, yet they are not in his faith ; these things argue the infirmity of his faith indeed ; but under all this, faith is fighting for the victory ; and as much faith in Christ as the man hath in exercise, so much confidence will he have anent the outmaking of the promise to him in particular ; and according to the degree of one's crediting the promise

with application to himself, so much confidence and
persuasion will he have.

But now, that I may clear this act of faith, or of
trusting in the Lord Jesus, a little farther to you, I
shall endeavour to illustrate it by two or three similitudes.

1. Then, it is just such another trust, as when you
trust a man of undoubted veracity and faithfulness.
When an honest man gives you his word, his promise,
whether it be a verbal word, or his written and sub-
scribed word, for any thing, you all know what it is in
such a case to trust him ; if a day of payment be spe-
cified in the promise, you are confident and persuaded
of payment against that day ; if there be no day named,
yet still you are confident, that in due time he will
make out his promise. After this manner Abraham,
the father of the faithful, believed the promise of God,
Rom. iv. 20, " He staggered not at the promise of
God through unbelief ; but was strong in faith, giving
glory to God. O sirs, have you trust and confidence to
put in the word of a man, will you take his promise,
and rest upon it with assured confidence ; and shall we
have no trust to put in the man Christ Jesus, in whose
mouth guile was never found, or in the report or record of God concerning him, for whom it is impossible
to lie ! Allow me to tell you, that every mere man,
whom you have trusted since you came into the world,
will stand in judgment and condemn you, saying, you
had confidence to put in me, but you had no confidence to put in a promising God in Christ. Will not
Christ say at the day of reckoning to unbelievers,
You trusted such a man's word, when he made a promise to you, but though you had my word, my oath,
my covenant, sealed with my blood, and though the
Three that bear record in heaven attested the truth of
the promise that I gave you ; yet you had no trust or
credit to give unto me, I could never obtain that
trust from you that you gave unto very ordinary persons, you treated me and my Father as though we had

been liars, dissemblers, and disingenuous? O how will the unbeliever be confounded at the day of reckoning when this shall be laid home to his door, by the great Judge of all the earth, the man Christ Jesus, the blessed Avenger of our blood upon Satan! he himself will then whet his glittering sword, and render vengeance to all that know not God, and obey not the gospel.

2. This trusting in Christ, is just such a trust as a man hath in a strong-hold or hiding-place to which he betakes himself for shelter and safety ; or such a trust as the chickens have under the wings of the hen, when she covers them with her feathers : Ruth ii. 12, " The Lord God of Israel reward thee, under whose wings thou art come to trust." Psal. xxxvi. 7, " How excellent is thy loving-kindness, O God! therefore the sons of men shall put their trust under the shadow of thy wings." Psal. xci. 4, " He shall cover thee with his feathers, and under his wings shalt thou trust: his truth shall be thy shield and buckler." O sinners, you lie exposed to the wrath of God, to the cruelty of Satan, that enemy and Avenger, that " goes about like a roaring lion, seeking whom he may devour ;" you are in danger of the curse of a broken law. Now to trust in Christ, is just to run in under the covert of his blood and righteousness, as the young chickens run in under the wings of the hen, or as the manslayer under the law did run into the city of refuge, and trusted that he was in safety there. O " turn to your strong-hold, ye prisoners of hope ;" for he is " a hiding-place from the storm and a covert from the tempest." Confide in his love, his promise, his providence, his righteousness, as a man doth in his house where he dwells, not being afraid of cold, or storm, or tempest, when he has got in under the roof of it.

3. This trusting in Christ our blessed Kinsman, is sometimes expressed by a leaning : Song viii. 5, " Who is this that cometh up from the wilderness, leaning upon her beloved ?" And so it alludes to a man lay-

ing his weight on a strong staff, which he knows will
not bow or break, or a man leaning upon the ground,
or upon a strong rock, which he knows is fully able to
bear his weight, and will not sink under him.

What Warrant we have to trust in Christ for Salvation.

1. The near relation that he stands under to you,
both by nature and office, may warrant and encourage
you to trust in him.   Will you not trust your Kinsman,
who, in resentment of your quarrel, has avenged you
upon the enemy that ruined you by bruising his head?
But Oh! say you, is he my Kinsman? I answer, He
is; for he is " God manifested in the flesh," his name
is " Immanuel, God with man, God with us;" he was
made of a woman, and took part of our flesh, and by
so doing has adorned our nature with a greater glory
than ever it had, while it shined with all the beauties and
glories wherewith it was adorned when it dropped out
of the Creator's fingers in innocency; yea, to a greater
glory than that of the angelical nature was ever advanced; for "he took not on him the nature of angels, but
the seed of Abraham."   And upon this ground let us
claim him as our Lord Jesus Christ, our Brother, our
elder Brother; for " he is not ashamed to call us brethren."   It is very remarkable, that Christ, while here
in a state of humiliation, commonly gloried in that
name of calling himself the Son of man, rather than
that of being the Son of God.   Why, what was the design of his making choice of that designation, but that
he might inculcate his relation upon us as our Kinsman, by virtue of his assuming our nature, that so we
might be encouraged to put our trust under the shadow of his wings?   But then, sirs, consider that Christ
is not only related to you by nature, but also by
office; he is the Prophet, Priest, and King of the
church; a Prophet to give wisdom to the ignorant;
a Priest to justify the guilty sinner; a King to subdue the enmity of the heart, and to deliver the

devil's captives; he is presented to us in the gospel
under each of these relative offices, that we, in a way
of believing, may be encouraged to trust him.   O sirs,
what is a Saviour for? is he not for a lost sinner?
Yea, surely, he himself tells us, that this was his very
errand, to "seek and save that which was lost; that
he came not to call the righteous but sinners to repentance."   What is a surety for, but for a broken bankrupt and dyvour?   And are you not such?   Yea,
surely, you and I are broken to all intents and purposes
in the first Adam, and to you he is presented in this
gospel upon this design, that you may, by trusting in
him, be put in a capacity to answer all the charges
that either law or justice have against you.   So then,
I say, let the near relation he stands under to you, both
by nature and office, encourage you to put your trust
under the shadow of his wings.

2. The express command of God may warrant and
encourage you to trust this blessed Kinsman and Relation of yours.   The Father commands you, by a proclamation from the excellent glory, saying, "Hear ye
him, for this is my beloved Son:" hence the apostle, 1
John iii. 23, speaks of this as the sum and substance of
all commands, yea as if this were the only command of God
to sinners, "This is his commandment, that ye believe
on the name of his Son Jesus Christ:" now, to believe
in Christ, and to trust him with our salvation, is one
and the same thing.   How frequently is this command inculcated, both in the Scriptures of the Old and
New Testament; and what is called believing in Christ
in the New Testament, is called trusting in the Lord
in the Old Testament: Is. xxvi. 4. "Trust ye in the
Lord for ever: for with the Lord JEHOVAH is everlasting strength.   Trust in him at all times; ye people,
pour out your hearts before him: God is a refuge for
us.   Selah."   O sirs, what can be a warrant for any
duty, if not the express command and authority of the
great God?   Do not imagine that it is presumption in
you to believe, or trust in the Lord Jesus (as described

before); no, no, a man can never be guilty of presumption in doing what God bids him do; yea, not
to do it, not to obey him in this matter, is to rush
upon his neck, to trample upon his authority. Do
not think that it is left optional to you whether
you trust him or not; no, the law is passed, and
you are concluded under its authority, and disobedience to it is as the sin of witchcraft. Do not
imagine there is no danger in sitting the command of
God in this matter; no, it is a command fenced with
the most severe penal sanction of any thing that ever
God commanded the children of men : " He that believeth not, is condemned already ; and the wrath of
God abideth on him."

3. Let the promise annexed unto believing or trusting engage you to trust your Kinsman, " He that believeth shall be saved. Whosoever believes in him
shall not perish, but have everlasting life." And therefore if you love your life, yea, the everlasting life of
your souls, incline your ears, come unto your Kinsman,
and intrust him with your everlasting all. This connection established between trusting and salvation,
makes on open door to every hearer of the gospel ; for
there is no doubt but faith is the duty of all by the
command of God, otherwise unbelief could not be their
sin ; now seeing the duty is to all, the promise of life
connected therewith must be to all likewise : so that is
true of every son of Adam, that if he believe he shall
be saved. But then consider, that the promise, yea,
all the promises of this glorious testament are indorsed
and directed to you as a warrant and encouragement
for you to trust in our blessed Kinsman. " To you is
the word of this salvation sent. The promise is unto
you, and to your seed, and to all that are afar off, and
to as many as the Lord our God shall call." I do not
think that the apostle's meaning was, that the promise
was theirs in possession before they believed it ; but it
was theirs in the exhibition, as a letter directed to a
person is his letter, because directed to him, even be-

fore it come to his hand, or before he break it up, and read the contents of it.

4. To encourage you to trust this blessed Friend, Kinsman, and Avenger, will you consider how pleasing and agreeable a thing it is to him to have poor sinners putting their trust under the shadow of his wings for safety. John vi. 26, says Christ there unto a company of men who were fond to know what the works of God were, that they might do the things that pleased him, "This (says he,) is the work of God, that ye believe in him, or trust in him whom he hath sent." As if he had said, God hath sent his Son upon an expedition unto this lower world, to satisfy justice, and to take vengeance upon the devil and his works, to rescue sinners from their bondage they are under to their enemies, and there is nothing so pleasing or agreeable unto him, yea, nothing can be pleasing to him unless you believe or trust in him for salvation from sin, Satan, and wrath. O sirs, never did a mother draw forth her breast to her sucking child with greater pleasure, when they were gorged and pained with great abundance of milk, than a God of love doth draw forth his grace, and mercy, and love to sinners in the gospel, that they may suck by faith and be satisfied with the abundance of his grace. O how is he pained at the heart till sinners come and suck the breasts of his grace, by putting their trust under the shadow of his wings! O Jerusalem, Jerusalem, how often would I have gathered thee, as a hen gathereth her chickens under her wings! How doth he expostulate with sinners for their aversion to come unto him! "O my people, what have I done unto thee? wherein have I wearied thee?" As if he had said, O what ails you at me? what harm have I done you? was I ever a barren wilderness, or a land of drought to you?

5. To encourage our faith and trust in this glorious Kinsman, and the Avenger of our blood, will you consider, that this is to answer the end of all that ever he did

or spake. Pray, tell me, why did God send his only
begotten Son into the world? Why did the only begotten Son of God come into the world? Why did
he assume our nature, take our place in law? Why
did he bruise Satan's head? Why did he die, rise
again, and ascend, and sit down at the right hand of
the Majesty on high? Why did he send forth his
apostles, and other ministers, as heralds to proclaim all
his glorious achievements unto a lost world? What
is the design of a preached gospel? Why has he given
you his statutes and testimonies, opened to you the
great things of his law and covenant, opened up the
love of his heart? And why are his bowels sending
out a sound to you who are running in the broad way
to ruin, saying, "As I live, I have no pleasure in the
death of the wicked, but rather that they turn unto
me and live?" What, I say, is the design of all this, but
just that sinners may trust, and rest, and believe in Christ
with assured confidence, that so they may not perish, but
have everlasting life? This is the very hinge on which
all religion turns, this is the white we should aim at in
preaching, and you in hearing, that you may be brought
to trust the Avenger of our blood. Now, seeing this
is the scope of the whole gospel revelation, and of all
that ever Christ did or said, does not this sufficiently
warrant you to believe and trust in him?

6. Consider the hazard and danger of not trusting
and believing in him. You do what in you lies to de-
feat the design of his whole undertaking, and the design of the whole gospel; you make God a liar in refusing to believe the record he hath given of his Son;
you must continue in a confederacy with Satan against
him if you do not believe, there is no mids, you lay
your souls open to inevitable ruin; for "there is no
name given under heaven whereby to be saved, but by
the name of Jesus." You make your kind Kinsman
your enemy, and draw the vengeance he designed in order
to your deliverance, upon your own heads; and there
is no vengeance so terrible as the vengeance of an in-

censed friend. O how terrible is the wrath of a slighted Saviour and Redeemer! 2 Thes. i. 8, " The Lord Jesus shall be revealed from heaven, with his mighty angels in flaming fire, taking vengeance on them that know not God, and that obey not the gospel." Consider this, ye that say now, " We will not have this man to rule over us."

7. Consider what glorious advantages shall redound to you by trusting and believing in this blessed Redeemer and Avenger.   Perfect peace shall be the fruit of it, a peace that passes all understanding : Is. xxvi. 3, " Thou wilt keep him in perfect peace whose mind is stayed on thee : because he trusteth in thee." Joy shall spring up in your bosoms upon your trusting in him, yea, a " joy unspeakable and full of glory ;" we are "filled with joy and peace in believing." Provision and food both for soul and body : Psal. xxxvii. 3, " Trust in the Lord, and do good, so shalt thou dwell in the land, and verily thou shalt be fed." Protection and safety in a time of danger ; protection from Satan, that cunning fowler, and all his birds of prey : Psal. xci. 2—4, " I will say of the Lord, He is my refuge, and my fortress ; my God, in him will I trust." And then it follows, " Surely he shall deliver thee from the snare of the fowler, and from the noisome pestilence.   He shall cover thee with his feathers, and under his wings shalt thou trust." Firmness and stability is the fruit of trusting in him, so as not to be shaken, like the trees of the wood, with the wind of temptation or affliction : " He that trusteth in the Lord shall be as mount Zion, which cannot be removed, but abideth for ever." King Jehoshaphat advises Israel under a shaking dispensation, " Believe in the Lord your God, so shall you be established ; believe his prophets, so shall ye prosper." You shall not be afraid of evil tidings, if your hearts be fixed, trusting in the Lord.   Increase and growth in grace is the fruit of trusting in him.   Would you have your souls in a lively flourishing condition, like the palm-tree and the cedar in Lebanon ?   Then trust your

this purpose, Jer. xvii. 7, 8, " Blessed is the man that trusteth in the Lord, and whose hope the Lord is. For he shall be as a tree planted by the waters, and that spreadeth out her roots by the river, and shall not see when heat cometh, but her leaf shall be green, and shall not be careful in the year of drought, neither shall cease from yielding fruit." But what shall I say more, everlasting life, and all that pertains to it, is the fruit of trusting in him : and he who believes in him shall never be confounded of his hope and expectation.

Special Seasons when we are more particularly called to Trust in Christ.

In general, there is no time unseasonable, yea, it is seasonable at all times, " Trust in him at all times ; ye people, pour out your hearts before him ;" there is not a moment of your life, there is not a turn of your pilgrimage here below, in which you do not stand in need of grace and mercy from your Kinsman to help you ; and therefore you need to trust him at all times, " To whom coming," by a lively trust and faith, " ye are built up a spiritual house," &c. But there are some special seasons in which we are called in a particular manner to exercise trust, faith, hope, and dependence upon him for his helping grace.

1. Under the arrests of the law as a covenant, or under the challenges of conscience supported by the law, craving the debt of obedience or punishment, according to the terms and tenor of the covenant : then we are called by faith to trust to him, and flee to him as " the end of the law for righteousness to every one that believes in him." O sinner, who art sinking under thy debt thou owes to justice, come put your trust in this Surety, he who bruised the head of the serpent in avenging your quarrel upon him, he will be sure to stand between thee and justice ; for " he brought in everlasting righteousness ; he magnified the law" as a covenant ; " he was made sin for us, for this very

end, " that we might be made the righteousness of God in him."

2. When thou art molested with a body of sin and death, I mean the workings of indwelling corruption, then trust your blessed Kinsman, that by the law of the Spirit of life which is in him, he may make you free from the law of sin and death. He is " made of God unto us sanctification ; and our old man is crucified with him, that the body of sin may be destroyed, that henceforth we might not serve sin." Atheism, enmity, unbelief, carnality, and other heart-evils under which thou art groaning, are his enemies as well as the enemies of thy soul ; and therefore he will wound the head of these his enemies ; all his enemies shall perish, into smoke shall they consume away ; he will waste, weaken, and wither that body of sin under which thou art groaning.

When thou art harassed with the fiery darts of Satan, tempting thee, perhaps, to the same sins of Atheism, distrust, and self-murder, unto which he had the impudence to tempt Christ himself when here upon earth, this is a season in which thou shouldst trust thy Friend, Kinsman, and Avenger. And to encourage thee to trust him in that case, remember that the day of vengeance is in his heart, his vengeance is in a peculiar manner pointed against that enemy ; and therefore he will be sure to join the poor soul that is groaning under his oppression, and crying to him for relief; and besides, he stands engaged by promise, that " he will not suffer thee to be tempted above what thou art able to bear, but with the temptation will provide a way to escape. He stands at the right hand of the poor ; he is the strength of the poor and needy in their distress, when the blast of the terrible ones is like a storm against the wall."

4. Art thou wrapt up among the dark and thick clouds of desertion ? This is a proper season of trust in thy Kinsman : Is. l. 10, " Who is this among you that feareth the Lord, that obeyeth the voice of his

servant, that walketh in darkness and hath no light?
let him trust in the name of the Lord, and stay
upon his God." Faith and trust is then especially to be exercised, when sense and reason can perceive nothing but anger and frowns; "for here
we walk by faith, and not by sight: and faith is the
substance of things hoped for, and the evidence of
things not seen." And to encourage thy trust in him,
in such a case, look to his promise, in which he has
said, that "though he forsake thee for a small moment,
yet he will return with everlasting kindness. Weeping endureth for a night, but joy cometh in the morning."

5. When thou art enjoying the sweet and sensible
manifestations of his love, that is a time for trusting, as
well as when under desertion and hidings. Never is the
believer in more danger, than when his sense is gratified
with a fill of the marrow and fatness, and wine of his
Father's house. Indeed sense is sweet, yea, it is the
suburbs of heaven; but, I say, the believer is never
more in danger, like Paul, of being lifted up above
measure, than when admitted unto the greatest sensible nearness; it is hard to carry a full cup with an
even hand: and therefore, I say, a time of special sensible nearness is a time proper for faith and trust in
the Lord, that he may help to the right improvement
of these visits of his love. And indeed this is one
great design of all the sensible glowings of divine love,
as well as of the displays that are made thereof in the
gospel-revelation, that the sons of men may be encour-
ed and engaged to "put their trust under the shadow
of his wings, Psal. xxxvi. 7.

6. When we are meeting with disappointments in the
world, as to these things in which we were expecting
satisfaction, that is a proper season for this duty of
trusting in Christ your glorious Kinsman. When
friends turn false and perfidious, it should teach us to
trust in that Friend that sticks closer than a brother.
So did David, when father and mother forsook him,

then he trusted that the Lord would take him up ; so Psal. cxlii. 4, 5, " I looked on my right hand, and beheld, but there was no man that would know me ; refuge failed me ; no man cared for my soul. I cried unto thee, O Lord, I said, Thou art my refuge, and my portion in the land of the living." When our worldly substance is withering, and our earthly possessions taken from us, either by force or fraud, that is a proper time of trusting our kind Kinsman and Avenger: Hab. iii. 17, 18, " Although the fig-tree shall not blossom, neither shall fruit be in the vines, the labour of the olive shall fail, and the fields shall yield no meat, the flock shall be cut off from the fold, and there shall be no herd in the stalls : yet I will rejoice in the Lord, I will joy in the God of my salvation." Sirs, God on purpose breaks our earthly comforts and cisterns in pieces, that by faith we may be brought to solace ourselves in him alone as an upmaking heritage for ever, saying with David, " My flesh and my heart faileth : but God is the strength of my heart and my portion for ever." Job, when he is swept naked of all he had in the world, cries out confidently, " I know that my Redeemer liveth :" and " Though he should kill me, yet will I trust in him."

The true Nature of the Church or Kingdom of Christ.

1. It is a spiritual kingdom. It is not of this world, as the Jews imagined, and as others imagine, who would fashion and mould it according to the kingdom of this world. The laws, the ordinances, the discipline, and whole of this kingdom is spiritual, and has a relation principally to the souls of men and women, and an eternal state to come. And seeing it is so, what a strange notion of the kingdom of Christ must men and judicatories among us have, who distinguish men in the affairs of Christ's kingdom by the gold ring, gay clothing, and worldly heritages. Alas ! true notions of the kingdom of Christ are generally lost among us

in this generation.   Some have no other notion of the
church of Christ, than a society of men meeting together, under the name of judicatories, under the protection of civil authority, whether they be acting according to the laws of Christ, or against them, for the
interest of the body of Christ, or to its hurt and prejudice ; whether they be holding Christ as a head, or
practically renouncing his headship, however they profess the contrary.   I make no difficulty to affirm, that a
church not holding the head, Christ, in all his offices, is
but an idol of man's making ; and zeal for such a church
is but like the zeal of those who cried, " The temple of
the Lord, the temple of the Lord, the temple of the
Lord are these," and yet were real enemies to the God
of the temple ; or like Ephraim, concerning whom it
is said, " Ephraim hath forsaken the Lord, and build-
eth temples."   I say then, that the kingdom of Christ
is of a spiritual nature, and it relates principally to the
soul, or the inner man : hence Christ declares concerning his disciples and followers, " The kingdom of God
is within you ;" and without this, it is little matter what
church or communion folk be of.
    2. Christ's catholic kingdom is of a large extent. It is
true, under the Old Testament dispensation, the kingdom of Christ was pent up within the confines of the
land of Judea, " To them belonged the adoption, the
covenants, the law, and the promises," while the generality of the Gentile nations were held as dogs, aliens
to Israel's commonwealth, &c.   But blessed be God,
now the waters of the sanctuary have run down to the
valley of Shittim, and the gospel is " preached unto all
nations, for the obedience of faith."   Psal. ii. 8,
" I will give him the heathen for his inheritance,"
&c.   Psal. lxxii. 8, " His dominion shall reach from sea
to sea, and from the river unto the ends of the earth."
    3. Although the kingdom of Christ, I mean his true
church, be of a large extent, yet it is but a little kingdom, I mean, it is not populous ; when compared with
the kingdom of the god of this world.   Christ's flock is

but a little flock, comparatively considered, Luke xii. 32, &c. They are but little in respect of their numbers. Indeed, abstractly considered, at the end of the day, they will make an "innumerable company, which no man can number;" but viewed in comparison of the wicked, they are but few: " strait is the gate, and narrow is the way that leadeth unto life, and few there be that find it;" like the gleanings after the vintage, " I will take them one of a city, and two of a family, and bring them unto Zion." They are but little in respect of quality. Christ's subjects are generally among the poorer sort of people : " God hath chosen the poor of this world, rich in faith, and heirs of the kingdom." 1 Cor. i. 26,—" Not many wise men after the flesh," &c. They are little in regard of esteem ; the world make but little account of them ; they are generally reckoned the dross and offscourings of the earth, 1 Cor. iv. 11—13 : but however little account the world may make of them, yet when Christ, at the end of the day, presents them unto his Father, they will shine like the stars, yea, like the sun in the kingdom of their Father.

4. The kingdom of Christ in this world is a kingdom of light. The church is called the " valley of vision," because of the light of the revelation that shines in it. Wherever Christ sets up his kingdom in a land, though it " sat in darkness," the people of it are made to " see great light." Light arises to them that " sat in the regions of the shadow of death." And all that are the true subjects of Christ's kingdom, they are " translated out of darkness into his marvellous light;" the light of the glory of God, in the face of Christ, shines into their hearts.

5. It is a heavenly kingdom. Matth. iii. 2, says John Baptist, when Christ was come to set up his standard, and sway his sceptre among the Jews, " Repent ye ; for the kingdom of heaven is at hand." And Heb. xii. 22, " Ye are come unto mount Zion, unto the heavenly Jerusalem." All the loyal subjects of the

kingdom are heaven-born, &c.; they are all pointing toward heaven in their way, and walk, and traffic, their "conversation is in heaven," and they are looking for "a better country," that is, an heavenly, Heb. xi. 16.

6. It is a regular and well governed kingdom : "Jerusalem is a city compactly built together." We have a description of the regularity and good order of the kingdom of Christ under the notion of a city built foursquare, Rev. xxi. See to this purpose, Eph iv. 16. There are many irregularities and disorders in the church of Christ, as she is managed by the hands of men, as sad experience testifies among us, at this day ; but as she is under the administration of the great King that God has set in the midst of her, there is nothing but beauty and order. If the church of Christ were, even his visible militant church, governed exactly according to Zion's laws by her pretended officers, there would be nothing but order and beauty in the whole kingdom ; but when men go about to make other laws than the laws of Christ, and to make their will the standard of government, rather than the will of the great King, this casts all into confusion, and yet even these confusions are managed by the King for the advantage of his true kingdom and subjects, and in due time he will bring light out of darkness, and order out of confusion.

7. The true kingdom of Christ is a kingdom that is much hated by the devil and the world. She is just the eye-sore of hell, and all its confederates ; hence we are told in the beginning of this psalm, that when Christ comes to set up his kingdom, " The heathen rage, the people imagine mischief, the kings of the earth, and princes thereof take counsel" how to suppress this kingdom of Christ. The gates of hell wage war against the kingdom of Christ. The world loves its own, who are under the government of the " god of this world," and who " walk according to the course of this world ;" but they hate the laws, the or-

dinances, the discipline, and subjects of Christ's kingdom; they are intolerable unto them, and therefore they are always trying to make themselves rid of them : hence are all the reproaches, afflictions, persecutions, and massacres of the followers of Christ, that we read of both in sacred and profane history.

8. Notwithstanding of this, the kingdom of Christ is a stable, firm, and everlasting kingdom ; it is like the little stone cut out of the mountain, that dashes all the kingdoms of the earth in pieces, and yet itself is not dashed or broken. As the King of Zion is himself the everlasting God, so his kingdom is an "everlasting kingdom, and of his dominion there shall be no end." He shall "rule over the house of Jacob for ever and ever."

9. The kingdom which Christ governs is a holy kingdom. The church of Christ, even his visible church, is a sanctified society federally holy ; you see in the text it is called "the holy hill of Zion." All the members of the visible church are dedicated to God in baptism, in which ordinance we renounce all filthiness both of the flesh and spirit, and are solemnly engaged to wage war against sin, and to "resist it even unto blood." The design of all church discipline, and of all ordinances, ministers, officers, and judicatories, is to preserve the church, or kingdom of Christ from corruption, either in principle or practice, that she may be a holy lump unto him. Whenever any scandal breaks out in a church, it is to be purged out by the discipline of Christ's appointment, lest that leaven, leaven the whole lump, and provoke the Lord, the Holy One of Israel, to depart from her. 1 Cor. iii. 17, the church is called "the temple of God :" "The temple of God is holy ; and if any man defile the temple of God, him will God destroy."

Marks of the Remnant of God's Heritage.

1. God's remnant are a people unto whom Christ is exceeding precious. His very name is unto them "as ointment poured forth;" they love to hear of him, they love to speak of him, and their meditations of him are sweet; "the desire of their soul is unto him, and the remembrance of his name; and they are ready to say with David, "Whom have I in heaven but thee?" &c. or with Paul, "I count all things but loss for the excellency of the knowledge of Christ Jesus my Lord."

2. God's remnant are a people that do not reckon themselves at home while they are here-away. This is not their proper country; but "they look for a better country, that is an heavenly," Heb. xi. 16. They "look for a city that has foundations, whose builder and maker is God," ver. 10. See this to be the character of God's remnant, ver. 13; the apostle tells us of these worthies, that they "confessed they were strangers and pilgrims on the earth." This confession David makes, Psal. cxix. 19, "I am a stranger in the earth, hide not thy commandments from me." So then, sirs, if your home be here, ye are none of God's remnant; if your thoughts and affections be confined within the narrow limits of time. God's remnant are a people that are coming up from the wilderness; they are always ascending and mounting heavenward, in their affections and desires: they "look not at the things that are seen, but at the things that are not seen."

3. God's remnant are a people that speak and think much on God. See this to be their character, Mal. iii. 16, "Then they that feared the Lord, spake often one to another, and a book of remembrance was written before him for them that feared the Lord, and that thought upon his name." Try yourselves by this. It is the character of the wicked, that "God is not in all their thoughts;" and he is as seldom in their mouths, except in a way of profanation. But God's remnant,

I say, they think much on God; and the thoughts of God, O how precious are they unto their souls! Psal. cxxxix. 17 ; and out of the abundance of their hearts their mouth speak honourably and reverently of him. They will speak to one another of his word, of his works, of his providences, and of his ordinances ; their "lips are like lilies, dropping sweet smelling myrrh."

4. God's remnant are a praying people: Psal. xxiv. 6, " This is the generation that seek thy face, O Jacob, or, O God of Jacob :" whereas it is given as the character of the wicked, Psal. xiv. 4, that they "call not upon God." They either live in the total neglect of this duty ; or, if they do it all, it is in a hypocritical, formal, and overly manner. But God's remnant they seek the face of God ; they seek him with fervency, with truth in the inward parts ; they seek him believingly ; they seek him constantly and perseveringly, which the hypocrite will not do: Job xxvii. 10, " Will he delight himself in the Almighty? will he always call upon God ?"

5. God's remnant are a mourning people. They mourn over their own sins in the first place : Ezek. vii. 16. The remnant of Jacob "that escape, they shall be on the mountains like doves of the valleys, every one mourning for their iniquity." They mourn over the errors of their hearts, and the iniquity of their lives, and are ready to cry out, " Innumerable evils have compassed me about, mine iniquities have taken hold on me," &c. And then they mourn, not only for their own personal sins, but for public sins ; the sins of others, whereby the land is defiled : " Rivers of waters run down mine eyes, because they keep not thy law ; I beheld transgressors and was grieved." That this is the character of God's remnant, ye may see from Ezek. ix. 4, " Go through the city, and set a mark upon the foreheads of the men that sigh, and cry for all the abominations done in the midst thereof." And then they mourn for the calamities and desolations of Zion, when

they see the bear out of the wood wasting her, and the
wild beasts out of the forest devouring her : Psal.
cxxxvii. 1, " By the rivers of Babylon we sat down
and wept when we remembered Zion." And then
they mourn when they see ordinances corrupted, or
God's candlestick in any measure removed, the
Lord's people deprived of their wonted freedom and
liberty in waiting upon him in these galleries : Zeph.
iii. 18, " I will gather them that are sorrowful for the
solemn assembly, to whom the reproach of it was a burden."

6. God's remnant are a people that will rather venture upon suffering than sinning. They rather venture to run the risk of displeasing kings and queens,
potentates and parliaments, than venture upon the displeasing of God : they can rather venture on the
rack of outward torments, than upon the rack of an
accusing conscience. See this to be the character of
God's remnant in the three children, Dan. iii. &c. ;
and Moses, Heb. xi. 27, "forsook Egypt, not fearing the
wrath of the king." Many other marks of God's remnant might be insisted upon. They are a people that
cannot live without Christ, and fellowship and communion with him, Cant. iii. 1. Job. xxiii. 3, " O that
I knew where I might find him ! that I might come
even to his seat !" They are a people that will not
rest in their attainments, but press towards the uttermost of grace and holiness, Phil. 3, 12. They press
after more nearness unto Christ, Cant. viii. 1. They
love holiness for itself, Psal. cxix. 140, Christ for
himself; yea, they love heaven for Christ and holiness. In a word, they love holiness, be the event
what it will.

*Concerning the Variety of the Saving Influences of the
Holy Spirit.*

1. THERE are the convincing influences of the Spirit ;
John xvi. 8, " When he is come, he will convince the

world of sin." This is what I conceive we are to understand by the north wind, Cant. iv. 16, which is
commonly boisterous, cold, chill, and nipping. The
elect of God by nature lie fast asleep within the
sea-mark of God's wrath, upon the very brink of everlasting ruin, crying, Peace, peace, to themselves ; the
Spirit of the Lord comes like a stormy north wind,
blows hard upon the sinner's face, and awakens him,
breaks his carnal peace and security, brings him to himself, and lets him see his danger, fills him with remorse
and terror. Hence, Is. xxviii. 17, the hail is said to
"sweep down the refuge of lies," before the sinner
come to settle upon the foundation that God hath laid
in Zion. Acts ii. 37, it is said, "they were pricked
in their heart," and then they cried out. "Men and
brethren, what shall we do ?'

(2.) There are the enlightening influences and breathings of the Spirit. Hence he is compared unto eye-
salve, Rev. iii. 18, "Ye have received an unction from
the Holy One, whereby ye know all things," 1 John ii.
20. We read, Is. xxv. 7, of a vail and face of a covering that is spread over all nations. The wind of the
HolyGhost must blow off this vail of ignorance and unbelief; and then the poor sinner comes to see a new
world of wonders that he never saw before ; a wonderful great God, a wonderful Redeemer, a wonderful
covenant, and a wonderful holy law. Hence we are
said to be "translated out of darkness into a marvellous light. The Spirit searcheth all things, yea, even
the deep things of God." And, 1 Cor. ii. 12, "By
the Spirit we know the things that are freely given to
us of God."

(3.) There are the renewing influences of the Spirit.
We are said to be "saved by the washing of regeneration, and renewing of the Holy Ghost," Tit. iii. 5.
Hence he is called "a new spirit." He renews the
will, and "makes old things to pass away, and all things
to become new."

(4.) There are the comforting influences of the Spirit.

This is the south-wind, as it were, gentle, and easy, and refreshing; and therefore he is called the Comforter. And indeed his consolations are strong consolations; they put more gladness into the heart than corn, wine, and oil in abundance; fill the soul with a joy that is "unspeakable and full of glory." And then,

(5.) There are the corroborating and strengthening influences of the Spirit. By the breathings of the Spirit the feeble are made "like David, and as the angel of God before him." It is he that "gives power to the faint, and increases strength to them that have no might." It is by him that worm Jacob is made to thresh the mountains, and to beat them small, and to make the hills as chaff. And then,

(6.) There are the drawing and enlarging influences of the Spirit: "Draw me, (says the spouse,) we will run after thee." The poor believer lies many times, as it were, wind-bound, that he is not able to move one step in the way of the Lord: but, O! when the Spirit of the Lord comes, then comes liberty and enlargement: "I will run the way of thy commandments (says David,) when thou hast enlarged my heart," to wit by the influences of thy Spirit. He is like oil to their chariot wheels; and when he comes, they are as the chariots of Amminadib, or a willing people.

(7.) There are the sin-mortifying and sin-killing influences of the Spirit: we through the Spirit are said to "mortify the deeds of the body, that so we may live." When this wind of the Holy Ghost blows upon the soul, he not only makes the spices to revive, but he kills the weeds of sin and corruption, making them to wither and decay; so that the poor believer, who was crying, "Wretched man, what shall I do to be delivered from this body of death!" he is made sometimes to tread upon the neck of these enemies, as a pledge of his complete victory at last. And then,

(8.) There are the interceding influences of the Spirit: Rom. viii. 26, "The Spirit maketh intercession

for us with groanings which cannot be uttered." **He**
intercedes in a physical and efficient way.   He makes
us to wrestle and pray, therefore he is called "the Spirit
of grace and supplications." Zech. xii. 10. He fills
the believer's heart and mouth with such a heavenly
rhetoric, that God is not able to withstand it.   Hence
Jacob "had power with the angel, and prevailed;"
for "he wept, and made supplication unto him."   And
then,

(9.) There are the sealing and witnessing influences
of the Spirit : He "witnesseth with our spirits, that
we are the sons of God." He bears witness of the
glorious fulness and suitableness of Christ to the soul :
" The Spirit shall testify of me," John xv. 26. And he
is said to "seal believers to the day of redemption;"
and his seal is the earnest of glory : Eph. i. 13, 14,
" Ye are sealed by the Holy Spirit of promise, which is
the earnest of the inheritance."   But let us speak a
little to the manner of the acting or operation of these
influences, or how it is that this wind blows upon the
soul?

1. The wind of the Holy Ghost blows very freely ;
the Spirit acts as an independent sovereign, John iii.
8.   It doth not stay for the command, nor stop for the
prohibition of any creature. So the breathings of the
Spirit are sovereignly free as to the time of their dona-
tion, free as to their duration and continuance, free as
to the measure, and free as to the manner of their working.   And then,

2. He breathes on the soul sometimes very surpris-
ingly : "Or ever I was aware (says the spouse,) my
soul made me like the chariots of Amminadib."   Can
thou not seal this in thy experience, believer, that sometimes, when thou hast gone to duty in a very heartless
and lifeless condition, perhaps beginning to raze foundations, and to say with Zion, "The Lord hath forsaken, and my God hath forgotten," a gale from heaven has in a manner surprised thee, and set thee upon
the high places of Jacob, and made thee to cry with

the spouse, " It is the voice of my beloved ! Behold, he cometh leaping upon the mountains, skipping upon the hills? His anger endureth but for a moment; in his favour is life : weeping may endure for a night, but joy cometh in the morning."

3. These breathings and influences of the Spirit, they are sometimes very piercing and penetrating. The cold nipping north wind, ye know, it goes to the very quick. The sword of the Spirit "pierces even to the dividing asunder of soul and spirit, and of the joints and marrow, and is a discerner of the thoughts and intents of the heart." Wind, you know, is of a very seeking, penetrating nature ; it seeks through the closest chambers. So the Spirit, which is the candle of the Lord, " searcheth the lower parts of the belly :" he makes a discovery of these lusts and idols that skulk in the secret chambers of the heart.

4. The breathings of this wind are very powerful, strong, and efficacious. Who can oppose the blowings of the wind ? Some winds they have such a mighty force with them, that they bear down, overturn, and overthrow every thing that stands in their way. So the Spirit of the Lord sometimes, especially at first conversion, he breaks in upon the soul like the rushing of a mighty wind, as he did upon the apostles, breaking down the strong-holds of iniquity, casting to the ground every high thought and towering imagination of the soul, that exalteth itself against Christ, with a powerful and triumphant efficacy. He masters the darkness of the mind, the contumacy and rebellion of the will, and the carnality of the affections : the enmity of the heart against God, and all the spiritual wickednesses that are in the high places of the soul, are made to fall down at his feet, as Dagon did before the ark of the Lord.

5. Although he act thus powerfully and irresistibly, yet it is with an overcoming sweetness, so as there is not the least violence offered unto any of the natural faculties of the soul : for whenever the Spirit comes with

his saving influences, he sweetly overcomes the darkness of the mind ; the sinner becomes a volunteer, and content to enlist himself a soldier under Christ's banner : Psal. cx. 3, " Thy people shall be willing in the day of thy power." No sooner does Christ by the Spirit say to the soul, " Follow me, but immediately they arise and follow him. Behold we come unto thee, for thou art the Lord our God." Then,

6. There is something in the breathing of this wind that is incomprehensible by reason : John iii. 8, " Thou hearest the sound thereof, but canst not tell whence it cometh, and whither it goeth (says Christ) : so is every one that is born of the Spirit." There is something in the operation of the eternal Spirit, and his influences beyond the reach, not only of natural, but of sanctified reason. Who can tell " how the bones are formed in the womb of her that is with child ?" so far less can we tell how the Spirit forms the babe of grace in the heart ; how he preserves, maintains, and cherishes the smoking flax, that is not quite extinguished. We may in this case apply the words of the psalmist in another case, and say, " Thy way is in the sea, and thy path in the great waters, and thy footsteps are not known ;" and that of the apostle, " How unsearchable are his judgments, and his ways past finding out."

7. These influences of the Spirit, they are sometimes felt before they be seen ; as you know a man will feel the wind and hear it, when he cannot see it. So it is with the Lord's people many times, on whom the Spirit breathes ; they feel his actings, they are sensible that he has been dealing with them ; and all that they can say about it is, with the man that was born blind, " One thing I know, that whereas I was blind, now I see." The kingdom of heaven comes not with observation.

The Necessity and Seasons of the Influences of the Holy Spirit.

THE necessity of these influences will appear, 1. From the express declaration of Christ, John xv. 5, " Without me ye can do nothing ;" that is, without the aid and influences of my Spirit. He doth not say, Without me ye cannot do many things, or great things; but, " Without me ye can do nothing."

2. It is evident from the express acknowledgment of the saints of God upon this head : 2 Cor. iii. 5, " We are not, (says the apostle) sufficient of ourselves to think any thing as of ourselves : but our sufficiency is of God." It is he that must work all our works in us and for us.

3. It is plain from the earnest prayers of the saints for the breathings of this wind : Cant. iv. 16, " Awake, O north wind, and come, thou south, and blow upon my garden." Psal. lxxxv. 6, " Wilt thou not revive us again : that thy people may rejoice in thee?" They are promised in the covenant, and therefore necessary : Is. xliv. 3, " I will pour water upon him that is thirsty, and floods upon the dry ground : I will pour my Spirit upon thy seed," &c. Ezek. xxxvi. 27, " I will put my Spirit within you, and cause you to walk in my statutes." Now, there is not a mercy promised in the covenant that can be wanting. But,

2. To what are these breathings necessary ? I answer, they are necessary,

1. To the quickening of the elect of God, when they are stark dead in trespasses and sins. Can ever the dry bones live unless this omnipotent wind blow upon them? It is strange to hear some men that profess Christianity, talking of the power of their own wills to quicken and convert themselves. They may as well say, that a dead man may take his grave in his two arms, and lay death by him, and walk. " No man (says Christ,) can come to me, except the Father which hath sent me draw him." Oh ! what a dead weight is

the sinner, that a whole Trinity must draw! for both Father and Son draw the sinner by the breathings of the Holy Ghost.

2. These influences are necessary for the suitable discharge of every duty of religion. You cannot read, you cannot hear, you cannot pray or praise, you cannot communicate to any advantage, unless the wind of the Holy Ghost blow upon you. It is the Lord that must enlarge our steps under us, and make your feet like hind's feet in the ways of the Lord.

3. They are necessary for accomplishing our spiritual warfare against sin, Satan, and the world. We will never be able to combat with our spiritual enemies, if he do not help us: it is he only that must " teach our hands to war, and our fingers to fight, so as bows of steel may be broken in pieces by us." Without the Spirit we will fall before every temptation; like Peter, curse and swear, that we never knew him.

4. They are necessary to the exercise of grace already implanted in the soul. As we cannot work grace in our hearts, so neither can we exercise it without the renewed influences of the Holy Ghost, Cant. iv. 16. When this wind blows, then, and never till then, do the spices flow out. But I shall not stand on this: the Spirit's influences are necessary to all the uses mentioned upon the second head; for conviction, illumination, renovation, consolation, enlargement, mortification of sin, for assurance of our adoption.

As to the seasons of these influences observe, 1. The Spirit's reviving influences, they blow very ordinarily in a day of conversion. This, as you were hearing, is a season when this wind breathes on the soul, Ezek. xxxvi. 26, when God takes away the stony heart, and gives the heart of flesh. He puts his Spirit within them, when the soul is first espoused unto Christ. So Jer. ii. 2, " I remember thee the kindness of thy youth, the love of thine espousals when thou wentest after me in the wilderness, in a land that was not sown."

2. When the soul has been deeply humbled under a sense of sin and unworthiness. When Ephraim is brought low, and is smiting on his thigh, acknowledging his sin and folly, then the Spirit of the Lord comes with a reviving gale upon his spirit. "Is Ephraim (says the Lord) my dear son? is he a pleasant child? for since I spake against him, I do earnestly remember him still : therefore my bowels are troubled for him ; I will surely have mercy upon him, saith the Lord."

3. After a dark night of desertion, when the Lord returns again, it is a time of sweet influences. After Zion had been crying, " The Lord hath forsaken me, my God hath forgotten me ;" upon the back of it comes a sweet gale of the Spirit, " Can a woman forget her sucking child, that she should not have compassion on the son of her womb? yea, they may forget, yet will not I forget thee."

4. Times of earnest prayer and wrestling ; for he giveth his Spirit to them that ask it. This is agreeable to the promise, Ezek. xxxvi. 37.

5. Times of serious meditation are times of sweet influences of the Spirit: Psal. lxiii. 5, 6, 8, " When I remember thee upon my bed, and meditate on thee in the night-watches, my soul is satisfied as with marrow and fatness, and my soul followeth hard after thee."

6. Communion-days are sometimes days of sweet influences. Some of the Lord's people can attest it from their experience, with the spouse, that " while the King sat at his table, the spikenard sent forth the smell thereof :" and when they " sat down under his shadow, they found his fruit sweet to their taste. He brought me to the banqueting-house, and his banner over me was love."

7. The day of death has sometimes been found to be a day of such pleasant gales of the Spirit, that they have been made to enter into the haven of glory with the triumphant song in their mouth, saying, " Thanks be to God, which giveth us the victory, through our

Lord Jesus Christ." Thus David, "Although my house be not so with God; yet he hath made with me an everlasting covenant, ordered in all things, and sure; for this is all my salvation, and all my desire." Thus Simeon, thus Paul, &c.

Trial whether the Saving Influences of the Spirit have ever yet Breathed upon our Souls.

1. IF these breathings have blown upon thy soul, man, woman, then he has blown away the vail and face of the covering that was naturally upon thy mind and understanding. He has given you other views of spiritual and divine things, than you can have by any natural or acquired knowledge. The Spirit of the Lord, he is called "the Spirit of wisdom and revelation," Eph. i. 17, because he reveals these things to the soul which flesh and blood is not able to receive or understand. So then, has the Spirit testified of Christ unto you? has he "who commanded the light to shine out of darkness, shined into your heart, to give the light of the knowledge of the glory of God, in the face of Jesus Christ?" And as a fruit and consequent of this,

2. If the wind of the Holy Ghost has blown upon thy soul, he has blown away some of the filth of hell that did cleave to thy soul, and has transformed thee into his own image: 2 Cor. iii. 18, "Beholding as in a glass the glory of the Lord, thou art changed into the same image, from glory to glory, even as by the Spirit of the Lord." If you have the Spirit, the "same mind will be in you, which was also in Christ Jesus; for he that is joined unto the Lord is one spirit." You will imitate and resemble him in his imitable perfections, in his holiness, meekness, self-denial, patience. He is a holy God, and wherever he comes he works holiness, and makes the soul holy.

3. If this wind has blown upon your souls, then it has driven you from your lying refuges, and made you take sanctuary in Christ. He has driven you from the

law, and made you consent to the method of salvation through the righteousness of the Son of God : " I through the law (says the apostle) am dead to the law, that I might live unto God." This is the design of all the Spirit's influences, to lead sinners off from sin, off from self, off from the law, that they may rest in Christ only.

4. If ever you felt any of the reviving gales of this wind of the Spirit, you will long for new gales and breathings of it ; and when these breathings are suspended and withheld, your souls will be like to faint, as it were, like a man that wants breath. You will pant for the air of the Spirit's influences, like David, Psal. lxiii. 1, " My soul longeth for thee in a dry and thirsty land, where no water is ;" and Psal. lxxxiv. 2, " My soul longeth, yea, even fainteth for the courts of the Lord : my heart and my flesh crieth out for the living God :" Oh for another gale of his Spirit in public ordinances !

5. If you have felt the breathings of this wind, you will not snuff up the east wind of sin and vanity : John iv. 14, " Whosoever drinketh of the water that I shall give him, shall never thirst." You will not thirst immoderately after things of time ; no, no ; you will see them to be but mere trash and vanity. You will " choose that good part which shall not be taken away from you." You will " seek those things which are above, where Christ sitteth on the right hand of God."

6. If this wind has blown upon thy soul, then you will follow the motion of this wind ; you will not run cross to this wind, but will go along with it. I mean, you will yield yourselves up to the conduct of the Spirit speaking in his word ; " For as many as are led by the Spirit of God, they are the sons of God."

But, say you, How shall I know if I be led by the Spirit of God ? I answer,

1. If ye follow the Spirit, then you will not fulfil the lusts of the flesh ; but, on the contrary, you will

study to " crucify the flesh, with the affections and lusts." You will be ready to cut off your right-hand, and to pluck out the right-eye sins at the Lord's command.

2. Then the way wherein you walk will be a way of holiness, for he is a Spirit of sanctification ; and a way of truth, for the Spirit of the Lord, he is a Spirit of truth, and he leads into all truth : a way of uprightness: Psal. cxliii. 10, " Thy Spirit is good, lead me into the land of uprightness."

3. Ye know leading imports willingness. There is a great difference between leading and drawing: between being driven by the wind, and following the motion of the wind. Sometimes indeed the wicked, a hypocrite, a natural man, by a strong north-wind of conviction may be driven on to duty through the force of terror. But the believer, he is a volunteer, he freely yields himself to the Spirit's conduct, he rejoices to work righteousness, and to remember God in his ways. Whenever he hears the Spirit whispering in his ears, and saying, " This is the way, walk ye in it," presently he complies. When the Spirit of the Lord says, Come, he immediately echoes back again, and says, " Behold, I come unto thee, for thou art the Lord my God." Now, try yourselves by these things.

The Gospel plan of a Sinner's Justification in the sight of God.

1. Then, you would know, that God having made man a rational creature, capable of moral government, he gave him a law suited to his nature, by which he was to govern himself in the duties he owed to God his great Creator. This law was delivered to man in the form of a covenant, with a promise of life upon the condition of perfect obedience, and a threatening of death in case of disobedience, Gen. ii. 17. Thus stood matters between God and man in a state of innocency.

2. Adam, and all his posterity in him, and with him,

having broken the covenant, are become liable to the
curse, and penalty of it; so that our salvation is become absolutely impossible, until justice be satisfied,
and the honour of the broken law be repaired. The
law and justice of God are very peremptory, and stand
upon a full satisfaction and reparation, otherwise heaven's gates shall be shut, and eternally barred against
man and all his posterity. The flaming sword of justice turns every way, to keep us from access unto the
paradise that is above.

3. While man in these circumstances was expecting
nothing but to fall an eternal sacrifice unto Divine justice, the eternal Son of God, in his infinite love and
pity to perishing sinners, steps in as a Mediator and
Surety; offering not only to take our nature, but to
take our law-place, to stand in our room and stead:
whereby the whole obligation of the law, both penal and
preceptive, did fall upon him; that is, he becomes liable
and obliged both to fulfil the command, and to endure
the curse of the covenant of works, which we had violated.
And here, by the way, it is fit to advertise you, that it
was an act of amazing grace in the Lord Jehovah, to
admit a Surety in our room; for, had he stood to the
rigour and severity of the law, he would have demanded a personal satisfaction, without admitting of the satisfaction of a Surety: in which case Adam, and all
his posterity, had fallen under the stroke of avenging
justice through eternity. But glory to God in the
highest, who not only admitted of a Surety, but provided one, and laid help upon one that is mighty.

4. Christ, the eternal Son of God, being in "the fulness of time, made of a woman, and made under the
law," as our Surety, he actually, in our room and stead,
fulfilled the whole terms of the covenant of works;
that is, in a word, he obeyed all the commands of the
law, and endured the curse of it, and thereby brings
in a complete law-righteousness; whereby guilty sinners are justified before God. And this is the righteousness by which we are exalted. By his active and

passive obedience, he "magnifies the law, and makes it honourable," and the Lord declares himself to be "well-pleased for his righteousness' sake."

Although Christ obeyed the law, and satisfied justice, and thereby brought in an everlasting law-righteousness for a whole elect world ; yet the elect of God are never exalted by virtue of this righteousness, till, in a day of power, they be brought to receive it by faith, and submit to it for justification before God. We disclaim that Antinomian error, of an actual justification from eternity, or yet of a formal justification, bearing date from the death of Christ. We own, indeed, with all Protestant sound divines, that it was the purpose of God to justify his elect from eternity, and that all the elect were represented by Christ in his obedience unto the death ; but that they are actually justified before conversion, or before their application by faith unto the blood of Jesus, is impossible ; because the sentence of the broken law stands always in force against them, till they actually believe in the Son of God ; for " he that believeth not is condemned already." And how can they be both justified and condemned at the same time ? Till then, they are " children of wrath even as others."

6. This righteousness of the Surety is conveyed unto us by imputation ; as is abundantly plain from many places of scripture, particularly Rom. iv. 6, 11, 12, 23, 24. God reckons what the Surety did in our room unto us ; so that his righteousness becomes as much ours for justification before God, as though we had obeyed the law, and satisfied justice in our own person. Now, this imputation of the Surety's righteousness runs principally upon these two or three things. (1.) Upon the eternal transaction between the Father and the Son, wherein the Son of God was chosen and sustained as the Surety of an elect world. Then it was that he gave bond to the Father, to pay their debt in the red gold of his blood, saying, " Sacrifice and offering thou didst not desire :—Lo, I come :—I delight to

do thy will." (2.) It is grounded upon the actual imputation of our sins unto him : the Lord, laid on him
the iniquity of us all." There is a blessed exchange
of places between Christ and his people : he takes on our
sin and unrighteousness, that we may be clothed with
the white robe of his righteousness : 2 Cor. v. 21,
" He was made sin for us, who knew no sin ; that we
might be made the righteousness of God in him." (3.)
This imputation goes upon the ground of the mystical
union between Christ and the believer. When the
poor soul is determined in a day of power to embrace
the Lord Jesus in the arms of faith, Christ and he in
that very moment do coalesce into one body. He becomes a branch of the noble vine ; a member of that
body whereof Christ is the glorious Head of eminence,
influence, and government. And being thus united to
Christ, the long and white robe of the Mediator's righteousness is spread over him ; whereby he is not only
freed from condemnation, but for ever sustained as
righteous in the sight of God : 1 Cor. 30, "But of
him are ye in Christ Jesus, who of God is made unto
us wisdom, and righteousness, and sanctification, and
redemption."

Reproof to those who endeavour to exalt themselves in their own
Righteousness.

THERE are some of the hearers of the gospel, who
exalt themselves in a negative righteousness : they are
not so bad as others : they are free of gross out-break-
ings, being no common drunkards, swearers, or Sabbath-
breakers ; and therefore conclude that all is right with
them. But, sirs, the Pharisee could make this brag :
and Paul before conversion could say, that " touching the law he was blameless ;" and yet when God
opened his eyes he found himself lying under the arrest
of justice ; for " when the commandment came, sin revived, and he died." Others are exalting themselves
in a moral kind of righteousness; they not only cease

to do evil, but do many things that are materially
good : they are sober, temperate, just in their dealings,
liberal to the poor, good peaceable neighbours; they
love every body, and every body loves them ; they
keep the commandments as well as they can : and this
is the ground they are standing upon.   But I may say
to you, as Christ said to the young man, who told him,
" All these things have I kept from my youth up, Yet
lackest thou one thing."   O what is that ? say you.   I
answer, It is to be brought off from the rotten bottom
of a covenant of works that ye are standing upon.   Ye
want to see that ye are spiritually dead, in trespasses and sins, and that ye are legally dead, condemned
already, and the wrath of God abiding on you.   Ye
want to see that " all your own righteousness is as filthy
rags," and to be made to say, with the church, " Surely in the Lord have I righteousness and strength."
Others will go farther than bare morality ; they will
abound in the duties of religion, read, hear, pray, communicate, run from sermon to sermon, from sacrament
to sacrament; and upon these things they rest.   All
these things are good in their proper place ; but if you
build your hope of acceptance here, you are still upon
a covenant of works bottom, seeking righteousness, as
it were by the works of the law ; and while you do so,
you do but seek the living among the dead.   All your
works are but dead works, till you be in Christ ; and
they will but stand for cyphers in God's reckoning,
till you be brought to submit to this righteousness, by
which alone guilty sinners can be exalted.   Others
rely upon a mixed kind of righteousness : they will
freely own, that their duties and performances will
never exalt them into favour and acceptance with God ;
but, O, say they, it is Christ and our duties, Christ
and our prayers, he and our tears and repentance that
must do it.   But believe it, sirs, Christ and the idol of
self will never cement ; these old rotten rags will never
piece in with the white and new robe of the righteousness of the Son of God : and if you adventure to

mingle them together, Christ shall profit you nothing,"
Gal. v. 2, 3, 4.   Others again, they will pretend to renounce all their works and duties, and own with their
own mouths, that it is by faith in Christ only that they
hope to be accepted : but though they own this with their
mouth, yet still their hearts cleave fast unto a covenant
of works ; they were never through the law, dead to
the law ; and when nothing else will do, they will make
their own act of believing the righteousness on which
they lean for acceptance ; which is still a seeking righteousness in themselves : whereas, if ever we be justified before God, we must have it in the Lord Jesus,
saying, "In him will we be justified, and in him alone
will we glory." Faith carries the soul quite out of itself ;
yea, faith renounces its own act in the point of justification.
All these, and many other rooms and lying refuges,
hath the devil and our own hearts devised, to lead us
off from Christ.   But, O sirs, believe it, these are but
imaginary sanctuaries, and the hail will sweep them
away.   Nothing but the doing and dying of the Surety,
apprehended by faith, will ever exalt you into favour
and fellowship with God, or acquit you from the curse
and condemnation of the broken law.   And unless
ye betake yourselves to the horns of this blessed altar,
to this refuge of God's appointing, you are undone ;
and you may read your doom, Is. l. 11, "Behold, all
ye that kindle a fire, that compass yourselves about
with sparks ; walk in the light of your fire, and in the
sparks that ye have kindled." This shall ye have of
mine hand, ye shall lie down in sorrow."

Advices concerning the Attainment of Gospel Lowliness
Humility.

1. Go to the law as a schoolmaster ; read the ten
commandments, and Christ's spiritual commentary
upon them, Matth. v.   View the law of God in its utmost extent and spirituality ; for it is exceeding broad.
This would make the proudest heart to lie in the dust :

Rom. vii. 9, "I was alive without the law once: but when the commandment came, sin revived, and I died." The feathers of his pride and legal righteousness soon fell, when the law in its spirituality was set before his eyes.

2. Get Christ to dwell in your heart by faith; for the reigning power of this evil is never broken, till Christ come by the power of his Spirit, bringing down the towering imaginations of the heart, and erect his throne there. The more of Christ, the more humility; and the less of Christ, the more pride. When the Spirit of Christ enters into the heart, he stamps the likeness and image of Christ there. O then if you would have this humility and lowliness of spirit, "lift up the everlasting-doors, that the King of glory may come in:" he brings a glorious retinue of graces with him, whereof this is one of the first.

3. Be much in viewing the glorious perfections of the Majesty of heaven, as they are displayed in the works of creation and providence; but especially as they shine in the face of Jesus Christ, and the glorious work of redemption through him. When the prophet Isaiah saw the Lord high and lifted up, and his train filling the temple, he cries out, "Woe is me, for I am undone, because I am a man of unclean lips." See Job xlii. 5, 6, "I have heard of thee (says he,) by the hearing of the ear: but now mine eye seeth thee. Wherefore I abhor myself, and repent in dust and ashes."

4. Be much in viewing the rock whence ye were hewn, and the hole of the pit whence ye were digged; I mean your original corruption and depravation; how you are conceived in sin, and brought forth in iniquity. And O how much of this cleaves even to believers themselves, while they are on this side of eternity! There is a "law in the members continually warring against the law of the mind." This laid the great apostle Paul in the dust notwithstanding of his high attainments.

5. Be much in viewing the vanity of the creature,

and all things below. " Vanity and vexation of spirit," is written in legible characters upon all things under the sun. " The fashion of this world is passing away." Be much in viewing the bed of the grave, where you must lie down shortly, and where rottenness and corruption shall cover you : let this make you say, with Job, " to corruption, Thou art my father ; and to the worm, Thou art my mother, and my sister." View an awful tribunal, and an endless eternity, that is to follow on the back of death, where you and I shortly shall stand pannels, and receive a sentence from the righteous Judge, which shall determine our state for ever.

6. *Lastly*, Be much in eyeing these patterns of lowliness and humility which I have already mentioned. God, angels and saints, have cast you a copy of it. But especially be much in viewing the humility and humiliation of the Son of God, which is proposed as the great pattern, Phil. ii. 5, 6, 7, 8, " Let this mind be in you, which was also in Christ Jesus : who being in the form of God, thought it not robbery to be equal with God : but made himself of no reputation, and took upon him the form of a servant, and was made in the likeness of men : and being found in fashion as a man, he humbled himself, and became obedient unto death, even the death of the cross."

What sort of Works they are which may properly be called Good Works.

In general, considering the law as a covenant, or an abstracted rule of righteousness, as contradistinct from the gospel, there are no works done by men that can be called good works ; for " there is none that doth good, (in this respect,) no not one : In many things we offend all." The most blameless and perfect actions of the most consummate believer that ever drew breath in God's air, while in this state of sin and imperfection, cannot perform a work legally good, because of the mixture of sin that attends his best performances.

And hence it is, that we find the saints in scripture owning, that they could not stand, if God should mark iniquity; that all their righteousness is as filthy rags; that their goodness extendeth not to him. O sirs, if God should lay judgment to the line, and righteousness to the plummet, we and all our good works, would be for ever rejected, like reprobate silver. And therefore we have little reason to think or imagine, that God is a debtor to us for any thing we do, or that our good works do procure the favour of God, his acceptation, or a title unto life. But our works are called good works, as having a respect unto the law, considered as a rule of duty, in the sweet hand of a Mediator. He makes his yoke easy, and his burden light, to his people, by accepting of their weak mints and endeavours, through his perfect obedience and satisfaction, as good, though attended with manifold imperfections. Now, to constitute an action good in an evangelical sense, there are several things requisite.

1. To make a work a good work, it must be done by a good and holy person, renewed by the Spirit of Christ, and justified by his merit. It is beyond all dispute and controversy, that the person must first be accepted of God, and reconciled to him in Christ, before the work can be accepted. Abel's person was accepted of God, and then his offering. And hence it is, that the sacrifices of the wicked are said to be an abomination to the Lord. The very ploughing of the wicked is sin. The matter is this; God is angry with their persons, and he hates and loathes them while out of Christ; and therefore nothing that comes from them, or that is done by them, can be acceptable. And therefore I say, to make works good and acceptable unto God, they must be done by a person that is in a gracious and reconciled state.

2. To make a work a good work, it must be a thing required and called for by the law of God. The reason of this is plain, because it is God's will that makes any thing sin or duty; and if it be not agreeable to his

revealed will, he may say unto us, " Who hath required this at your hand ?"   Hence Christ taxeth the Pharisees, saying, " In vain do they worship me, teaching
for doctrines the commandments of men." And therefore if you would do any work acceptable to God, you
must take care that the thing you do be required and
commanded of God.   Indeed there are some actions
that are of an indifferent nature ; that is, God has left
men at a perfect liberty, whether to do them or not.
But then it would be remembered, that these actions,
in the case of offence or edification, they cease to be
indifferent, and fall under some commandment of the
moral law.   In which case Paul says, 1 Cor. viii. 13,
" If meat make my brother to offend, I will eat no
flesh while the world standeth." It was a thing indifferent, whether Paul did eat flesh or not ; but when
offence was like to follow his eating, he would abstain
from it as much as though it were expressly forbidden
in the law of God, because, in that case, it became a
breach of the law of love and charity.

3. To make a work a good work, it must be done
out of a right principle.   It must be done out of a
principle of faith, as was already hinted ; for no work
can be acceptable without this, Heb. xi. 6.   And
there is a twofold faith requisite in a good action. (1.)
A general faith or persuasion, that the thing we do
may be done lawfully.   And of this the apostle speaks,
when he says, " Whatsoever is not of faith, is sin,"
Rom. xiv. 23.   And, (2.) a particular justifying faith,
believing the acceptance of what we do, only through
the Lord Jesus Christ, and his merit and mediation.
Again, a good work must be done out of a regard unto
the authority of God commanding : and that not simply with a respect unto the authority of a God Creator : for thus a Heathen, or a Mahometan, may obey
God, and do good actions ; but out of a respect unto
the authority of a God in Christ.   We must eye the
authority of the Creator, in our obedience, as coming
in this blessed channel, otherwise it is not a true Chris-

tian obedience: for we Christians are "under the law to Christ;" and when we are so, we are "not without law to God," seeing God hath commanded us to hear his voice and to obey him, as our Lord, King, and Lawgiver. And whatsoever we do in word or deed, we are to do all in the name and authority of the Lord Jesus Christ, to the glory of God by him. And further, good works must be done with simplicity and godly sincerity, avoiding hypocritical and Pharisaical ostentation in the discharge of duty: for "his soul which is lifted up, is not upright in him," Hab. ii. 4.

4. To make a work a good work it must be done to a right end. It must be done to the glory and honour of God, this being the principal and ultimate end of our being, according to that of the apostle, 1 Cor. x. 31, "Whether ye eat or drink, or whatsoever ye do, do all to the glory of God." It must be done as a declaration of our gratitude to God for redeeming love. We are bought with a price; therefore we are to "glorify him in our souls and bodies, which are his." They must be done also with a view to the edification of others, Matth. v. 16.

Concerning the Influence which Faith hath upon Good Works, or in producing Holiness in all manner of Conversation.

1. TRUE faith it unites the soul to Christ, who is the very root and fountain of all holiness. "From me (saith the Lord,) is thy fruit found. Except ye abide in me, and I in you," to wit, by faith, "ye cannot bring forth much fruit." Indeed a person in a state of nature may bring forth many fruits that are morally and materially good; but, without union with Christ we can do no work that is spiritually good and acceptable; for, "as the branch cannot bear fruit of itself, except it abide in the vine; no more can ye, except ye abide in me." We may as well gather grapes of thorns, or figs of thistles," as expect works that are spiritually

good from a person out of Christ. Why? The reason of it is plain : his root is but rottenness, while he grows upon the old Adam ; and therefore his blossom shall go up as dust. While a man is growing upon the old Adam, he is married to the law as a covenant ; and therefore all his works they are but dead works : and can ever dead works be acceptable to the living God? We must be " dead to the law by the body of Christ," and married unto that better husband, before we can " bring forth fruit unto God," Rom. vii. 4.

2. Faith works by love ; and love is the fulfilling of the law. Love to God in Christ is the next and immediate fruit of true and saving faith. Now, the heart being oiled with the love of God in Christ, this makes the man to abound in good works: " The love of Christ constraineth us," says the apostle. Love makes a man to keep God's commandments. Love will make a man to run through fire and water for him. " Many waters cannot quench love," &c. Cant. viii. 7, " Who shall separate us from the love of Christ?" Rom. viii. 35.

3. Faith is a shield to quench the fiery darts of Satan. When temptation without, and corruption within, are forming a conspiracy against the work of grace in the soul, whereby the whole work is endangered, then faith breaks the plot, and countermines it. When Adonijah's conspiracy had carried the whole strength of the kingdom of Israel, it was broken by making application unto David, " Hast thou not said, that Solomon shall reign?" So, when temptation and corruption have carried the matter to a great height, the conspiracy is broken by faith's application to Christ : O Lord, hast thou not said that grace shall reign, and that " sin shall not have dominion over me?" And thus the soul is made to go on its way, " rejoicing to work righteousness."

4. Faith applies the promises of the new covenant, and fetches grace from thence, for obeying the precept of the law. So that faith, as it were, travels between

the precept and the promise : it carries the man from the precept unto the promise, and from the promise to the precept. As, for instance, when the law says, " Thou shalt love the Lord thy God with all thy heart, and with all thy soul, and with all thy strength, and with all thy mind ;" faith runs to the promise, where God hath said, " I will circumcise their hearts to love me." . When the law says, " Thou shalt fear the Lord thy God, and make him thy dread ;" faith, in that case, runs to the promise for the grace of fear, " I will put my fear in their hearts, that they shall not depart from me." Does the law say, Thou shalt know the Lord and acknowledge him for thy God ? Well, faith looks to the promise, " I will give them a heart to know me, that I am the Lord." Does the law oblige us to keep all his commandments ? Faith runs to the promise, and applies it, " I will put my Spirit within you, and cause you to walk in my statutes."

5. Faith hath influence on good works, as it beholds the authority of a God in Christ interposed in every commandment of the law. The eye of natural reason may see, as was hinted, the authority of a God-Creator, as is plain in the case of the heathens ; but it is only the eye of that faith, which is of God's operation, that can behold the authority of a God in Christ, and receive the law out of his hands. In this respect we are told, " that no man can call Jesus Lord, but by the Holy Ghost." And when the law is received from his mouth. it does not reflect dishonour upon God as a Creator. O ! when a God in Christ is viewed by faith, the soul cannot but cry out, " He is my King of old, working salvation in the midst of the earth : His commandments are not grievous : His yoke is easy, and his burden is light :" for I see it no more a covenant of works to me, but a rule of obedience, sweetened with redeeming love and grace.

In what respects Good Works are Profitable unto Men.

1. Then, they are not at all profitable unto men for justification or acceptance before God ; for " by the works of the law (says the apostle,) shall no flesh be justified." Our justification and acceptance, both as to our persons and our works, goes upon a quite other ground, namely, upon the everlasting righteousness, the obedience and death, of the Son of God, as our Surety, apprehended by faith. It is in him " that all the seed of Israel shall be justified, and shall glory." Indeed the generality of men, that are trained up in a protestant country, will tell you, that they do not expect to be justified by their own righteousness, but only by the righteousness of Christ. But, alas ! how few are they that do really and actually submit unto this righteousness ! There is a cursed bias in the heart of man to lean to something in himself. Is not this the language of thy heart many times ? O ! if I had such a frame, such a melting heart, such love, such a degree of humility and obedience, then I think God would accept of me, and love me on that account. But sirs, let me tell you, that it is not on the account of any thing wrought in you, or done by you, that God accepts of you, but only on the accout of the doing and dying of the Son of God. I may say to all legalists, that are looking for acceptance with God on the ground of the law, and their own obedience, as the prophet Isaiah says to a set of men in his day, Is. lix. 6, " Their webs shall not become garments, neither shall they cover themselves with their works." So, then, good works are not at all profitable to righteousness and justification. Hence is that, Is. lvii. 12, " I will declare thy righteousness, and thy works, for they shall not profit thee."

2. Good works are not at all profitable to found a claim or title unto heaven, or yet to any blessing and mercy promised in the whole covenant of grace ; for heaven, and all the blessings that lie on this side of it,

they come to us in the way of a free gift. God gives Christ his unspeakable gift, and with him he freely gives us these things: "The gift of God is eternal life, through Jesus Christ our Lord." I own indeed, that in God's covenant of promise there is a connection and order established, for conferring of these promised blessings unto us, so that when God gives one thing, it is a pledge of another thing a-coming: when he gives grace, to be sure he will give glory; when he gives a mourning heart, it is a sign that comfort is a-coming, because that is God's method and way, "to give the oil of joy for mourning, and to revive the heart of the humble." But though the tears of gospel-mourning be a sign and evidence of comfort a-coming, yet they are not the condition for which God bestows comfort. So God has connected faith and salvation together in the covenant; so that "he that believeth shall be saved:" but it is not our faith that entitles us unto salvation; no, but faith unites the soul to Christ, in whom we recover our right to the forfeited inheritance. It is by virtue of the soul's union with Christ by faith, that it is entitled to all the promised blessings. Hence all the promises are said to be "in him yea, and in him amen." There is no promise in the Bible, but it is made in the first instance to Christ as the head, and in him to the members of his mystical body. Just as it was in the first covenant, to wit, the covenant of works; the promise of life upon condition of perfect obedience, was made directly to Adam as the covenant-head, and, in him, to his posterity: so in the new covenant, of which Christ is the head, the promise of life, and every thing belonging to it, is first made to him; and in him, to all his spiritual seed and offspring: and in this respect all the promises are yea and amen in him. Christ is the first heir of all things; and the title of the younger brethren is only through him, or by virtue of their union with him. Thus, good works, I say, are not profitable unto men, in order to found a title to heaven and eternal life.

3. Our good works, as they are not profitable unto men in any of these respects, so neither are they profitable unto God, as though he had any advantage by them : Job. xxii. 2, 3, " Can a man be profitable unto God, as he that is wise may be profitable unto himself? Is it any pleasure to the Almighty, that thou art righteous? or is it gain to him, that thou makest thy ways perfect?" Hence David acknowledgeth, that " his goodness extended not to the Lord." Alas! we are ready to think, that God is much indebted unto us when we do this or that : Have we fasted and prayed, mourned and repented, kept the Sabbath, attended ordinances, and performed this or the other duty ; and yet will not God be pleased with all? No, no ; do not mistake it, sirs, you that bring these things as a price in your hands, to recommend you to God, all your duties are but like the cutting off of a dog's neck, and the offering of swine's blood upon his altar. And therefore he will say to you, as he said to Israel, Is. i. 11, " To what purpose is the multitude of your sacrifices unto me."

But now, you may perhaps say to me, By this way of speaking you make good works profitable for nothing at all. What strange doctrine is this? I answer, although they be not at all profitable in any of these respects, but wholly unprofitable and pernicious ; yet good works, when done out of a principle of faith, they are really profitable on many other accounts. As,

1. They are profitable, as they are the fruits and evidences of a true and lively faith : Jam. ii. 18, " Yea, a man may say, Thou hast faith and I have works : show me thy faith without thy works, and I will show thee my faith by my works." And ver. 22, " Seest thou how faith wrought with his works, and by works was faith made perfect?" From whence it is plain, that works are profitable, as the fruits and evidences of true faith. We know that there is sap and life in the tree by the fruits, the leaves, and blossoms, that

it puts forth ; so we know our faith, to be a true faith, by the fruits of holiness and good works. Yea, our good works will be brought forth at the last day, as the evidence of our faith ; and therefore it is said, Rev. xx. 12, " They were judged according to their works." Works are not a ground of confidence, but an evidence ; they are not the foundation of faith, but the fruits of it : and the believer's comfort may be increased by the sight of good works, though it is not built on them. In a word they manifest our claim and title to the crown, but do not at all found or merit the same. We have peace with God and with conscience, by the righteousness of Christ ; and by holiness, or good works, our peace of conscience is maintained and evidenced unto us.

2. They are profitable, as they are testimonies and evidences of our gratitude unto God for the wonders of his grace and love, manifested in and by Jesus Christ. Hence is that of David, Psal. cxvi. 12, 13, " What shall I render unto the Lord, for all his benefits towards me ? I will take the cup of salvation, and call upon the name of the Lord." 1 Pet. ii. 9, " Ye are a chosen generation, a royal priesthood, a holy nation, a peculiar people ; that ye should show forth the praises of him who hath called you out of darkness into his marvellous light." The works of obedience, they are, as it were, thank-offerings unto God for the benefits bestowed on us ; and when men have not a conversation suitable unto their mercies, they despise the goodness of God. Hence is it that the Lord complains of such, saying, " Do ye thus requite the Lord, O foolish people and unwise ?"

3. They are profitable and needful for strengthening our assurance: 1 John ii. 3, " Hereby we do know that we know him if we keep his commandments." And ver. 5, " Whoso keepeth his word, in him verily is the love of God perfected : hereby know we that we are in him." 2 Pet. i. 5, to ver. 10. From all which you see, that assurance is strengthened and confirmed by

the fruits of holiness and good works. We read, that
" the Spirit beareth witness with our spirit, that we are
the children of God :" and it is well, when, with the
witness of the Spirit, we have that of water, that is,
sanctification and purity of heart and life.

4. They are profitable, as they are edifying unto
others : Matth. v. 16, " Let your light so shine before
men, that they may see your good works, and glorify
your Father which is in heaven." Christ does not
there encourage vain-glory and boasting, but proposeth
the true end of our visible or external holiness, namely,
that others may have matter of praise to God, for his
grace abounding toward us ; and that they may be also
engaged to the study of holiness and practical religion
by our example. It was a saying of Hierom, " That
he loved Christ dwelling in Austin." So we ought
so to walk, as others may love Christ dwelling in us.
It is an exhortation to believing wives, 1 Pet. iii. 1,
so to walk, that their husbands may be won to the
Lord. So that, I say, good works are edifying to
others.

5. They are profitable, as they serve to adorn the
profession of the gospel : 1 Tim. vi. 1, " Let as many
servants as are under the yoke, count their own masters worthy of all honour ; that the name of God, and
his doctrine be not blasphemed." Tit. ii. 5, 9, 10, 11,
12. Thus they serve to adorn religion. The church
is the Lord's garden ; and you know the fruitfulness of
the trees of the garden serve exceedingly to adorn it ;
whereas barrenness, or bad fruit, is a disgrace, and
makes the garden to be ill spoken of. When men,
professing godliness, have not a walk and conversation
suitable, it makes enemies and strangers to conclude,
that all religion is but a fraud or cheat, and that there
is no reality in it ; whereas a fruitful conversation stops
the mouths of the enemies of religion : 1 Pet. ii. 15,
" So is the will of God, that with well-doing ye may
put to silence the ignorance of foolish men."

6. They are profitable, as they manifest our implan-

tation or ingrafting into Christ: Eph. ii. 10, " We are his workmanship, created in Christ Jesus unto good works, which God hath before ordained that we should walk in them."

7. There is an analogy and proportion between good works and glory : Rom. vi. 22, " But now being made free from sin, and become servants to God, ye have your fruit unto holiness, and the end everlasting life."*

Arguments to urge Sinners to Embrace Christ, together with Answers to Objections.

1. CONSIDER the absolute need ye have of this Christ whom we offer unto you. Without him ye are condemned already ; without him ye are without God in the world ; God is angry with you every day ; the law and justice of God, like the avenger of blood, is pursuing you. And therefore, O sinners, flee to a Saviour, " Turn ye to your strong-hold, ye prisoners of hope."

2. Consider the matchless excellency of that Saviour whom we call you to embrace. Angels and men are at an everlasting stand to speak of his worth and glory; he is best known by his own or his Father's testimony concerning him: and if ye would know the record of God concerning him, search the Scriptures, for these are they that testify of him ; it is in this glass that " we behold his glory, the glory as of the only begotten of the Father, full of grace and truth." I despair that ever a sinner will embrace Christ, till there be an uptaking of his personal excellency, as Immanuel God-man. There is a seeing of the Son, which, in order of nature, although not in order of time, goes before the soul's believing in him, John vi. 40.

3. Consider the ability and sufficiency of this Sa-

* See more on this important subject, in " Evangelical Lectures and Essays," by the Editor, page 45, &c.

viour whom we call you to embrace." Take the Father's testimony of his ability, Psal. lxxxix. 20, " I have laid help upon one that is mighty." Take his own testimony, Is. lxiii. 1, " I that speak in righteousness, mighty to save." Take the Spirit's testimony, in the mouth of the apostle Paul, Heb. vii. 25, declaring him "able to save them to the uttermost, that come unto God by him." Thus ye have the three that bear record in heaven, attesting this sufficiency of the Saviour. O then " set to your seal, that God is true, by believing the record that God gives of his Son ;" for if ye do not, your unbelief gives the lie unto a whole Trinity, 1 John v. 10, 11.

4. Consider that this sufficient Saviour is " the sent of God." This is a designation given to Christ thirty or forty times in the gospel according to John, and the ordinary argument with which Christ persuades sinners to embrace and receive him. And nothing could have greater influence than this designation, if the weight of it were but duly weighed. O consider in what quality and capacity his Father has sent him : shall not God's Ambassador-extraordinary get a hearing among a company of condemned rebels? He is sent as a Redeemer to liberate captives ; and shall not captives embrace him ? He is sent as a Surety ; and will not dyvours and bankrupts embrace a cautioner ? He is sent as a Physician ; and will not the wounded and diseased sinner embrace him, and his healing balm ? &c.

5. Consider, that his heart and his arms are open and ready to embrace all that are willing to be embraced by him. O may the soul say, fain would I embrace him, but I doubt of his willingness to embrace me. I tell you good news, he is more willing to embrace you by far than you are to be embraced by him.

He says he is willing, and you may believe his word, for he is " the Amen, the faithful and true Witness ;" and he says, that he will cast out none that come unto him : he swears he is willing, and will ye not believe his oath ? Ezek. xxxiii. 11, " As I live, saith the

Lord God, I have no pleasure in the death of the wicked, but that the wicked turn from his way and live." Pray tell me, why did he engage from eternity, and voluntarily give his hand to the Father in the council of peace, saying, Lo, I come ;—I delight to do thy will, O my God ?" Why did he assume the nature of man, and the sinless infirmities thereof? Why did he that is the great Lawgiver, subject himself unto his own law? Why did he that is the Lord of life and glory, submit to the stroke of death ignominiously upon a cross? Why doth he send out his ministers to you, with call upon call ? Why doth he wait all the day long, saying, " Behold me, behold me ?" Why doth he expostulate the matter with you? Why is he grieved at the obstinacy of your hearts, if he be not willing that ye should embrace him ? For the Lord's sake therefore consider these things, and do not reject the counsel of God against yourselves.

6. Consider what a glorious train and retinue of blessings come along with him, when he is embraced in the arms of faith : such as pardon of sin ; Heb. viii. 12.; peace with God, Rom. v. 1; a complete justifying righteousness, Rom. viii. 3, 4.; adoption and sonship, John i. 1 ; sanctification, both in the root and fruit of it, 1 Cor. i. 30 ; saving knowledge of God, and the mysteries of his covenant, 2 Cor. iv. 6.; the crown of eternal glory at last, John iii. 16. All these might be particularly enlarged on ; but I do not insist, but proceed to obviate some objections that some may make against complying with this exhortation.

Object. 1. Some poor soul may be ready to say, Gladly would I embrace Christ with my very soul; but still I entertain a jealousy of my right and warrant to meddle with the unspeakable gift of God; he is such a great good, that I am afraid it is but presumption in me to attempt the embracing of him. Now, for removing any jealousies of this nature, I shall lay before you a few of these warrants, upon which a lost sinner may receive and embrace this Saviour.

1. Let desperate and absolute necessity be your warrant.   Ye must either do or die; there is no mids:
" He that believeth, shall be saved ; but he that believeth not, shall be damned." Do not stand to dispute
the matter ; there is no time, no, not one moment of
time, wherein a man is allowed to toss this question in
his breast, after the revelation of Christ to him in the
gospel, Shall I believe, or shall I not ? Or if ye will
dispute the matter, will ye argue as the Samaritan
lepers did : " If we sit still here, we perish ; but if we
go into the camp of the Assyrians, peradventure we
shall live."   So we, if we sit still in this sinful and miserable condition, without God and without Christ in
the world, we unavoidably perish ; but if we throw ourselves into the arms of a Redeemer, and upon the mercy of God in him, beyond peradventure we shall be
saved.   And therefore, I say, let absolute necessity be
your warrant.

2. Venture to embrace this Saviour in the arms of
faith, upon the warrant of the very design of his incarnation.   Why, is there a Saviour provided ?   Why was
he manifested in the flesh ?   Upon what errand was
he sent into the world, but to seek and save that which
was lost ?   Well, since this is the very design of God
in giving a Saviour, that sinners might be saved by him,
what can be more agreeable unto him, or his Father
that sent him, than that a lost sinner should embrace
and receive him ?

3. Let the revelation of this incarnate Deity, in the
glorious gospel, be your warrant to embrace and receive him : a bare revelation of a Saviour, without any
more, is enough to induce a sinner to believe in him.
Why was the brazen serpent in the wilderness lifted up
on the pole, but that every one in the camp of Israel,
who were stung with the fiery serpents, might look unto it, and be healed ?   The very lifting up of the brazen serpent was a sufficient warrant to any man to look
to it : so the Son of man his being lifted up on the pole

of the everlasting gospel, warrants every man to believe him, John iii. 14, 15.

4. Besides the revelation of Christ, ye have a full, free, and unhampered offer of him in the external call of the gospel ; and this directed to every one without exception, Is. lv. 1—3. Rev. xxii. 17. Mark xvi. 15. Prov. viii. 4. Sirs, we offer a Christ to you, and the whole fulness of grace and glory, merit and Spirit, that is in him, as the free gift of God, without the money and price of your own works and qualifications ; if ye bring any such price, to make a purchase of the pearl of great price, ye shall lose him for ever : God loves to give his Christ freely, but he scorns to receive any thing for him. Let this then be your warrant, that Christ is gifted and offered of God in this gospel : and let it be remembered that in the matter of a gift, there is no difference between man and man ; the poorest as well as the richest, may receive a gift presented unto him : a condemned malefactor has as good a right to receive a gift presented unto him by the king, as the greatest favourite in the court ; his being a guilty criminal is no prejudice at all to his receiving a gift ; yea, his being so, qualifies him for receiving the pardon. So here Christ's being the gift of God freely offered and presented, warrants the sinner to receive him, without respect to any qualifications but that of his being a sinner. Hunger is the best disposing qualification for meat, nakedness fits a man for clothing, &c. And that Christ seeks no other qualifications is evident from his counsel to Laodicea, Rev. iii. 17, 18,—"Thou art wretched, and miserable, and poor, and blind, and naked. I counsel thee to buy of me gold tried in the fire, that thou mayest be rich ; and white raiment that thou mayest be clothed, and that the shame of thy nakedness do not appear ; and anoint thine eyes with eyesalve that thou mayest see."

5. Ye have not only an offer of Christ, but an express command requiring you to embrace him, for your warrant : John iii. 23, " This is his commandment, that

we should believe on the name of his Son Jesus Christ."
Sirs, it is not a thing left optional to you to embrace
Christ or not, as ye please ; no, ye are concluded under a law fenced with the severest penalty, " He that
believeth not is condemned already, and the wrath of
God abideth on him." The unbelieving sinner counteracts the authority of heaven ; and thus rushes upon
" God's neck, upon the thick bosses of his bucklers."
Ye have no reason to doubt but that the command of
believing is to you ; for if ye were not commanded to
believe, your unbelief could not be your sin : " Where
no law is, there is no transgression." Ye do not doubt,
but ye are commanded by the word of God, to read,
hear, pray, sanctify the Sabbath, and to perform the
other duties of the moral law ; and because they are
commanded, ye mint at obedience. Now believing is
as peremptorily enjoined, yea, rather more than any other
duty, inasmuch as the successful and acceptable performance of all other duties depends upon it. And
therefore do not stand disputing your warrant, against
the express authority of Heaven.

6. Besides the command of God, ye have a promise
of welcome to encourage you in believing : John vi.
37, " Him that cometh to me, I will in no wise cast
out." John iii. 16, " Whosoever believeth in him,
shall not perish, but have everlasting life." But, say
ye, these promises may be to others, and not to me. I
answer, The promise is indorsed to you, directed to
you, in the external call and dispensation of the gospel, Acts ii. 39. There the apostle is preaching to a
company of men, whose hands had lately been dipped
in the blood of the Son of God. He calls them to faith
and repentance. By what argument does he enforce
the exhortation ? Why, he tells them, " The promise
is unto you, and to your children, and to all that are
afar off, even as many as the Lord our God shall call."
Where it is plain, the promise is extended, first to the
Jews, and then to the Gentiles, who at that time were
afar off ; and then indefinitely, both to Jew and Gen-

tile, to whom the call of the gospel should reach; the external call which is only here intended, howsoever, the Spirit of the Lord did internally concur, being the alone foundation upon which the promise is to be received, and not the internal call of one person, which can never be a warrant of believing to another. And therefore, as the apostle said to them, so say I to you, in the name of God, "the promise is unto you," I mean, the promise of welcome: "Whosoever of you believeth, shall not perish." This promise is not made to believers exclusively of others, but to every one that hears this gospel; for if so, we could call none to believe but such as have believed, which is most absurd. Well then, let God's promise warrant you to believe in Christ: and if ye do not think this sufficient, take his promise of welcome, ratified with his oath, Ezek. xxxiii. 11, these being the "two immutable things wherein it is impossible for God to lie."

7. Let the indefinite and absolute nature of the covenant of grace be your warrant for embracing the Lord Jesus. The covenant of grace, as it lies in the external dispensation of the gospel, is conceived in the form of a blank bond, or testamentary deed, where there is room left to every man to fill up his name, by the hand of faith. The strain and tenor of it is, " I will be their God, and they shall be my people: I will take away the stony heart out of their flesh, and will give them an heart of flesh: I will sprinkle clean water upon them: I will put my Spirit within them: I will be merciful to their unrighteousness: I will subdue their iniquities." Where, you see, the grant runs in an indefinite way; no man's name mentioned, neither any by name excluded. Why, what is the design of this, but that every man may be encouraged to subscribe his name, or to make application thereof to his own soul, in a way of believing, by which we are said to take hold of God's covenant? O sirs! the covenant of grace, as it lies in the external dispensation of the gospel, (for now I abstract from his secret purposes,

which are not at all the measure or rule of faith,) is
just like a rope cast in among a company of drowning
men ; he that throws it in, cries to every one of them
to take hold of the rope, promising to draw them safe
to shore : so God in the gospel-dispensation proposes
his covenant to every one as a ground of faith, assuring them, that whosoever takes hold of his covenant,
and receives his Christ, whom he hath "given for a
covenant of the people, shall not perish, but have everlasting life." For the Lord's sake do not put this rope
of salvation away from you, under a pretence that ye
know not if it be designed for you. Would not you
reckon it ridiculous madness in any of these drowning
men now mentioned, to fall a-disputing whether the
rope were cast in to them, when they are at the very
point of sinking to the bottom ? Would not every one
of them gripe at it with the utmost strength and vigour, without putting any question ? Now this is the
very case, O sinner ; thou art going down to the pit
of eternal misery ; God, by his ministers, cries to
you to take hold of this rope of salvation : O then !
" see that ye refuse not him that speaketh from heaven ;" do not dispute yourselves away from your own
mercy.

8. Let the welcome that others have met with in
coming to Christ be your encouragement to venture
also. Never any that really came to him, but they met
with a kindly reception. Ask the prodigal son, ask
Mary Magdalene, Paul, and others, what entertainment they met with from this Saviour ; they will be
ready to tell you that they "obtained mercy." Now
the same mercy that saved them, is as ready to save
you. You do not doubt but Moses, David, Peter,
Paul, and other saints that are now in glory, had sufficient warrant to believe. Sirs, you have the same
grounds of faith as ever they had ; the same God, the
same Saviour, the same Bible, the same covenant, the
same promises, the same faithfulness of God to lean to,
as ever they had ; and these grounds of faith are so

firm, that they never disappointed any that leaned to
them : and therefore be encouraged to believe, as they
did.   O how will it gall and torment unbelieving sinners in hell for ever, when they see others, who believed upon the same grounds that were common to them
also, sitting down in the kingdom of heaven, and themselves shut up in utter darkness, with devils and damned spirits, because of their unbelief!   And how will
the devil himself upbraid unbelievers in hell, when fallen under the same condemnation with himself, that
they had such fair warrants to believe in Christ which
he never had.

Object. 2. You bid me embrace Christ ; but, alas !
he is far away out of my reach : Christ is in heaven,
how shall I win at him ?

Answ. Seeing ye cannot come up to Christ, Christ
is come down to you ; and we bring him near to you, in
this word of salvation which we preach : Is. xlvi. 12,
13, " Hearken unto me, ye stout-hearted, that are far
from righteousness.   I bring near my righteousness :
it shall not be far off, and my salvation shall not tarry."
And therefore, say not in thine heart, Who shall ascend
into heaven ? (that is, to bring Christ down from
above ;) or, Who shall descend into the deep ? (that is,
to bring Christ up again from the dead) : for the word
is nigh thee, even in thy mouth, and in thy heart :
that is the word of faith which we preach," Rom. x.
6—8.   Sirs, Christ is in this gospel, this word of faith
and grace, which we, in the name of God, deliver unto
you ; and your faith must terminate immediately upon
this word, otherwise you can never embrace him.   As
I believe or trust a man by his verbal or written promise ; so I embrace Christ by the word of faith, or
promises in the gospel.   Suppose a sponsible man re-
siding in America, should send me his bill for any sum
of money, that man and his money are brought near to
me by his bill and security which he sends me : so here,
though Christ be in heaven, and we upon earth, yet
the word of faith which we preach, brings him, his

kingdom, righteousness, salvation, and whole fulness, nigh unto every one of us, so that we need not ascend into heaven, or descend into hell, in quest of him.

On the Reign of Grace.

1. Grace reigns and is displayed in the contrivance of this righteousness ; for it is the device of infinite wisdom, animated and inspired by free grace. When man had fallen under the sentence of the law, justice was ready to execute judgment upon him : but grace cries, Stop, and stay thy hand, for " I have found a ransom." 2 Sam. xiv. 14, "God doth devise means, that his banished be not expelled." Our first parents, they provoked God to drive them out of paradise, and accordingly they were actually driven out of his presence ; but infinite wisdom, actuated and animated by the bowels of mercy, contrives a way how banished man may be brought home again in a consistency with justice, and that is by the righteousness of the Messiah.

2. Grace reigns and is displayed in the acceptation of this righteousness. What but infinite love and grace could prevail with inexorable justice, so far to dispense with the rigour of the law, as to admit of a surety's righteousness in the room of the sinner ! But this I touched upon already. And therefore,

3. Grace reigns in the impetration of this righteousness ; for " God (in his amazing grace) sent forth his Son, made of a woman, made under the law, to redeem them that were under the law." That righteousness whereby we are justified, is the very righteousness of God in our nature, he wrought it by his doing and dying. O how does grace reign here ! Faith's views of this may fill us all with wonder, and make us cry with the church, Is. lxiii.1, " Who is this that cometh from Edom, with dyed garments from Bozrah ? this that is glorious in his apparel, travelling in the greatness of his strength ?"

4. Grace reigns in the revelation of this righteousness. Grace was not content to contrive and bring about this righteousness, but the news of it must be published and proclaimed to a lost world, as it were by sound of trumpet. Hence the apostle, Rom. i. 17, when he would give us an account of the sum and substance of the gospel, he does it in one word, "The gospel is the power of God unto salvation ; for therein is revealed the righteousness of God." O how forward was the grace of God, to have the proclamation anent the satisfaction of justice by a surety, issued out! Adam had scarce sinned, till grace intimates the plot unto him in the first promise, " The seed of the woman shall bruise the head of the serpent." The Messiah is scarce born in Bethlehem, till an angel is despatched from heaven to notify it to the shepherds, " Unto you is born this day, in the city of David, a Saviour, which is Christ the Lord."

5. Grace reigns and is displayed in the appropinquation, or the bringing near of this righteousness to the sinner in a preached gospel. Not only does grace reveal the righteousness of God, but it brings it near to the sinner, in order to be accepted and received : Is. xlvi. 12, 13, " Hearken unto me, ye stout-hearted, that are far from righteousness. I bring near my righteousness : it shall not be far off," &c. It is brought near to the sinner, just as the manna was brought near to Israel, when it fell in about the tent doors; they had not far to go for it.

6. Grace reigns and is displayed in the imputation of this righteousness. And indeed there is a great mystery of grace here, that cannot be expressed in words; how a guilty sinner, that has violated the law, and is obnoxious to justice, comes to be sustained in the sight of God as though he had fulfilled the law, and satisfied justice in his own person, and to be put in case to say, " Who shall lay any thing to my charge ? It is God that justifieth: who is he that condemneth ?"

7. Grace reigns in the soul's acceptation of this righteousness by faith. There is nothing in all the world that runs so cross to proud nature, as to renounce all its own righteousness, its obedience, duties, endeavours, its own grace and holiness, in point of acceptance, and to submit to the righteousness of another, and to be obliged to the doing and dying of the Son of God alone. This was a stone of stumbling to the Jews; they could never imagine any other way of justification before God, but by the works of the law ; and therefore they " went about to establish a righteousness of their own, and would not submit unto the righteousness of God." Now, I say, to unhinge a sinner from this legal bottom, to bring down these towering imaginations of a righteousness in ourselves, to cast down the refuge of lies, and to bring the proud, conceited sinner that length, as to own and acknowledge, that his own righteousness is but as filthy rags, saying " Surely in the Lord only have I righteousness and strength ; in him will I be justified, and in him alone will I glory." I say, grace reigns, and is wonderfully displayed in all this.

8. Grace reigns through righteousness, inasmuch as that it is by the revelation of this justice-satisfying righteousness, that grace conquers and powerfully subdues sinners, brings them under its own government and dominion. The apostle, speaking of believers, Rom. vi. 14, says, " Ye are not under the law, but under grace ;" that is, ye are brought in under the government and administration of grace. But what way is it that grace conquers them? what is the great engine made use of for this end? it is just the revelation of the righteousness of Christ in the gospel, Rom. i. 15, " The gospel is the power of God unto salvation." What way? Mark the expression, ver. 17, " For therein is the righteousness of God revealed from faith to faith." From which it is plain, that the preaching of an imputed righteousness, as the alone ground of a sinner's acceptance, is the very pith and marrow of the

gospel. Some, now-a-days, they have got a way of preaching, which, I believe, will never convert a soul; they deliver fine elegant harangues of morality, adorning them with all the flowers of rhetoric; but, in the meantime, they do but stink in the nostrils of a solid Christian. Why? Because though they preach us a moral righteousness, yet they have little or nothing of the righteousness of Christ, which is the very basis and foundation of a throne of grace: and when that is wanting, they want the true Shibboleth of the gospel; for the gospel is a revelation of " the righteousness of God;" and this makes it to be " the power of God unto salvation."

Here I judge it not amiss, to subjoin a quotation from the great and judicious Owen to this purpose, in his Commentary on the Hebrews, chap. v. 7, " Some are of the mind," says he, " that the whole business of ministers, is to be conversant in and about morality. For this fountain and spring of grace," the righteousness and satisfaction of Christ; " this basis of eternal glory; this evidence and demonstration of divine wisdom, holiness, righteousness, and love; this great discovery of the purity of the law and vileness of sin; this first, great, principal subject of the gospel, and motive of faith and obedience; this root and cause of all peace with God, all sincere and incorrupted love toward him, of all joy and consolation from him,—they think it scarcely deserves a place in the objects of their contemplation, and are ready to guess, that what men write and talk about it, is but phrases, canting and fanatical. But such as are admitted into the fellowship of the sufferings of Christ, will not so easily part with their immortal interest and concern therein. Yea, I fear not to say, that he is likely to be the best, the most humble and the most holy and fruitful Christian, who is most sedulous and diligent in spiritual inquiries into this great mystery, of the reconciliation of God unto sinners by the blood of the cross, and in the exercise of faith about it. Nor is there any such powerful means of preserving the soul in a constant abhorrence of sin, and watchfulness against it, as a due apprehension of what it cost to make atonement for it."

Sinners Flying to Christ, both Pleasing and Surprising.

1. IT is pleasant to God the Father, Son, and Holy Ghost, and to all the angels and glorified saints; for there is joy in heaven, when a sinner on earth takes a flight into Christ by faith. It is pleasant to all honest minis-ters who travail in birth till Christ be formed in sinners; and it is pleasant to God's whole family; all his house rejoices when the prodigal comes home.

I will tell you some things that make it a pleasant sight to see sinners fly into Christ, "as doves to their windows." 1. It cannot but be pleasant, because it is a fulfilling of God's purpose of grace and love from all eternity. He has loved his own with an everlasting love; he loved them when he saw them in their blood. Now must it not be pleasant to see the election of God obtaining and taking place; to see his everlasting love breaking out in the drawing of his own with loving-kindness? 2. It must be pleasant, because the flight of sinners to Christ is just the travail of Christ's soul, Is. liii. "He shall see of the travail of his soul, and shall be satisfied." It is a satisfaction to Christ to see the fruit of his sore travail, when he said, "Now my soul is exceeding sorrowful, even unto death;" and what is so pleasant unto Christ himself, cannot but be plea-sant unto all that love him. 3. It is the day of his es-pousals, the day of Christ's marriage and coronation, and therefore must be very pleasant to the bride, and the friends of the Bridegroom, Cant. iii. 11, "Go forth, O ye daughters of Zion, and behold king Solomon with the crown wherewith his mother crowned him in the day of his espousals," &c. 4. Because then the prisoners are released, "the captives of the mighty are taken away, and the prey of the terrible is delivered," &c. 5. It is pleasant, because then the head of the old serpent gets a new bruise, and his works are destroyed more and more, " The strong man is then bound and spoiled of his goods."

2. I come to tell you, that the flight of the sinner to Christ is not only pleasant, but surprising and amazing. And this will appear, if we consider,

1. The state and condition that the sinner is into before he fly to Christ. He is dead in sin, wholly destitute of any principle of spiritual life. Now, is it not surprising to see God showing wonders among the dead? to see a dead sinner rising and taking a flight to Christ within the vail? The sinner is afar off; and is it not surprising to see the man that was " afar off, made nigh by the blood of Jesus?" The sinner is by nature full of enmity against God and his Christ, yea, enmity itself: and is it not surprising to see the enmity of the heart broken, and the man brought to a state of peace and reconciliation with God.

2. The flight of the sinner to Christ is surprising, considering the strong opposition that arises against it from within. The ignorance of the mind lies in the way; for we are " alienate from the life of God through the ignorance that is in us,"and it is impossible, while this stands in its power and reign, that ever the sinner can fly to Christ, because faith is founded in knowledge, even " the light of the knowledge of the glory of God in the face of Jesus Christ." The obstinacy and hardness of the heart stands in the way. The will is inflexible, and will bend to nothing but the almighty power of God ; and is it not surprising to see this iron sinew bended and made pliable by the rod of the Mediator's strength ? &c. The legal bias of the heart opposes the sinner's flight unto Christ : the man is married to the law as a covenant, and nature can never think of another way of acceptance before God than by doing or working ; and is it not surprising to see the sinner that was wedded to the law, and to his own righteousness, crying, " I through the law am dead to the law, that I may live unto God," through the righteousness

of Christ ; and saying with Paul, " What things were gain to me, those I counted loss for Christ ; yea, doubtless, I count all things but dung, that I may win Christ, and be found in him, not having mine own righteousness," &c. Again, the guilt that is upon the conscience opposes the sinner's flight to Christ ; for we find a guilty Adam flying from the presence of God ; and the natural language of a guilty conscience, when it is awakened, is, O there is no mercy for me, there is no hope of acceptance. Now is it not surprising to see the sinner, that was flying from God under a sense of guilt, flying to him through Christ, and crying, " Pardon mine iniquity, for it is great," &c. Again, the carnality of the affections lie in the way of the sinner's flight. The man was flying after vanity, and crying, " O, who will show me any good ?" who will give me riches, honours, pleasures in a world ? This is the natural run of the affections ; they spend themselves upon things that cannot profit ; and is it not surprising to see the man turning his back upon all these things ? saying with Solomon, "All is vanity," and seeking and " setting his affections on things that are above, where Christ is at the right hand of God."

3. The flight of the sinner to Christ is surprising, if we consider how active Satan is to keep the sinner under his power. He is called the strong man, and he keeps the house ; he rules in the hearts of the children of disobedience, and leads them about in the chains of their own lusts. Now, is it not surprising to see Christ coming in a day of his power, " spoiling the strong man of his prey ;" and not only so, but arming the poor captive of the devil as a soldier under his own banner, to resist that enemy, and put him to flight, and by the shield of faith, quenching the fiery darts of the enemy ?

4. It is surprising, if we consider the entanglements of an ensnaring world. The devil is called the god of this world, because ever since the entry of sin, Satan

has got so much power over the good things and bad
things of it, as that they are all his tools for ruining
the souls of sinners, and for detaining them in his service.   Hence is it that we see most part of the world
dancing to the devil's pipe, and selling their souls for
profits, for pleasures, for riches, for honours, and the
like. These are just the devil's baits, whereby he trains
men and women on, until he has brought them to hell,
where he is sure he has them fast through eternity.
Now, is it not surprising to see a sinner that has been
decoyed and deceived all his days with the things of
the world, casting them all behind his back, and trampling on them like the woman, Rev. xii. 1, who hath the
moon under her feet, &c.

In a word, is it not surprising to see the dry bones
getting life, and flesh, and strength ? to see the Ethiopian washed and made whiter than snow ? the seed of
the serpent that licked the dust taking a flight from
earth to heaven ?

What those who have Fled to Christ, have certainly Found in Him.

IF you have really fled to Christ as doves to their
windows, there are some things you have found in him,
which you could never find any where else.   1. Thou
hast found the life of thy soul in him : Our "life is hid
with Christ in God : He that hath the Son hath life,"
&c.   2. Thou hast found rest to thy soul in him :
Thou triedst to find this and the former in lying refuges,
but was aye disappointed in thy expectation, but now,
now, thou hast found it according to his promise,
Matth. xi. " Come unto me, all ye that labour and are
heavy laden, and I will give you rest," O glorious rest!
Is. xi. 10.   3. Thou hast found soul-health in him, like
the woman that spent all her means upon other physi-
cians to no purpose, till she came and touched the hem
of Christ's garments, and then the bloody issue was
stayed.   So can not thou say upon thy coming to
Christ ; thou foundst his countenance to be thy health ;

" healing is under his wings," Mal. iv. 2. Psal. ciii. 3,
" He healeth all my diseases," &c. 4. Thou hast found
food to thy soul in him: His "flesh is meat indeed, and his blood is drink indeed, &c. O taste and
see that the Lord is good," &c. 5. Thou hast found
clothing to thy naked soul in him: you was trying,
like our first parents, to cover thy nakedness with fig-
leaves; but now thou castest these away, and taking
the skin of the word to cover thee with, which God
provided, and upon thy being thus clothed with the
righteousness of Christ, thou hast been made to sing
that song, Is. lxi. 10, " He hath clothed me with the
garments of salvation, he hath covered me with the
robe of righteousness," &c. 6. You have found riches,
and unsearchable riches, in him, that do not rot in the
grave, gold better than the gold of Ophir, to make you
up for all eternity. 7. In one word, you have found
your God in him, whom you lost in the first Adam;
for God is in Christ, and you have found him as your
own God: and now you will be ready to say, he is
" my God, and I will prepare him a habitation, even
the God and Father of our Lord Jesus Christ; and
therefore I will exalt him. Our God is the God of
salvation," &c.

*Exhortations to Sinners to Fly to Christ, with Answers to
Objections.*

THAT you may fly to Christ, consider, 1. God commands you to fly to Christ, " This is his commandment, That we should believe on the name of his Son
Jesus Christ," &c.

2. He invites you to fly to his Christ, " Behold my
servant whom I uphold," &c.

3. He entreats and beseeches you to fly to him, " We
pray you in Christ's stead, as though God did beseech
you by us, be ye reconciled to God," &c.

4. He expostulates with you, because of your back-

slidings, to fly to him, "O my people! what have I done unto thee?" &c.

5. He assures you of welcome by his promise, "Come to me who will, I will in no wise cast out," &c. And by his oath, "As I live, I have no pleasure in the death of the wicked, but rather that the wicked turn from his way and live," &c.

6. All things in his house are ready to give entertainment unto you, behold, "all things are ready, come to the marriage," Proverbs, 8th and 9th chapters.

7. Fly, the windows are open, the heart of Christ is open, &c. His arms are open and stretched out, &c. His covenant is open to you to take hold of it, &c.

8. Consider what is behind you. (1.) The roaring lion, ready to devour you. (2.) The curse of the broken law is behind you, &c. (3.) The wrath of God is behind you. O! who knows the power of it? &c.

9. There is no safety for you in heaven nor earth, if you do not fly from sin: "There is no other name under heaven given among men, whereby we must be saved," &c. "How shall we escape if we neglect so great a salvation: they that despised Moses' law died without mercy," &c.

10. The time of flying will be gone within a little; no flying out of hell; none to come to you there to cry, "Turn ye to your strong-holds," &c. "He that lives for ever and ever, has sworn, with his hand lifted up to heaven, that time shall be no more," &c. "And therefore to-day, if ye will hear his voice," &c.

11. Fly, or else you will lose your soul for ever; "He that believeth not shall be damned." And "what is a man profited, if he shall gain the whole world, and lose his own soul," &c.

Object. 1. You bid us fly, but to what purpose? you tell us we are dead in sins. *Answ.* It is the glory of sovereign grace to show wonders to the dead; see what he did among the dry bones, Ezek. xxxvii. 3, &c. Can these dry bones live? Yea, if the Spirit of the

Lord breathe upon them, God has bidden prophesy upon dry bones to cry to the dead, to arise and fly ; and therefore we must do it.   And if God would bid me say to the mountains, Remove, to the rocks, and trees, and grass piles, Arise and live, I would do it, and I would believe that God would make it effectual.

Object. 2. You bid me fly, but alas ! I want wings to fly, " O that I had wings like a dove, for then would I fly," &c.   *Answ.* If there be a will to fly, and a hearty desire to fly, thou hast got wings : and if you want even that, seek wings from him that bids you fly, for he gives power to the faint, and then they mount up with wings as eagles, &c.

Object. 3. I have a load of sin upon my back, I cannot get up.   *Answ.* " Cast thy burden upon the Lord," and if you cannot fly, rest you with your load upon him ; for as faith is a flying, so it is a resting, &c.

Object. 4. Christ is so far away, that I will never reach him.   *Answ.* Do not say so, for he is near, Rom. x. 8, &c.

Object. 5. When I attempt to fly, the devil, and the world, and my own heart, pull me back again into the mire, and then I am just where I was.   *Answ.* From that moment that thou makest an attempt to fly to Christ, the devil, the world, and corruption, will be upon thee to harass thee.   But though they may do thee many an ill turn, yet they shall never pull thee out of Christ, if once thou hast fled to him ; no man " shall pluck them out of my hand, my Father who gave them me is greater than all (says Christ), and none shall pluck them out of my Father's hand."   Many a pluck the enemy gives at Christ's doves, but they shall never pluck them away from him.

Quest. You bid me fly like a dove into Christ, and his windows ; but will you give me your advice in order to it ? *Answ.* 1. Be much in viewing the holiness of the law, and of the Lawgiver, " for it is a schoolmaster to bring us to Christ," &c.   2. Be much in viewing your danger while out of Christ, condemned already, &c.   3. Be much in studying the gospel, Christ in his person, nature, and offices ; the freedom of the covenant, and the fulness and suitableness of the gospel remedy, &c.   4. Be persuaded of the Lord's willingness to take you in to himself, at his windows, his bowels sound towards sinners, &c.   5. Cry for the wind of the Spirit to blow, that thereby you may be set a-flight, for he testifies of Christ, and joins the sinner to him, &c.   6. Make at Christ, through the window of prayer, and of faith in prayer ; wrestle, cry, seek, and knock, for to such shall it be opened, &c.

Explanation of Psal. lxviii. 31.—*" Ethiopia shall soon stretch out her hands unto God."*

This psalm was penned, probably, upon the occasion of David's carrying up the ark from the house of Obed-edom, to the tent he had pitched for it in Mount Zion, whereby was typified the ascension of Christ, and the erection of his spiritual kingdom and government in the world, by the preaching of the everlasting gospel. You see his ascension and exaltation spoken of, ver. 18. " Thou hast ascended on high, thou hast led captivity captive, thou hast received gifts for men, yea, for the rebellious also, that the Lord God might dwell amongst them."   And in the following part of the psalm is foretold the erection of his kingdom over the belly of all opposition that should be made thereunto, either by hell or earth.

The words read (not to insist in the entry) are a declaration of the success of the gospel among the Gentile nations : Ethiopia, Egypt, and other places of the world, would submit unto his royal sceptre, when it should be swayed among them in the dispensation of the gospel, " Princes shall come out of Egypt, Ethiopia shall soon stretch out her hands unto God."   It is only the latter clause I am to speak to : Where,

1. We have a solemn act of divine worship, and that is, the stretching out of the hands.   The actions of the

body are the expressions of the actions of the soul
or mind, Psal. cxliii. 6. says the Psalmist, " I stretch
forth my hands unto thee, my soul thirsteth after thee,
as a thirsty land, Selah." So Psal. cxli. 2. " Let my
prayer be set forth before thee as incense, and the lifting up of my hands as the evening sacrifice." So that
the internal worship of the soul is the thing intended by the lifting up of the hands. And in every act
of worship, faith, which is the hand of the soul, is the
leading and principal part, insomuch that, "without
faith, it is impossible to please God."

2. We have the object of this worship, or to whom
the hand is to be lifted up : it is unto God ; to " God
in Christ, reconciling the world to himself, not imputing their trespasses unto them." An absolute God
cannot be the object of a sinner's faith, hope, trust,
and confidence, but, on the contrary, the object of his
terror and amazement. Hence, like our father Adam,
before the revelation of the promised seed, we fly from
him, and do not love to retain the knowledge of him
in our thoughts ; as it is said of the heathen world,
Rom. i. 28, who want the knowledge of Christ.

3. In the words we may notice, who they are that
stretch out their hands unto God; Ethiopia, which
may be understood either literally or figuratively. If
we take it figuratively, it is to be understood of the
Gentile nations in general, a part being put for the
whole. God the Father had said to the Son, Psal. ii.
" Ask of me, and I shall give thee the heathen for
thine inheritance, and the uttermost parts of the earth
for thy possession." And accordingly, upon his resurrection and ascension, the gospel came to be preached to the Gentiles, according to the commission given
to the apostles, Mark xvi. 15, " Go ye into all the
world, and preach the gospel unto every creature"
under heaven, that is, unto all nations of the world,
without distinction. And thereupon Ethiopia, with
the rest of the Gentile nations, did receive the word
of the gospel, and did obeisance unto the Son of God.

And how the leaven of the gospel came to be spread unto Ethiopia, in particular, we have some account, Acts viii. 27, to the close, where we are told of the conversion of the Ethiopian eunuch, by the ministry of Philip, who after a profession of his faith in Christ, being baptized in his name, went on his way towards his own country rejoicing ; and, no doubt, would spread the glad tidings of salvation through Christ in his own country, some of the fruits whereof are said to remain among the Abyssinians of Inner Ethiopia unto this day.

4. We have the ready and cheerful obedience that is given by Ethiopia, or the Gentile nations, unto the call of the gospel ; they soon stretch out their hands unto God, that is, they will do it without delay, and with readiness of mind ; a literal accomplishment of which you will see, Acts xiii. 40, 47, 48, where when the Jews rejected the gospel, the apostle tells them, that seeing they put the word of God from them, " lo, we turn to the Gentiles, for so hath the Lord commanded us, saying, I have set thee to be a light of the Gentiles, that thou shouldst be for salvation to all the ends of the earth." And then it is added, " And when the Gentiles heard this, they were glad, and glorified the word of the Lord," that is, they entertained it with a ready mind.

5. We have the certainty of the event, they shall stretch out their hands unto God : as if he had said, However firmly they were rooted in their ignorance and idolatry, and other wickednesses, for many ages and generations, yet such shall be the efficacy of the gospel, and the victorious power of grace accompanying it, that they shall give up with their idols, and stretch out their hands in a way of worship and obedience unto the only living and true God. Much to this purpose is that word, Psal. cx. 3, " The Lord shall send the rod of thy strength out of Zion : Rule thou in the midst of thine enemies. Thy people shall be willing in the day of thy power ; or (orig.) in the day of thy armies."

Concerning the Great and Awful Day of Judgment

1. LET us all be warned, and while we have time, provide for that day ; yet, the weather is fair, we may frame an ark to save us from the flood ; yet are the angels at the gate of Sodom, and yet is Jonah in the streets of Nineveh ; yet the prophet laments, crying, "O Judah ! how shall I entreat thee ;" yea, the apostle prays, nay, we pray you in Christ's stead that ye be reconciled unto God.   But here a question will arise, How will Christ appear?

I answer, He who, as man, once appeared to be judged, will then appear to judge all mankind.   Consider this, ye that are going to the bar ; what a dreadful sight will this be to the faithless Jews, stubborn Gentiles, and wicked Christians, when every eye shall see him, and they also that pierced him ?   This is the man, shall they say, that was crucified for us, and again crucified by us.   Why, alas ! every sin is a cross, and every oath is a spear ; and when that day is come, you must behold the Man, whom thus you do crucify by your daily sin ; sure this will be a fearful sight. Where is the bloody swearer, that can tear his wounds, heart, and blood ?   At that day, all these words will appear, the heart be visible, and the body and the blood be sensible of good and evil : then shall the fearful voice proceed from his throne, Where is the blood thou spilled ?   Here is the woeful and terrible judgment, when thou that art the murderer, shalt see the slain Man be thy Judge.   What favours canst thou think to expect at his hand, whom thou hast so vilely and treacherously used by thy daily sins ?   Be sure, the Son of man shall come, as it is written, " but woe unto that man by whom the Son of man is betrayed ; it had been better for that man he had never been born," Matth. xxvi. 24.

As Christ shall appear in the form of a man, so this Man shall appear in a glorious form.   O sinner, look about you, the Judge is coming : a fire devours before him, and behind him a flame burns : on every side the people tremble, and all faces shall gather blackness. Here is a change indeed! He that was at the bar now sits on the throne, and that for ever and ever. Then Christ stood as a lamb before Pilate ; now Pilate stands as a malefactor before Christ. He that was made the footstool of his enemies, must now judge, till he has made his enemies his footstool. Where shall they run ? and how shall they seek the clefts of the rocks and hollow places ? The glory of his majesty will kindle a flame, while the heavens and the earth shall flee away from the presence of the powerful Judge.

But if here be the Judge, where is the guard ? Behold him coming from above with great power and glory ! Would you know his habit ? He is indeed clothed with majesty. Would you know his attendants ? They are a host of holy angels ; nay, yet a much longer train, even the souls of the saints descending from their imperial seats, and attending the Lamb, with great glory. Never was there any judge, lord of such a circuit : His footstool is in the clouds, his feet are in the rainbow ; his judges are saints, his officers, angels and archangels. The trumpet proclaims a silence, whilst a just sentence cometh from his mouth upon all the world. Thus you see the assize begun. "I beheld till the throne was cast down, (saith the prophet,) and the Ancient of days did sit, whose garments were white as snow, and the hair of his head like pure wool : his throne was like the fiery flame, and the wheels as burning fire," Dan. vii. 9.

This is the Judge, whose coming is so fearful, and ushered in by a fiery cloud, and apparelled in snowy white, carried in his circuit on burning wheels, and attended with thousands of thousands. O, ye Jews, behold the Man whom before ye crucified as a malefactor ! behold him on his throne, whom ye said his disciples had stolen away by night out of his grave! Matth. xxviii. 13. Behold him in his majesty, him upon whom you would not look in his humility! This is he at whose appearance the kindreds of the earth shall mourn. Such a shout of fury follows the sight of his majesty, that the vaults shall echo, the hills resound, the earth shall shake, the heavens shall pass away, and be turned to confusion. Then shall the wicked mourn, then shall they weep and wail, yet their tears shall not serve their turn ; their sins past betray them, and their shame condemns them, and their torments to come confound them : Thus shall the wicked bewail their miserable, hapless, unfortunate birth, and cursed end. O fearful Judge! terrible as an army with banners! The kings of the earth shall be astonished, and every eye shall see this Judge, and tremble at his sight. Lo, but conceive the guilty prisoner come to his trial. Will not the red robes of this Judge make his heart bleed for his blood shed. Thus have I showed you how Christ will appear in a glorious manner.

1. Think now, O sinner, what shall be thy reward, when thou shalt meet this Judge. The adulterer for a while may flatter beauty, the swearers grace their words with oaths, the drunkards kiss their cups, and thank their bodily healths, till they drink their souls to ruin : but let them remember, " for all these things God will bring them into judgment." A sad comfort in the end. Now shall the adulterer satisfy lust when he lies on a bed of flames? The swearer shall have enough of wounds and blood, when the devil shall torture his body and rack his soul in hell. The drunkard shall have plenty of his cups, when scalding lead shall be poured down his throat, and his breath draw flames of fire instead of air. As is thy sin, so is thy punishment ; this Judge will give just measure in the balance of his indignation and wrath.

For comfort to all that are the Judge's favourites, now is the day, (if ye are God's servants,) that Satan shall be trodden under your feet, and you, with your Master Christ, shall be carried into the holy of holies.

You may remember, how all the men of God in their greatest anguish here below, have fetched comfort from the eyes of faith. It was at this mountain Job rejoiced, being cast on the dunghill, that his Redeemer lived, and that he should see him at the last day stand on the earth. So likewise the evangelist John longed and cried, " Come, Lord Jesus, come quickly," Rev. xxii. 20. " Now little children, abide in him, that when he shall appear, we may have confidence, and not be ashamed at his coming. And this is the promise that he hath promised us, even eternal life," 1 John ii. 28, 29. But I proceed.

The persons to be judged are a world of men, good and bad, elect and reprobate.

(1.) There is a summons, and this every man must hear, and this shall be the voice of the last trumpet, " Arise, ye dead, and come to judgment." O what a fearful and terrible voice will this be to all the wicked! How will they tremble at his voice, which makes the earth to tremble! Even at this voice the graves of the dead shall be opened, and every soul re-united to its own body ; the dark pit of hell shall be shaken, when the dreadful soul shall leave its place of terror, and once more re-enter into its stinking carrion, to receive a greater condemnation, John v. 28, 29. The voice of Christ is a powerful and strong voice ; The dead shall hear his voice, and they shall come forth, they that have done good unto the resurrection of life, and they that have done evil to the resurrection of condem- nation.

Thus much for the summons, you hear it given, and every man must appear. Death must now give back all that he hath taken from the world. What a ghastly and shocking sight shall this be to see all the graves open, and to see dead men arise out of their graves, and the scattered flying on the wings of the wind till they meet together in one body, Ezek. xxxvii. 6, " The dry bones shall live." Behold, the power of God Almighty, out of the grave and the dust of the earth, from these chambers of death and darkness, shall raise the bodies of the buried, Rev. xx. 12, 13, " I saw the dead (saith St John,) small and great, stand before God : and the sea gave up the dead which were in it ; and death and hell delivered up the dead that were in them ; and they were judged every man according to his works." He that said to corruption, Thou art my father, and to the worm, Thou art my sister and mother, said also, " I know that my Redeemer liveth, and mine eyes shall behold him." O good God! how wonderful is thy power! Joel iii. 11, 12, " Assemble yourselves and come, all ye heathen, to the valley of Jehoshaphat, for there will I sit to judge all the heathen round about."

Thus have you an account of the dead being raised ; they are all brought together, and now we must put them asunder ; the sheep shall be put on the right hand, and the goats on the left hand. And now see the parties thus summoned, raised, gathered, and set apart. Is not here a world of men to be judged all in one day ! All tongues, all nations and people of the earth, shall appear in one day : We shall then behold each son of Adam, and Adam shall then see all his posterity. Consider this, ye that are high and low, rich and poor, one with another, " for with God there is no respect of persons." Hark, O beggar! petitions are out of date, yet thou needest not fear, for thou shalt have justice done thee this day. All causes shall be heard, and thou, though ever so poor, and even despised in the world, must with the rest receive thy sentence. Hark, O farmer! now are the lives and leases together finished ; this day is the new harvest of the Judge, who gathers in his wheat, and burns up his chaff with fire unquenchable : no bribes, no prayers, no tears : but as thou hast done, so thou art sentenced. Hark, O landlord! where is thy purchase to thee and thy heirs for ever? This day makes an end of all ; and unhappy were thy soul, if thou hadst not better land than a barren rock, to cover and shelter thee from the presence

of the Judge.   Hark, O captain ! how vain is the hope
of man to be saved by the multitude of a host.   Thou
hast commanded all the armies of the earth and hell,
yet canst thou not resist the power of heaven.   Hark,
the trumpet sounds, and the alarm summons thee ;
thou must appear : all must appear,—the beggar, the
farmer, the captain, the prince, and the greatest potentates of the world ; nay, all shall receive their reward according to their deserts.

(2.) This is for terror to the wicked ; every man
must appear : O that every man would but think of
it !   Would you know the man that shall at this day
be blessed ?   It is he that thinks on this day, and prepares for it.   O then, I beseech you, meditate every
day, that you and every man must one day appear before the Judge of the quick and dead, and receive
according to your works.

And now, having brought the prisoners to their
trial, I must tell you how this trial must be ; for your
works : Faith justifies, but it is by works we are judged.
Mistake me not, he shall be judged according to his
works, as being the best witness of his inward righteousness.   But the better to acquaint you with this
trial, we come to consider,

1. How all men's works shall be manifested to us.

2. How all men's works shall be examined by God.

1. Of the manifestation of every man's works : Rev.
xx. 12.   " I saw the dead, small and great (saith St
John,) stand before God : and the books were opened ;
and another book was opened, which is the book of
life : and the dead were judged out of these things
which were written in the books, according to their
works."   Remember this, O forgetful sinner ; thou
mayest commit sin after sin, and multiply your sins ;
but be sure God keeps a just account, and none of
your sins, though ever so secret, shall be forgot.
There is a book of God's memory ; it is called a book
of remembrance, Mal. iii. 16, " A book of remembrance was written before God, for them that feared

the Lord, and called upon his name." This is that which manifests all secrets; this is that which reveals all doings, whether good or evil. In these records are found at large Abel's sacrifice and Cain's murder, Absalom's rebellion and David's devotion, the Jews' cruelty and the prophets' innocency. Nothing shall be hid when this book is opened, for all may run and read it. " God will bring every man into judgment, with every secret thing, whether it be good, or whether it be evil," Eccles. xii. 14. Wail, ye wicked, and tremble in astonishment. Now your closet sins must be disclosed, and your private faults laid open.

Imprimis, For adultery, envy, blasphemy, drunkenness, oaths, violence, murder, sabbath-breaking, lying, and every other sin from the beginning to the end, from your birth to your death, the total sum is eternal death and damnation. But there is another book, that shall give a more fearful evidence than the former, and the secretary is the soul of man : No man can commit a sin, but the soul that is privy to the fact will write it in this book. What a woeful case will thy poor heart then be in ! What a strong terror of trembling must it then stand possessed with, when this book shall be opened, and thy sins revealed ? This book is now perhaps shut up and sealed : but in the day of judgment it shall be opened, and what will be the evidence that will be brought in ? There is a private session to be held in the breast of every sinner ; the memory is the record, truth is the law, damnation is the judgment, hell is the prison, devils are the jailors, and conscience both the witness and the judge to pass sentence upon thee. What hopes can he have at the general assize, whose conscience hath condemned him before he appears ? Consider this, O thou impenitent sinner !

But yet there is another book we read of, and that is the book of life, wherein are written all the names of God's elect from the beginning of the world unto the end thereof. This is the precious book of heaven, wherein if we be registrated, not all the powers of

darkness, death, or devils, can blot us out again.
Therefore, to make some useful applications,

1. Consider now, O sinner, what books one day
must be set before thee.   The time will come, when
every word of thy mouth, every glance of thine eye,
every moment of thy time, every sermon thou hast
heard, every thing thou hast left undone, all shall be
seen, and laid open before men, angels, and devils;
thou shalt then and there be horribly and everlastingly
ashamed.   Never go about then to commit sin, though
ever so secretly, though at midnight, and all the doors
locked about thee, yet at this great day it shall be
brought to light.

2. As you intend the good of your souls, amend
your lives, call yourselves to an account, while it is
called to-day; search and examine all your thoughts,
words, and deeds ; prostrate yourselves before God,
with broken and bleeding affections ; pray that your
name may be written in the book of life ; and if you
do so, God is not unrighteous to forget your labour
of love, and all your good works : for at that great day,
the book shall be opened, our works manifested, and,
as we have done, so we must be rewarded ; for then
shall he reward every man according to his works.
But a little to recall ourselves.

The prisoners are tried, the verdict brought in, the
indictments are found, and the Judge now sits upon
life and death, even ready with sparkling eyes to pronounce the sentence.   The Lord grant, that, when
this day comes, the sentence may be for us, and we be
saved, to our everlasting comfort.   O now hold up
your heads, all ye saints of the most high God, for
this shall be a blessed day for you ; for then shall ye
hear the sweet heavenly voice of Christ saying, " Come,
ye blessed of my Father, inherit the kingdom prepared
for you."   I cannot express what joy it will be to the
righteous, when they shall hear Christ say, Come, ye
blessed soul, who hath been bathed in repenting tears.
Here is a sentence able to revive the dead, much more

the afflicted. Are you sorrowing for your sins, leave it a while, and meditate with me on this ensuing melody. Hark! yonder is the choir of angels sounding to the Judge while he is pronouncing thy sentence. Now is the day of your coronation; now shall ye be made perfectly happy, and that for ever. Come, saith Christ, you that have suffered for me, now you shall have your reward; you shall have your souls filled to the brim with joy, such as is unspeakable, and full of glory.

But I must return to the left hand, and show another crew, prepared for another sentence. And O what a terrible sentence will that be, which will make all ears glow and tingle! "His lips (saith the prophet) are full of indignation, and his tongue like a consuming fire," Is. xxx. 27. What fire is so hot as that fiery sentence, Matth. xxv. 41, " Depart from me, ye cursed, into everlasting fire, prepared for the devil and his angels."

1. They must depart. This seems nothing to the wicked: now they are content to be gone; they have much more delight in sin, than in God's service. But whither must they go? "From me." If from me, then from all my mercies, my glory, and my salvation. But whither, O Lord, shall the cursed go, that depart from thee? Into what haven shall they arrive? What master shall they serve? It is thought a great punishment to be banished from our native soils? What then is it to be banished from the Almighty God? But whither must they go? Into everlasting fire. O what bed is this! no feathers but fire, no friends but furies, no ease but fetters, no day-light but darkness, no clocks to pass away the time, but endless eternity, fire eternal, always burning, and never dying. O who can endure everlasting flame! it shall not be quenched night nor day; the smoke thereof shall go up for ever and ever. The wicked shall be crowded together, like bricks in a fiery furnace. But for whom was this fire prepared? For the devil and his angels. These must be your companions. The last sentence is now pronounced.

What! Go, (who?) ye cursed, into everlasting fire, to crews of devils. O take heed, that you live in the fear of God, lest that, leaving his service, he give you this reward, "Depart from me, ye cursed," &c.

2. Consider, then, what fearful trembling will seize on your souls, that have their sentence for eternal flames: O which way will they turn? How will they escape the Almighty's wrath? To go backward is impossible, to go forward is intolerable. Whose help will they crave? God is their Judge, heaven their foe; the saints deride them, angels hate them. Good Lord, what a world of miseries hath seized on miserable souls. Their executioners are devils, the dungeon hell; the earth stands open, and the furnace burning, ready to receive you. O how will these poor souls quake and tremble! Every part of their body will bear a part in their doleful ditty; eyes weeping, hands wringing, breasts beating, hearts aching, with voices crying. Now, O man of the earth, what shall thy wealth avail thee; one drop of water, to cool thy tongue in the flames, is worth more than all the pleasures of the world.

Thus you have heard the sentence of the just and wicked; and the Judge is risen from his glorious seat. The saints guard him along, and the sentenced prisoners are delivered to the jailors; shrieks of horror shall be heard. What woes and lamentations shall be uttered, when devils and reprobates, and all the damned crew of hell, shall be driven into hell, never to return. Down they go howling, shrieking, and gnashing their teeth: the world leaves them, the earth forsakes them, hell entertains them; there they must live, and yet not live nor die; but dying live, and living die.

O miserable must these be, if the drowning of the world, the swallowing up of Korah, and the burning of Sodom with brimstone, were attended with such terror and hideous outcries; how infinitely, to all possibility of conceit, and trembling of that red fiery day; in a word, what wailing, weeping, roaring, and yelling, filling both heaven, earth, and hell! O most miserable wretches, Matth. xxii. 12, "Take them away, and cast them into utter darkness : there shall be weeping and gnashing of teeth." A darkness indeed! They must for ever be debarred from the light of heaven. Sunshine never peeps within these walls, nothing is there but smoke and darkness ; and such is the portion of sinners, and the reward of the wicked.

THE END.

GLASGOW: W. G. BLACKIE AND CO., PRINTERS, VILLAFIELD.

SELECTED BIBLIOGRAPHY
ON EBENEZER AND RALPH ERSKINE

Addison, William. *The Life and Writings of Thomas Boston of Ettrick*. Edinburgh: Oliver and Boyd, 1936.

Baker, Frank. "The Erskines and the Methodists." *The London Quarterly and Holborn Review* 27 (1958):36-45.

Barnett, T. Ratcliffe. *The Makers of the Kirk*. Boston: T.N. Foulis, 1913, pp. 243-55.

Bavinck, Herman. Introduction to *Levengeschiedenis en Werken van Ralph en Ebenezer Erskine*, pp. 1-13. Doesburg: J.C. van Schenk Brill, 1904.

Beaton, Donald. "'The Marrow of Modern Divinity' and the Marrow Controversy." *The Princeton Theological Review* IV, 3 (1906): 317-338.

Bell, M. Charles. *Calvin and Scottish Theology: The Doctrine of Assurance*. Edinburgh: Handsel Press, 1985.

Blaikie, W.G. *The Preachers of Scotland from the sixth to the nineteenth century*. Edinburgh: T. & T. Clark, 1888.

Boorman, David. "Ebenezer Erskine and Secession." In *Diversities of Gifts*, pp. 86-101. The Westminster Conference, 1980. Swansea: Howard Jones, 1981.

Boston, Thomas. *The Complete Works of the Late Rev. Thomas Boston, Ettrick*. 12 vols. Ed. Samuel M'Millan. London: William Tegg, 1855; reprint, Wheaton, Ill.: Richard Owen Roberts, 1980. (See especially, "The Marrow of Modern Divinity, with notes by Thomas Boston," vol. 7.)

Brienen, Teunis. "Het Avondmaal in de Gereformeerde Schotse Kerken, speciaal in de preken van de Erskines." In *Bij Brood en Beker*, ed. Willem van't Spijker. Kampen: De Groot Goudriaan, 1980, pp. 226-47.

Brown, James Campbell. *The Annals of Portmoak during the Ministry of the Rev. Ebenezer Erskine from 1703 to 1731, gathered from the Session Book*, published in Kinross-shire Advertiser, 1889.

Brown, John (of Whitburn), ed. *Gospel Truth Accurately Stated and Illustrated, by the Rev. Mess. James Hog, Thomas Boston, Ebenezer and Ralph Erskine, and Others. Occasioned by the Republication of the Marrow of Modern Divinity*. Edinburgh: J. Pillans and Sons, 1817.

Bruggink, Donald J. "The Theology of Thomas Boston, 1676-1732." Ph.D. dissertation, University of Edinburgh, 1956.

Burleigh, J.H.S. *A Church History of Scotland*. Edinburgh: Hope Trust, 1988.

Cowan, Henry. "Erskine, Ebenezer." In *The New Schaff-Herzog Encyclopedia of Religious Knowledge*, ed. Samuel Macauley Jackson, IV:171. Reprint, Grand Rapids: Baker, 1977.

Cunningham, John. *The Church History of Scotland, from the commence-*

ment of the Christian era to the present century, vol. II. Edinburgh: Adam & Charles Black, 1882.

Drummond, A.L., and Bulloch, J. *The Scottish Church 1688-1843. The Age of the Moderates.* Edinburgh: The Saint Andrew Press, 1973.

Erskine, Ebenezer. *God's Little Remnant Keeping their Garments Clean in an Evil Day.* Edinburgh: Patrick Walker, 1725.

_____.*The Whole Works of Ebenezer Erskine.* 3 vols. Philadelphia: Wm. S. & A. Young, 1836. (Includes memoir by Donald Fraser, pp. iii-xxx.)

Erskine, Ralph. *Faith no Fancy, or Treatise of Mental Images.* Edinburgh, 1745.

_____.*The Sermons and Other Practical Works of Ralph Erskine.* 7 vols. Aberdeen: George and Robert King, 1862; reprint vols. 1-6, Glasgow: Free Presbyterian, 1991. (Vol. 7, which contains Erskine's *Poetical Works*, includes memoir by John Brown of Whitburn, pp. v-xxxvi.)

Fawcett, Arthur. *The Cambuslang Revival, the Scottish Evangelical Revival of the Eighteenth Century.* London: Banner of Truth Trust, 1971.

Fraser, Donald. *The Life and Diary of the Reverend Ebenezer Erskine.* Edinburgh: William Oliphant, 1831.

Fraser, Donald. *The Life and Diary of the Reverend Ralph Erskine.* Edinburgh: William Oliphant, 1834.

Gentleman, Ebenezer. "Memorials of Erskine Church." In *Stirling Natural History and Arch. Soc. Transactions* XXX-XXXI (1907-1908).

Gib, Adam. *The Present Truth: A Display of the Secession-Testimony in the three periods of the rise, state and maintenance of that Testimony.* 2 vols. Edinburgh, 1774.

Gordon, Alexander. "Erskine, Ebenezer" and "Erskine, Ralph." In *Dictionary of National Biography,* ed. Leslie Stephen and Sidney Lee, VI: 822-25, 851-52. London: Oxford, 1921.

Graafland, Cornelis. "De spiritualiteit van de Puriteinen (inzonderheid van Ebenezer en Ralph Erskine en haar invloed in Nederland)." In *Spiritualiteit,* ed. Willem van't Spijker. Kampen: De Groot Goudriaan, 1993, pp. 209-229.

_____. *Van Calvijn tot Comrie. Oorsprong en ontwikkeling van de leer van het verbond in het Gereformeerd Protestantisme.* Zoetermeer, 1993.

Grier, W.J. "Erskine, Ebenezer" and "Erskine, Ralph." In *The Encyclopedia of Christianity,* IV: 89-90. Ed. Philip E. Hughes. Marshallton, Del.: National Foundation for Christian Education, 1972.

Harper, James, et al. *Lives of Ebenezer Erskine, William Wilson, and Thomas Gillespie, Fathers of the United Presbyterian Church.* Edinburgh: A. Fullarton, 1849. (On Ebenezer Erskine, pp. 1-88.)

Hetherington, W.M. *History of the Church of Scotland from the introduction of Christianity, to the period of the Disruption, May 18, 1843.* Edinburgh: Johnstone and Hunter, 1852.

Jenkins, Gordon, F.C. "Establishment and Dissent in the Dunfermline Area 1733-1883." Ph.D. dissertation, University of Edinburgh, 1988.

Ker, John. "The Erskines: Ebenezer and Ralph." In *Scottish Nationality and other Papers*. Edinburgh: Andrew Elliot, 1887, pp. 64-108.

Lachman, David. "Erskine, Ebenezer" and "Erskine, Ralph." In *Dictionary of Scottish Church History & Theology*, ed. Nigel M. de S. Cameron. Downers Grove, Ill.: InterVarsity Press, 1993, pp. 298-302.

_____. *The Marrow Controversy, 1718-1723: An Historical and Theological Analysis*. Rutherford Studies Series One: Historical Theology. Edinburgh: Rutherford House, 1988.

_____."The Marrow Controversy: An Historical Survey with special reference to the Free Offer of the Gospel, the Extent of the Atonement, and Assurance and Saving Faith." Th.M. thesis, Westminster Theological Seminary, 1973.

Leckie, J.H. *Secession Memories, the United Presbyterian Contribution to the Scottish Church*. Edinburgh: T & T Clark, 1926.

McCain, Charles Rodgers. "Preaching in Eighteenth Century Scotland: A Comparative Study of the Extant Sermons of Ralph Erskine, John Erskine, and Hugh Blair." Ph.D. dissertation, Edinburgh, 1949.

M'Clintock, John, and Strong, James, eds. "Erskine, Ebenezer" and "Erskine, Ralph." In *Cyclopedia of Biblical, Theological, and Ecclesiastical Literature*, III: 282-83. New York: Harper & Brothers, 1894.

M'Crie, C.G. *The Church of Scotland: her Divisions and her Reunions*. Edinburgh: MacNiven & Wallace, 1901.

_____. *The Confessions of the Church of Scotland, their Revolution in History*. Edinburgh: MacNiven & Wallace, 1907.

M'Crie, Thomas, Jr. "Account of the Controversy respecting the Marrow of Modern Divinity." *The Edinburgh Christian Instructor* XXX (August, October, December 1831); New Series, I (February 1832).

_____."'The Marrow' Controversy: with Notices of the State of Scottish Theology in the beginning of last Century." *The British and Foreign Evangelical Review* II (June 1853):411-40.

_____.*The Story of the Scottish Church from the Reformation to the Disruption*. Glasgow: Bell and Bain Ltd., 1875.

MacEwen, A.R. *The Erskines*. Edinburgh: Oliphant Anderson & Ferrier, 1900.

McIntyre, D.M. "First Strictures on 'The Marrow of Modern Divinity.'" *The Evangelical Quarterly* X (January 1938): 61-70.

MacKenzie, Robert. *John Brown of Haddington*. London: Hodder and Stoughton, 1964.

M'Kerrow, John. *History of the Secession Church*. 2 vols. Edinburgh: William Oliphant and Son, 1839.

Macleod, John. *Scottish Theology*. Reprint, London: Banner of Truth Trust, 1974.

M'Millan, Samuel, ed. *The Beauties of the Rev. Ebenezer Erskine, being a Se-*

lection of the Most Striking Illustrations of Gospel Doctrine Contained in His Whole Works. Glasgow: Blackie & Son, 1850.

M'Millan, Samuel, ed. *The Beauties of the Rev. Ralph Erskine, being a Selection of the Most Striking Illustrations of Gospel Doctrine Contained in His Whole Works.* 2 vols. Edinburgh: A. Fullarton, 1850. (Includes memoir, pp. xiii-xxxvi.)

Mathieson, William Law. *The Awakening of Scotland: A History from 1747 to 1797.* Glasgow, 1910.

Mechie, Stewart. "The Marrow Controversy Reviewed." *The Evangelical Quarterly* XXII (January 1950): 20-31.

Mitchell, James. "Ebenezer Erskine." In *Scottish Divines 1505-1872,* pp. 149-88. Edinburgh: Macniven and Wallace, 1883.

Muirhead, Andrew T.N. "Religion, Politics and Society in Stirling during the ministry of Ebenezer Erskine, 1731-1754." M.Litt. thesis, University of Stirling, 1983.

_____. "A Secession Congregation in its Community: The Stirling Congregation of the Rev. Ebenezer Erskine, 1731-1754." *Records of the Scottish Church History Society,* XXII (1989): 211-223.

_____. "Stirling 1734." *Forth Naturalist and Historian,* 11 (1986): 105-120.

Murray, John J. "The Marrow Controversy—Thomas Boston and the Free Offer." In *Preaching and Revival,* pp. 34-56. The Westminster Conference, 1984. Colchester, Essex: Christian Design & Print, 1985.

Philip, Adam. *The Devotional Literature of Scotland,* London: James Clarke & Co., n.d.

Philpot, J.C. *Reviews,* 2:483-91. London: Frederick Kirby, 1901.

Roxburgh, Kenneth B.E. *Thomas Gillespie and the Origins of the Relief Church in 18th Century Scotland.* New York: Peter Lang, 1999.

Scott, David. *Annals and Statistics of the Original Secession Church: till its disruption and union with the Free Church of Scotland in 1852.* Edinburgh: Andrew Elliot, 1886.

Scott, E. Erskine. *The Erskine-Halcro Genealogy. The ancestors and descendants of Henry Erskine, minister of Chirnside, his wife, Margaret Halcro of Orkney, and their sons, Ebenezer and Ralph Erskine.* Edinburgh, 1895.

Scott, Hew. *Fasti Ecclesiae Scoticanae. The Succession of Ministers in the Church of Scotland from the Reformation.* 7 vols. Edinburgh, 1915-1928.

Scott, Kenneth B. *Ebenezer Erskine, the Secession of 1733, and the Churches of Stirling.* Edinburgh, n.d.

Sell, Alan. "The Message of the Erskines for Today." *Evangelical Quarterly* 60, 4 (1988): 299-316.

Small, Robert. *History of the Congregations of the United Presbyterian Church.* 2 vols. Edinburgh, 1904.

Smeaton, George. "The suitableness of Erskine's writings to a period of religious revivals." In *The Beauties of Ralph Erksine*, ed. Samuel M'Millan. Edinburgh: A. Fullarton, 1829, pp. xxxi-xxxviii.

Stewart, Alexander. *Reminiscences of Dunfermline and Neighbourhood.* Edinburgh, 1886.

Taylor, William M. *The Scottish Pulpit from the Reformation to the Present Day.* London: Harper and Brothers, 1887.

Thomson, Andrew. *Historical Sketch of the Origin of the Secession Church.* Edinburgh: A. Fullarton, 1848.

_____. "On the characteristics of Ralph Erskine's ministry." In *The Beauties of Ralph Erskine*, ed. S. M'Millan. Edinburgh: A. Fullarton, 1829, pp. xv-xxx. Reprinted in *Free Presbyterian Magazine* XXXVIII, 11-12 (1934):459-64, 493-99.

_____. *Thomas Boston of Ettrick: His life and Times.* Edinburgh: T. Nelson and Sons, 1895.

Tyerman, Luke. *The Life of the Rev. George Whitefield.* 2 vols. London: Hodder and Stoughton, 1890.

Van der Groe, Theodorus. "Voorrede, handelende over het schadelijke misbruik van eene algemeene overtuiging, tot een valschen grond van rust voor de ziel." In *Al de werken van R. en E. Erskine*, deel 8, stuk 1. Amsterdam, 1855, pp. iii-xxiv.

_____. "Voorrede aan den christelijken lezer." In *Al de werken van R. en E. Erskine*, deel 7, stuk 1. Amsterdam, 1855, pp. iii-xxxi.

_____. "Voorrede, waarin omstandig gehandeld wordt over de noodige voorbereidselen, wezenlijke eigenschappen en onafscheidelijke gevolgen van het ware zaligmakende geloof." In *Al de werken van R. en E. Erskine*, deel 5, stuk 1. Amsterdam, 1854, pp. iii-lxxxvi.

_____. "Voorrede handelende over het opregt geloovig aannemen en gebruik maken van de beloften des H. Evangelies, tot ontdekking van de tijd- en waangeloovigen, en tot bevestiging van de ware geloovigen." In *Al de werken van R. en E. Erskine*, deel 4, stuk 1. Amsterdam, 1854, pp. iii-xlvi.

_____. "Voorrede of verhandeling over den pligt van het lezen der H. Schrift en andere godgeleerde boeken." In *Al de werken van R. en E. Erskine*, deel 3, stuk 1. Amsterdam, 1854, pp. iii-lxviii.

Van der Linde, Simon. "Ebenezer en Ralph Erskine." In *Christelijke Encyclopedie*, 2:630-31. Kampen: J.H. Kok, 1957.

Van Harten, Pieter Hendrik. *De Prediking van Ebenezer en Ralph Erskine: Evangelieverkondiging in het spanningsveld van verkiezing en belofte.* 's-Gravenhage: Boekencentrum, 1986.

Van Valen, L.J. *Herauten van het kruis: Leven en werk van Ralph en Ebenezer Erskine.* Houten: Den Hertog, 1995.

_____. *Thomas Boston: een visser der mensen.* Houten: Den Hertog, 1990.

Walker, James. *The Theology and Theologians of Scotland*. Edinburgh: T. & T. Clark, 1888.

Watson, Jean L. *Life of Ralph Erskine*. Edinburgh: James Gemmell, 1881.

Watt, Hugh. "Ebenezer Erskine, 1680-1754." In *Fathers of the Kirk: Some Leaders of the Church in Scotland from the Reformation to the Reunion*, ed. R. S. White. Oxford: University Press, 1960, pp. 106-118.

Webber, F. *A History of Preaching in Britain and America*, 2:161-76. Milwaukee: Northwestern Publishing House, 1952.

Woodside, D. *The Soul of a Scottish Church, of the Contribution of the United Presbyterian Church to Scottish Life and Religion*. Edinburgh, n.d.

Young, D., and Brown, J. *Memorials of Alexander Moncrieff, M.A., and James Fisher, Fathers of the United Presbyterian Church*. Edinburgh, 1849.